Getting Started with Citrix XenApp 6.5

Design and implement Citrix farms based on XenApp 6.5

Guillermo Musumeci

BIRMINGHAM - MUMBAI

Getting Started with Citrix XenApp 6.5

Copyright © 2012 Packt Publishing

All rights reserved. No part of this book may be reproduced, stored in a retrieval system, or transmitted in any form or by any means, without the prior written permission of the publisher, except in the case of brief quotations embedded in critical articles or reviews.

Every effort has been made in the preparation of this book to ensure the accuracy of the information presented. However, the information contained in this book is sold without warranty, either express or implied. Neither the author, nor Packt Publishing, and its dealers and distributors will be held liable for any damages caused or alleged to be caused directly or indirectly by this book.

Packt Publishing has endeavored to provide trademark information about all of the companies and products mentioned in this book by the appropriate use of capitals. However, Packt Publishing cannot guarantee the accuracy of this information.

First published: June 2011

Second Edition: July 2012

Production Reference: 1160712

Published by Packt Publishing Ltd.
Livery Place
35 Livery Street
Birmingham B3 2PB, UK.

ISBN 978-1-84968-666-2

www.packtpub.com

Cover Image by Jarosław Blaminsky (`milak6@wp.pl`)

Credits

Author
Guillermo Musumeci

Reviewers
Christopher Buford
Shankha Mukherjee
Peter Nap

Acquisition Editor
Dilip Venkatesh

Lead Technical Editor
Kedar Bhat

Technical Editor
Madhuri Das

Project Coordinator
Yashodhan Dere

Proofreader
Mario Cecere

Indexer
Monica Ajmera Mehta

Production Coordinator
Aparna Bhagat

Cover Work
Aparna Bhagat

About the Author

Guillermo Musumeci is a Windows Infrastructure Architect, specialized in Citrix and Virtualization, with 17 years of experience and passion for designing, building, deploying, and supporting enterprise architectures using Citrix, Microsoft, and VMware products.

He worked as Project Manager and Consultant in medium to large Citrix and virtualization projects in America and Europe, and now he works as Citrix SME (Subject Matter Expert) for one of the world's top financial companies in Asia, where he lives with his wife and two kids.

Guillermo is the founder and developer of the popular site CtxAdmTools, which provides free Citrix, VMware, and Microsoft automation tools to manage Citrix environments, Active Directory, Virtual Machines, and more. Also, he is the author of the book *Getting Started with Citrix XenApp 6.0*.

He holds more than 25 Citrix, Microsoft, and VMware certifications, and has passed more than 50 certification exams.

When he is not working he loves to cook with his son, particularly homemade Italian food, or walking around Singapore with his family, tasting new food, and clicking pictures.

Acknowledgement

This book is dedicated to my beautiful wife Paola and my amazing kids, Stefano and Ornella. All of you are my number one source of happiness. I love you all!

Also I want to dedicate this book to my grandparents, Vicenta, Sarito, Nino, and Lorenza, and my parents, Carolina and Juan Carlos. Thank you for teaching me important values that made me who I am.

Also, I want to thank my sisters, our families, and friends for their support.

In particular I want to give a big thank you to all our new friends in Singapore!

Finally I want to thank all the people from Packt Publishing, who helped me on this book, principally the Project Coordinator, Yashodhan Dere, for their amazing help. Thank you!

About the Reviewers

Christopher Buford is a Citrix Certified Enterprise Engineer in Virtualization (CCEE) and Citrix product consultant, with 13 years of experience with Citrix products.

His experience includes XenApp, XenDesktop, NetScaler, Provisioning Server, Universal Profile Manager, Business Practices, and Technical Documentation. He also has experience in architecting, designing, and implementing Citrix Solutions. He has worked with several Fortune 500 companies as well as small to mid-sized Businesses as a Citrix subject matter expert.

He is currently a Citrix consultant for SMB Technology Solutions, LLC. SMB Technology Solutions, LLC is an Atlanta, GA-based boutique virtualization consulting company, specializing, in the small-midsized business arena. SMB Technology Solutions focuses on the South Eastern United States.

He really loves the ability to bring historically enterprise-level technologies to the SMB market. He feels great to be able to apply years of enterprise experience to the small business market. They are instrumental in helping level the playing field for the smaller guys.

Christopher was also chosen as a reviewer for the forerunner of this book, *Getting Started with Xenapp 6*.

Acknowledgement

I would like to thank the following individuals for my success.

First of all, I would like to thank my Lord and Savior Jesus Christ.

I would also like to thank my loving family; my beautiful wife Carol Buford, for her support. My children, who are the main reasons for my pressing towards the goal, daughters Ceterra, Chrisha, Christiana, and Taliyah, and grandson Jordan, and of course my parents, Mr. and Mrs. O.J. Buford, for their guidance and for always being there for me.

I would also like to thank the following mentors, friends, and colleagues for driving me towards excellence:

Mr. Alonzo James III — Zo, "Technological Genius" you are one of the very few people who have technical brilliance along with "real world" common sense. Thanks for sharing the knowledge, and thanks for being such a great friend.

Mr. Dexter Oliver — Thanks Dex, "I.T. Manager Extraordinaire" for your guidance, mentoring, and wisdom, and for keeping me spiritually grounded and assisting me in keeping focus on what really counts.

Mr. Scott Tucker (Citrix Technology Consultant) — Scott, I have learned so much from you in our technology battles and ("hashing" things out) conversations, Thanks a bunch buddy.

Shankha Mukherjee has five years experience in Citrix XenApp (new name for Presentation Server). He has worked on almost all the versions of Citrix XenApp, starting from Metaframe XP. He is currently working as a Level-2 administrator for WINTEL (Windows Intel / Citrix XenApp / VMware), giving support to client infrastructure, remotely.

Shankha Mukherjee is a B-Tech Engineer in Information Technology.

He has also reviewed the book, *Getting Started with Citrix XenApp 6*.

> I am thankful to Yashodhan Dere and Amey Kanse for providing me this opportunity.

Peter Nap is a very experienced Server Based Computing Consultant and Infrastructure Architect. He is 38 years old, lives in the Netherlands, and is currently employed as an Infrastructure Architect for Logica. He has 13 years of work experience in various large and small businesses, including Ministry of Defense and Ministry of Justice of the Netherlands.

Last year, Peter was migrating a company to XenApp 6.5 in combination with Citrix Provisioning 6.1 and hosted on physical blades.

www.PacktPub.com

Support files, eBooks, discount offers and more

You might want to visit www.PacktPub.com for support files and downloads related to your book.

Did you know that Packt offers eBook versions of every book published, with PDF and ePub files available? You can upgrade to the eBook version at www.PacktPub.com and as a print book customer, you are entitled to a discount on the eBook copy. Get in touch with us at service@packtpub.com for more details.

At www.PacktPub.com, you can also read a collection of free technical articles, sign up for a range of free newsletters and receive exclusive discounts and offers on Packt books and eBooks.

http://PacktLib.PacktPub.com

Do you need instant solutions to your IT questions? PacktLib is Packt's online digital book library. Here, you can access, read and search across Packt's entire library of books.

Why Subscribe?

- Fully searchable across every book published by Packt
- Copy and paste, print and bookmark content
- On demand and accessible via web browser

Free Access for Packt account holders

If you have an account with Packt at www.PacktPub.com, you can use this to access PacktLib today and view nine entirely free books. Simply use your login credentials for immediate access.

Instant Updates on New Packt Books

Get notified! Find out when new books are published by following @PacktEnterprise on Twitter, or the *Packt Enterprise* Facebook page.

Table of Contents

Preface	**1**
Chapter 1: Getting Started with Citrix XenApp 6.5	**7**
Introducing XenApp 6.5	**8**
XenApp feature overview	**12**
System requirements	**13**
Data store databases	15
Citrix AppCenter console	16
License server	17
Clients	17
Summary	**18**
Chapter 2: Designing a XenApp 6.5 Farm	**19**
Case study: Brick Unit Constructions	**19**
Farm terminology and concepts	**20**
Infrastructure servers	23
Virtualization infrastructure	24
Access Infrastructure	25
Designing a basic XenApp architecture	**26**
The pilot plan	**28**
Designing Active Directory integration	30
Building a small test farm	30
Creating a list of applications to publish in our XenApp farm	33
Testing the list of applications	34
Microsoft Office applications	36
Java	37
Summary	**38**

Chapter 3: Installing XenApp 6.5 — 39

- Installing and configuring XenApp 6.5 — 39
- Configuring Windows components — 40
  - Configuring Windows Firewall — 41
  - Configure IE ESC (Enhanced Security Configuration) — 43
- Installing XenApp using the Wizard-Based Server Role Manager — 44
- Installing License Server and Web Interface roles in server BRICKXA65-01 — 47
- Configuring Citrix License Server — 48
- Installing Citrix Licenses — 50
- Configuring XenApp Using the Wizard-based Server Configuration Tool — 56
  - Configuring the first XenApp server of the farm — 57
    - Installing Data Stores — 58
      - Microsoft SQL Server 2008 Express Database Server — 59
      - Microsoft SQL Server 2008 Database Server — 60
      - Oracle Database Server — 62
      - Configuring XenApp — 62
  - Installing and configuring XenApp 6.5 on BRICKXA65-03 — 65
- Configuring Citrix Web Interface server — 67
  - Creating a XenApp Web Site — 68
  - Creating a XenApp Services Site — 73
- Configure Remote Desktop Licenses — 74
  - Configuring Remote Desktop licensing mode by using Group Policy — 76
- Managing XenApp Farms — 77
- Summary — 78

Chapter 4: Advanced XenApp Deployment — 79

- Unattended install of XenApp 6.5 — 79
  - Unattended install of XenApp Components — 80
- Customizing Citrix Web Interface Server — 86
  - Changing the header section color — 88
  - Changing the header Citrix logo — 88
  - Changing horizontal page upper section color — 89
  - Changing the product name image — 89
  - Changing devices image — 90
  - Changing horizontal page lower section color — 91
  - Changing the tagline text — 91
  - Changing the footer Citrix logo — 92
  - Changing the HDX logo — 93
  - Changing the Footer section — 93
- Summary — 94

Chapter 5: Using Management Tools — 95
Management Consoles — 95
Citrix AppCenter Console — 95
License Administration Console — 98
Citrix Web Interface Management Console — 104
Other Administration Tools — 112
Citrix SSL Relay Configuration Tool — 112
Shadow Taskbar — 113
SpeedScreen Latency Reduction Manager — 114
Managing Citrix Administrators — 114
Adding a Citrix administrator — 114
Disabling a Citrix administrator — 118
Modifying Administrator properties — 119
Summary — 119

Chapter 6: Application Publishing — 121
Publishing applications — 121
Choosing the best method to deliver applications — 123
Publishing a hosted application using the Publish Application wizard — 124
Publishing a streaming application using the Publish Application wizard — 136
Publishing content using the Publish Application wizard — 147
Publishing a server desktop using the Publish Application wizard — 152
Configuring content redirection — 162
    Enabling content redirection from server to client — 162
    Configuring content redirection from client to server — 163
Associating published applications with file types — 163
Updating file type associations — 165
Enabling or disabling content redirection — 167
Summary — 169

Chapter 7: Application Streaming — 171
Application streaming — 171
System requirements for application streaming — 173
Components for application streaming — 175
Choosing which plug-in to use for application streaming — 176
Profiling Microsoft Office 2010 — 177
Installing a profiler workstation — 178
Customizing the Office 2010 installation — 179
Profiling Microsoft Office 2010 — 187
Publishing Office 2010 on the farm — 197
Specifying trusted servers for streamed services and profiles — 202
Summary — 204

Table of Contents

Chapter 8: Managing XenApp Policies — 205
Understanding XenApp policies — 205
- Working with XenApp policies — 206
- Best practices for creating XenApp policies — 207
- Guidelines for working with policies — 208

Working with management consoles — 208
- Using the Group Policy Management Console — 209
- Using the AppCenter Console — 209
- Using the Local Group Policy Editor — 211

Creating XenApp policies — 213
- Creating a policy using consoles — 213

Applying policies to sessions — 217
- Unfiltered policies — 218
- Using multiple policies — 219

Using Citrix policies templates — 220
- Creating a new Citrix Policy template — 221
- Importing and exporting policy templates — 222

Using Worker Groups to assign policies — 223
- Creating Worker Groups — 224

Troubleshooting policies — 227
- Using the Citrix Policy Modeling Wizard — 228
- Simulating connection scenarios with XenApp policies — 228
- Citrix settings precedence over Windows settings — 233
- Searching policies and settings — 233
- Importing and migrating existing policies — 235

Summary — 236

Chapter 9: Printing in XenApp Environments — 237
Windows printing concepts — 237
- Print job spooling — 238

Printing on Citrix XenApp — 239
- Printing pathway — 240
- Client local printing — 241
- Client network printing — 242
- Server network printing — 243
- Assigning network printers to users — 243
  - Adding session printers settings to a Citrix policy — 244
  - Setting a default printer for a session — 244
  - Modifying settings of session printers — 245
- Server local printers — 246
  - Configuring server local printers — 247

[iv]

Managing printer drivers	**247**
Controlling printer driver automatic installation	248
Modifying the printer driver compatibility list	249
Replicating print drivers in XenApp	251
Using the Citrix Universal Printer	**252**
Setting up an auto-create generic universal printer	255
Setting up universal driver preference	256
Configuring the Universal printer driver usage on sessions	257
Setting up universal printing preview preference	258
Universal printing EMF processing mode	259
Universal printing image compression limit	259
Universal printing optimization defaults	260
Universal printing print quality limit	261
Changing the default settings on the Universal Printer	262
Implementing Printers	**262**
Auto-creation	262
Auto-creating client machine printers	263
Auto-creating network printers	263
Configuring printer auto-creation settings	264
Configuring legacy client printer support	265
User provisioning	265
Publishing the Windows Add Printer wizard	266
Publishing the ICA Client Printer Configuration tool	267
Storing users' printer properties	267
General locations of printing preferences	269
Printing for mobile users	**270**
Smooth Roaming	271
Proximity printing	271
Configuring printers for mobile users	271
Improving printing performance	272
Limit printing bandwidth	273
Third-party printing solutions	**273**
Summary	**274**
Chapter 10: Multimedia Content in XenApp	**275**
Description of Citrix HDX technologies	**276**
Using HDX 3D technologies to improve image display	**276**
Using HDX 3D Image Acceleration to reduce bandwidth	277
Using HDX 3D Progressive Display to improve the display of images	279
Reducing CPU usage by moving processing to GPU	281
Using HDX Broadcast Display settings	**281**

Table of Contents

Using HDX MediaStream Multimedia Acceleration	**285**
Using Citrix policies to configure multimedia settings (HDX MediaStream)	286
Configuring echo cancellation	290
Using HDX MediaStream for Flash to optimize Flash content	**291**
System requirements for HDX MediaStream for Flash	292
Enabling HDX MediaStream at server side	292
Configuring HDX MediaStream for Flash settings	295
Setting up Flash Acceleration	295
Setting up Flash background color list	296
Setting up Flash backwards compatibility	297
Enable Flash event logging	297
Setting up Flash intelligent fallback	298
Setting up Flash latency threshold	299
Setting up Flash server-side content fetching URL list	300
Setting up Flash URL Blacklist	301
Setting up Flash URL compatibility list	301
Configuring HDX MediaStream for Flash on the client machine	302
Install/uninstall HDX MediaStream for Flash	304
Configuring audio using policies	**305**
Enabling Audio Plug N Play	306
Setting up audio quality	306
Setting up Client audio redirection	307
Setting up Client microphone redirection	308
Bandwidth policy settings	**308**
Setting up Audio redirection bandwidth limit	309
Setting up Audio redirection bandwidth limit percent	309
Setting up HDX MediaStream Multimedia Acceleration bandwidth limit	310
Setting up HDX MediaStream Multimedia Acceleration bandwidth limit percent	310
Configuring audio for user sessions	**311**
HDX Experience Monitor for XenApp	**311**
Summary	**313**
Chapter 11: Managing Sessions	**315**
Understanding sessions	**315**
Monitoring XenApp sessions	**317**
Managing XenApp sessions	**319**
Disconnecting, resetting, and logging off sessions	320
Terminating processes in a user session	321
Sending messages to users	322

Viewing XenApp sessions	**323**
Viewing sessions using the Shadow Taskbar	324
Starting the Shadow Taskbar	325
Initiating shadowing	325
Ending a shadowing session	326
Enabling logging for shadowing	327
Enabling user-to-user shadowing	328
Creating a shadowing policy	328
Maintaining session activity	**331**
Configuring Session Reliability	331
Configuring automatic client reconnection	332
Configuring ICA Keep-Alive	335
Customizing user environments in XenApp	**336**
Controlling the appearance of user logons	336
Controlling access to devices and ports	337
Mapping drives	338
Redirecting COM ports and audio	338
Limiting concurrent connections	**339**
Limiting the number of sessions per server	339
Limiting application instances	340
Logging connection denial events	341
Sharing sessions and connections	342
Preventing user connections during farm maintenance	344
Optimizing user sessions for XenApp	**344**
Mouse click feedback	344
Local text echo	345
Configuring SpeedScreen Latency Reduction	346
Redirection of Local Special Folders in sessions	**347**
Enabling Special Folder Redirection in the Web Interface	349
Enabling Special Folder Redirection for the Citrix Receiver or Citrix Online Plug-In	350
Using Group Policy to redirect Special Folders	350
Summary	**353**
Chapter 12: Scripting Programming	**355**
MFCOM and PowerShell	**355**
Installing XenApp Commands on XenApp Servers	**356**
Installing Citrix XenApp 6.5 PowerShell SDK	357
Installing PowerShell XenApp Commands	357
Using PowerShell for basic administrative tasks	**358**
Installing Citrix XenApp Commands snap-in	359
Using PowerShell for farm management	360

Table of Contents

Using PowerShell Commands from .NET applications	**366**
Creating a sample VB.NET application	366
Adding references	367
Creating and opening a runspace	368
Running a cmdlet	369
Displaying results	369
Passing parameters to cmdlets	371
Creating a sample C#.NET application	371
Adding references	372
Creating and opening a runspace	373
Running a cmdlet	373
Displaying results	374
Passing parameters to cmdlets	376
Using MFCOM on XenApp	**376**
Convert MFCOM scripts to PowerShell	**376**
Summary	**378**
Chapter 13: Receiver and Plug-Ins Management	**379**
Introduction to Citrix Receiver	**379**
Citrix Receiver features	380
Citrix Receiver Plug-In compatibility	380
Citrix Receiver system requirements and compatibility	382
Citrix Receiver for Windows	382
Citrix Receiver for Macintosh	382
Setting up Citrix Merchandising Server 2.2	**383**
Installing Merchandising Server software	383
Merchandising Server System requirements	383
Importing the virtual appliance into VMware vSphere	384
Importing the virtual appliance into Citrix XenServer	386
Setting up Merchandising Server	388
Configuring administrator users	390
Installing Plug-Ins	392
Creating recipient rules	393
Creating deliveries	395
Configuring SSL certificates	398
Creating a self-signed SSL certificate	399
Creating a Certificate Signing Request	400
Importing SSL certificates	400
Creating a signing request for Microsoft certificate services	402
Installing SSL certificates on client machines	402

Installing Citrix Receiver	**403**
Deploying Citrix Receiver for internal users with administrative rights	403
Installing Citrix Receiver for Windows	404
Installing Citrix Receiver on XenApp servers	405
Installing Citrix Receiver for Macintosh	405
Deploying Citrix Receiver for internal Windows users without administrative rights	406
Summary	**407**
Chapter 14: Virtualizing XenApp Farms	**409**
Deploying XenApp 6.5 in a virtualized environment	**409**
Virtual machine performance and host scalability	411
Choosing the right virtualization platform	**413**
Deploying XenApp 6.5 on Citrix XenServer	**414**
Creating a new XenApp 6.5 VM in XenServer	415
Deploying XenApp 6.5 on Microsoft Hyper-V	**419**
Creating a new XenApp 6.5 VM in Hyper-V	420
Deploying XenApp 6.5 on VMware vSphere	**424**
Creating a new XenApp 6.5 VM in VMware vSphere	426
Virtual machines optimizations	**433**
Cloning XenApp 6.5 virtual machines	**433**
Summary	**437**
Index	**439**

Preface

XenApp is the leader in application hosting and virtualization delivery, allowing users from different platforms such Windows, Mac, Linux, and mobile devices to connect to their business applications. Using XenApp, you can deploy secure applications quickly to thousands of users.

XenApp 6.5 brings with it exciting new features such as a brand new management console, Instant App access, Multi-stream ICA, Single Sign-on and SmartAuditor enhancements, and more.

Getting Started with Citrix XenApp 6.5 provides comprehensive details on how to design, implement, and maintain Citrix farms based on XenApp 6.5. Additionally, you will learn to use management tools and scripts for daily tasks such as managing servers, published resources, printers, and connections.

Getting Started with Citrix XenApp 6.5 starts by introducing the basics and new features of the brand new version such as installing servers and configuring components, and then teaches you how to publish applications and resources on the client device before moving on to configuring content redirection.

Author Guillermo Musumeci, includes a use case throughout the book to explain advanced topics like creating management scripts and deploying and optimizing XenApp for Citrix XenServer, VMware vSphere, and Microsoft Hyper-V virtual machines. It will guide you through an unattended installation of XenApp and components on physical servers.

By the end of this book, you will have enough knowledge to successfully design and manage your own XenApp 6.5 Farms.

What this book covers

Chapter 1, *Getting Started with XenApp 6.5*, provides an introduction to XenApp 6.5 and discusses the new features in the product. This chapter also covers the requirements to deploy XenApp 6.5.

Chapter 2, *Designing a XenApp 6.5 Farm*, explains Citrix farm terminologies and concepts, and how to design a basic XenApp architecture and a basic pilot plan to deploy XenApp. Also, how to choose applications and implement them on XenApp is discussed with the help of a case study.

Chapter 3, *Installing XenApp 6.5*, describes how to install and configure XenApp 6.5, including XenApp, Licensing Service, and Web Interface roles using the new XenApp Server Role Manager. Configuring Remote Desktop Services, installing the new Citrix AppCenter management console, and learning about Controller and Session-host modes are also discussed in this chapter.

Chapter 4, *Advanced XenApp Deployment*, explains unattended install of XenApp servers and customizing the Web Interface.

Chapter 5, *Using Management Tools*, presents the Citrix AppCenter Console, License Administration, and Citrix Web Interface Management Consoles. It shows other tools like Citrix SSL Relay Configuration tool, Shadow taskbar, and SpeedScreen Latency Reduction Manager. Finally, it shows how to create and manage Citrix administrator's accounts.

Chapter 6, *Application Publishing*, discusses how to publish different types of resources in XenApp: hosted and streamed applications, content and server desktops. Also, it discovers content redirection, from server to client and client to server, and explains how to set up and update file type associations.

Chapter 7, *Application Streaming*, explains the installation, configuration, and delivery of streaming applications. It describes system requirements and components for application streaming. It chooses plugins for application streaming and describes how to profile and publish Microsoft Office 2010 on a XenApp farm.

Chapter 8, *Managing XenApp Policies*, describes XenApp policies and how to create, manage, and apply Citrix policies. It explains the use of the Group Policy Management Console, Citrix AppCenter Console, and Local Group Policy Editor to manage Citrix Policies. Also, troubleshooting Citrix Policies is discussed in this chapter.

Chapter 9, *Printing in XenApp Environments*, describes Windows and Citrix XenApp printing concepts. It explains how to assign network printers to users using Citrix policies. It presents the new XenApp Printing Optimization Pack. It shows how to manage printer drivers, use the Citrix universal printer, and implement printers. It also explains printing for mobile users.

Chapter 10, *Multimedia Content on XenApp*, explains how to optimize user sessions for XenApp using different Citrix HDX features like HDX MediaStream Multimedia Acceleration, HDX 3D Technologies to improve image display, HDX MediaStream for Flash, and more. It describes how to configure HDX MediaStream for Flash on the Server and different multimedia, audio, and video settings using Citrix policies.

Chapter 11, *Managing Sessions*, describes sessions and explains how to manage and monitor sessions using Citrix AppCenter Console, including viewing and shadowing of sessions. It discusses how to customize user environments in XenApp and limit concurrent connections. It also shows how to optimize user sessions, redirect local Special folders in sessions, and maintain session Activity using Session Reliability, Auto Client Reconnect, and ICA keep-alive.

Chapter 12, *Scripting Programming*, shows how to install and configure PowerShell to manage XenApp farms and how to use cmdlets to manage XenApp servers. It explains how to use PowerShell commands from inside VB.NET and C#.NET code. It discusses how to convert MFCOM scripts to PowerShell and access MFCOM objects and manage previous versions of XenApp from PowerShell.

Chapter 13, *Receiver and Plugins Management*, presents Citrix Receiver, including features and compatibility, and explains how to install Citrix Receiver for Windows and Macintosh. It describes how to deploy a Citrix Merchandising Server on VMware, XenServer Virtual Machines, and configure Merchandising Server and Receiver Plugins.

Chapter 14, *Virtualizing XenApp Farms*, explains how to deploy XenApp 6.5 in a virtualized environment, including advantages and disadvantages of virtualization, virtual machine performance, host scalability, and more. It describes how to deploy XenApp 6.5 on Citrix XenServer, Microsoft Hyper-V, and VMware vSphere virtual machines, and how to clone XenApp 6.5 virtual machines.

What you need for this book

The following are the software requirements for this book:

- Microsoft Windows Server 2008 R2 and Citrix XenApp 6.5 are required to install and configure XenApp 6.5 servers
- Optional: dedicated database server running Microsoft SQL Server 2005 or later or Oracle 11g R2 is required in *Chapter 3, Installing XenApp 6.5*
- Microsoft Office 2010 is required to setup Application Streaming for *Chapter 7, Application Streaming*
- Microsoft Visual Basic.NET or Microsoft C#.NET to create applications in *Chapter 12, Scripting Programming*
- One hypervisor like Citrix XenServer, Microsoft Hyper-V, and VMware vSphere to create virtual machines discussed in *Chapter 14, Virtualizing XenApp Farms*

Who this book is for

If you are a system administrator or consultant who wants to implement and administer Citrix XenApp 6.5 farms, then this book is for you. This book will help both new and experienced XenApp professionals to deliver virtualized applications.

Conventions

In this book, you will find a number of styles of text that distinguish between different kinds of information. Here are some examples of these styles, and an explanation of their meaning.

Code words in text are shown as follows: "We can use `ServerManagerCmd.exe` command, PowerShell cmdlets or Microsoft DISM (Deployment Image Servicing and Management) tool to deploy prerequisites such as IIS or .NET Framework."

A block of code is set as follows:

```
Command myCommand = newCommand("Get-XAServer");
myCommand.Parameters.Add("ZoneName", "US-ZONE")
pipeLine.Commands.Add(myCommand);
```

Any command-line input or output is written as follows:

```
Disable-XAServerLogOn-ServerName "BRICKXA65-02"
```

New terms and **important words** are shown in bold. Words that you see on the screen, in menus or dialog boxes for example, appear in the text like this: "To install the Citrix AppCenter console (or the Citrix Delivery Services Console in XenApp 6.0) on a computer, from the XenApp Autorun menu, select **Manually Install Components | Common Components | Management Consoles**."

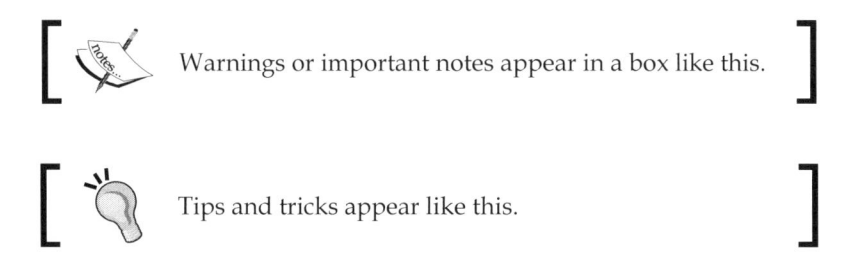

> Warnings or important notes appear in a box like this.

> Tips and tricks appear like this.

Reader feedback

Feedback from our readers is always welcome. Let us know what you think about this book—what you liked or may have disliked. Reader feedback is important for us to develop titles that you really get the most out of.

To send us general feedback, simply send an e-mail to `feedback@packtpub.com`, and mention the book title via the subject of your message.

If there is a topic that you have expertise in and you are interested in either writing or contributing to a book, see our author guide on `www.packtpub.com/authors`.

Customer support

Now that you are the proud owner of a Packt book, we have a number of things to help you to get the most from your purchase.

Downloading the example code

You can download the example code files for all Packt books you have purchased from your account at `http://www.PacktPub.com`. If you purchased this book elsewhere, you can visit `http://www.PacktPub.com/support` and register to have the files e-mailed directly to you.

Errata

Although we have taken every care to ensure the accuracy of our content, mistakes do happen. If you find a mistake in one of our books—maybe a mistake in the text or the code—we would be grateful if you would report this to us. By doing so, you can save other readers from frustration and help us improve subsequent versions of this book. If you find any errata, please report them by visiting `http://www.packtpub.com/support`, selecting your book, clicking on the **errata submission form** link, and entering the details of your errata. Once your errata are verified, your submission will be accepted and the errata will be uploaded on our website, or added to any list of existing errata, under the Errata section of that title. Any existing errata can be viewed by selecting your title from `http://www.packtpub.com/support`.

Piracy

Piracy of copyright material on the Internet is an ongoing problem across all media. At Packt, we take the protection of our copyright and licenses very seriously. If you come across any illegal copies of our works, in any form, on the Internet, please provide us with the location address or website name immediately so that we can pursue a remedy.

Please contact us at `copyright@packtpub.com` with a link to the suspected pirated material.

We appreciate your help in protecting our authors, and our ability to bring you valuable content.

Questions

You can contact us at `questions@packtpub.com` if you are having a problem with any aspect of the book, and we will do our best to address it.

1
Getting Started with Citrix XenApp 6.5

Citrix XenApp is the leader of application virtualization or application delivery. Several years ago, when the word Virtualization didn't exist, people used to talk about application hosting. Citrix was founded in 1989 and they developed the first successful product in 1993 called WinView. It provided remote access to DOS and Windows 3.1 applications on a multi-user platform. Citrix licensed Microsoft's Windows NT 3.51 source code from Microsoft; and in 1995 they shipped a multiuser version of Windows NT based on the MultiWin engine, known as WinFrame. This allowed multiple users to logon and execute applications on a WinFrame server. In 1996 Citrix licensed the MultiWin technology to Microsoft, establishing the foundation of Microsoft's Terminal Services.

I remember perfectly the first time I was in touch with application hosting was in 1997, and I was working at Microsoft in Argentina as Technical Support Engineer. I was invited for MCSE certification training on a Saturday morning. We had been building a lab with several machines, when I saw several Microsoft Beta CDs on a table.

I took one of them called **Hydra** and I asked the guy in charge of the training about it, and he told me that the CD contained an application to convert a Windows NT 4.0 into a sort of mainframe. I asked him if we could install it on a machine and he told me we did not have enough RAM to install it. I recall walking inside empty offices to open computers and remove the RAM so that we could install Hydra on a computer.

It was couple of years later, in 1999, when I discovered that Hydra is Windows 4.0 Terminal Server Edition. I was working with my first Citrix server and that was when I first fell in love with application hosting.

In this chapter we will learn:

- New XenApp 6.5 features
- System requirements for the installation of XenApp 6.5

Introducing XenApp 6.5

When Citrix introduced XenApp 6.0 in March 2010, they rewrote the code completely for the Windows 64-bit platform (2008 R2). This job provided a great opportunity to optimize the code for performance and scalability and to provide new features. Now with XenApp 6.5, released in August 2011, Citrix has introduced more features, performance improvements and the new faster application launch.

XenApp 6.5 looks like an enhanced version of XenApp 6.0, but there are several differences in the farm architecture, so there is no direct upgrade from XenApp 6.0 to 6.5, forcing us to create a new farm for XenApp 6.5 servers.

Here are some of the highlights of the new XenApp 6.5:

- **Role-based Setup Wizard**: This wizard, introduced on XenApp 6.0, simplified server deployment and reduced installation time. The new redesigned setup makes installation simple, fast, and intuitive. Now we can install XenApp 6.0 or 6.5 in a few clicks. Also, by separating the install from configuration Citrix simplified XenApp deployments using Citrix Provisioning Services or other image management solutions. We will use the Role-based Setup Wizard in *Chapter 3, Installing XenApp 6.5*, to install our first XenApp 6.5 servers.

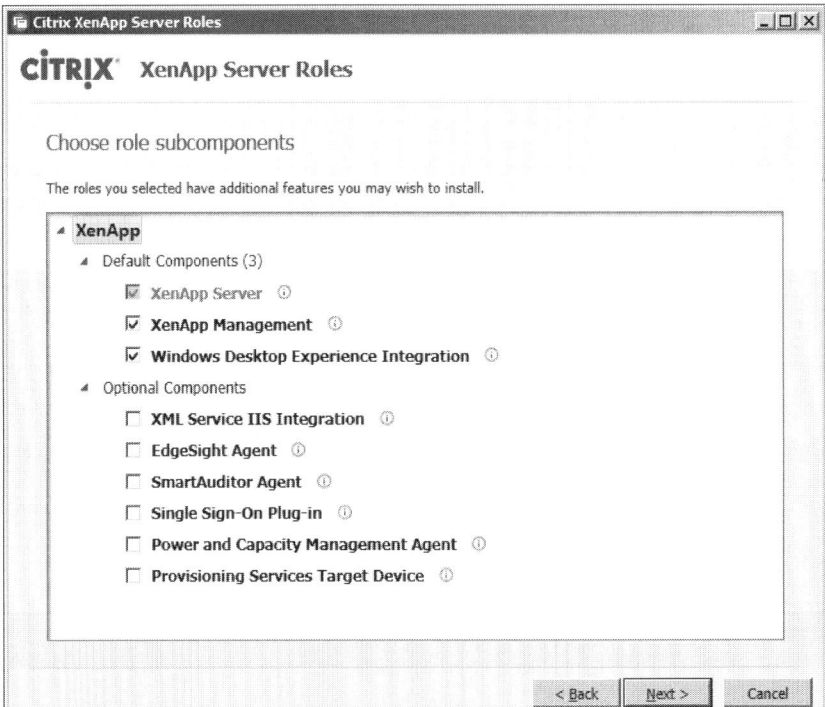

- **Instant App Access**: This new feature introduced on XenApp 6.5, also known as Session Pre-Launch, is the favorite for both XenApp customers and administrators. This new feature will reduce the launch time of sessions.

  On previous versions of XenApp when a user opens the first session, they will need to wait several seconds until the login script is processed, policies are applied, and profile is loaded. If the user opens a second application in the server, this application launches almost instantly.

  This is the idea behind the **Session Pre-Launch** feature. When a user logs on into the farm (or by XenApp policy) a pre-launch session is created on the XenApp server, just waiting for the user to log on.

  The same happened when the user closed the session. Session is kept open for a specific amount of time (defined by Session Limit policy).

  Enabling these policies XenApp reduces delay, improving the user experience, but also consumes hardware resources (memory and CPU) and use licenses. We are going to discuss this feature in the next chapter.

- **Windows Desktop Experience Integration**: This new XenApp 6.5 feature is installed by default when we install the XenApp server role. This feature gives XenApp 6.5 a Windows 7 appearance. This option was available on the XenApp 6.0 Service Provider Automation Pack and provides PowerShell scripts to manage multiple desktop options (Themes, Wallpaper, Start Menu and Taskbar, and so on).

- **PowerShell Support**: We can use Microsoft PowerShell to automate common XenApp management tasks. Citrix dropped support for MFCOM (the programming interface for the administration of XenApp servers and farms on previous versions) on XenApp 6.0 and added PowerShell 2.0 support. The new Citrix XenApp 6.5 PowerShell SDK introduced several improvements, including the ability to run cmdlets remotely, *Chapter 12, Scripting Programming*, is dedicated to scripting programming using PowerShell.

Getting Started with Citrix XenApp 6.5

- **New Management Console**: Only one console is something all administrators asked for years. Citrix introduced the Citrix Delivery Services Console in XenApp 6.0, and then replaced it by the new AppCenter on XenApp 6.5. The new management console has been completely redesigned. We still need a separate console to manage Web Interface servers and Licensing. We are going to explore the new AppCenter in *Chapter 4, Advanced XenApp Deployment*, and *Chapter 5, Using Management Tools*.

- **Citrix HDX Technologies**: Introduced in XenApp 6.0 and improved in XenApp 6.5, HDX technologies provides better multimedia and high-definition experience with support for more USB devices than ever before. Citrix HDX offers great improvements in both audio and video quality. New video conference capabilities and advanced Adobe Flash support are included too. Also, HDX provides multi-monitor support, improving application compatibility when we use multiple monitor. *Chapter 11, Managing Sessions*, is dedicated to improving the multimedia experience of users using Citrix HDX technologies.

- **Improved Printing Performance**: The XenApp Printing Optimization Pack for XenApp 6.0, released in October 2010, is now included in XenApp 6.5. This feature improves printing speed, reduces bandwidth required for printing, and improves the user experience when printing to redirected client printers. We are going to talk about printing in *Chapter 9, Printing in XenApp Environments*.

- **Multi-stream ICA**: Another new feature included in XenApp 6.5 is the option of delivering XenApp ICA traffic over up to four TCP/IP streams. Now instead of prioritizing the entire ICA pipeline over HTTP traffic, we can apply a granular control for QoS (Quality of Service) routing. This feature is extremely useful to optimize network for audio and visual applications.

- **Active Directory group policy integration**: Another great addition on XenApp 6.0. Now we can manage XenApp policies and configure XenApp servers and farm settings using Active Directory Group Policies (GPO). *Chapter 9* is dedicated to XenApp policies and provides extensive information on how to use Group Policy Management Console to manage Citrix policies.

- **Windows Service Isolation for streamed applications**: This new feature, included on XenApp 6.0, allows applications to install Windows services and so that they can be profiled and streamed. This new option increases the number of streamed applications supported. Applications such as Microsoft Office 2010 or Adobe Creative Suite install a windows service. Now we can profile and stream them and other applications, using the new service isolation technology. We can learn about Application Streaming in *Chapter 7, Application Streaming*.

- **Improved support for Windows Portable USB Devices**: This feature allows users to plug in their USB devices such as cameras, scanners, and other devices and access them from their published applications on XenApp 6.0 and XenApp 6.5.

- **Microsoft App-V integration** allows us to manage and deliver both Citrix and Microsoft application delivery from a single point. Also App-V managed applications can now be delivered via Citrix Dazzle. Administrators can now distribute App-V Plug-In to end point devices using Citrix Receiver.

- **Multi-lingual User Interface (MUI)**: MUI is another feature introduced in XenApp 6.0. This feature allows multinational companies to deploy one XenApp server to serve users who need access to their applications in their local language.

- **Citrix Receiver**: The new Citrix Receiver 3.0 for Windows supports several languages and provides support for new Plug-Ins including Single Sign-On, WAN Acceleration, App-V, and more. This new version includes support for Session Pre-Launch, Internet Explorer 9.0, and more. Also, there is a new Receiver for Mac and mobile users. We can use Receiver on the iPhone, iPad, Android, Blackberry, or other devices to access applications hosted on XenApp 6.0 or 6.5. We are going to learn about Citrix Receiver in detail in *Chapter 11*.

- **Citrix Dazzle:** Citrix called Dazzle the first self-service "storefront" for enterprise applications. Dazzle allows corporate employees 24x7 self-service access to the applications they need to work. End users now can subscribe to XenApp applications (including App-V packages) using Dazzle on PC or Mac.

In addition to these major features and enhancements, XenApp 6.5 includes other features like updated Web Interface, Single Sign-on and SmartAuditor enhancements, new 32-bit color support, Windows 7 smart card support, and so on.

XenApp feature overview

This section provides summary descriptions of some of the most popular XenApp features. This section will help new Citrix customers to understand major features on last versions of XenApp (XenApp 4.5, 5.0, 6.0, and 6.5).

- **Access applications from any device, anytime, anywhere**: We can deliver any published Windows application to an extensive variety of user devices and operating system, including Windows, Mac, Linux, UNIX, DOS, Java, and mobile devices such as iPhone, iPad, Blackberry, and Android.
- **Active Directory Federation Services Support**: We can use ADFS to provide business partners access to published applications.
- **Application Gateway**: Citrix provides SSL-proxy, using both hardware (Citrix NetScaler and Citrix Access Gateway) and software (Citrix Secure Gateway) solutions, to allow remote users to access published applications in XenApp, securely.
- **CPU Utilization Management**: This feature prevents users and their processes from utilizing the CPU too much and guarantees a consistent performance level for all users on the XenApp server.
- **Installation Manager**: This feature allows us to remotely install applications to multiple XenApp servers simultaneously.
- **Network Management Console Integration:** XenApp supports SNMP monitoring and integration with third-party network management tools, including: Microsoft System Center Operations Manager (SCOM), Microsoft Operations Manager (MOM), IBM Tivoli, HP OpenView, CA Unicenter.
- **Novell eDirectory and NDS Support:** XenApp now provides support for Novell eDirectory and Domain Services for Windows, allowing XenApp to authenticate Novell users.

- **Power and Capacity Management**: We can create system policies to manage server power consumption. This feature can turn on/off XenApp servers. As users log off and idle resources increase, idle servers are shut down. When users arrive in the morning and they log on to the farm, servers are powered up. Also, we can schedule times for powering on and powering off servers.
- **Single Sign-On**: This feature (formerly known as Password Manager) provides single sign-on access to Windows, Web, and terminal emulator applications. The self-service password reset feature included on Single Sign-On allows users to reset their domain password or unlock their Windows account.
- **SmartAuditor**: Utilize policies to allow us to record the on-screen activity of any user's session, over any type of connection, from any server running XenApp. SmartAuditor records, catalogs, and archives sessions for review.
- **Web Interface**: The Web Interface allows users access to published applications and content on XenApp through a standard Web browser or Citrix Plug-In. Web Interface provides built-in support for two-factor, RADIUS and Smart Card authentication, simple customization through the management console and multilingual support, for the following languages: English, German, Spanish, French, Japanese, Chinese (simplified and traditional), and Korean.

System requirements

The most obvious requirement to install XenApp 6.5 is a 64-bit operating system. No more 32-bit operating systems are supported. XenApp 6.0 was only available for Microsoft Windows Server 2008 R2, and XenApp 6.5 is available for Microsoft Windows Server 2008 R2 and Microsoft Windows Server 2008 R2 Service Pack 1 with two exceptions: Web Server and Core editions. We cannot install XenApp in these two Windows versions.

If we want to deploy XenApp on Microsoft Windows Server 2003 or Microsoft Windows Server 2008 R1 (x86 and x64) we must choose to use XenApp 5.0. Citrix XenApp 6.5 does not support mixed farms. Mixed farms are XenApp farms that contain more than one server operating system version.

Until previous versions Citrix supported XenApp farms that contained different versions of Windows and/or of XenApp. XenApp 6.5 cannot co-exist with any previous versions in the same farm, even with XenApp 6.0. We can have two separated farms and use web interface to provide users access to both farms using one single interface.

We can keep XenApp 5.0 or 6.0 and 6.5 servers together on the same farm for a migration, but this is not recommended (and supported) by Citrix for a long term implementation.

During the wizard-based installation, the XenApp Server Role Manager automatically installs prerequisites for the selected roles. Also, we can choose to install XenApp from command-line installations or using unattended scripts. In that case, we must deploy the prerequisites before starting XenApp role installation.

We can use `ServerManagerCmd.exe` command, PowerShell cmdlets or Microsoft's DISM (Deployment Image Servicing and Management) tool to deploy prerequisites such as IIS or .NET Framework.

The XenApp Server Role Manager deploys the following software, if it is not already installed:

- .NET Framework 3.5 SP1 (this is a prerequisite for the XenApp Server Role Manager and it is deployed automatically when we choose XenApp server role).
- Windows Server Remote Desktop Services role (if we do not have this prerequisite installed, the Server Role Manager installs it and enables the RDP client connection option; we will be asked to restart the server and resume the installation when we log on again).
- Windows Application Server role.
- Microsoft Visual C++ 2005 SP1 Redistributable (x64).
- Microsoft Visual C++ 2008 SP1 Redistributable (x64).

If the server already has the IIS role services installed, the Citrix XML Service IIS Integration component is selected by default in the wizard-based XenApp installation, and the Citrix XML Service and IIS share a port (the default port is 80).

If the IIS role services are not installed, the Citrix XML Service IIS Integration component is not selected by default in the wizard-based installation. In this case, if we select the checkbox, the Server Role Manager installs the following IIS role services. (If we do not install these services, the Citrix XML Service defaults to standalone mode with its own port settings, which we can configure using the XenApp Server Configuration Tool.)

- **Web Server (IIS) | Common HTTP Features | Default Document**. **Selecting** this role automatically selects **Web Server (IIS) | Management Tools | Management Console** (not required for XenApp installation)

[14]

- **Web Server (IIS) | Application Development | ASP.NET**. Choosing this role automatically selects **Web Server (IIS) | Application Development | .NET Extensibility**.
- **Web Server (IIS) | Application Development | ISAPI Extensions**.
- **Web Server (IIS) | Application Development | ISAPI Filters**
- **Web Server (IIS) | Security | Windows Authentication**
- **Web Server (IIS) | Security | Request Filtering**
- **Web Server (IIS) | Management Tools | IIS 6 Management Compatibility** (which includes IIS 6 Metabase Compatibility, IIS 6 WMI Compatibility, IIS 6 Scripting Tools, and IIS 6 Management Console)

Data store databases

The data store database is a repository of persistent XenApp farm information, including server's information, published applications, administrators, and more static data.

The following databases are supported for the data store:

- Microsoft SQL Server 2008 Express SP3 (the new XenApp Server Configuration Tool can install it when creating a new XenApp farm)
- Microsoft SQL Server 2008 R2 Express
- Microsoft SQL Server 2008 R2
- Microsoft SQL Server 2008 SP2 or later
- Microsoft SQL Server 2005 SP4 or later
- Oracle 11g R2 32-bit Enterprise Edition

For more information about supported database versions, see Document ID CTX114501 at `http://support.citrix.com/article/CTX114501`

We are going to use Microsoft SQL Server to configure the Citrix data store in this book because it is the most popular option. We are going to install and configure a SQL Server as data store database in *Chapter 3*.

Citrix AppCenter console

The Citrix AppCenter, formerly known as Citrix Access Management Console in XenApp 4.5 and 5.0 and Citrix Delivery Services Console in XenApp 6.0, is a tool that integrates into the Microsoft Management Console (MMC) and enables us to execute management Using Citrix AppCenter. We can set up and monitor XenApp servers and farms, published resources and sessions, configure policies, and provide users access to applications.

Also we can manage load balancing, troubleshoot alerts, diagnose problems in our farms, view hotfix information for our Citrix products, and track administrative changes.

By default, the console is installed on the same XenApp server where we install the XenApp server role; but we can install and run the console on a separate computer.

If we want to administer multiples farms of the different XenApp versions, we need to install multiple versions of management consoles on the same computer.

To install the Citrix AppCenter console (or the Citrix Delivery Services Console in XenApp 6.0) on a computer, from the XenApp Autorun menu, select **Manually Install Components | Common Components | Management Consoles**. We are going to install the Citrix AppCenter Console in *Chapter 3*.

We can install Citrix AppCenter Console or Citrix Delivery Services Console in the following operating systems:

- Microsoft Windows XP Professional SP3 (32-bit) and SP2 (64-bit) editions
- Microsoft Windows Vista SP2 (Business, Enterprise, and Ultimate versions), 32-bit and 64-bit editions
- Microsoft Windows 7 SP1 (Professional, Enterprise, and Ultimate versions), 32-bit and 64-bit editions
- Microsoft Windows Server 2003 SP2 (Standard, Enterprise, and Datacenter versions), 32-bit and 64-bit editions
- Microsoft Windows Server 2003 R2 (Standard, Enterprise, and Datacenter versions), 32-bit and 64-bit editions
- Microsoft Windows Server 2008 SP2 (Standard, Enterprise, and Datacenter versions), 32-bit and 64-bit editions
- Microsoft Windows Server 2008 R2 and Microsoft Windows Server 2008 R2 SP1 (Standard, Enterprise and Datacenter versions)

Also, the XenApp Server Role Manager deploys the following software, if it is not already installed:

- Microsoft .NET Framework 3.5 SP1
- Microsoft Windows Installer (MSI) 3.0
- Microsoft Windows Group Policy Management Console
- Microsoft Visual C++ 2005 SP1 Redistributable (x64)
- Microsoft Visual C++ 2008 SP1 Redistributable (x64)
- Microsoft Visual C++ 2008 SP1 Redistributable
- Microsoft Visual C++ 2005 SP1 Redistributable
- Microsoft Primary Interoperability Assemblies 2005

> If we install the AppCenter Console on a computer that previously contained the Microsoft Group Policy Management Console (GPMC) and an earlier version of the Delivery Services Console, we may also need to uninstall and reinstall the Citrix XenApp Group Policy Management Experience (x64) program in order to use the GPMC to configure Citrix policies.

License server

The Citrix License Server is a small component required in every XenApp deployment. It can be installed on a XenApp server or shared XenApp infrastructure server (more about this in the next chapter) for testing or smaller environments or on large environments, in one dedicated server.

Citrix licenses are **required** to allow users to connect to the XenApp farm.

We can download and install the latest Citrix License Server or use the version included on the ISO of XenApp 6.5. Minimum license server version number is **11.9**.

We are going to install and configure the Citrix License Server in *Chapter 3*.

Clients

Citrix XenApp Receiver (formerly known as Citrix Plug-In and ICA Client) is a light software client that allows us to access published applications and desktops on XenApp farms and servers from almost any client device, including Windows and Macintosh computers and mobile devices such as Android and Blackberry phones, Apple iPhone and iPad devices.

We need to install the most recent version of any Citrix Receiver to guarantee availability of all features and functionality of XenApp 6.5 to our users. XenApp Receiver version **13.0** is the minimum version recommended to use all features of XenApp 6.5.

To install Citrix Receiver, we need to connect to `www.citrix.com` and then go to **Downloads** option. We need to choose **Citrix Receiver**, and then install the right **Citrix Receiver** for our platform.

Summary

In this chapter, we learned some new features about XenApp 6.5. Specifically:

- Role-based setup wizard
- Session Pre-Launch (Instant App Access)
- Citrix AppCenter management console
- Enhanced scalability and performance
- Citrix Receiver and Citrix Dazzle
- Windows service isolation for streamed applications
- Multi-lingual User Interface
- Citrix HDX technology
- Active Directory Group Policy integration
- PowerShell support

We discussed these new exciting features and in particular the Citrix AppCenter console, the 64-bit support, the new installation process using roles-based setup and more. Also, we enumerated system requirements.

In the next chapter, we are going to discuss how to design a XenApp 6.5 farm and how to implement some of these new features.

2
Designing a XenApp 6.5 Farm

Now that we have learned about the features of XenApp and the new features of XenApp 6.5, it's time for us to start the design of our XenApp 6.5 farm. The most important step before any XenApp deployment is, to understand the features of the product and design the architecture.

In this chapter, we will take a look at the case study that we will use in the book to implement XenApp 6.5: Brick Unit Constructions.

In this chapter we will cover the following topics:

- Learning XenApp Farm terminology and concepts
- Designing a basic XenApp architecture
- Designing a basic Pilot plan
- Creating a list of applications to publish in our XenApp farm
- Reviewing a list of applications and deciding the best method to deliver them

Case study: Brick Unit Constructions

John Charles Empire established a small construction company near Washington DC in 1973. His company started building small homes in the state of Maryland and currently is one of the most important construction companies in the area. In the last 10 years, they increased the revenue, the amount of employees, and construction sites, and now they have several construction sites around the state.

Designing a XenApp 6.5 Farm

Managing the software installed on computers and other devices in the field is a nightmare for the small IT department of the company and their manager, William Empire, son of John Charles.

When William read about the new XenApp 6.5, he thought the product could help the company manage the distributed and complex environment of Brick Unit Constructions.

Farm terminology and concepts

Now is the moment to define the terminology which we are going to use in this book. If you are new in the XenApp world, please pay attention to this section. Except when noted, all following terminology applies to both XenApp 6.0 and XenApp 6.5.

- **Multi-user environment** is when applications are published on servers running Microsoft Remote Desktop Services and/or Citrix XenApp accessed by multiple users simultaneously.
- **XenApp server** is the main software component of the Citrix Application Delivery Infrastructure. The objective of XenApp servers is to deliver applications to user devices.
- **XenApp application servers** are the farm servers that host published applications, desktop, or content.
- **XenApp infrastructure servers** are the farm servers that host services such as a license server or Web Interface. Usually, they do not host published applications.
- **Remote Desktop Services**, formerly known as **Terminal Services**, is one of the components of Microsoft Windows Server 2008 and 2008 R2 that allow a user to access applications and data on a remote computer over a network. We need to install this component (and appropriate licenses) to set up and run XenApp servers. XenApp extends the functionality of Microsoft Remote Desktop Services, adding flexibility, manageability, security, and performance to RDS.

Applications can be made available by installing in the server or streaming to the client. Both XenApp 6.0 and 6.5 supports only Windows 32-bit or Windows 64-bit applications. Running 16-bit applications is *not* supported.

XenApp offers three methods for delivering applications to user devices, servers, and virtual desktops:

- **Server-Side application virtualization**: Applications run on the XenApp servers. XenApp shows the application interface on the user device or client, and transmits user actions from the device, such as keystrokes and mouse actions, back to the application.
- **Client-Side application virtualization**: XenApp streams applications on demand to the user device from the XenApp farm and runs the application on the user device.
- **VM hosted application virtualization**: Problematic applications or those requiring specific operating systems run inside a desktop on the XenApp server. XenApp shows the application interface on the user device or client, and transmits user actions from the device, such as keystrokes and mouse actions, back to the application. The application runs a XenDesktop or XenApp Server.

XenApp server farm is a logical collection or group of XenApp servers that can be managed as a single entity. Usually Citrix define three types of farms:

- **Design validation farm**: Design validation farm is set up in a laboratory, typically as the design or blueprint for the production farm. Usually the preferred method to build a design validation farm today is using virtual machines.
- **Pilot farm**: Pilot farm is a preproduction farm used to test a farm design and applications before deploying the farm across the company. The pilot must include users from the entire organization and role. These users should access the farm for their everyday needs.
- **Production farm**: Production farm is in regular use and accessed by all users in the organization.

Farm architecture defines the plan for the design of the server farm and zones based on current requirements and considers future expansion plans. Farm architecture requires a strong understanding of the network topology, scalability, failover, and geographic location of the sites and users in the company.

- **Zones**: Zones are used to control the aggregation and replication of data in the farm. A farm should be divided into zones based upon the network topology, where major geographic regions are assigned to separate zones. Each zone elects a data collector, which aggregates dynamic data from the servers in its zone and replicates the data to the data collectors in the other zones. Citrix recommends to create no more than 25 Zones.

- **Worker Group**: A Worker Group is a new feature introduced on XenApp 6.0, also available on XenApp 6.5. It is a collection of XenApp servers in the same farm. Worker Groups allow a set of similar servers to be grouped together and managed as one. Worker groups are closely related to the concept of application silos (silos usually are servers dedicated to run critical or resource intensive applications). All servers in the Worker Group share the same list of published applications and identical XenApp server settings.

- **Server roles**: XenApp 6.5 introduces new server roles: session-host (also known as session-only) and session-host and controller (also known as controller) roles and the ability to create either controller or session-host only servers. In previous versions of XenApp, including version 6.0, all servers were having/must have both roles and we can't split them.

    When we choose the controller mode, servers act like previous versions of XenApp: they can host sessions, the XML services, provide application enumeration, force data collector elections, and so on.

    On another hand, running XenApp servers in session-host mode improves start-up and join performance, which is especially recommended for servers running in different zones, branch office, or remote sites. This is because servers running in Session-only mode require less read/writes to the Data store during a join or sync process, which reduces bandwidth and resource usage on the Data store server. We are going to continue learning about server roles in the next chapter.

- **Data Collector**: Data Collector server stores information about server load and published applications inside a zone and acts as a gateway between Data Collector servers in other zones. In large XenApp server farm environments, it is a good idea to have a primary dedicated data collector server and backup data collector. Also it is recommended to restrict the primary data collector from delivering applications. A dedicated Data Collector improves load balancing decisions and reduces session logon time. We can use a small virtual machine or small server for the dedicated data collector role. XenApp 6.5 introduces the controller role (see above) and when designing our farm, data collectors must be set always as controller role.

User device is where the client software is installed to access data anywhere:

- **Citrix Receiver**: Citrix Receiver is the first universal client for IT service and netbooks (PC or Mac).With Citrix Receiver installed on a device, IT can deliver applications and desktops as an on-demand service with no need to manage, own or care about the physical device or its location. Citrix Receiver is a lightweight software client with an extensible browser-like "Plug-In" architecture. Citrix Receiver was formerly known as Citrix ICA Client.

- **Citrix Dazzle and the Self-service storefront**: Citrix Dazzle, the self-service enterprise application storefront, offers a personal and easy-to-use interface for subscribing to applications. Administrators can distribute the Dazzle plugin using Citrix Receiver, and users can choose their published application subscriptions. Dazzle also downloads and pre-caches streamed applications. The self-service storefront is available for both Windows and Mac users.
- **Merchandising Server** provides easy management, setup and distribution of Citrix Receiver and related plugins and updates. Users simply point any browser to the setup site included with Merchandising Server and within two clicks the setup process starts. Merchandising Server software is **delivered as a virtual appliance for Citrix XenServer or VMware**.

Infrastructure servers

Infrastructure servers are farm servers that host services such as a license server or web interface. Usually, they do not host published applications.

XenApp farms have two types of infrastructure servers:

- **Virtualization infrastructure** consists of the XenApp servers that deliver virtualized applications and VM hosted applications, and roles that support sessions and administration, such as the data store, data collector, Citrix XML broker, Citrix License Server, Configuration Logging database (optional), Load Testing Services database (optional), and Service Monitoring agents, and so on.
- **Access Infrastructure** consists of roles such as the Web Interface, Secure Gateway (optional), and Access Gateway (optional) that provide access to users.

In small deployments, we can group one or more roles together. In large deployments, we can provide services on one or multiple dedicated servers.

Virtualization infrastructure

Virtualization infrastructure represents a series of servers that control and monitor application environments.

Now, we will see different types of infrastructure servers:

- **Citrix Licensing**: A Citrix License Server is *required* for all XenApp deployments. Install the license server on either a shared or standalone server, depending on our farm's size. After we install the license server, we need to download the appropriate license files from the `MyCitrix.com` website and install them in the license server. We can share a license server with multiple Citrix products. We are going to install and configure a license server in the next chapter.

- **Data Store database**: Also known as IMA Data store, is a repository of persistent farm information, including server's information, published applications, administrators, printers, and so on. We can host the Data Store database on a SQL Server Express database running on one of our XenApp servers in a small or test farm, or use a dedicated SQL Server or an Oracle database server in medium to large farms. If XenApp servers are running in multiples zones, we need to host the Data store in the largest site. We are going to install and configure a Data Store in the next chapter.

- **Citrix XML Broker** acts as an intermediary between the Web Interface and other servers in the farm. When a user logs in into the Web Interface, the XML Broker receives the user's credentials from the Web Interface and queries the server farm for a list of published applications that the user has permission to access. The XML Broker obtains this application set from the IMA (Independent Management Architecture) system and returns it to the Web Interface.

- **Citrix XML Service**: The XML Broker is a component of the Citrix XML Service. By default, the XML Service is installed on every server during XenApp setup. However, only the XML Service on the server specified in the Web Interface acts as the broker. In a small farm, the XML Broker runs on a server with multiple infrastructure functions. In a large farm, the XML Broker might be configured on one or more dedicated servers. Configuring a dedicated XML server is a simple task, we need to set up a dedicated XenApp server without any published applications.

- **Single Sign-on** (**optional**): Single Sign-On provides password management for published applications. Single Sign-on can use Active Directory or a NTFS share to store password information. Single Sign-on was formerly known as **Password Manager** and requires a Platinum license. Installation and configuration of Single Sign-on is beyond the scope of this book.

- **Service Monitoring (optional)** is based on **Citrix Edgesight** and enables the administrator to collect, monitor, and report server resource metrics to estimate servers required to deploy a XenApp farm or to analyze the load of production servers. This feature requires a Platinum license. Installation and configuration of Edgesight is beyond the scope of this book.

- **Provisioning Services (optional)** assist administrators to manage the entire XenApp farm of application hosting servers, both physical and virtual, using one or multiple standardized server image(s). PVS can rollback to a previous working image in the time it takes to reboot. This feature requires a Platinum license. Installation and configuration of Provisioning Services is beyond the scope of this book.

- **SmartAuditor (optional)** allows administrator to record the onscreen activity of any user's session, over any type of connection, from any server running XenApp. SmartAuditor uses policies to record, catalog, and archive sessions for retrieval and playback. This feature requires a Platinum license. Installation and configuration of SmartAuditor is beyond the scope of this book.

- **Power and Capacity Management (optional)** enables administrators to reduce power consumption and manage server capacity by dynamically scaling the number of online servers or powering on/off servers based on specific times. This feature requires a Platinum license. Installation and configuration of Power and Capacity Management is out the scope of this book.

Access Infrastructure

Access Infrastructure represents a series of servers deployed within the local network or the DMZ (Demilitarized Zone) to provide access to different types of users (local or remote) to resources published on XenApp servers.

XenApp farms have three types of access infrastructure servers:

- **Web Interface** provides users access to resources published on one or multiple XenApp farms through a standard Web browser or through the Citrix Receiver (formerly known as Citrix Online Plug-I). The new Citrix CloudGateway released in January 2012 is going to replace Web Interface on upcoming versions of XenApp. Web Interface end of life is planned for 2015.

- **Access Gateway (optional)** is a universal SSL VPN appliance that can be used to secure client connections to XenApp farms and provide secure access to other internal network resources. XenApp Platinum Edition licenses include a universal Access Gateway license, which can be used with any Access Gateway edition. The Access Gateway appliance, also known as **NetScaler** must be purchased separately.

- **Secure Gateway (optional)** assists administrators to secure access to enterprise network computers running XenApp and provides a secure Internet gateway between XenApp farms and client devices. The Secure Gateway transparently encrypts and authenticates all user connections to help protect against data tampering and theft. All data traversing the Internet between a remote workstation and the Secure Gateway is encrypted using the SSL (Secure Sockets Layer) or TLS (Transport Layer Security) protocol. The Secure Gateway is an application that runs as a service on a server that usually is deployed in the DMZ. The free Access Gateway VPX available as Virtual Machine is the natural replacement for Secure Gateway.

Designing a basic XenApp architecture

Let's learn more about Brick Unit Constructions. The HQ of the company is located near Frederick in Maryland. The company had around 120 users working there. Currently, they have 17 sites under construction around the state located in a 150 mile radius of HQ. Each of these sites has 10 to 25 computers, accessing applications installed on the site server or in each user computer. So we have around 400 users between HQ and the construction sites. Almost 20 percent of these users utilize laptops, work on a few projects at the same time, and travel between sites. All these sites are connected in a MPLS network between HQ and sites using T1 links.

Usually these projects are short-term, between six months to two years. When the project is completed, IT department needs to take a full back up of every machine and the server and reassign them to a new project.

None of these sites has its own IT personnel, so the management of these servers and computers (backups, install new applications, printers, and so on) is centralized from HQ, making the administration very complicated.

Users with laptops are having issues with printers and access to files located on different servers. William wants to resolve these issues moving all data in remote file servers to a centralized file server on a NAS (Network Attached Storage) device, and migrate all printer queues located on remote sites to a new printer server on HQ. The migration of printers will help him to clean up print server drivers and check the compatibility of current printers with XenApp.

The other issue these users are having is related to an in-house developed financial application installed on construction site servers. Users must have these applications installed multiple times (one per site).

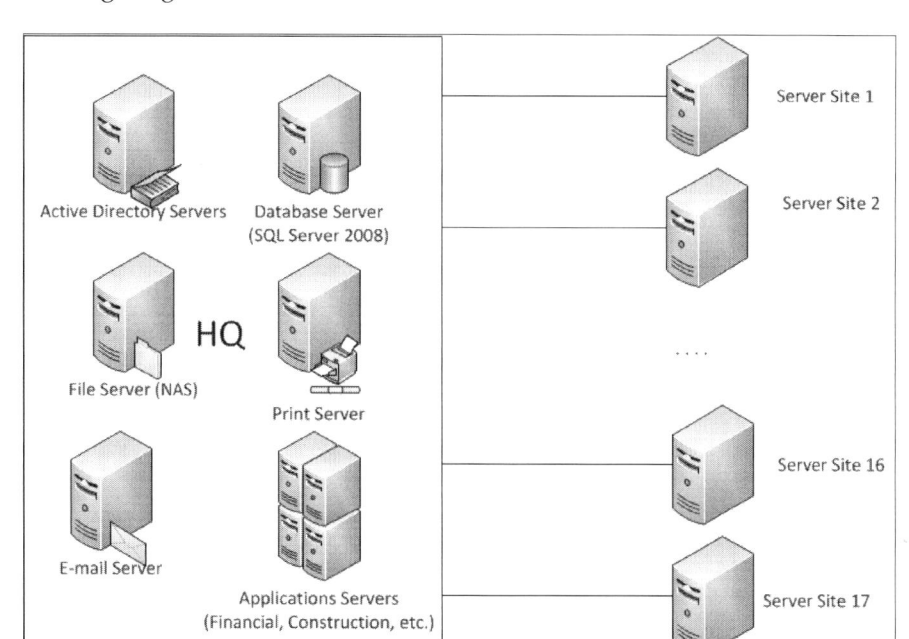

The following diagram is the Brick Unit Construction's current infrastructure:

William is concerned about the following:

- Deciding whether he wants to run XenApp on virtual machines or physical servers
- Budget: The cost of all Remote Desktop Services (Terminal Server) and Citrix licenses will require a large expenditure
- Virtual machines will provide a lot of benefits, but will require a large investment in a SAN (Storage Area Network), the increase of memory RAM of existing servers and the cost of the virtualization server software

William's idea is to move all applications installed on a client's machine or servers in remote sites to a XenApp farm, migrate all data in these sites to the HQ file and print servers, remove servers from field, and reuse them (these servers are pretty new) to build more XenApp servers or virtualization hosts to run XenApp on virtual machines.

Moving all applications to XenApp will help IT to reduce the license cost of applications and simplify the deployment of new versions and manage applications centrally.

Centralizing all data in a NAS file server will help to reduce backup cost (hardware and software) and simplify administration. Also, it will reduce the time required to restore information.

Currently, the most popular option to implement XenApp 6.5 is using virtual machines and William decided to use it for the deployment of Brick Unit's farm. We are going to learn how to implement XenApp on virtualized environments in *Chapter 14, Virtualizing XenApp Farms*.

The pilot plan

William wants to build a very simple infrastructure to test the product with some users and later add more features (and servers) to the deployment.

Hence, he creates a basic task list to deploy **the XenApp design validation farm**:

1. Design Active Directory integration.
2. Build a small test farm in the lab with three servers to test XenApp and applications and get some experience with the product.
3. Create a list of applications to publish in the XenApp farm.
4. Test the list of applications and decide the best method to deliver them.

If we are satisfied with the results, the next step will be to create a XenApp pilot farm or extend our XenApp design validation farm, and provide some users access to the farm. This will be discussed in more detail in the next chapter. However, a few tasks are described as follows:

- Estimate the amount of XenApp applications Servers: In this step we need to calculate the number of XenApp application servers required. We can obtain an estimate based on the amount of memory and CPU required per user when they are executing the applications. Then we can add extra servers based on how critical these applications are and the future growth of the company. The pilot phase will confirm if these estimations are realistic or not.

- Are we going to enable Instant App Access (also known as Session Pre-Launch) on our XenApp farm? Introduced in XenApp 6.5, the new feature improves launch time, BUT also requires more hardware resources because to improve launch times, XenApp creates pre-launch on advance and keeps closed sessions open. This session will require some testing to figure out the appropriate settings for our environment.

- Determine the number of XenApp infrastructure servers we need for our farm. Based on the size of the farm (and our budget) we need to estimate how many XenApp infrastructure servers we need. One Web Interface server is enough or do we need at least two? Are we going to use one (or more) dedicated Data Collectors?

- Define the installation processes: In this step we need to decide the method to build the XenApp servers. Are we going to use Microsoft WDS (Windows Deployment Services), unattended scripts, or a manual process to install the operating system in physical servers? Or are we going to use virtual machines and just clone the template?

- Build and test XenApp applications servers: In this step we are going to choose how to build the application servers. Are we going to use virtual machines and deploy a template with all applications? Clone and deploy images to physical servers with all applications installed? Use Active Directory GPOs or script to install applications? Are we going to set all our XenApp servers as session-only to improve performance or set some of them as controller mode to use as backup just in case our main controller gets down?

- Design, build, and test XenApp infrastructure servers: Here we need to decide the appropriate way to build infrastructure servers. Are we going to build these servers as virtual machines or use physical servers? Can some infrastructure servers run small or old servers? Can we reuse any existing servers?

- Create and test a preproduction pilot farm based on our farm design. In this phase, after we have our servers ready, a small amount of users, usually from the IT department test applications on XenApp servers.

- Select and make a list of pilot users from different business groups. In this step, managers from every area of the company will select a few users from each department to test the farm and applications.

- Provide access to pilot users to the pilot farm. In this phase, we need to create Active Directory groups and assign the pilot users selected in the previous phase to these groups. After that, we will assign these groups to published applications and users can start the pilot phase.

- Release the server to production. In this final phase, after we successfully test the farm for several weeks or months, and all errors and issues are resolved, we can provide access to all users in the organization to the new farm.

Designing Active Directory integration

The Active Directory design is very important for a successful XenApp implementation and now in XenApp 6.5 (and 6.0) more than ever because XenApp policies and farm and servers settings have been added to Active Directory group policies.

Following is a check list of the basic recommendations:

- Put all XenApp servers in their own AD OUs (Organizational Units), this will help us easily manage servers using Worker Groups.
- If we use dedicated servers for some applications (silos), we need to create an OU for each of them, and keep servers organized in their own OUs.
- All XenApp servers must reside in the same domain.
- The server farm needs to be in a single Active Directory forest. If our XenApp farm has servers in more than one forest, users cannot log on using UPNs (user principal names). UPN logons use the format *username@UPN*.

XenApp supports Active Directory Federated Services (ADFS) when used with the Citrix Web Interface. If we provide access to published applications to a business partner, ADFS will provide a great alternative to creating multiple new user accounts on our AD domain.

Building a small test farm

Installing a small test farm is the first step to gain some experience with the product.

We have two options:

- Build a single server test farm. If we want to learn about XenApp 6.5 or deploying a very small internal farm for a few users, we can install all these components in a single server. The following is a list of steps required to build a single server small test farm:
    - Install Windows Server 2008 R2 SP1 on the server. Requirements are already mentioned in *Chapter 1*, *Getting Started with XenApp 6.5*.
    - Join the server to the Active Directory domain. Although we can run XenApp on a workgroup, I don't recommend it.
    - Follow the instructions in *Chapter 3*, *Installing XenApp 6.5*, to configure Windows components such as Windows Firewall and IE ESC (Enhanced Security Configuration).

- Using instructions in *Chapter 3, Installing XenApp 6.5*, to install and configure these components on the server: Web Interface, License Server, and XenApp.
- When XenApp setup asks about the database, we need to choose New Database. This option will install SQL Server 2008 Express Edition on the same server.
- After the setup is completed and server rebooted, we need to download and install a XenApp Evaluation licenses from www.citrix.com. Instructions are provided in *Chapter 3, Installing XenApp 6.5*.
- Optionally we can set up Remote Desktop license. This step is not required if we are going to use this test environment for less than 120 days.

- Build a multiple server test farm. If we are planning a pilot farm for a medium or large company, we would probably want to build a few XenApp servers, usually a separate Web Interface server (or two if we want some redundancy), and install the License server on one of the Web Interface Server. Also, we probably want to use a separate SQL Server. This scenario is covered in detail in *Chapter 3, Installing XenApp 6.5*.

William wants to test basic features of XenApp 6.5. Later, he can add more infrastructure servers for other roles or increase redundancy.

The following diagram shows a graphic of the components of a small XenApp farm:

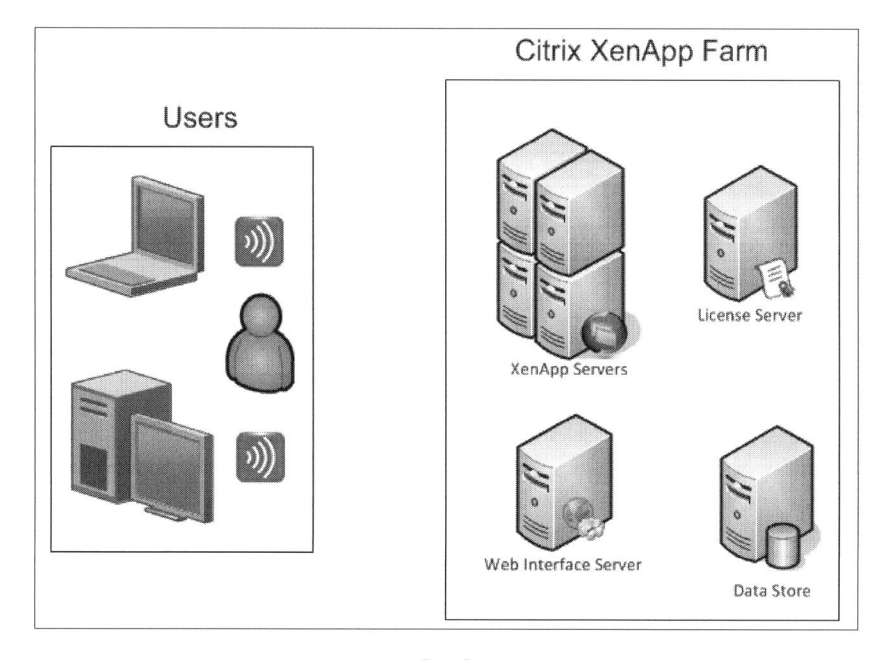

Designing a XenApp 6.5 Farm

There are three roles he will use in the test farm: Citrix XenApp, Citrix Web Interface, and Citrix License Server.

William will reuse two existing servers with two CPUs (Quad Core) and 16 GB RAM, and at least two hard drives with RAID 1 (more about disk configuration is discussed in the next chapter) for XenApp testing servers.

Here he is facing two options:

- Build test servers on physical servers
- Use these two servers to deploy hypervisors and create virtual machines

William chooses to deploy XenApp using my favorite option for test environments: download a free hypervisor like Citrix XenServer, VMware ESXi, or Microsoft Hyper-V Server and create virtual machines. Using virtual machines to build a lab provides a lot of benefits, including the ability to take snapshots and roll back changes, very useful to the learning process, faster server delivery, and more. We are going to talk about running XenApp on virtual machines in *Chapter 14, Virtualizing XenApp Farms*.

As Brick Unit Construction had one existing SQL Server 2008 dedicated server, William will create the Citrix data store on it.

This is the new proposed architecture of infrastructure servers at Brick Unit Construction:

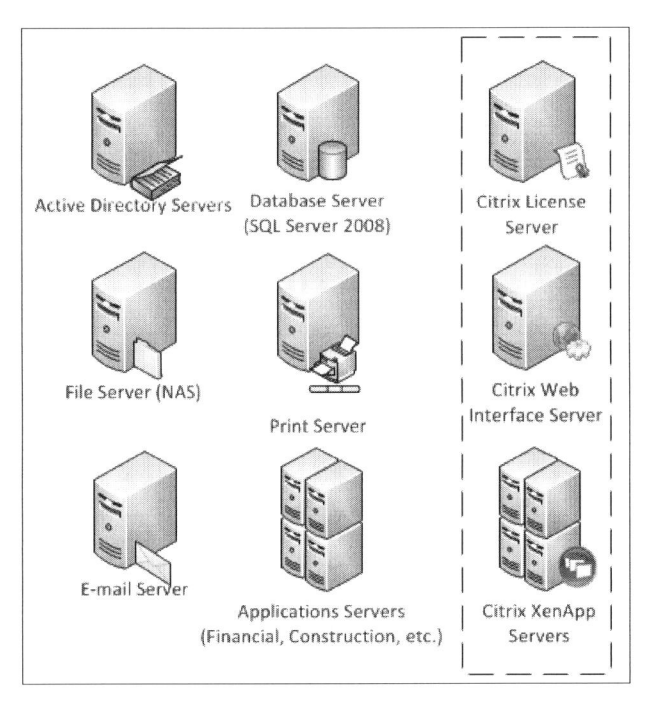

Creating a list of applications to publish in our XenApp farm

The first step to deploy applications on a multi-user environment is to decide which applications we want to run on XenApp.

XenApp is especially useful when we have applications that are old and infrequently used, difficult to manage, or frequently updated.

The following are some parameters we can use to select applications we want to move to our XenApp 6.5 farm:

- Citrix XenApp lets us efficiently deploy and maintain software in an enterprise environment. We can easily deploy applications from a central location (our datacenter). As we install the programs on the XenApp server and not on the client computer, programs are easier to upgrade and to maintain.
- Testing new versions of a new application is easy and we can run multiple versions of the same application at the same time, using multiple servers or streaming the application to the client. For example, we can run Office 2007 and Office 2010 or both 32-bit and 64-bit versions of Microsoft Office 2010 at the same time.
- Are we going to provide remote access to applications published on XenApp in the near future? Remote users can access programs that are running on XenApp farm from devices such as home computers, kiosks, mobile devices, and operating systems other than Windows, such as MAC and Linux.
- Applications accessing remote databases or data stores can improve its performance and reduce network utilization, moving the application from branch offices or remote sites to our datacentre.
- Reducing license expenses is the other advantage that we will have when we move applications to a XenApp farm. We can limit the amount of sessions of a specific application.

William decided to move all Microsoft Office suite applications in use in the company (Microsoft Word, Microsoft Excel, Microsoft Outlook, Microsoft PowerPoint, Microsoft Project, and Microsoft Visio) to the XenApp farm. This decision will reduce the time the IT department spends updating Office in remote machines and simplify the license management of Microsoft Project and Microsoft Visio.

Brick Unit Constructions doesn't have enough licenses of Microsoft Project and Microsoft Visio for all employees, and usually the change of roles of several users makes license management complicated and deployment of these applications slow. The creation of the Active Directory group for all project managers will simplify the Microsoft Project and Microsoft Visio management and provide instant access for users of these applications.

Moving the Microsoft Office suite to XenApp will simplify printing and file storage and management, too.

The next application William picks to move to XenApp is the financial application used in each construction site. This is an in-house application known internally as **BrickFin**. This application is very difficult to deploy because it requires the company to install a client in every computer and then manually set up multiple connections to access financial information for the site.

Brick Unit Constructions uses another in-house application for architects and engineers. This is an offline application used in the construction site in laptops, to take notes and photos and document the project. This application is called **BrickDocProject**.

Finally, the company has two more applications; one for time tracking called **BrickTime** and another used for expenses tracking called **BrickExpenses** used for all users. These applications are web applications, so publishing them in the farm is pretty easy.

Testing the list of applications

The next step is to test the list of applications and decide the best method to deliver them.

Most Windows 32-bit programs will work on the 64-bit version of Windows like Windows Server 2008 R2. One of the exceptions is antivirus programs. They use 32-bit kernel-mode device drivers and 32-bit drivers don't run on 64-bit operating systems.

The same applies to any device driver. Printers will require 64-bit print drivers. We will talk later about printing on a XenApp 6.5 environment in *Chapter 9, Printing in XenApp Environments*.

The WOW64 (known as **Windows 32-bit** on **Windows** 64-bit) subsystem allows 32-bit Windows-based applications to run flawlessly on 64-bit Windows operating systems.

Some 32-bit programs may run slower on Windows Server 2008 R2 than they would on 32-bit versions of Windows Server 2003/2008.

The WOW64 subsystem isolates 32-bit binaries from 64-bit binaries by redirecting registry and file system calls. The WOW64 subsystem isolates the binaries to prevent a 32-bit binary from accidentally accessing data from a 64-bit binary. For example, a 32-bit binary that runs a `.DLL` file from the `%systemroot%\System32` folder might accidentally try to access a 64-bit `.DLL` file that is not compatible with the 32-bit binary. To prevent this, the WOW64 subsystem redirects the access from the `%systemroot%\System32` folder to the `%systemroot%\SysWOW64` folder. This redirection prevents compatibility errors because it requires the `.DLL` file to be specifically designed to work with 32-bit programs.

Running 32-bit applications on a 64-bit operating system can cause overload because WOW64 creates a 32-bit environment for any application to load 32-bit DLLs and isolate it from 64-bit applications.

> For more information about this topic, see the "Running 32-bit Applications" in the 64-Bit Windows section of the Microsoft Platform SDK documentation.
> http://msdn2.microsoft.com/en-us/library/aa384249.aspx

One of the best practices for installing applications is to install related applications or applications that have dependencies on other local applications on the same XenApp servers.

If the application has compatibility issues or excessive use of resources that might affect other programs on the same server, deploy it on silo servers using **Worker Groups**.

Before installing any application on a Remote Desktop Server (Terminal Server) or XenApp server, is a good idea to check the vendor website to ensure the application can run on multi-user environment. If the application has issues, vendors usually provide compatibility scripts or fixes. If the application is not supported on multi-user environment, we must try to stream the application to the client.

Websites that use old ActiveX controls in Microsoft Internet Explorer must run on the 32-bit version of Microsoft Internet Explorer.

After testing, if any of these solutions do not work, we might need to try finding and fixing the root cause of the issue.

To identify root application issues, we need to consider using free tools such as the Microsoft Application Compatibility Toolkit (ACT) or Microsoft Sysinternals tools such as Process Monitor. Also we can buy Citrix AppDNA.

Sysinternals tools are available at `http://technet.microsoft.com/sysinternals`

Examples of common issues include the following:

- Custom or in-house applications developed with hardcoded paths in the registry.
- Applications that use the computer name or the IP address as credential or for identification purposes.
- `.INI` files that contain hardcoded file path names, database connection settings, and read/write file.
- 32-bit applications that use 16-bit DLLs.

Microsoft Office applications

The Microsoft Office suite is one of the most popular products delivered in XenApp environments. Here we have some advice to deliver them successfully:

- If we have an application that requires Microsoft Excel to export results, install them on the same server.
- Install all Microsoft Office applications (Microsoft Office, Microsoft Project, Microsoft Visio, and so on) on the same server. Microsoft Office shares a lot of components between different products. Avoid mixing different versions of Microsoft Office products on the same server (for example Office 2003 and Visio 2007 on the same server).
- If you need to deliver multiple versions of Office products (Office 2003, Office 2007, and Office 2010) at the same time and you can't use a dedicated server for each one, use application stream.
- Office 2010 is the first edition of the suite released on both native 32-bit and 64-bit versions. Curiously, Microsoft recommends installing the 32-bit version instead of the 64-bit version. Installing 32-bit Office 2010 applications that run on 64-bit operating systems allow for better compatibility with Active X controls, COM add-ins, and VBA code.

- Some Microsoft Office 2010 compatibility issues on the native 64-bit version:
    - **Microsoft Access MDE/ADE/ACCDE** files created on the 32-bit version cannot run on 64-bit editions of Office 2010 and vice versa.
    - **ActiveX controls and COM DLLs add-ins** that were written for 32-bit Office will not work in a 64-bit version. The workaround for resolving this issue is to obtain 64-bit compatible controls and add-ins or to install Office 2010 32-bit (WOW).
    - **Inserting an object** into an Office 2010 application document might fail, if we try to insert a 32-bit object in a 64-bit Office 2010 application document.
    - **Visual Basic for Applications (VBA)** code that uses the Declare statement to access the Windows Application Programming Interface (API) or other DLL entry points will see differences between 32-bit and 64-bit versions.

Java

Windows Server 2008 R2 comes with both 32-bit and 64-bit Internet Explorer browsers. 32-bit IE comes as a default. There are different versions of Java software available for download depending on whether you are using 32-bit or 64-bit IE browsers.

If we are using:

- 32-bit Internet Explorer (IE), we need to download and install 32-bit Java.
- 64-bit IE, we need to download and install 64-bit Java.
- Both 32-bit and 64-bit IE, we need to download and install both 32-bit and 64-bit Java versions.

William and his team installed and tested all selected applications, and took the following decision to deliver them:

- Microsoft Office suite: They will deploy Office 2010 64-bit. Brick Unit Construction talked with several users and reviewed documents and they found users don't have any VBA code or 32-bit add-ins and nobody uses Microsoft Access. Using the native 64-bit version will reduce the amount of resources used on XenApp servers.
- BrickFin: Installing the application in a XenApp server and creating multiple icons (one for each site) will simplify access to this application. This application requires Excel to export financial results to Excel, so IT will deploy it on the same XenApp server as Microsoft Office.

- BrickDocProject: IT decided to stream it to client computer because it requires offline access.
- Web applications: William and his team tested these two web applications and found one of them used to manage expenses using an old 32-bit ActiveX so they need to run it on Internet Explorer 32-bit version. This web application uses lots of resources on the XenApp server because users sometimes left it open and updated the time several times a day. That might affect other programs on the same XenApp server, so they think they will deploy it on silo servers.

Summary

In this chapter, we learned how to design a Citrix XenApp 6.5 (and 6.0) farm and discovered Brick Unit Construction. Specially:

- Common XenApp farm terminology and concepts used in the Citrix world and some new names used on XenApp 6.5
- Designing a Basic XenApp Architecture
- Writing a simple pilot plan
- Designing Active Directory integration
- Building a small test farm, used as a design validation farm
- Creating a list of applications to publish on the new farm
- Testing the list of applications and deciding the best method to deliver them

Designing and building a basic XenApp 6.5 farm, is the first step for a successful deployment of the product. Installing and testing applications will help us understand the features of the products and gain experience with them.

In the next chapter, we will leave words aside and we will start building our first XenApp 6.5 servers!!!

3
Installing XenApp 6.5

In the last chapter, we learned about common Citrix farm terminologies, concepts, and discovered our case study, Brick Unit Construction. We discussed how to design a simple Citrix XenApp 6.5 farm and wrote a simple pilot plan. Now, we are going to install our first XenApp 6.5 servers.

Installing and configuring XenApp 6.5

Now, let's take a look at the lab created by William to build the pilot farm at Brick Unit Construction, to test XenApp 6.5. Except where noted, most of these steps also can be applied to XenApp 6.0. He had two existing servers, an Active Directory domain controller, and a database server running on SQL Server 2008. He will deploy three new XenApp servers.

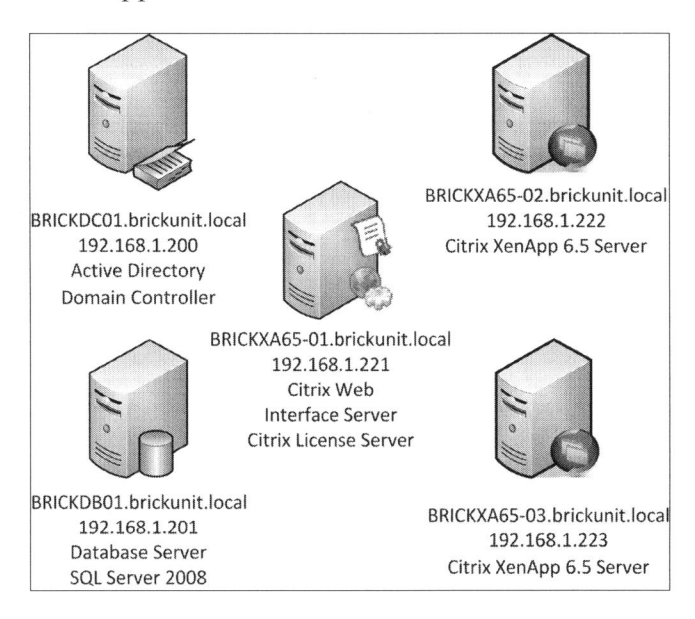

BRICKDC01.brickunit.local
192.168.1.200
Active Directory
Domain Controller

BRICKXA65-02.brickunit.local
192.168.1.222
Citrix XenApp 6.5 Server

BRICKXA65-01.brickunit.local
192.168.1.221
Citrix Web Interface Server
Citrix License Server

BRICKDB01.brickunit.local
192.168.1.201
Database Server
SQL Server 2008

BRICKXA65-03.brickunit.local
192.168.1.223
Citrix XenApp 6.5 Server

Installing XenApp 6.5

He will deploy Citrix Web Interface and Citrix License Server on one of the servers called BRICKXA65-01. Later, he will install Citrix XenApp 6.5 on servers BRICKXA65-02 and BRICKXA65-03.

The following is his plan to deploy the pilot farm:

1. Install Windows Server 2008 R2 SP1 on all servers. Windows Server 2008 R2 or Windows Server 2008 R2 SP1 is required for all XenApp Applications servers, but he can use existing Windows Server 2008 R1 32-bit or 64-bit for database server, license server, and Web Interface servers.
2. Join servers to the Active Directory domain.
3. Configure Windows components (Windows Firewall and IE ESC).
4. Install Citrix Licensing Server and Citrix Web Interface on BRICKXA65-01.
5. Configure Citrix Licensing Server.
6. Install Citrix Licenses.
7. Install and configure XenApp 6.5 on BRICKXA65-02 using Wizard-Based Server Role Manager (first server of the farm).
8. Install and configure XenApp 6.5 on BRICKXA65-03.
9. Configure Citrix Web Interface.
10. Configure Remote Desktop Licensing (formerly known as Terminal Server Licensing).

Configuring Windows components

Before installing XenApp 6.5, he had two components that depend on the environment that he probably wants to configure:

- Windows Firewall
- IE ESC (Enhanced Security Configuration)

In previous versions of XenApp, he needed to install Remote Desktop Services (formerly known as Terminal Server) before the XenApp setup. In XenApp 6.5 (and 6.0), the setup process will install Remote Desktop Services automatically.

Configuring Windows Firewall

He had multiple options to configure Windows Firewall:

- **Configure Windows Firewall using Active Directory Group Policies (GPO)**.

    Open **Group Policy Management Editor** and expand **Computer Configuration | Policies | Administrative templates | Network | Network Connections | Windows Firewall | Domain Profile**. Modify appropriate settings.

- **Disable Windows Firewall**.

    Open command prompt and type:

    `Netsh advfirewall set allprofiles state off`

    Also, he can disable Windows Firewall from Windows interface. Open **Control Panel** and choose **Windows Firewall**.

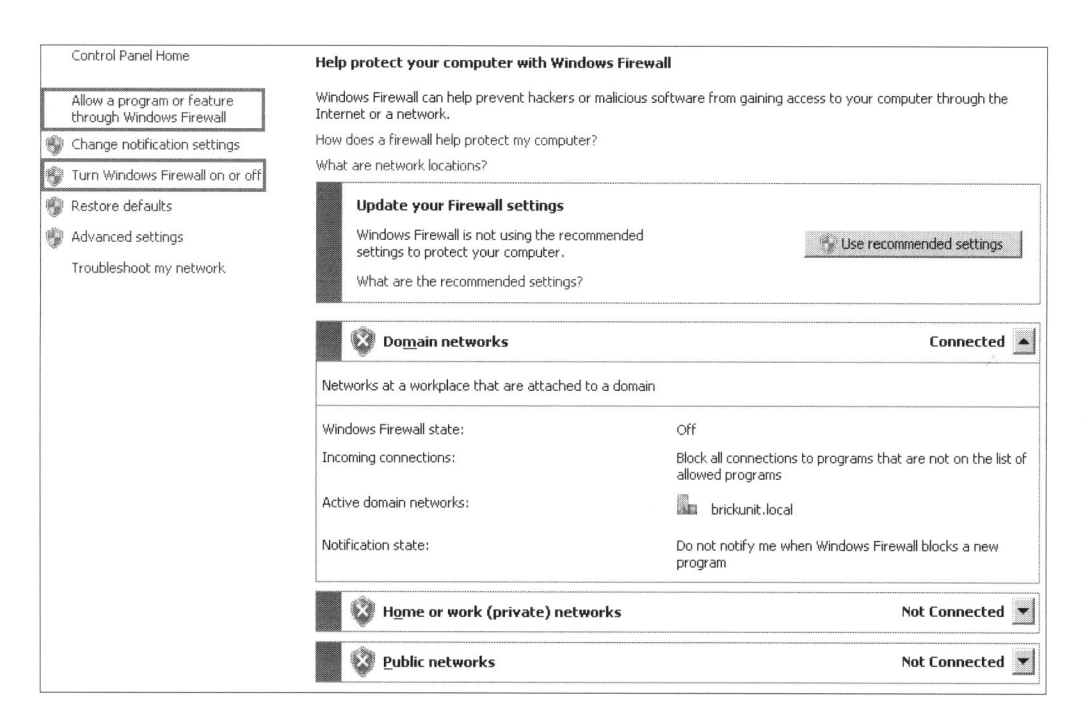

Installing XenApp 6.5

Select **Turn Windows Firewall on or off** option and then select **Turn off Windows Firewall (not recommended)** for all profiles.

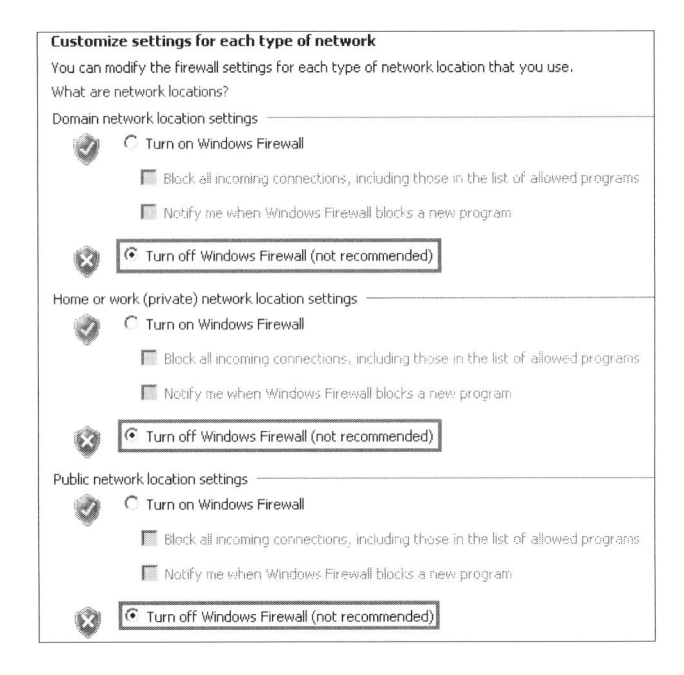

- **Configure Windows Firewall for XenApp**:

    In order to keep Windows Firewall running after installation of XenApp 6.5, he needs to configure XenApp ports. Open **Control Panel** and select **Windows Firewall**. In the **Windows Firewall** main page, click on **Allow a program or feature through Windows Firewall** option and verify that Citrix ports checkboxes for all profiles are enabled.

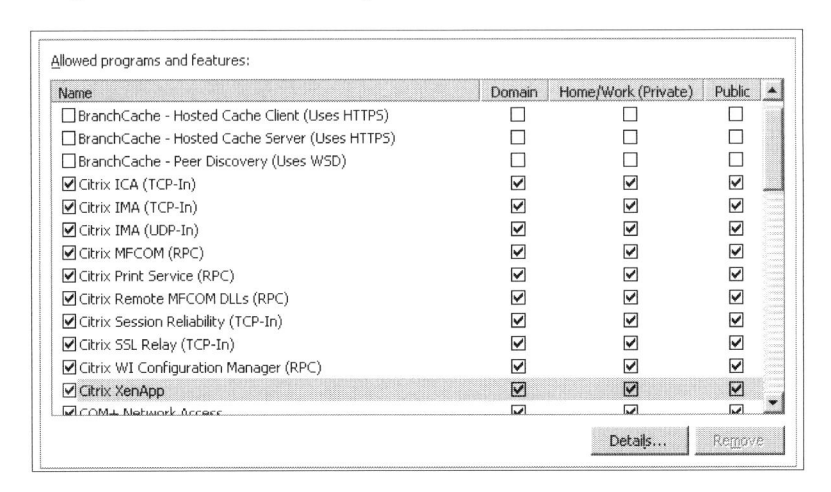

Chapter 3

Configure IE ESC (Enhanced Security Configuration)

Microsoft recommends as a best security practice, administrators must have limited access to the Internet to avoid the possibility of an attack on the server by malicious websites. This is a good practice for critical servers like domain controllers or databases servers, but impractical for Terminal Servers and XenApp servers.

To disable IE ESC, open **Server Manager** (**Start button | All Programs | Administrative Tools | Server Manager**) and click on **Configure IE ESC**.

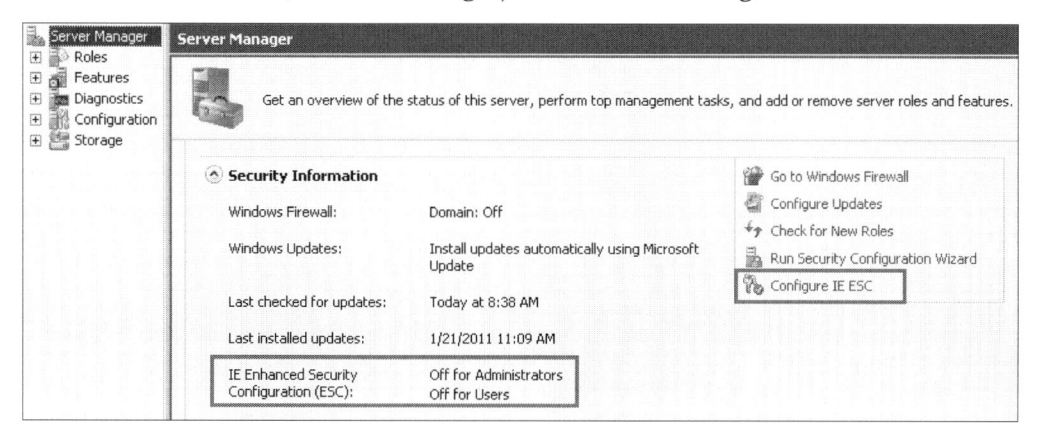

Select **Off** for both **Administrators** and **Users**, and click on the **OK** button.

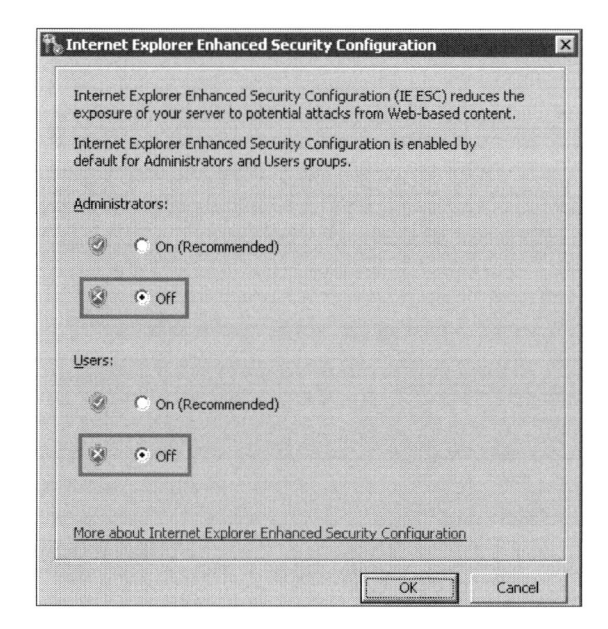

Installing XenApp using the Wizard-Based Server Role Manager

There are two different ways to deploy XenApp 6.5 servers: using the **Wizard-Based Server Role Manager** or the command line. Usually the first option is the preferred one when we need to deploy one or two specific roles and the second option is the best when we need to deploy multiple (and identical) servers using scripts. We are going to learn more about deploying an entire server using unattended scripts in *Chapter 4, Advanced XenApp Deployment*.

This step is common to all setup processes. To start the setup William needs to open the DVD or mount the .ISO file (if he is using a Virtual Machine or a remote console) and run the file autorun.exe in the root of the disk.

1. After autorun.exe has been executed, the Citrix XenApp installation menu is displayed.
2. He selects **Install XenApp Server**.

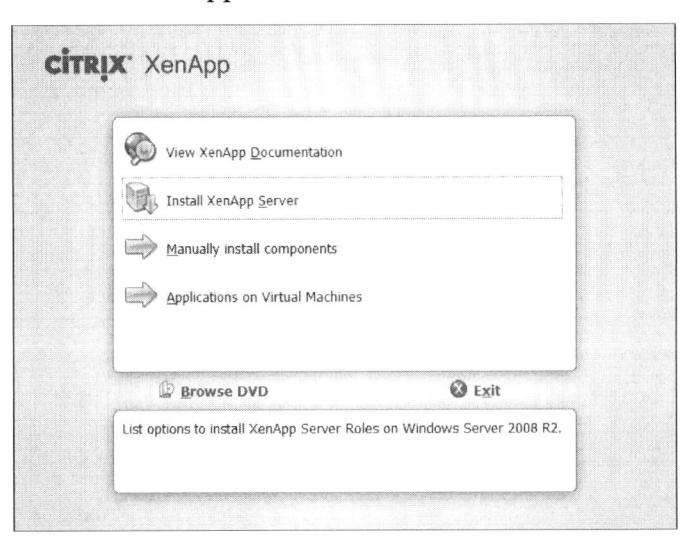

3. If .NET Framework 3.5 SP1 is not installed on the server, XenApp wizard will launch the setup of the .NET Framework 3.5. The following pop-up will be displayed:

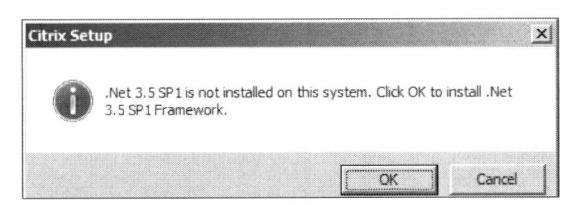

Chapter 3

4. Click on **OK** to install it.
5. After .NET Framework 3.5 SP1 installation is completed, he needs to click again on **Install XenApp**. Then Citrix XenApp Server Role Manager will be displayed.
6. Click on **Add server roles** to start the setup of the XenApp server.

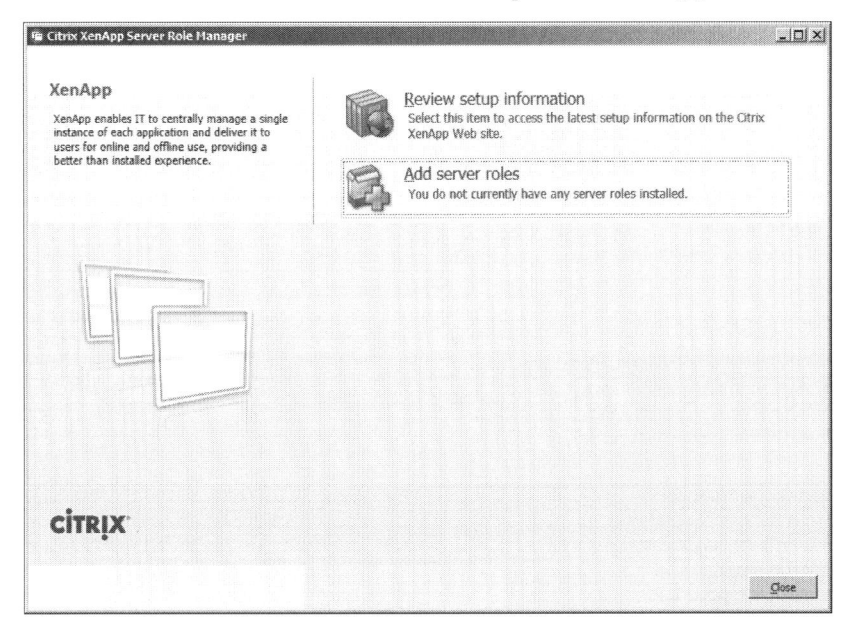

7. Choose XenApp edition. Features available to install will vary. If you want to test the new XenApp 6.5 using a 90 day evaluation license, choose **Platinum Edition**, because you can test all features. We are going to use **Platinum Edition** licenses in this Pilot lab.

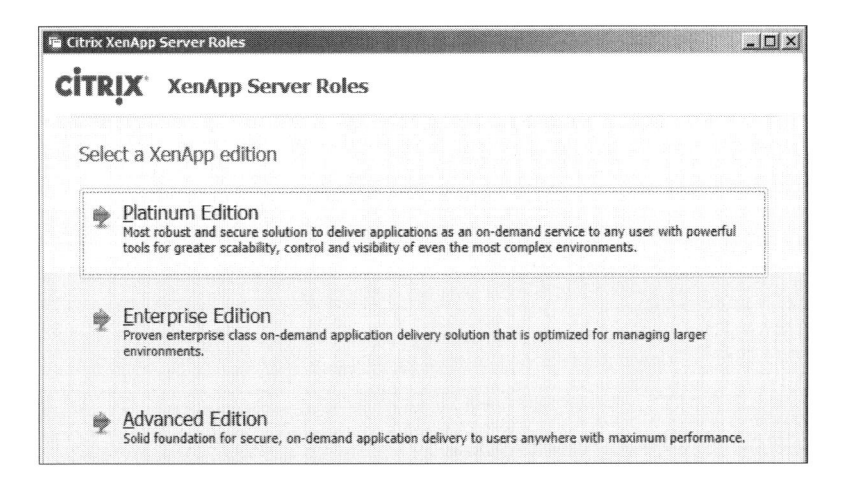

Installing XenApp 6.5

> If we have a single server or just want to test the product, we can install all common roles (License Server, XenApp, and Web Interface) in one server. In his Pilot, William is going to build multiple XenApp servers, but in *Chapter 2*, *Designing a XenApp 6.5 Farm*, there is a list of steps required to build a single server pilot.

8. After he accepts the Citrix License Agreement, he can choose the roles he wants to install on the XenApp server.

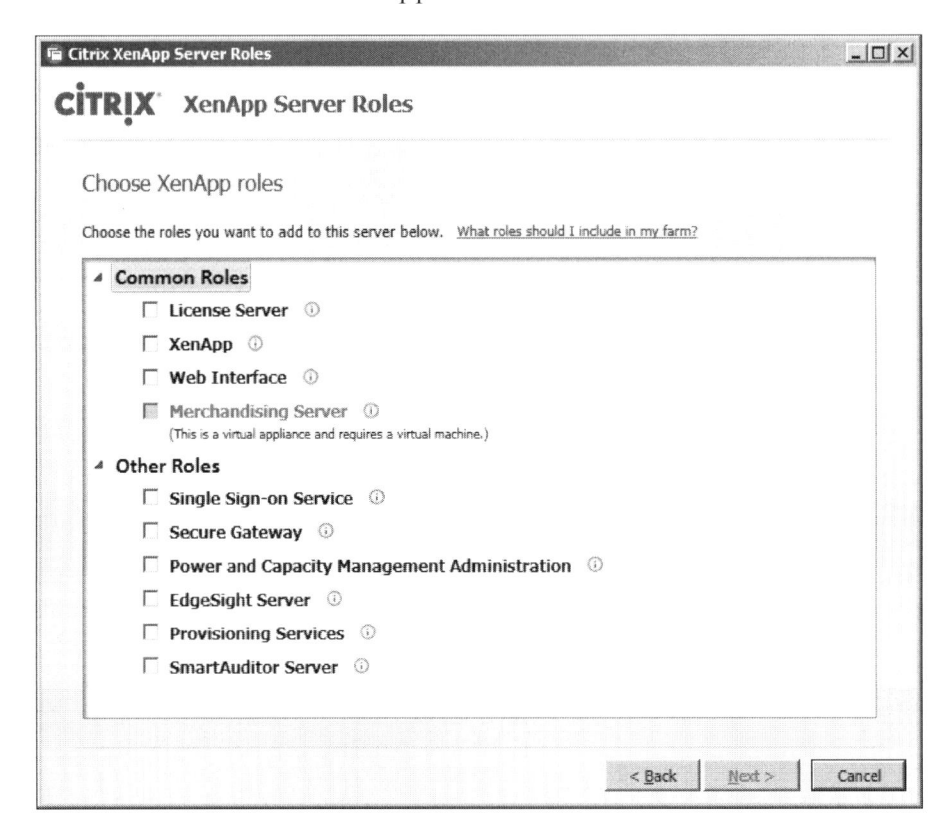

![Citrix XenApp Server Roles dialog showing Choose XenApp roles with Common Roles (License Server, XenApp, Web Interface, Merchandising Server) and Other Roles (Single Sign-on Service, Secure Gateway, Power and Capacity Management Administration, EdgeSight Server, Provisioning Services, SmartAuditor Server)]

[46]

Installing License Server and Web Interface roles in server BRICKXA65-01

Now William is going to start with the deployment plan, and the first step is to install both roles on the server BrickXA65-01. He needs to follow the instructions given in the preceding section, then choose **License Server** and **Web Interface** roles and click on **Next** button to see the role subcomponents:

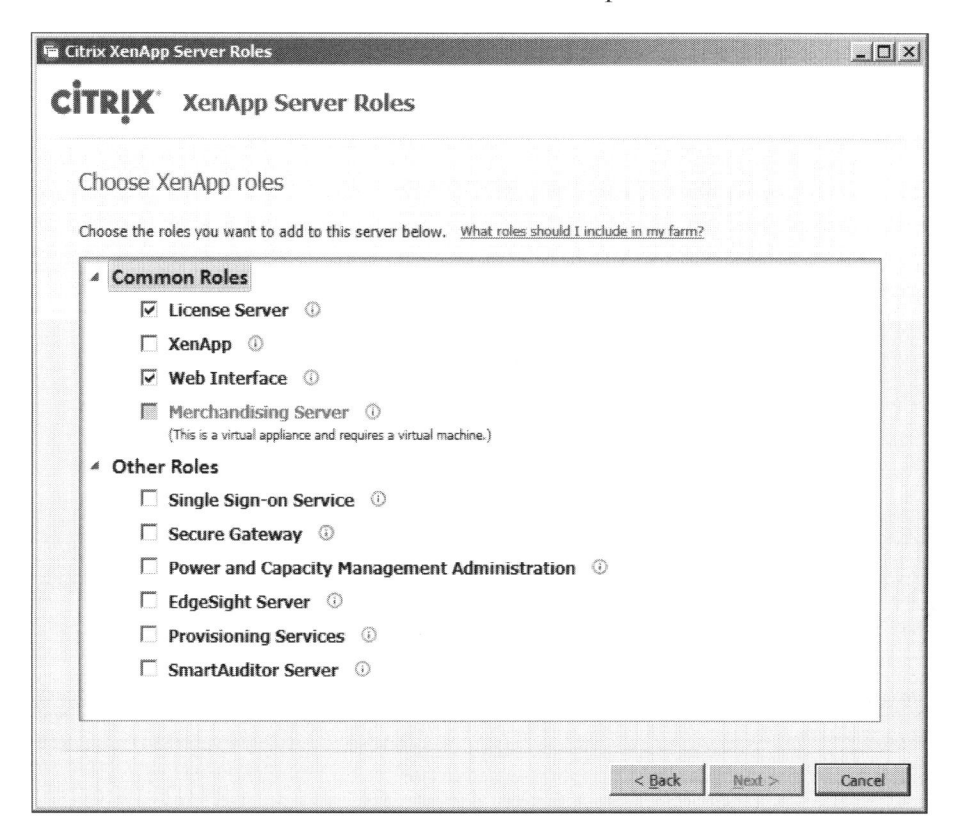

At this moment, XenApp Setup will install missing prerequisites. Click on the **Next** button to continue.

Click on the **Install** button to start the setup process.

Once the installation is complete, click on the **Finish** button to close the window.

In this window, the setup process shows both components installed and ready to be configured.

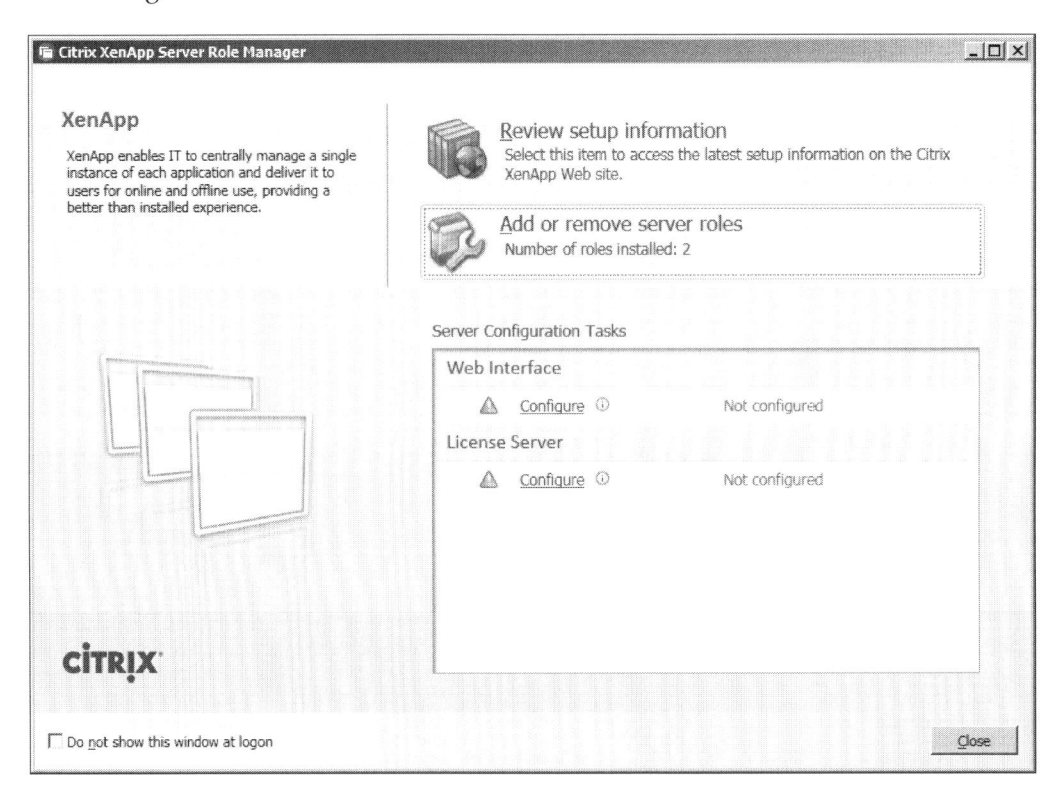

Configuring Citrix License Server

To configure the license server, William clicks on **Configure** link under **License Server** option. This process will open a window. He needs to enter a password and confirm it. He can change ports of services (optional) and click on the **OK** button to apply changes.

The default license server port is **27000** and the **Management Console Web port** is **8082**. He needs to verify these ports are open in the firewall. The XenApp setup process will open the required ports on Windows Firewall.

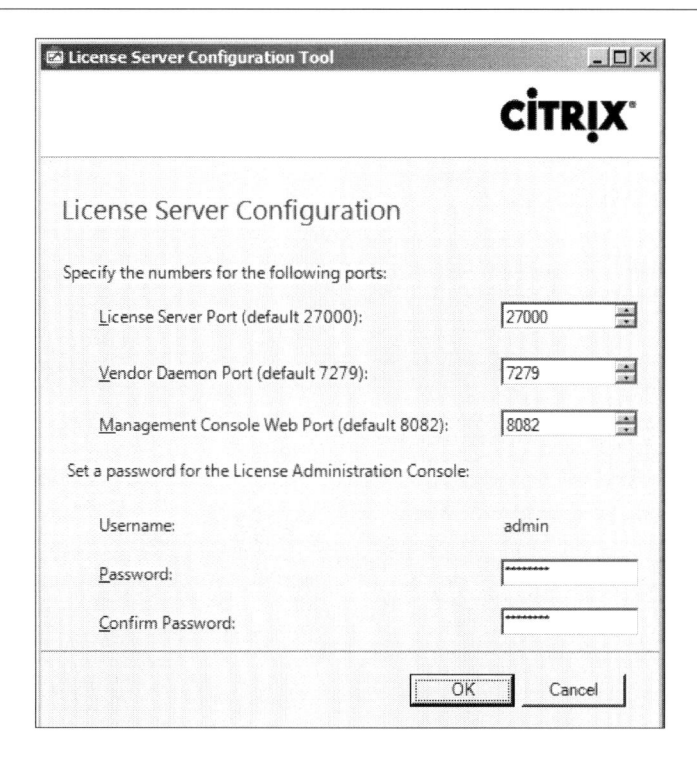

The following screenshot shows that the License Server is configured:

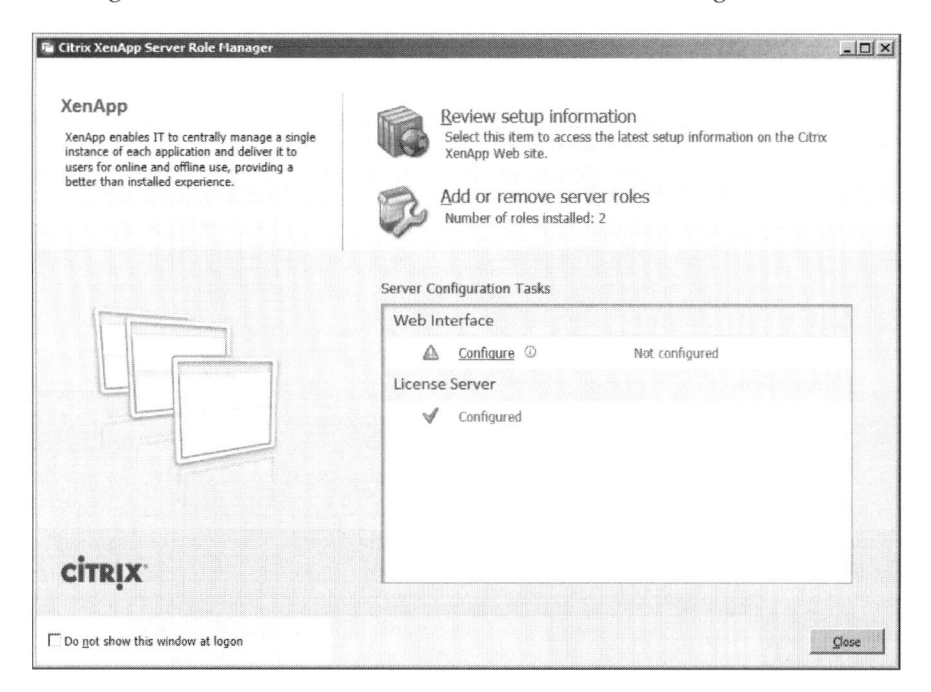

Installing XenApp 6.5

Installing Citrix Licenses

Now we are going to install Citrix Licenses on our License server. We are going to install XenApp Evaluation Licenses. These licenses are valid for 90 days and they are perfect to evaluate XenApp.

The first step is to log in at www.citrix.com/mycitrix (this requires a MyCitrix account) and in the **Choose a Toolbox** menu select **Previews/Betas – License Retrieval**:

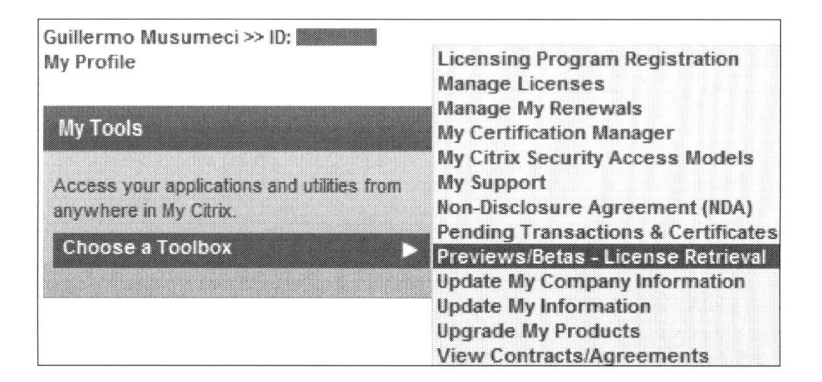

Then select **XenApp Evaluation** in the horizontal menu.

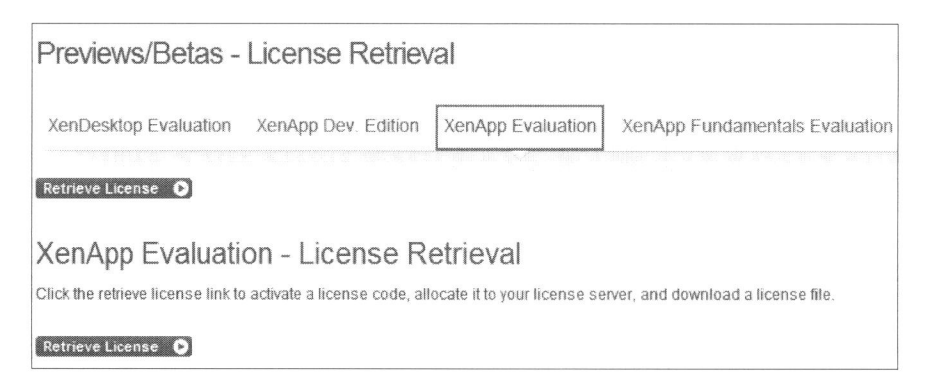

In this page, we need to click on the hyperlink of one of the serial numbers to start the activation process.

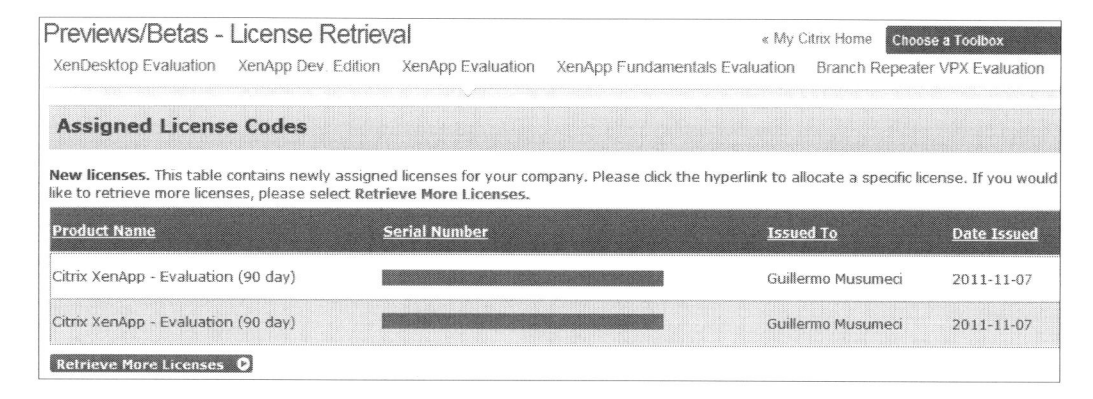

Next, we need to enter the hostname of Citrix License Server.

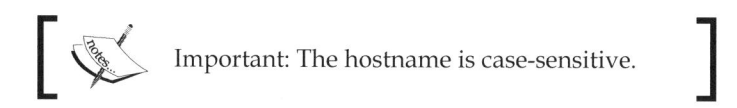

> **Important**: The hostname is case-sensitive.

To determine the hostname, on our license server machine, we need to open a command prompt window and type **hostname**.

The hostname returned will be in case-sensitive format. Copy this name to the hostname field box in MyCitrix.

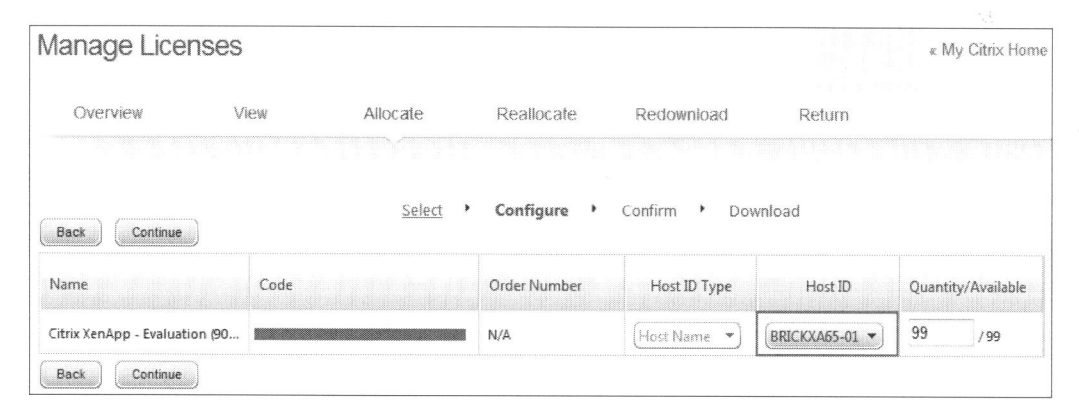

[51]

Installing XenApp 6.5

The site then confirms the license allocation and tells us we can download the license.

And finally we are ready to download the license.

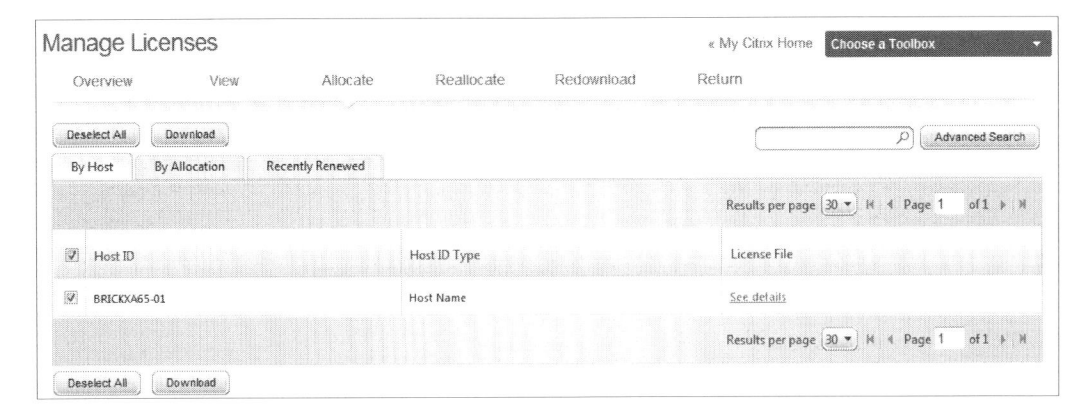

After we download the license and copy it to our license server, we need to install it using the Citrix License Administration Console. We need to click on the **Import License** button located on the **Vendor Daemon Configuration** tab. Detailed information about this procedure is available in *Chapter 5, Using Management Tools*. Restarting the licensing service or even rebooting the server is recommended.

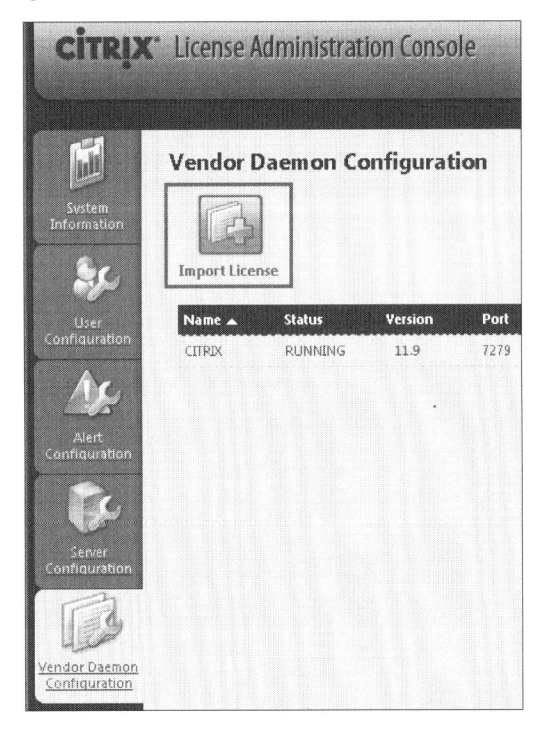

Chapter 3

Install and configure XenApp 6.5 on BRICKXA65-02 using Wizard-Based Server Role Manager (first server of the farm)

The next step in the deployment plan is to install the first XenApp server. On the **Choose XenApp roles** page, William needs to select only the **XenApp** role.

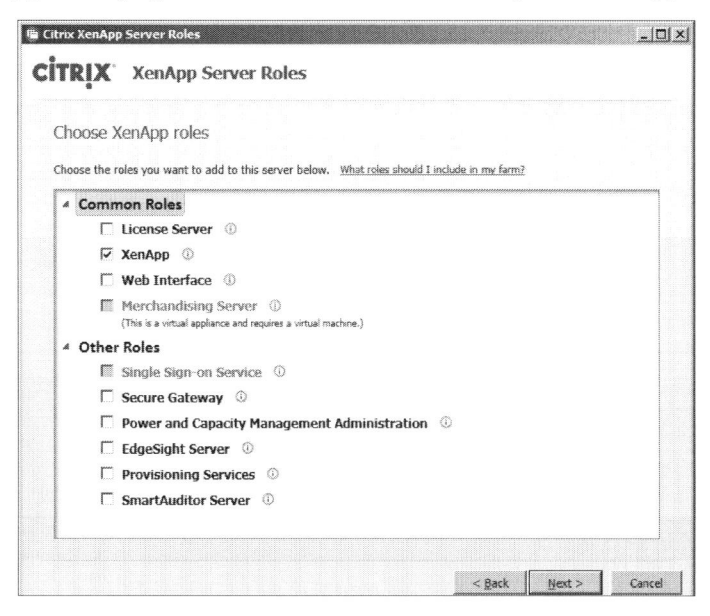

He can choose to install default components or remove **XenApp Management**.

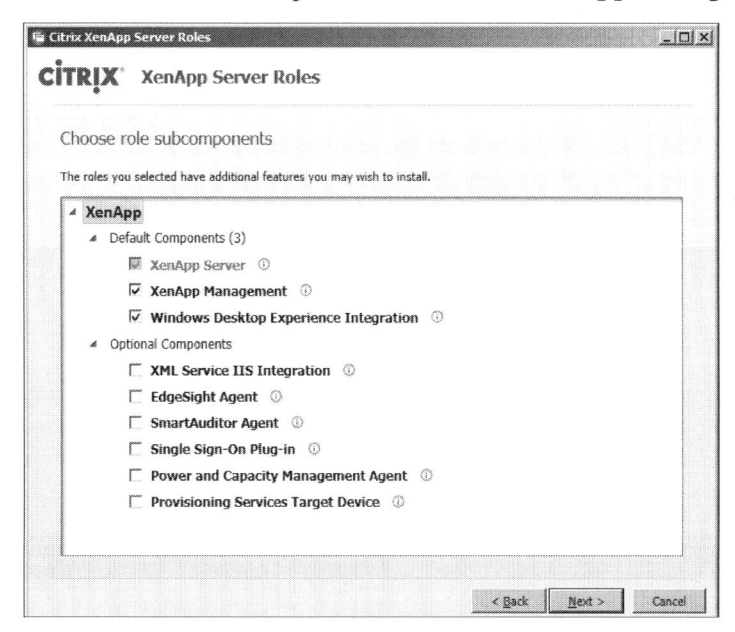

[53]

Installing XenApp 6.5

Now, XenApp Setup will install for us the missing prerequisites. William clicks on the **Next** button to continue. One of these prerequisites is **Remote Desktop Services** (formerly known as Terminal Server), XenApp 6.5 (and XenApp 6.0) will install it automatically, if required.

Once he is ready to install all components, he clicks on the **Install** button to continue.

When all components are installed, he needs to restart the server to continue the setup and click on the **Finish** button.

He then clicks on the **Reboot** link to restart the server to complete prerequisite installation and configuration:

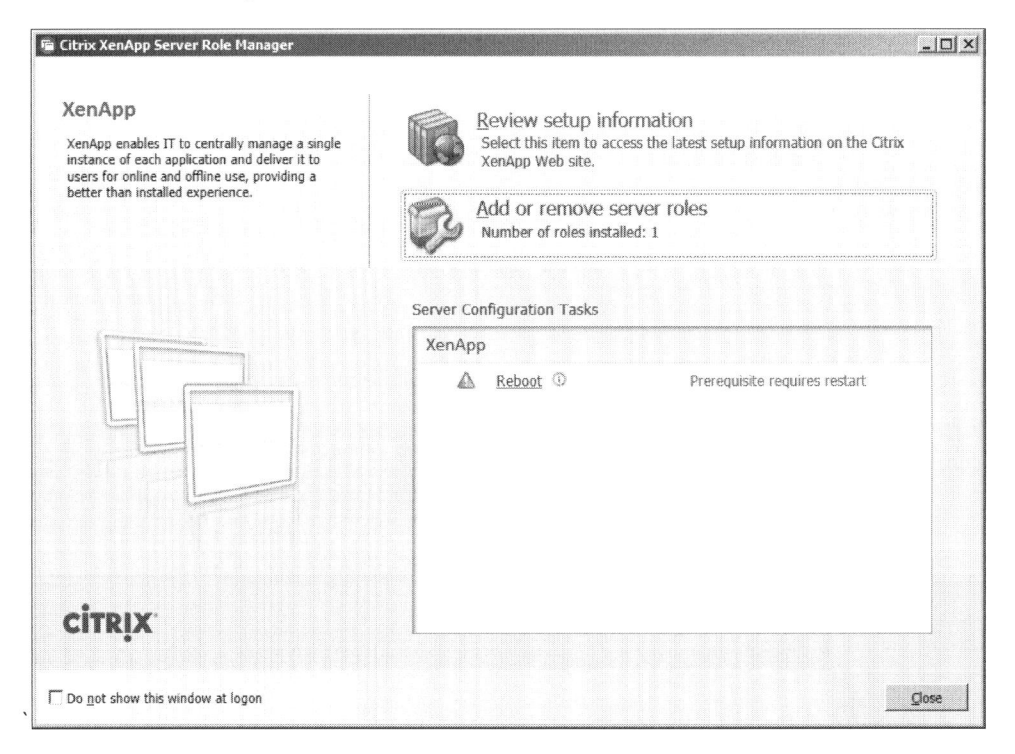

After restarting the BRICKXA65-02 server, the **XenApp Server Role Manager** is presented. On **Server Configuration Tasks**, William clicks on the **Resume Install** link to continue the XenApp installation.

[54]

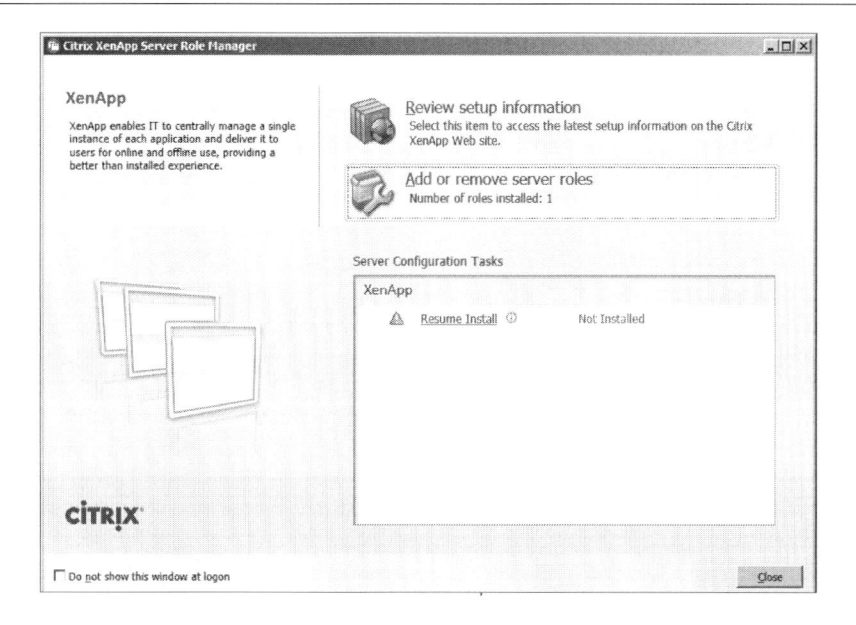

After the list of prerequisites is reviewed, he clicks on the **Install** button to install them.

Once the installation is complete, he clicks on the **Finish** button to continue:

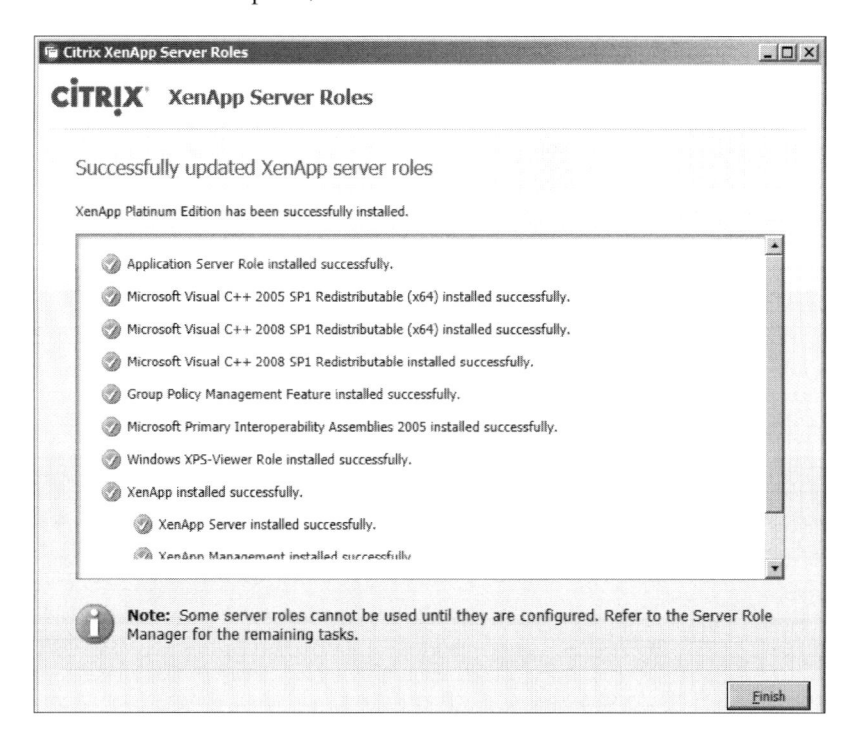

Configuring XenApp Using the Wizard-based Server Configuration Tool

Once XenApp is set up, it is time to configure the server. William needs to click on the **Specify Licensing** link to configure license server.

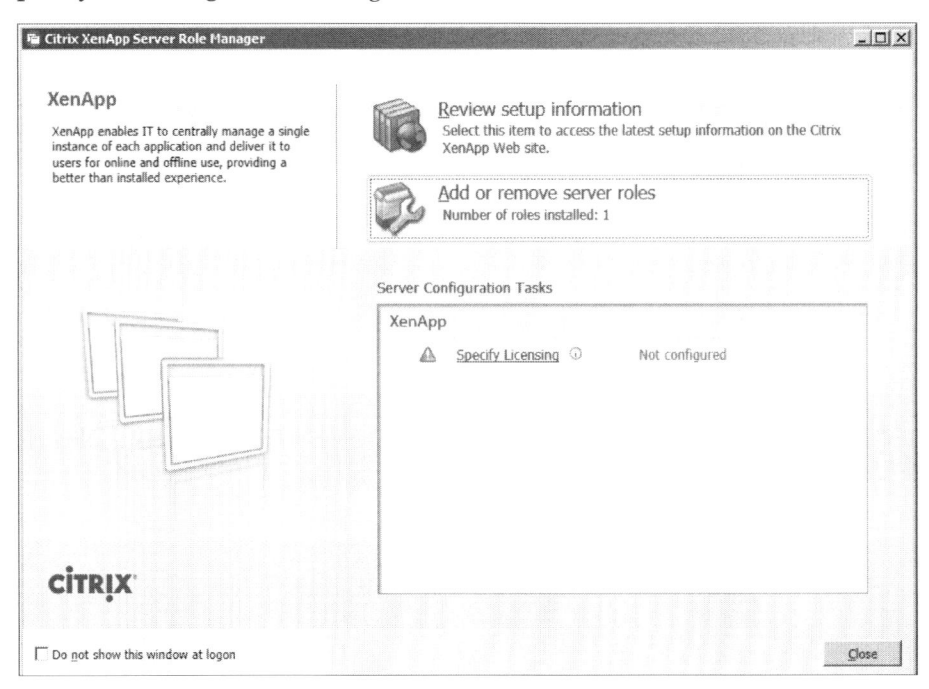

In this step, he can enter the Citrix License Server Name, if it is already set up. Also, he can set up the license server later using a policy. We are going to learn how to create a policy to set the license server in *Chapter 8, Managing XenApp Policies*.

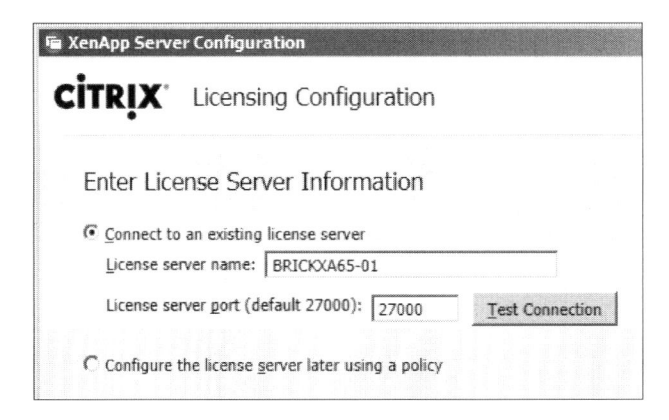

Once he enters the license server and clicks on the **Next** button, he will choose the **License Model**.

After that he needs to click on the **Configure** link to start the configuration process.

During the setup procedure, he can choose to create a new Citrix farm, or join the server to an existing Citrix farm and set up the Citrix data store.

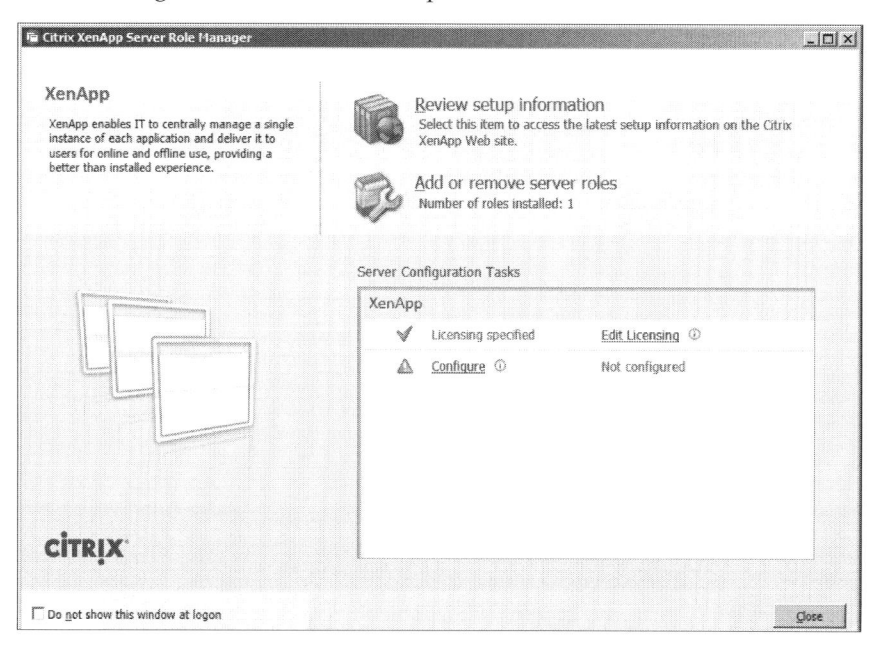

Configuring the first XenApp server of the farm

At this point, William can select if he wants to **Create a new server farm** or **Join an existing server farm**. In his case, because this is the first XenApp server in his environment, he needs to choose **Create a new server farm**.

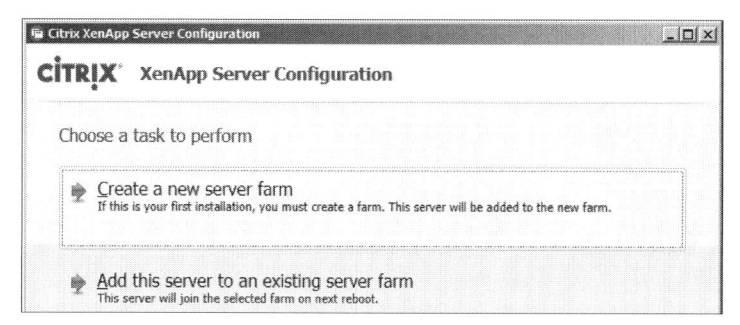

Here, he needs to enter the name of the new Citrix farm and the first Citrix administrator account: here he enters a domain account. In some cases (for example, single test server on a workgroup) we can use a local account.

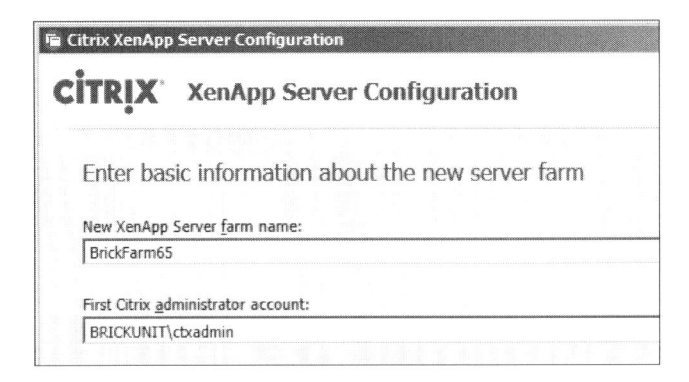

Installing Data Stores

The next step in the installation process is to choose where we can install his Citrix data store.

We have three options here:

- **New database**: This option will install and set up a Microsoft SQL Server 2008 Express Edition on the current machine. This option is appropriate when we want to build a test or small XenApp Farm, but is not recommended for medium to large farm or multi-zone farms.
- **Existing Microsoft SQL Server database**: This option will install the data store on an *existing* SQL Server database. You must check with your DBA to create one in advance or check http://xenapp6.musumeci.com.ar for detailed instructions to create a new database on a Microsoft SQL Server 2008. For more information about supported databases versions, take a look at the document **CTX114501** at http://support.citrix.com/article/CTX114501
- **Existing Oracle database**: This option will install the data store on an *existing* Oracle database. You must check with your DBA to create one in advance. For more information about supported database versions, take a look at the document **CTX114501** at http://support.citrix.com/article/CTX114501

> The **Existing Oracle database** option is visible only if you previously installed the **32-bit (x86) Oracle client** on your XenApp server.

In this Lab, William is going to use SQL Server 2008 Standard server, but we are going to see how to install both versions (Express and Standard).

Microsoft SQL Server 2008 Express Database Server

This limited version of Microsoft SQL Server 2008 is perfect for test or small environments because it is free and migration to other versions of Microsoft SQL Server is easy and fast. Express Edition is also recommended for evaluation or PoC (Proof of Concept) implementation because it's easy to set up and doesn't require an extra server.

The configuration process of Microsoft SQL Server Express is pretty simple. Select **New database** and click on **Next** button and the setup will install SQL Server and create a new database for us.

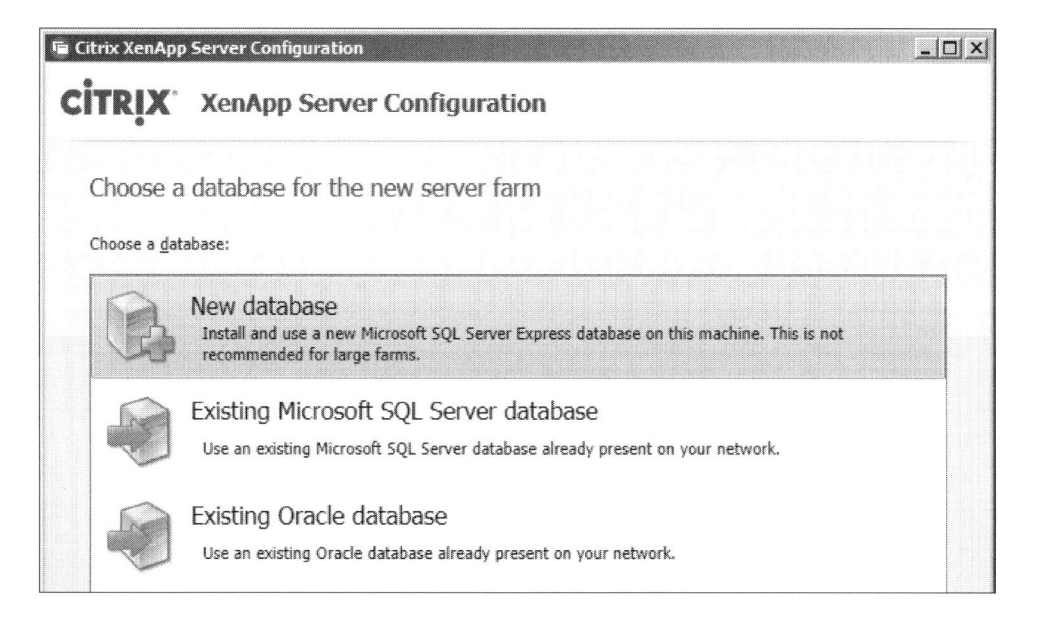

In the following screen William needs to click on the **Enter Credentials** button, type the administrator username and password and click on the **OK** button.

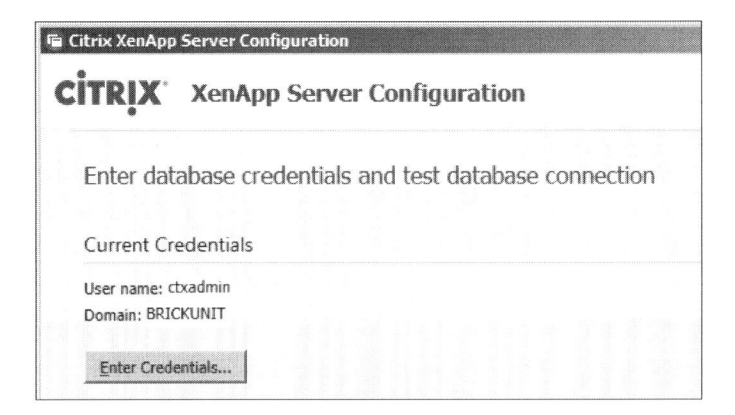

Microsoft SQL Server 2008 Database Server

Deploying Microsoft SQL Server Standard or Enterprise Edition versions is the preferred option for medium to large Citrix implementations.

In this screen, William selects the **Existing Microsoft SQL Server** database option and clicks on the **Next** button.

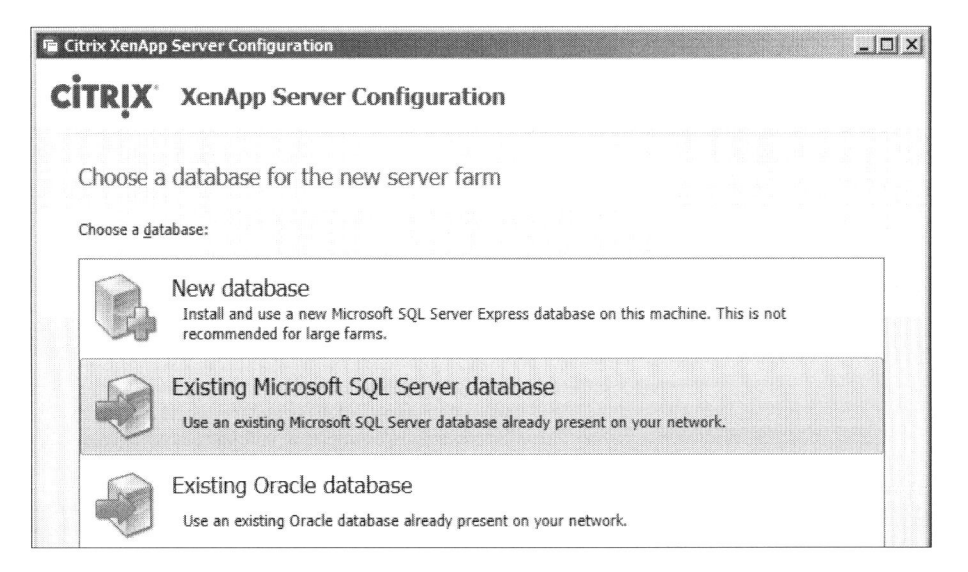

Here he needs to enter the **Database server name** and the **Database name**. The database *must* exist before the setup.

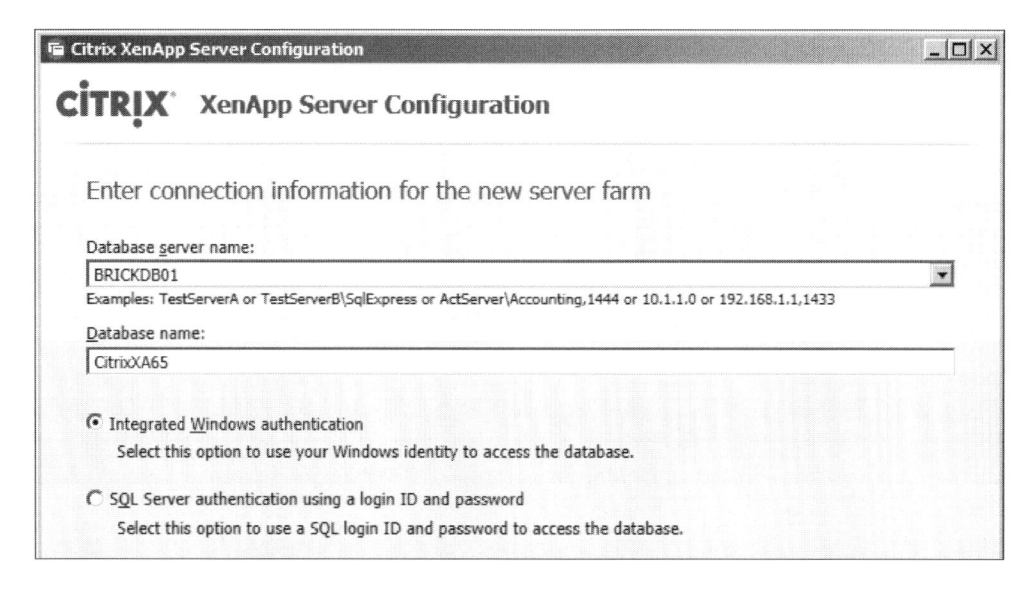

He enters credentials with permissions to access the database specified in the last step, and clicks on the **OK** button.

When **Test Connection** button returns a **Test Completed Successfully** message, he clicks on the **Next** button to continue with the setup process.

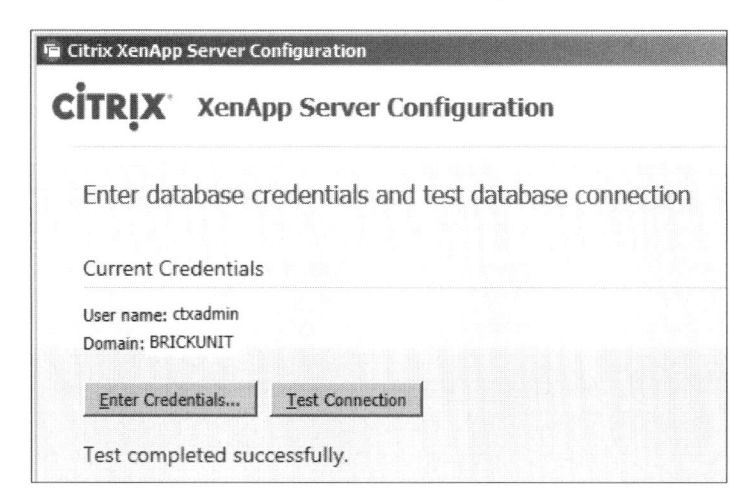

Installing XenApp 6.5

> If you have issues with the Test Connection process, try to use the server name followed by "1433" where 1433 is the port of SQL Server. Also, you can try using the IP address of the database server and verify that the firewalls on both machines (SQL Server and XenApp server) are not blocking traffic in the SQL port.

Oracle Database Server

We are going to use Microsoft SQL Server to setup the Citrix Data Store in this book because it is the most popular method to deploy Citrix data stores, and also the setup of an Oracle database is complex and out the scope of this book.

Configuring XenApp

The data store is now ready and it's time to continue with our configuration process.

Configuring shadowing permits Citrix administrators to take control of the user's sessions. On the screen, William enables **Force a shadow acceptance popup** and **Force logging of all shadow connections** checkboxes. Enabling the first option will not request shadow permissions to users and enabling the second option will allow logging of all shadow activities.

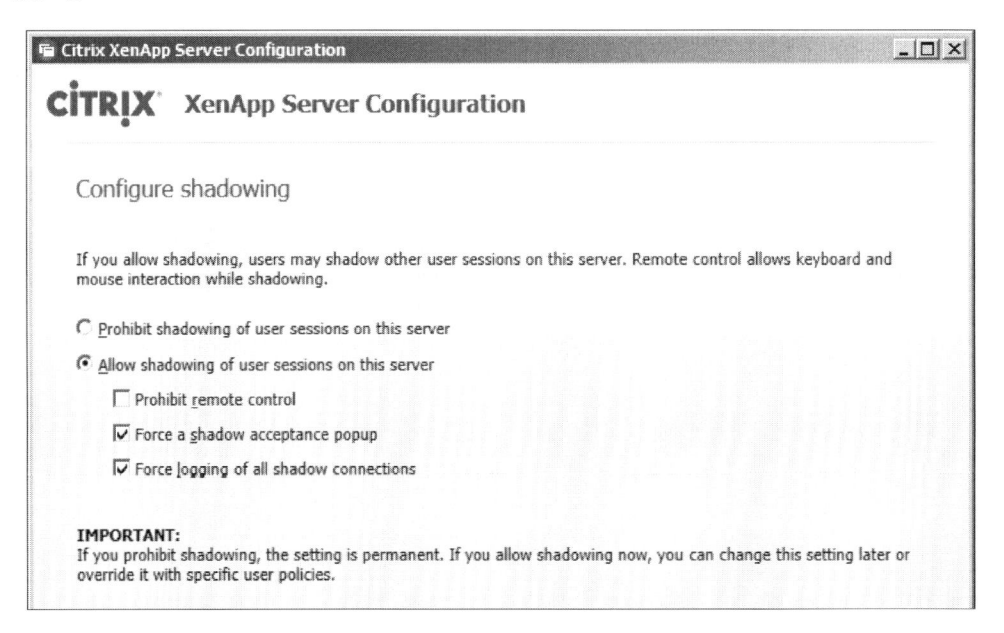

Now it is time to review advanced server settings, and discover one of the new features introduced on XenApp 6.5. As we discussed in the previous chapter, XenApp 6.5 introduces new server roles: Session-host (also known as Session-only) and Session-host and controller (also known as controller) roles and the ability to create either controller or Session-host only servers. In the previous versions of XenApp, including version 6.0, all servers are running both roles.

When we Choose the controller mode, servers act like previous versions of XenApp: they can host sessions, the XML services, provide application enumeration, force data collector elections, and so on.

On the other hand, running XenApp servers in Session-host mode improves start-up and join performance, which is especially recommended for servers running in different zones, branch office or remote sites. This is because servers running in Session-only mode require less read/writes to the Data store during a join or sync process, which reduces bandwidth and resource usage on the Data store server.

We can't configure the first server of the XenApp farm, and the server is set as Controller, to guarantee at least one data collector on the XenApp farm.

Also, here William can enter a custom **Zone name** for the new server. Zones are useful in complex environments where large numbers of servers are located in geographically dispersed locations, but multiple zones generate more network traffic. It is not recommended to create multiple zones, if you are installing a test or small farm.

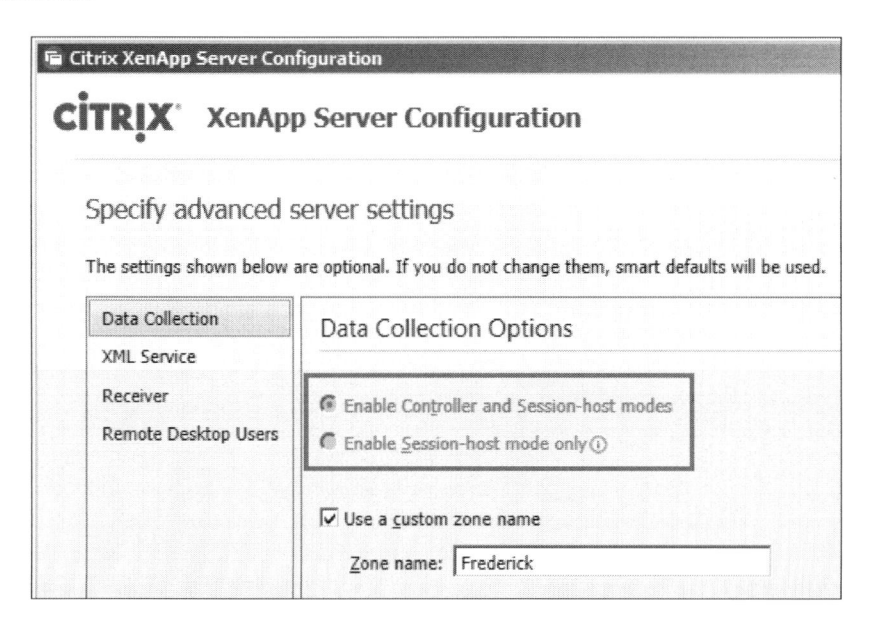

Installing XenApp 6.5

Here he can change the XML port (optional). If he changes this port, he needs to specify it later when he sets up the Web Interface server. Citrix recommends to change the port to 8080.

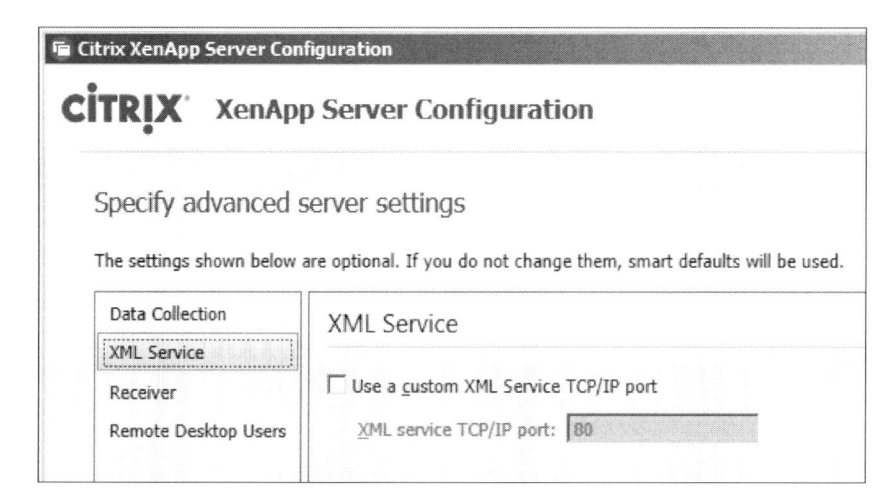

Now, William can enter the **Web Interface server name** (optional).

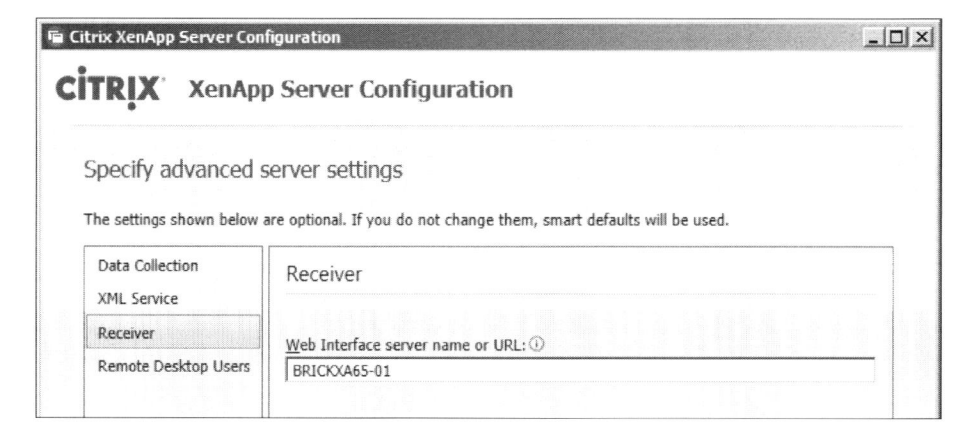

In this screen we provide permissions to **Remote Desktop Users** (optional). By default, the **Add Anonymous users** checkbox is enabled, we need to disable it except if we need it.

Chapter 3

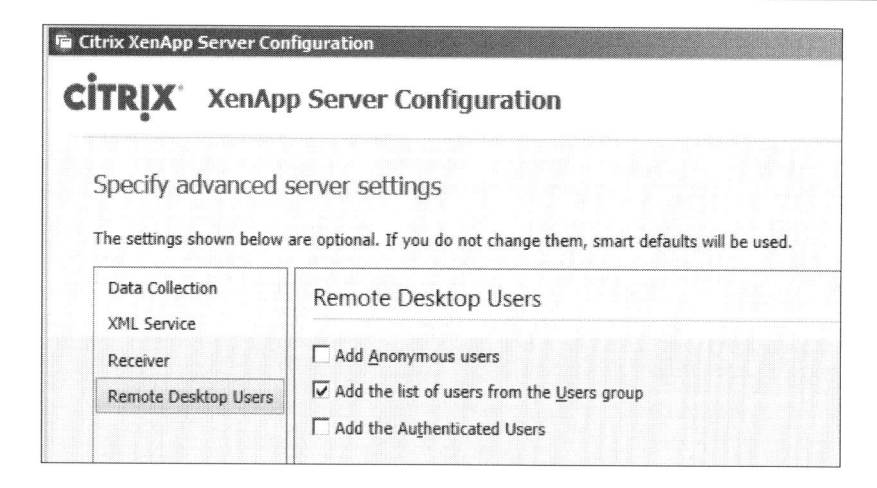

[Screenshot: Citrix XenApp Server Configuration – Specify advanced server settings, with Remote Desktop Users tab showing "Add the list of users from the Users group" checked.]

He clicks on the **Apply** button to finish the configuration.

Then he clicks on the **Finish** button to complete the setup.

A reboot is required to complete the installation process. He clicks on the **Reboot** link to restart the server.

Installing and configuring XenApp 6.5 on BRICKXA65-03

Now, continuing with the deployment process, William adds a new XenApp server to the XenApp farm. This process is pretty similar to the installation of the first server of the farm. For this process he must:

1. Select the **Add this server to an existing server farm** option to continue.

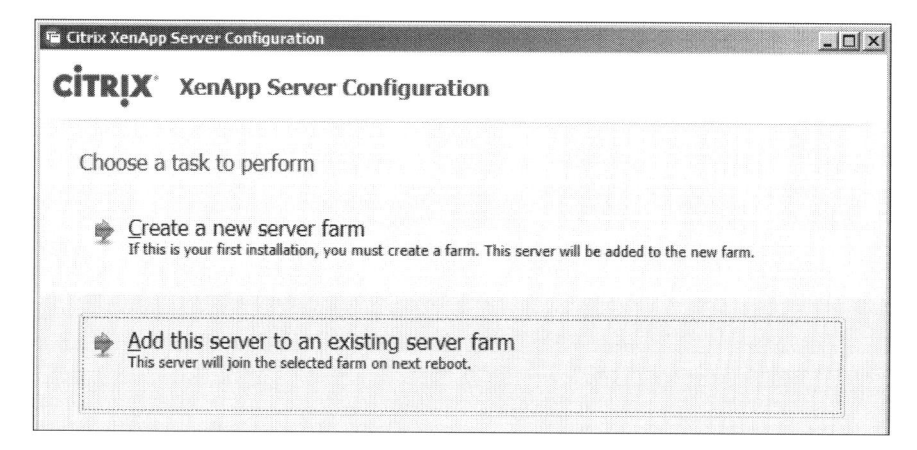

[Screenshot: Citrix XenApp Server Configuration – Choose a task to perform, with options "Create a new server farm" and "Add this server to an existing server farm".]

Installing XenApp 6.5

2. He then selects the **Existing Microsoft SQL Server database** option and clicks on the **Next** button.

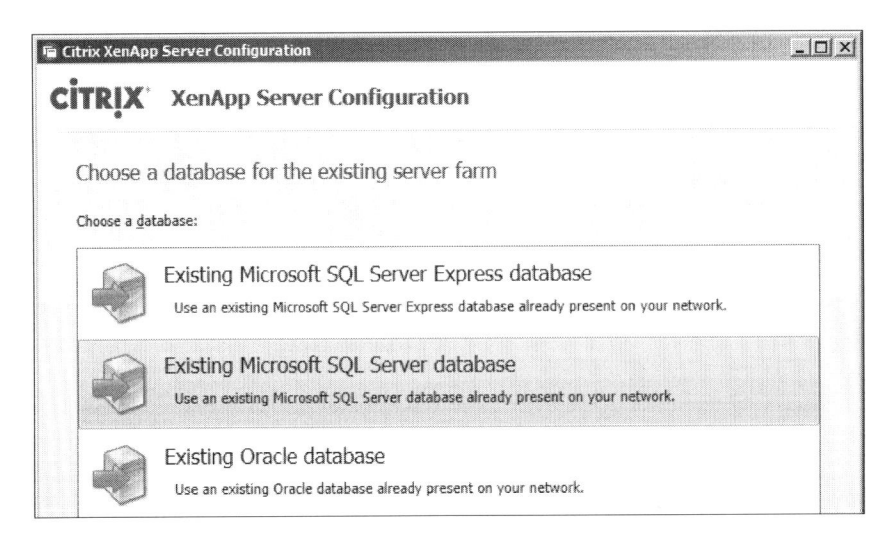

3. He enters the database server name, database name, and credentials, and tests the connection.
4. He sets up the Shadowing.
5. Now he sets the server mode. He can choose the **Enable Controller and Session-host modes** option (this is the default option, similar to previous XenApp versions) or select **Enable Session-host mode only** option. The second option provides better performance, for application servers only.

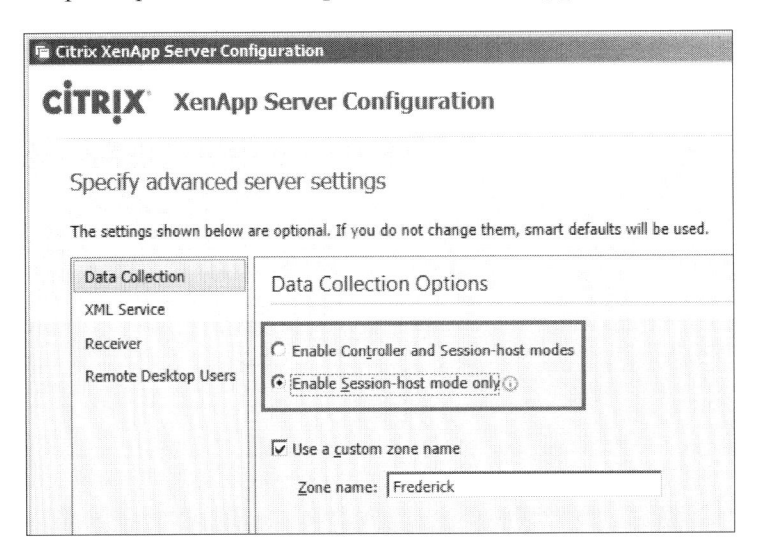

Now, the configuration process continues in the same way as described in the *Configuring the first XenApp server of the farm* section.

Configuring Citrix Web Interface server

The Web Interface server is the server used by the client to access applications. We can find two types of XenApp Sites on the Web Interface servers:

- **XenApp Web Sites**: These sites are used when users access applications, desktop, and content published on the XenApp farm (and also virtual desktop (VDI) running XenDesktop) using a web browser. Once authenticated, users can access online and offline applications using a Citrix client.

- **XenApp Services Sites**: These sites are used to integrate resources with users' desktops. Citrix Online Plug-In provides access to applications, virtual desktops, and online content by clicking icons on the **Start** menu or shortcuts in their desktop. XenApp Services Sites was formerly known as Program Neighborhood Agent site.

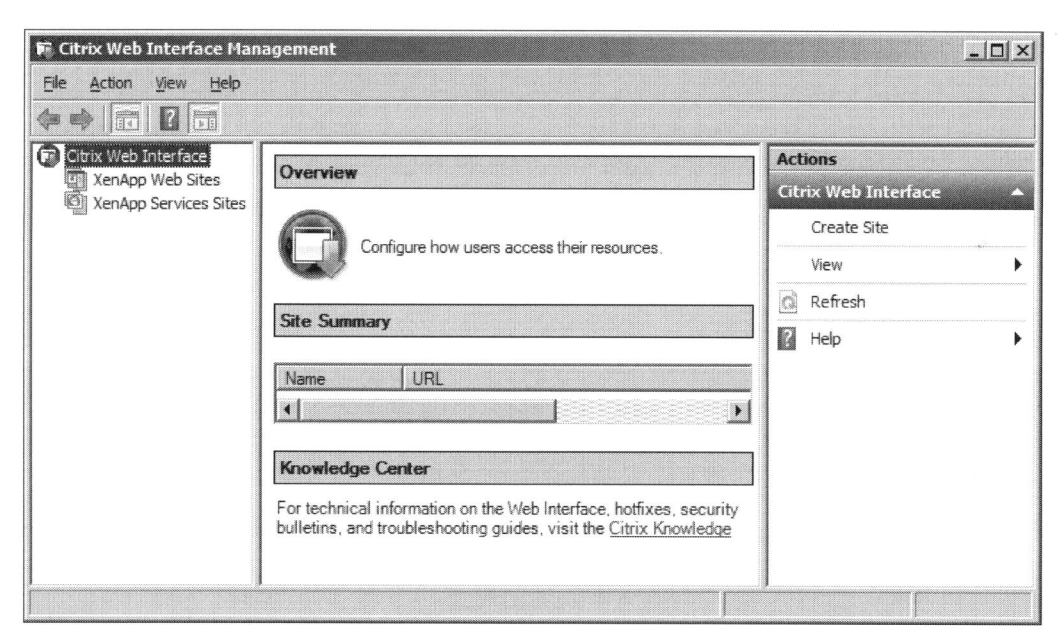

Creating a XenApp Web Site

To create a new site, William needs to open the **Citrix Web Interface Management** console, click on **XenApp Web Site**, and then click on **Create Site** on the right-hand side panel. The **Set as the default page for the IIS site** checkbox is used if we have multiple sites.

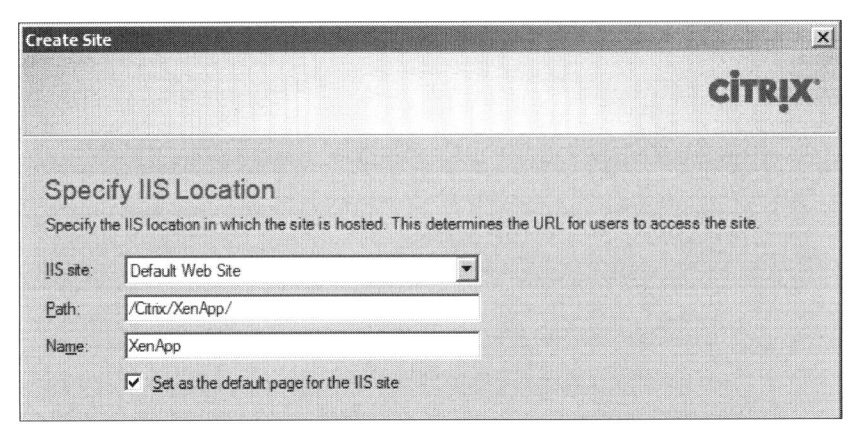

Here he can leave the default authentication (at Web Interface) because he is going to access the Web Interface internally only. Then, he clicks on the **Next** button to continue.

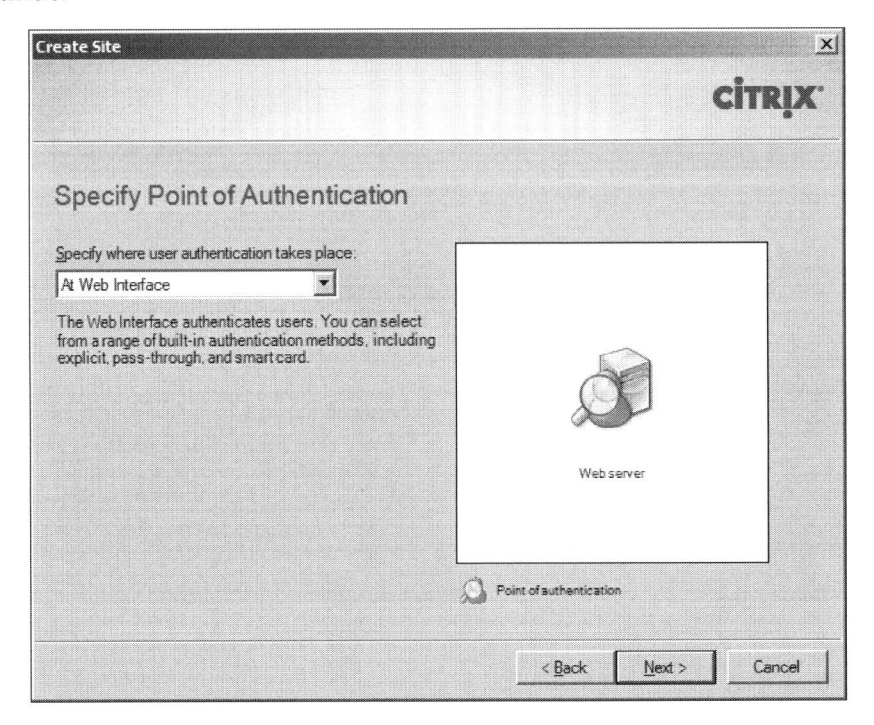

Chapter 3

He clicks on the **Next** button until the site is successfully created.

Now, William needs to enter the **Farm Name** and the name of at least one XenApp server running the XML service. William can only add server defined as **Controller** (Session-host and controller role) through the XenApp setup.

In small or medium production environments, it is recommended to have two or more XML servers. In large farms, Citrix recommends at least two or more dedicated XML servers.

Check the XML Service port is the right for your environment (usually XML port is 80 (default) or 8080 (recommended by Citrix).

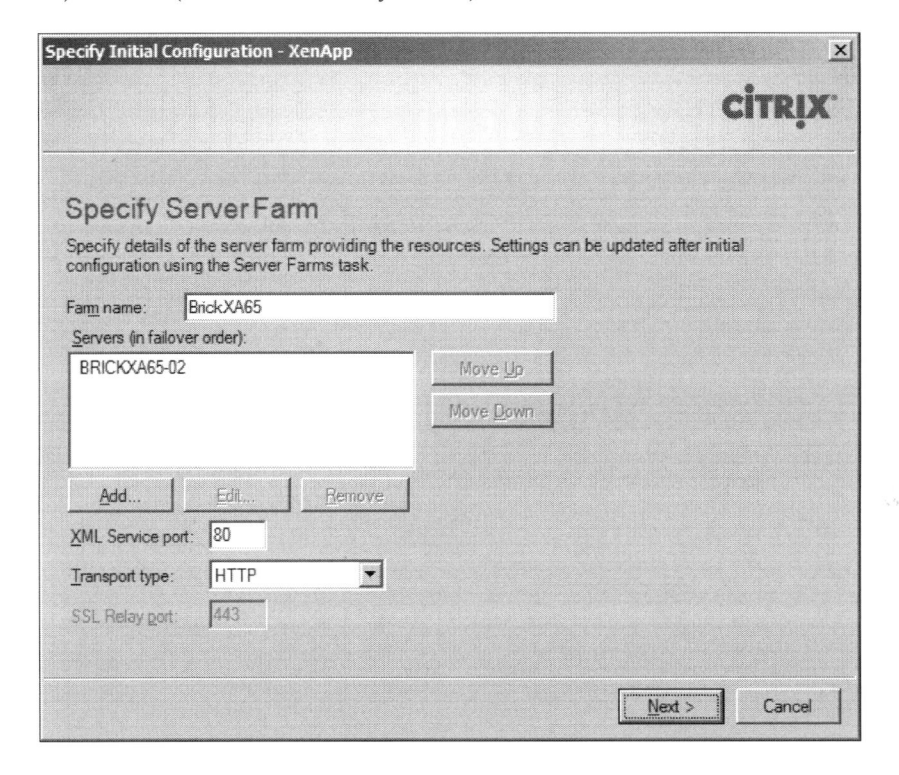

Now he needs to configure Authentication Methods:

Explicit (XenApp Web sites) or Prompt (XenApp Services sites): Users need to log in using a username and a password. Authentication options are User Principal Name (UPN), Microsoft domain-based authentication, and Novell Directory Services (NDS).

Pass-through: Users can authenticate using the credentials they provided when they logged on to their Windows desktop machines. The Citrix Client sends their credentials to the Web Interface server and their resource set appears automatically.

Pass-through with smart card: Users are authenticated by inserting a smart card in a smart card reader attached to the user desktop machine or mobile device. If users have installed the Citrix Receiver 3.x (formerly Citrix Online Plug-In on XenApp 6.0), they are prompted for their smart card PIN when they log in to the client device. After logging in, users can access their resources without additional logon prompts. Users accessing XenApp Web sites are not asked for a PIN.

Smart card: Users use a smart card to authenticate. The user is asked for the smart card PIN.

Anonymous: Anonymous users can log on without providing a username and password, and access resources published only for anonymous users. This is a pretty uncommon scenario and is not recommended.

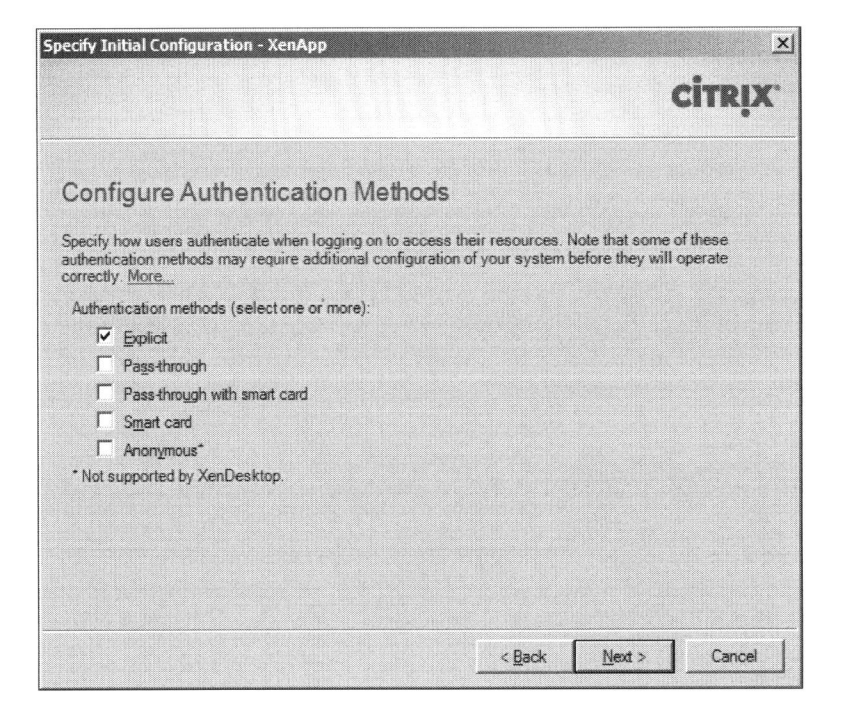

William can restrict the list of domains with permissions to login to the Citrix Web Interface, as shown in the following screenshot. When we set **Domain Restriction**, the Web Interface will only ask for username and password. This option is useful to simplify user login.

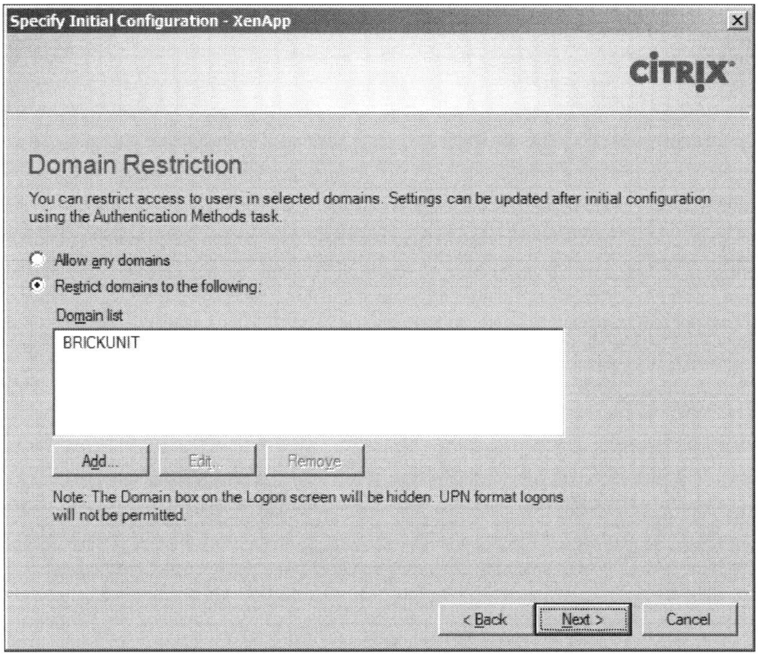
Specify Initial Configuration - XenApp
CITRIX
Domain Restriction
You can restrict access to users in selected domains. Settings can be updated after initial configuration using the Authentication Methods task.
Allow any domains
Restrict domains to the following:
Domain list
BRICKUNIT
Add...
Edit...
Remove
Note: The Domain box on the Logon screen will be hidden. UPN format logons will not be permitted.
< Back
Next >
Cancel

Here, he needs to choose the **Logon Screen Appearance**: the default option is **Minimal**. He decides to use the **Full** version for his Lab.

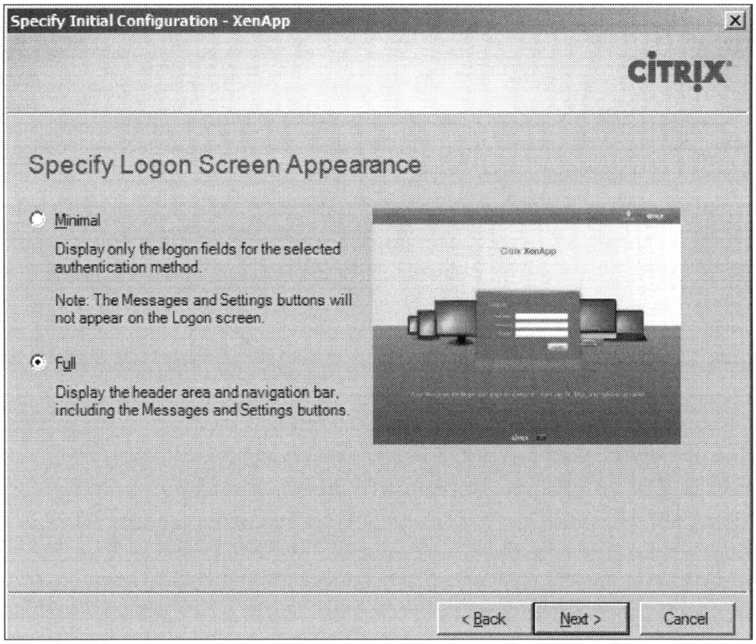
Specify Initial Configuration - XenApp
CITRIX
Specify Logon Screen Appearance
Minimal
Display only the logon fields for the selected authentication method.
Note: The Messages and Settings buttons will not appear on the Logon screen.
Full
Display the header area and navigation bar, including the Messages and Settings buttons.
< Back
Next >
Cancel

Installing XenApp 6.5

Now he needs to choose the **Published Resource Type** option supported by the site. Options are as follows:

Online: Users access applications, content, and desktops hosted on remote servers. Users need a network connection to XenApp servers to access their resources.

Offline: XenApp streams applications to their desktops and opens them locally. Users need a network connection to log on to the site and start their applications. When the applications are running, the network connection is not required.

Dual mode: Users access both online and offline applications, content, and desktops.

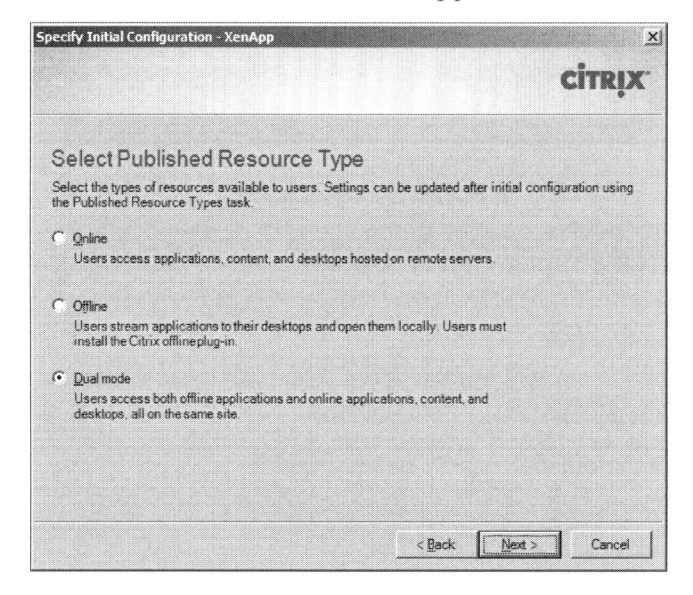

William clicks on the **Finish** button to complete the configuration.

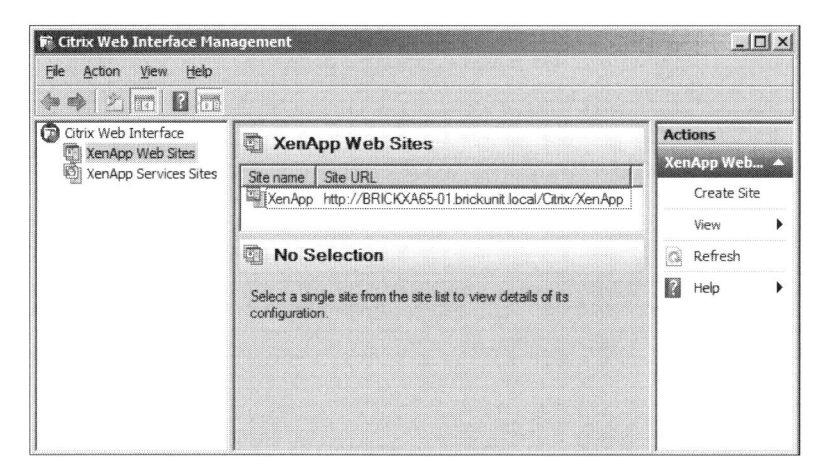

Creating a XenApp Services Site

To create a new site, William needs to open the **Citrix Web Interface Management** console, click on the **XenApp Services Site**, and then click on **Create Site** in right panel.

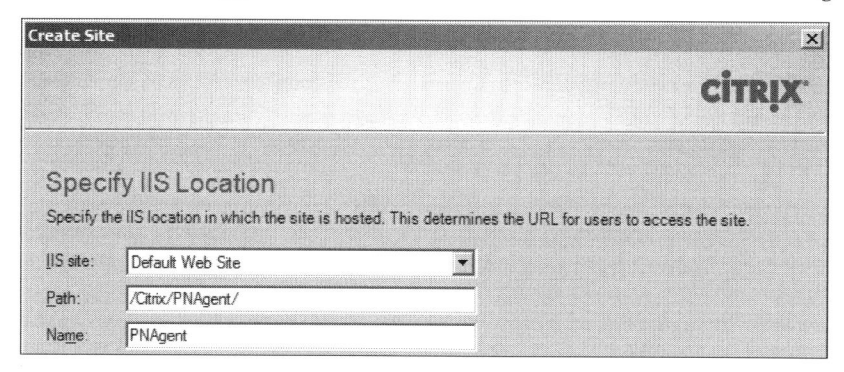

He clicks on the **Next** button, until the site is successfully created.

He needs to enter the **Farm Name** and the name of at least one XenApp server running the XML service. As we mentioned before, William can only add a server defined as **Controller** (Session-host and controller role) through the XenApp setup.

In small or medium production environments, it is recommended to have two or more XML servers. In large farms, Citrix recommends at least two or more dedicated XML servers.

Check if the XML Service port is right for your environment (usually XML port is 80 or 8080).

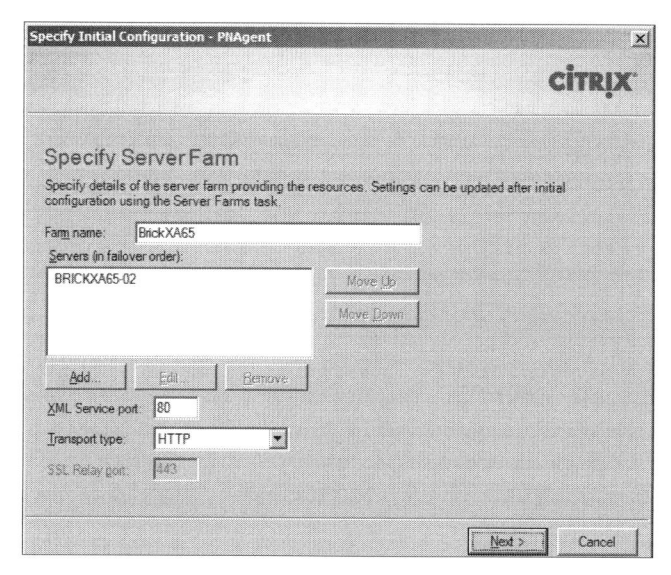

Installing XenApp 6.5

Now, he needs to choose **Published Resource Types** supported by the site. The options are the same as that to those XenApp Web Site.

He clicks on the **Finish** button to complete the configuration.

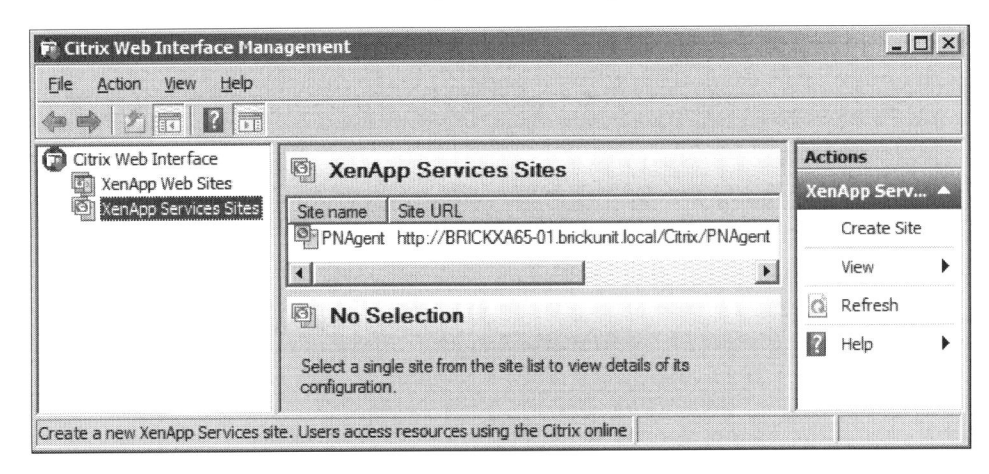

Configure Remote Desktop Licenses

The last step to finish the setup of the pilot XenApp farm is the configuration of the Remote Desktop Licensing.

When he logs in to XenApp servers before the Remote Desktop licenses are configured, he will see a balloon in the Windows taskbar, similar to the one shown in the following screenshot. The grace period for a Remote Desktop license setup is 120 days.

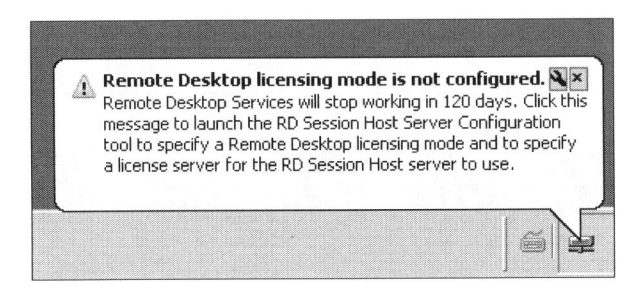

William needs to install the Remote Desktop Licensing Role Service, activate a Remote Desktop license server, and install Remote Desktop Services client access licenses (CAL) on a Windows Server 2008 or Windows Server 2008 R2 on the Active Directory Domain (or test server if we are testing the product on one single test server).

> To install **Remote Desktop Licensing Role Service** and Remote Desktop licenses, contact your Active Directory administrator or follow the instructions available at `http://xenapp6.musumeci.com.ar`

To specify the Remote Desktop licensing mode on XenApp Servers, he needs to use the **Remote Desktop Session Host Configuration** console. To open **Remote Desktop Session Host Configuration**, he clicks **Start | Administrative Tools | Remote Desktop Services | Remote Desktop Session Host Configuration**.

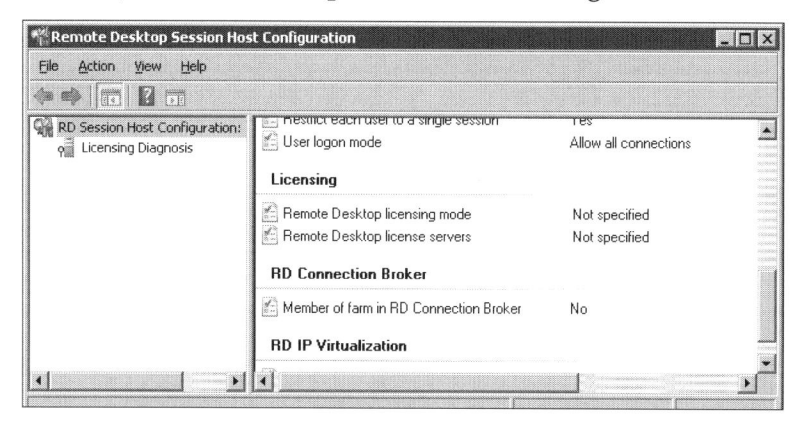

Under **Licensing**, he double-clicks on the **Remote Desktop licensing mode** option.

We can select either **Per Device** or **Per User**, depending on our environment.

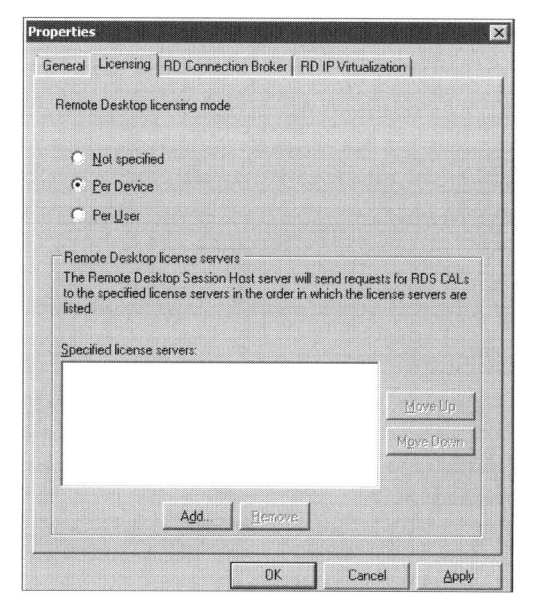

Installing XenApp 6.5

He clicks on the **Add** button, selects decided License servers and clicks on the **OK** button.

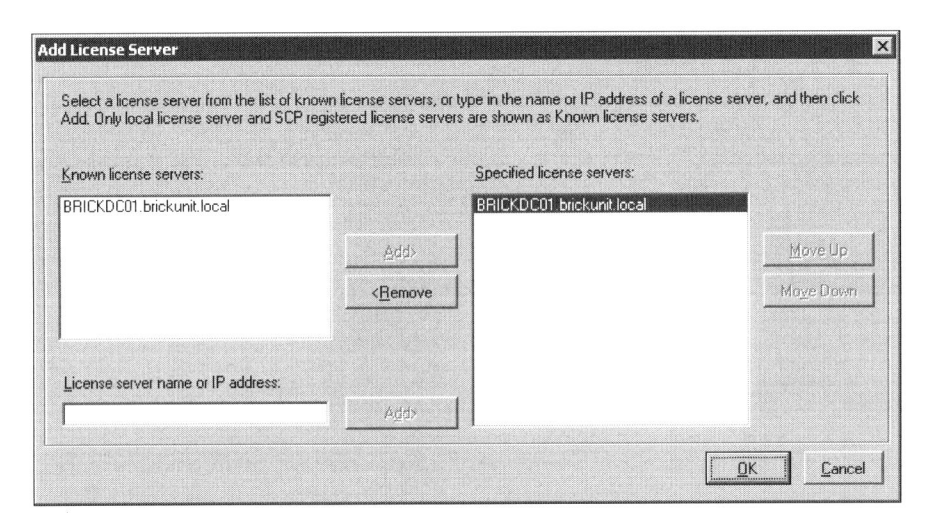

Licensing configuration is now complete. The resulting window will look like the one shown in the following screenshot:

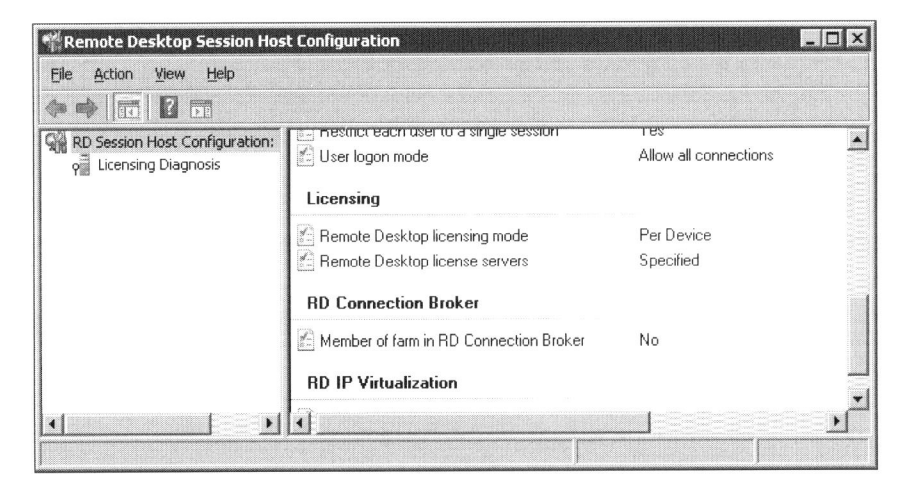

Configuring Remote Desktop licensing mode by using Group Policy

To specify the Remote Desktop licensing mode by using Group Policy (GPO), William (the administrator) enables the **Set the Remote Desktop licensing mode** GPO.

This GPO setting is located under **Computer Configuration | Policies | Administrative Templates | Windows Components | Remote Desktop Services | Remote Desktop Session Host | Licensing**.

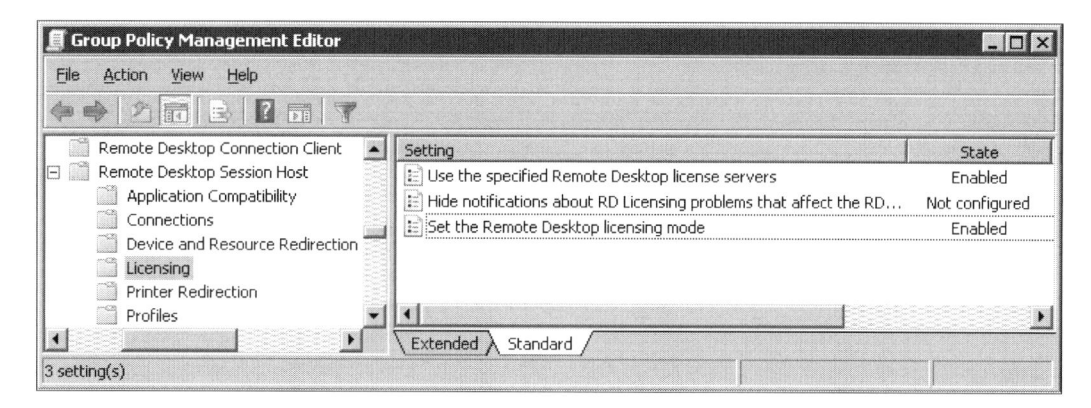

> This GPO setting will overwrite the setting configured in Remote Desktop Session Host Configuration.

To configure this GPO setting, William can use the **Group Policy Management Console** (**GPMC**) in Active Directory environments, or the **Local Group Policy Editor** to configure the GPO setting locally on our XenApp server or workgroup. Using an Active Directory GPO is the preferred method to configure Remote Desktop licensing.

This is the end of our deployment plan. Now we are ready to start with our pilot plan.

Managing XenApp Farms

William can manage his new Citrix XenApp 6.5 farm from his desktop machine or management server installing the Citrix AppCenter management console.

To start the setup, William needs to open the DVD or mount the `.ISO` file (if he is using a Virtual Machine or a remote console) and run the file `autorun.exe` in the root of the disk.

1. After `autorun.exe` has been executed, the Citrix XenApp installation menu is displayed.
2. He selects the **Manually Install** components option.

3. He selects **Common Components** and then **Management Console** on the next window.

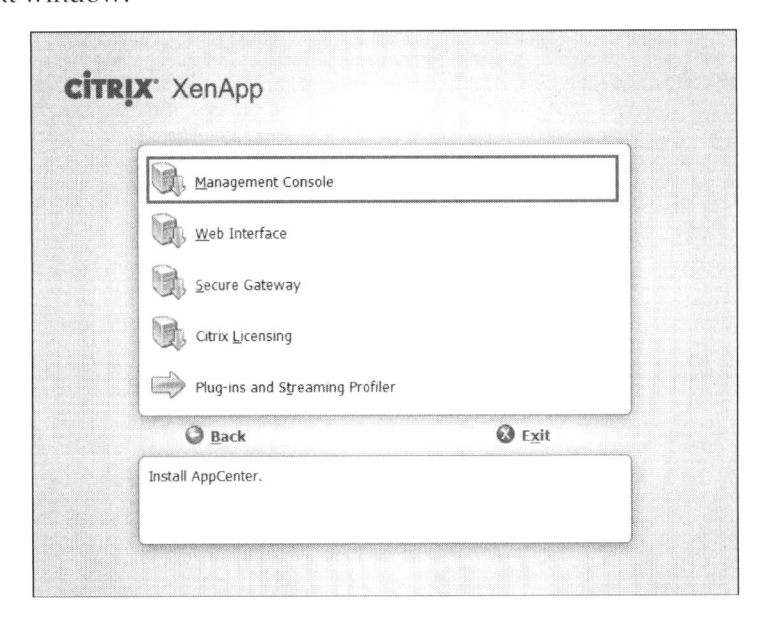

4. He then clicks on the **Next** button to launch the setup.
5. He clicks on the **Next** button to continue.
6. He clicks on the **Finish** button to complete the setup.

Summary

In this chapter, we learned how to install and configure XenApp 6.5 related components. Specifically:

- Install and configure Citrix Licensing Server
- Install and configure Citrix Web Interface
- Install and configure XenApp servers using the Wizard-Based Server Role Manager
- Configure Remote Desktop Licensing (formerly known as Terminal Server Licensing) using Remote Desktop Session Host Configuration console and Active Directory Group Policy
- Install the Citrix AppCenter management console on non-Citrix servers

In the next chapter, we are going to talk about how to use advanced XenApp deployment options, including unattended installation of XenApp.

4
Advanced XenApp Deployment

The last chapter was a very hands on chapter. We set up a Citrix data store based on Microsoft SQL Server 2008 and talked about different data store options.

We configured Remote Desktop Licensing (formerly known as Terminal Server Licensing) using Remote Desktop Session Host Configuration console and Active Directory Group Policy.

We learned how to install different Citrix XenApp 6.5 components, and particularly the XenApp 6.5 license server and Web Interface Server, and discussed how to configure these three XenApp roles using the Wizard-based Server Configuration Tool.

Finally, we learned how to install the Citrix AppCenter Management Console on non-Citrix servers or administration servers/desktops.

Now, we are going to talk about advanced XenApp deployment, including:

- Unattended install of XenApp 6.5
- Customizing Citrix Web Interface Server

Unattended install of XenApp 6.5

An unattended installation (also called silent installation) is one that does not require user interaction. Sometimes an unattended installation is called silent installation when it does not display any indication of status or progress. Mostly people use one or the other name to refer to automatic deployments.

Advanced XenApp Deployment

> This process also, can be used to deploy XenApp 6.0 servers.

In XenApp 6.5, we can use two different commands to set up the server in unattended mode:

- **XenAppSetupConsole.exe**: Is used to install XenApp components.
- **XenAppConfigConsole.exe**: Is used to configure XenApp, join server to a farm, configure authentication, and so on.

We can use the following unattended install instructions to automatize the deployment of both physical and virtual XenApp servers.

Unattended install of XenApp Components

We learned how to install XenApp 6.5 in *Chapter 3, Installing XenApp 6.5*. We also found detailed information there. Let's take a quick look at the list of tasks used by William to prepare the server to install XenApp in unattended mode:

1. Install and configure Microsoft Windows Server 2008 R2 SP1.
2. Join the server to domain (if required). He can use the `netdom` command on a CMD script or the command `Add-Computer` on PowerShell.

   CMD Script:
   ```
   Netdom join /domain:brickunit.local BrickXA03
   ```

   PowerShell:
   ```
   Add-Computer -DomainName brickunit.local -Credential brickunit\wempire -Passthru
   ```

3. Disable Windows Firewall, using the following command:
   ```
   Netsh advfirewall set allprofiles state off
   ```

4. Disable IE ESC (Enhanced Security Configuration), with the following scripts:

   Off for Administrators:
   ```
   REG ADD "HKEY_LOCAL_MACHINE\SOFTWARE\Microsoft\Active Setup\Installed Components\{A509B1A7-37EF-4b3f-8CFC-4F3A74704073}" /v "IsInstalled" /t REG_DWORD /d 0 /f
   ```

Off for Users:

```
REG ADD "HKEY_LOCAL_MACHINE\SOFTWARE\Microsoft\Active Setup\
Installed Components\{A509B1A8-37EF-4b3f-8CFC-4F3A74704073}" /v
"IsInstalled" /t REG_DWORD /d 0 /f
```

5. Disable UAC (User Account Control) to avoid issues with unattended scripts. He can re-enable later, if he needs. He disabled UAC by clicking on **Start | ControlPanel | UserAccounts | ChangeUserAccountControlSettings** and set UAC to **Nevernotify** or use the following scripts:

   CMD Script:

   ```
   REG ADD HKLM\SOFTWARE\Microsoft\Windows\CurrentVersion\Policies\
   System /v EnableLUA /t REG_DWORD /d 0 /f
   ```

   PowerShell Script:

   ```
   Set-ItemProperty -Path registry::HKEY_LOCAL_MACHINE\Software\
   Microsoft\Windows\CurrentVersion\policies\system -Name EnableLUA
   -Value 0
   ```

   After the setup and post installation configuration of the operating system is completed, he needs to add required Windows roles and install and configure XenApp 6.5 on the server. The following is the process used by William to install and configure XenApp:

6. Add required Windows roles using PowerShell. He opens a Windows PowerShell command and types the following command:

   ```
   Import-Module Servermanager
   ```

   This cmdlet will load the Server Manager module into the Windows PowerShell session (also he can create a PowerShell script with this and following cmdlets).

7. Then he adds the required roles (GPMC, .NET Framework 3.51, and Remote Desktop) using the following PowerShell cmdlets:

   ```
   Add-WindowsFeature AS-NET-Framework
   ```

   ```
   Add-WindowsFeature NET-Framework
   ```

   ```
   Add-WindowsFeature GPMC
   ```

   ```
   Add-WindowsFeature RDS-RD-Server –restart
   ```

   The last cmdlet will force a restart of the server.

Advanced XenApp Deployment

> If we want to add an extra role, and we do not know the command name of the role or feature, we can use the PowerShell cmdlet `Get-WindowsFeature` to show a list of all roles and features available. We need to use the command in the `Name` column.

Also, William can install roles from the command line, using the command `ServerManagerCmd.exe`. This command is depreciated and replaced by the previously explained PowerShell cmdlet `Add-WindowsFeature`, and is not guaranteed to work in future versions of Windows Server.

To install roles or features using `ServerManagerCmd.exe`, he can use the following command:

```
ServerManagerCmd -install AS-NET-Framework
ServerManagerCmd -install NET-Framework
ServerManagerCmd -install GPMC
ServerManagerCmd -install RDS-RD-Server -restart
```

If William wants to add an extra role, and he doesn't not know the command name of the role or feature, he can use the following command:

```
ServerManagerCmd -query
```

This command will show a list of all roles and features available (and their names) and which of them are installed.

8. Prerequisite installations are completed. William needs to extract the XenApp 6.5 ISO file downloaded from the Citrix site to a folder in the server or mount the XenApp 6.5 DVD in the server.

9. The next step for William is to install XenApp running `XenAppSetupConsole.exe` file from the folder `\Xenapp Server Setup\Bin` in the local server folder or the XenApp 6.5 DVD, using the following command:

```
XenAppSetupConsole.exe /install:XenApp /Platinum
```

The `/install` parameter is used to select features to install. He can install multiple features using commas. Valid options are:

- **EdgeSightServer**: Installs EdgeSight Server role
- **Licensing**: Installs Citrix Licensing Server role
- **MerchandisingServer**: Installs Merchandising Server role
- **PCMAdmin**: Installs Power and Capacity Management administration components

- **Provisioning**: Installs Provisioning Services
- **SecureGateway**: Install Secure Gateway
- **SmartAuditorServer**: Install SmartAuditor server
- **SsonService**: Install Single sign-on service
- **WebInterface**: Install Web Interface role
- **XenApp**: Install XenApp server role

If he chooses the **XenApp** feature, the Citrix AppCenter Console, Windows Desktop Experience Integration, Citrix Receiver for Windows (formerly known as Online Plug-in), and Citrix Offline Plug-in are installed by default.

Also he can use the /exclude parameter to omit the installation of the same XenApp Role components. Options are:

- **XA_Console**: Omits the installation of the Citrix Delivery Services Console
- **XA_IISIntegration**: Omits the installation of the XMLS IIS Integration feature if the server has IIS role services installed
- **XenAppEnhancedDesktopExperience**: Omits the installation of the Windows Desktop Experience Integration feature (this option is new in XenApp 6.5 and is not available on XenApp 6.0)

He used the /Platinum parameter to set the edition of XenApp to Platinum. If we don't specify an edition option, the Platinum edition is set by default. Other options available are:

- /Enterprise: Sets the edition of XenApp to Enterprise
- /Advanced: Sets the edition of XenApp to Advanced

> More information about XenAppSetupConsole.exe is available at http://support.citrix.com/proddocs/topic/xenapp65-install/ps-install-command-line.html

10. Once the XenApp installation is complete, he is ready to join the XenApp server to existing farm and configure XenApp 6.5, using the `XenAppConfigConsole.exe` tool, located at `C:\Program Files (x86)\Citrix\XenApp\ServerConfig` folder of XenApp 6.5. If we are running XenApp 6.0, the file is located at `\XenApp Server Configuration Tool` folder.

    The following command will join the server to the existing XenApp farm and using the information stored in the SQL Server using a DSN file (instructions to create the file are below):

    ```
    XenAppConfigConsole.exe /ExecutionMode:Join /FarmName:BrickFarm65
    /DSNFile:c:\XA65\BrickFarm65.dsn /OdbcUsername:brickunit\
    administrator /odbcPassword:Passw0rd /ZoneName:Frederick /
    LicenseServerName:BrickXA01.brickunit.local /Log:C:\XA65\
    XA65Config.log
    ```

    ```
    C:\Program Files (x86)\Citrix\XenApp\ServerConfig>XenAppConfigConsole.exe /Execu
    tionMode:Join /FarmName:BrickFarm65 /DSNFile:c:\XA65\BrickFarm65.dsn /OdbcUserna
    me:brickunit\administrator /odbcPassword:Passw0rd /ZoneName:Frederick /LicenseSe
    rverName:BrickXA01.brickunit.local /Log:C:\XA65\XA65Config.log
    Citrix XenApp Server Configuration Tool [Version 1.2]
    Copyright (c) 2010 Citrix Systems, Inc.  All rights reserved.

    Exit Code: Successful

    C:\Program Files (x86)\Citrix\XenApp\ServerConfig>
    ```

    > Use the `/Confirm` parameter to show a confirmation message before configuring the XenServer server. This option is very useful for testing an unattended script.

    The `/ExecutionMode` parameter sets the task we want to execute. William can use this option to create a XenApp farm, join or remove the XenApp from an existing farm, using the following options:

    - **Create**: Creates a new XenApp farm
    - **Join**: Joins a XenApp server to an existing farm
    - **Leave**: Removes the XenApp server from the farm. This option is valid *only* if we previously joined the XenApp server to an existing farm
    - **ImagePrep**: Prepares the XenApp server for imaging. This option is valid only if we previously joined the XenApp server to an existing farm

The `/FarmName` parameter specifies the XenApp farm name.

The `/DSNFile` parameter is used to set the path to the DSN file used to connect to the XenApp data store hosted on a SQL Server (or an Oracle database).

To create the DSN for the unattended install, William needs to open the `mf20.dsn` file located at `C:\Program Files (x86)\Citrix\Independent Management Architecture` folder of an existing XenApp server. Then he copies the content to a new DSN file located on local hard drive of the new XenApp server or in a network file server.

The DSN file should look like this:

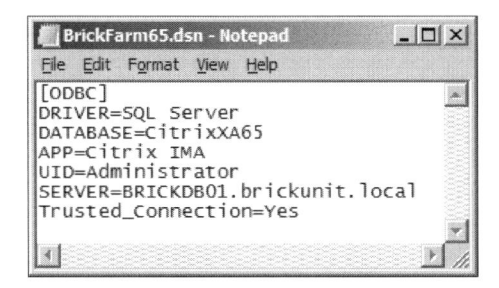

```
BrickFarm65.dsn - Notepad
File Edit Format View Help
[ODBC]
DRIVER=SQL Server
DATABASE=CitrixXA65
APP=Citrix IMA
UID=Administrator
SERVER=BRICKDB01.brickunit.local
Trusted_Connection=Yes
```

The `/OdbcUserName` parameters are used to set the data store user name in format DOMAIN\USER.

The `/OdbcPassword` parameters specify the data store password.

The `/ZoneName` parameter is used to set the Zone Name.

The `/LicenseServerName` parameter is used to specify the name of the Citrix license server.

The `/Log` parameter saves the progress of the configuration to the log file specified.

> More information about `XenAppConfigConsole.exe` is available at `http://support.citrix.com/proddocs/index.jsp?topic=/xenapp6-w2k8-install/ps-config-command-syntax.html`

Advanced XenApp Deployment

11. After the configuration process is completed successfully, William needs to reboot the server to complete the process. He can automatize this step, using the following command:

    ```
    Shutdown /r /t 0
    ```

Customizing Citrix Web Interface Server

One of the common tasks, almost every customer wants is the customization of Citrix Web Interface and William is no exception. He wants to remove all Citrix branding logos and change color to corporate colors (blue and red). The following is a screenshot of the original Citrix Web Interface Logon page and its different parts.

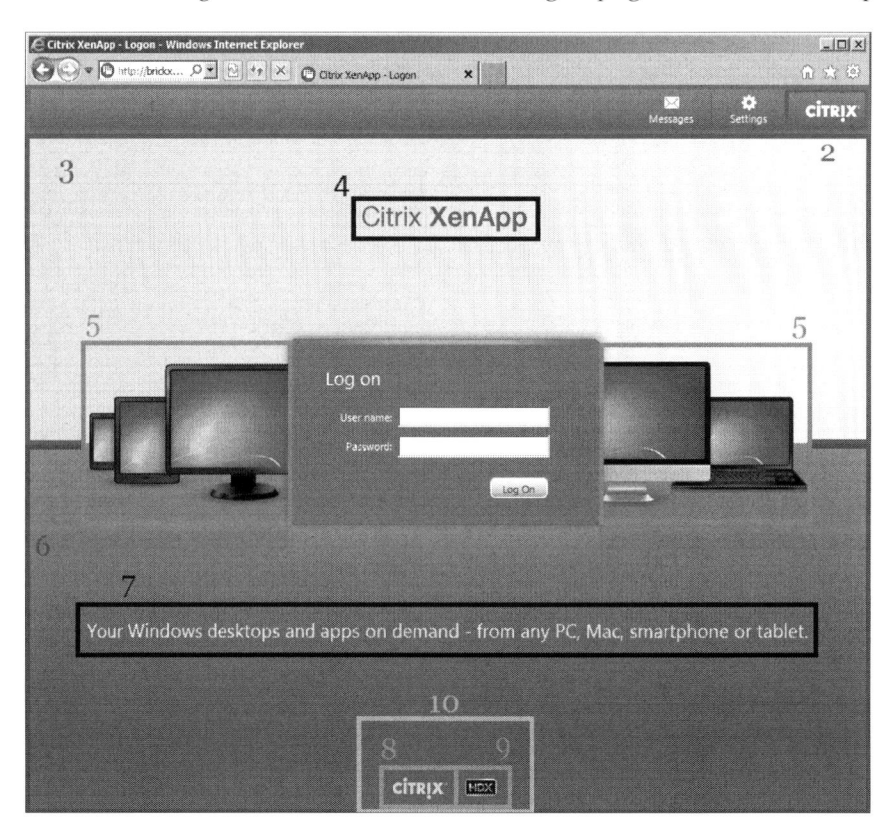

1. Header section
2. Header Citrix logo
3. Horizontal Page Upper section
4. Product Name logo

5. Device image
6. Horizontal Page Lower section
7. Tagline text
8. Footer Citrix logo
9. Footer HDX logo
10. Footer section

Now, let's help William to customize the Web Interface. The process will require:

- Backup of Web Interface folder
- Basic knowledge of HTML and CSS to understand and/or customize changes

The first step is creating a backup of Web Interface folder, just in case. He needs to back up the folder `C:\inetpub\wwwroot\Citrix\XenApp`, where `XenApp` is the folder of the XenApp Web Site's site.

Also, if the site got corrupted after any change, we can repair the site, using the following steps. Note, that all previous changes will be lost.

1. Open **CitrixWebInterfaceManagement**.
2. Click on **XenAppWebSites**.
3. Right-click on the site name.
4. Select **SiteMaintenance**.
5. Choose **RepairSite**.

After the backup is done, William is ready to modify the Login page.

Original image files are located at the `[XenApp Site folder]\media` folder, and usually there are two files: one `.PNG` to display on new browsers and one `.GIF` for older browsers.

Similarly, we can find files ended with `loggedoff`. These files are displayed when the user is logged off.

Changing the header section color

To change the color of the header (Part #1), William needs to open the file `fullStyle.inc`, located at `[XenApp Site folder]\app_data\include` folder, search for `#headerWrapper` and `#header` sections and replace the following line on the background CSS property `<%=Branding.getBrandingColor ( wiContext.getConfiguration ()) %>url(<%=Branding.getBrandingImageURL ( wiContext.getConfiguration ())%>)` to a color name (example: blue) or a color code (example: #456789), similar to the following example:

```
<%
// Header area
%>
#headerWrapper {
    background: blue repeat-x bottom left;
    width: 100%; /* needed for the header wrapper to fill the
entire width in IE6 on the login page. Alternative fix is to
remove "position: relative" from the body (for IE6) */
}

#header {
    background: blue repeat-x bottom left;
    margin: 0 auto;
    width: <%=wiContext.getString("PageWidth")%>;
    color: <%=Branding.getHeaderFontColor
(wiContext.getConfiguration()) %>;
}
```

Changing the header Citrix logo

To remove the Citrix Logo from Header (Part #2), William needs to open the file `fullStyle.inc`, located at the `[XenApp Site folder]\app_data\include` folder, search for the `#headerLogo` section and add the bolded text:

```
#headerLogo {
    padding: 11px 0 11px 18px;
    display: none;
}
```

Here, William added the CSS property `display` to `#headerLogo` section. He set display to the value `none`. This setting hides an element, but it will not take up any space on the page.

Alternatively, he can use a custom image file instead of the default logo. To accomplish this, he needs to modify the following files:

- `[XenApp Site folder]\media\CitrixLogoHeader.png`
- `[XenApp Site folder]\media\CitrixLogoHeader.gif`

Changing horizontal page upper section color

To change the horizontal page upper section color (Part #3), the area that contains the Product name image (Part #4) and the Device name image (Part #5), William needs to search for `#horizonTop` section in the file `fullstyle.inc`, located at the `[XenApp Site folder]\app_data\include` folder and replace the following line `#FDFDFDurl("../media/HorizonBgTop.png")` on the background CSS property to a color name (example: red) or a color code (example: #456789), similar to the following example:

```
#horizonTop {
    width: 100%;
    height: 325px;
    background: red no-repeat top left;
    text-align: center;
}
```

Changing the product name image

To remove the product name image (Part #4), William needs to search for the `#horizonTopimg` section and add the bold text, similar to the following example, to the file `fullstyle.inc`, located at the `[XenApp Site folder]\app_data\include` folder.

```
#horizonTop img {
    padding-top: 75px;
    display: none;
}
```

Here, William added again the CSS property `display` to `#horizonTopimg` section. He set display to the value `none`. This setting hides an element but it will not take up any space on the page.

Also, he can use a customized image file and replace the original one.

> Depending on our environment, we can have a XenApp or XenDesktop image.

Advanced XenApp Deployment

To replace the **XenApp** image, he needs to replace following files:

- `[XenApp Site folder]\media\CitrixXenApp.gif`
- `[XenApp Site folder]\media\CitrixXenAppLoggedoff.gif`
- `[XenApp Site folder]\media\CitrixXenApp.png`
- `[XenApp Site folder]\media\CitrixXenAppLoggedoff.png`

To replace the **XenDesktop** image, he needs to replace following files:

- `[XenApp Site folder]\media\CitrixXenDesktop.gif`
- `[XenApp Site folder]\media\CitrixXenDesktopLoggedoff.gif`
- `[XenApp Site folder]\media\CitrixXenDesktop.png`
- `[XenApp Site folder]\media\CitrixXenDesktopLoggedoff.png`

Changing devices image

To remove the devices image (Part #5) located at left and right of the login window (in fact, it is just one single image file), William needs to search for `.horizonPage.mainPane` section on the file `fullstyle.inc`, located at the `[XenApp Site folder]\app_data\include` folder and modify the text on bold:

```
.horizonPage .mainPane {
    position: relative;
    top: -120px;
    background: none;
    color: white;
    padding: 0;
    overflow: auto;
}
```

Here, William takes a different approach to remove the image. He modifies the CSS property `background` and changes the value to `none`. No background image will be displayed when he uses this setting.

To replace the devices image with a custom image, he needs to modify the following files:

- `[XenApp Site folder]\media\Devices.gif`
- `[XenApp Site folder]\media\DevicesLoggedoff.gif`
- `[XenApp Site folder]\media\Devices.png`
- `[XenApp Site folder]\media\DevicesLoggedoff.png`

Changing horizontal page lower section color

To change the horizontal page lower section color (Part #6), the area that contains the Tagline text (Part #7) and Footer section (Part #10), William needs to search for `.horizonPage` section in the file `fullstyle.inc`, located at the `[XenApp Site folder]\app_data\include` folder and replace the line `#566169 url("../media/HorizonBgBottom.png")` in the background CSS property to a color name (example: blue) or a color code (example: #456789), similar to following example:

```
.horizonPage {
    background: blue repeat-x left 325px;
}
```

To replace the background image with a custom image, he needs to modify the following file:

- `[XenApp Site folder]\media\HorizonBgBottom.png`

Changing the tagline text

To remove the tagline "Your Windows desktop and apps on demand – from any PC, MAC, smartphone or tablet" (Part #7), William needs to search for the `#horizonTagline` section in the file `fullstyle.inc`, located at the `[XenApp Site folder]\app_data\include` folder and modify the text on bold:

```
#horizonTagline {
    color: #F2F2F2;
    font-size: 180%;
    font-weight: normal;
    margin: 50px 0 0 0;
    padding-bottom: 10px;
    text-align: center;
    display: none;
}
```

Here, William added again the CSS property `display` to `#horizonTagline` section. He sets display to the value `none`. This setting hides an element but it will not take up any space on the page.

Advanced XenApp Deployment

If later, William wants to display the tagline, he needs to search for the `HorizonTagline` entry in the file `accessplatform_strings.properties` located at `C:\Program Files (x86)\Citrix\Web Interface\5.4.0\languages` folder and modify the text on bold:

```
DisasterRecoveryInUse=The Web site could not connect to the
resources you normally use. Some of your resources may behave
differently or may not be available.
HorizonTagline=Welcome to Brick Unit Constructions
```

> The file `accessplatform_strings.properties` contains messages in English only. If we are going to customize the Citrix Web Interface for different languages, we must edit the appropriate file for our language. For example, we need to edit the file `accessplatform_strings_ES.properties` if we are planning to change the Spanish message file.

Changing the footer Citrix logo

To remove the Citrix logo from Footer (Part #8), William needs to open the file `fullstyle.inc`, located at the `[XenApp Site folder]\app_data\include` folder, search for the `#footer img` section and add the bolded text:

```
#footer img
{
    padding: 0 8px;
    vertical-align: middle;
    display: none;
}
```

Here, William added the CSS property `display` to `#footer img` section. He sets `display` to the value `none`. This setting hides an element but it will not take up any space on the page.

Alternatively, he can use a custom image file instead of the default logo. To accomplish this, he needs to modify the following files:

- `[XenApp Site folder]\media\CitrixWatermark.png`
- `[XenApp Site folder]\media\CitrixLogoDarkLoggedOff.png`
- `[XenApp Site folder]\media\CitrixWatermark.gif`
- `[XenApp Site folder]\media\CitrixLogoDarkLoggedOff.gif`

Changing the HDX logo

To remove the HDX logo from Footer (Part #9), William needs to open the file `fullstyle.inc`, located at the `[XenApp Site folder]\app_data\include` folder, search for the `.horizonPage #hdxLogo` section and change the bolded text:

```
.horizonPage #hdxLogo {
    display: none;
}
```

Here, William changed the CSS property `display` in `.horizonPage #hdxLogo` section to the value `none`. This setting hides an element but it will not take up any space on the page.

Alternatively, he can use a custom image file instead of the default logo. To accomplish this, he needs to modify the following files:

- `[XenApp Site folder]\media\HDX.gif`
- `[XenApp Site folder]\media\HDXLoggedoff.gif`
- `[XenApp Site folder]\media\HDX.png`
- `[XenApp Site folder]\media\HDXLoggedoff.png`

Changing the Footer section

The Footer (Part #10) section is composed of the Footer Citrix logo (Part #8) and Footer HDX logo (Part #9) areas. To remove the whole Footer section, William needs to open the file `fullstyle.inc`, located at the `[XenApp Site folder]\app_data\include` folder, search for the `#footer` section and add the bolded text:

```
<%
  // Footer area
%>
#footer
{
    text-align: center;
    padding-bottom: 10px;
    display: none;
}
```

Here, William added the CSS property `display` to the `#footer` section and set the value to `none`. This setting hides an element but it will not take up any space on the page.

After all these changes, we can see the final result:

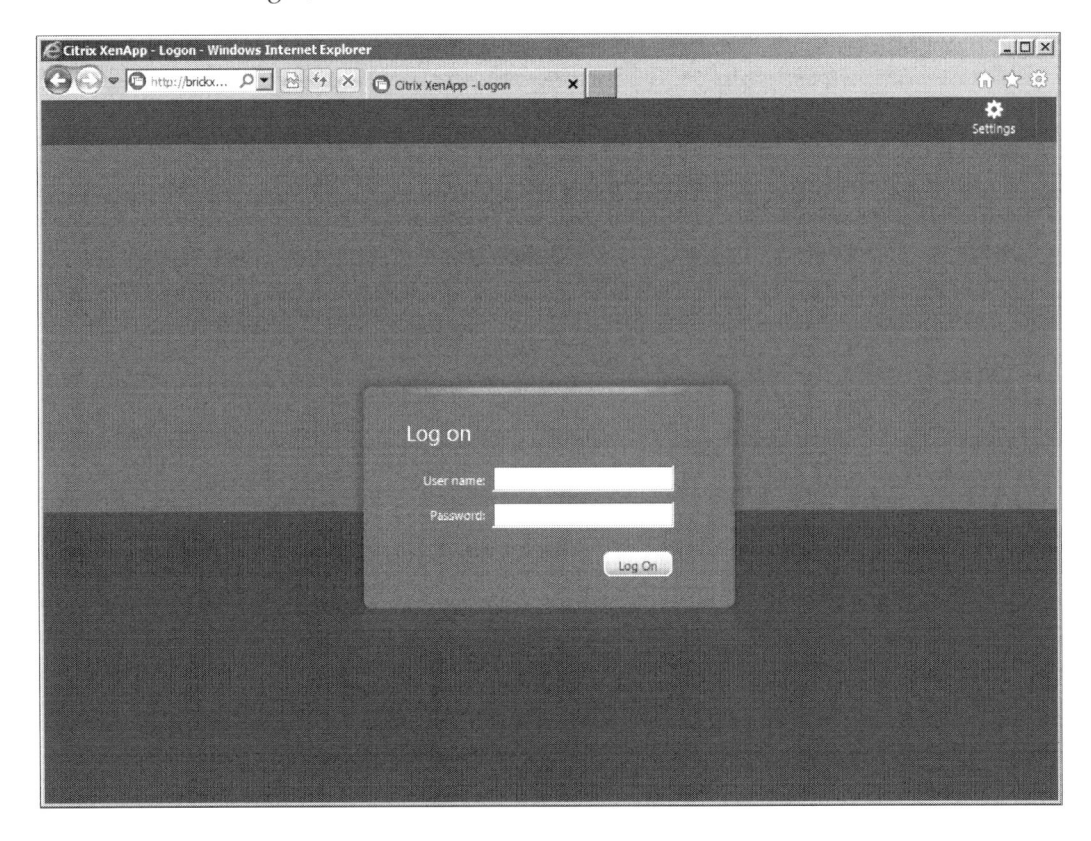

Summary

In this chapter, we learned some advanced XenApp 6.5 deployment tasks. Specifically:

- Installing and configuring Citrix XenApp 6.5 in unattended mode
- Installing and configuring Citrix XenApp 6.5 from command line
- Customization of the Citrix Web Interface.

In the next chapter, we are going to talk on about how to use the new Citrix AppCenter management console to manage our XenApp farms and provide access to other administrators to access all or some specific administration features.

5
Using Management Tools

In the previous chapter, we used unattended scripts to deploy XenApp 6.5 or install XenApp from the command line and we learned how to customize the Citrix Web Interface, change colors, and remove branding.

Now, we are going to help William Empire from Brick Unit Construction to manage Citrix components using Citrix management tools, and in particular, we will work with the following:

- Citrix AppCenter Console
- License Administration Console
- Citrix Web Interface Management Console
- Citrix SSL Relay Configuration tool
- Shadow taskbar
- SpeedScreen Latency Reduction Manager
- Managing XenApp administrators accounts

Management Consoles

Citrix offers a complete set of tools for managing servers, farms, published resources, and connections.

Citrix AppCenter Console

The **Citrix AppCenter**, formerly known as **Citrix Delivery Services Console** in XenApp 6.0 and **Citrix Access Management Console** in previous XenApp versions is a tool that integrates into the Microsoft Management Console (MMC) and enables us to execute management tasks.

Using Management Tools

Using Citrix AppCenter console, we can set up and monitor servers, server farms, publish resources and sessions, configure policies and printers, and configure application access.

We can manage load balancing, troubleshoot alerts, diagnose problems in our XenApp farms, view hotfix information for our Citrix products, and track administrative changes.

> The Citrix AppCenter console is pretty similar to Citrix Delivery Services Console in XenApp 6.0, so most of the tasks in this chapter are similar, but we will find a few differences.

Now, let us look at what happens when William opens his Citrix AppCenter console for the very first time.

To open the console, he clicks on **Start | All Programs | Citrix | Management Consoles | Citrix AppCenter**.

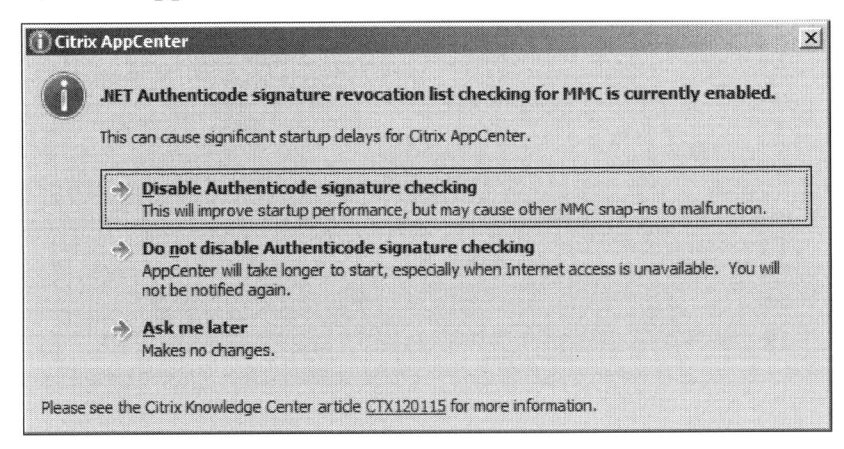

A pop up window appears if .NET Authenticode signature for the MMC console is enabled. He chooses the **Disable Authenticode signature checking** option as Citrix recommends it to improve startup performance.

> Follow the instructions on http://support.citrix.com/article/CTX120115 to disable the **Authenticode signature checking** in multiple machines

In the following screen, he needs to choose **XenApp** from **Select Products or Components** and click on the **Next** button. He can add more components later from the console by clicking on **XenApp** and then using the option **Configure and run discovery** task from the **Actions** pane of the Citrix AppCenter Console.

[96]

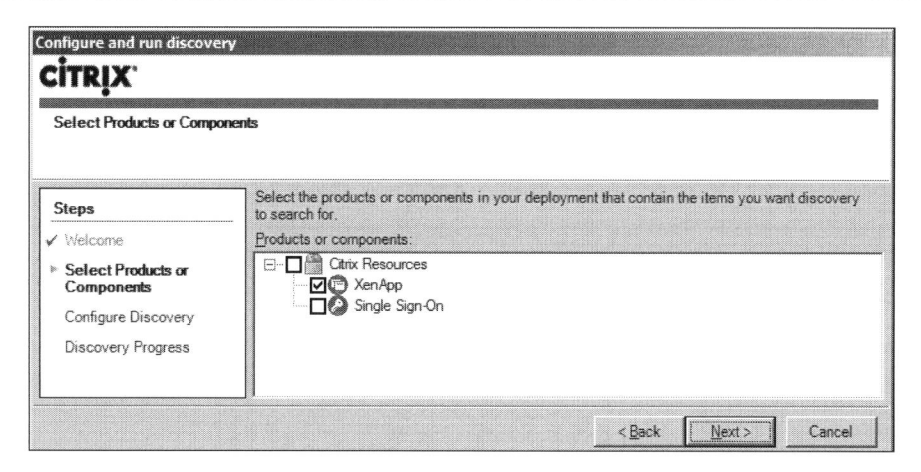

Chapter 5

[Screenshot: Configure and run discovery — Select Products or Components, with XenApp checked under Citrix Resources]

Now he needs to add at least one XenApp 6.5 server. He can use the **Add Local Computer** button to add current server or use the **Add** button to add a different server and click on the **Next** button to continue.

Remember, at the very beginning in XenApp 6.5, we can set up the server in **Session-Host Only** or **Session-Host and Controller** mode. This XenApp server selected should be configured as **Session-Host and Controller** (also known as Controller) role server. As we have mentioned before, the first server of the farm is a session-host and controller server, so if we are not sure of which server is running XML service, choose the first server of the farm.

[Screenshot: Configure and run discovery — Select Servers, with BRICKXA65-02 listed]

[97]

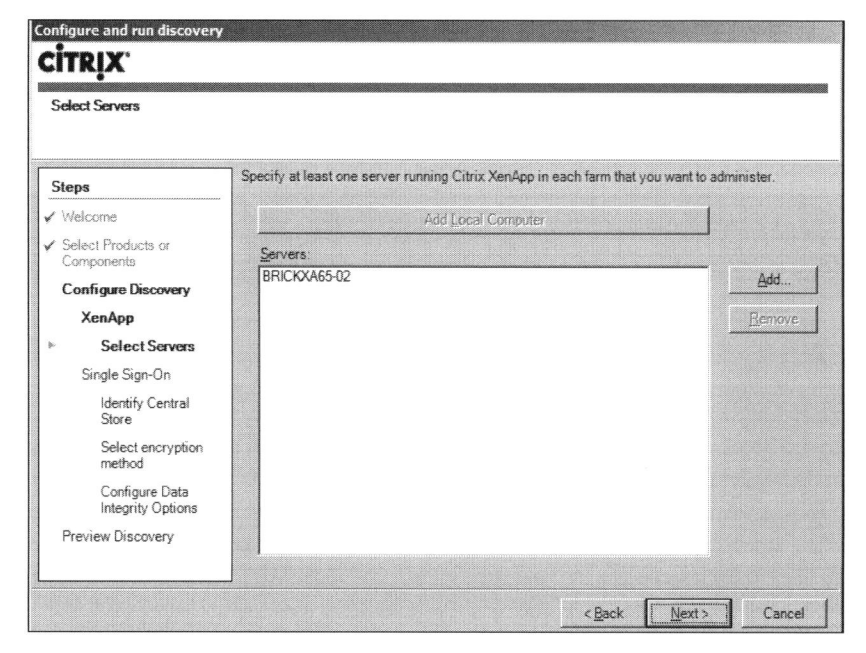

Using Management Tools

The console is ready to use as soon as the discovery is successful.

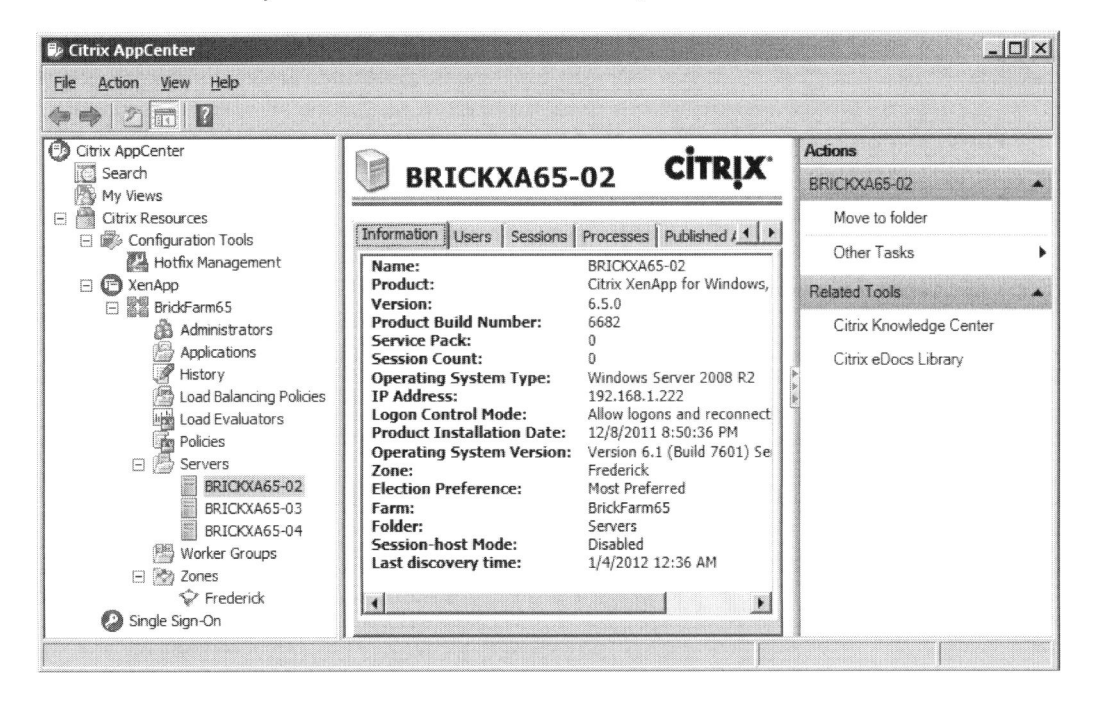

License Administration Console

William can use this console to add, manage, and track Citrix licenses using a web browser.

A web browser can be used to open the console on a remote server using one of the following URL options:

`http://license-server-name:port` or `http://brickxa65-01:8082`

`http://license-server-IP-address:port` or `http://192.168.1.222:8082`

where:

- **license-server-name** is the name of the license server.
- **license-server-IP-Address** is the IP address of the license server.
- **port** is the port number for the console's Web service. The default Web service port for the console is **8082**.

In order to open the **License Administration Console**, on the machine on which it is installed, William clicks on **Start | All Programs | Citrix | Management Consoles | License Administration Console**:

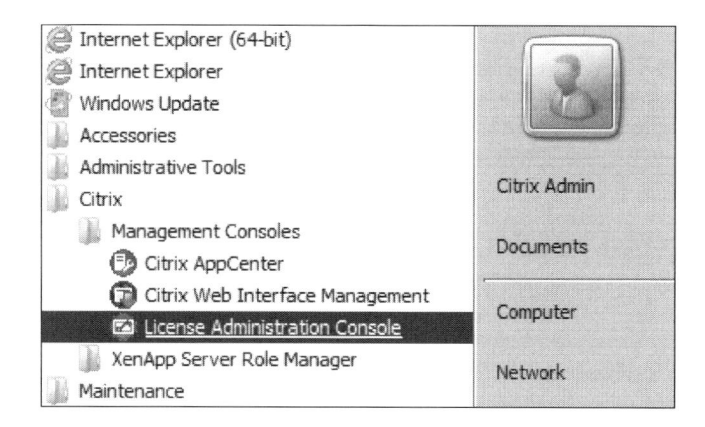

This is the default view when he opens **Citrix License Administration Console**:

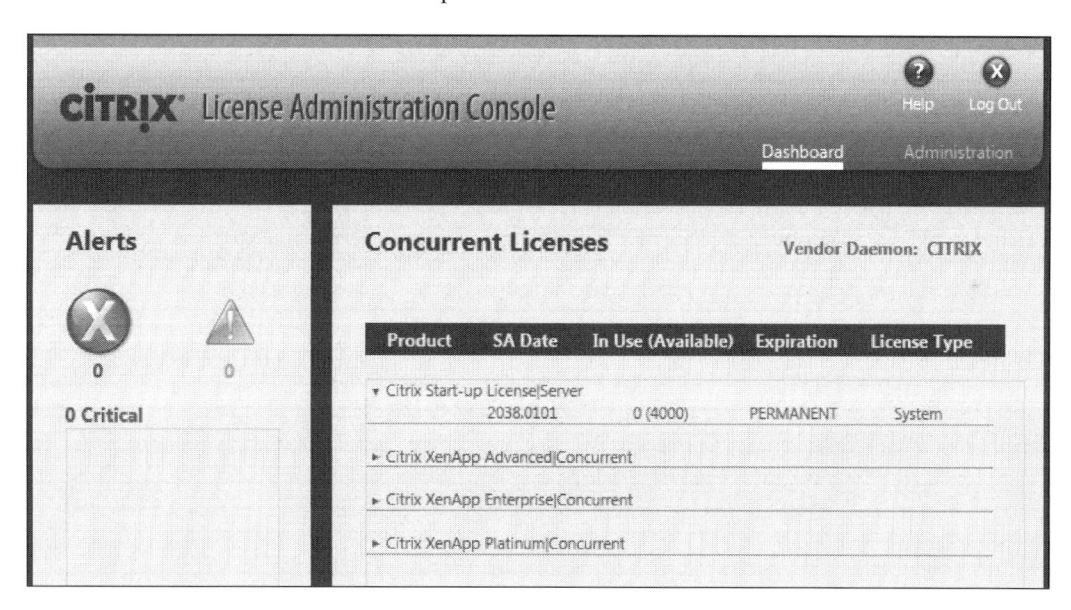

The console includes two areas to view and manage licenses: **Dashboard** and **Administration** areas. He can switch between both views using links in the top-right area of the console.

He can use the **Dashboard** to monitor licenses, license activity, and alerts.

Using Management Tools

He can use the **Administration** area to view system information, add and administer licenses, configure users and alerts, log license management activities, secure the console server, and more.

To log in to the console, he needs to click on the **Administration** area, enter the username (default is **admin**), password, and choose **Display Language** (optional).

The **System Information** tab provides very useful information such as **Release Version** and **Host Name**. The host name is used when he needs to assign Citrix licenses.

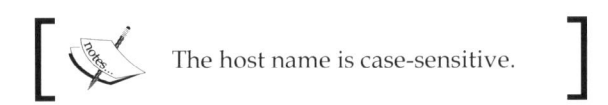

> The host name is case-sensitive.

For more information on how to install Citrix licenses, refer to *Chapter 3, Installing XenApp 6.5*.

The **User Configuration** tab is where William can add or manage users. Now let us help William create a new account for himself. He needs to click on the **New User** icon to create a new user for himself:

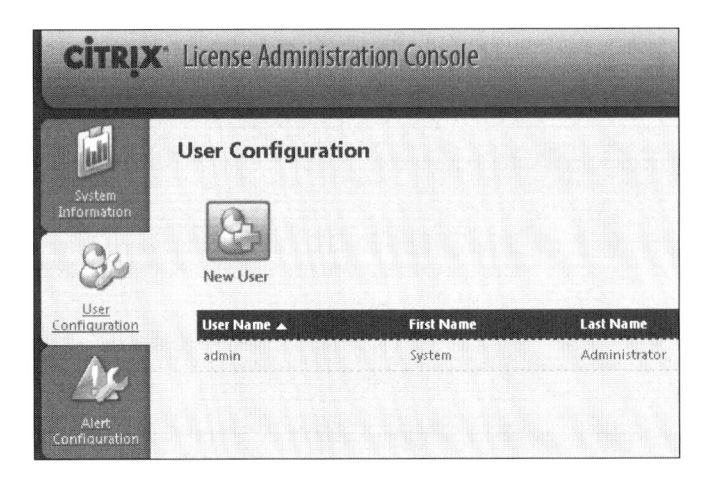

In the **New User** screen, he needs to enter **User Name**, **First Name**, **Last Name**, and **Password**. Also, he needs to choose the role between **User** and **Administrator**. He will choose **Administrator**, so he can install and manage licenses. The **User** role is useful to check the configuration of the license server or to check the available licenses.

Chapter 5

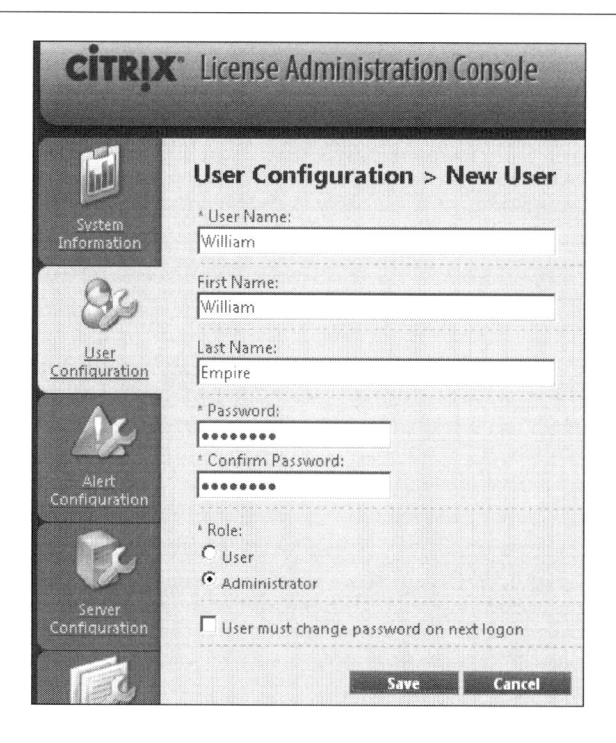

The following screenshot shows the list of users, including the new user created by William:

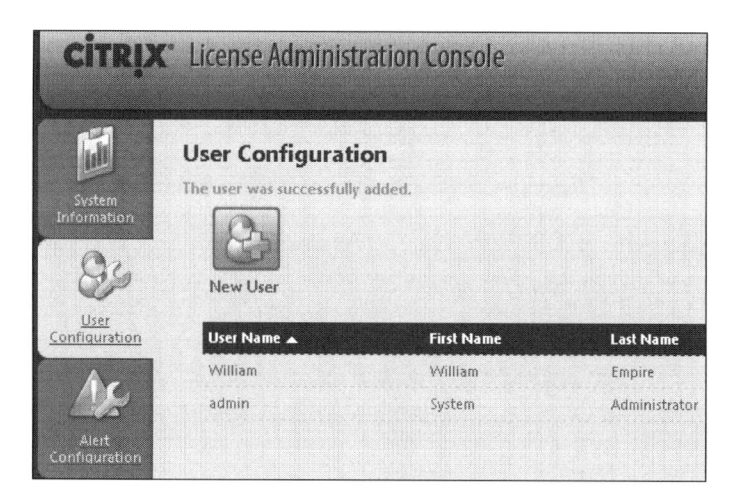

Using Management Tools

In the **Alert Configuration** tab, William can select the alerts he wants to display on the Dashboard and determines the threshold to trigger the alert.

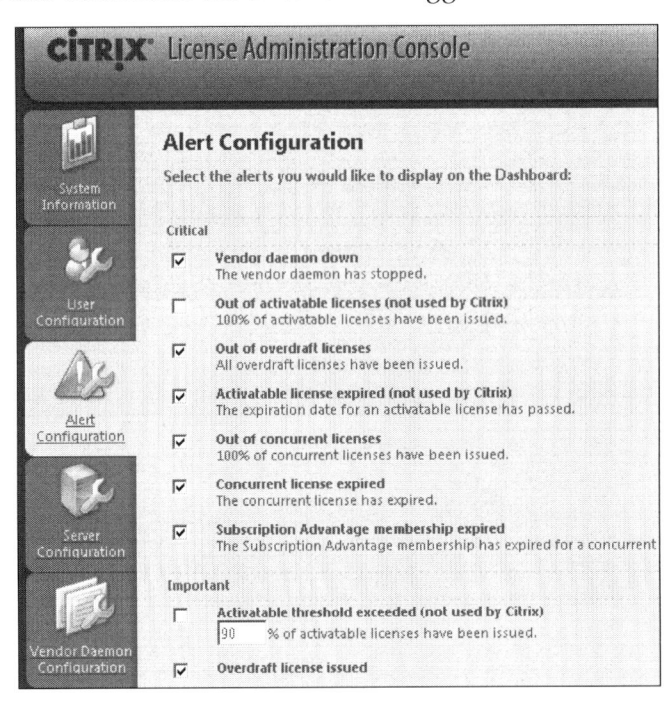

The **Server Configuration** tab helps him to change License Port, enable HTTPS protocol and install Web certificates, configure License Server Manager Port, change Log Level, and adjust User Interface settings.

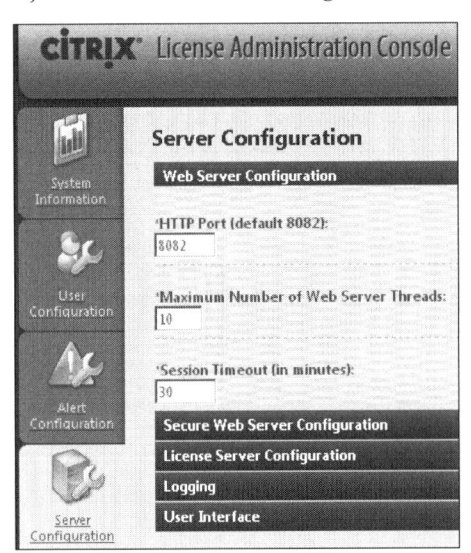

Chapter 5

The **Vendor Daemon Configuration** tab is used to check the status of Citrix License server. This is the first place he needs to check if he experiences any license issue. The status must be **Running**.

This tab is the place he uses to install and manage licenses. To install new licenses we need to click on the **Import License** icon.

If added licenses are not shown in the console, it is recommended to restart all Citrix Licensing services on the License Server or even restart the machine.

> An alternative method to install licenses is to manually copy the .LIC file into C:\Program Files (x86)\Citrix\Licensing\MyFiles folder and restart the **Citrix Licensing service**.

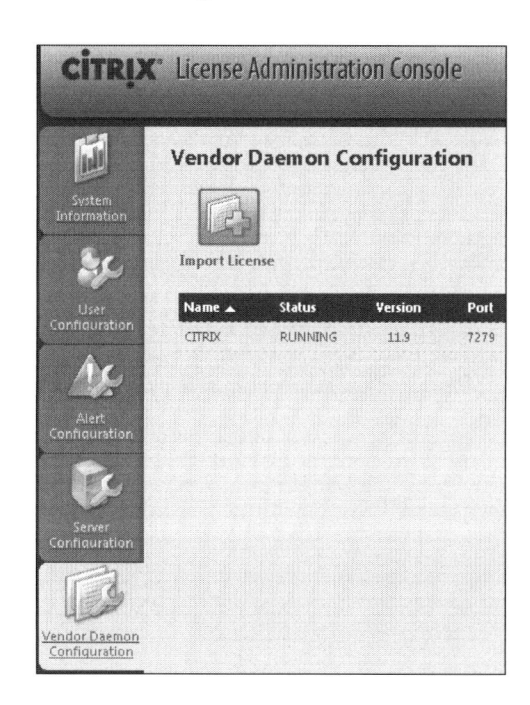

[103]

Using Management Tools

Citrix Web Interface Management Console

The Web Interface provides users with access to XenApp applications, desktops, and content. Users access their resources using a web browser or Citrix Receiver (formerly known as Citrix Online Plug-in or Citrix Client).

William has two options to configure Web Interface sites:

- He can create and configure Web Interface sites on Microsoft Internet Information Services (IIS) using the **Citrix Web Interface Management** console.
- He can edit manually the site configuration file `webinterface.conf` to manage and administer Web Interface sites. Usually, this file is located at `C:\inetpub\wwwroot\Citrix\<SiteName>\conf` folder, where `<SiteName>` is the name of the site. Restarting the IIS web server using IISRESET from the command line is recommended but not required. Please back up the file before making any changes on the web interface. Installing or upgrading a new version of web interface will overwrite changes.

> Important: Editing the `.conf` file and copying the file to multiple servers using a script is a common practice in environments with multiple or personalized web interface servers, but if your environment just involves one or two web interface servers, you would probably want to modify the site configuration from the console.

The following screenshot is a view of the **Citrix Web Interface Management** console. Using the **Actions** pane of the MMC console, William can **Create Site** or **Edit Settings** of the selected site.

Chapter 5

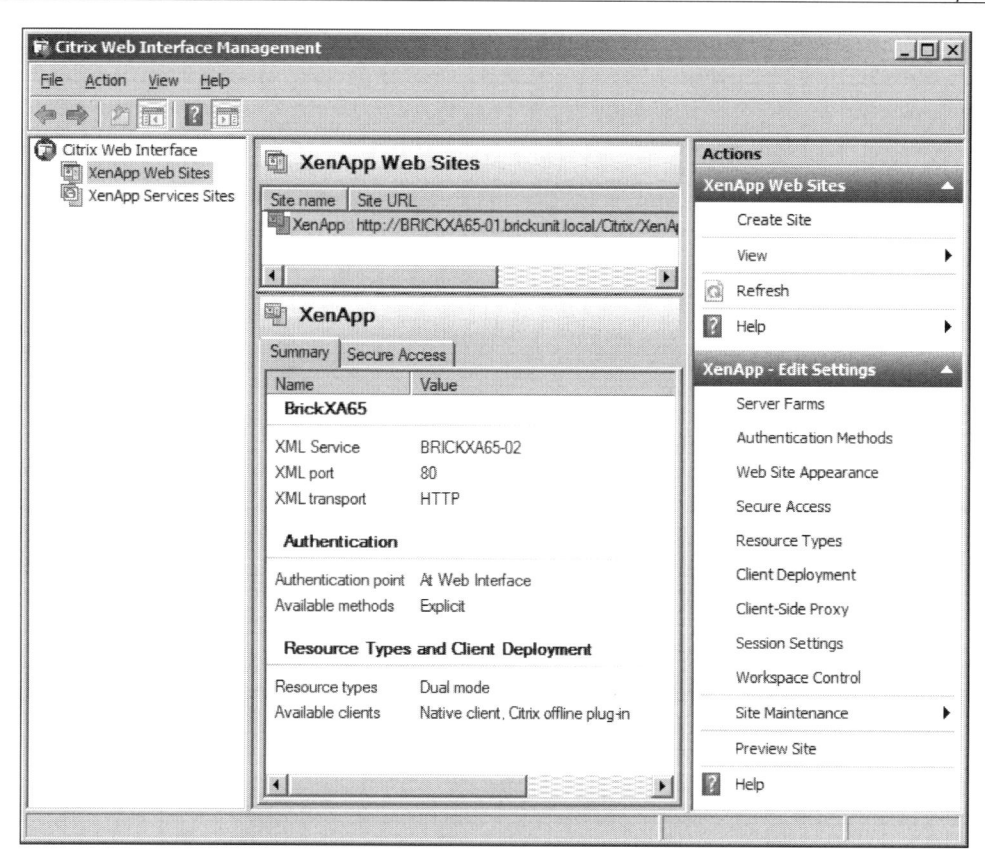

![Citrix Web Interface Management screenshot showing XenApp Web Sites configuration with Summary tab displaying BrickXA65 farm details including XML Service BRICKXA65-02, XML port 80, XML transport HTTP, Authentication settings, and Resource Types. Actions pane on the right shows options like Create Site, View, Refresh, Server Farms, Authentication Methods, Web Site Appearance, Secure Access, Resource Types, Client Deployment, Client-Side Proxy, Session Settings, Workspace Control, Site Maintenance, Preview Site, and Help.]

The **Server Farms** option on the **Edit Settings** pane helps us to set up XML Broker(s) and Citrix farm(s) accessible to the web interface.

The XML Broker (also referenced as XML service or XML server) and web interface work together to offer the users access to applications.

The web interface uses the XML Broker to display a list of applications based on the user's permissions. After a user receives applications and launches one of them, the XML Broker provides a list of servers in the farm that hosts this application. The XML Broker chooses one of them based on several rules and returns the address of this server to the web interface.

Using Management Tools

Choosing the appropriate XML Broker is critical for our farm. If we have one single XML Broker configured in the web interface and this server is down, users will be unable to launch any applications. You must consider having multiple or at least two XML Broker servers for redundancy.

In a small farm, with a few servers, the XML Broker is hosted on one or two servers used for multiple infrastructure functions. Also, sometimes for redundancy purposes, the least used XenApp application server is added as the XML Broker.

In a large farm, the XML Broker is usually configured on one or more dedicated servers, usually dedicated data collectors or most preferred servers to become data collector in the zone.

Remember, only servers set as **Session-Host and Controller** (also known as Controller) role are running the XML service.

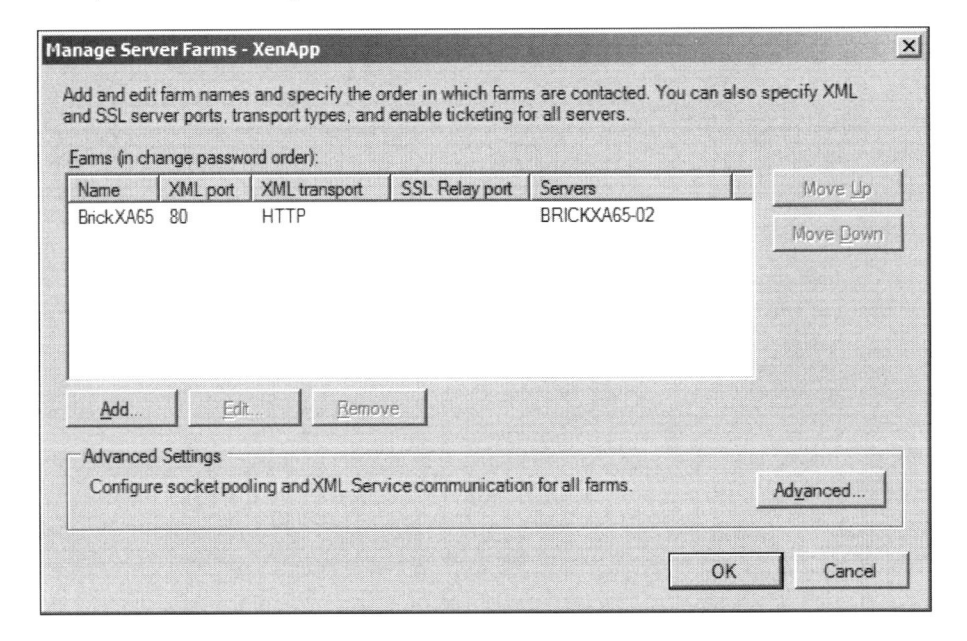

> When we have two Data Collector servers (XenApp servers configured as Session-Host and Controller), we can use them as a XML Broker. A best practice here would be to use the Primary Data Collector as XML Broker 2 and Backup Data Collector server would be XML Broker 1.

The **Authentication Methods** option on **Edit Settings** pane is where William needs to specify how users authenticate in the Web Interface. Authentication methods are explained in *Chapter 3, Installing XenApp 6.5*.

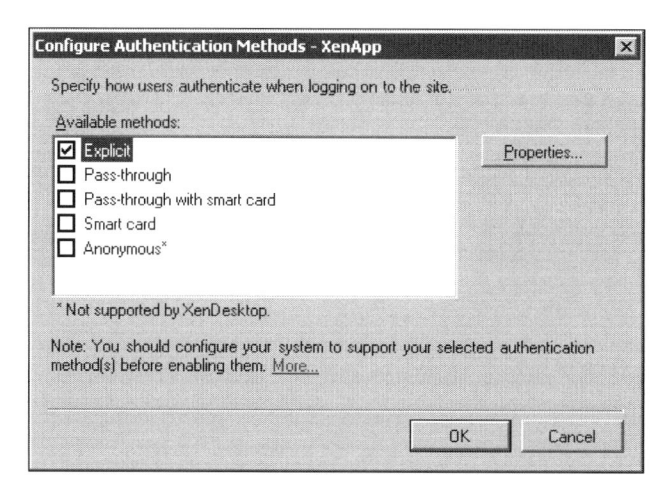

We use the **Secure Access** option on the **Edit Settings** pane to determine how users connect to a server farm. Access methods are explained as follows:

- **Direct**: Citrix Receiver or Citrix Online Plug-In connects to the actual IP address of the XenApp server. This method is used when our users are located in a LAN or access our network using the Access Gateway Plugin.

- **Alternate**: The Alternate method is similar to the Direct method, but users connect to an alternate IP address, defined on each XenApp server using the command **ALTADDR**, instead of the actual IP address of the XenApp server.

- **Translated**: The Translated method is similar to the Alternate method, except that the alternate address for each XenApp server is defined in the web interface configuration instead of using `ALTADDR` on each XenApp server.

- **Gateway direct**: The Gateway direct method is used for remote users accessing the LAN through Access Gateway (or Secure Access). The user connects to the URL of Access Gateway and the Receiver or Online Plug-In initiates an SSL (Secure Sockets Layer) connection to the Access Gateway, which creates a connection to the actual address of the XenApp server. This method requires one or multiple STA (Secure Ticket Authority) server to validate incoming connections. This is the preferred method for users connecting through Access Gateway.

- **Gateway alternate**: The Gateway alternate method is similar to the Gateway direct method, except Access Gateway makes a connection to the alternate address, defined using the command `ALTADDR` of the XenApp server.

Using Management Tools

- **Gateway translated**: The Gateway translated method is similar to the Gateway alternate method, except Access Gateway makes a connection to the alternate address, defined in the web interface configuration of the XenApp server.

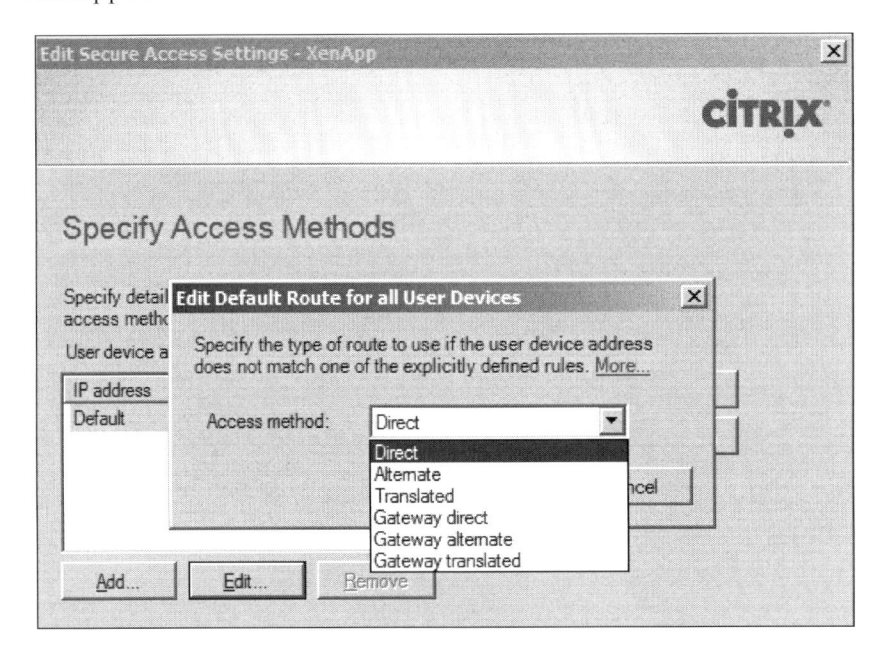

The **Resource Types** option on the **Edit Settings** pane sets up how users will access **Online** resources (applications, content, and desktops) through a web browser or the Citrix Receiver or Citrix Online Plug-In. The **Offline** application feature enables users to stream applications to their desktops and open them locally and **Dual Mode** provides access to both options described before.

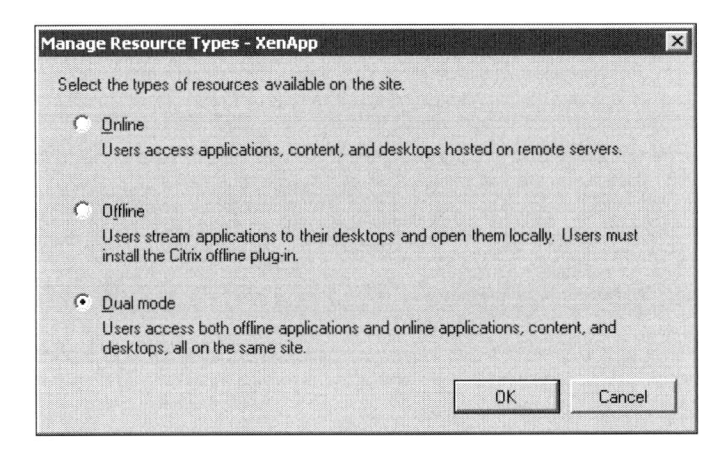

To access published resources (applications, content, and desktops), users must have, at least, either a supported Citrix Receiver (also known as Citrix Client or Citrix Plug-In) or a supported web browser. We can use the **Client Deployment** task in the Web Interface Management Console to configure web-based client deployment. We can specify which Citrix clients are offered to users for download and installation.

Citrix recommends having the latest version of the Receiver or Plug-In installed. Later in this book, there is a chapter, where we talk about the Citrix Receiver and Plug-Ins.

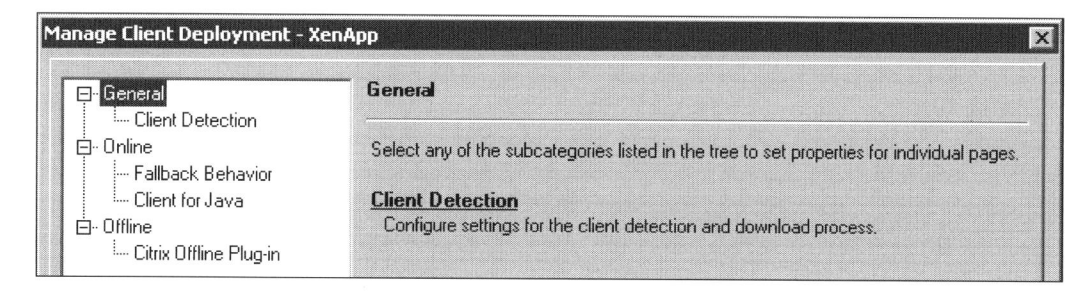

We can use the **Client-side Proxy** task to configure if Citrix Plug-Ins must communicate or not with the server running XenApp through the proxy server.

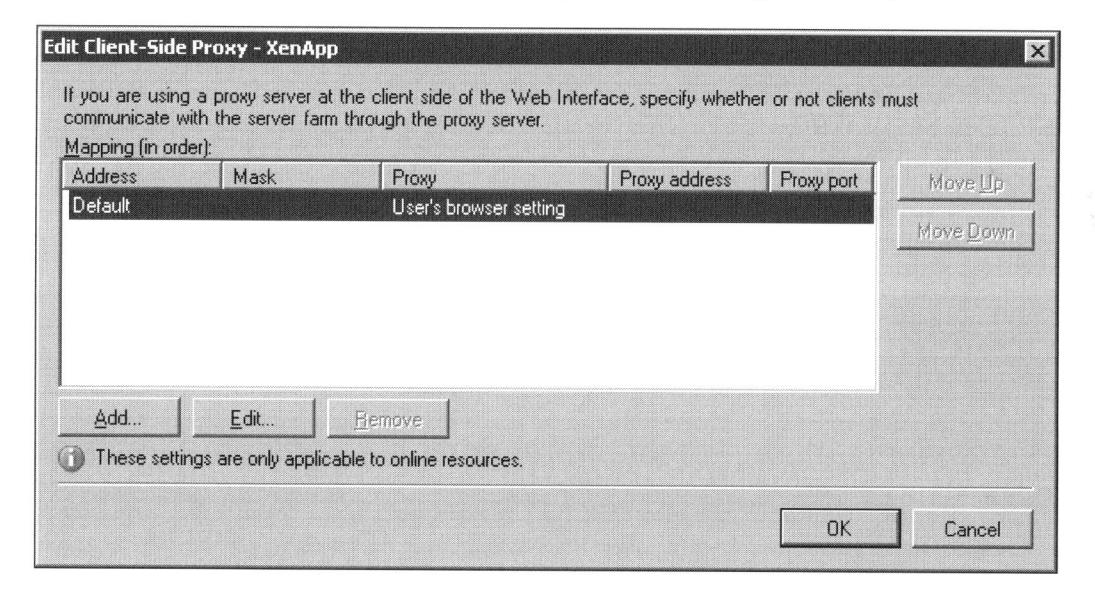

Using Management Tools

We can use the **Manage Session Preferences** task to specify the settings that users can change. We can also use this task to specify the time after which inactive users are logged off from the Web Interface, manage **User Customizations**, adjust **Connection Performance**, and **Display** settings. We can set up whether the Web Interface should override the Plug-In name in the case of published resources hosted on remote servers.

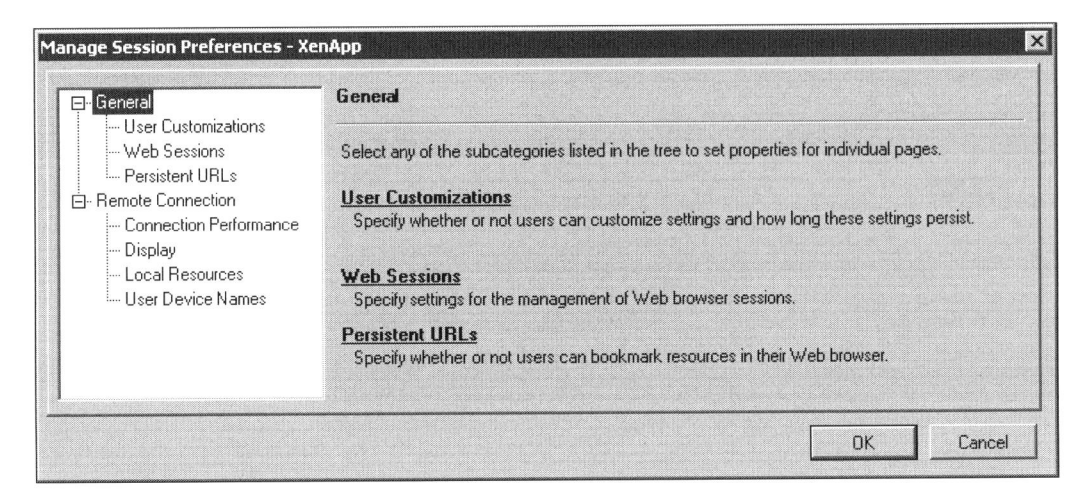

Manage Session Preferences - XenApp

- General
  - User Customizations
  - Web Sessions
  - Persistent URLs
- Remote Connection
  - Connection Performance
  - Display
  - Local Resources
  - User Device Names

General

Select any of the subcategories listed in the tree to set properties for individual pages.

User Customizations
Specify whether or not users can customize settings and how long these settings persist.

Web Sessions
Specify settings for the management of Web browser sessions.

Persistent URLs
Specify whether or not users can bookmark resources in their Web browser.

> Settings you specify in the Remote Connection items *overrule* Farm and Client settings. For example, color depth and client drive mappings. Therefore, pay attention to these settings. If you disable sound here, you cannot turn it on elsewhere.

Enable workspace control for XenApp Services sites using the **Workspace Control** task, which lets us configure automatic reconnection when users log on, configure the **Reconnect** button, and allows users of XenApp Web Sites to log off from both the Web Interface and active sessions or from the Web Interface only.

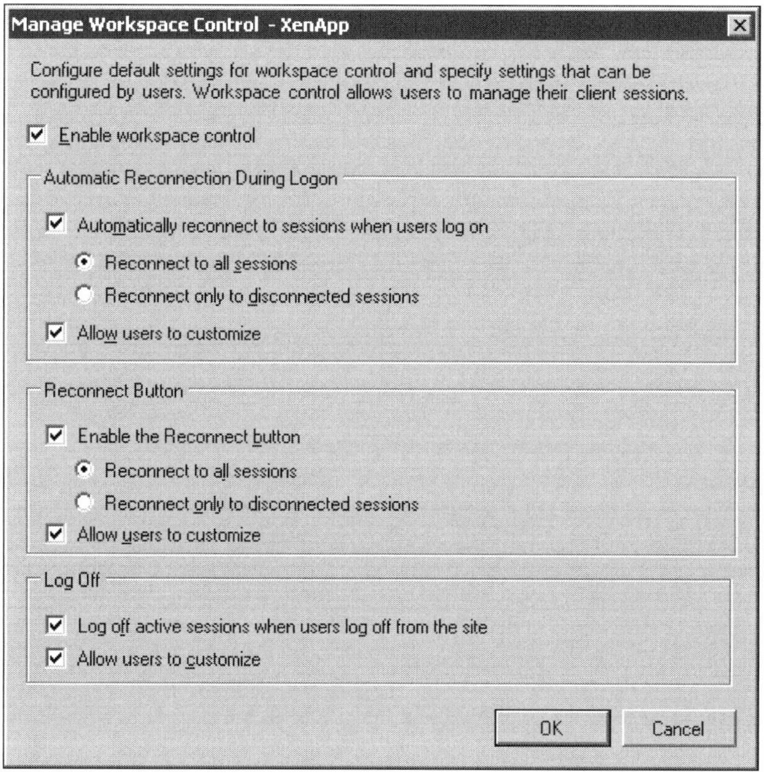
Manage Workspace Control - XenApp
Configure default settings for workspace control and specify settings that can be configured by users. Workspace control allows users to manage their client sessions.
Enable workspace control
Automatic Reconnection During Logon
Automatically reconnect to sessions when users log on
Reconnect to all sessions
Reconnect only to disconnected sessions
Allow users to customize
Reconnect Button
Enable the Reconnect button
Reconnect to all sessions
Reconnect only to disconnected sessions
Allow users to customize
Log Off
Log off active sessions when users log off from the site
Allow users to customize
OK
Cancel

The **Site Maintenance** task opens a menu with the following four options:

- We need to use the **Manage IIS Hosting** task to change the location of our Web Interface site on MS IIS.
- **Repair Site** will repair the site and rebuild the original site content.
- **Uninstall Site** task removes sites. Uninstalling a site removes it from the system.

- The **Diagnostic Logging** task helps us to increase system security for error logging. We can suppress identical events from being logged recurrently and configure how many duplicate events are logged and how frequently.

> Important: If we have created any images or custom scripts for our Web Interface site and we run the **Repair Site** task, all these customized files, included the `webinterface.conf` are removed. All customized files are also removed when we use the **Manage IIS Hosting** task.

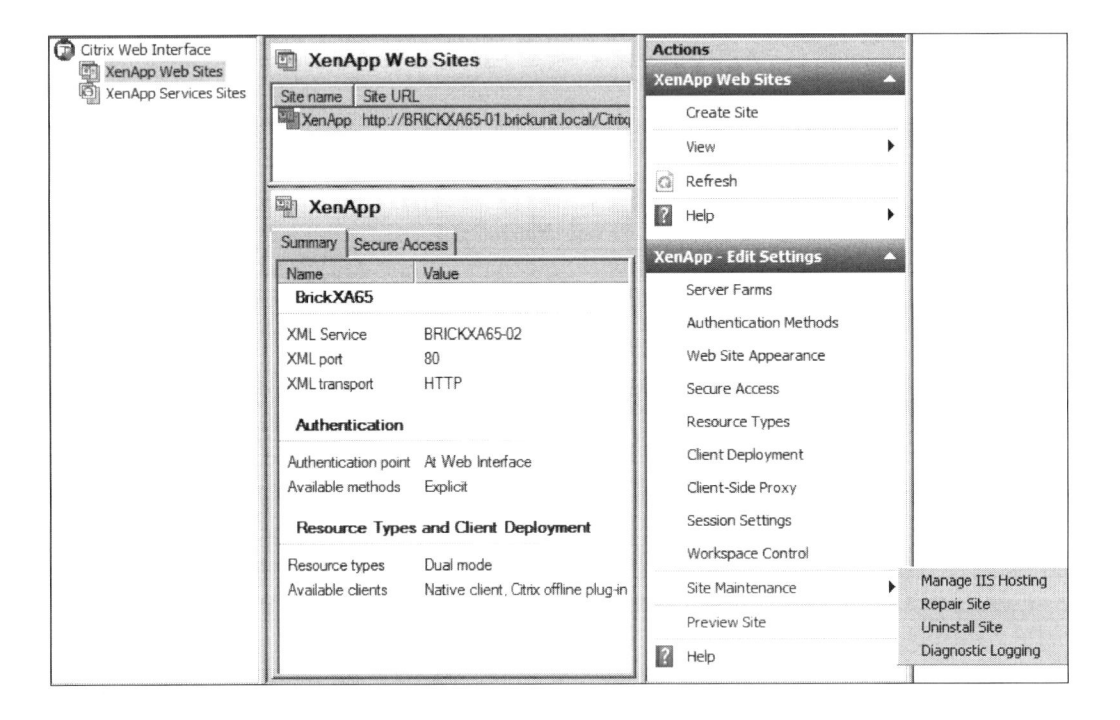

Other Administration Tools

Now we are going to talk about a few extra management tools included in XenApp 6.5 (and previous versions). These tools are rarely used, except for the Shadow taskbar, but can be useful for some specific deployments.

Citrix SSL Relay Configuration Tool

We can use this tool to secure communication using SSL protocol between a server running the Web Interface and our XenApp farm.

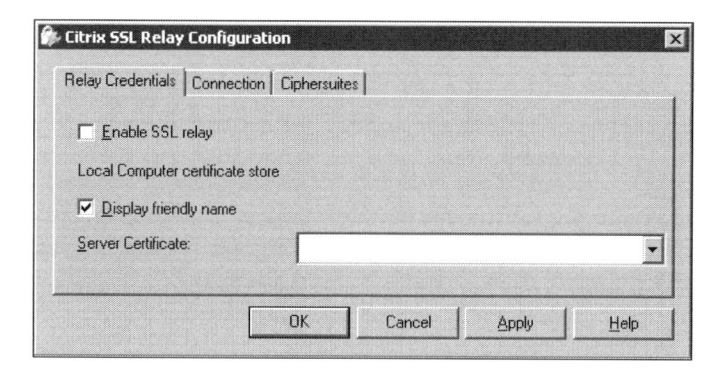

Shadow Taskbar

Shadowing allows administrators or other users to view and control other users' sessions remotely. Use the **Shadow Taskbar** to shadow sessions and to switch among multiple shadowed sessions. We can shadow ICA sessions within the **Citrix AppCenter** and on previous versions of XenApp on the **Citrix Delivery Services Console** or **Citrix Access Management Console**, too.

> Shadowing of sessions with multi-monitors is not supported. If we need to shadow multi-monitor sessions, we can use the Remote Assistance feature. Also, shadowing of sessions when Desktop Experience is installed is not supported. More info at http://support.citrix.com/article/CTX125693

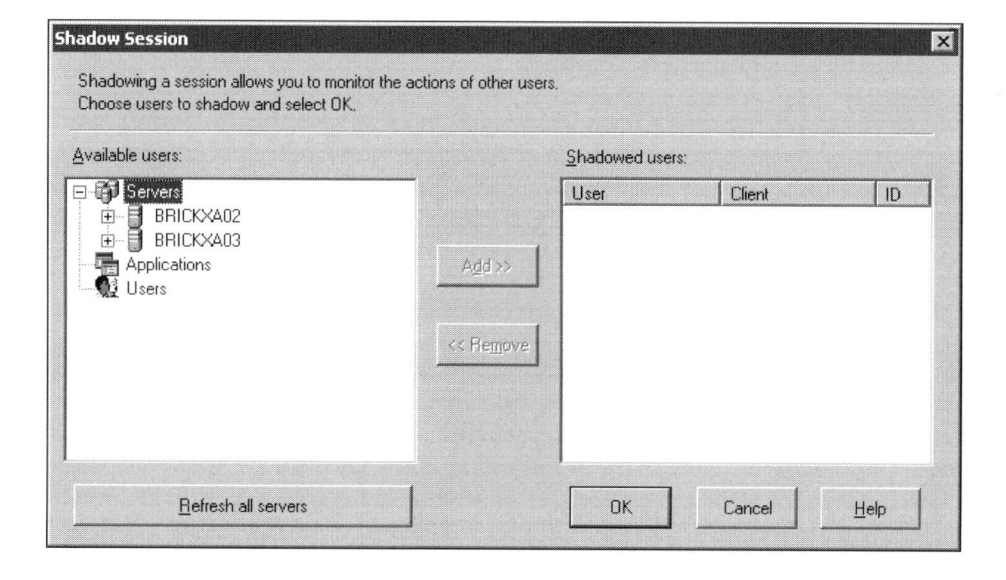

SpeedScreen Latency Reduction Manager

We can use this tool to configure local text echo and other features that improve the user experience on slow networks. **SpeedScreen Latency Reduction Manager** includes the following two technologies:

- **Local Text Echo** speeds up the display of the input text on the client machine on high latency networks
- **Mouse Click Feedback** provides visual feedback to a user updating the mouse pointer, to avoid the user clicking the mouse several times

We can use the configuration wizard to configure latency reduction settings for the XenApp server or an application.

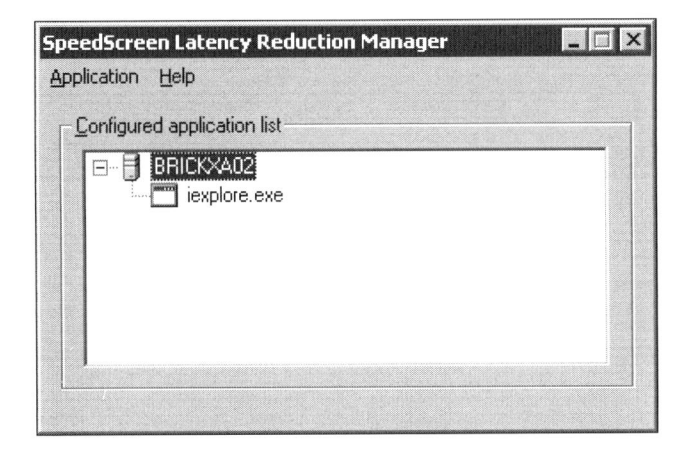

Managing Citrix Administrators

Citrix provides a very simple (and powerful) approach to manage Citrix Administrators. We can assign the Citrix Administrator role to existing Active Directory accounts for both users and groups.

Adding a Citrix administrator

Now we are going to help William Empire from Brick Unit Construction create a full administrator for himself.

From the **Start** menu, he selects **All Programs | Citrix | Management Consoles | Citrix AppCenter** if it's XenApp 6.5 or the Citrix Delivery Services Console if it's XenApp 6.0.

In the left pane, he needs to expand **Citrix Resources** and then **XenApp**, click on farm name, and then on the right pane, he needs to select **Action | Add administrator**.

Finally, he needs to click on the **Add** button and select the desired user or user group account. In this case, he is going to add the wempire account as a Citrix administrator.

On the **Privileges** page, he needs to select the privilege level he wants to grant to his own user account. He has three options:

- **View Only**: Administrators can view all areas of XenApp farm but they cannot modify them
- **Full Administration**: Administrators can view and modify all areas of the XenApp farm and create and manage other administrators' accounts
- **Custom**: Administrators can view and/or modify almost all areas of the XenApp farm but they can't create and manage other administrators' accounts

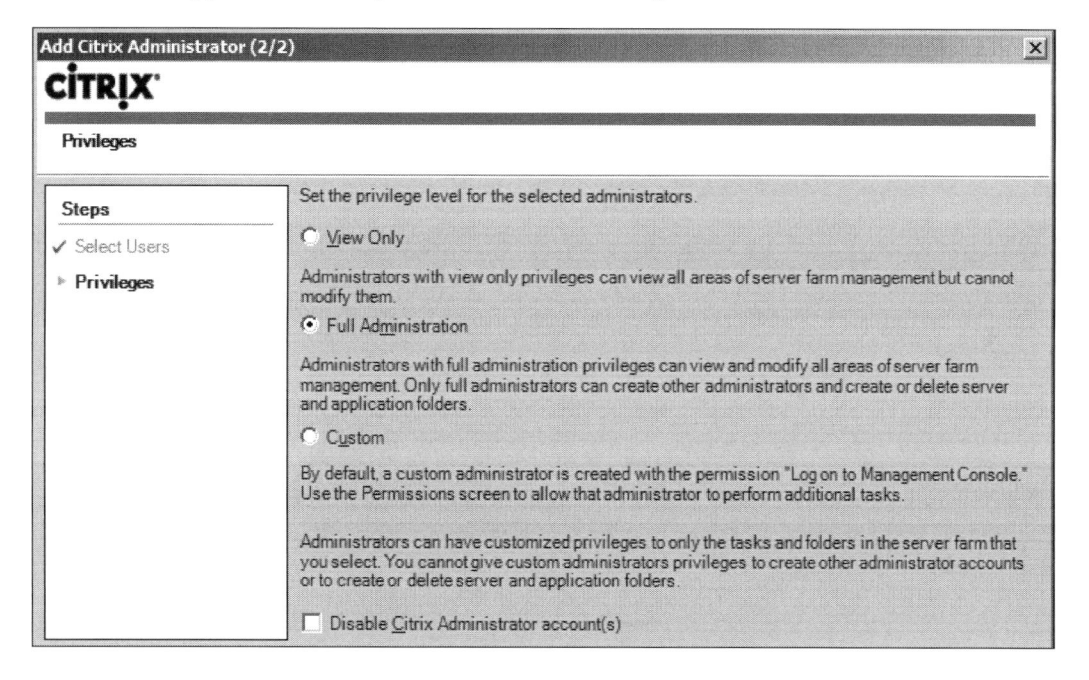

Using Management Tools

At this time, we are going to help William Empire to assign custom administrator permissions to the Helpdesk group account at Brick Unit.

First, he needs to choose the group account.

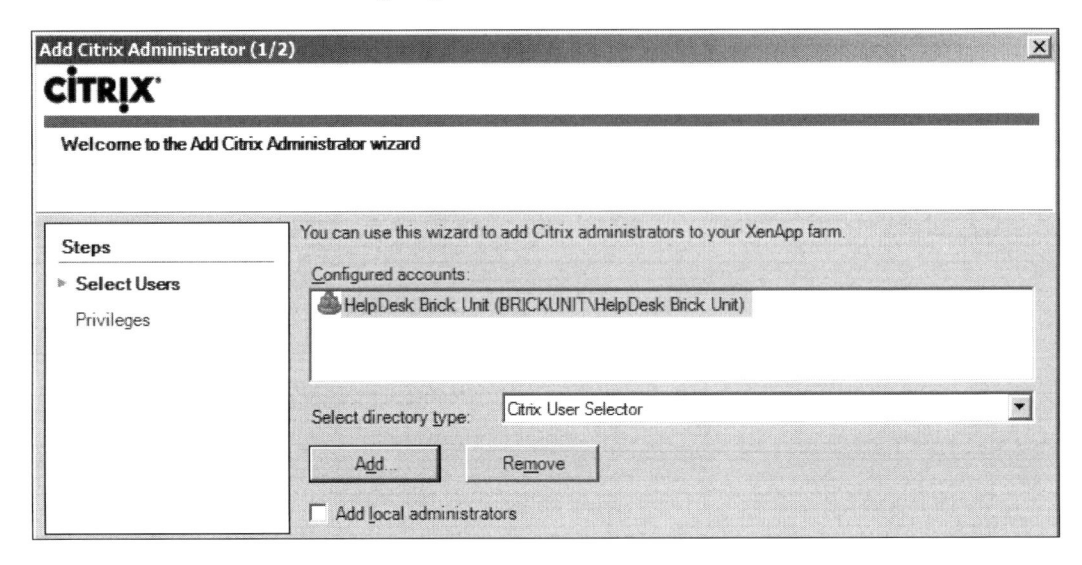

Then he needs to select the **Custom** privilege level:

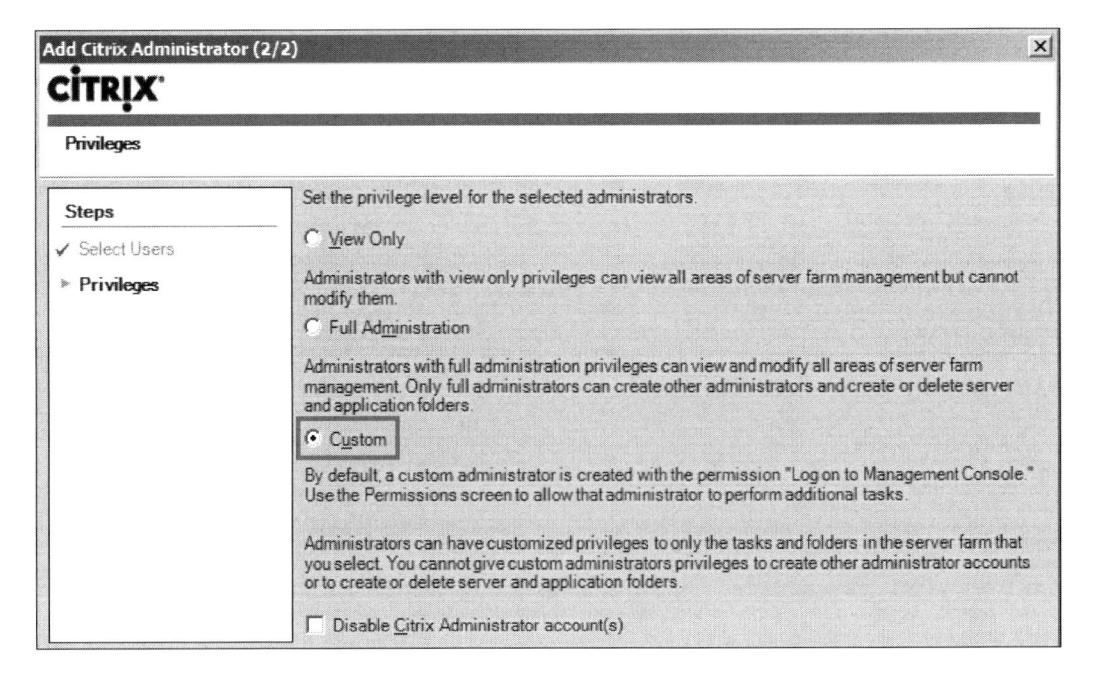

Finally, he can use granular tasks to set permissions:

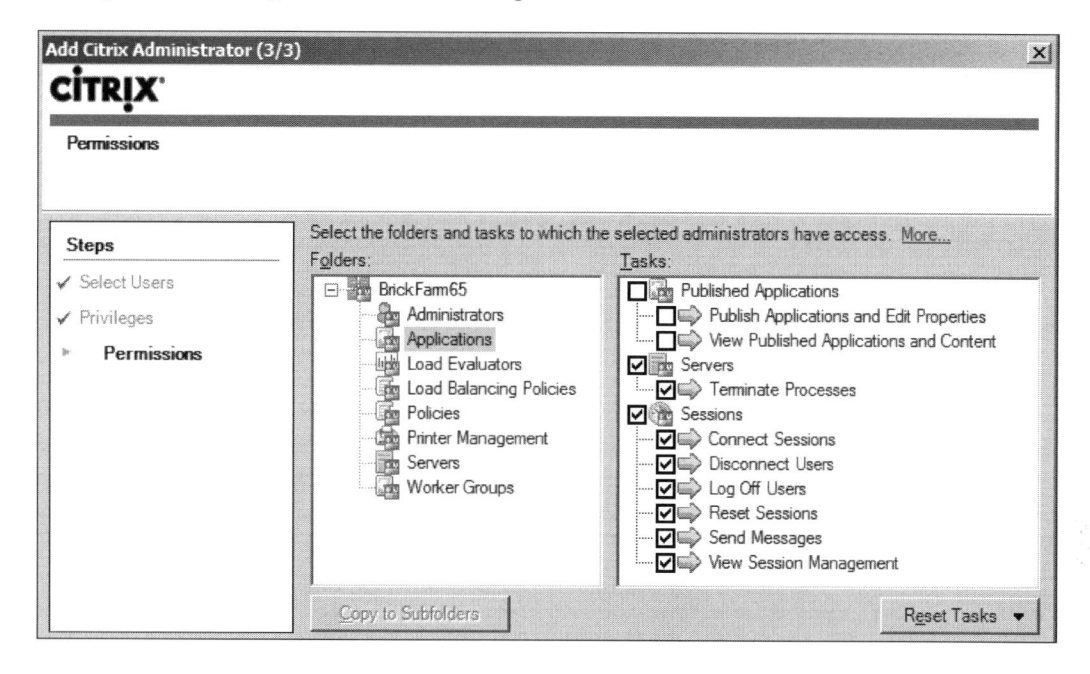

And here is the result, now we can see the console accounts of both William and Helpdesk group.

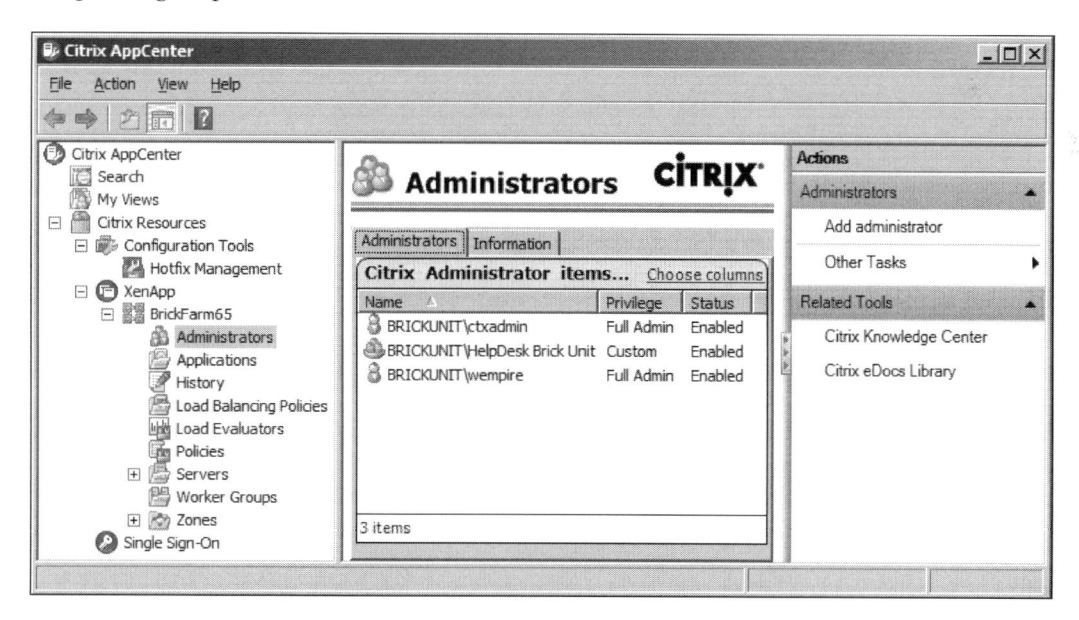

Using Management Tools

Disabling a Citrix administrator

If we ever need to disable a Citrix XenApp administrator, for example, to temporarily remove access for an administrator, but we want to retain the account and settings, we need to click on the administrator account whose privileges we want to disable.

On the **Actions** pane or **Action** menu, click on the **Disable** button:

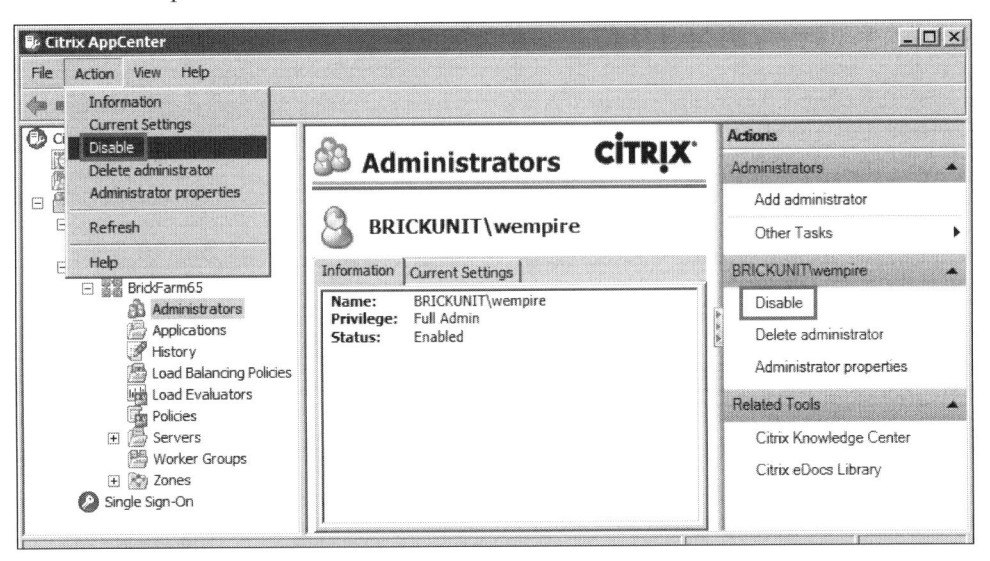

When an administrator account is disabled, the administrator icon appears in grey.

On the **Actions** pane or **Action** menu, click on **Enable**, to enable the account:

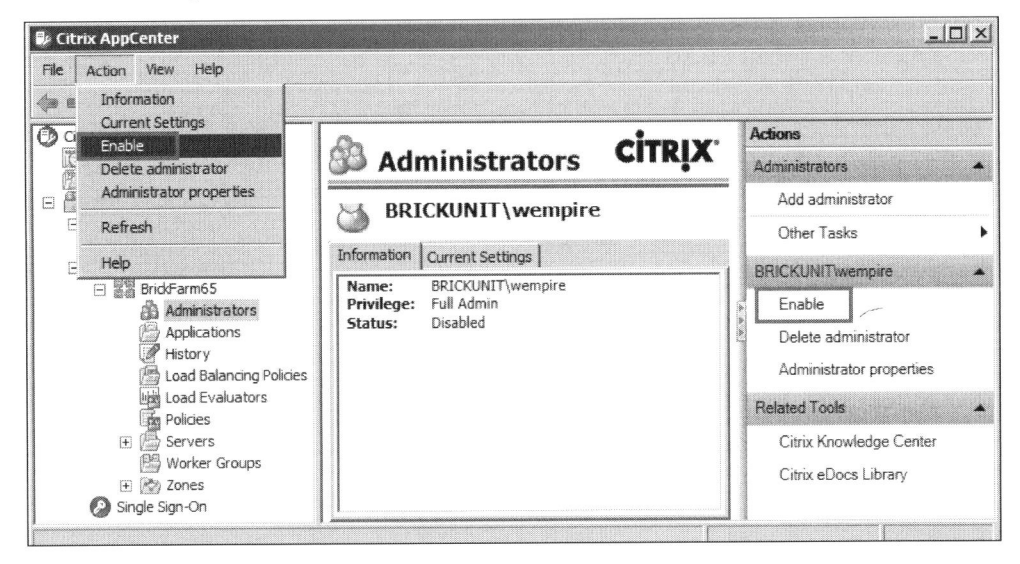

Modifying Administrator properties

First we need to select the administrator account whose privileges we want to modify.

On the **Actions** pane or **Action** menu, click on **Administrator properties**.

Then we need to select **Permissions**:

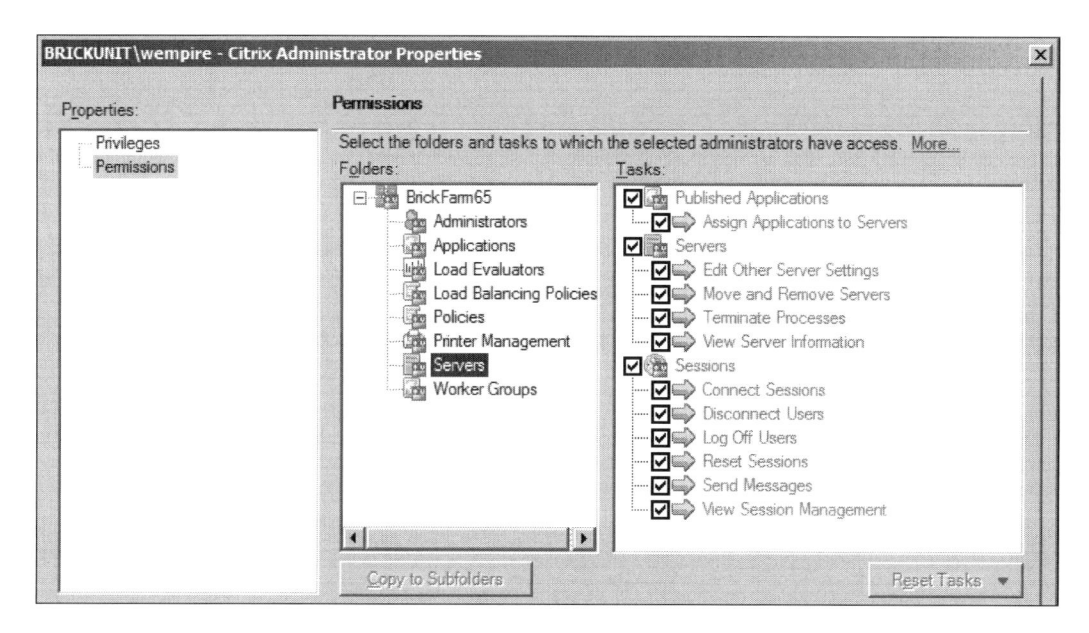

Summary

In this chapter, we have learned about different management tools provided by Citrix in XenApp 6.5. Specifically the following:

- Citrix AppCenter Console, the main management console
- License Administration Console
- Citrix Web Interface Management Console
- Other management tools, including Citrix SSL Relay Configuration tool, Shadow taskbar, and SpeedScreen Latency Reduction Manager
- Creating and managing administrators' accounts

In the next chapter, we will see how to use the Citrix AppCenter Console to publish and manage applications on the XenApp farm.

Application Publishing

6

In the previous chapter, we discussed the XenApp Management tools. In this chapter, we will use them to publish applications and resources so that users can start using our XenApp farm.

In this chapter we are going to learn about:

- Choosing the best method to deliver applications
- Publishing a hosted application using the Publish Application wizard
- Publishing a streaming application using the Publish Application wizard
- Publishing a server desktop using the Publish Application wizard
- Publishing content using the Publish Application wizard
- Configuring content redirection

Publishing applications

Building a XenApp farm is an expensive solution, so we need to test all applications in a pilot environment to make sure all the applications can run on Remote Desktop Services (formerly known as Terminal Server) and on Citrix XenApp servers.

We need to decide on the appropriate application publishing method. Intensive testing of applications is critical for the success of XenApp farm deployment.

We can provide access to several types of published resources in XenApp to the users:

- **Hosted applications** are installed locally on servers running XenApp. When users access them, the published applications are executed on the servers, but appear to be running locally on client machines. Hosted applications only run when users are connected to XenApp servers.

Application Publishing

- **Streamed applications** are installed in application profiles and are stored on a file server in our App Hub, published using the XenApp publishing wizard, and delivered to any client desktop or server on demand. Streaming applications can run online or offline.
- **Content**: We can publish documents, data files such as Excel spread sheets or Word documents, media files, web pages, and URLs.
- **Server desktops**: Users can access all of the resources available on the server. Usually, this feature is used for administrators, but is not a recommended practice for common users. In that case, we need to secure server desktops to prevent user access to sensitive areas of the operating system.

When we publish an application, configuration information for the application is stored in the data store of the XenApp farm. This information includes the types of files that are associated with the application, which users can connect to the application, client-side session properties such as window size and resolution, encryption level and audio settings, and more.

When delivered to users, published applications appear very similar to applications running locally on the client machine. This is the ultimate goal for Citrix: Provide a better-than-local experience to users.

When users start applications, configuration is based on the delivery options we configured in the publishing wizard and on the XenApp Plug-in they run on their client machine.

One best practice for application publishing is to give access to Active Directory groups instead of users when we publish applications. For example, an application published to 300 users requires **Independent Management Architecture** (**IMA**) to validate 300 objects. The same application published to a single group of 500 users requires IMA to validate only one object.

> Citrix defines the IMA as a server-to-server infrastructure that provides robust, secure, and scalable tools for managing server farms of any size. Among other features, IMA enables centralized, platform-independent management, an ODBC-compliant data store, and management products that plug into a management console. The following link gives more information on it:
>
> http://community.citrix.com/display/edgesight/Report+Counters+Glossary

The new Citrix AppCenter console available in XenApp 6.5 is almost the same product, with a few differences, as Citrix Delivery Service Console on XenApp 6.0, so instructions are valid for both XenApp 6.5 and XenApp 6.0 products.

Choosing the best method to deliver applications

Selecting the appropriate delivery method for an application is the first step of publishing it. There is a big discussion around this subject. Some people prefer streaming applications and some people prefer hosted applications.

There is no magic formula to choose the appropriate way to publish an application; testing and more testing is the real way to figure it out.

A common scenario is to use hosted applications and if they don't work well, use streaming applications, but again this decision is related to the application, the size of the farm and type, and location of users. The following are some rules to help us decide the right way to publish an application:

- **Patching and upgrade**: Application streaming simplifies delivery by allowing us to set up and configure an application on one (or multiple) file servers for delivery to client machines. To patch or upgrade the application, we make the updates only in the location where we stored the application. If we have a hosted application, we have more options to patch or upgrade the application, depending on how many servers we have. If we have just a few servers, we can manually deploy updates, or use scripts to update them. If we have a medium to large farm, we can use Microsoft System Center Configuration Manager (SCCM), formerly known as Microsoft Systems Management Server (SMS) to deploy a patch or upgrade package, using Citrix Installation Manager or the preferred option included in the Platinum license of XenApp 6.5, using the Provisioning Server to have a single or multiple images of the XenApp 6.5 server. When we are using Provisioning server, we need to update just the master image to update all servers.
- **Network connectivity** may be a big factor in our decision on whether to host or stream applications. If users are located in branch or are accessing applications remotely, hosted applications are the preferred option. Streaming applications are recommended if users are close to the server where the application's profiles are located. We can deploy streaming applications on multiple servers and XenApp will use the closest file server based on the IP address of the client machine.
- **Client machine type** is another aspect to help decide the type of published resource. If we need to run a CPU-intensive application and we are using a Thin Client or very old computer, we need to choose hosted applications. Sometimes we can stream this CPU-intensive application to client machines to avoid overloading our XenApp servers, affecting other applications. If the user accessing the application is a mobile user, we can use streaming applications, and the client can run the application offline.

- **Multiple versions** of the same software on the same server sometimes are not possible or extremely complex to set up on hosted applications. So, in this scenario, using streaming applications is the preferred option.
- **Application compatibility** is another factor in choosing streaming applications over hosted applications. For example, if we have multiple applications requiring different versions of Oracle clients, Crystal Reports, or any shared component.

There are more reasons, but again, most of these considerations will depend on our applications and the size of the environment, so we need to check how our clients are going to access our applications, and test and re-test them.

Publishing a hosted application using the Publish Application wizard

William decided to deploy Microsoft Project 2010 on the farm. Project is one of the most important applications for Architects and Project Managers and is one of the first applications he wants to try on XenApp 6.5. The company bought 35 licenses of Microsoft Project 2010, but there are around 45 users of Project. These users are not concurrent, so he needs to limit the amount of concurrent licenses.

The first step is to install the applications for all users on XenApp 6.5 servers:

1. He needs to open a command prompt with Administrator privileges.
2. He right-clicks on the command prompt shortcut on the **Start** menu and selects **Run as Administrator**:

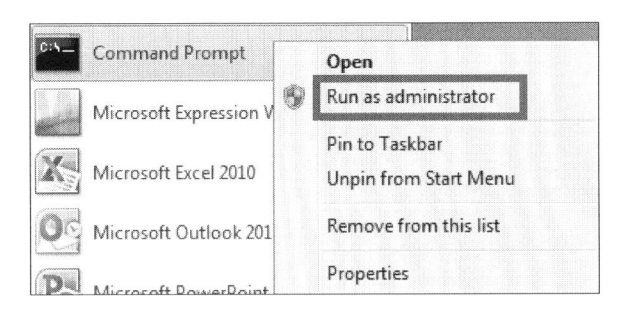

3. Another option is to execute the command prompt using the RUNAS command as administrator. For example, William will use the following command:

   `C:\> RUNAS /user:brickunit\wempire CMD`

4. Now that he is executing the command prompt as the administrator, he can run the following command in a command prompt:

   `C:\ > change user /install`

5. He will receive a message to confirm he is running Remote Desktop Services on Install mode:

   `User session is ready to install applications.`

6. If he wants to see the Remote Desktop Services mode, he needs to run the following command:

   `C:\ >change user /query`

7. Now he can run the setup of the application from the command prompt:

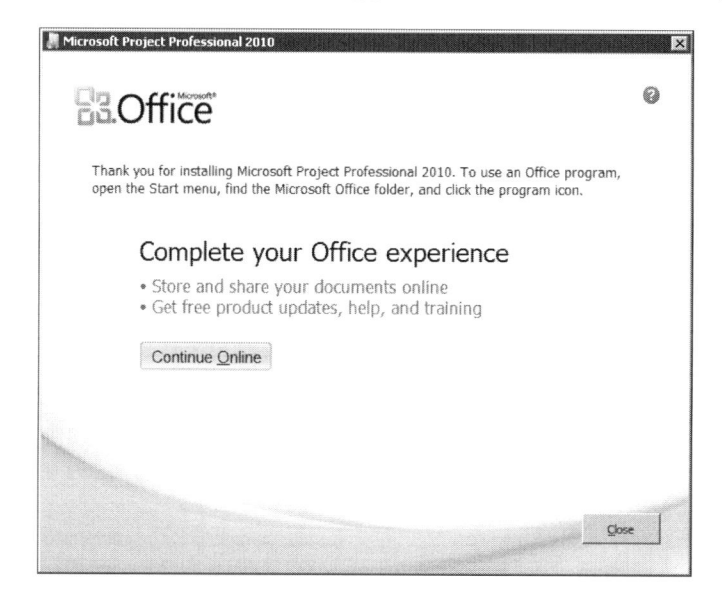

8. The setup of the Microsoft Project 2010 is complete. He can proceed to install the application on other servers if he needs it.

   > When we install an application on multiple XenApp servers, we always need to install it in the *same* directory.

9. Now it's time to return the Remote Desktop Services to execute mode. From the command prompt, he needs to type the following command:

   `C:\ >change user /execute`

Application Publishing

Also, William can install applications using the option **Install Application on Remote Desktop Server** from the **Control Panel**.

In order to publish Microsoft Project 2010, he needs to open **Citrix AppCenter Console** (formerly called Citrix Delivery Service Console on XenApp 6.0).

From the AppCenter console, under the **XenApp** node, he needs to expand the farm or server to which he wants to publish the application.

He needs to select the **Applications** node.

> We can use the **Actions** pane and choose **Create folder**. We need to name the folder for the application we are publishing. This step is optional if we have a few applications, but will be necessary to create folders to keep applications organized, if we have dozens or hundreds of applications. These folders are visible only to XenApp Administrators and not visible to standard users.

He needs to select the folder he created before (optional) and from the **Actions** pane choose **Publish Application**.

In the **Publish Application** wizard, on the **Name** page, he needs to provide a **Display name** (maximum 256 characters) and **Application description**. The name appears on client machines when users access the application and on the console for the farm applications. XenApp supports application names that use Latin-1 and Unicode character sets, including characters used in Japanese, Chinese, and Korean.

On the **Type** page, he needs to specify the type of resource we want to publish and the delivery method. He has three types of resources to be published (server desktop, content, and application).

He needs to choose **Application**, then select **Accessed from a server** for **Application** type, and then choose **Installed application** to publish a hosted application:

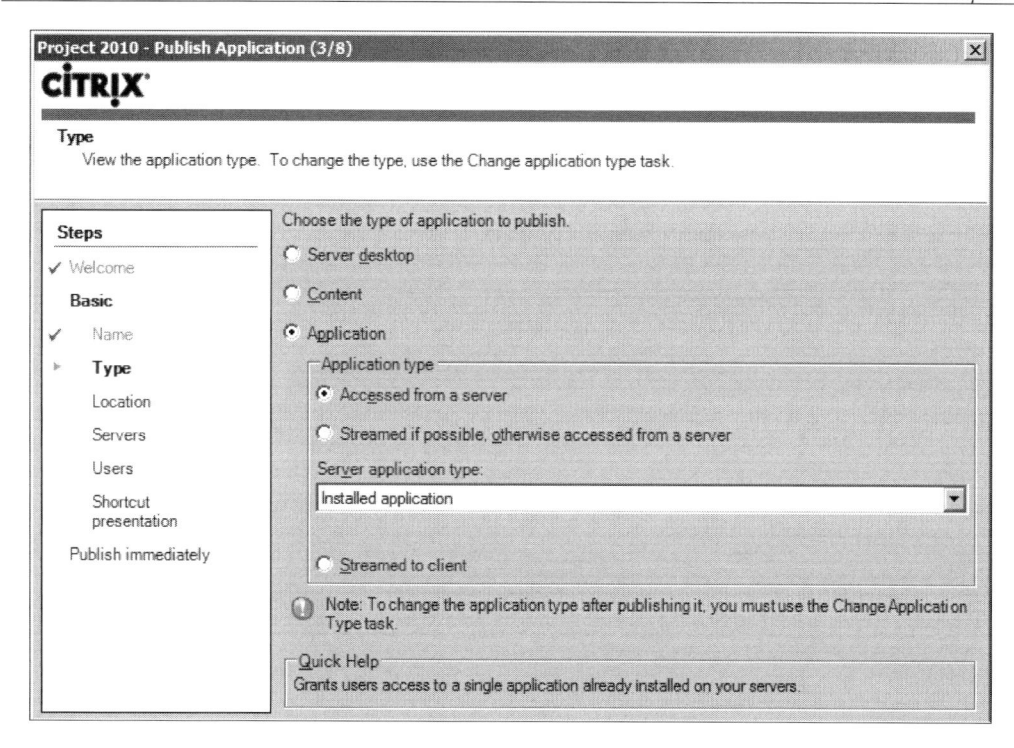

On the **Location** page, he needs to type or use the **Browse** button to set the command line and working directory (optional). As we discussed before, when we publish the same application on multiple servers, we *must* install the application in the same path and the folder in all servers or the application will fail.

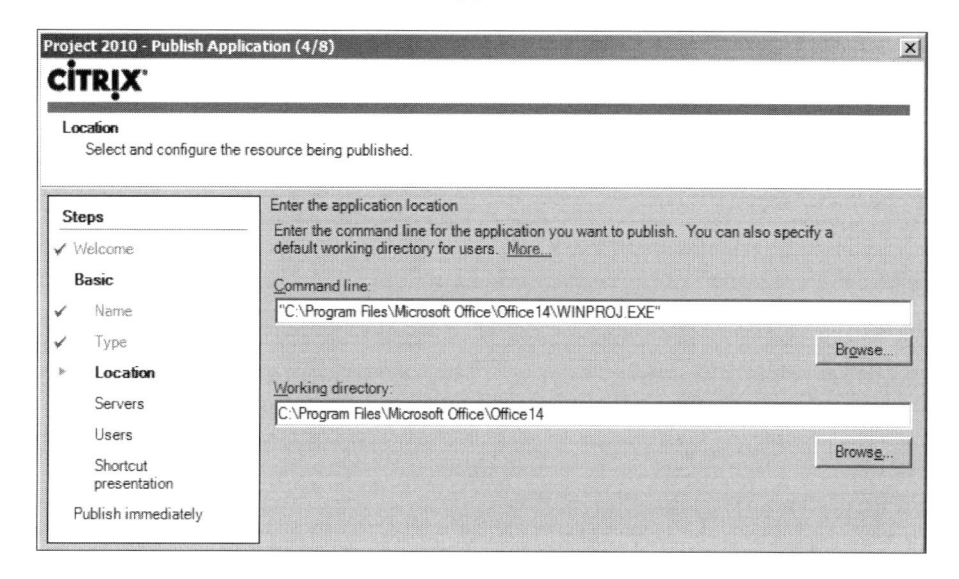

Application Publishing

On the **Servers** page, William needs to add the individual servers or worker groups on which the published application runs.

> To add a server to the list of servers for a published desktop or application (after publishing the application), drag-and-drop the server onto the published desktop or application in the left-hand side pane of the console. We can also drag-and-drop the published desktop or application onto the server.

In the following screenshot, William decided to use a Worker Group called Production Servers, which contain several servers.

> When we use Worker Groups, we need make sure that all the XenApp servers in the Worker Group have the application publishing installed and also that it is installed on the same folder.

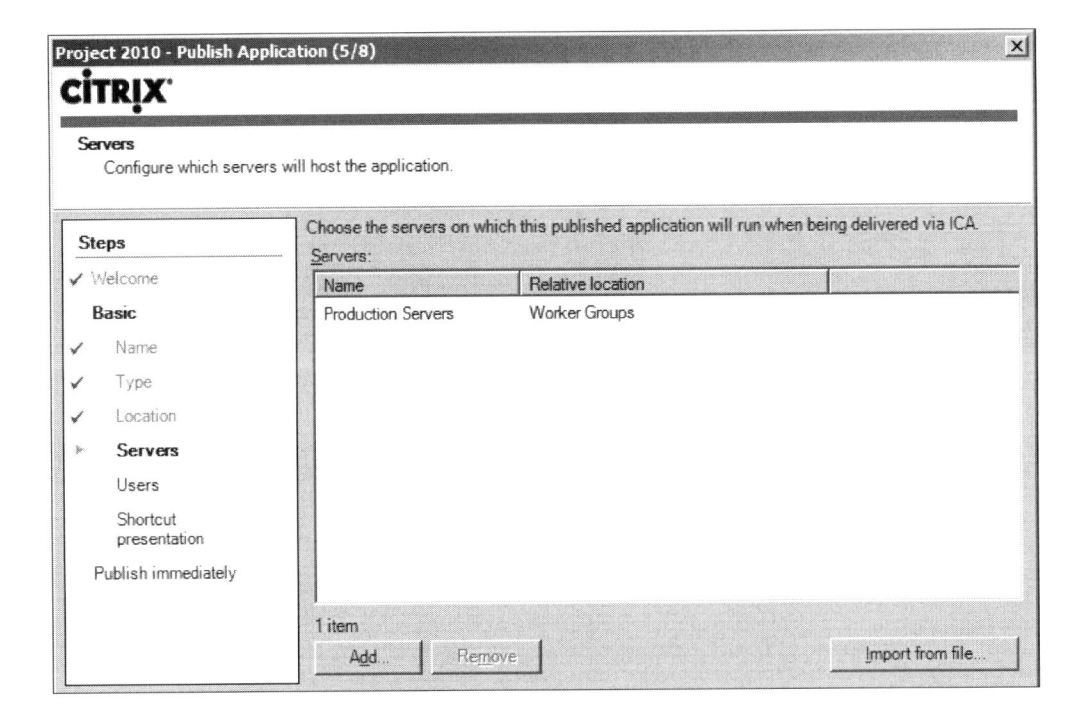

Project 2010 - Publish Application (5/8)

CITRIX

Servers
Configure which servers will host the application.

Steps
- ✓ Welcome
- **Basic**
- ✓ Name
- ✓ Type
- ✓ Location
- ▸ **Servers**
- Users
- Shortcut presentation
- Publish immediately

Choose the servers on which this published application will run when being delivered via ICA.

Servers:

Name	Relative location
Production Servers	Worker Groups

1 item

Add... | Remove | Import from file...

On the **Users** page, he needs to add users or groups who have access to the application and he can allow access only to configured user accounts or to anonymous users.

William assigned permissions to the **BU Project Managers** and **Domain Admins** groups.

Usually, it is a good practice in medium to large environment to create a **Test Group** and avoid using the **Domain Admins** group for testing purposes.

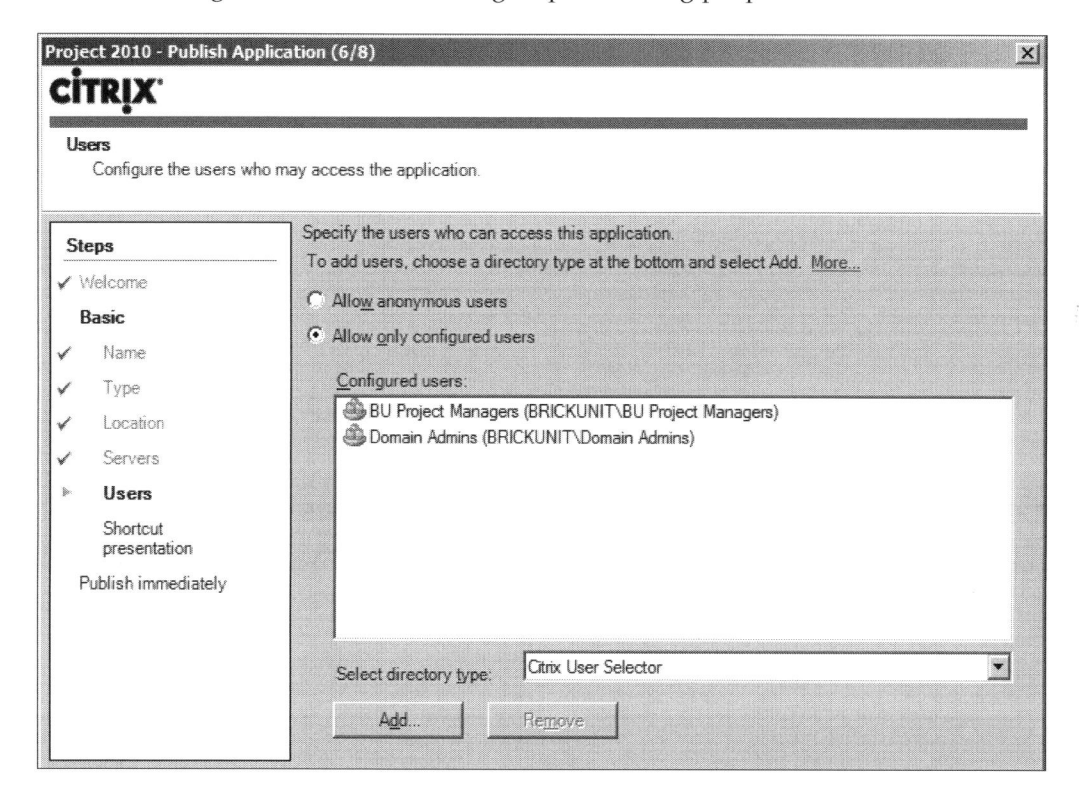

On the **Shortcut presentation** page, he selects the icon for the application and chooses how the application is enumerated on the client machine.

The client application folder is used when we need to organize applications inside folders. This is a recommended practice, if we have a lot of applications.

Application Publishing

Both **Add to the client's Start menu** and **Add shortcut to the client's desktop** options are used when client machines utilize the XenApp Plug-in to connect to the XenApp farm.

> The console has a limit of 1,000 unique application icons. When that limit is exceeded, the console displays a generic icon for all new applications.

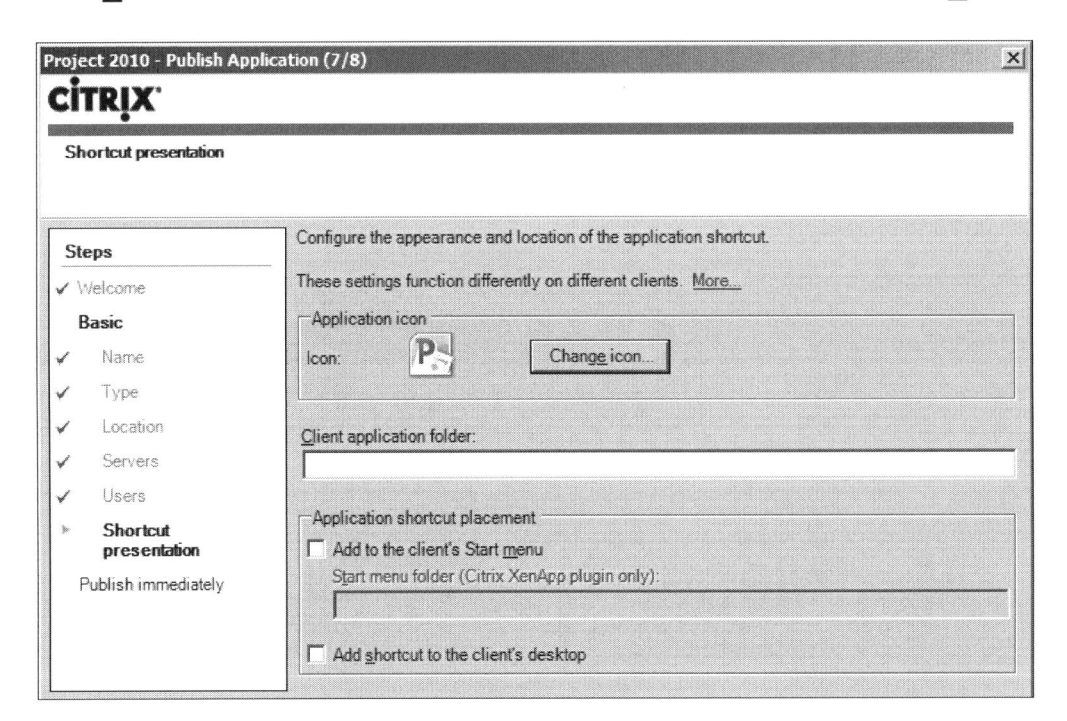

On the **Publish immediately** page, he needs to select **Disable application initially**, if he wants to prevent users from accessing the application. Later, he can manually enable it through application properties.

To view and select **Advanced** options, he needs to check the **Configure advanced application settings now** option. Alternatively, he can modify the **Advanced** settings using the application properties.

Chapter 6

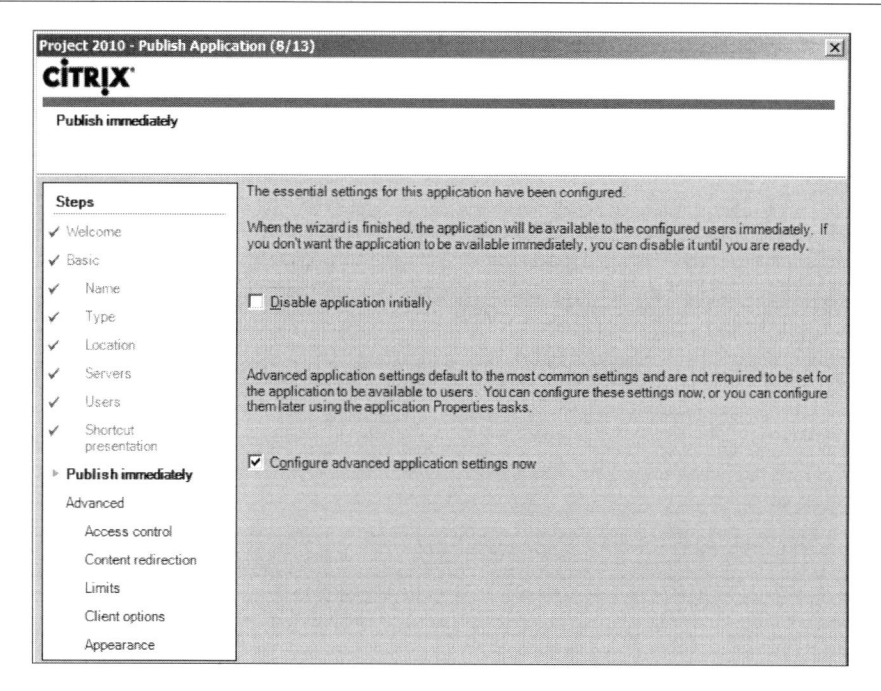

On the optional **Access control** page, William can configure the access to this application using **Access Gateway Advanced Edition**, the Citrix SSL VPN solution was used to provide farm access to remote users.

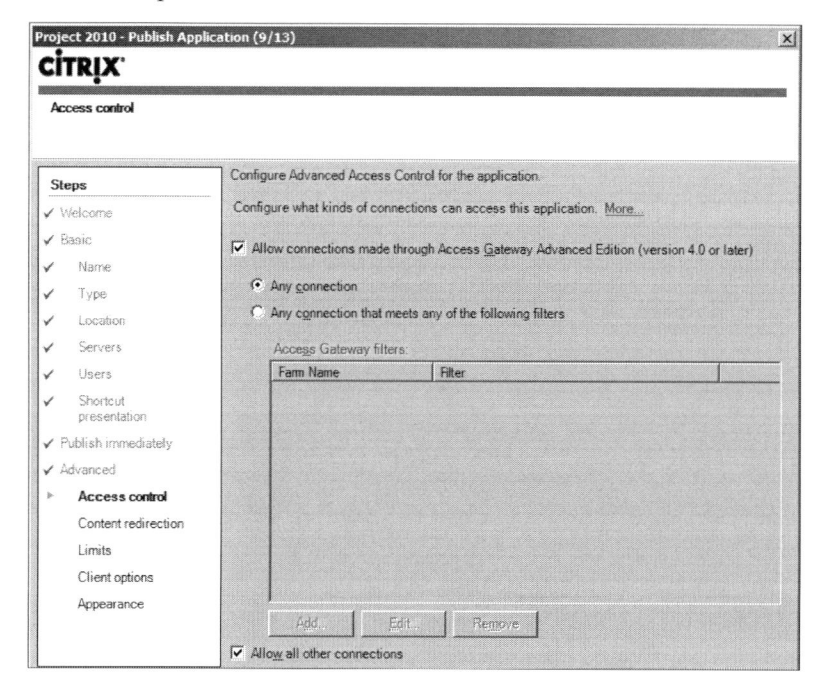

On the **Content redirection** page, he can configure the file types associated with the application. We will talk about content redirection at the end of this chapter.

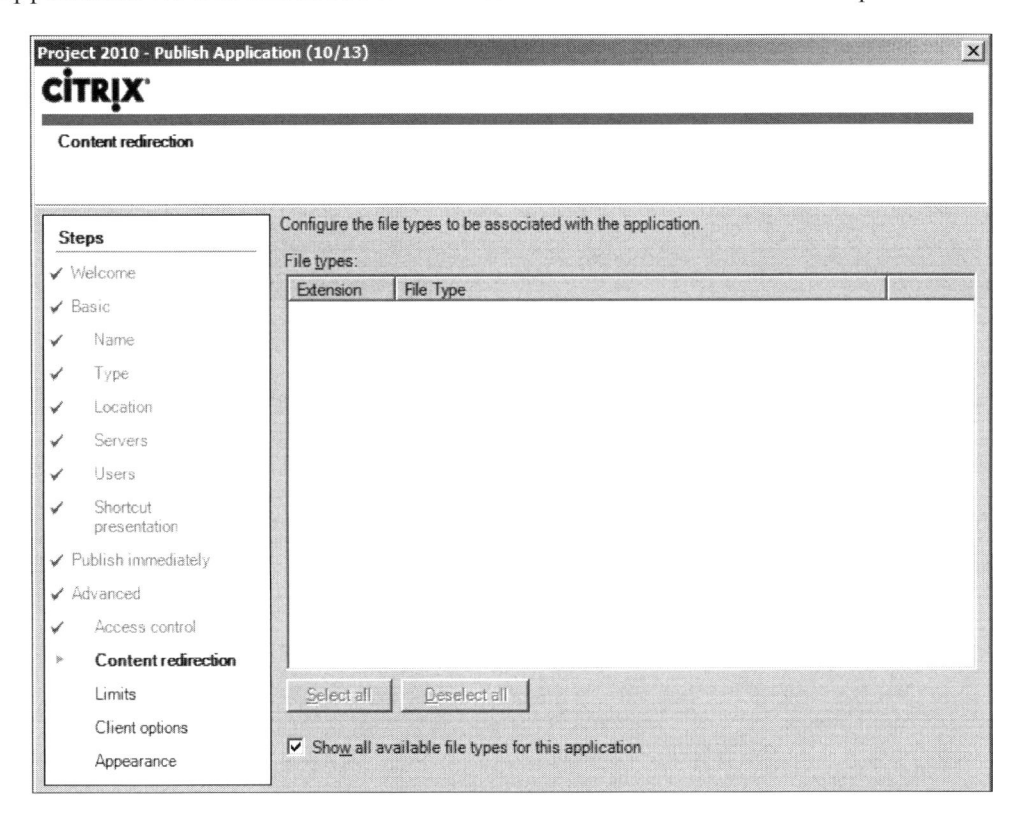

On the **Limits** page, he needs to configure application limits. William enables the **Limit instances allowed to run in server farm** checkbox and sets the **Maximum instances** option to 35, because this is the amount of Microsoft Project licenses the company owns.

William also enabled the checkbox **Allow only one instance of application for each user** to avoid one user using more than one license at the same time.

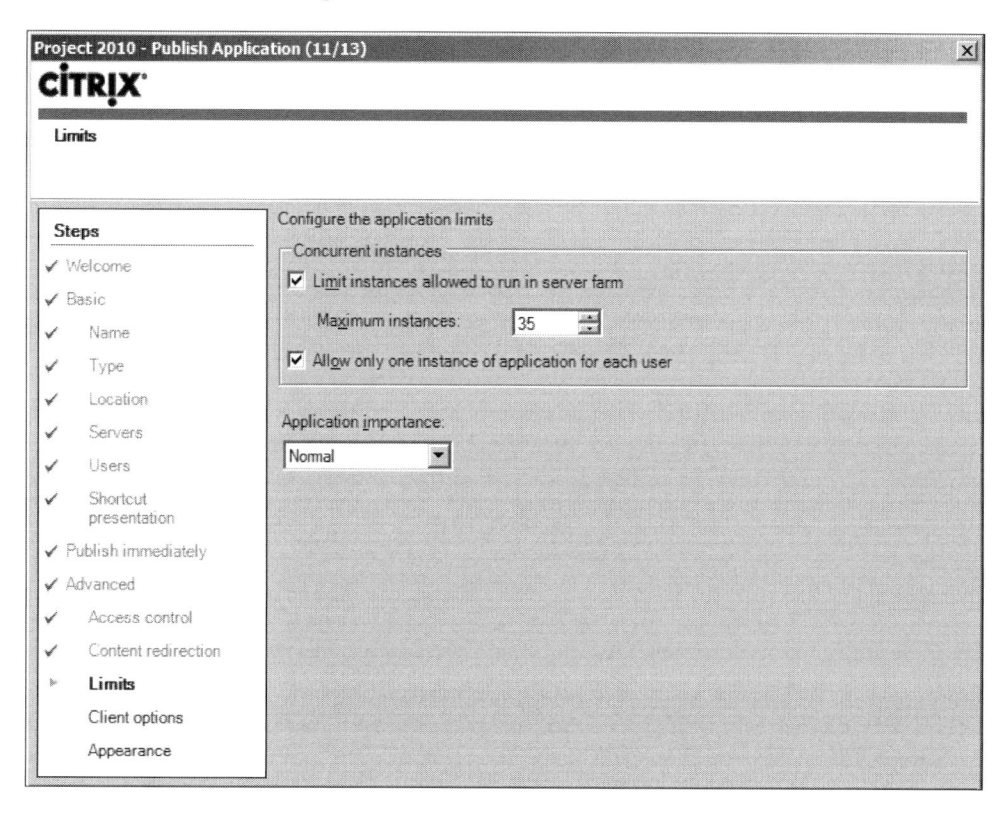

On the **Client options** page, he can configure multiple settings, such as **Client Audio Connection encryption levels**, and **Printing**.

Application Publishing

Enabling the **Start this application without waiting for printing to be created** option improves the logon speed, but sometimes can cause an issue, if a user has a lot of printers and the user tries to print before all printers are created.

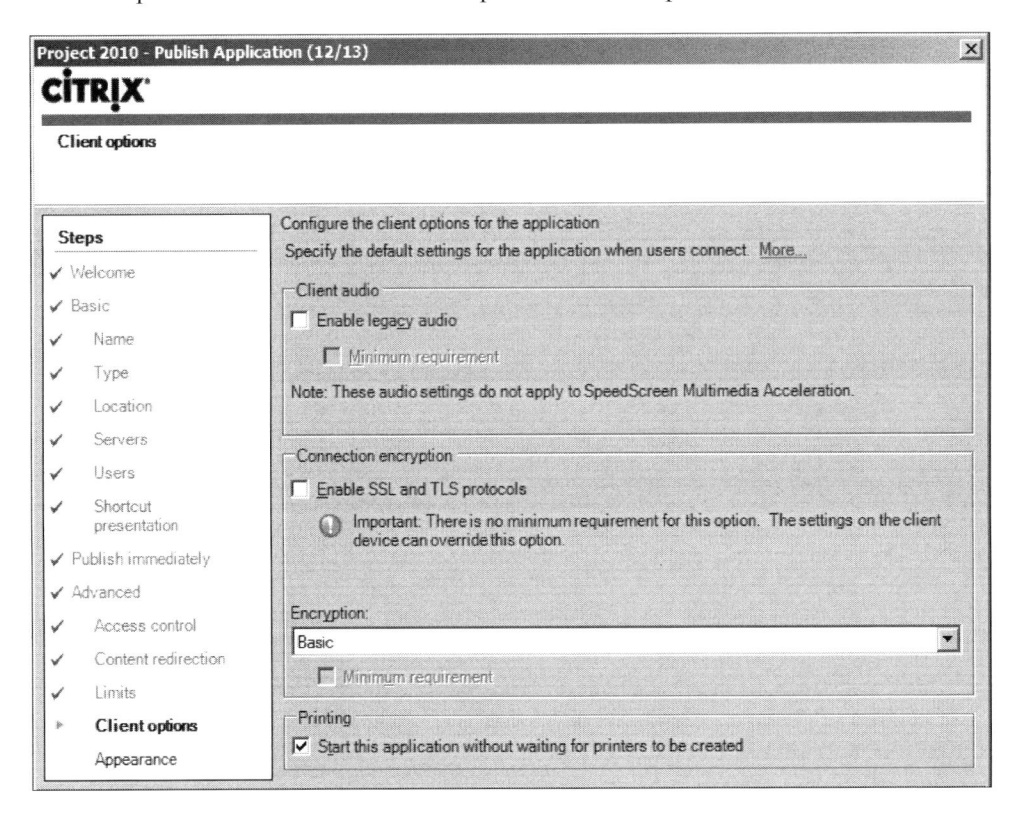

On the **Appearance** page, he can configure the visual setting of the application, such as **Session window size**, **Maximum color quality**, and so on:

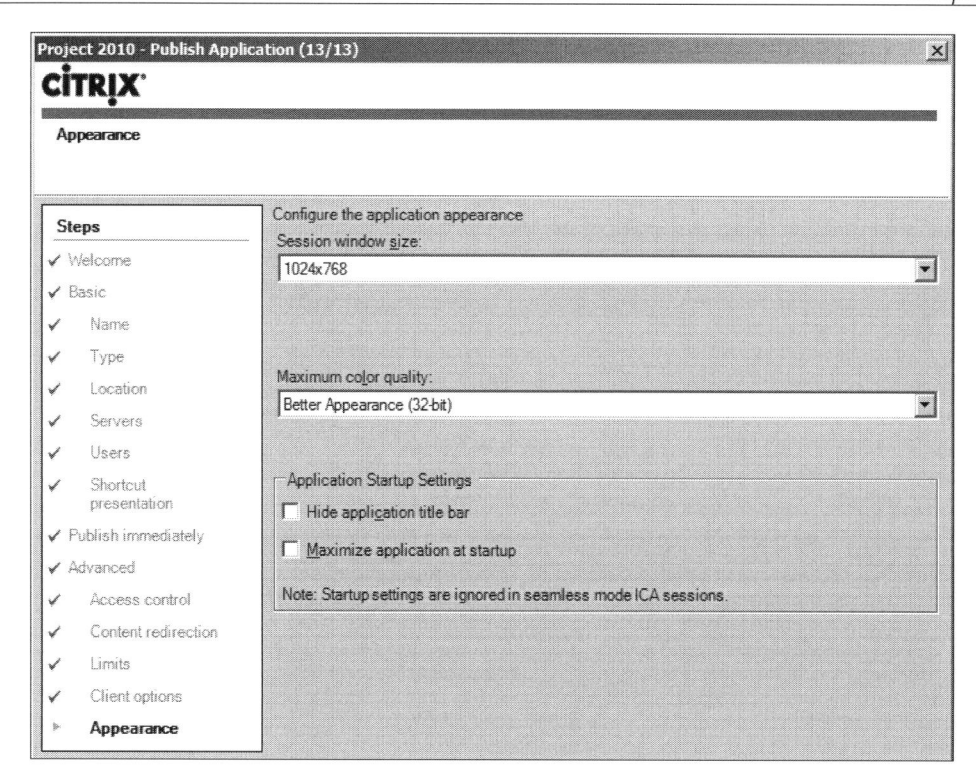

When he finishes the wizard, the published hosted application (unless he disables it on the **Publish immediately** page) is available for users.

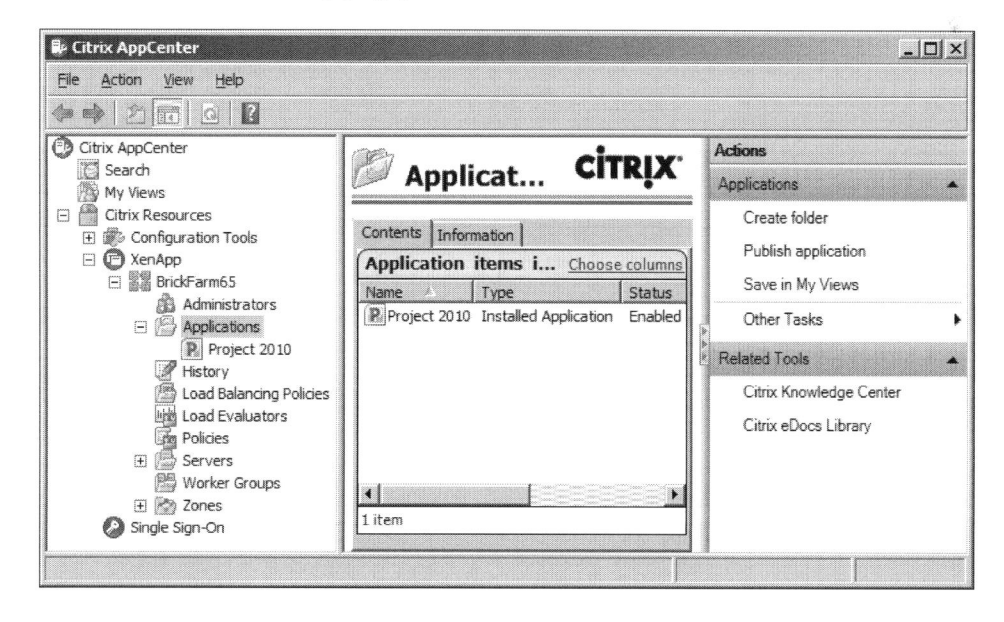

Also, he can use PowerShell to publish a hosted application. Detailed information to set up XenApp Commands on PowerShell can be found in *Chapter 12, Scripting Programming*.

```
New-XAApplication -BrowserName "Project 2010" -ApplicationType
"ServerInstalled" -DisplayName "Project 2010" -Enabled $true -
CommandLineExecutable "C:\Program Files\Microsoft Office\Office14\
Winproj.EXE" -WorkingDirectory "C:\Program Files\Microsoft Office\
Office14" -AnonymousConnectionsAllowed $false –AddToClientStartMenu $true
-InstanceLimit "-1" -WindowType "1024x768" -ColorDepth "Colors256"
```

Publishing a streaming application using the Publish Application wizard

William decided to publish Microsoft Visio 2010 as a streaming application. This decision is based on the need of architects and project managers to take some notes and make diagrams, when they are visiting clients or construction sites, and they need to run Visio on their notebooks. The ability to run Visio in both online and offline mode is critical for both the groups.

The first step is to profile Microsoft Visio 2010 and copy the application profile to the file server. We are going to cover how to install and configure streaming applications in detail in the next chapter.

When the application profile process is completed and the profile is copied to the file server, William needs to open the **Citrix AppCenter** console. The following steps are almost the same on the Citrix Delivery Service Console on XenApp 6.0.

From the XenApp console, under the **XenApp** node, he needs to expand the farm or server to which he wants to publish the application.

He needs to select the **Applications** node and from the **Actions** pane he chooses **Publish Application**.

In the **Publish Application** wizard, on the **Name** page, he needs to provide a **Display name** (maximum 256 characters) and **Application description**. The name appears on client machines when users access the application and on the console for the farm applications. XenApp supports application names that use Latin-1 and Unicode character sets, including characters used in Japanese, Chinese, and Korean.

Chapter 6

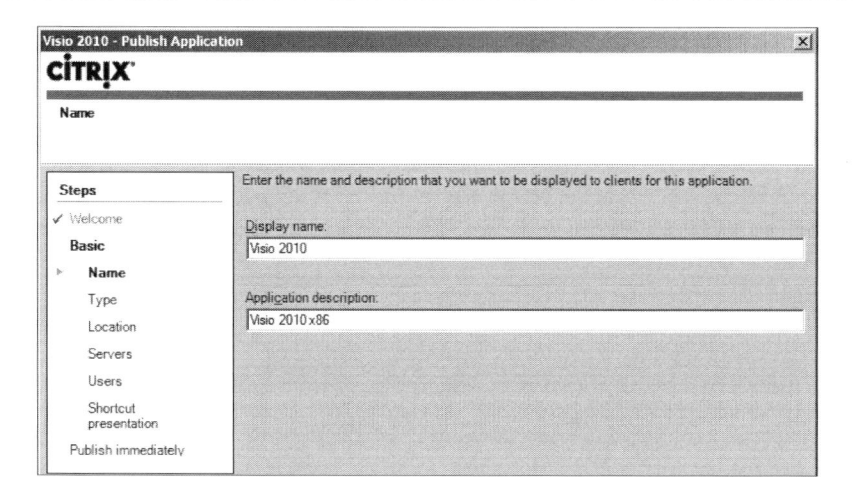

On the **Type** page, William needs to specify the type of resource he wants to publish and the delivery method. He had three types of resources to be published (server desktop, content, and application).

He needs to choose **Streamed to client** to publish a streaming application. An alternative option is to choose **Streamed if possible, otherwise accessed from a server**, but this option will require installing (or streaming) the application on the XenApp server too.

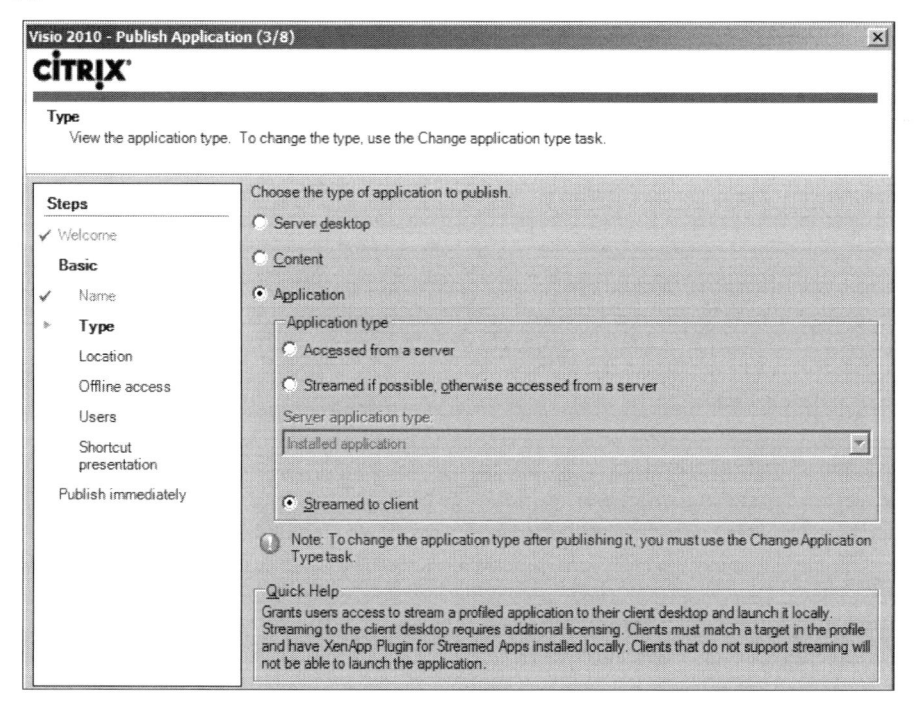

[137]

Application Publishing

On the **Location** page, he needs to type or use the **Browse** button to set **Citrix streaming application profile address**, and then he needs to choose the **Application to launch from the Citrix streaming application profile**. He can also set **Extra command line parameters** for the application.

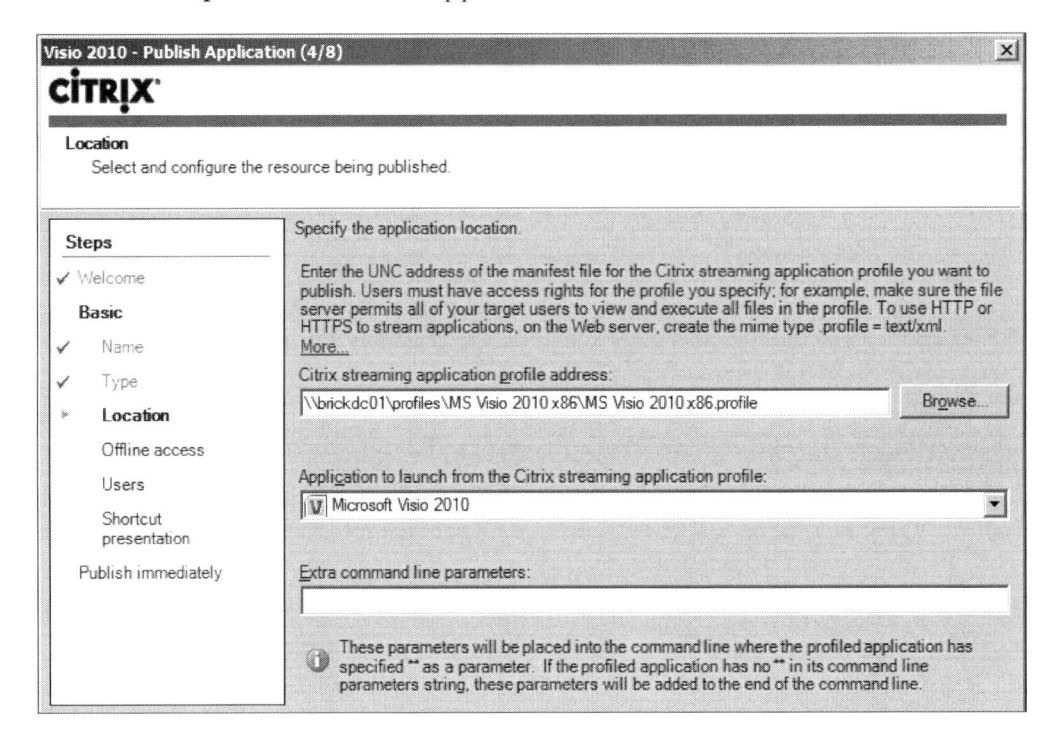

On the **Offline access** page, William can configure streamed applications for offline access.

The server fully caches applications enabled for offline access on client machines; the entire application is sent to client machines while the user is online so that the user can launch the application offline and have full functionality of the application. By default, applications are cached when a user logs on to the system.

When William clicks on the **Enable offline access** checkbox on the **Offline access** page, he needs to configure the **Cache preference**:

- **Pre-cache application at login** caches the application when the user logs on (selected by default). However, concurrent logons may slow network traffic. Pre-caching is also possible using third-party tools, such as Microsoft System Center Configuration Manager (SCCM) or similar.
- **Cache application at launch time** caches the application when users launch it. Use this option if the number of users logging on at the same time (and pre-caching their applications) could overload the network.

The offline access option requires the Citrix Receiver or Citrix Offline Plug-in to be installed on the client machine.

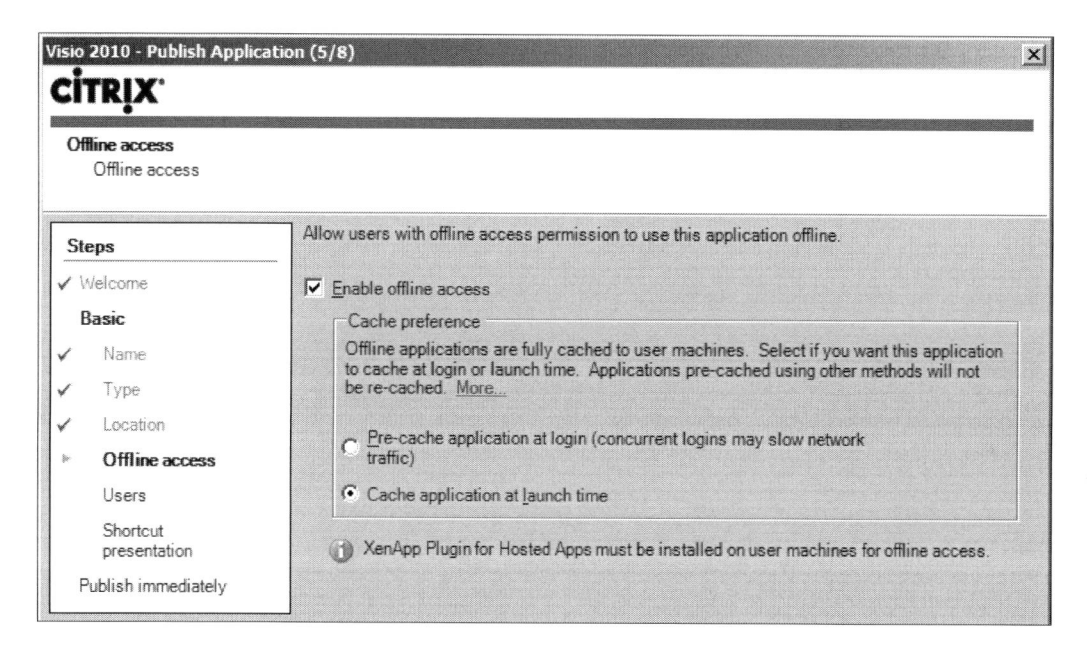

On the **Users** page, he needs to add users or groups who have access to the application and he can allow access only to configured user accounts or to anonymous users.

Application Publishing

William assigned permissions to **BU Project Managers** and **Domain Admins** groups:

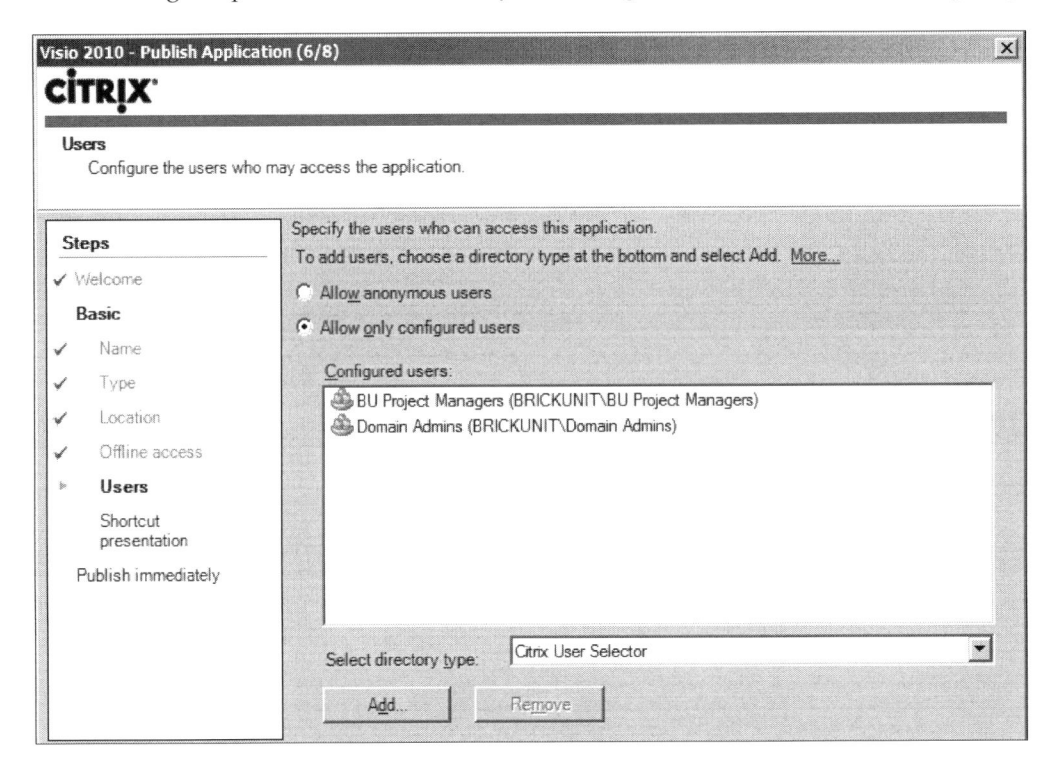

On the **Shortcut presentation** page, William selects the icon for the application and chooses how the application is enumerated on the client machine.

The client application folder is used when he needs to organize applications inside folders. This is a recommended practice, if we have a lot of applications.

The **Add to the client's Start menu** option creates a shortcut under the `Programs` folder of the local **Start** menu. If a folder structure is specified in the **Start menu Folder** textbox, the folder structure is created within the local `Programs` folder. If no folder structure is specified, the application is available from the top level of the **Start** menu.

This option provides a real integration of the streamed application in the client machine and looks like the application is installed locally.

The **Add shortcut to the client's desktop** option creates a shortcut to this application on the user's local desktop.

> The console has a limit of 1,000 unique application icons. When that limit is exceeded, the console displays a generic icon for all new applications.

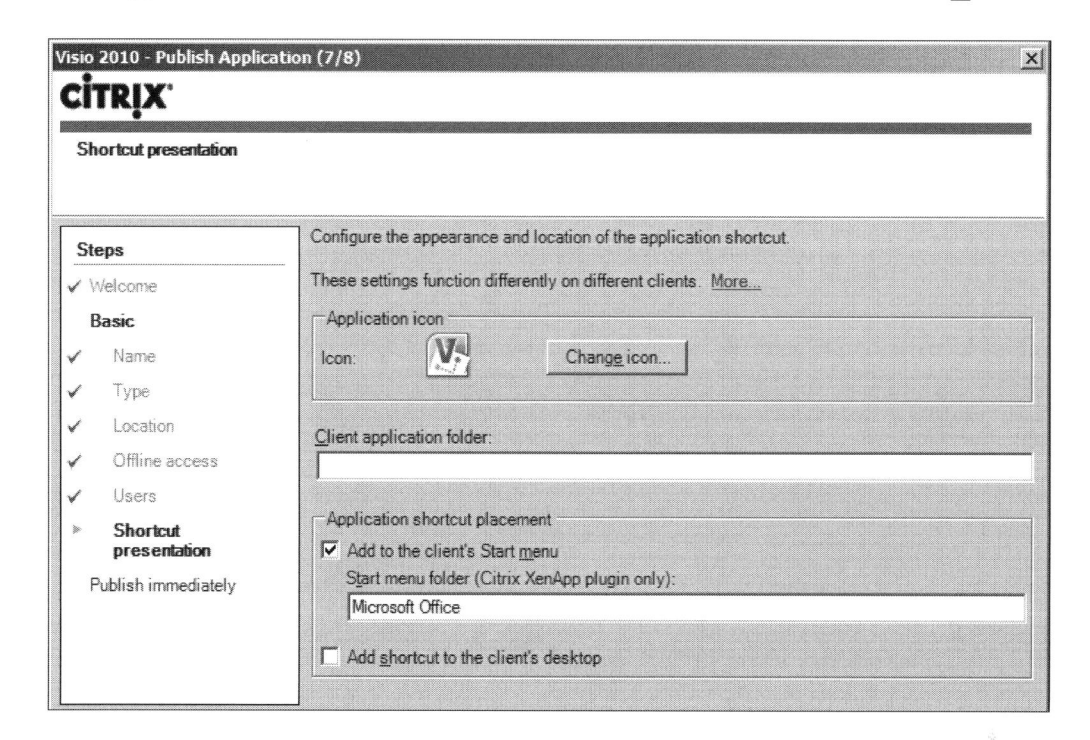

On the **Publish immediately** page, he needs to select **Disable application initially**, if he wants to prevent users from accessing the application. Later, he can manually enable it through application properties.

Application Publishing

To view and select **Advanced** options, he needs to enable the **Configure advanced application settings now** option. Alternatively, he can modify the **Advanced** settings using the application properties.

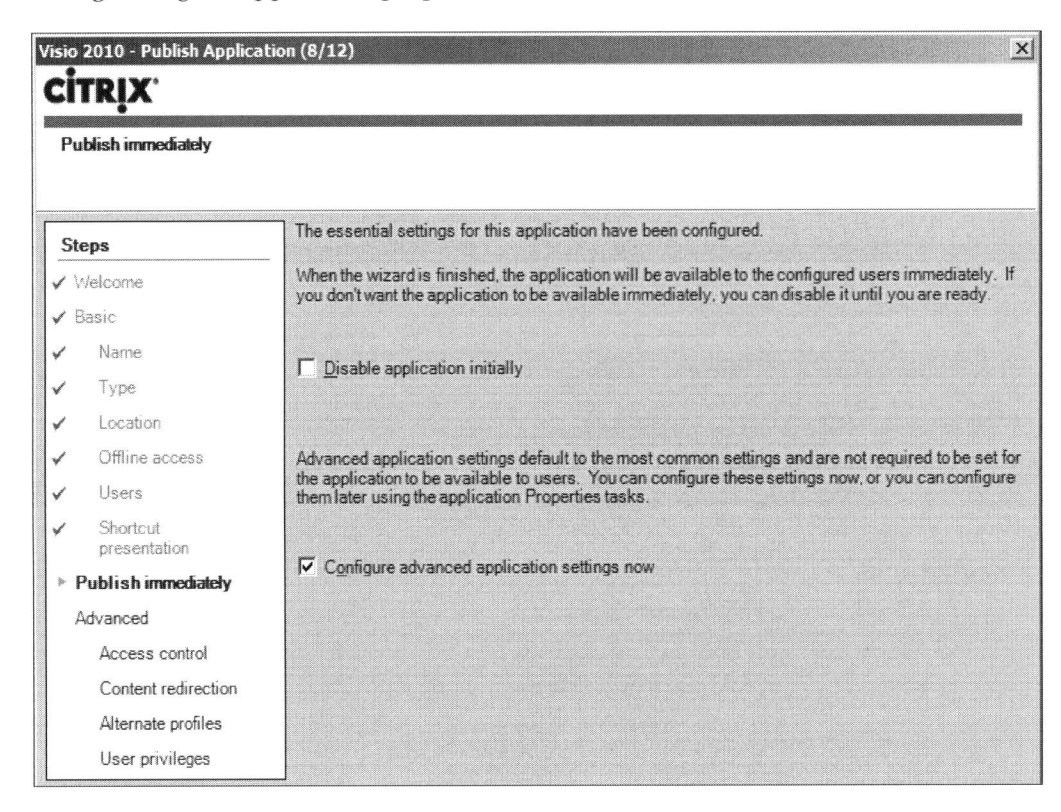

On the optional **Access control** page, he can configure the access to this application using **Access Gateway Advanced Edition**, the Citrix SSL VPN solution was used to provide access to the farm to remote users.

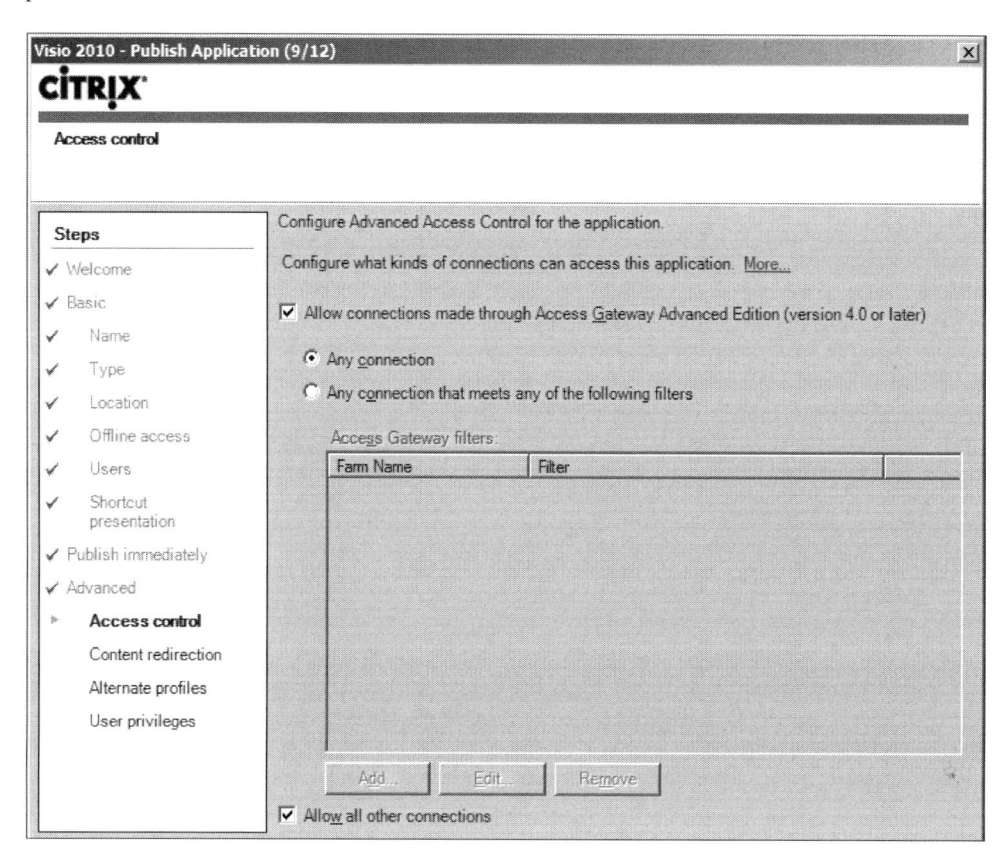

Application Publishing

On the **Content redirection** page, he can select the file types associated with the application.

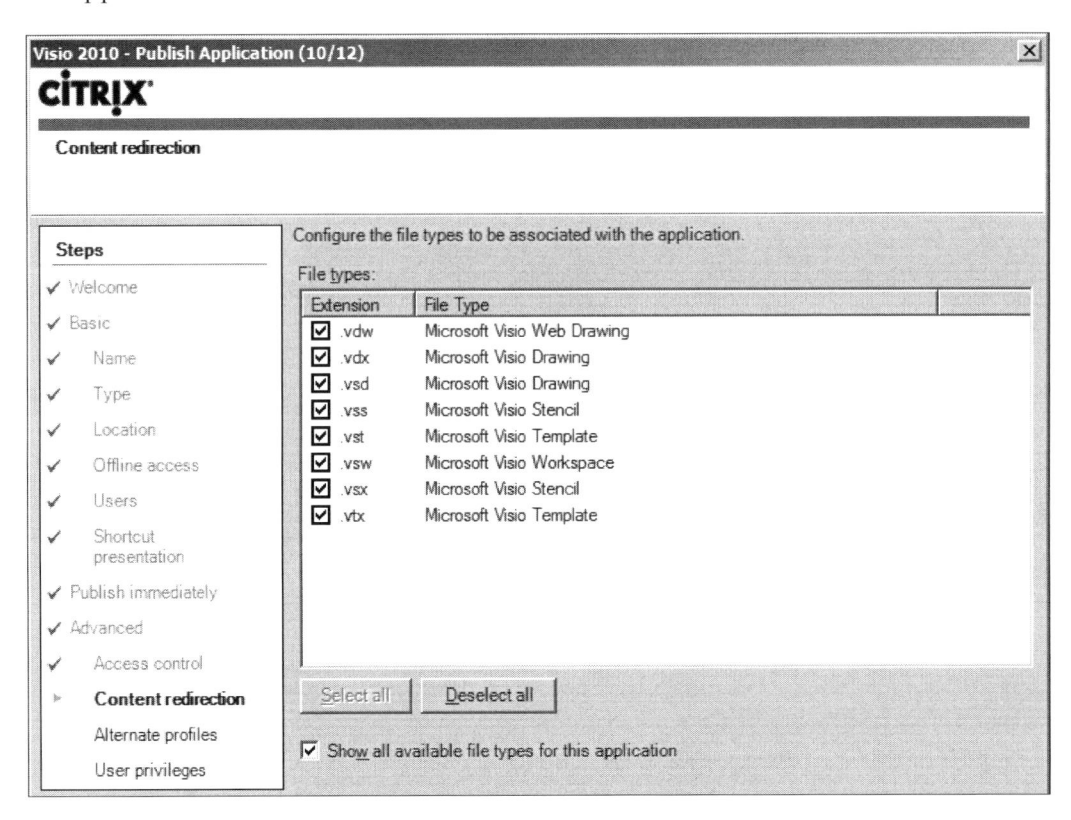

On the **Alternate profiles** page, he can add an alternate profile for connections that come from specific IP addresses. For example, William can use an alternate profile to allow users in remote branches to access one published application using file servers on their location, increasing performance and reducing loading delays.

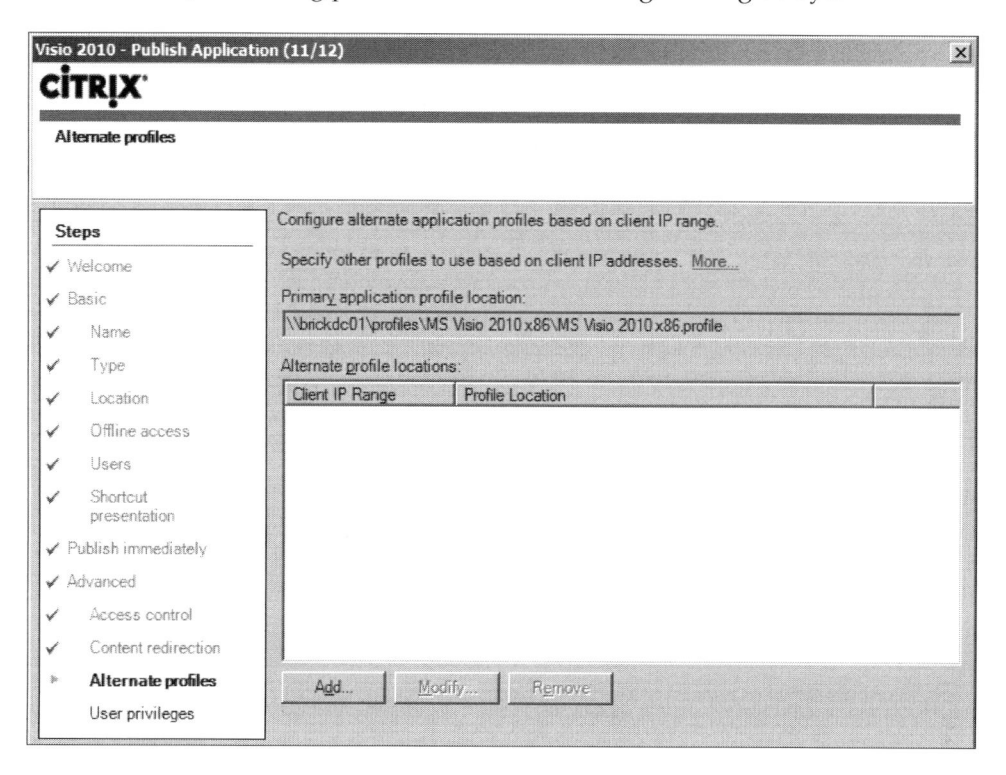

On the **User privileges** page, he can set up the level of privileges when the application runs on the client machine.

Application Publishing

When the checkbox **Run application as a least-privileged user account** (not selected by default) is enabled, all users, even those with an administrator account, run the application with normal user privileges.

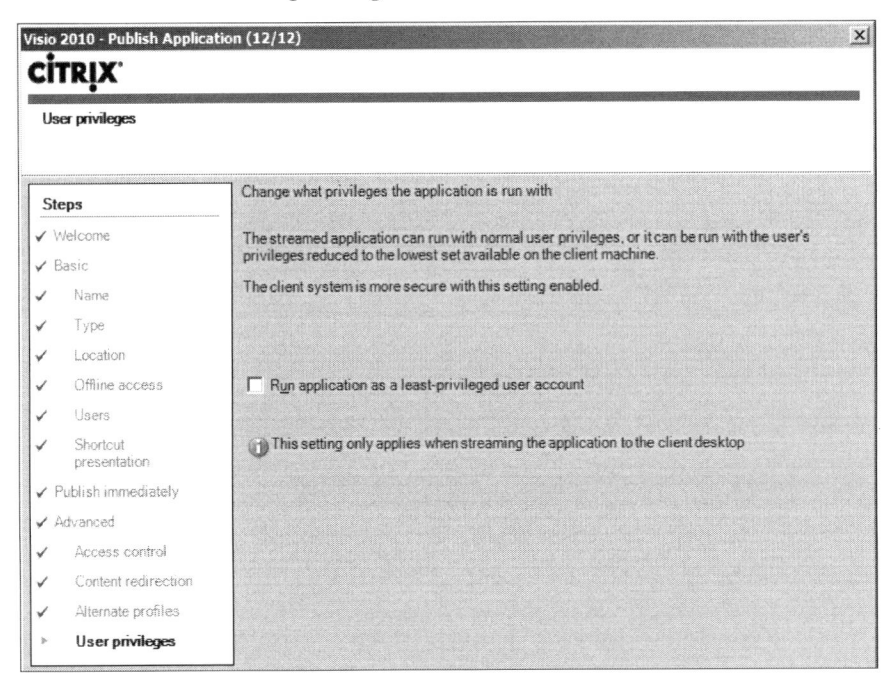

When he finished this wizard, the published streamed application (unless he disables it) is available for users.

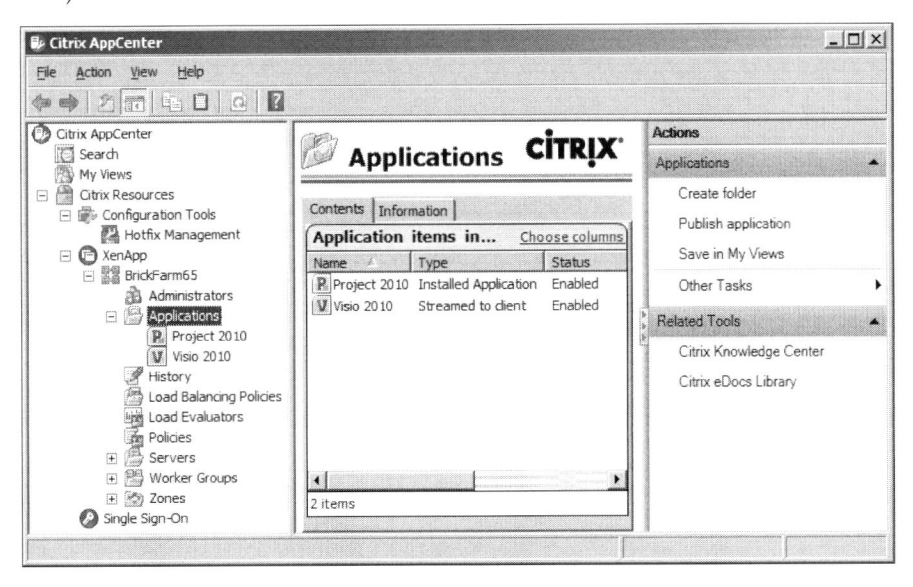

Publishing content using the Publish Application wizard

William will publish the **CtxAdmTools** website to administrators. CtxAdmTools is a popular site for free tools of Citrix, Microsoft, and VMware tools, featured on the Citrix community website.

To publish content, William needs to open the **Citrix AppCenter** console (formerly known as Citrix Delivery Service Console on XenApp 6.0).

From the AppCenter console, under the **XenApp** node, he needs to expand the farm or server to which he wants to publish the content.

He needs to select the **Applications** node and from the **Actions** pane, he chooses **Publish Application**.

In the **Publish Application** wizard, on the **Name** page, William needs to provide a **Display name** (maximum 256 characters) and **Application description**. The name appears on client machines when users access the application and on the console for the farm applications. XenApp supports application names that use Latin-1 and Unicode character sets, including characters used in Japanese, Chinese, and Korean.

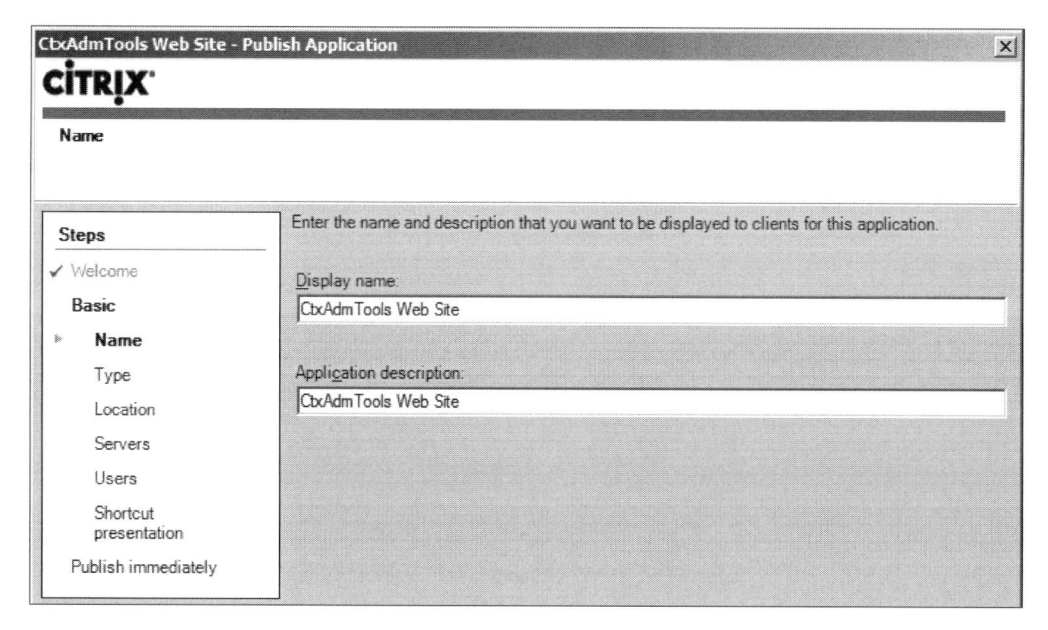

Application Publishing

On the **Type** page, he needs to specify the type of resource he wants to publish and the delivery method. He has three types of resources to be published (server desktop, content, and application).

William will choose the **Content** option to publish a website.

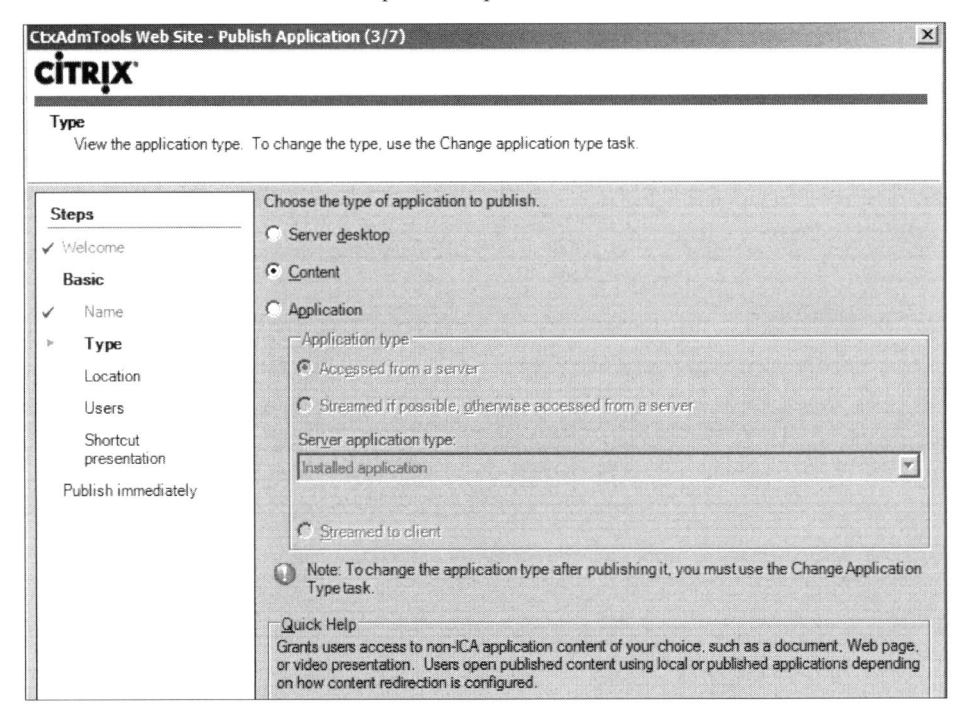

On the **Location** page, he needs to type or use the **Browse** button to set the path of the file or the URL of the resource, `http://ctxadmtools.musumeci.com.ar`.

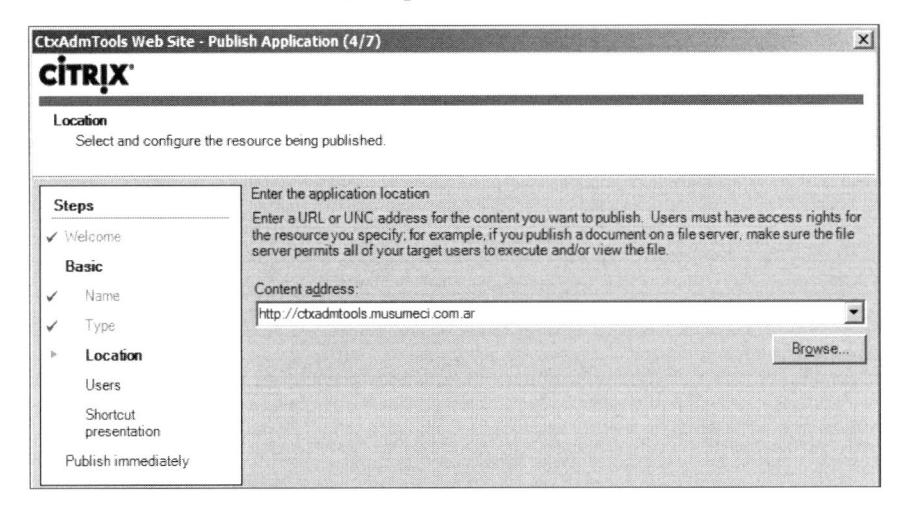

On the **Users** page, he needs to add users or groups who have access to the application and he can allow access only to configured user accounts or to anonymous users.

William assigned permissions to the **Domain Admins** group because CtxAdmTools is a website for free Citrix, Microsoft, and VMware tools, and only administrators will access the site:

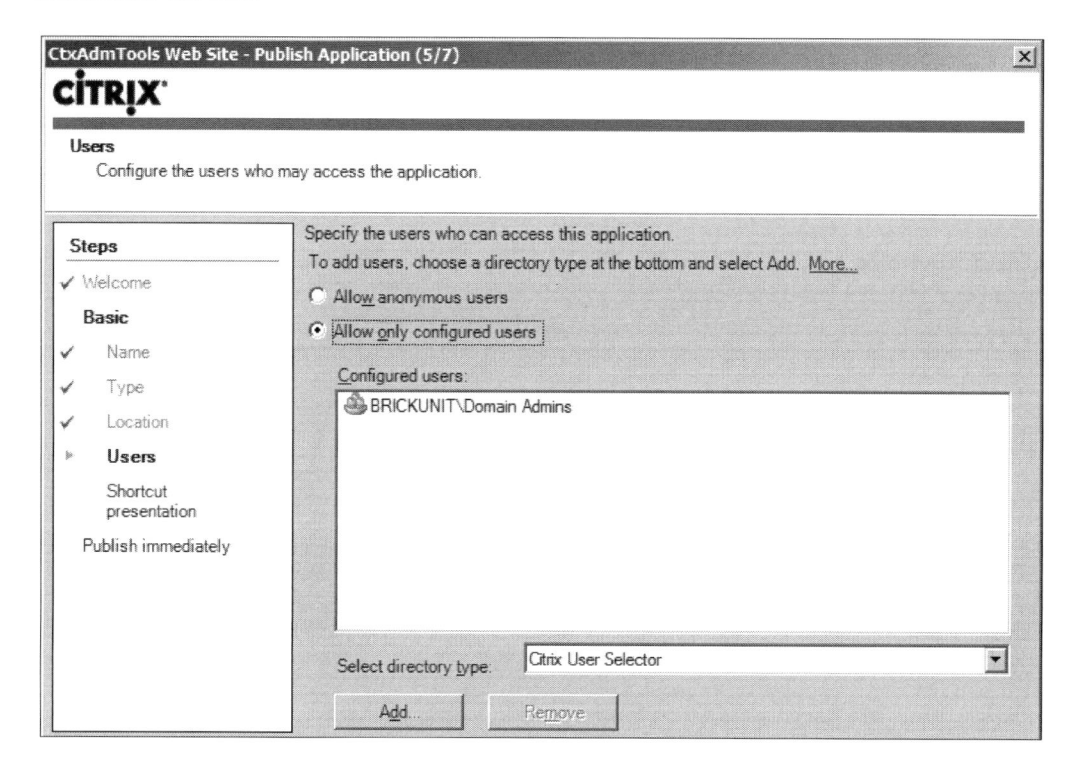

On the **Shortcut presentation** page, select the icon for the application and choose how the application is enumerated on the client machine.

The client application folder is used when we need to organize applications inside folders. This is a recommended practice, if we have a lot of applications.

Application Publishing

Usually both **Add to the client's Start menu** and **Add shortcut to the client's desktop** are used when clients utilize the XenApp Plug-in to connect to the XenApp farm.

> The console has a limit of 1,000 unique application icons. When that limit is exceeded, the console displays a generic icon for all new applications.

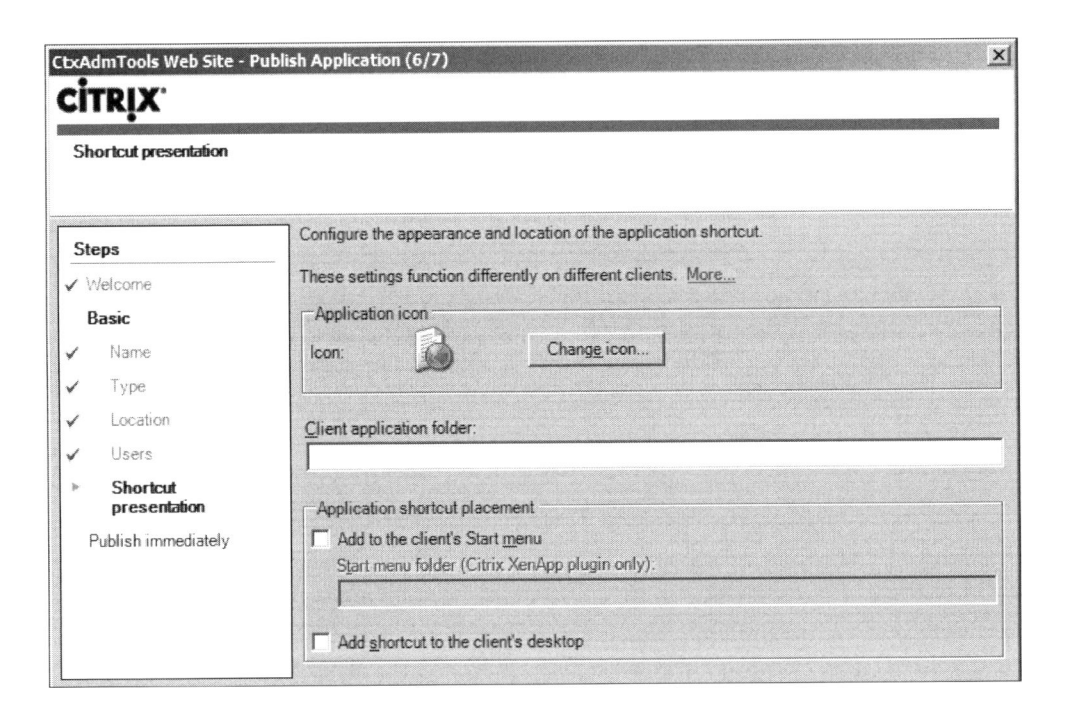

[Screenshot: CtxAdmTools Web Site - Publish Application (6/7) - Shortcut presentation step showing Application icon, Client application folder, and Application shortcut placement options including "Add to the client's Start menu" and "Add shortcut to the client's desktop"]

On the **Publish immediately** page, he needs to select **Disable application** initially, if he wants to prevent users from accessing the application. Later, he can manually enable it through application properties.

To view and select **Advanced** options, he needs to enable the **Configure advanced application settings now** option. Alternatively, he can modify the **Advanced** settings using the application properties:

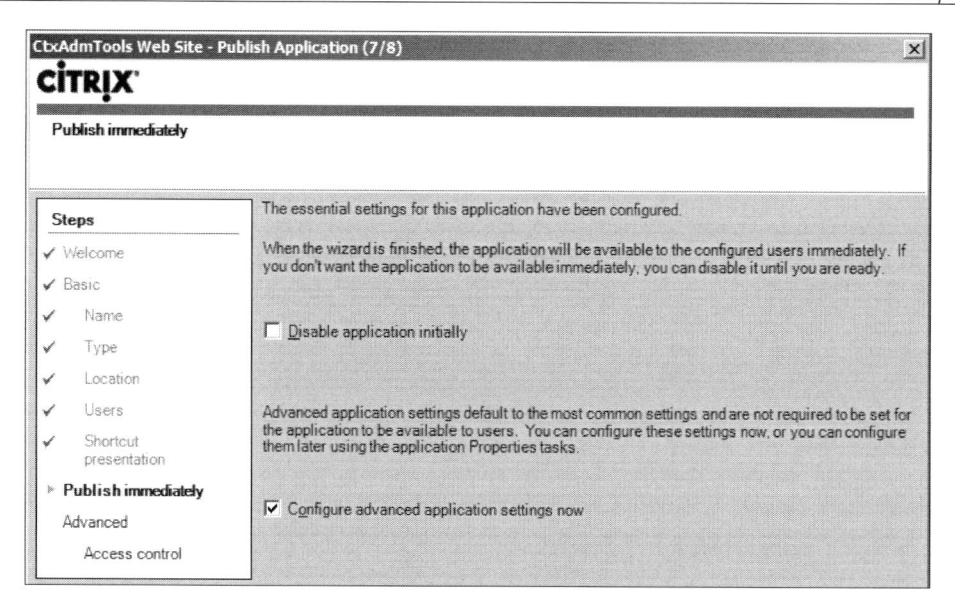

Chapter 6

[Screenshot: CtxAdmTools Web Site - Publish Application (7/8) - Publish immediately step]

On the optional **Access control** page, he can configure access to this application using Access Gateway Advanced Edition, the Citrix SSL VPN solution was used to provide access to the farm to remote users:

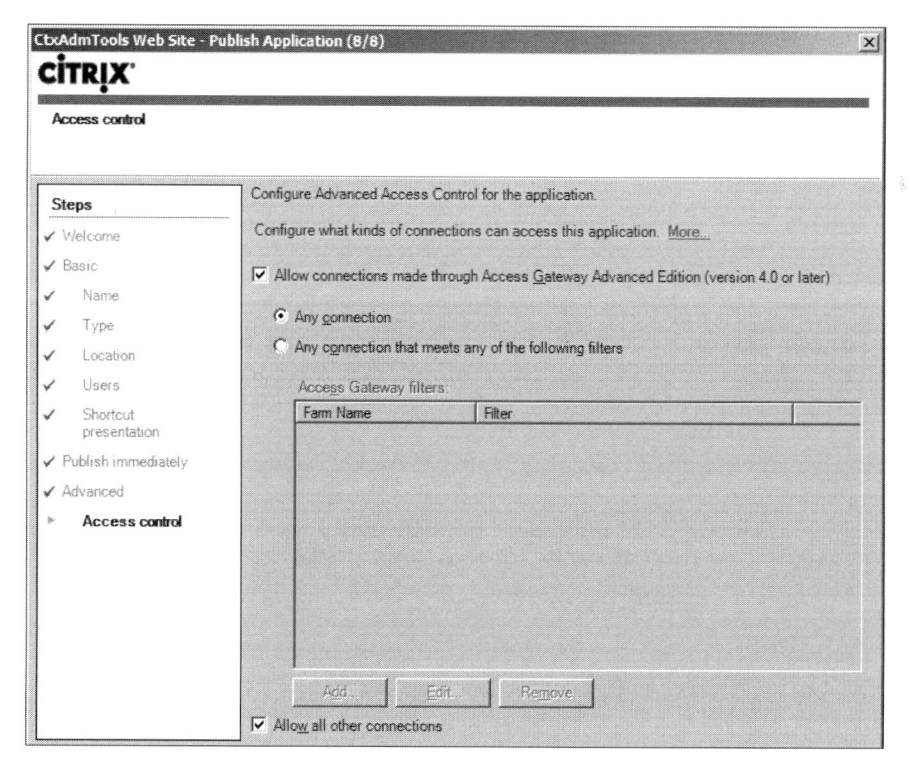

[Screenshot: CtxAdmTools Web Site - Publish Application (8/8) - Access control step]

Application Publishing

When he finished the wizard, the published content (unless he disabled it) is available for users:

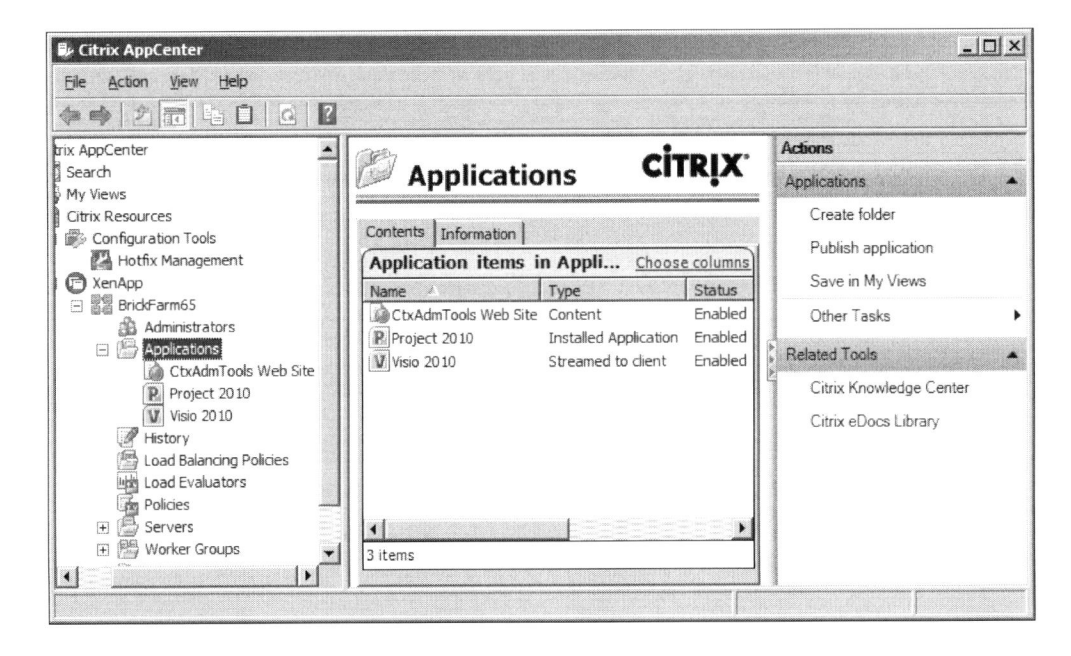

Publishing a server desktop using the Publish Application wizard

William will publish server desktops of XenApp servers to help administrators manage servers. To publish a server desktop, he needs to open the Citrix AppCenter console (or Citrix Delivery Services Console on XenApp 6.0).

From the AppCenter console, under the **XenApp** node, William needs to expand the farm or server to which he wants to publish the application.

He needs to select the **Applications** node.

> We can use the **Actions** pane and choose **Create folder**. We need to name the folder for the application we are publishing. This step is optional if we have a few applications, but will be necessary to create folders to keep applications organized, if we have dozens or hundreds of applications. These folders are visible only to XenApp Administrators and not visible to standard users.

He needs to select the (optional) folder if he created one before; if not, just click on the root **Applications** node and from the **Actions** pane, choose **Publish application**.

In the **Publish Application** wizard, on the **Name** page, he needs to provide a **Display name** (maximum 256 characters) and **Application description**. The name appears on client machines when users access the application and on the console for the farm applications. XenApp supports application names that use Latin-1 and Unicode character sets, including characters used in Japanese, Chinese, and Korean.

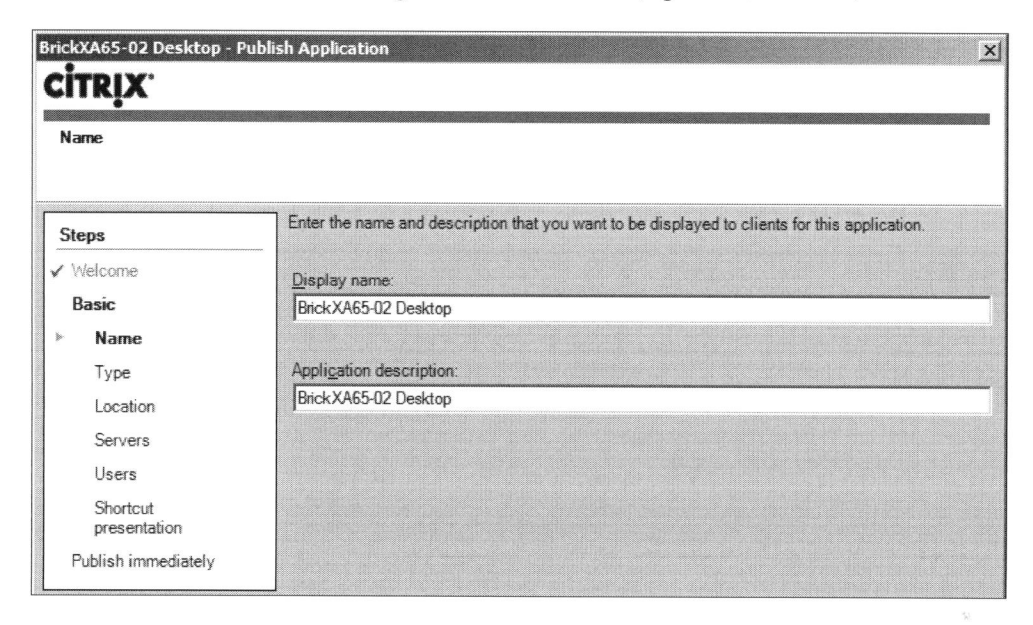

On the **Type** page, he needs to specify the type of resource he wants to publish and the delivery method. He has three types of resources to be published (server desktop, content, and application).

He needs to choose **Server desktop**.

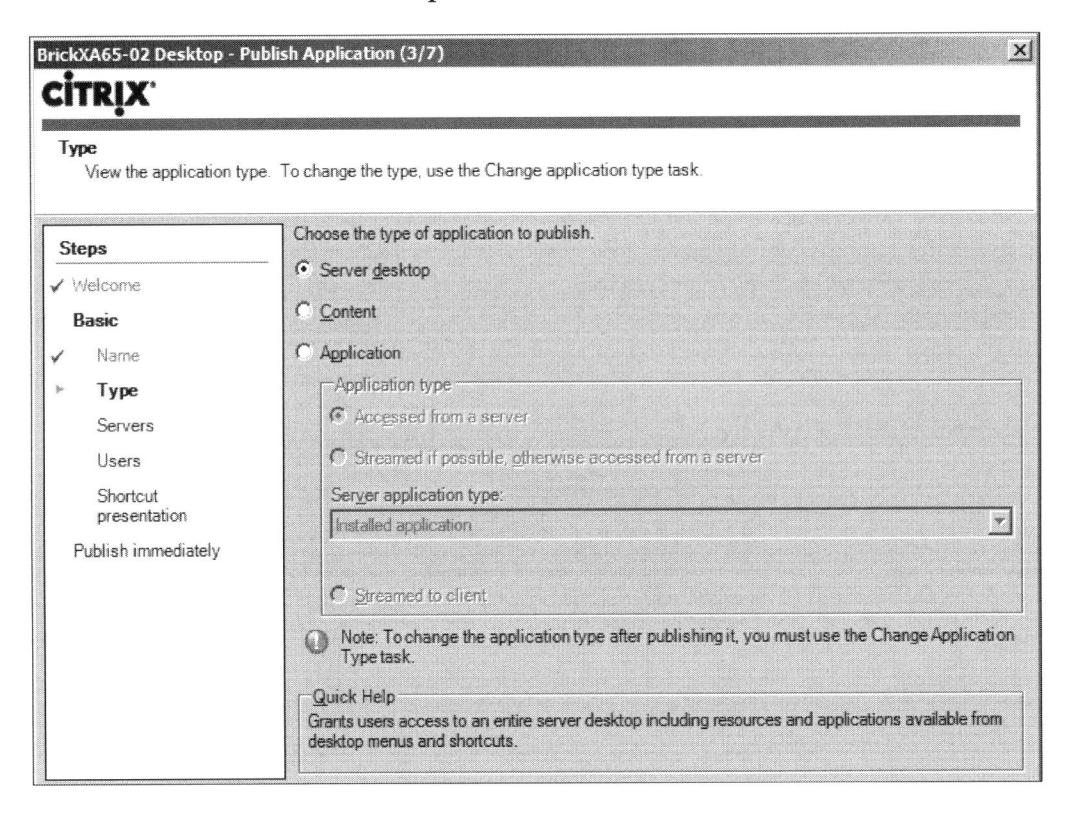

On the **Servers** page, he needs to add the individual servers or worker groups on which the published application runs.

Creating one published server desktop for each XenApp server for administration purposes is a common practice, in most of the environments.

> To add a server to the list of servers for a published desktop or application (after publishing the application), drag-and-drop the server onto the published desktop or application in the left-hand side pane of the console. We can also drag-and-drop the published desktop or application onto the server.

Chapter 6

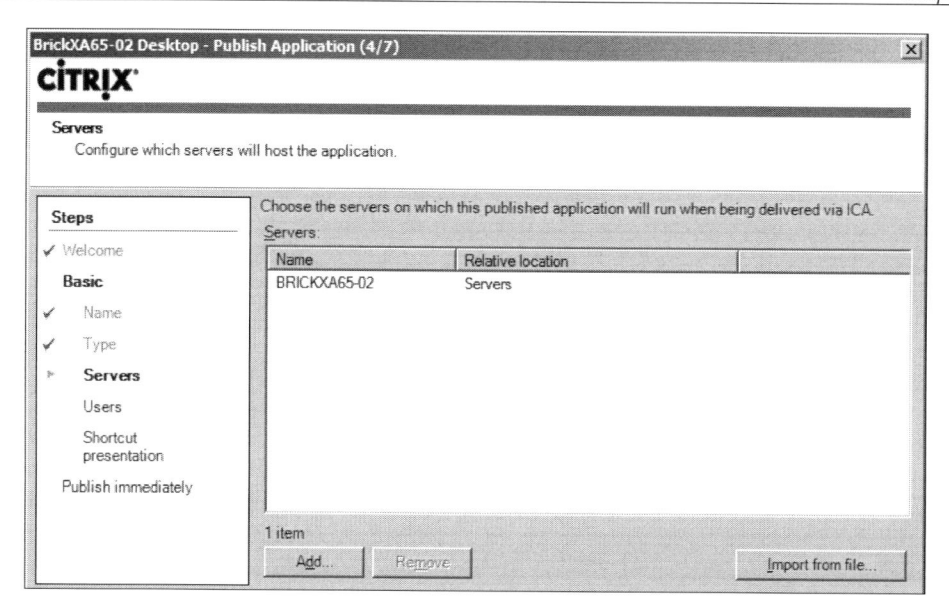

On the **Users** page, he needs to add users or groups who have access to the application and he can allow access only to configured user accounts or to anonymous users.

William assigned permissions to the **Domain Admins** group, because only administrators will access the server desktop.

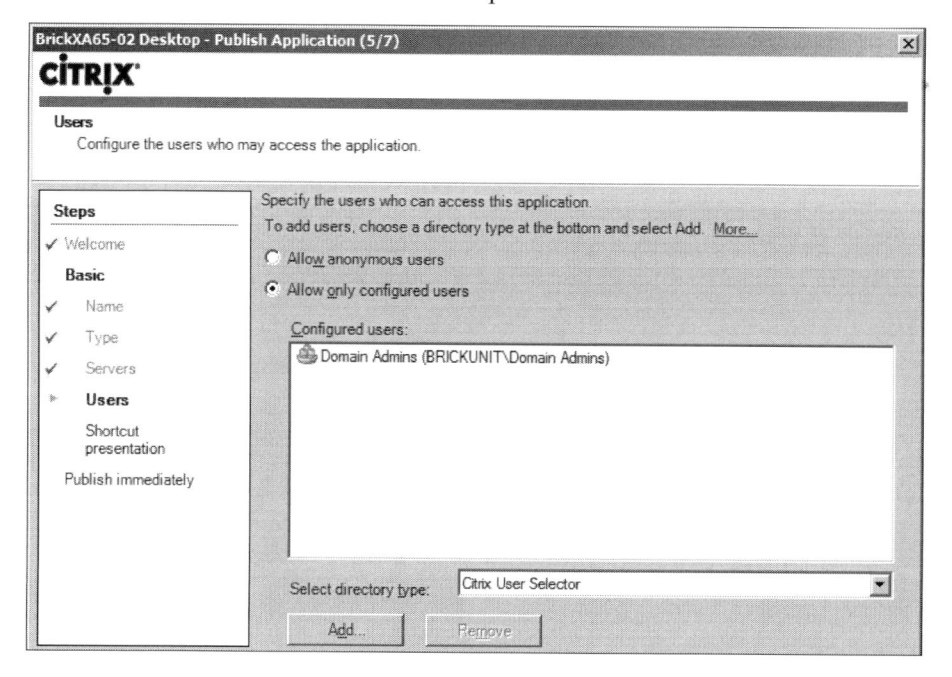

Application Publishing

On the **Shortcut presentation** page, he selects the icon for the application and chooses how the application is enumerated on the client machines.

The client application folder is used when he needs to organize applications inside folders. This is a recommended practice, if he had a lot of applications.

Usually both **Add to the client's Start menu** and **Add shortcut to the client's desktop** options are used when clients utilize the XenApp Plug-in to connect to XenApp farm.

> The console has a limit of 1,000 unique application icons. When that limit is exceeded, the console displays a generic icon for all new applications.

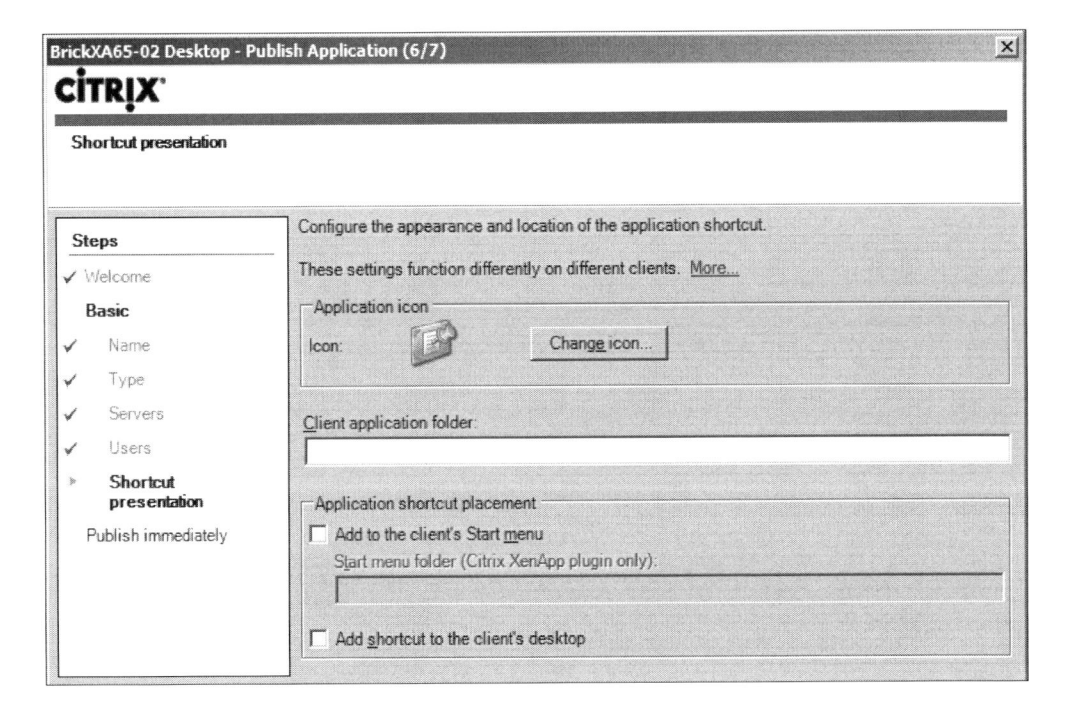

[156]

On the **Publish immediately** page, he needs to select **Disable application initially**, if he wants to prevent users from accessing the application. Later, he can manually enable it through application properties.

To view and select **Advanced** options, he needs to enable the **Configure advanced application settings now** option. Alternatively, he can modify the **Advanced** settings using the application properties.

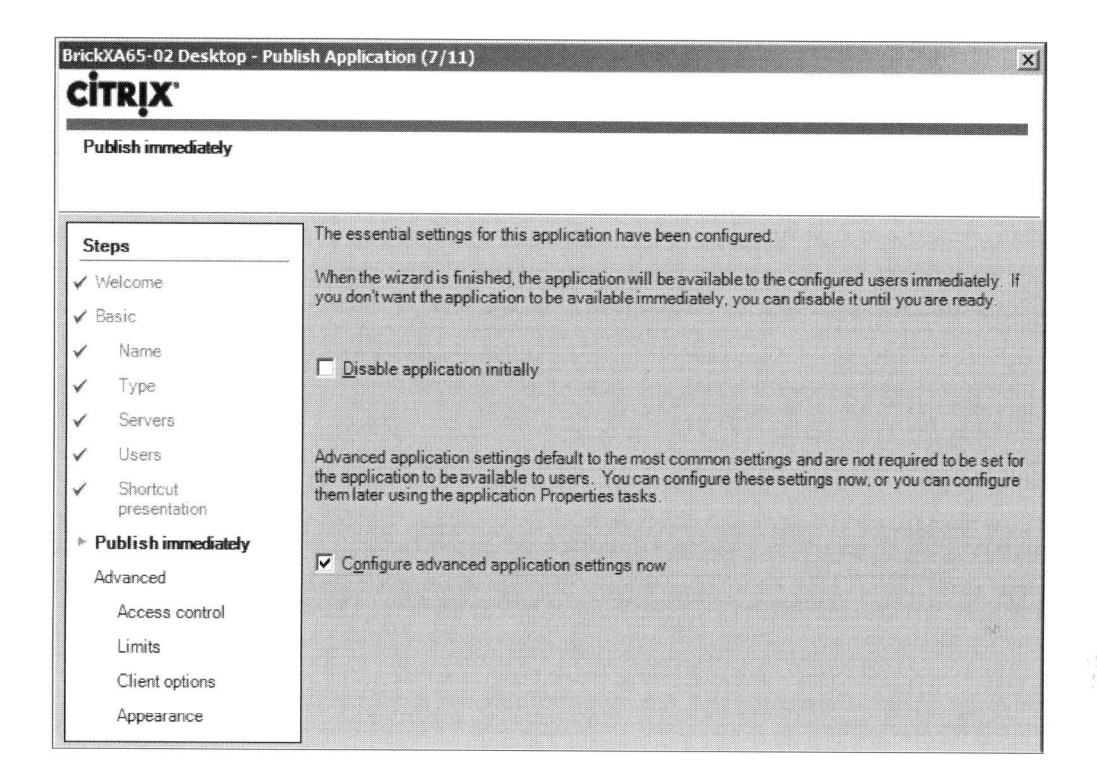

Application Publishing

On the optional **Access control** page, he can configure the access to this application using Access Gateway Advanced Edition, the Citrix SSL VPN solution was used to provide access to the farm to remote users.

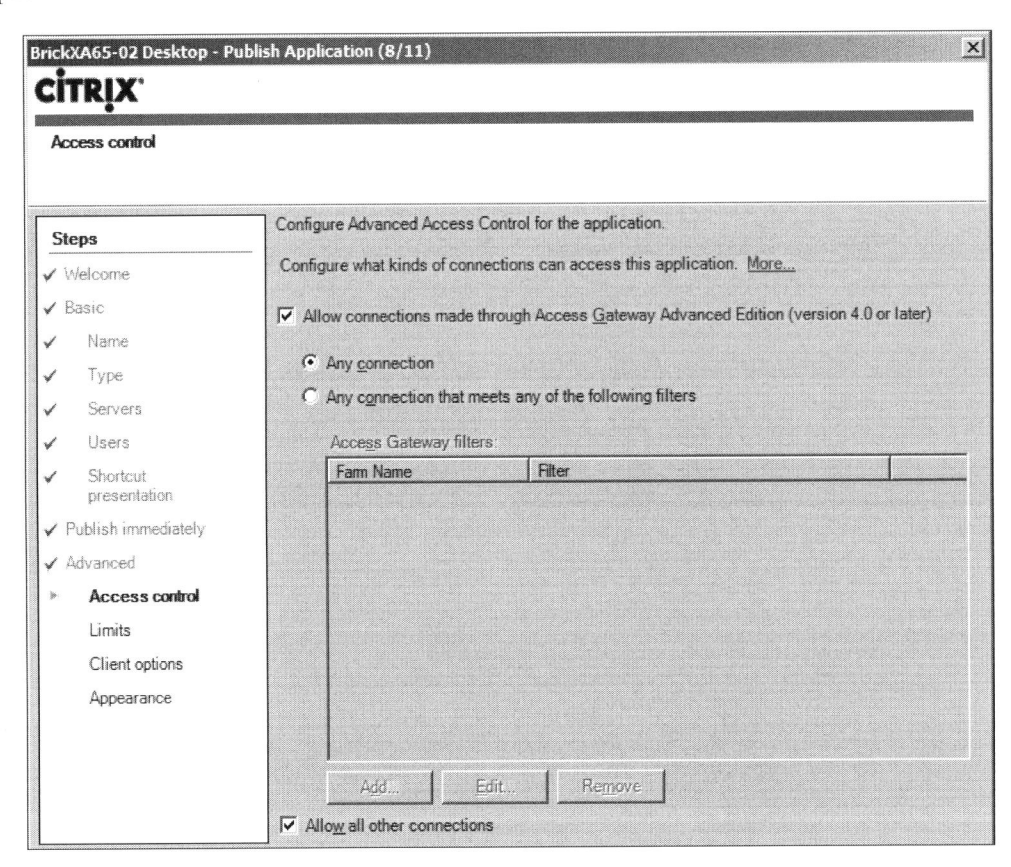

On the **Limits** page, he needs to configure application limits. William doesn't enable the **Limit instances allowed to run in server farm** checkbox and **Maximum instances** checkbox, because there is no need to limit the amount of simultaneous connections.

William also keeps the checkbox **Allow only one instance of application for each user** disabled.

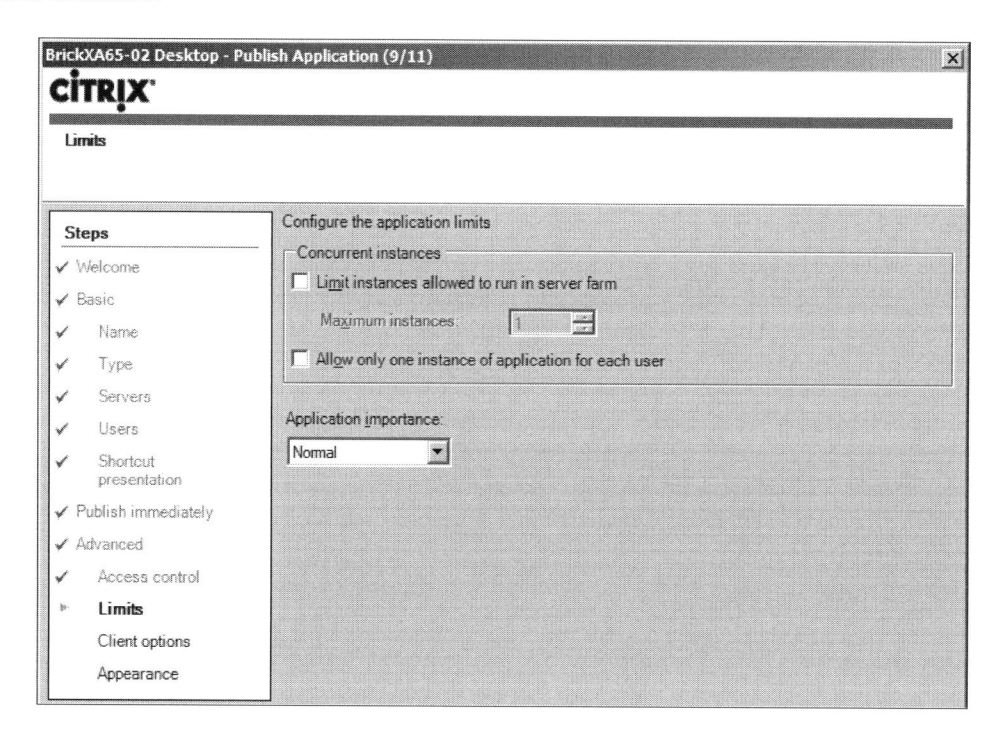

On the **Client options** page, he can configure multiple settings, like Client Audio, Connection encryption levels, and Printing.

Enabling the **Start this application without waiting for printing** to be created option improves the logon speed but sometimes can cause issues, if a user has a lot of printers and he tries to print before all printers are created.

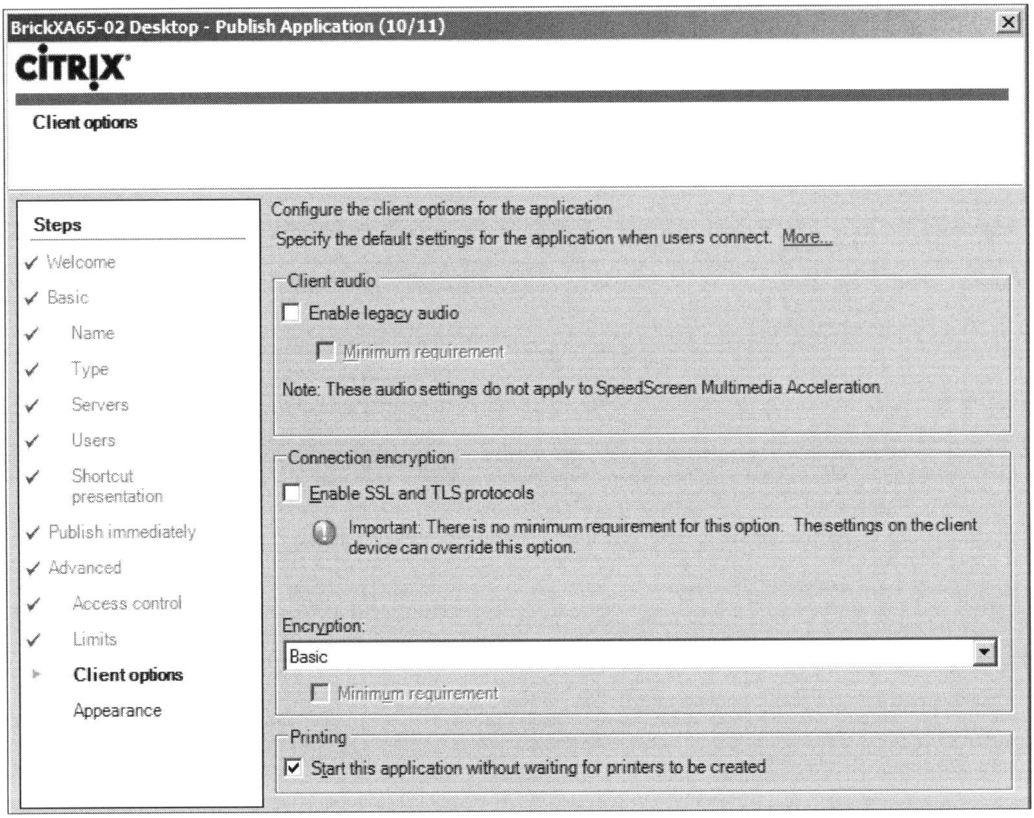

On the **Appearance** page, he can configure the visual setting of the application, like Session window size, color quality, and so on.

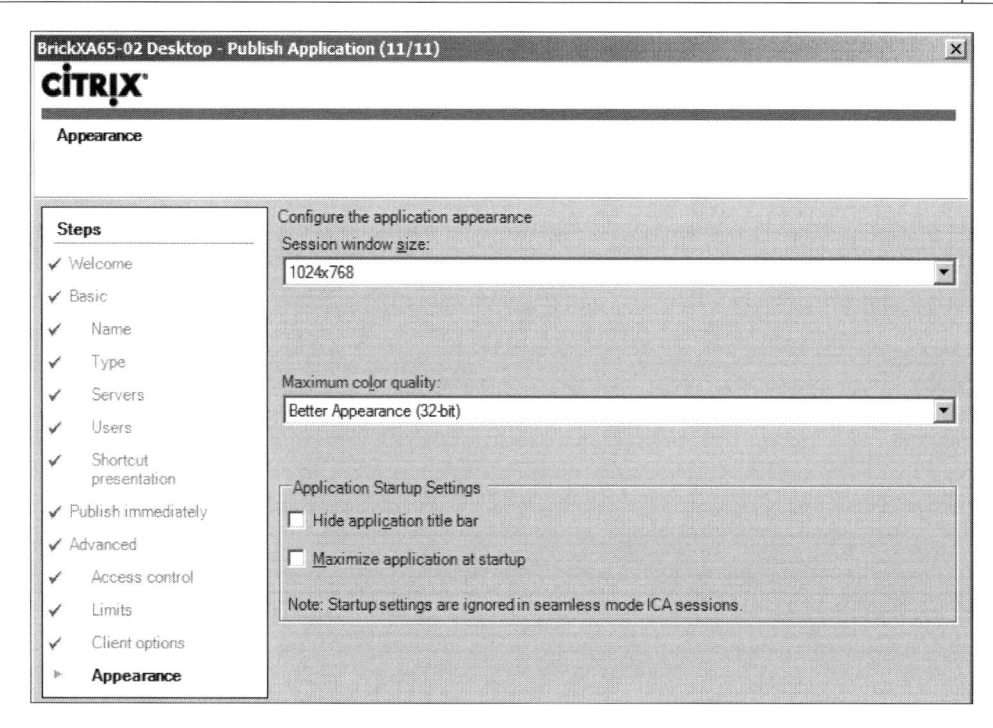

When he finishes the wizard, the published desktop is available for users, unless he disabled it before.

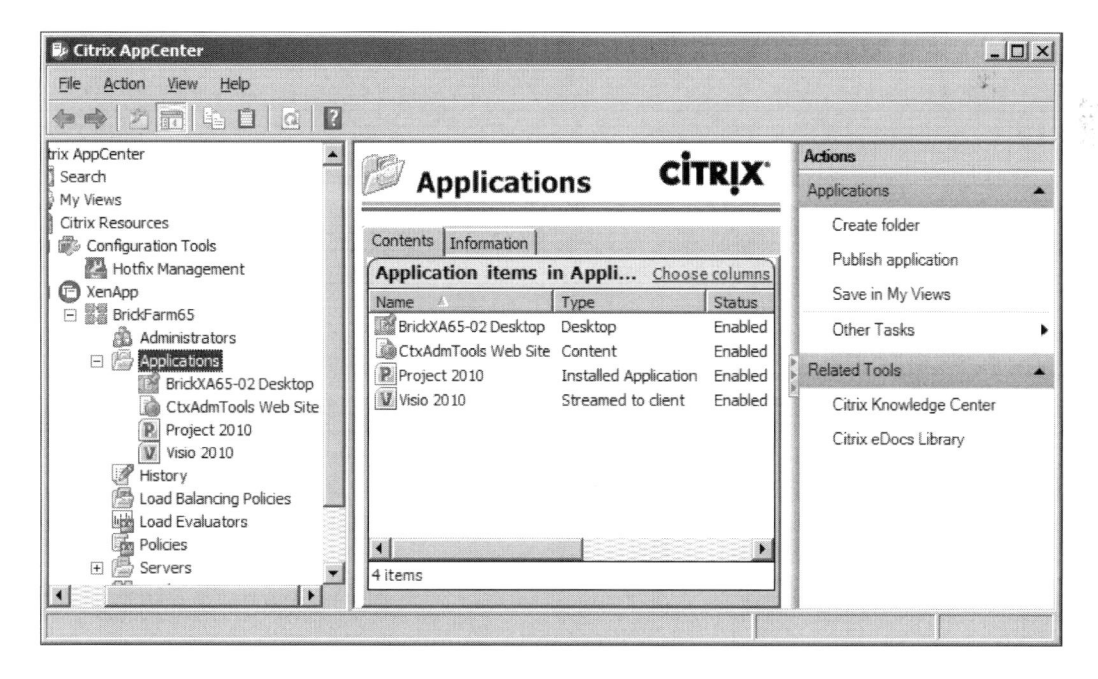

Configuring content redirection

The capability to redirect application and content launching from server to client or client to server is referred to as **content redirection**.

Content redirection allows us to manage whether users access information with applications published on servers or with applications running locally on client machines.

Enabling content redirection from server to client

When we enable server to client content redirection, the XenApp server intercepts embedded URLs and sends them to the client machine and the web browser, or multimedia players, on the client machine open these URLs. This feature reduces the usage on servers from processing these types of requests by redirecting application launching for supported URLs from the server to the local client machine. The browser locally installed on the client machine is used to navigate to the URL. Users cannot disable this feature. Accessing published content with local client desktops does not use XenApp resources or licenses because local viewer applications do not use XenApp sessions to display the published content.

For example, users can access a training website with a lot of graphics and sound in their client machines, without overloading servers. Multimedia sites, such as training sites with intensive graphics, usually run better on client machines.

> If the client machine fails to connect to a URL, the URL is redirected back to the server.

The following URL types are opened locally through client machines for Windows and Linux when this type of content redirection is enabled:

- HTTP (Hypertext Transfer Protocol)
- HTTPS (Secure Hypertext Transfer Protocol)
- RTSP (Real Player and QuickTime)
- RTSPU (Real Player and QuickTime)
- PNM (Legacy Real Player)
- MMS (Microsoft Media Format)

If content redirection from server to client is not working for some of the HTTPS links, we need to verify that the client machine has an appropriate certificate installed. If the appropriate certificate is not installed, the HTTP ping from the client machine to the URL fails and the URL is redirected back to the server.

Configuring content redirection from client to server

When we configure client to server content redirection, users running the XenApp Online Plug-in open all files of the associated type using applications published on the server. Content redirection from client to server is available only for users connecting with the XenApp Online Plug-in.

For example, Brick Unit Construction doesn't have enough licenses of Project 2010 for all client machines. However, occasionally, some users receive a project file attached in an e-mail. When users double-click project attachments on the e-mail application running locally, the attachment opens in a Project 2010 session that is published on the server.

When we configure content redirection from client to server, context menu commands available from within Windows Explorer function differently than on client machines that do not use this feature. For example, if we right-click a file in Windows Explorer on a client machine with content redirection from client to server enabled for the file type, the **Open** command opens the file with the remote application on XenApp. For a streamed application, the file could be opened either on the client machine or on the XenApp server, depending on the delivery configuration.

Most commands on the Windows Explorer context menu are unaffected. Context menu items are generally defined by each application when installed.

Associating published applications with file types

When we publish applications, we associate the published item with certain file types present in the Windows registry on the server. We can associate published applications with file types initially from the **Publish Application** wizard.

Application Publishing

To modify the file types, first William needs to select the application from the **Action** menu, he selects **Application properties**, and then **Content redirection**.

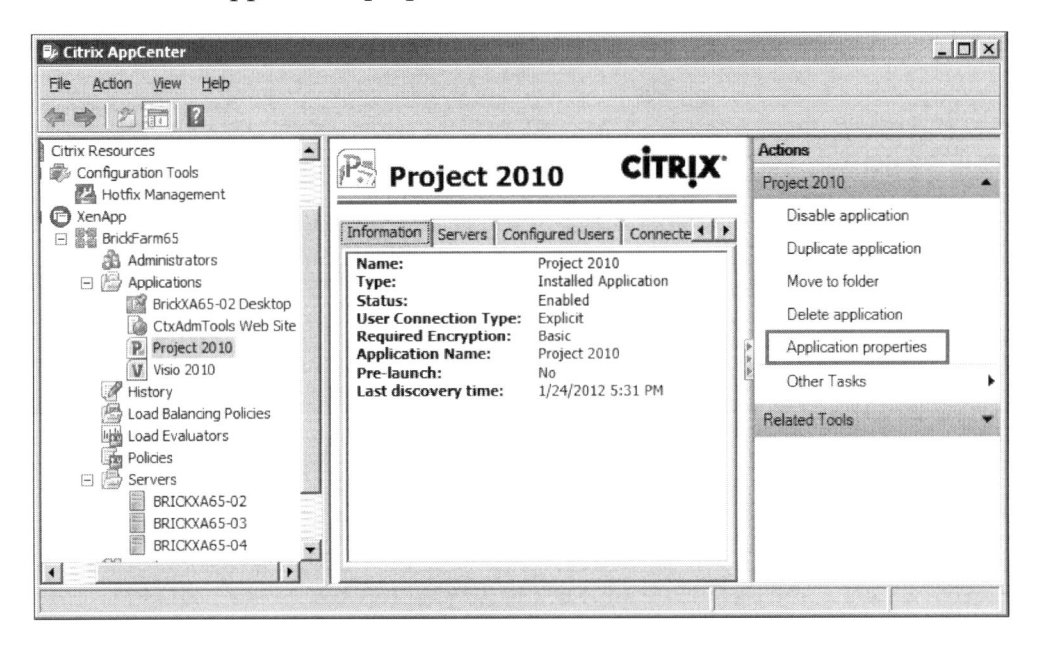

He enables the **Show all available file types for this application** checkbox and the selects one or multiple file types.

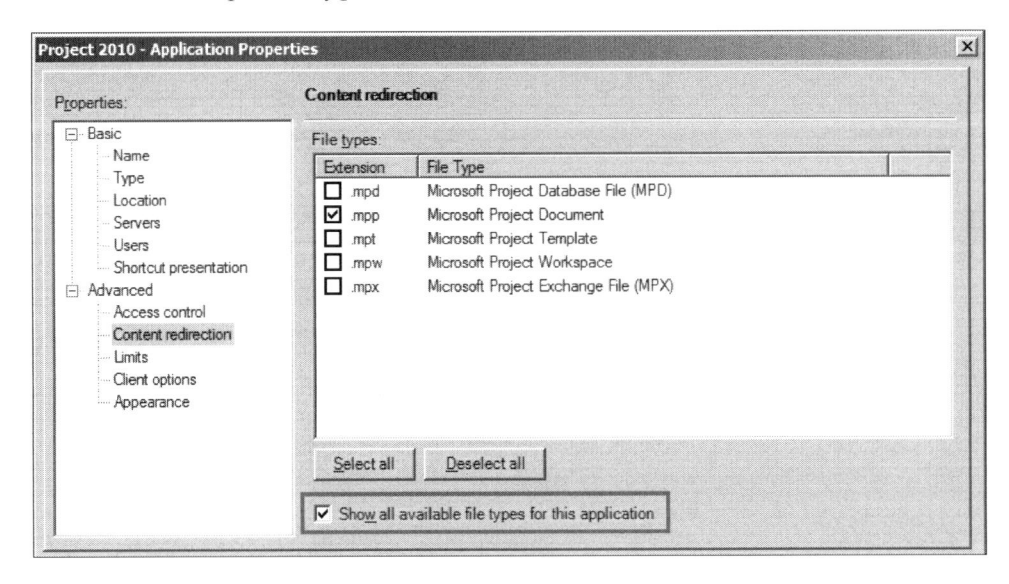

> If we enable the **Show all available file types for this application** checkbox, and the **File types** list still empty, update file type associations (details are in the next section) and try again.

Updating file type associations

File types are associated with applications in a server's Windows registry. If we set up and then publish applications after installing XenApp 6.5, we need to update the file type associations in the Windows registry on the server.

To verify which file types are associated with a published application, we need to select the application and then from the **Action** menu, we select **Application properties** and then **Content redirection**.

Use **Update file types** to associate these file types with the application in the XenApp farm's data store.

> Updating the file type association data for a farm can take a long time. This time depends on the amount of servers, the number of streamed applications, and the availability of the streamed application file shares.

We need to update the file type associations in the data store if:

- We installed a new application, but we have not published it yet.
- We plan to enable content redirection from client machine to the server or have users open published content using the application.
- The data store does not already contain the file type associations. If we updated the file types from the registries of other servers hosting the application, the data store already contains the associations.

Now we can help William to update file types for the farm or for an individual server:

Application Publishing

In the console, he needs to select a farm in the left-hand side pane and from the **Actions** menu, select **Other Tasks** and then **Update file types**:

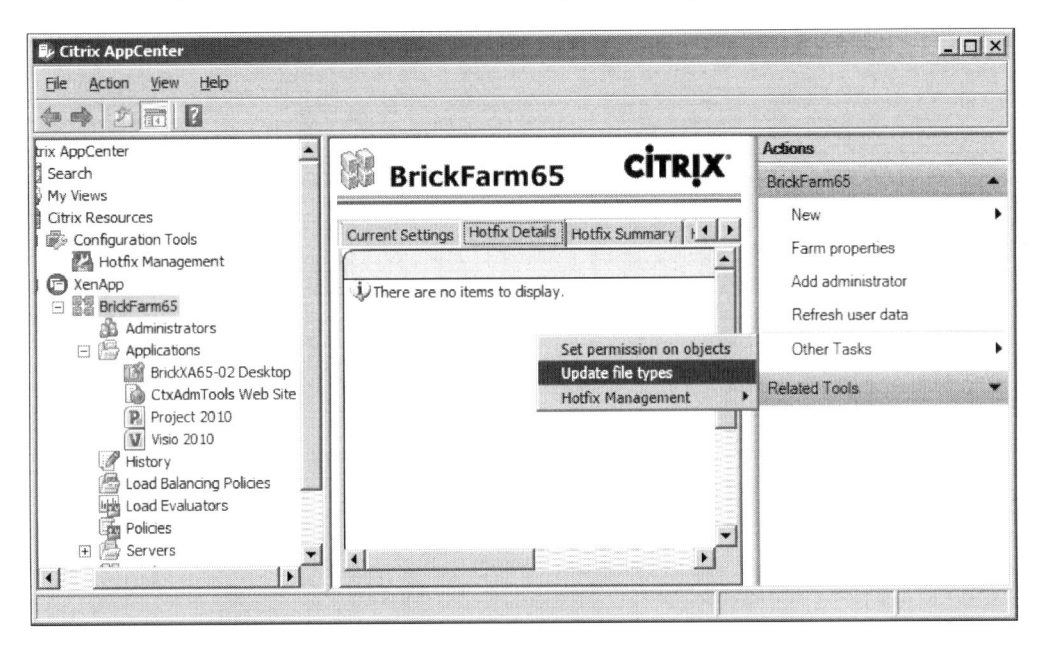

He selects a server in the left-hand side pane and from the **Actions** menu, select **Other Tasks** and then the **Update file types from registry** option:

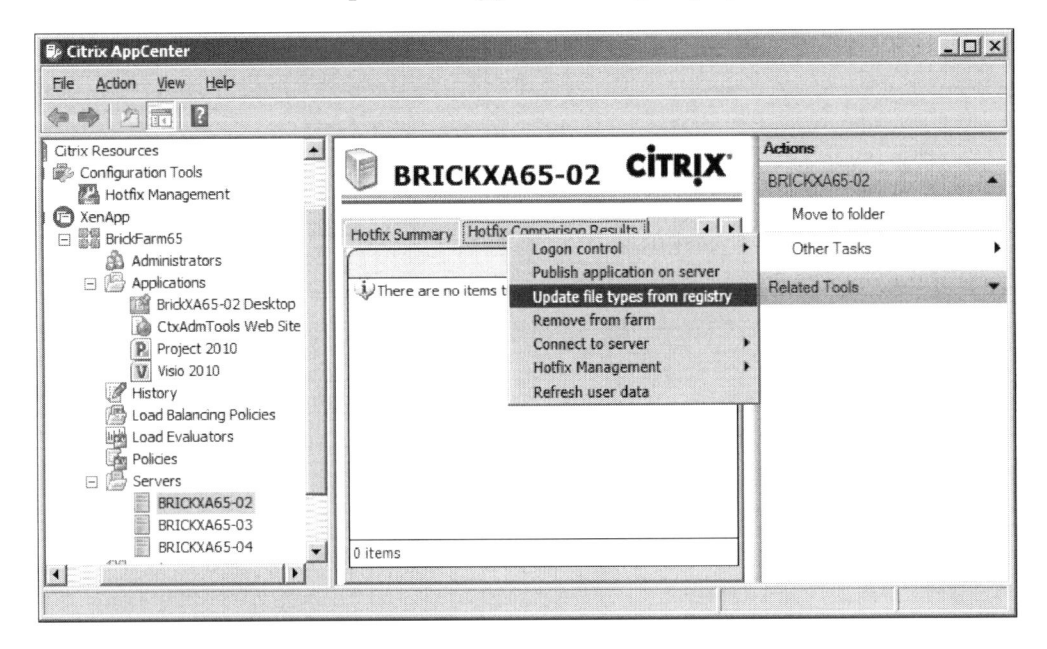

William needs to choose which file types are opened with a published application. When he publishes an application, a list of available file types appears on the **Content redirection** page. This list is current only if the data stored was updated with the file type associations for the application.

If he publishes applications to be hosted on more than one XenApp server, he needs to update the file types on each server.

Enabling or disabling content redirection

William needs to log in to the Citrix Web Interface server and then open the **Citrix Web Interface Management** console.

He selects **XenApp Services Sites** and in the **Actions** pane, he clicks on **Server Farms**:

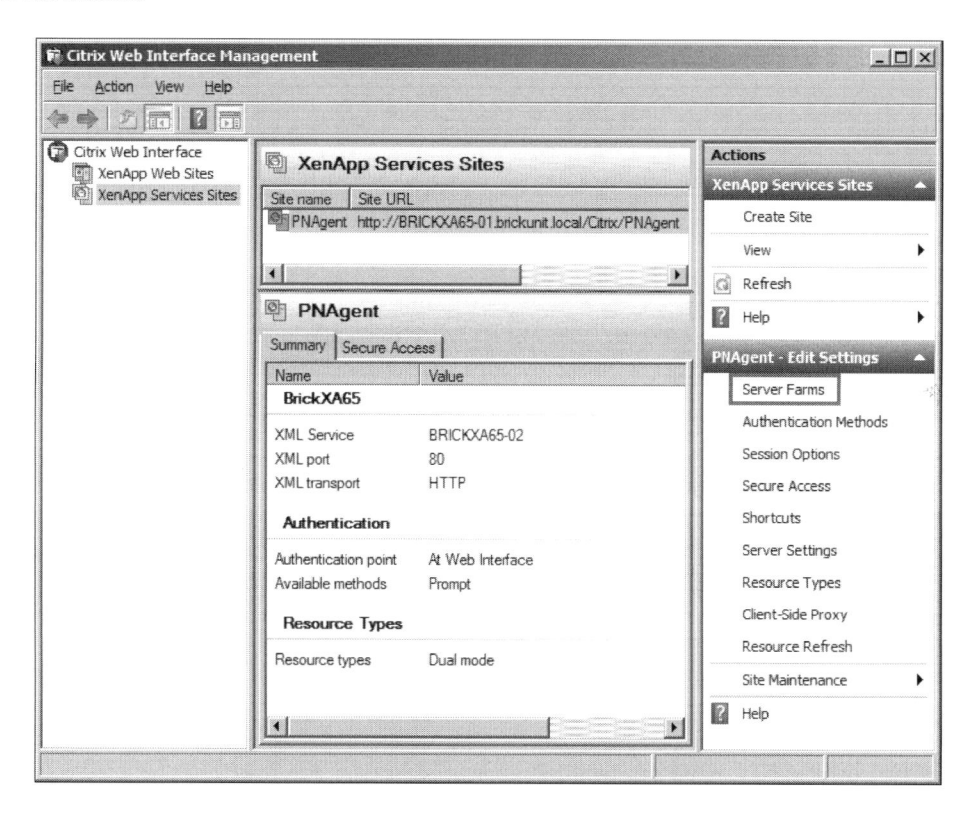

Application Publishing

On the **Manage Server Farms** window, he needs to click on the **Advanced** button:

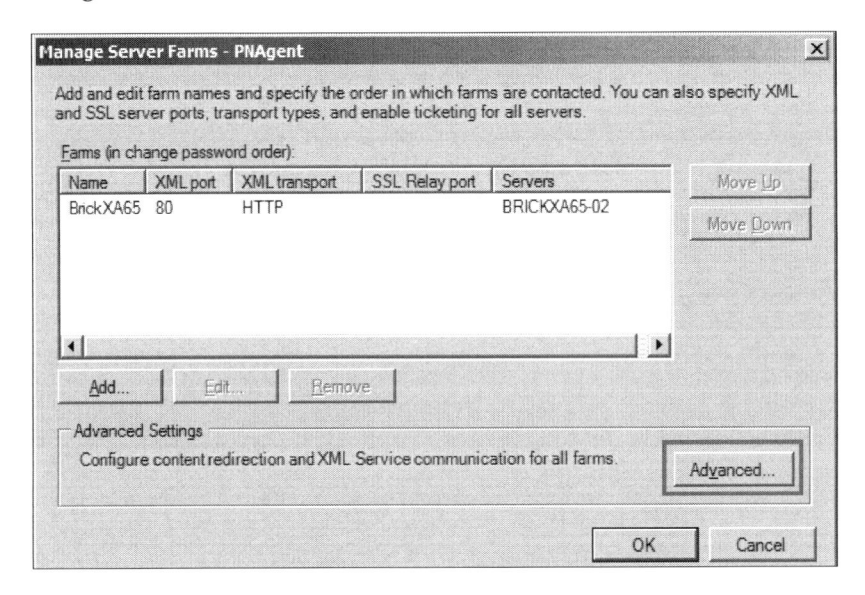

William can use the **Enable content redirection** checkbox to enable or disable content redirection:

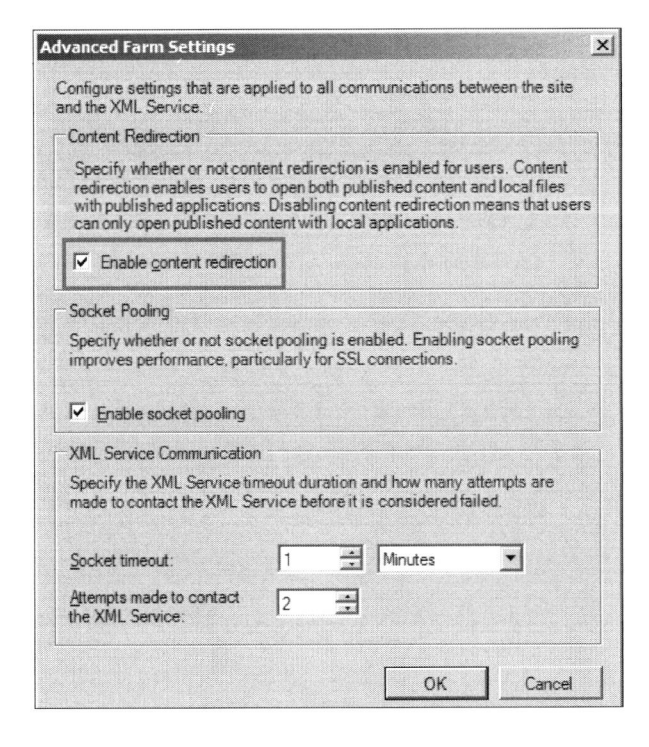

Summary

In this chapter, we learned how to publish different types of resources in XenApp. In particular:

- Hosted applications
- Streamed applications
- Content
- Server desktops

Also, we covered content redirection, from server to client and client to server, and we learned how to set up and update file type associations.

In the next chapter, we are going to learn how to install and configure streaming applications in detail.

Application Streaming

In the previous chapter, we learned how to publish different types of resources in XenApp. In particular, we installed and published; hosted and streamed applications, and server desktops.

Also, we talked about content redirection, from server to client and client to server, and how to configure it and update file type associations.

In this chapter, we are going to cover the installation, configuration, and delivery of streaming applications. By the end of this chapter, you will have learned:

- Application streaming
- System requirements for application streaming
- Components for application streaming
- Choosing which plug-ins to use for application streaming
- How to profile and publish an application on the XenApp farm

Application streaming

Application streaming simplifies application delivery to users by virtualizing applications on client machines. We can install and configure an application centrally and deliver it to any XenApp server or client machine on demand. One of the major features of application streaming is the ability to run multiple versions of an application on the same client; for example, we can run Office 2007 and Office 2010 on the same client machine. Also, application streaming is useful to run applications that can't run on XenApp.

Using streamed applications provides a lot of benefits, including:

- The ability to install an application once on a profiler workstation and copy and replicate to fileservers within the company.
- Use of streamed applications reduces patching complexity in large environments.
- Updates to a streamed application don't require re-profiling applications.
- All streamed applications run within isolated environments that keep the applications from interfering with others running on the same client machine.
- Application files can be cached on the client machine to allow faster access the next time the application is launched.
- A wide range of target environments can host streamed applications. Specifically, supported versions include Windows XP Professional, Windows Server 2003 and 2008, Windows Vista, and Windows 7.
- We can configure XenApp to stream software to client machines or run the application on the client machine from a XenApp server.
- Streamed applications that can be accessed through the server appear next to other applications that the user is familiar with, either within the web interface, Citrix Plug-ins, or on the desktop; giving a consistent end-user experience. The user does not have to know where and how the application is executing.
- When a streamed application is configured and delivered, applications can be accessed even when the user is offline. The only requirement is that the Citrix Offline Plug-in is installed on the client machine.
- Streamed applications can easily be delivered to a XenApp farm. When publishing applications in a farm, we can choose to run applications from XenApp. Instead of installing applications on our farm servers, we can stream them to XenApp servers from a central file share in our App Hub. When we update the application in the central location, we update the application on all the farm servers.
- Streamed applications allow easy disaster recovery because the profiles can be easily backed up, and XenApp servers and client machines can be replaced easily.

System requirements for application streaming

The Citrix Offline Plug-in and the Citrix Streaming Profiler (we used version 6.5 of both products for this book) are supported on the following Microsoft operating systems:

- Microsoft Windows XP Home and Professional editions, 32-bit and 64-bit, with the last service pack
- Microsoft Windows Vista (Home, Business, Enterprise, and Ultimate editions), 32-bit and 64-bit editions, with Service Pack 1
- Microsoft Windows 7, 32-bit and 64-bit (Enterprise, Professional, Ultimate)
- Microsoft Windows Server 2003 R2, 32-bit and 64-bit editions
- Microsoft Windows Server 2008, 32-bit and 64-bit editions
- Microsoft Windows Server 2008 R2

The current Citrix Offline Plug-in supports Citrix Receiver versions 1.x, 2.x, and 3.x.

We need to have a dedicated machine, usually called a profiler workstation. The profiler workstation must provide an environment that is as close to our users' environment as possible, such as the same or similar operating system and platform (x86, x64).

We need to install the application on the profiler workstation on the same disk partition of client machines. Don't install applications on the D drive, if client machines only have a C drive.

The profiler workstation should also include standard programs that are a part of the company image, such as an antivirus program or hotfixes. Same User Account Control setting is also recommended.

> **Important**: Do not install the Citrix Offline Plug-in on the profiler workstation.

To stream Microsoft Office 2007 or 2010 programs or to stream profiles enabled for inter-isolation communication, install .NET Framework 2.0 (3.0 or 3.5 optional). Without .NET Framework, streaming will fail.

Application Streaming

Citrix defines inter-isolation communication as a feature that links individual profiles, so applications in separate profiles can communicate with each other when they are launched on the client machine. Also, this feature can be used if a streamed application fails because it needs data from another streamed application, but cannot detect it because both are running in isolation environments.

When we create a profile enabled for inter-isolation communication, applications launched on the client machine can interact with other applications, but applications stay isolated from the system and from other isolated applications.

> Install the profiler in a path with single-byte characters only. Double-byte characters in the installation path are not supported. Examples of not supported characters include Japanese, Korean, and Chinese.

The client machine must meet the following requirements:

- A network connection to the XenApp farm always, or the first time, when Offline access is enabled.
- A supported browser such as Microsoft Internet Explorer 6.0, 7.0, 8.0, and 9.0.
- Uninstall any previous version of the Streaming Client and Program Neighborhood Agent on the client machine.
- Install the most recent version of the Citrix Receiver (formerly known as Citrix Online Plug-in) and the Citrix Offline Plug-ins.
- To stream applications to client machines, install both the Citrix Offline Plug-in and Citrix Receiver (or Citrix Online Plug-in on XenApp 6.0) on the client machines.
- To stream applications to a server, install the Citrix Receiver (also known as Citrix Online Plug-in or Citrix Client) on the server.
- To stream Microsoft Office 2007 or 2010 programs or to stream profiles enabled for inter-isolation communication, we need to install .NET Framework 2.0 on the client machine (3.0, 3.5, and 4.0 are optional).
- The Citrix Offline Plug-in is not required, unless we are planning to run offline streamed applications.

> The examples in this book are based on Citrix Receiver for Windows v3.1 and Citrix Offline Plug-in v6.5.

Chapter 7

If we are streaming from a web interface site, we need to add the site to the list of trusted sites. We can use a GPO to add the web interface site to the list of trusted sites.

The Group Policy setting can be found at the following location:

Computer Configuration | Administrative Templates | Windows Components | Internet Explorer | Security Zones: Use only machine settings

Components for application streaming

Citrix provides multiple components that support virtualization on the client machine, including the XenApp server, Citrix licensing, streaming profiler workstation, file servers, web interface, and Citrix Plug-ins. These components can be separated into four different categories as follows:

- **Licensing**: The licensing component includes the license server and License Management Console. We use the License Management Console to manage licensing. To install Citrix licensing, please refer to *Chapter 3, Installing XenApp 6.5*.

  > For detailed information about licensing, read through Application Streaming Licensing explained at http://support.citrix.com/article/CTX112636

- **Administration (server farm)**: Consists of the following components:
    - XenApp servers
    - IMA database
    - Web Interface servers
    - The Citrix AppCenter Console (also known as Citrix Delivery Services Console on XenApp 6.0), used to configure, manage, and publish applications on the farm

- **Citrix Streaming Profiler**: Citrix Streaming Profiler is used to create and manage streaming application profiles. The streaming profiler is an independent application that enables us to profile Windows applications, web applications, browser plug-ins, files, folders, and registry settings that can be streamed to user machines and/or servers.

  We can profile one application to one or more targets (operating systems) within an application profile. This creates a single profile that can be used for multiple user platforms.

- **Citrix Plug-ins**: The Citrix Offline Plug-in (formerly known as the Streaming Client) is used to stream applications to the client machine and provide offline access to applications. We need to install both Citrix Offline Plug-in and Citrix Receiver (formerly known as Citrix Online Plug-in) on client machines to support dual-mode streaming. When a user clicks on a published application in a web interface site, the plug-in finds the correct target in the profile in the App Hub, sets up the isolation environment on the user machine, and then streams the application from the profile location to the safety of the isolation environment set up on the client machine.

Choosing which plug-in to use for application streaming

The plug-ins that our users must install on their client machines are determined by the method of streaming:

- **Streamed to client desktops**: When streaming applications directly to client desktops, some of the application files are cached locally and the applications run using the resources of the client machine.

    We need to install both Citrix Receiver and Citrix Offline Plug-in on client machines running `CitrixReceiver.exe` and `CitrixOfflinePlugin.exe`.

    This enables us to:

    - Provide dual-mode streaming. When we select **Streamed if possible, otherwise accessed from a server** and **Streamed to server**, if streaming to the client machine fails, applications automatically are streamed to a XenApp server and then launch from it using Citrix Receiver.

    - Enumerate published applications located on the **Start** menu and create shortcuts on the desktop of the client machine.

    - Configure applications and users for offline access. This is because the entire application is fully cached on the client machine. Users can use the application for the time specified in the offline license, even if they are disconnected from the network.

- **Accessed from a server**: The profile is streamed from the App Hub to the XenApp server, where the Citrix Offline Plug-in is installed by default. The Offline Plug-in is not required on the client machine and the application runs on the client machine using the Citrix Receiver.

   When we publish applications as **Accessed from a server** and **Streamed to server**, users will access the applications using the Citrix Receiver. This method does not support desktop integration or offline access to applications.

Profiling Microsoft Office 2010

William Empire is the IT Manager of Brick Unit Construction. William decided to stream Office 2010 from XenApp servers to client machines. We will help him profile Office 2010 and then publish it to all users in Brick Unit Construction.

> Microsoft Office 2010 SP1 is *not* supported in XenApp 6.0 or 6.5.

The following process of configuring and profiling Office 2010 is based on the 32-bit version of Office 2010 (64-bit applications are not supported by Citrix Profiler 6.0 and 6.5).

William will use a KMS server to activate Office 2010 licenses. MAK license activation currently is not supported by Citrix.

> Latest Microsoft products such as Windows 7, Windows Server 2008 R2, Windows Vista, Windows Server 2008, and Microsoft Office 2010, use a new type of product activation called Volume Activation (VA). To activate these operating systems or applications with VA, we can use either a Multiple Activation Key (MAK) or Key Management Service (KMS), requiring a KMS server.

For more information on KMS server setup and configuration for Office 2010, please visit http://xenapp6.musumeci.com.ar.

Once the KMS server is installed and configured, the next step is installing a profiler workstation.

Installing a profiler workstation

The profiler workstation is a dedicated (and clean) machine to profile applications. This machine should have the same or similar operating system (such as Windows 7 and Windows Vista) as the one we are going to stream to. If we need to stream the application to both 32-bit and 64-bit client machines, we have to profile the application on two different machines, one for 32-bit clients and other for 64-bit clients. We cannot profile a package on a 32-bit operating system and stream the profile to a 64-bit operating system and vice versa.

William will start the profiling process by installing the latest version of Streaming Profiler on the profiler workstation (currently version 6.5). The minimum version required to profile Office 2010 is version 6.0 (included on XenApp 6.0). The previous versions of the profiler don't support streaming of services.

His preferred option is to use a virtual machine for the Profiler Workstation machine. So he can take a snapshot before making any changes and easily rollover any modifications in seconds.

Operating systems earlier than Microsoft Windows Vista require some Microsoft hotfixes. He needs to install the following hotfixes on the profiling computer and client machines:

- For Microsoft Windows XP SP3, we need to install hotfix KB978835, available at http://support.microsoft.com/kb/978835.
- For Microsoft Windows XP x64 and Microsoft Windows Server 2003 x64: KB973573 available at http://support.microsoft.com/kb/973573.
- MSXML 6: This file installs Microsoft Core XML Services (MSXML) 6.0 Service Pack 1 in the profile. MSXML 6 is included in Windows 7 and Windows 2008 R2.
- MSVCR80.DLL: Search for the file MSVCR80.DLL and keep a copy of the last version of this file in a folder (this requirement is applied to XenApp 6.0).
- To profile and stream Microsoft Office applications to Windows Server 2003, William needs to install the Windows Data Execution Prevention (DEP) hotfix on the server and in the profiler workstation. This hotfix is available for download at http://support.microsoft.com/kb/931534.
- Download and install the hotfix http://support.microsoft.com/kb/2359223 on the Streaming Profiler workstation with Windows 7 (32-bit and 64-bit) only. This hotfix requires a computer restart.
- For Windows Server 2008 and Windows Server 2008 R2, we need to enable the Desktop Experience feature if profiling and streaming OneNote 2010 on XenApp 6.0 is not enabled on XenApp 6.5.

The streaming profiler can be installed from the XenApp DVD or downloaded from the Citrix website. Always check the Citrix website for the latest version.

Installing the Citrix Streaming Profiler is really simple:

1. William needs to run the `.exe` file, follow the Installation Wizard, and reboot the machine.
2. He clicks on the **Next** button and then he types the appropriate program folder name. Then he clicks on the **Install** button.
3. Finally, he clicks on the **Finish** button to complete the setup and reboots the Profiler workstation.

Customizing the Office 2010 installation

William starts the process mounting the Microsoft Office 2010 DVD on the profiler workstation and copies the installation files to the local drive.

Then he opens a command prompt, navigates to the Microsoft Office 2010 installation directory, and types:

`setup /admin`

The `/admin` switch starts the Microsoft Office Customization Tool that allows him to pre-configure the installation options in order to perform an unattended installation. All customized settings are stored in an `.msp` file that must be saved in the `Updates` subfolder in the Microsoft Office 2010 installation directory.

He selects the **Create a new Setup customization file for the following product** option and then clicks on the **OK** button:

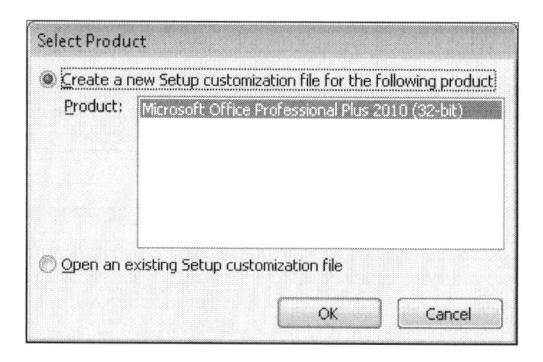

Under **Setup, Install location and organization name**, he needs to enter the organization name. Also, he can change the default installation path, if he wants.

Application Streaming

Under **Setup, Licensing and user interface**:

1. William selects **Use KMS client key** (default) and enables the **I accept the terms in the License Agreement** checkbox.

2. Then he selects **Basic** for **Display Level** and enables the **Suppress modal** checkbox for a silent installation. (We could also keep the **Full** option (default), useful for a test installation).

3. Under **Features | Modify user settings** he must:
    - Expand **Microsoft Office 2010** and click on **Global Options**.
    - Select **Enabled** in the **Use ClearType** option.

   then:
    - He expands **Privacy** and chooses **Trust Center**.
    - Then he selects **Enabled** in the **Disable Opt-in Wizard on first run** option.

Chapter 7

4. Under **Features | Set feature** installation states:
   - He clicks the drop-down menu for **Microsoft Office**, selects **Run all from My Computer**, and then he unchecks specific features or products that he won't need. Also, it is recommended to remove **Microsoft SharePoint Workspace 2010** because there are lot of issues reported:

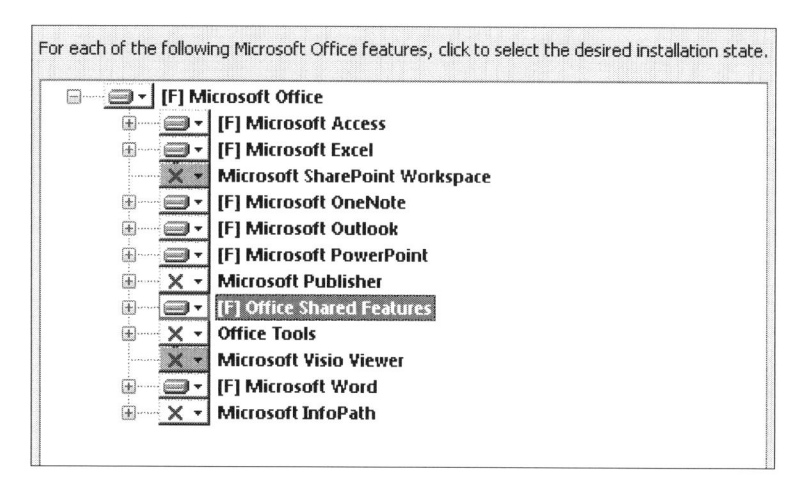

   ```
   For each of the following Microsoft Office features, click to select the desired installation state.
       [F] Microsoft Office
           [F] Microsoft Access
           [F] Microsoft Excel
           X  Microsoft SharePoint Workspace
           [F] Microsoft OneNote
           [F] Microsoft Outlook
           [F] Microsoft PowerPoint
           X  Microsoft Publisher
           [F] Office Shared Features
           X  Office Tools
           X  Microsoft Visio Viewer
           [F] Microsoft Word
           X  Microsoft InfoPath
   ```

5. Under **Additional Content**, select **Add registry entries**.
6. Add the following registry entries to prevent pop-up windows, disable first-run dialogs, and set the KMS server name and port.

   > **Warning**: This section, method, or task contains steps that tell you how to modify the registry. However, serious problems might occur if you modify the registry incorrectly. Therefore, make sure that you follow these steps carefully. For added protection, back up the registry before you modify it.

   - **Disabling Office Welcome Screen**: This registry prevents the Office Welcome Screen from asking for the user information:
     - Set the value of **Root** as **HKEY_CURRENT_USER**
     - Set **Data type** as **REG_DWORD**
     - Set **Key** as `Software\Microsoft\Office\14.0\Common\General`

[181]

Application Streaming

- Set **Value name** as `ShownOptIn`
- Set **Value data** as `00000001`

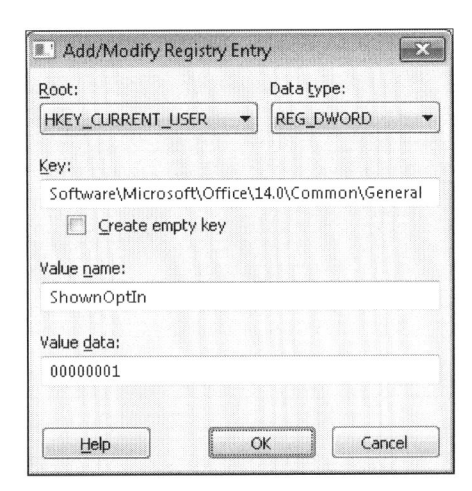

○ Disabling some Office popups: This registry key prevents some Outlook windows from being shown:

- Set **Root** as **HKEY_CURRENT_USER**
- Set **Data type** as **REG_SZ**
- Set **Key** as `Software\Microsoft\Office\14.0\Outlook\Option\General`
- Set **Value name** as `PONT_STRING`
- Set **Value data** as `60`

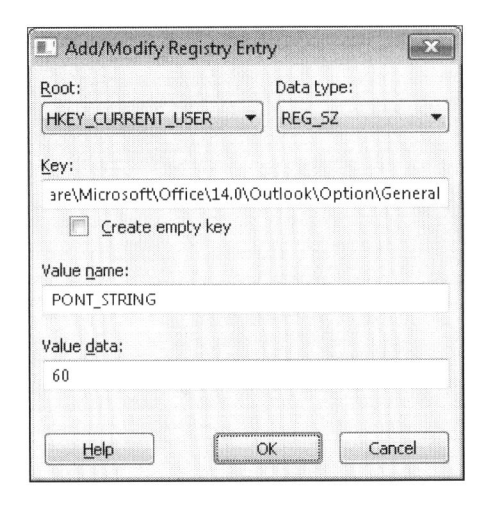

Chapter 7

- **Setting the KMS server name (32-bit target device)**: This registry key sets the KMS server name on 32-bit machines:
    - Set **Root** as **HKEY_LOCALMACHINE**
    - Set **Data type** as **REG_SZ**
    - Set **Key** as `Software\Microsoft\OfficeSoftwareProtectionPlatform`
    - Set **Value name** as `KeyManagementServiceName`
    - Set **Value data** as name or IP address of KMS License Server

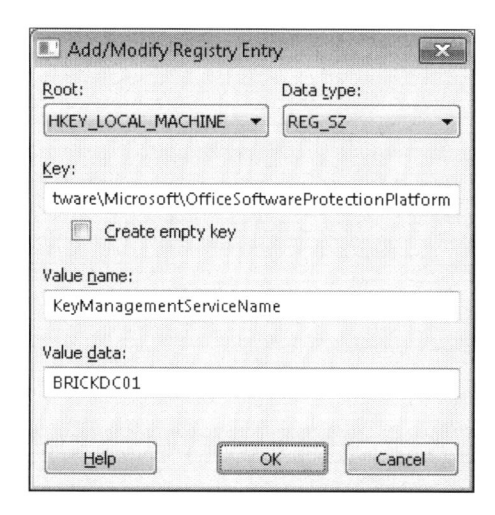

- **Setting the KMS server name (64-bit target device)**: This registry key sets the KMS server name on 64-bit machines:
    - Set **Root** as **HKEY_LOCALMACHINE**
    - Set **Data type** as **REG_SZ**
    - Set **Key** as `Software\Wow6432Node\Microsoft\OfficeSoftwareProtectionPlatform`
    - Set **Value name** as `KeyManagementServiceName`

Application Streaming

- Set **Value data** as name or IP address of KMS License Server

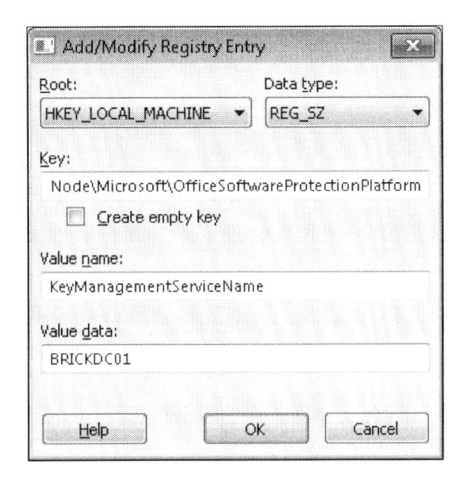

   ○ **Setting the KMS port number (32-bit target device)**: This registry key sets the KMS port number on 32-bit machines:
      - Set **Root** as **HKEY_LOCALMACHINE**
      - Set **Data type** as **REG_SZ**
      - Set **Key** as `Software\Microsoft\OfficeSoftwareProtectionPlatform`
      - Set **Value name** as `KeyManagementServicePort`
      - Set **Value data** as `1688`

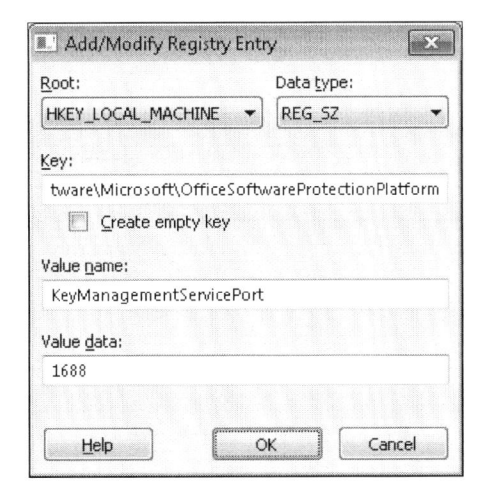

Chapter 7

- ○ **Setting the KMS port number (64-bit target device)**: This registry key sets the KMS port number on 64-bit machines:
    - Set **Root** as **HKEY_LOCALMACHINE**
    - Set **Data type** as **REG_SZ**
    - Set **Key** as `Software\Wow6432Node\Microsoft\OfficeSoftwareProtectionPlatform`
    - Set **Value name** as `KeyManagementServicePort`
    - Set **Value data** as `1688`

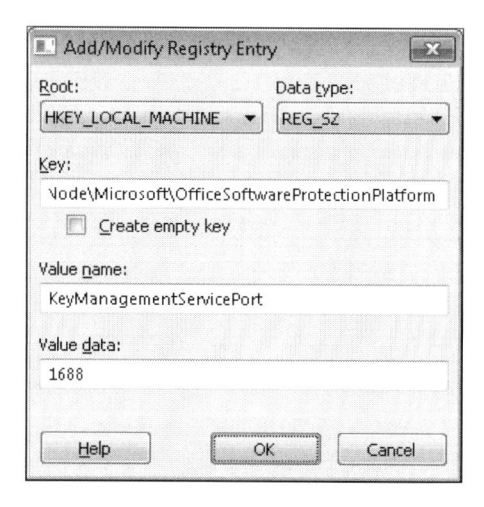

The following window will show all registry keys added by William to the Office Setup:

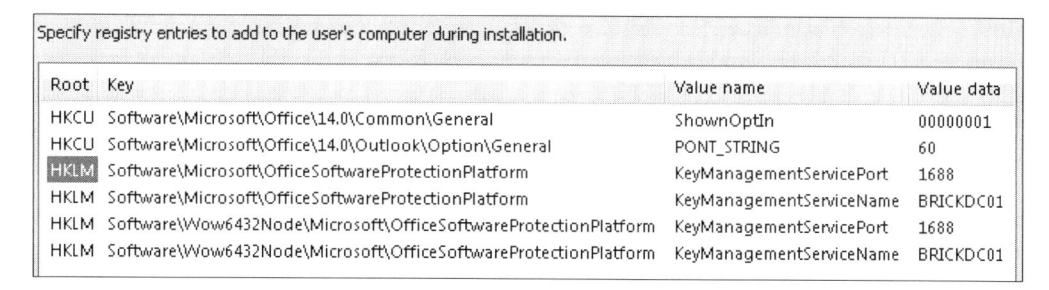

Root	Key	Value name	Value data
HKCU	Software\Microsoft\Office\14.0\Common\General	ShownOptIn	00000001
HKCU	Software\Microsoft\Office\14.0\Outlook\Option\General	PONT_STRING	60
HKLM	Software\Microsoft\OfficeSoftwareProtectionPlatform	KeyManagementServicePort	1688
HKLM	Software\Microsoft\OfficeSoftwareProtectionPlatform	KeyManagementServiceName	BRICKDC01
HKLM	Software\Wow6432Node\Microsoft\OfficeSoftwareProtectionPlatform	KeyManagementServicePort	1688
HKLM	Software\Wow6432Node\Microsoft\OfficeSoftwareProtectionPlatform	KeyManagementServiceName	BRICKDC01

Application Streaming

7. Under **Outlook | Outlook Profile**, he sets up Microsoft Exchange accounts.
    ○ He selects **Modify Profile**:

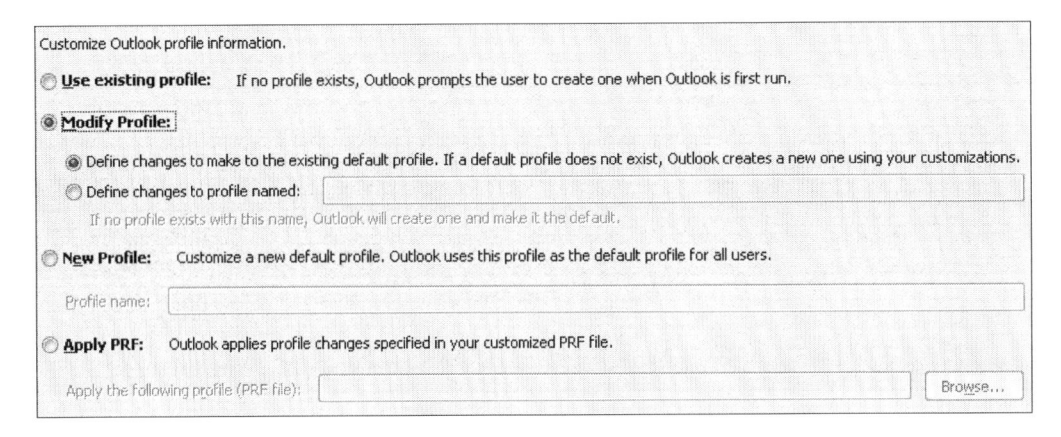

    ○ Then, William clicks on **Add accounts**
    ○ He selects **Customize additional Outlook profile and account information**
    ○ He clicks on **Add**
    ○ He selects **Exchange** to set up a Microsoft Exchange Server account:
    ○ Then he enters an **Account Name**, and he leaves **User Name** as `%UserName%` and enters the **Exchange Server** name:

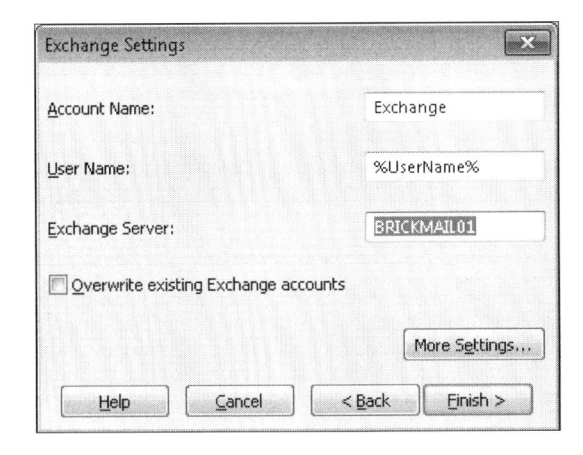

    ○ The **More Settings…** button includes alternative options such as **Cached Mode**
    ○ Save the customization file:

He clicks in **File** option in the menu bar and selects **Save**

He browses to the **Updates** folder in the **Microsoft Office 2010** installation directory and enters a filename such as **StreamingConfig** while saving it

Profiling Microsoft Office 2010

William completed the customization of Microsoft Office 2010. Now, he must open the Citrix Streaming Profiler and start profiling the application setup.

He clicks on the **New Profile** button, and at the Wizard introduction notification, he clicks on the **Next** button:

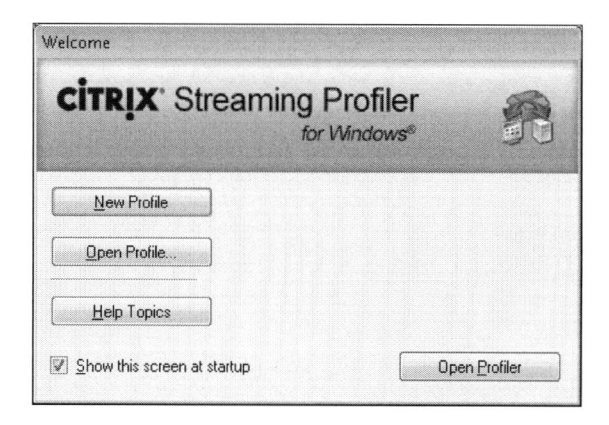

In the **Name Profile** page, William enters a name for the profile (Office2010) and clicks on the **Next** button:

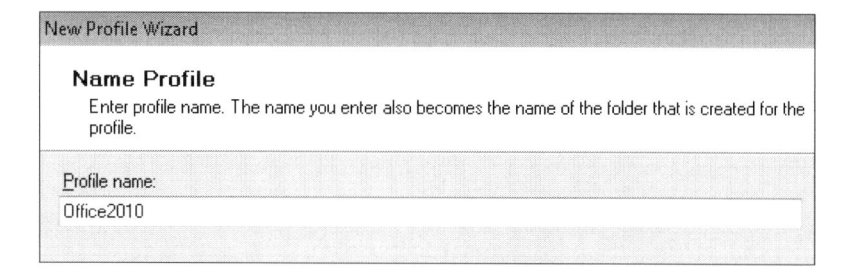

Application Streaming

In the **Enable User Updates** page, he keeps both checkboxes unchecked:

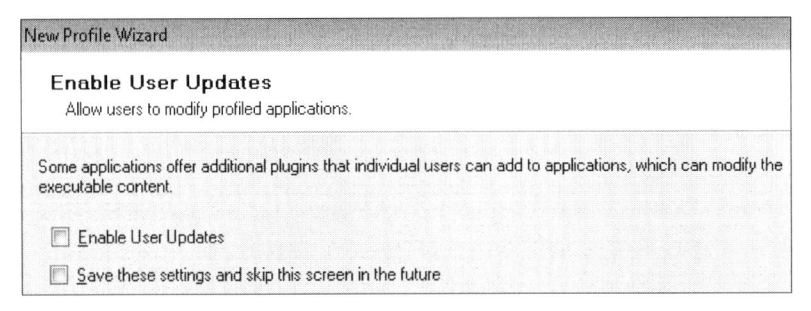

New Profile Wizard

Enable User Updates
Allow users to modify profiled applications.

Some applications offer additional plugins that individual users can add to applications, which can modify the executable content.

☐ Enable User Updates
☐ Save these settings and skip this screen in the future

The new **Support Legacy Offline Plug-ins** page provides an option to **Enable support for 6.0 Offline Plug-Ins**. He keeps the checkbox unchecked.

If we are building a new farm and there are no Citrix Offline Plug-ins deployed, we can keep them unchecked. But if we have existing clients deployed using version 6.0, we need to enable the checkbox, to keep the compatibility. After all clients have moved to Citrix Offline Plug-In 6.5, we need to uncheck the option.

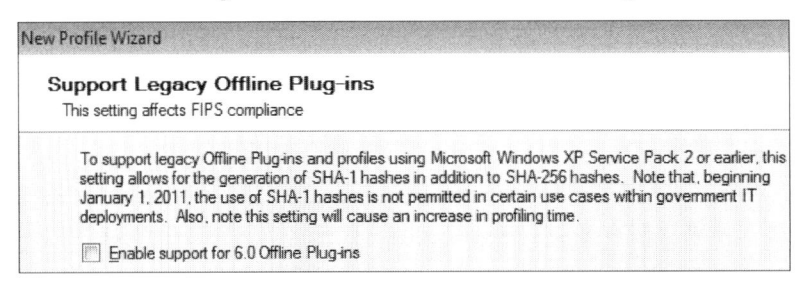

New Profile Wizard

Support Legacy Offline Plug-ins
This setting affects FIPS compliance

To support legacy Offline Plug-ins and profiles using Microsoft Windows XP Service Pack 2 or earlier, this setting allows for the generation of SHA-1 hashes in addition to SHA-256 hashes. Note that, beginning January 1, 2011, the use of SHA-1 hashes is not permitted in certain use cases within government IT deployments. Also, note this setting will cause an increase in profiling time.

☐ Enable support for 6.0 Offline Plug-ins

The **Set up Inter-Isolation Communication** page, helps us to configure communication with previously profiled application. This is useful, for example to allow a financial application to generate Excel reports or access Adobe Acrobat documents generated by a CRM application.

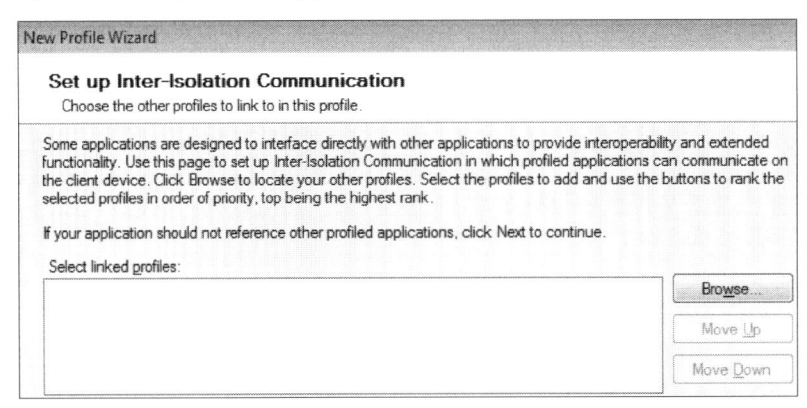

New Profile Wizard

Set up Inter-Isolation Communication
Choose the other profiles to link to in this profile.

Some applications are designed to interface directly with other applications to provide interoperability and extended functionality. Use this page to set up Inter-Isolation Communication in which profiled applications can communicate on the client device. Click Browse to locate your other profiles. Select the profiles to add and use the buttons to rank the selected profiles in order of priority, top being the highest rank.

If your application should not reference other profiled applications, click Next to continue.

Select linked profiles:

[Browse...]
[Move Up]
[Move Down]

Chapter 7

On the **Set Target Operating System and Language** page, William accepts the default target operating system and target language.

The target machine must be run on a compatible operating system and processor architecture (32-bit or 64-bit) of the operating system; so, if we create a profile or an application on a 32-bit operating system, we can stream this application only to a similar 32-bit operating system.

After he selects all the required operating systems, he clicks on the **Next** button to continue as shown in the following screenshot:

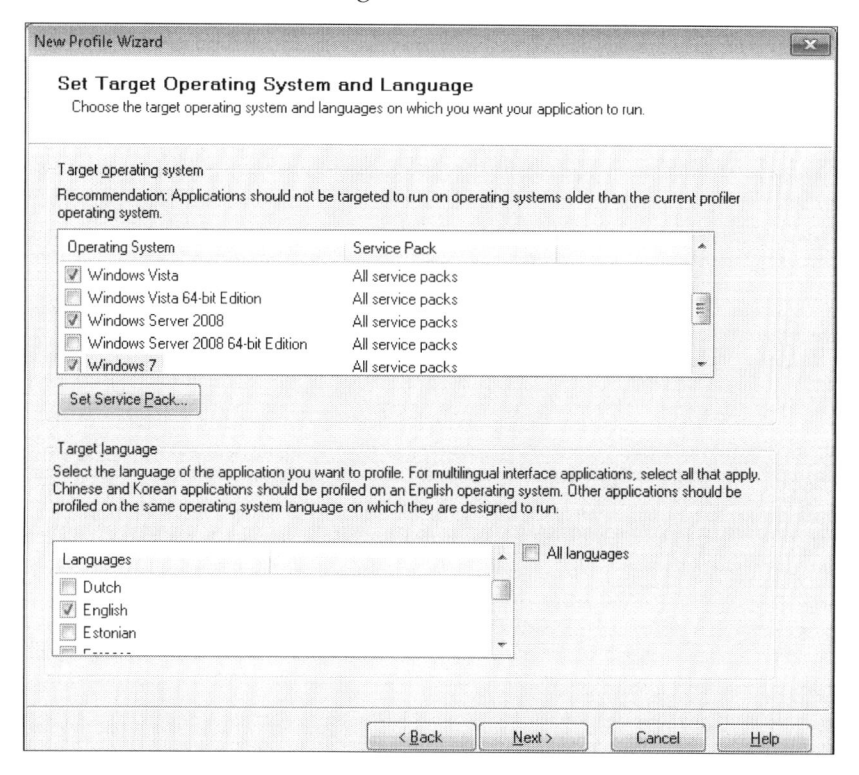

Now, in the **Select Install Option** page, he chooses **Advanced Install** and then clicks on the **Next** button.

This is an optional step required if we are running Windows 2000 Service Pack 4, Windows Server 2003 Service Pack 1, or Windows XP Service Pack 2. We need to install Microsoft XML support before Microsoft Office 2010.

1. We need to download the MSXML6 package to a folder in the profiler workstation.
2. Select **Run install program or command line script** and then click on the **Next** button.

Application Streaming

3. We need to browse for the previously downloaded file (`msxml6_x86.msi`) and then click on the **Next** button.
4. Click on **Launch Installer**.
5. Click on the **Finish** button when the installation completes.
6. At the **Select Next Step** dialog, we need to select **Perform additional installations** and then click on the **Next** button.

Now William is ready to install Microsoft Office 2010:

1. He selects **Run install program or command line script** and clicks on the **Next** button.
2. In the **Choose Installer** page, William browses to the Microsoft Office 2010 installation folder, selects `setup.exe` file, and then clicks on the **Next** button:

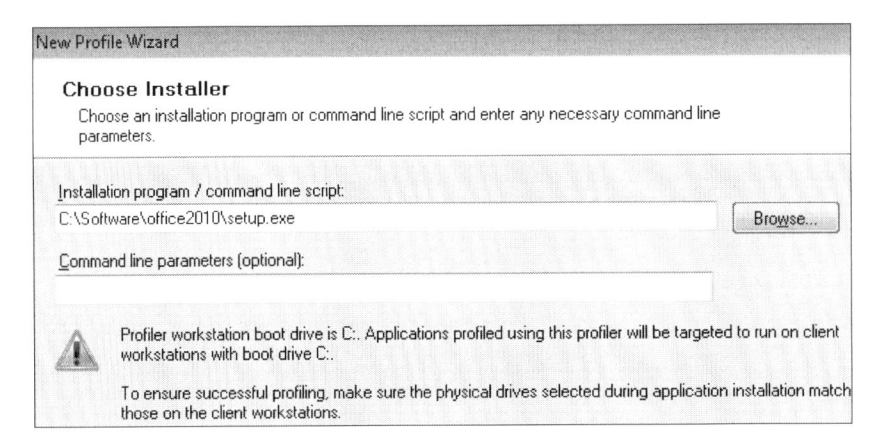

3. In the **Run Installer** page, he clicks on the **Launch Installer** button.
4. Once the Microsoft Office 2010 setup process starts, he clicks on the **Install Now** button to continue.
5. When the Office 2010 installation is complete, he needs to click the **Next** button to run the installer.
6. Now, a virtual reboot is required to complete the setup as shown in the following screenshot:

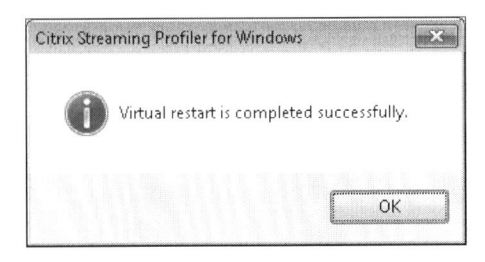

Chapter 7

Now, he needs to install additional required files:

1. He selects **Perform additional installations** and then clicks on the **Next** button:

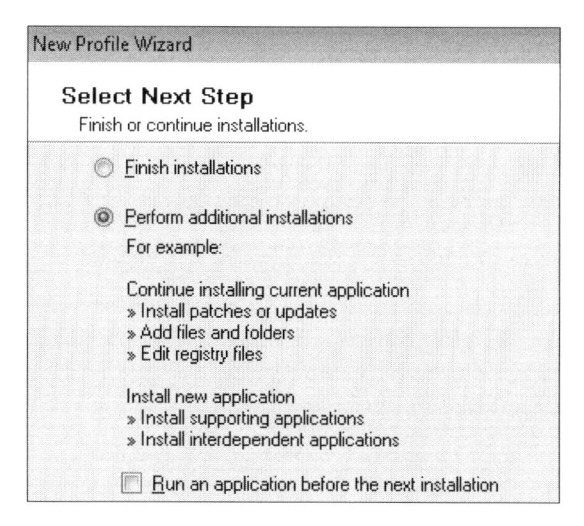

2. William clicks on **Select files and folders** and then he clicks on the **Next** button.

The following four files are to be added to the package:

- **MSVCR80.DLL** (Required by Microsoft C Runtime Library and Visual Studio).

    Located in several places.
    - 32-bit target copy to `C:\Program Files\Microsoft Office\Office14`
    - 64-bit target copy to `C:\Program Files (x86)\Microsoft Office\Office14`

- **MLCFG32.CPL** (Required to set up Exchange accounts in Outlook).

    Located in folder `C:\ctxpackager\<Target>\device\c\Program Files\Microsoft Office\Office14`
    - 32-bit target copy to `C:\Windows\system32`
    - 64-bit target copy to `C:\Windows\SysWOW64`

Application Streaming

- **CMD.EXE** (Windows Command Prompt).

    Located at `C:\Windows\system32folder`
    - 32-bit target copy to `C:\Windows\system32`
    - 64-bit target copy to `C:\Windows\SysWOW64`

- **CONTROL.EXE** (Windows Control Panel).

    Located in `C:\Windows\system32` folder
    - 32-bit target copy to `C:\Windows\system32`
    - 64-bit target copy to `C:\Windows\SysWOW64`

For each of these files, he needs to:

1. Browse for the file on the left-hand pane.
2. Select the target folder on the right-hand pane.
3. Click the green arrow icon to copy the file.

> Also, you can drag-and-drop files to right-hand side pane.

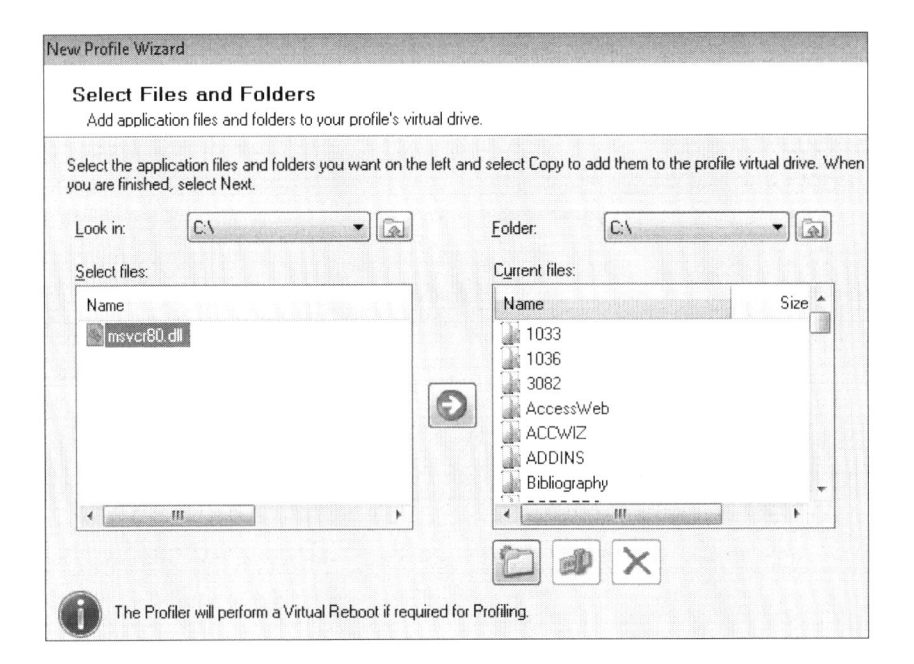

Then he clicks on the **Next** button to return to the **Select Next Step** screen. Here William chooses the **Finish installations** option.

On the **Run Application** screen, he needs to keep the **Application Not Run** option for all applications and clicks on the **Next** button:

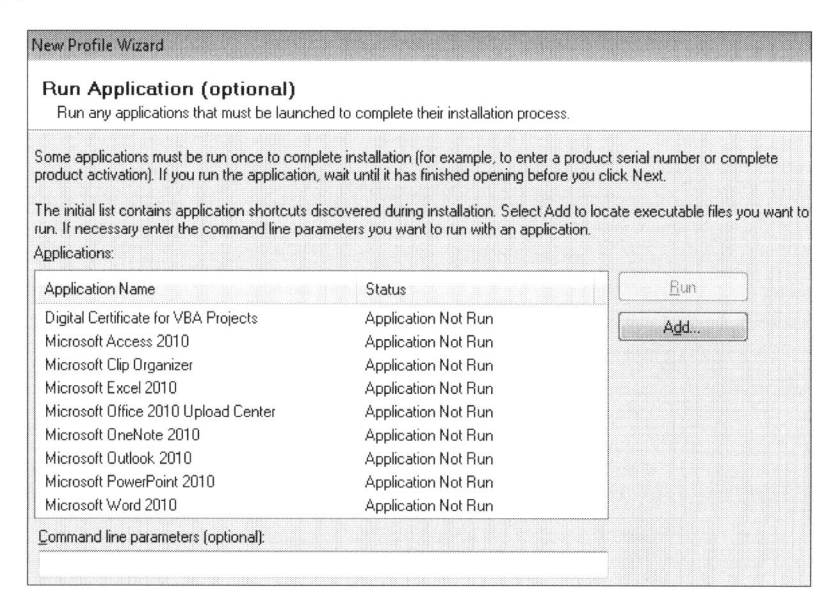

In the **Select Applications** page, William can see the list of applications available to publish using the Citrix AppCenter Console (Citrix Delivery Services Console on XenApp 6.0). He can add or delete applications, if he needs to. He decides to add one extra application, the **Outlook Profile Editor** from the **Select Applications** page:

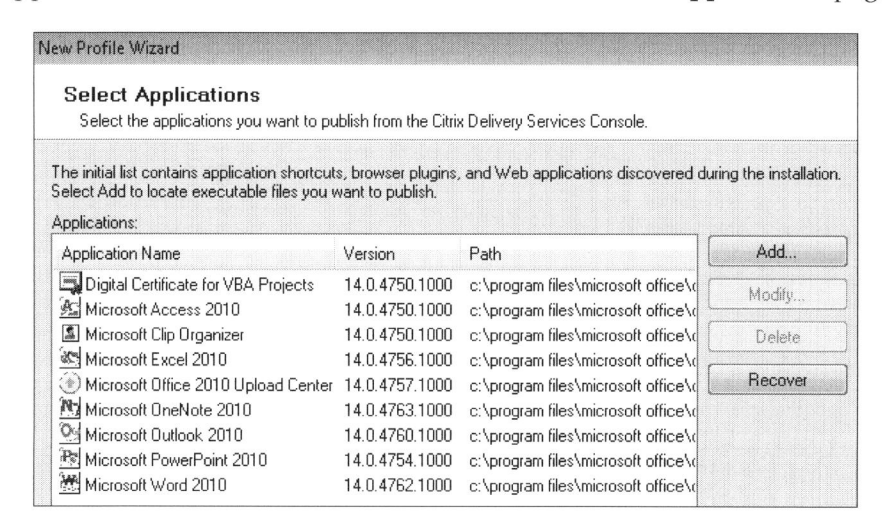

Application Streaming

On the **Select Applications** page, he clicks on the **Add** button, and then he enters the information as shown in the following screenshot:

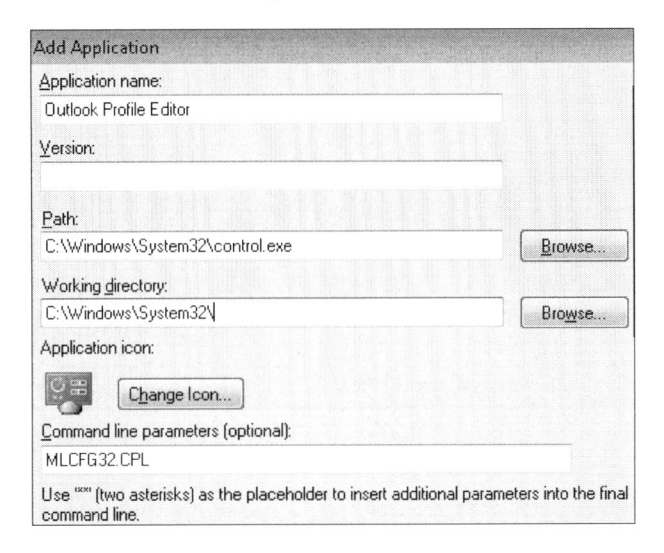

*[Screenshot: Add Application dialog showing Application name: Outlook Profile Editor; Version: (blank); Path: C:\Windows\System32\control.exe; Working directory: C:\Windows\System32\; Application icon with Change Icon button; Command line parameters (optional): MLCFG32.CPL. Use "**" (two asterisks) as the placeholder to insert additional parameters into the final command line.]*

In the **Add Virtual Hard Disk (VHD)** page (a new feature introduced in Citrix Streaming Profiler v6.5), William had the option to create a virtual hard disk for the target. Using VHD can improve the launch performance. Here William will keep the checkbox unchecked:

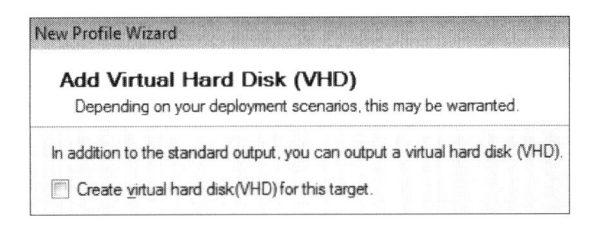

[Screenshot: New Profile Wizard — Add Virtual Hard Disk (VHD). Depending on your deployment scenarios, this may be warranted. In addition to the standard output, you can output a virtual hard disk (VHD). ☐ Create virtual hard disk(VHD) for this target.]

In **Sign Profile** page, he chooses the **Do not sign profile** option and then clicks on the **Next** button.

> If you need to sign the profile, please read the document CTX110304 at http://support.citrix.com/article/CTX110304

[194]

In the **Process Are Still Running** page, he clicks on the **Terminate All** button to end all running processes (such as `OSPPSVC.exe`):

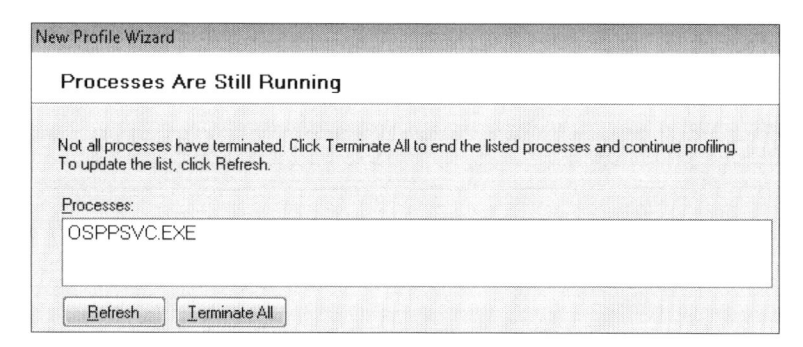

The profiling process is almost complete; William needs to click on the **Finish** button to generate the profile.

The following steps are optional, but will be necessary if we receive an error. One common error we can receive is related to security permissions. So sometimes we need to reset the permissions of all files inside the profile, using the following process:

1. Open the **Windows Explorer**, select the `CtxPackager` folder.
2. Right-click on this folder and select **Properties**.
3. Click on the **Security** tab and then on the **Advanced** button.
4. Click on the **Owner** tab, then the **Edit** button.
5. Enable the **Replace owner on subcontainers and objects** checkbox.

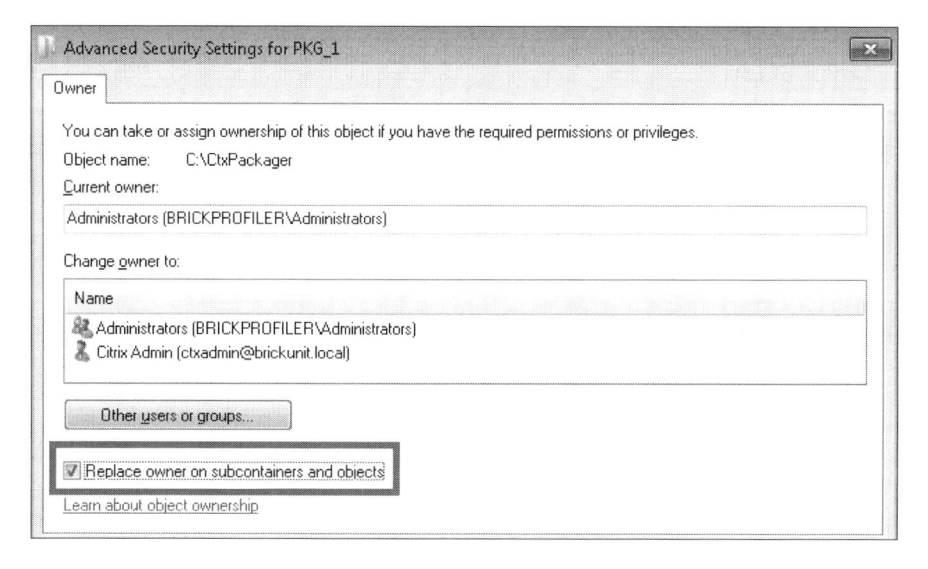

Application Streaming

Now, he clicks on the **Finish** button to complete the process!

Once the profile is created, William needs to set services to start automatically:

1. Expand the profile.
2. Right-click on the target name.
3. Browse to **Properties**.
4. Click on **Services**.
5. Click on **Modify** for each service and change the **Start Type** to **Automatic**:

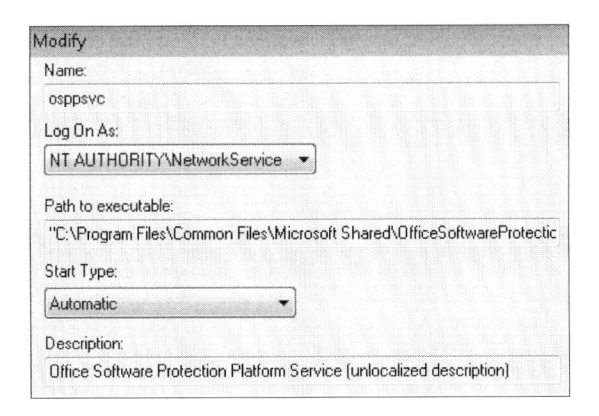

Here, the following screenshot shows us that both services are changed to **Automatic**:

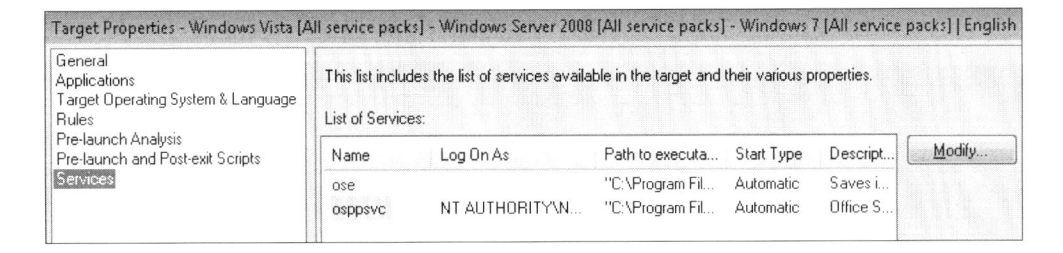

After that, William saves the profile to the network file:

1. He clicks on **File | Save As**.
2. He enters or browses to the file share where profiles will be stored.

3. He clicks on the **Save** button:

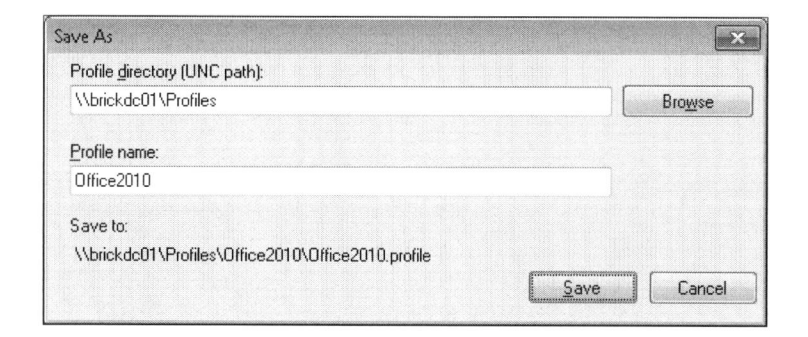

> When using SMB CIFS file shares, we should optimize for best performance, especially for profile streaming. Take a look at this link for more information: http://blogs.citrix.com/2010/10/21/smb-tuning-for-xenapp-and-file-servers-on-windows-server-2008

Publishing Office 2010 on the farm

William is now ready to publish Microsoft Office 2010 applications in the XenApp farm using the Citrix AppCenter Console (Citrix Delivery Services Console on XenApp 6.0). For detailed information about the Application Publishing process, please refer to *Chapter 6, Application Publishing*.

> This process is very similar on XenApp 6.0, using Citrix Delivery Services Console

William needs to open the Citrix AppCenter Console.

From the XenApp console, under the XenApp node, he needs to expand the XenApp farm or server to which he wants to publish the application.

After that, he needs to select the **Applications** node, and from the **Actions** pane, he chooses **Publish application**.

Application Streaming

In the **Name** page, he types the name of the application, **Word 2010** in the **Display name** and **Application description**:

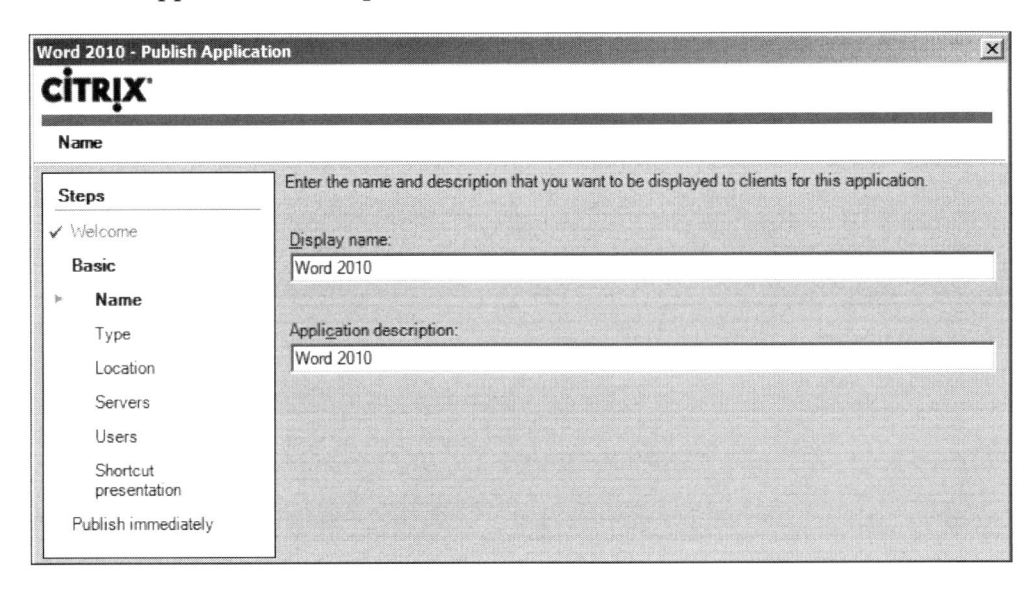

On the **Type** page, he needs to specify the type of resource he wants to publish and the delivery method. He chooses **Application** and **Streamed to client** to publish a streaming application:

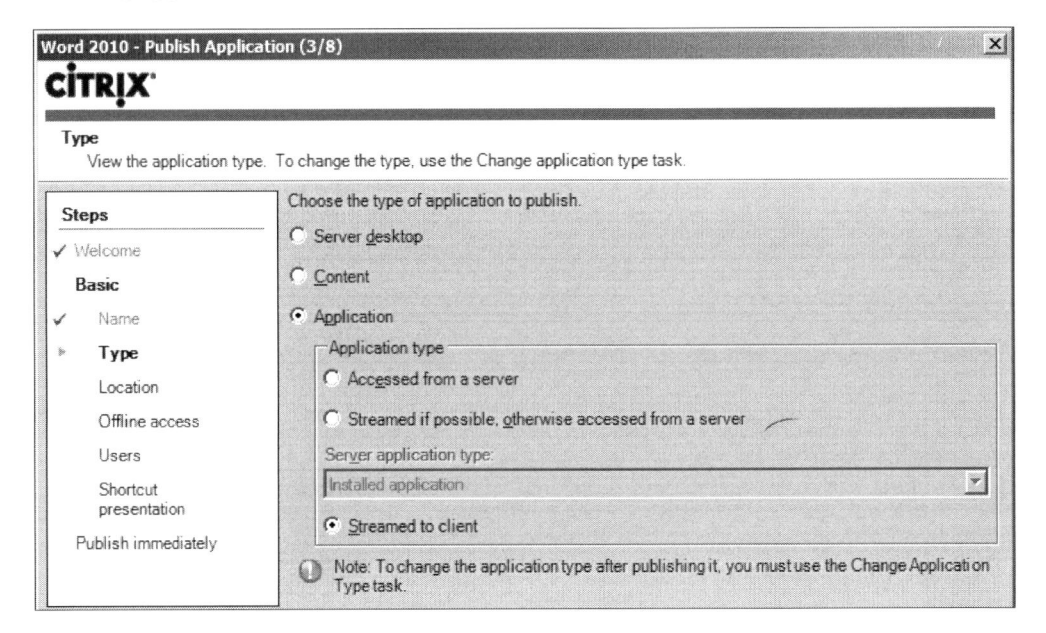

On the **Location** page, William needs to type or use the **Browse** button to set **Citrix streaming application profile address**, this is generally UNC of the file share, and then he needs to choose **Microsoft Word 2010** from the **Application to launch from the Citrix streaming application profile** drop down. He can also set **Optional parameters for the application**.

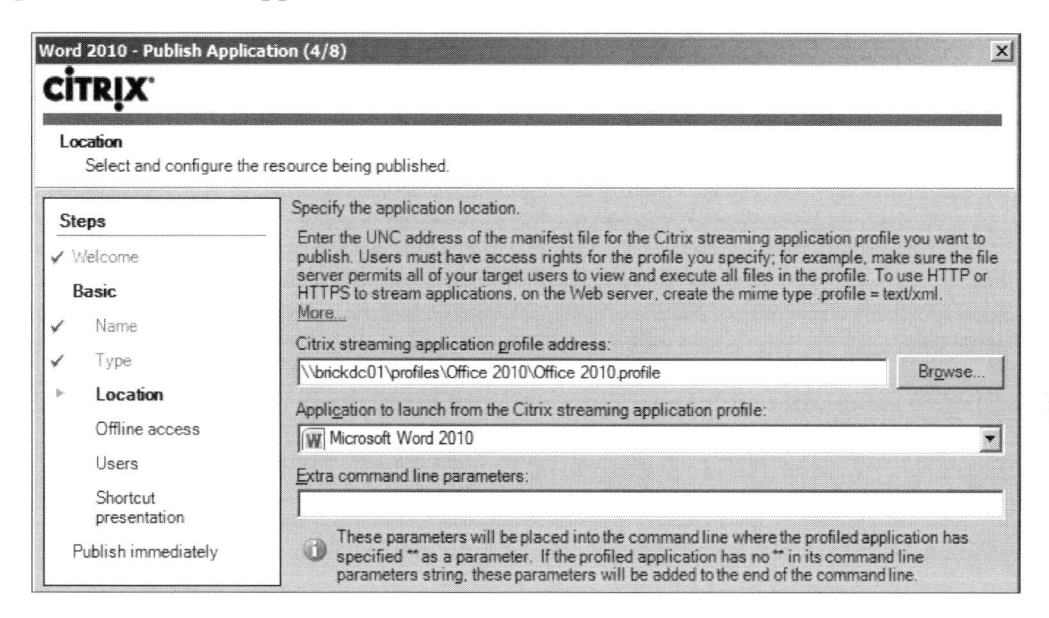

On the **Offline access** page, he can configure streamed applications for offline access.

The server fully caches applications enabled for offline access on client machines; the entire application is sent to user devices while the user is online so that the user can launch the application offline and have full functionality of the application. By default, applications are cached when a user logs on.

When he clicks on the **Enable offline access** checkbox on the **Offline Access** page, he needs to configure the **Cache preference**:

- **Precache application at login**: Caches the application when the user logs on (selected by default). However, concurrent logons may slow network traffic. Precaching is also possible using third-party tools, such as Microsoft System Center Configuration Manager (SCCM) or similar.
- **Cache application at launch time**: Caches the application when users launch it. We can use this option if the number of users logging on at the same time (and precaching their applications) could overload the network.

Application Streaming

The offline access option requires the Citrix Receiver (formerly known as Citrix Offline Plug-in) to be installed on the client machine.

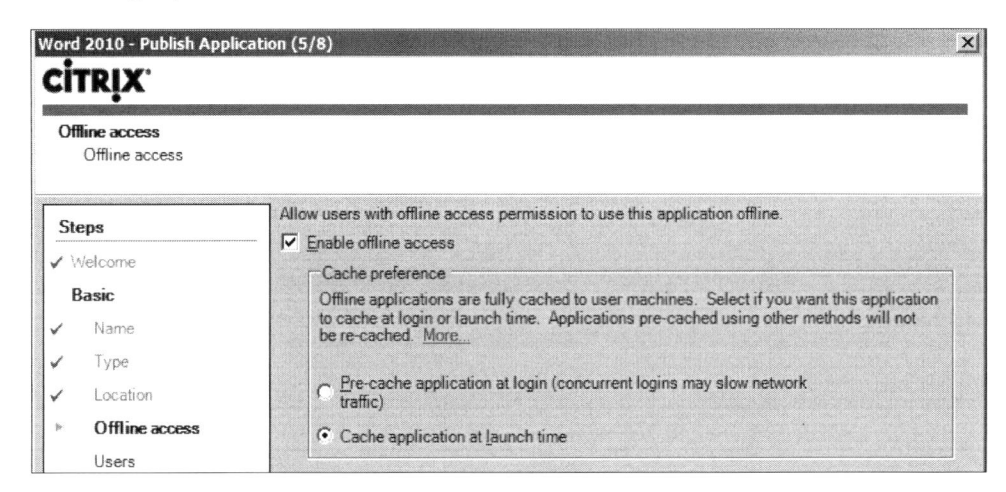

On the **Users** page, he needs to add users or groups who have access to the application and he can allow access to anonymous users or specified groups selecting **Allow only configured users** and add users or groups using the **Add** button.

William assigned permissions to the Domain Users group:

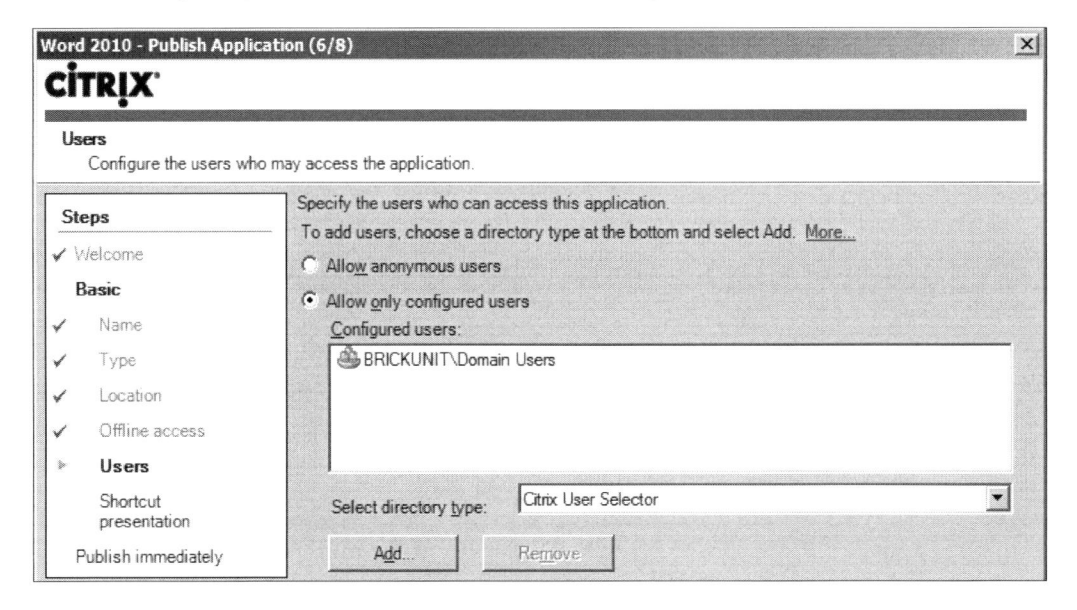

[200]

On the **Shortcut presentation** page, he can choose the icon for the application using the **Change icon** button.

The **Client application folder** is used when we need to organize applications inside folders. This is a recommended practice, if we have a lot of applications. William will keep it blank to display all applications together.

The **Add to the client's Start menu** option creates a shortcut under the `Programs` folder of the local **Start** menu. If a folder structure is specified in the `Start Menu Folder` textbox, the folder structure is created within the local `Programs` folder.

If no folder structure is specified, the application is available from the top level of the **Start** menu.

This option provides a real integration of the streamed application in the client machine and looks like the application is installed locally.

The **Add shortcut to the client's desktop** option creates a shortcut to this application on the client machine.

On the **Publishing immediately** page, William needs to select **Disable application initially**, if he wants to prevent users from accessing the application. Later, he can manually enable it through application properties.

To view and select advanced options, William needs to enable the **Configure advanced application settings now** checkbox. Alternatively, he can modify the advanced settings using the application properties later.

Application Streaming

In this step, William will configure file types associated with the application, on the **Content redirection** page. First he needs to check the **Show all available file types for this application** checkbox and then he selects one or multiple file types. This will allow users when they click on a file with any of these file types to launch the streamed application.

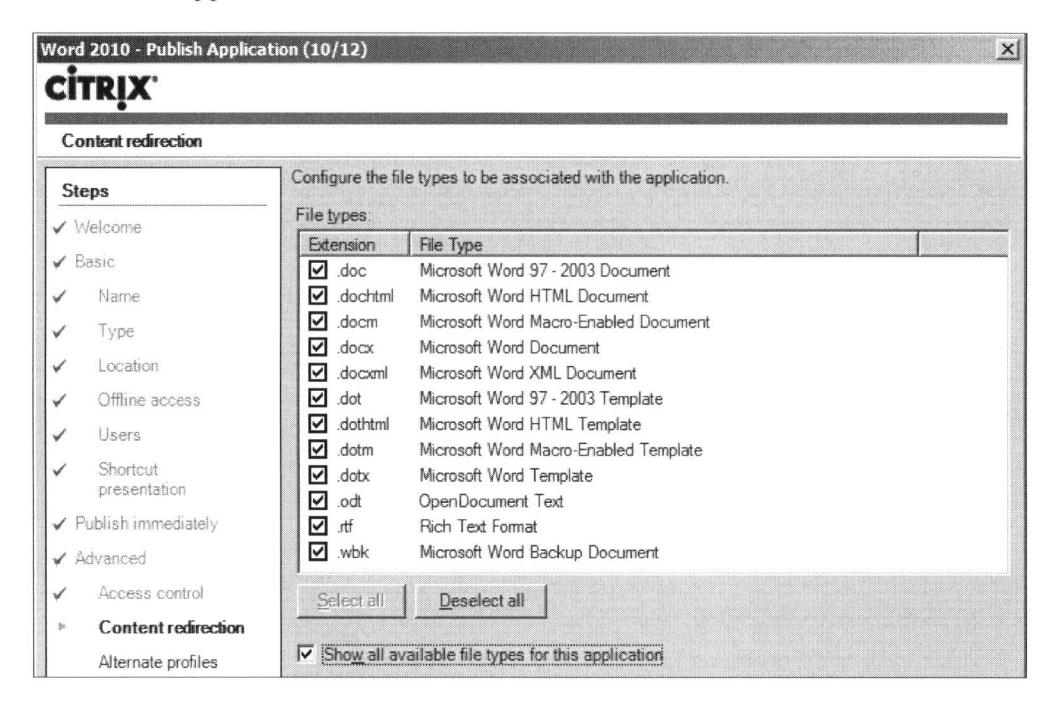

Specifying trusted servers for streamed services and profiles

The last step before users can start using Office 2010 on Brick Unit XenApp farm is to set up in all client machines or servers (if we are going to stream applications to servers) a registry key with the Application Hubs names.

In Citrix application streaming, the "Application Hub" is the place where streaming profiles are stored. The streaming profiler writes content to the Application Hub and the streaming client pulls content from the Application Hub at runtime. An Application Hub is the file server or web server where we stored our streaming application's profiles. The Application Hub supports all kinds of protocols and services such as SMB, CIFS, Samba, Novell, HTTP, HTTPS, Apache, or IIS.

To ensure that client machines run only approved services, William needs to edit the registry on client machines to enable a whitelist of approved server locations.

On the client machine, he creates the following registry location (the same for 32-bit and 64-bit systems), using `regedit.exe` or `regedt32.exe`:

- Key: **HKEY_LOCAL_MACHINE\SOFTWARE\Citrix\Rade**
- Value: **AppHubWhiteList**
- Type: **REG_SZ**

Then he adds server names (or local file system folder) in the registry value in a semicolon (;) delimited format, without spaces before or after the semicolon.

If the application has been streamed from a web location (also called HTTP streaming), the server name must be prefixed with HTTP (or HTTPS) in the AppHubWhiteList registry entry. Also, there is a clear distinction between HTTP and HTTPS servers.

If the profile location is `\\BRICKdc01\Profiles\Office2010\Office2010.profile`, then the **AppHubWhiteList** must contain BRICKDC01 or the IP Address of BRICKDC01:

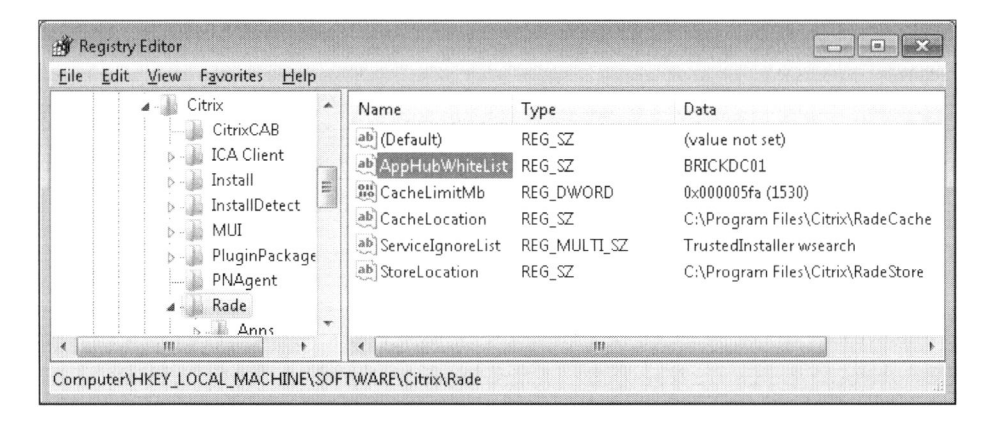

Also, William can use Active Directory GPO to set up the **AppHubWhiteList** registry key.

Summary

In this chapter, we learned about application streaming. In particular, we talked about:

- System requirements for application streaming
- Components for application streaming
- Choosing plug-ins to use for application streaming

Then we learned how to profile Microsoft Office 2010:

- Install a profiler workstation
- Customizing the Office 2010 installation
- Profiling Microsoft Office 2010
- Publish Office 2010 on the XenApp farm
- Specifying trusted servers for streamed services and profiles (AppHubWhiteList)

In the next chapter, we will discuss Citrix XenApp policies; in particular, we are going to learn about:

- Working with Citrix XenApp policies
- Creating and applying Citrix XenApp policies
- Troubleshooting Citrix XenApp policies

8
Managing XenApp Policies

In the last chapter, we learned about application streaming, including system requirements and components for application streaming, choosing plugins to use for application streaming, and profiling Microsoft Office 2010.

Now we are going to discuss XenApp policies, and in particular, we are going to cover the following in this chapter:

- Understanding XenApp policies
- Using the Group Policy Management Console, Citrix AppCenter Console, and Local Group Policy Editor to manage XenApp Policies
- How to create, manage, and apply XenApp policies
- How to create, import, and export Policies Templates
- Using Worker Groups on XenApp Policies
- Troubleshooting XenApp policies
- Working with Citrix policy templates
- Migrate policies between different XenApp farms

Understanding XenApp policies

In the Active Directory, a Group Policy contains two categories (also called nodes): **Computer Configuration** and **User Configuration** settings.

- The Computer Configuration node contains policy settings applied to computers and our XenApp servers, when we use GPO to manage servers.
- The User Configuration node contains settings applied to users accessing the machine, the XenApp server in our case the XenApp server, regardless from which client they log on.

XenApp policies also have the same categories: computer and user.

- Computer policy settings in Citrix are applied to XenApp servers. When the server is rebooted, these policies are applied to the server.
- User policy settings are used for the duration of the session and are applied to user sessions. Policy settings changes can also take effect when XenApp re-evaluates policies every 90 minutes.

XenApp policies are the preferred way to manage session settings or user access and the most effective method of controlling connection, security, and bandwidth settings on Citrix XenApp farms.

We can create and assign XenApp policies to users, groups, machines, or connection types, and each policy can contain one or several settings. Using policies allows us to turn on/off settings like:

- ICA session settings, such as Auto Client Reconnect, Keep Alive, Session Reliability, or Multimedia configuration
- Licensing configuration, such as license server hostname or port
- Mapping of local drivers, printer, and ports
- Server settings, such as Connections Settings, Reboot Behavior, and Memory/CPU Management
- Shadowing options and permissions

Working with XenApp policies

A policy is basically a collection of settings or rules. XenApp policies include the user, server, and environment settings that will affect XenApp sessions when the policy is enforced. Policy settings can be enabled, disabled, or not configured.

For some policy settings, we can enter a value or we can choose a value from a list when we add the setting to a policy.

We can set some policies to one of the following conditions to enable or permit a policy setting: **Enabled** or **Allowed** and we can use **Disabled** or **Prohibited** to turn off or disallow a policy setting.

Also, we can limit configuration of the setting by selecting **Use default value**. Selecting this option disables configuration of the setting and allows only the setting's default value to be used when the policy is enforced.

Chapter 8

If we create more than one policy in our environment, we need to prioritize the policies. The best way to track applied settings is to run a **Resulting Set of Policies Logging report** from the **Group Policy Management Console** or the **Citrix Policy Modeling Wizard**.

These reports will show all the Citrix settings configured via a policy, and which Group Policy Object, including the XenApp farm GPO, has actually won the merging calculation. We are going to talk about this in detail later.

Usually, XenApp policies will override the same or similar settings applied to the XenApp farm, specific XenApp servers, or on the client machine, except for the highest encryption setting and the most restrictive shadowing setting, which always overrides other rules or settings.

Policies are processed in the following order:

1. Local GPO
2. XenApp farm GPO (stored in the XenApp farm data store)
3. Site-level GPOs
4. Domain-level GPOs
5. Organizational Units

But, if we experience a policy conflict, policy settings that are processed last can overwrite those that are processed earlier. This means that policy settings take precedence in the inverted (next) order:

1. Organizational Units
2. Domain-level GPOs
3. Site-level GPOs
4. XenApp farm GPO (stored in the XenApp farm data store)
5. Local GPO

Best practices for creating XenApp policies

The following is a list of recommendations when configuring policy settings:

- **Reduce the amount of policies**: Avoid creating multiple policies for different groups of users. Create one policy and apply filters to it.
- **Disable unused policies**: Unused policies waste processing resources. If we are using Active Directory Group Policies, we can disable the unused part of the policy (Computers or User part).

- **Assign User policies to Active Directory groups**: If we assign policies to groups rather than a user, management is easy and can reduce processing time.
- **Assign Computer policies to Worker Groups**: We will discuss this item later in this chapter.
- **Remote Desktop Session Host Configuration** settings are similar to XenApp policy settings in a few ways. We need to avoid using Remote Desktop Session Host Configuration to reduce overlapping of settings.

> We can use Remote Desktop Session Host Configuration (formerly known as Terminal Services Configuration on Windows Server 2003) to configure settings for new connections, modify the settings of existing connections, and delete connections. We can configure settings on a per connection basis or for the server as a whole.

Guidelines for working with policies

The process for configuring policies is as follows:

- **Create and give a name to the policy**: We need to create and provide a name for the new policy.
- **Configure policy settings**: We need to choose if we are going to create a User Configuration or Computer Configuration policy and then set the policies.
- **Apply the policy to connections using filters**: Using filters we can choose to apply the policy to a specific group of users or computers.
- **Prioritize the policy**: In the final (and optional) step, we will assign priority so that policies will override or take precedence over other policies.

Working with management consoles

In previous versions of Citrix XenApp presentation, Citrix Presentation Server, and Citrix MetaFrame, policies were stored on the IMA and we managed XenApp policies from the Citrix Management Console.

Starting with XenApp 6, and continuing with XenApp 6.5, policies are stored in the Active Directory and we can manage XenApp policies through the Group Policy Management Console or Local Group Policy Editor in Windows, or using the Citrix AppCenter Console on XenApp 6.5, or the Citrix Delivery Services Console in XenApp 6.0 servers. Choosing the right console depends on our network environment and permissions.

Using the Group Policy Management Console

The Group Policy Management Console (shown in the following screenshot) allows us to view or create Active Directory policies. It also enables us to view the resulting policies applied to users or computers, which is very useful for troubleshooting (more about this is discussed later).

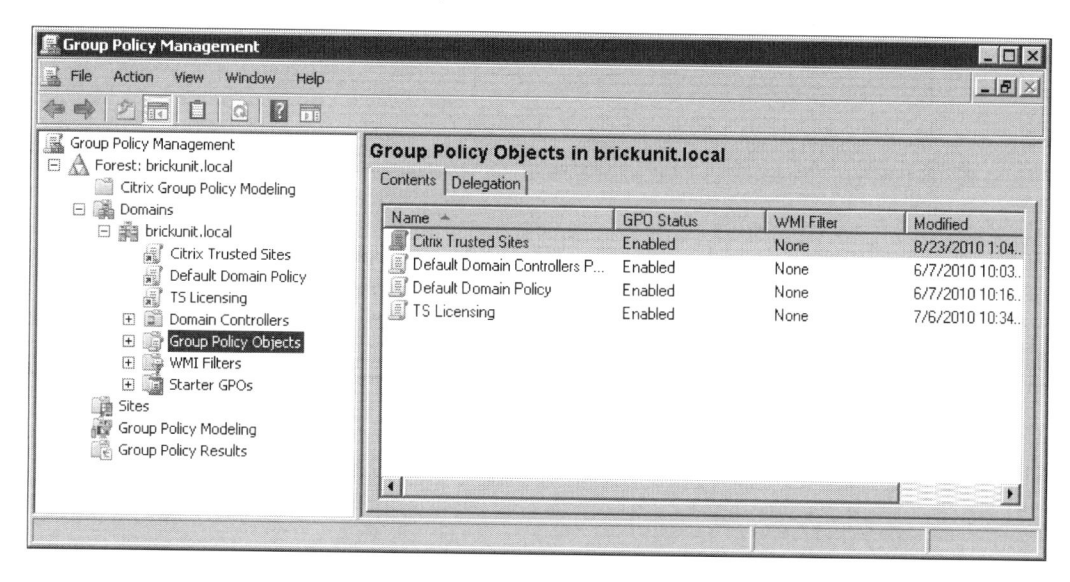

If our network environment is based on the Active Directory and we have the appropriate permissions to manage Group Policies (GPO), using the **Group Policy Management** Console to create policies for our XenApp farm is the preferred option.

The main reason to use the Group Policy Management Console over the Citrix AppCenter (or Citrix Delivery Service Console on XenApp 6.0) is because Active Directory GPOs take precedence over the farm GPO (also known as IMA GPO).

Using the AppCenter Console

The Citrix AppCenter Console (shown in the following screenshot), formerly known as the Citrix Access Management Console on Citrix Presentation Server and Citrix Delivery Service on XenApp 6.0, is a tool that integrates into the Microsoft Management Console (MMC) and enables us to execute management tasks, including creating and viewing XenApp policies. Detailed information about this console is covered in *Chapter 5, Using Management Tools*.

Managing XenApp Policies

If we don't have permissions to manage the Active Directory of our company or if our environment doesn't use the Active Directory, we need to use the Citrix AppCenter Console to create policies for our farm. Policies are stored in a farm GPO in the Citrix data store.

> Both Citrix AppCenter Console and Citrix Delivery Service Console are extremely similar, so all following steps are easy to reproduce on XenApp 6.0.

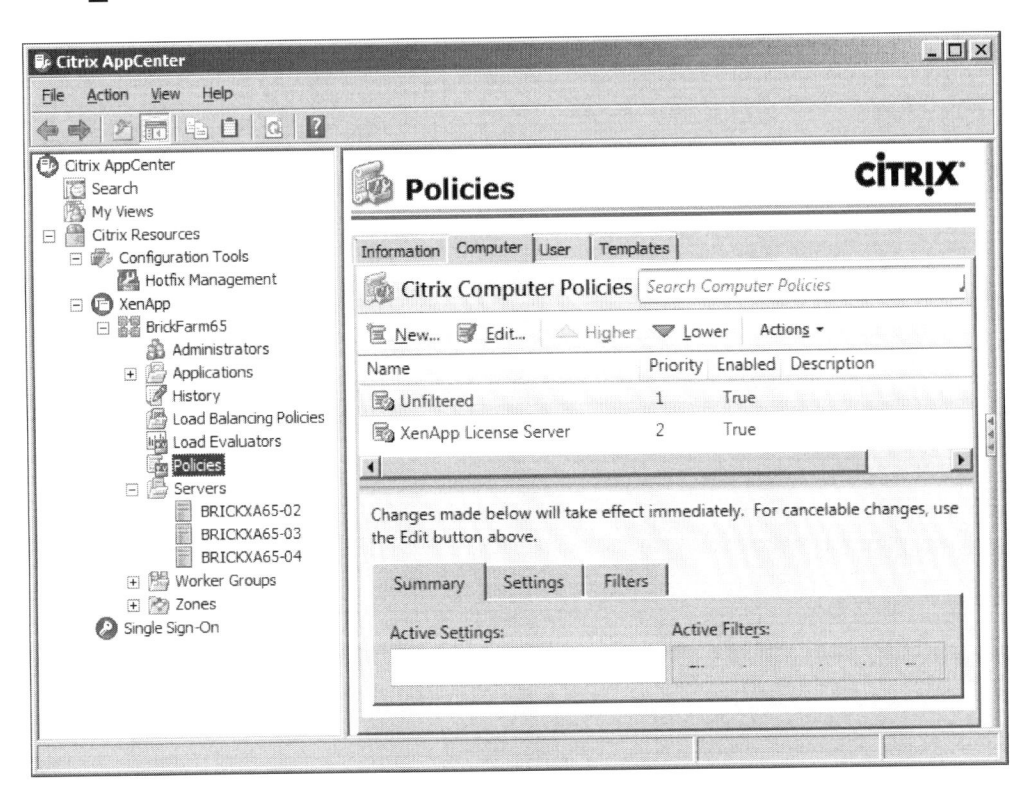

In the **Citrix AppCenter** Console, we can view the policies configuration by clicking on the **Policies** node, and then select either the **Computer** or **User** tabs in the middle pane.

When we click one of these two tabs, three more tabs will be displayed, as shown in the following screenshot:

- **Summary**: Shows the settings and filters configured for the selected policy
- **Settings**: Shows available and configured settings by category for the selected policy

- **Filters**: Shows the available and configured filters applied to the selected policy

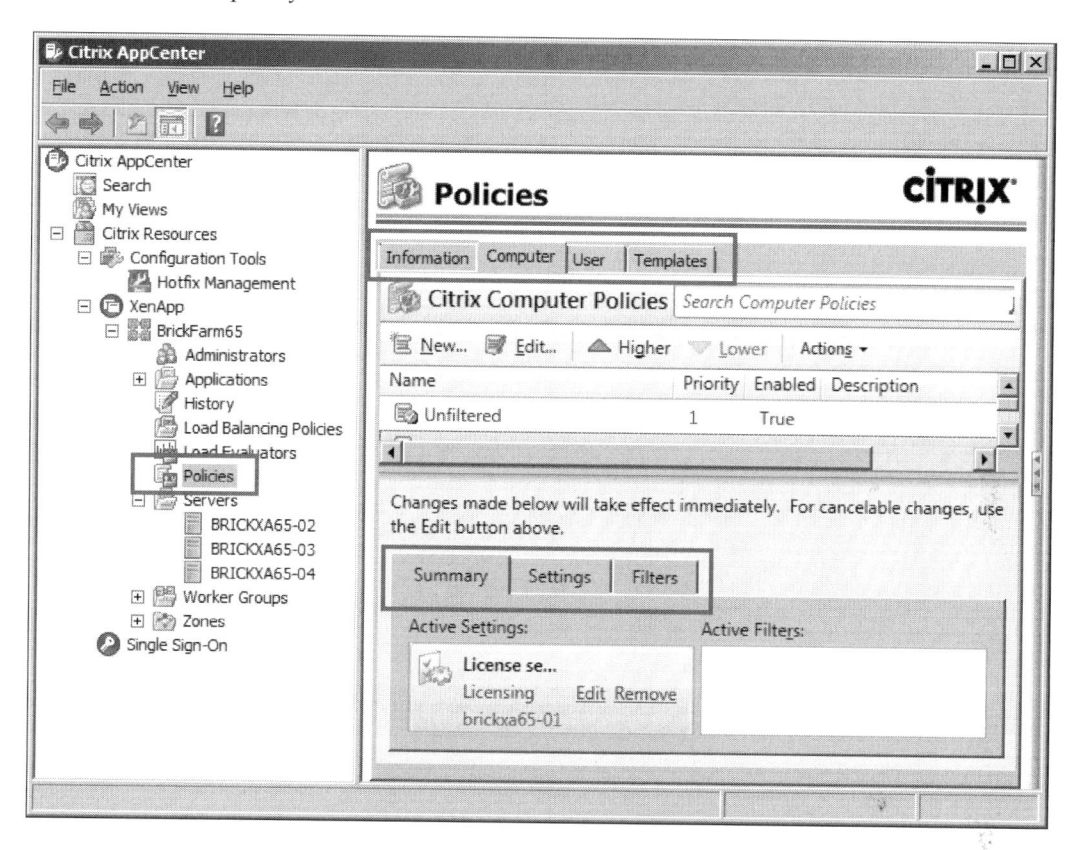

Using the Local Group Policy Editor

If we don't want to use the Citrix AppCenter Console, we don't have permissions to modify or create a GPO in the Active Directory, or we don't have an Active Directory domain (a NetWare network or workgroup, for example), we have another option. We can create a local GPO using the Local Group Policy Editor (shown in the following screenshot).

Managing XenApp Policies

If we type GPEDIT.MSC, from **Start | Run**, the Local Group Policy Editor will open. We can modify the local policy of a single server, so it is useful to create or edit a policy in one or maybe a couple of servers; for example, silo or test servers, but it is not useful for medium to large farms. The Local Group Policy will affect everyone who logs onto this machine—including users accessing via XenApp and administrators.

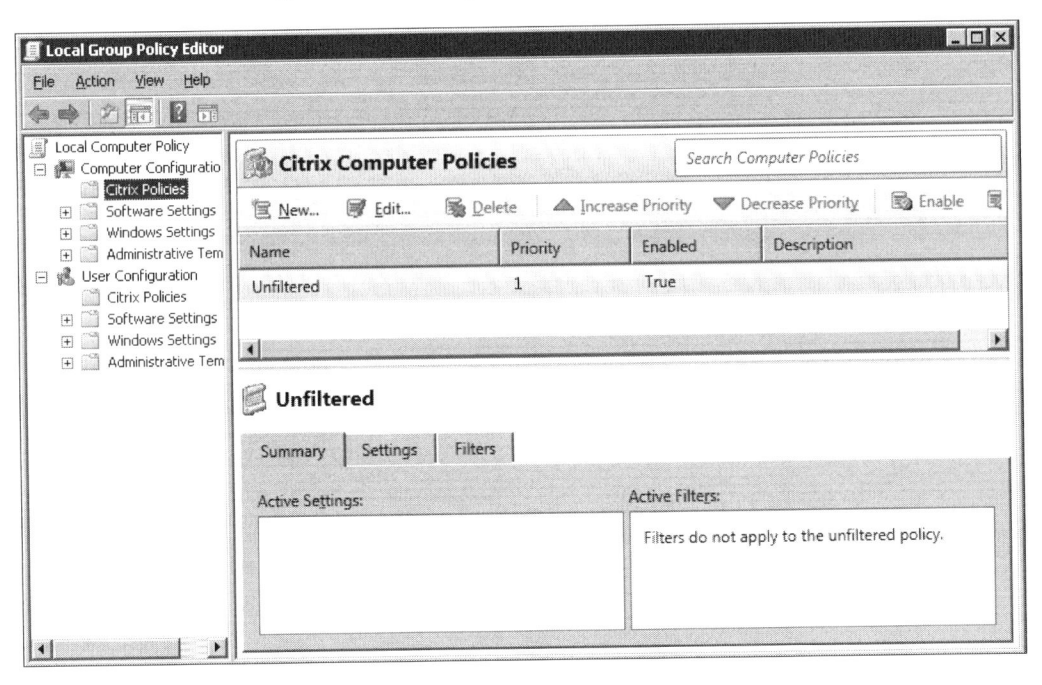

We can access policies and their settings in the **Local Group Policy Editor**, by clicking on the **Citrix Policies** node under **User Configuration** or the **Computer Configuration** in the tree pane, located on the left-hand side.

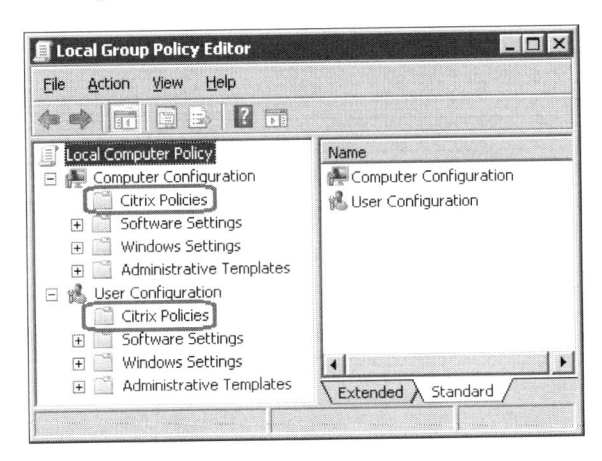

[212]

> Remember, Active Directory Group policies take precedence over farm GPO; and farm GPO takes precedence over Local Group policies.

Creating XenApp policies

William Empire from Brick Unit Construction is planning to use XenApp policies to manage the XenApp farm. He needs to decide which group of users, servers, or machines he wants to affect, before he creates the policy.

As Brick Unit Construction network infrastructure uses Active Directory, he can use existing Active Directory OU structure to create the XenApp policies.

Commonly, policies are based on geographic location (HQ, remote sites, and so on), connection type (local or remote users), server role, user role (IT, financial, and so on), and client machines (laptops, thin clients, and so on.)

Creating a policy using consoles

From the **Citrix AppCenter** Console, he selects the **Policies** node on the left-hand side pane and then selects the **Computer** or **User** tab and clicks on **New**. These policies are stored on the IMA data store.

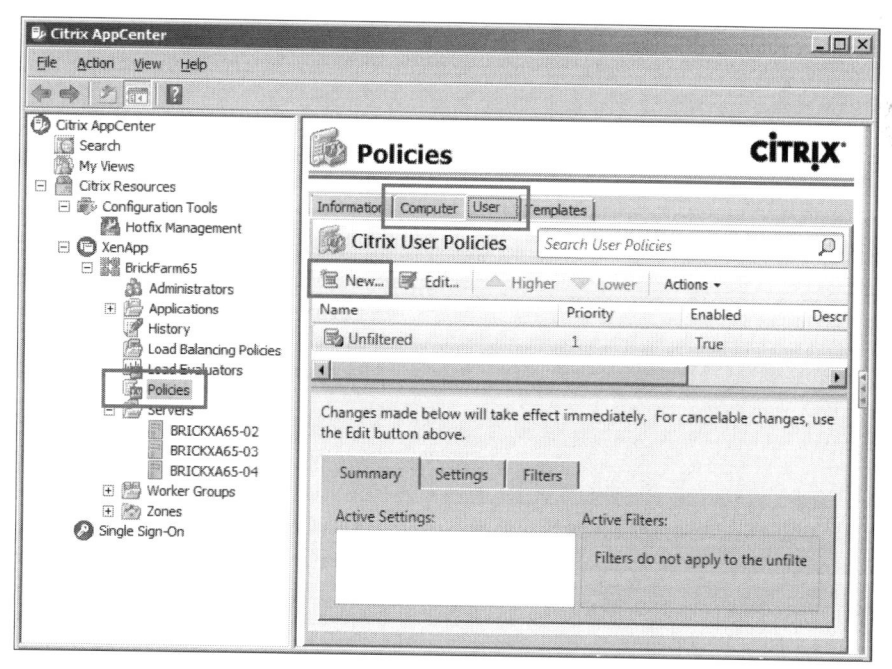

Managing XenApp Policies

William also can use the **Local Group Policy Editor** to create or modify local policies. He needs to select the **Computer Configuration** or **User Configuration** node, then **Citrix Policies**. He clicks on the **New** option to add a new policy. As we mentioned before, the policy is stored in local machine policy and can be used to add specific policies to a few servers.

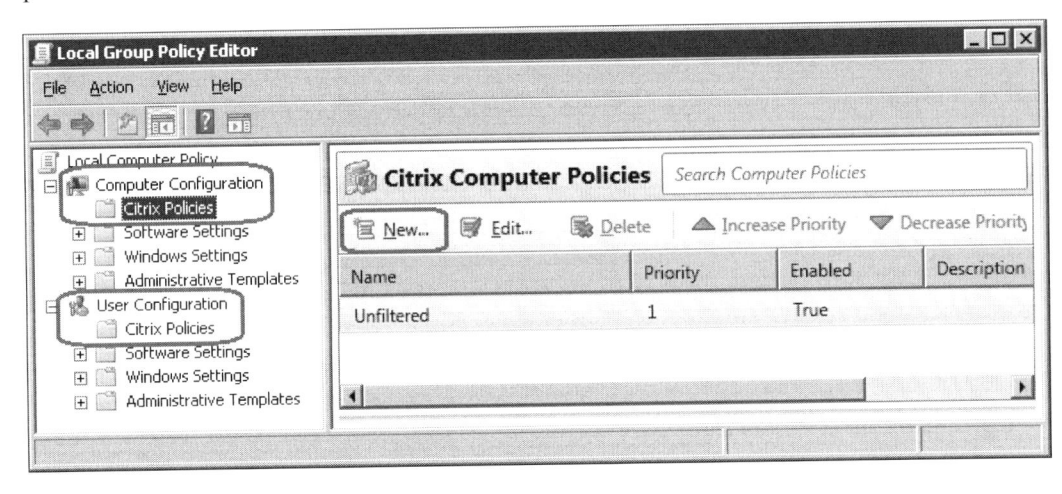

The last and preferred console is the **Group Policy Management Console**. William needs to select the container for the policy, **Group Policy Objects**, in this case. He right-clicks over the container and selects **New**. Finally, he gives the new GPO a name and clicks on the **OK** button.

Starting with this step, the following process is common to all consoles.

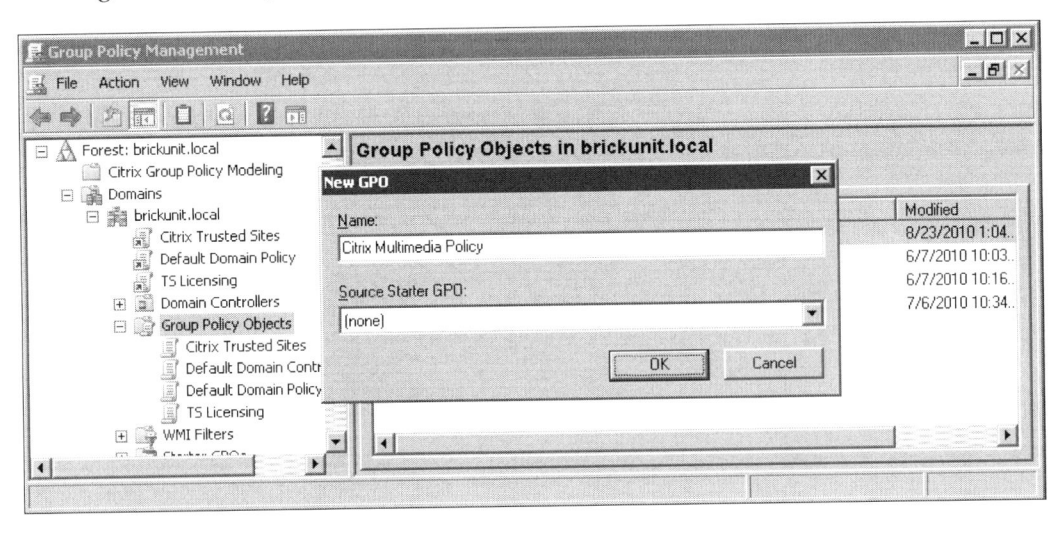

[214]

Chapter 8

After he gives the policy a name, he needs to select the **Computer Configuration** or **User Configuration** node, and then under **Policies**, click on **Citrix Policies**. Next, he clicks on **New** to add a new policy.

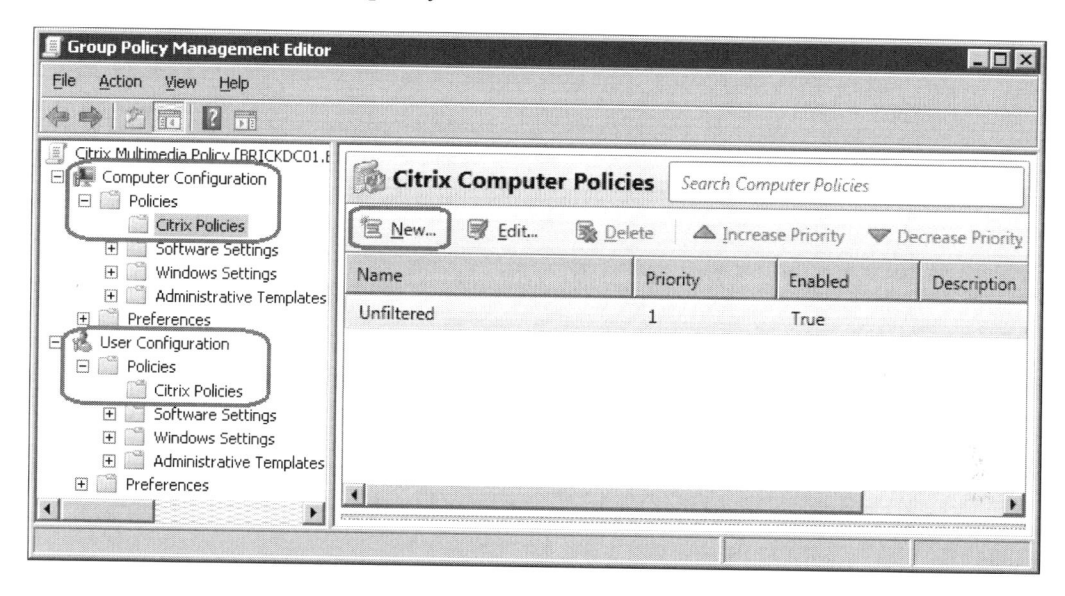

After the **New Policy** wizard appears, William adds a **Name** and **Description**, and clicks on the **Next** button. In this example, he is going to create a policy to manage multimedia policies.

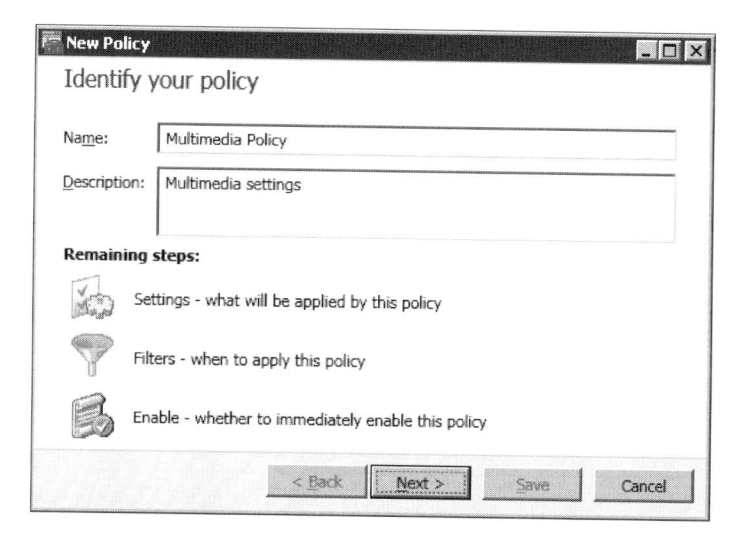

[215]

Managing XenApp Policies

He needs to choose the policy settings he wants to set up. In this case, he will enable the **HDX MediaStream Multimedia Acceleration** using the **Add** button:

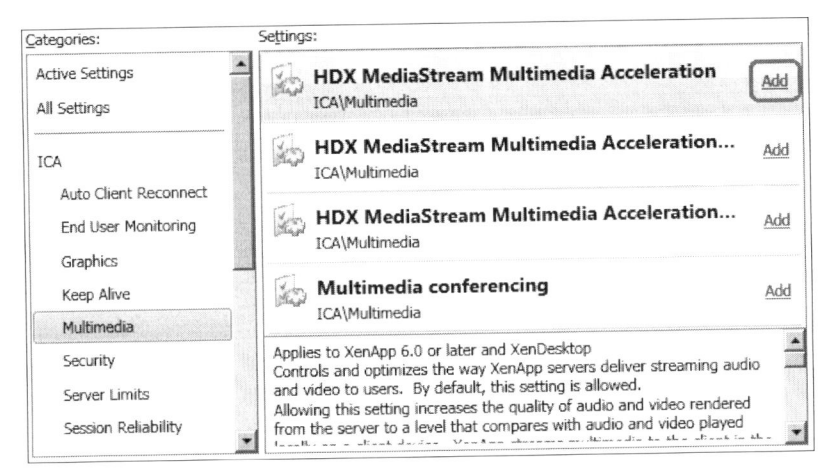

He chooses the **Allowed** option to enable **HDX MediaStream Multimedia Acceleration**:

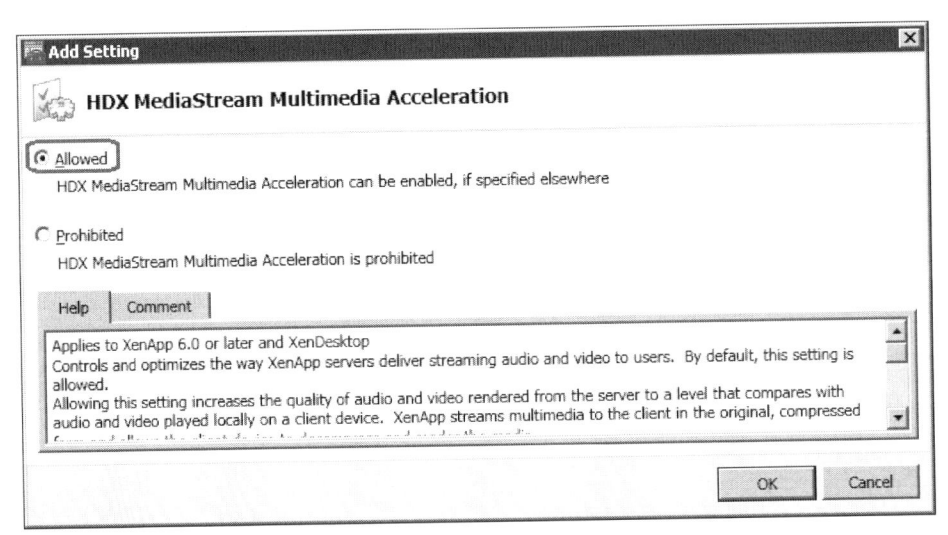

Then he needs to choose the filters he wants to apply to the policy. Here, he applies the multimedia policy to the **Training Devices** worker group, so all users using XenApp Servers machines in the training room (members of the **Training Devices Worker Group**) will improve the multimedia performance.

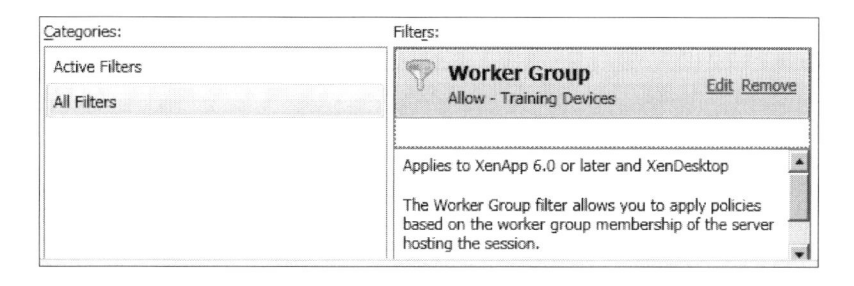

Categories:	Filters:
Active Filters	▽ **Worker Group** Edit Remove
All Filters	Allow - Training Devices

> Applies to XenApp 6.0 or later and XenDesktop
>
> The Worker Group filter allows you to apply policies based on the worker group membership of the server hosting the session.

In the final step, William selects the **Enable this policy** checkbox to leave the policy enabled; enabling the policy allows it to be applied immediately to users logging on to the farm. Also, he can clear the **Enable this policy** checkbox to disable the policy; disabling the policy prevents it from being applied.

> XenApp installs the Citrix Group policy engine, when the Citrix AppCenter Console or Citrix Delivery Services console is installed (on a XenApp 6.x server or standalone machine). The Citrix group engine provides integration between Active Directory group policies and XenApp policies.

Applying policies to sessions

When William creates a policy, their settings are applied to sessions. By default, the policy is applied to all sessions, if no filter is added.

He can use filters to apply a policy to a target group (for example users, groups, or computers).

When a user logs in to the farm, XenApp recognizes the policies that match the filters for the connection and applies them based on the priority ranking of the policy.

Some filters depend on whether we are applying a Computer or a User policy. The following list shows the available filters:

- **Access control**: The policy is applied based on a connection Citrix Secure Gateway. This filter applies only to User policies.
- **Client IP address**: The policy is applied based on the client's IP address (IPv4 or IPv6 address) used to connect to the XenApp farm. This filter applies only to User policies.
- **Client name**: The policy is applied based on the name of the client machine used to connect to the XenApp farm. This filter applies only to User policies.

- **User**: The policy is applied based on the user or group membership of the user. This policy can apply to local or Active Directory users. This filter applies only to User policies.
- **Worker group**: The policy is applied based on the worker group membership of the XenApp server hosting the session. This filter applies to either User policies or Computer policies.

> Disabled policy settings take precedence over a lower-ranked setting that is enabled and policy settings that are not configured are ignored.

Unfiltered policies

By default, XenApp provides Unfiltered policies for Computer and User policy settings. The settings added to this policy apply to all connections.

William will use the **Group Policy Management Console** to manage XenApp policies, and settings heading to the Unfiltered policy are applied to all farm servers and connections that are within the scope of the Group Policy Objects (GPOs) that contain the policy.

If he uses the Citrix AppCenter Console to manage XenApp policies, settings we add to the Unfiltered policy are applied to all servers and connections in the XenApp farm.

Now we are going to help William apply policies. He creates a test policy which he will apply to his account so that he can test it. From the policy wizard, he needs to select the **User** filter and click on the **Add** button:

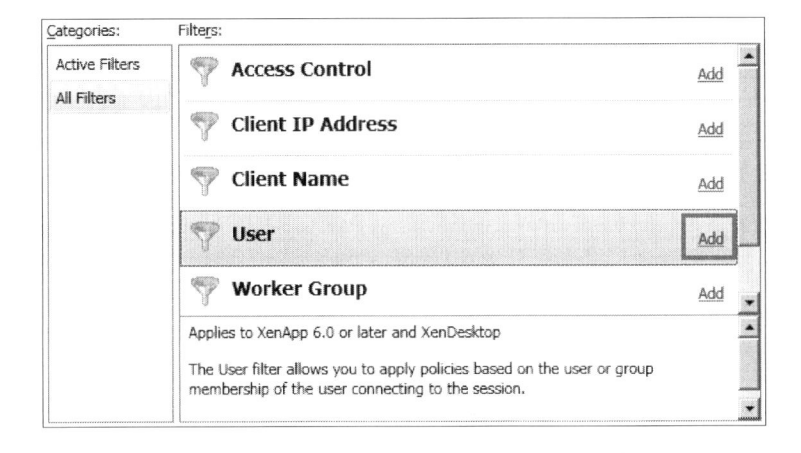

Categories:	Filters:	
Active Filters	Access Control	Add
All Filters	Client IP Address	Add
	Client Name	Add
	User	**Add**
	Worker Group	Add

Applies to XenApp 6.0 or later and XenDesktop

The User filter allows you to apply policies based on the user or group membership of the user connecting to the session.

From the **New User Filter** dialog box, he selects his account and clicks on the **Add** button:

Now, he can see all filters applied to the policy:

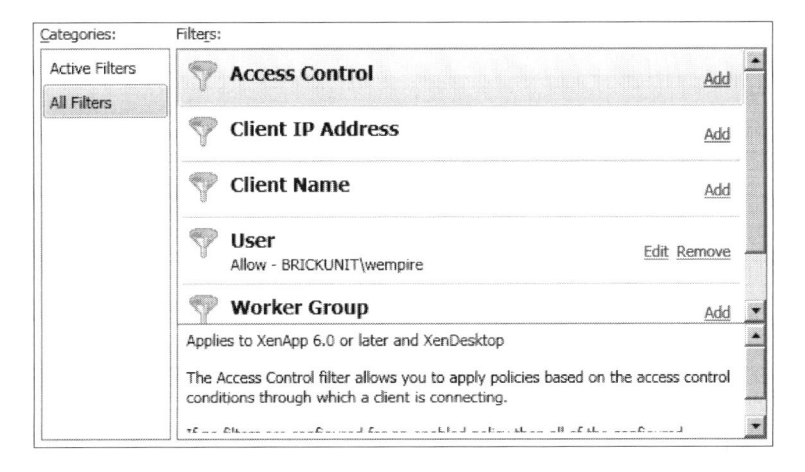

The policy is applied the next time William logs on to the XenApp farm.

Using multiple policies

We can use multiple policies to provide access to users based on their job functions, geographic locations, or connection types.

For example, William can create a policy that prevents remote users from mapping printers and local hard drives.

However, there is a group of project managers at Brick Unit Construction who are working from home and need access to their local drives and printers. So, William can create another policy and assign it to this group. Then he needs to prioritize the two policies to control which one takes precedence.

After William creates both policies, he needs to change the priority of policies.

From the console tree, he chooses to view **Citrix Computer Policies** or **Citrix User Policies**.

He created two policies: One called "Block Mapping Local Disks and Printers" is applied to all remote users. The second one, called "Enable Mapping Local Disks and Printers Project Manager", is applied to the project manager group.

From the middle pane, he selects the policy he wants to prioritize.

He needs to click the **Higher** or **Lower** buttons (**Increase Priority** or **Decrease Priority** buttons on XenApp 6.0) until the policy has the preferred rank. He needs to give more priority to the project manager policy.

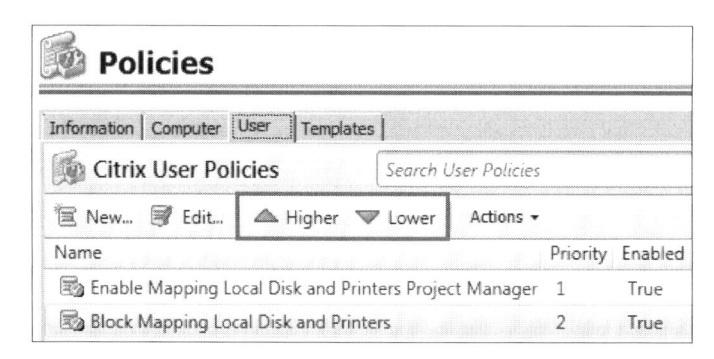

In general, policies override similar settings configured for the entire XenApp farm, for specific servers, or on the client machine. The exception is security. The highest encryption setting in our environment, including the operating system and the most restrictive shadowing setting, always overrides other settings and policies.

Using Citrix policies templates

A new feature introduced on XenApp 6.5 is the ability to use and create Citrix policy templates.

We can access the **Templates** tab in both in the **Citrix AppCenter Console** and the **Group Policy Management Editor**. We have two types of templates: **User** and **Computer** templates.

We can create our own templates from existing policies or use one of the four templates included on XenApp 6.5 as reference to start a new template. Included templates are listed here:

- **Citrix High Definition User Experience templates**: These templates contain both **Computer** and **User settings** to deliver optimal audio, graphics, and video to our users.
- **Citrix High Server Scalability templates** contain both **Computer** and **User settings** to allow us to run more user sessions per server.
- **Citrix Optimized Bandwidth for WAN templates** includes **Computer** and **User settings** to deliver XenApp applications to users connected to our XenApp farm with high latency or low bandwidth connections.
- **Citrix Security and Control templates** contain only **User settings** to lockout client machines, by not allowing port redirection, drive mapping, access to external devices (USB drives for example), and Flash acceleration.

Creating a new Citrix Policy template

We can create new policies from existing policies or existing templates. We need to choose between **Computer** and **User settings**, because templates cannot contain both types of settings together.

William is going to create a new template based on an existing template. He can use Citrix AppCenter console or Group Policy Management Editor.

1. He opens the **Citrix AppCenter console**, and then clicks on **Policies** node (left-hand side pane). If William decides to use the **Group Policy Management Editor**, he needs to expand the **Computer** or **User Configuration** nodes, then expand the **Policies** node, and then select **Citrix Policies**.

2. He clicks on the **Templates** tab and then selects the **Citrix High Server Scalability Computer Settings** template from which he wants to create his new template.

Managing XenApp Policies

3. Click on the **New Template** button:

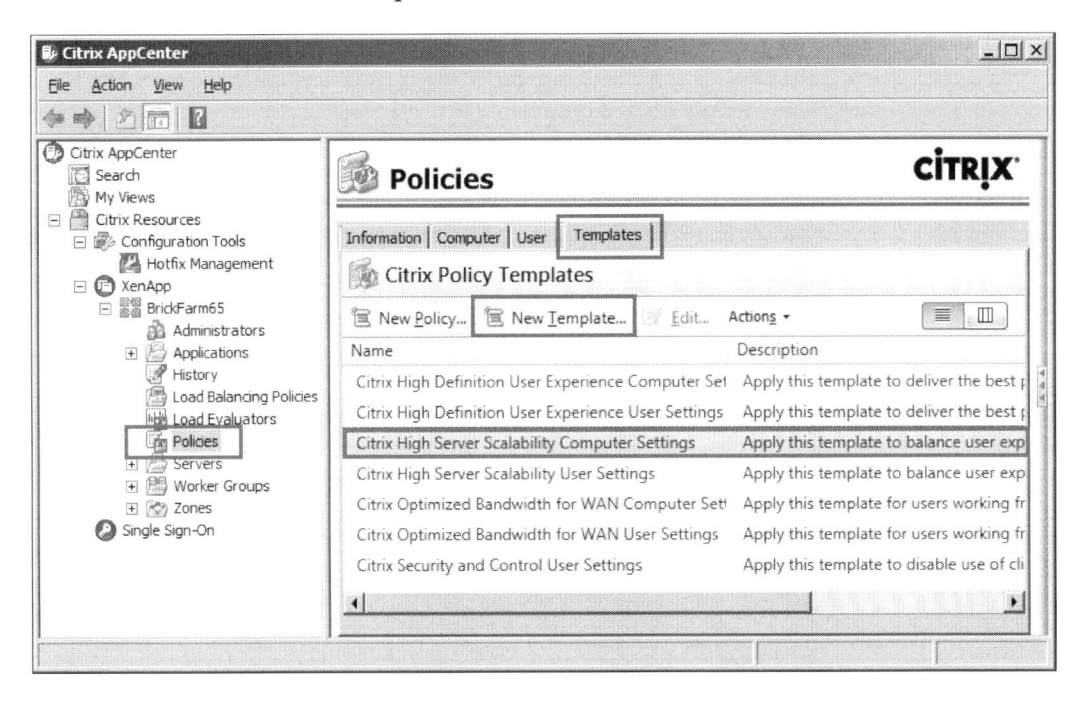

4. The **New Template** wizard appears. He enters a name for the template and clicks on the **Next** button.
5. On the **Choose the settings that will be applied** page, William needs to add or remove and configure the desired policy settings for the template.
6. When he is done with policy settings, he clicks on the **Create** button, and the new appears on the **Templates** tab.

Importing and exporting policy templates

The policy template created by William on the previous section is local to the server where the Citrix AppCenter console used to create the template is located.

So, he can import and export policy templates created in different servers or XenApp farms. This is one of the main reasons to use templates, to create a set of policies, and share with different XenApp farms and/or servers.

The second reason is to create a backup of new or existing templates.

The process to import or export a policy template is pretty simple:

1. William opens the **Citrix AppCenter console**, and then clicks on **Policies** node (left-hand side pane). If William decides to use the **Group Policy Management Editor**, he needs to expand the **Computer** or **User Configuration** nodes, then expand the **Policies** node, and then select **Citrix Policies**.
2. He clicks on the **Templates** tab, and then on the **Actions** drop-down menu:

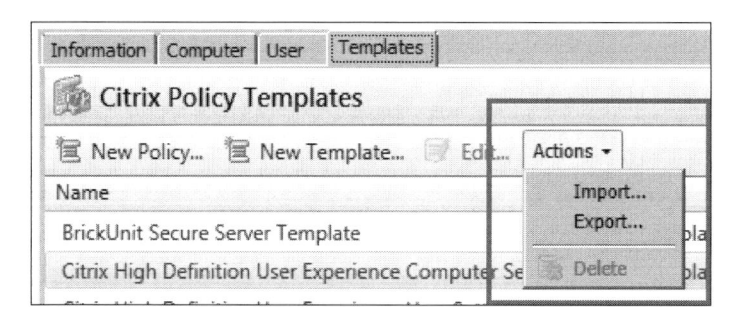

3. William chooses the **Import** or **Export** button and new dialog box appears. He selects the file if he is importing a template or types a file name if he is exporting it.

> Policy template uses the .gpt extension.

Using Worker Groups to assign policies

Worker Groups allow us to group related XenApp servers together and simplify the management of XenApp farms. We can group XenApp servers based on server role, application installed, or location.

Assigning policies to Worker Groups can reduce the time to deploy and publish new applications on XenApp servers.

Managing XenApp Policies

This is a feature introduced on XenApp 6.0. In previous versions, we can organize and group servers into two containers: zones and server folders. These containers still exist in XenApp 6.5, but Worker Groups provide extra features:

- We can create a Worker Group with one or several servers. Also, one server may belong to multiple worker groups. For example, we can create a worker group for all servers hosting specific applications and then create a worker group for each site. A server may belong to one or multiple worker groups for applications and one for the site.

- Worker groups can be dynamic. We can add AD containers instead of servers to a worker group, and when we add or remove servers from the AD container; changes are automatically replicated in the server's worker group memberships.

Creating Worker Groups

Now lets help William to create Worker Groups for his new XenApp farm. He has three servers running Office, two located on the Frederick site and one on the Washington site.

The two servers on the Frederick site are located on OU (Organization Unit) called Frederick and the remaining server on a OU called Washington. He needs to create a Worker Group for all servers running Office, and one Worker Group for each location.

1. He opens the **Citrix AppCenter Console** and expands the **XenApp** section. Then he expands the **XenApp** farm and clicks on the **Worker Groups** section. William clicks on the **Create worker group** action on the right-hand side.

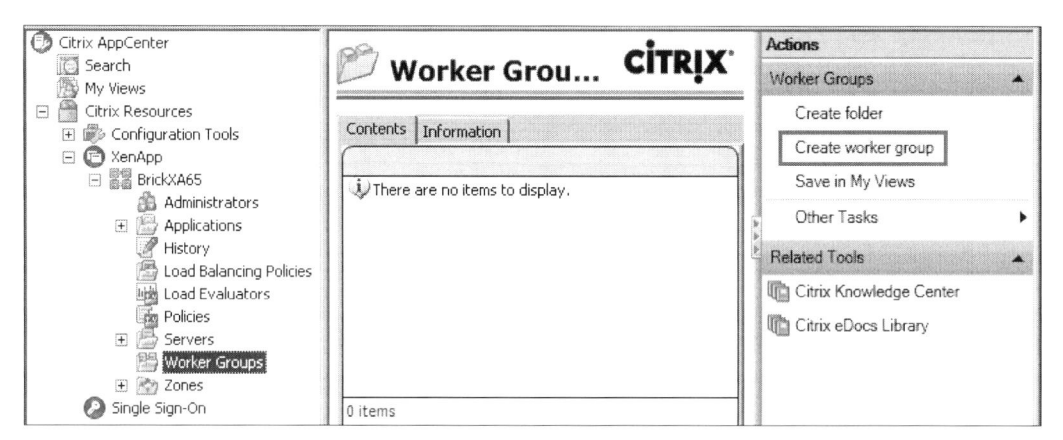

2. William types the **Name** and **Description** of **Worker Group** and then he selects the source. Available options are as follows:
    - **Active Directory Container**: Adds XenApp servers located on specific Active Directory OU.
    - **Active Directory Server Groups**: Adds XenApp servers members of specific Active Directory groups.
    - **Farm Servers**: Adds one or multiples XenApp servers. This option is useful if we have all our XenApp servers in a single OU, we are not using Active Directory group or we are not using Active Directory.

William selected the **Farm Servers** option, but he also he can add both OUs to the Worker Group. Both options are valid.

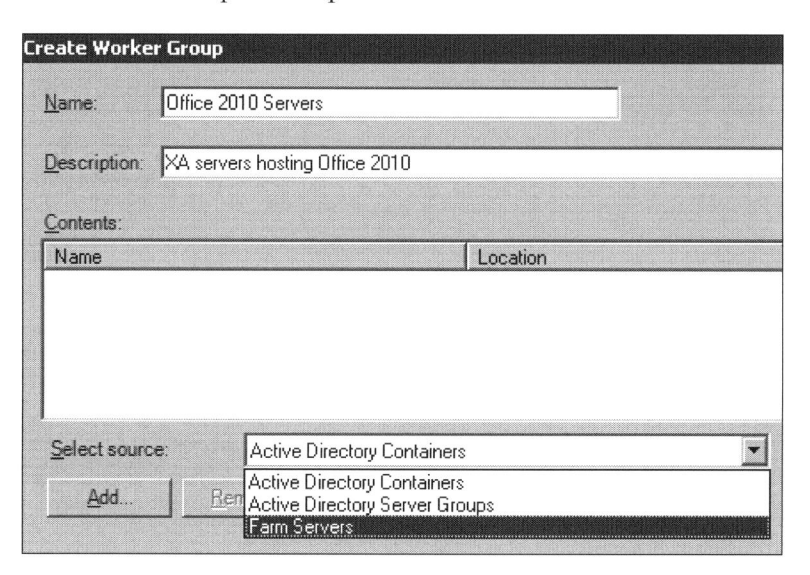

3. Here William can select all XenApp servers hosting Office using the **Add** or **Add All** buttons. Remember that the application (in this example Office) must be installed on the same drive and folder in all servers members of Worker Group. After that, he clicks on the **OK** button to create the Worker Group.

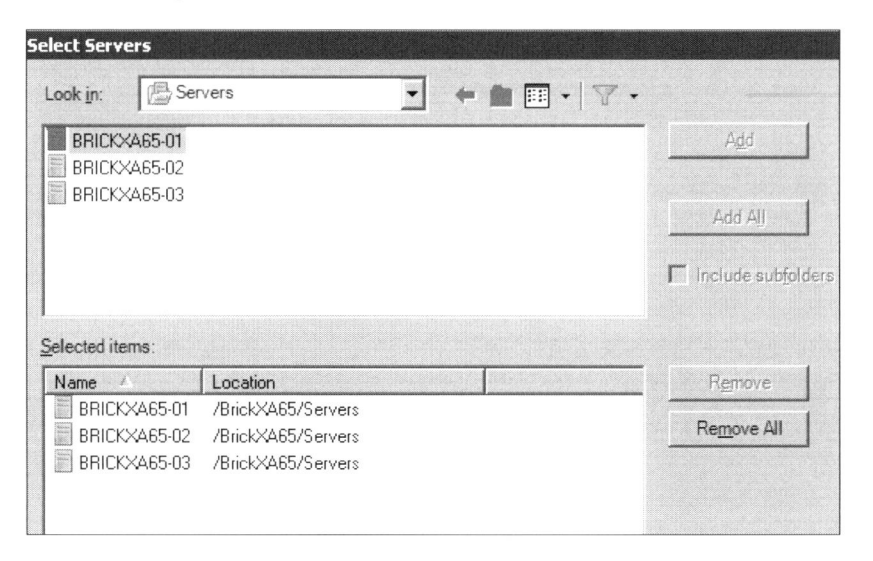

4. The next step for William is creating a new Worker Group for all XenApp servers located on the Frederick site. He creates a new Worker Group, types the **Name** and **Description** and then selects **Active Directory Containers** as source. The final step is to select the Frederick OU and click on the **OK** button to create the Worker Group.

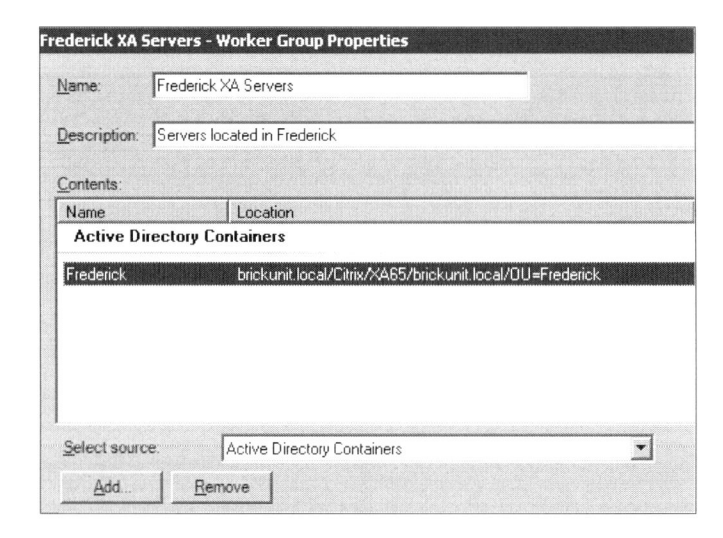

5. He repeats the process for the Washington OU, and the result is:

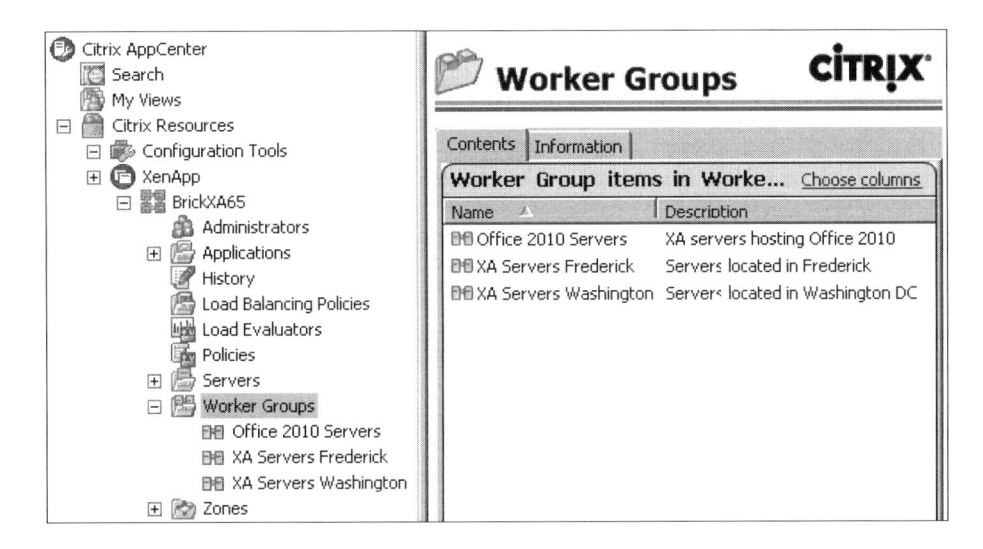

Now William can assign a policy to all XenApp servers located on Frederick using the **XA Servers Frederick** Worker Group:

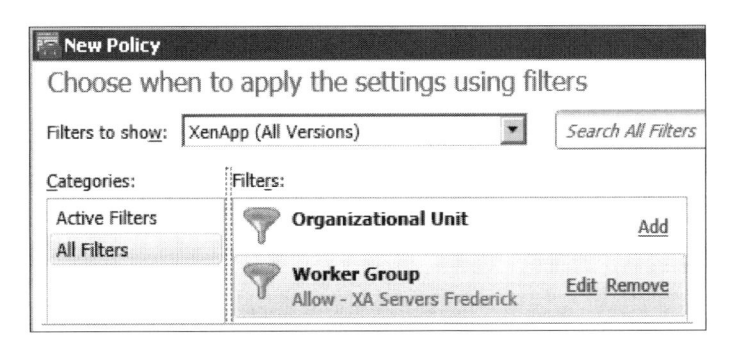

Troubleshooting policies

Occasionally, a connection does not respond as expected, because multiple policies are applied to the session. If a higher priority policy also applies to a session, it can override the settings we configured in the original policy. As we saw before, we can determine how the final policy settings are merged for a connection by calculating the **Resultant Set of Policy**. We can calculate the Resultant Set of Policy in the following ways:

- We can use the **Citrix Policy Modeling Wizard** to simulate a connection scenario and discern how XenApp policies might be applied.

- We can use Group Policy Results to produce a report describing the XenApp policies in effect for a given user and server.
- We can launch both tools from the **Group Policy Management Console** in Windows. If our XenApp environment doesn't use the Active Directory, we can launch the **Citrix Group Policy Modeling Wizard** from the **Actions** pane of the **Citrix AppCenter Console**.

Using the Citrix Policy Modeling Wizard

The Citrix Group Policy Modeling Wizard generates a report of XenApp policies applied to a particular environment such as domain controller, users, Citrix policy filter evidence values, and simulated environment settings such as slow network connection.

> Results of the wizard will be based on the user account we use and where we run it.

If we are logged on to the server with a domain account and our environment includes Active Directory, the wizard result will include Active Directory GPOs. If we run the wizard from the **Citrix AppCenter Console**, the farm GPO is included in the result too. However, if we are logged on to the server as a local user account and run the wizard from the **Citrix AppCenter Console**, the wizard calculates the **Resultant Set of Policy** using only the farm GPO.

Simulating connection scenarios with XenApp policies

Depending on our XenApp environment, we can use the **Citrix Group Policy Modeling Wizard** from the **Citrix AppCenter Console** (or **Citrix Delivery Services Console**) or the **Microsoft Group Policy Management Console**.

From the **Citrix AppCenter Console**, we need to click on the **Policies** node in the console tree and then click on **Run the modeling wizard** from the **Actions** pane.

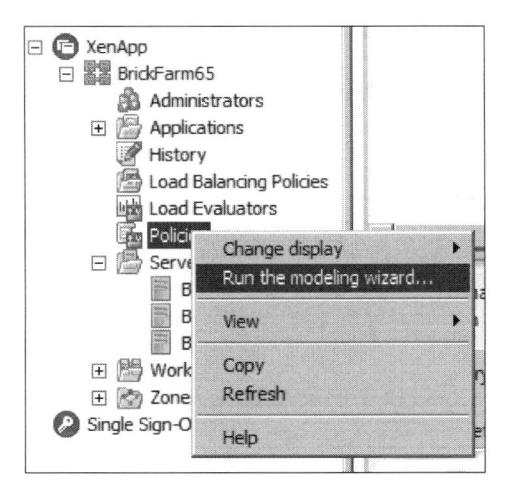

Now we are going to help William run the **Citrix Group Policy Modeling Wizard** from the **Group Policy Management Console**. He needs to right-click on the **Citrix Group Policy Modeling** node in the console tree and then select **Citrix Group Policy Modeling Wizard**:

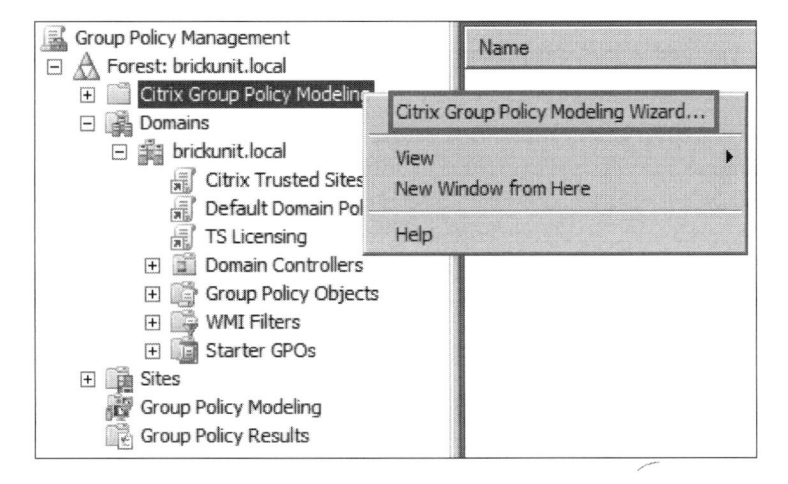

Managing XenApp Policies

The wizard starts with the welcome page. He then clicks on the **Next** button. He follows the wizard and selects the domain controller; users, computers, environment settings, and Citrix filter criteria he wants to use in the simulation.

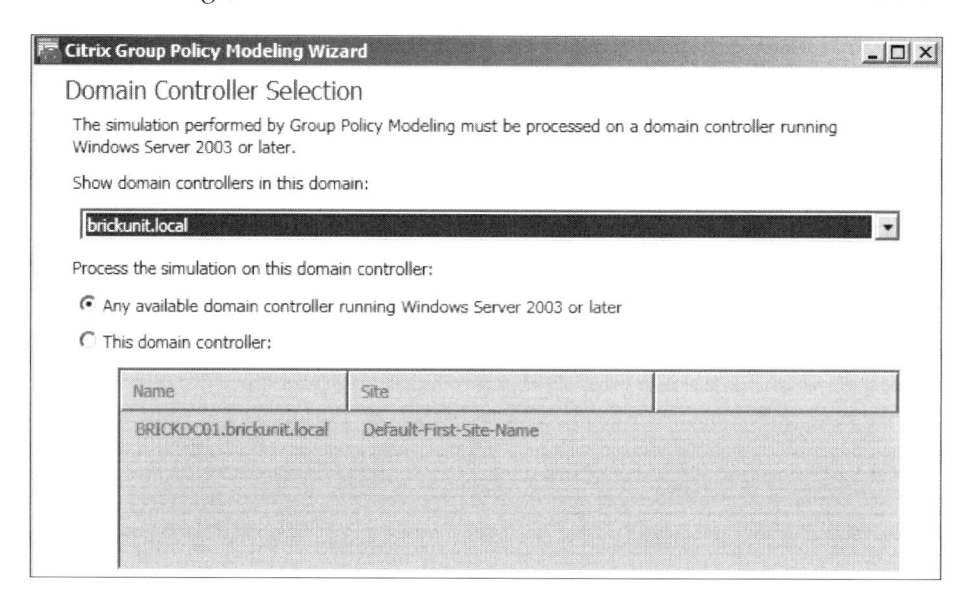

He selects his user and selects the computer container:

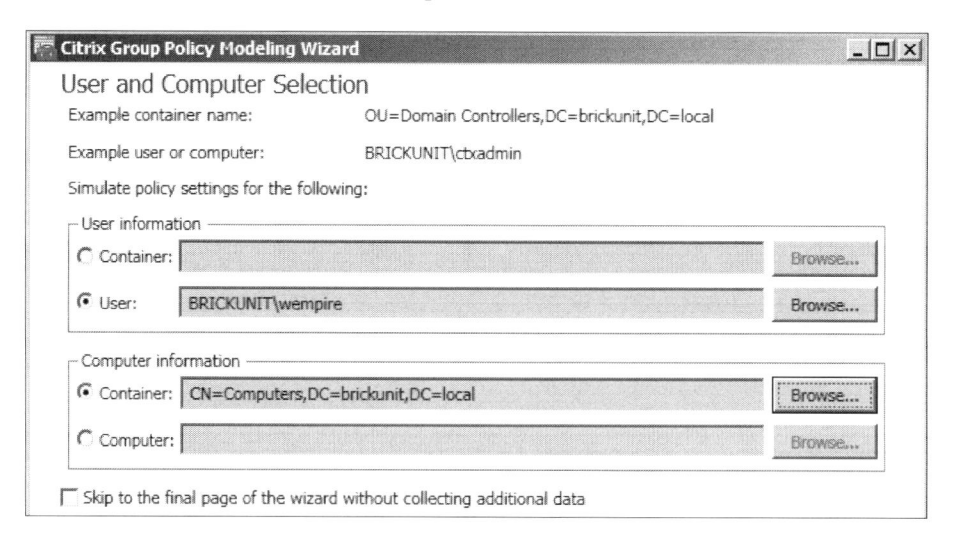

In the **Advanced Simulation Options** page, he keeps the default options.

In the **Alternate Active Directory Paths** page, he selects OU for the User location.

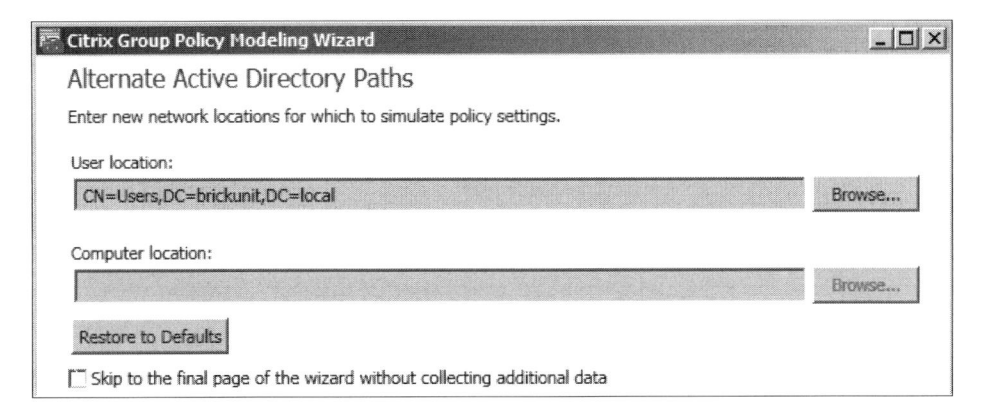

In the **Filter Evidence Selections** page, he enters the **Client IP address**:

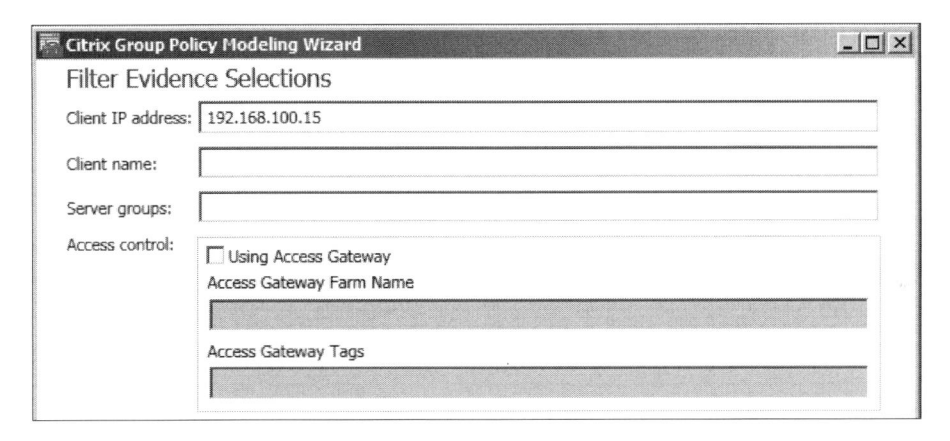

Managing XenApp Policies

In the **Summary of Selections** page, William clicks on the **Run** button.

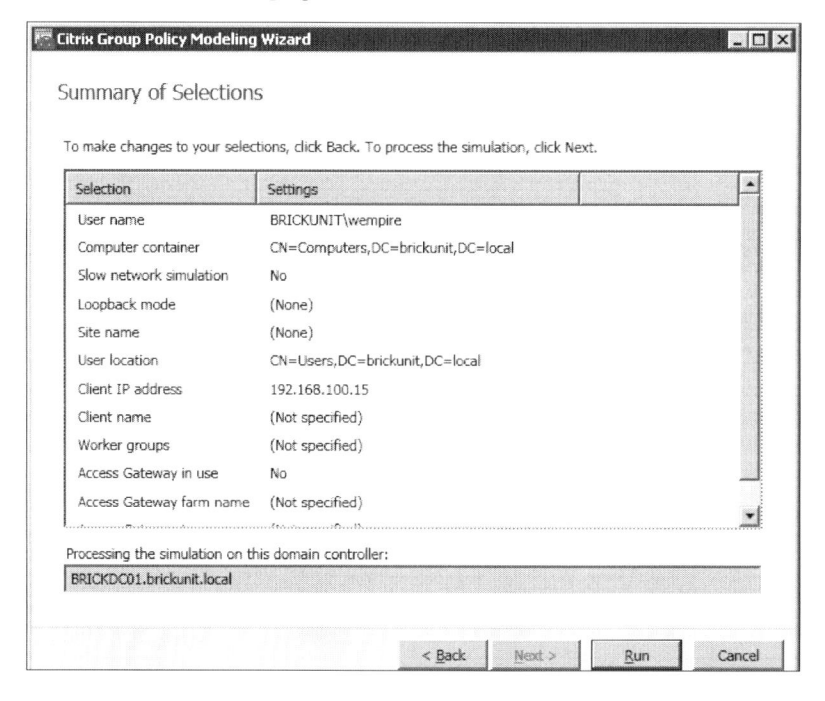

When he clicks on the **Close** button, the wizard produces a report of the modeling results. In the **Citrix AppCenter Console**, the report appears as a node in the console tree, underneath the **Policies** node. The **Modeling Results** tab in the middle pane displays the report, grouping effective Citrix policy settings under the **User Configuration** and **Computer Configuration** headings.

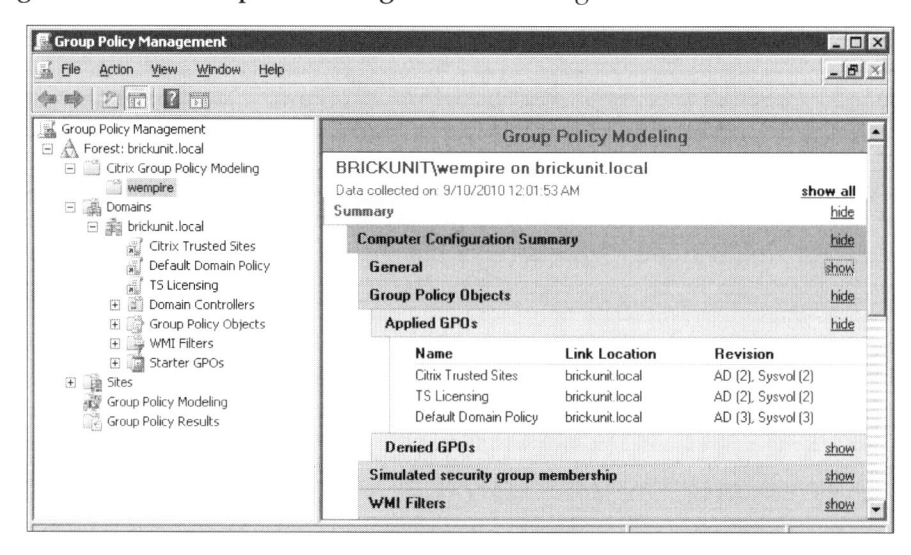

Citrix settings precedence over Windows settings

In a XenApp environment, Citrix settings override the same settings configured in an Active Directory policy or using Remote Desktop Session Host Configuration. This applies to settings that are related to Remote Desktop Protocol (RDP) client connection settings such as desktop wallpaper, menu animation, and so on.

Exceptions to this rule are settings for encryption and shadowing where the most restrictive settings are configured by Remote Desktop Session Host Configuration, Active Directory settings, application configuration, and Citrix settings.

Searching policies and settings

From the Citrix AppCenter Console (or Citrix Delivery Services Console on XenApp 6.0), we can search the policies and their settings and filters. Now we are going to help William Empire from Brick Unit Construction to search policies.

All searches find items by name as he types the policy name. He can perform searches from the following places:

- For searching policies, he can use the search box over the list of XenApp policies:

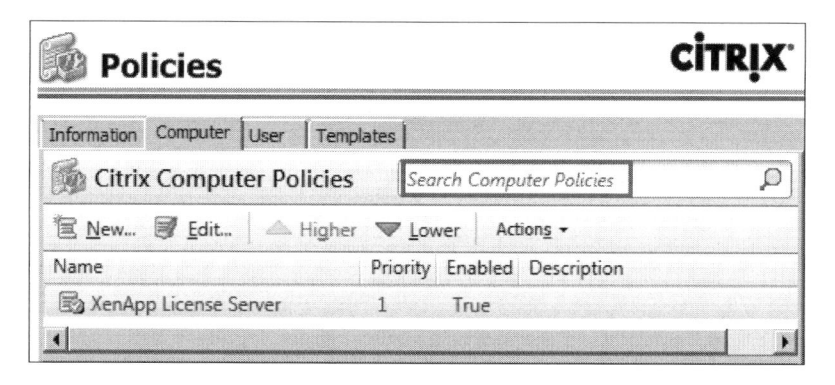

Managing XenApp Policies

- William can use the search tool on the **Settings** tab to search policy settings. He types `license` and all policies matching the word `license` are displayed:

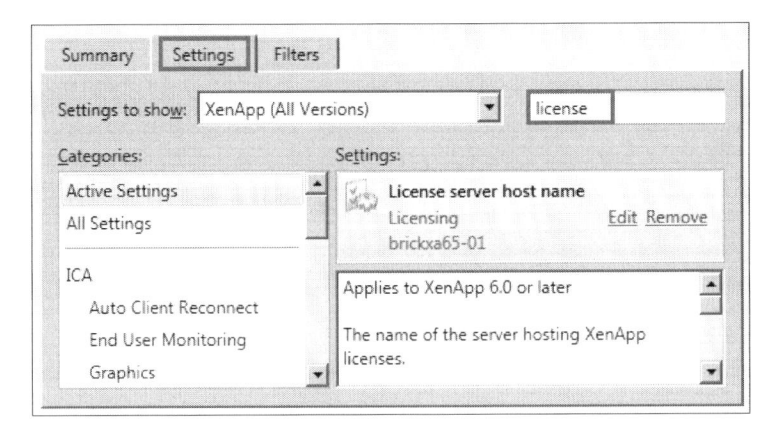

- For searching filters, he can use the search tool on the **Filters** tab:

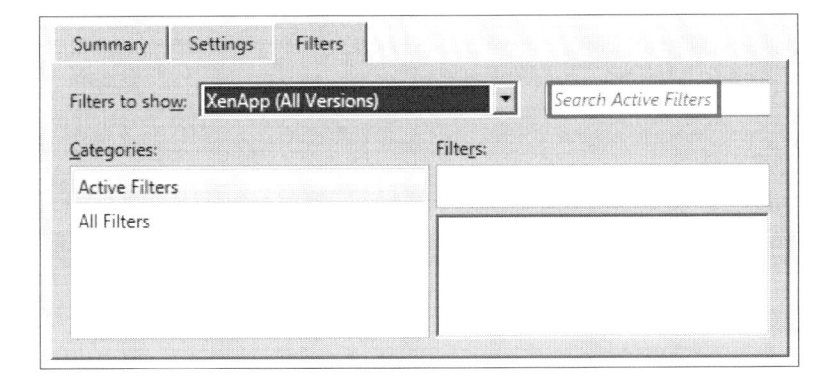

> When managing policies through the **Citrix AppCenter Console**, we need to avoid making frequent changes. It can adversely impact server performance. When we modify a policy, the XenApp server synchronizes its copy of the farm Group Policy Object (GPO) with the data store, propagating the change to other servers in the XenApp farm.
>
> For example, if we make changes to five policies, the server synchronizes the farm GPO five times. In a large farm with multiple policies, this frequent synchronization can result in delayed server responses to user requests.
>
> To ensure server performance is not impacted by needed policy changes, arrange to make these changes during off-peak usage periods.

Importing and migrating existing policies

The setup of XenApp 6.5 installed a new tool called **Citrix XenApp Migration Center**, which is extremely good to migrate policies and other settings (administrators, for example) from existing XenApp 5.0, 6.0, and 6.5 farms.

- The tool is available as a GUI tool or collection of PowerShell scripts.
- Both source and new XenApp farms must exist.
- If we are planning to migrate from XenApp 6.5 source farm, we need to choose a server running the controller role.

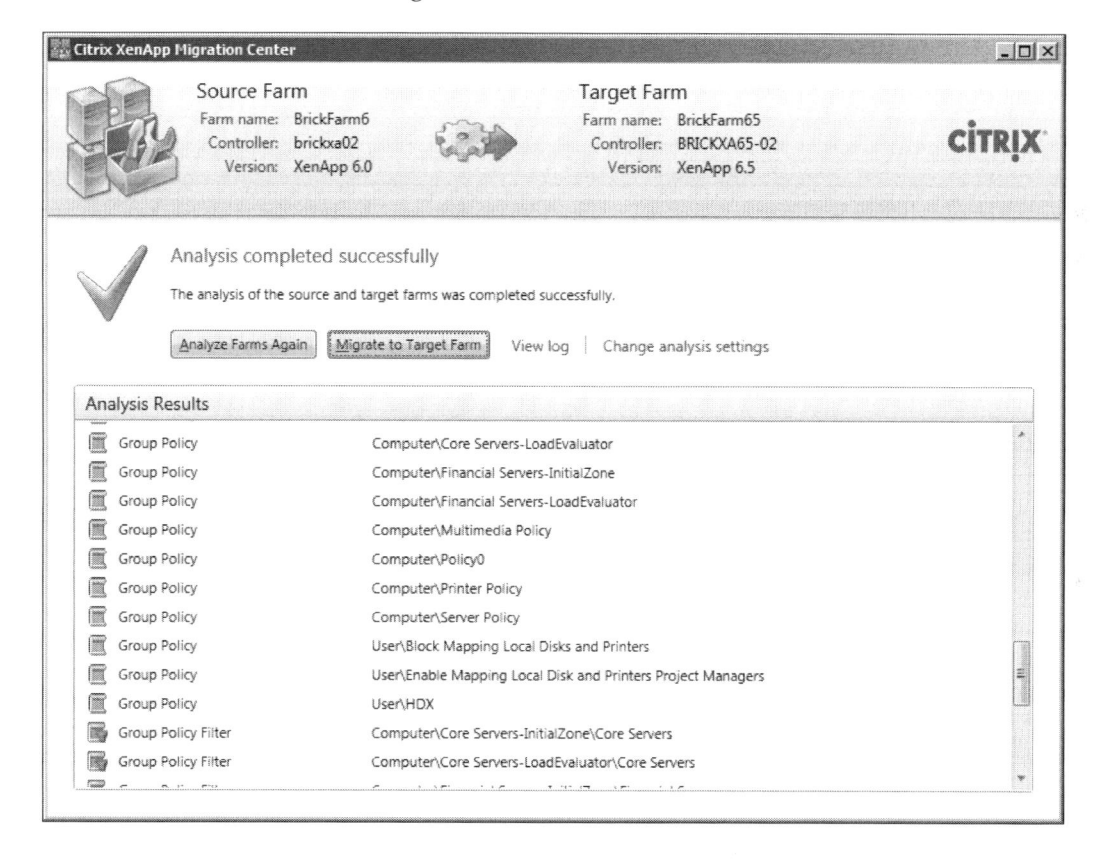

Also, Citrix releases a tool called **XenApp 6.0 to 6.5 Upgrade Utility**, to help us to migrate existing XenApp policies and worked groups from XenApp 6.0 to 6.5. This utility requires both XenApp 6.5 and 6.0 farms deployed in advance, to transfer the information.

The utility is available at `http://support.citrix.com/article/CTX130614`.

For XenApp 6.0, there are more migration tools available, for example **Citrix XenApp 6 Migration Tool** can help us to migrate settings (including XenApp policies) from XenApp 5.0 farms to XenApp 6.0 farms.

The Citrix XenApp 6 Migration Tool is available for download at `http://support.citrix.com/article/CTX125471`.

We can migrate our XenApp policies from farm GPOs to Active Directory GPOs using a PowerShell script available at `http://community.citrix.com/x/GQDPC`.

Summary

In this chapter, we have learned about managing policies on XenApp 6.5 (and XenApp 6.0). Specifically:

- Understanding XenApp policies
- Using the Group Policy Management Console, Citrix AppCenter Console (or Delivery Services Console on XenApp 6.0), and Local Group Policy Editor to manage XenApp policies
- Creating, managing, applying, and troubleshooting XenApp policies
- Working with Citrix policy templates
- Using Worker Groups on XenApp Policies
- Present tools to migrate XenApp policies

In the next chapter, we are going to talk about printing in a XenApp environment.

9
Printing in XenApp Environments

In the last chapter we learned about Citrix XenApp policies, how to create, manage, apply, and troubleshoot policies, using the Group Policy Management Console, Citrix AppCenter Console, and Local Group Policy Editor.

In this chapter, we are going to learn about printing in XenApp environments. This chapter will cover:

- Windows and Citrix XenApp printing concepts
- Assigning network printers to users using Citrix policies
- Managing printer drivers
- Using the Citrix Universal Printer
- Implementing printers
- Printing for mobile users

Windows printing concepts

The following is a list of basic printing concepts and components in the Windows environment.

We can print from our machine to a locally attached printer connected on USB or LPT port or we can print from a network printer that is managed by a print server.

- **Printing device**: A printing device is the physical printer (the hardware device) to which we send print jobs.
- **Printers**: This is the software representation of a printing device. Computers store information about printers, so they can find and interact with printing devices.

- **Printer driver**: Printer driver is the software program that lets the computer communicate with the printing device. The driver converts the information to be printed to a language that the printing device can understand and process appropriately.
- **Print job**: When a user sends a document to print, the data sent to the printer is known as a print job. Print jobs are queued to the printer in a specific sequence, controlled by the print spooler.
- **Print spooler**: This Windows service manages printer objects, coordinates drivers, helps us install new printers, manages the scheduling of print jobs, and determines where print jobs are processed. The print spooler also determines if the printer prints each page as it receives it or if the printer waits until it receives all pages to print the job.
- **Print queue**: The print queue keeps a list of the print jobs waiting to be printed in a specified order. The spooler maintains this list for each printer in the computer.
- **Print server**: Print server usually is a dedicated Windows server, hosting shared printers and managing the communications between client machines and printers. Also, print servers provide print drivers to client devices and keep print jobs in a print queue until the printer can print them. A print server acts like a remote print spooler.
- **Network printer**: A printer object connected to a wired or wireless network, usually accessed through a network print server.

Print job spooling

Spooling is the process of sending data to a spool. A spool can be a printer spool (the memory of the printer) or a document saved on the disk of a printer server, before being sent to the printer.

Print jobs can be spooled either remotely or locally. Typically, print jobs sent to locally attached printers are spooled locally, and jobs sent to network printers are spooled remotely. Where print jobs are spooled is where print jobs are processed.

The processing location can generate or reduce the network traffic and affect the time of processing and resources used on the device machine or print server.

The Windows machine processes the job when print jobs are spooled locally. The application creates a spooled print job. The local print spooler uses the printer driver to process the print job and sends the print job to the printing device (the physical printer).

In a Windows environment, printer drivers and settings are stored on the client machine itself.

When print jobs are spooled remotely, a Windows print server processes the print job.

A typical printing process for spooled print jobs is as follows:

- For local spooling, the application tells the local spooler to create a print job and an associated spool file on the local machine, or the application tells the remote spooler to create a print job and an associated spool file on the print server for remote spooling.
- On the local machine, Windows sends the application's drawing commands to the local spool file (local printing) or the remote spool file (remote spooling).
- Windows sends writing commands until the job is completely spooled.
- The local spooler or the remote spooler processes the print job with the print driver. This process is known as rendering.
- For local printing, the local spooler delivers the rendered data to the printing device (usually a local printer); or for remote printing, the print server delivers the rendered data to the printing device (usually a network printer).

When the client machine doesn't have enough resources available, such as thin clients, remote spooling is the best option because the print job is processed on the print server, causing little overhead on the client machine.

Unlike remote spooling, local spooling does not use the network servers like a print server. If the print jobs are spooled remotely across the WAN, and users are facing latency issues, local printing is the recommended option.

Printing on Citrix XenApp

The XenApp printing works on top of the Windows printing environment, so the first step is to configure the printers in the Windows environment. When users log in to a XenApp session, XenApp will create the appropriate printers. Printer drivers must be installed on the XenApp server.

Most XenApp printing functions are configured through the following **Citrix** User **policy** categories:

- **Bandwidth**: This category contains settings to limit the bandwidth allocated to printers
- **Printing | Client Printers**: These settings affect the client redirected printers and printing using the client printing pathway
- **Printing | Drivers**: These settings control driver management
- **Printing | Universal Printing**: These settings configure universal printers and drivers

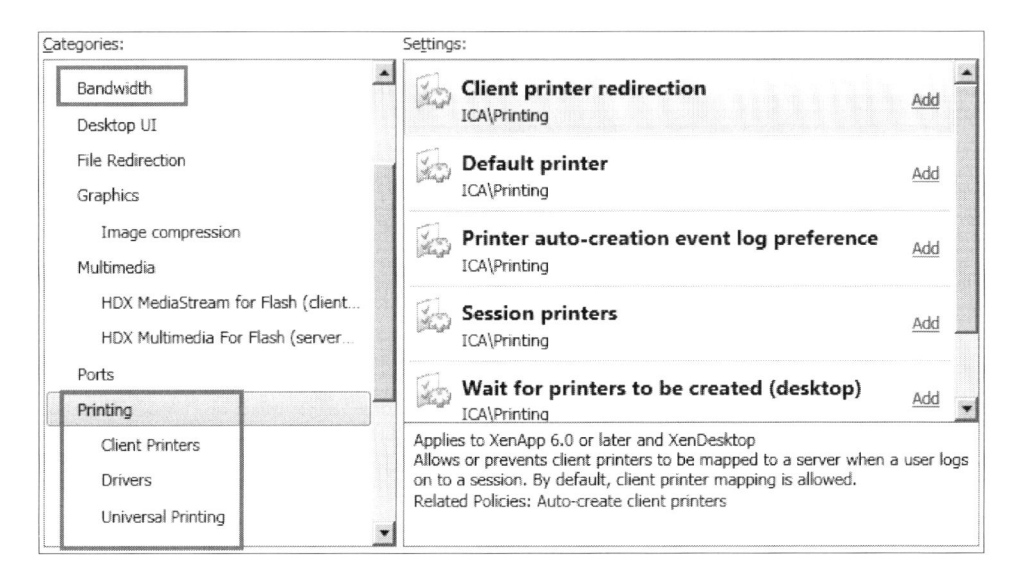

Printing settings are evaluated once the user logs on and stay the same throughout the session. Any new printers added to a policy or a client machine during a session do not appear in the session until the user logs off.

Please note that Citrix policies always take precedence over Windows policies in a XenApp environment.

Printing pathway

The printing pathway is a very important concept in XenApp 6.5 (and XenApp 6.0); it includes the path by which print jobs are routed and the location where print jobs are spooled. Both aspects of this concept are very important because routing affects network traffic, and spooling affects utilization of local resources (CPU, memory, and disk space) on the client machine that processes the job.

In XenApp, print jobs can use two different printing pathways:

- Client printing pathway
- Network printing pathway

The **client printing pathway** refers to print jobs that are routed, using the ICA protocol, through the client machine to the printer and spooled on the Citrix Receiver (formerly known Citrix Online Plug-in). The printer can be connected directly to the client machine or located in a print server.

When we use the client printing pathway, a virtual printer is constructed in the session that redirects to the printer object on the client machine, and then the client machine sends the print job to the printer. These jobs are spooled locally on the XenApp server. There are two different configurations of the client printing pathway: one for printers attached directly to the client machine (client local printing) and another for network printers (client network printing).

When the **network printing pathway** is used to print jobs that are routed from the XenApp server hosting the user's session to a print server and spooled remotely; there are two different configurations of the network printing pathway: one for network printers connected to the printer server (server network printing) and another for printers attached directly to XenApp (server network printing).

Client local printing

First, we need to install and configure the printer and printer driver on the client machine. Then we need to install and configure the printer driver on the XenApp server or enable the universal driver.

In client local printing, the print job spools from the XenApp server to the client machine and then to the printer installed on the client machine. An example of this environment is a remote user working from home or a small office without network printers.

This is the process when a print job is spooled in the client local printing environment:

- The published application tells the local spooler, on the XenApp server, where the application is located to create a print job and an associated spool file
- On the XenApp server, Windows writes the application's drawing commands to the local spool file until the job is completely spooled
- The local spooler processes the job using the printer driver in a process known as rendering

- The rendered data is delivered to the client machine through the ICA protocol
- The client machine sends the print data to the locally attached printer on the client machine

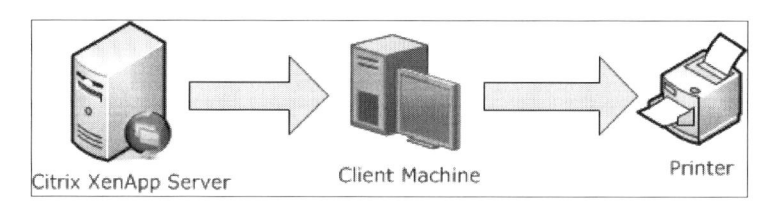

Client network printing

The process is almost the same to the client local printing device, but instead of sending the job to the printer attached to the client machine, the job is sent to the printer server.

The following is the process when a print job is spooled in the client network printing environment:

- The published application tells the local spooler on the XenApp server where the application is located to create a print job and an associated spool file
- The XenApp server sends the print job to the client machine for processing
- The client machine processes the spooled job and sends it to the print server for processing
- The print server then sends the print job to the appropriate network printer

Configuring the client printing pathway for network printing is useful for low bandwidth connections such as WANs. Also, the ICA connection provides traffic compression and we can limit traffic or restrict bandwidth assigned for print jobs.

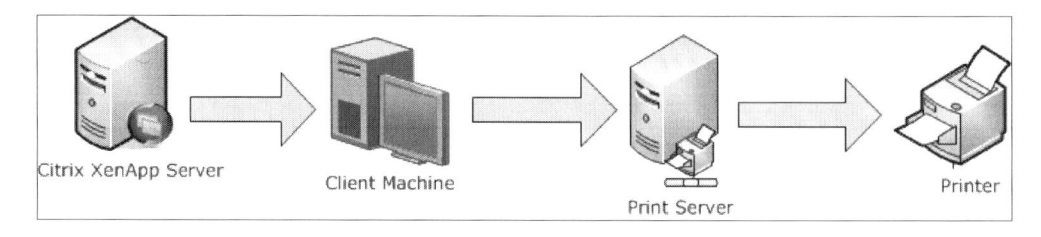

Server network printing

In a server network printing environment, the XenApp server sends the print job to the network print server and then to the printer.

To configure network printers, we need the printer drivers on the servers running XenApp. Then we can assign printers to users using the session printers policy. We can filter the policy by access control, client IP address, client name, server, or users and groups. For example, we can create a rule to assign a specific printer to all users in a specific floor of a building, based on the IP address of the client machine.

When a print job is spooled remotely, it uses the following process:

- The application on the XenApp server tells the remote spooler to create a print job and an associated spool file
- The Windows print provider sends the spool file to the print server
- The print server processes the spool file
- The print server sends the print job to the appropriate network printer

Assigning network printers to users

Automatic printer creation can fail for session printers or network printers on a client machine, usually because the right drivers are not installed automatically by Windows. Often, this is caused by a policy setting preventing auto-installation or because they are manufacturer drivers (drivers not available on the Windows distribution, usually we need to download from the manufacturer website). We can resolve this problem by installing the corresponding drivers to our XenApp servers manually or using a script if we have multiple print drivers. Later, we will learn how to work with print drivers on XenApp.

Now we are going to help William Empire from Brick Unit Construction to set up a session printer, used to assign a specific printer using Citrix policies.

Adding session printers settings to a Citrix policy

William opens the **Citrix AppCenter Console** (also he can use **Group Policy Management Console**), chooses **Policies | Create or edit a Citrix policy | User** tab | **New** | type a **Name** | **Printing** | **Session printers**, and adds a network printer using one of the following methods:

- He types the **Printer UNC path** using the format \\servername\printername.
- He uses the **Browse** button to browse for printers on a specific server. He can also type the server name using the format \\servername and click on **Browse**:

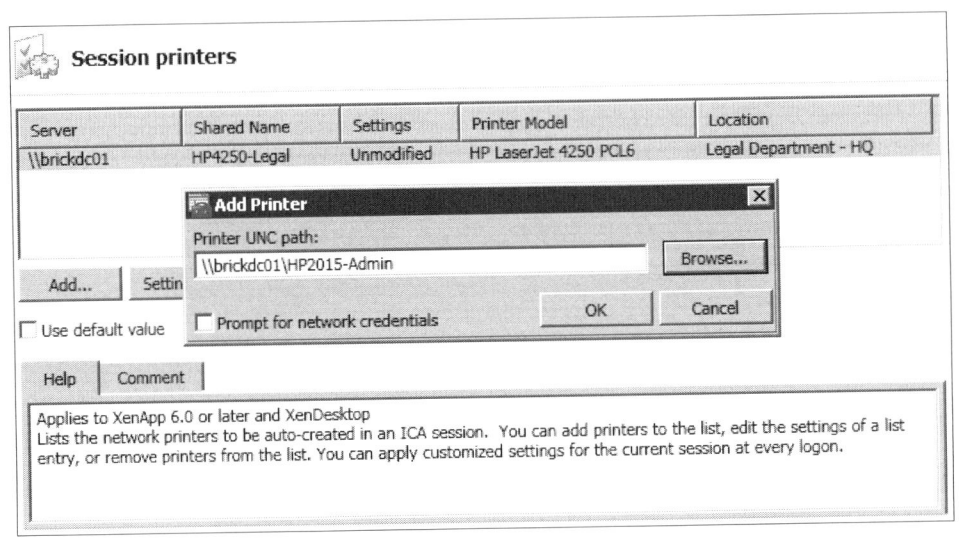

[The server merges all enabled session printer settings for all applied policies, starting from the highest to lowest priorities. When a printer is configured in multiple policies, the custom default settings are taken from only the highest priority policy object in which that printer is configured.]

Setting a default printer for a session

After adding a few printers to the session printer policy, William needs to specify a default printer, using the **Citrix User Policy** setting **Printing | Default printer** from the settings page; from the **Choose client's default printer** drop-down list, he chooses one of the following:

- **One printer created by a session printer rule**: Sets the default printer to an existing session printer.

- **Set default printer to the client's main printer**: Sets the default printer to the client's current default printer, if the client's main printer is mapped.
- **Do not adjust the user's default printer**: Uses the current **Remote Desktop Services** or Windows user profile setting for the default printer. Note that the default printer is not saved in the profile and it does not change according to other session or client machine properties:

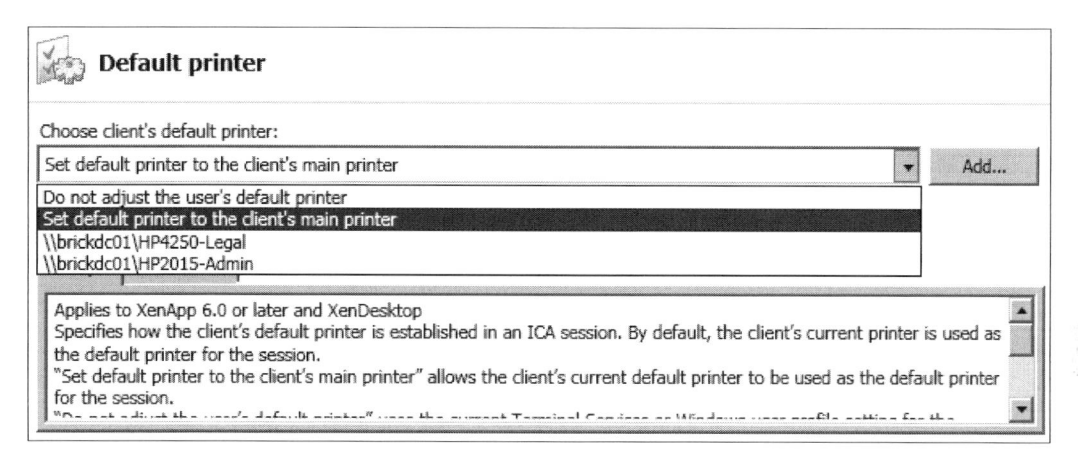

Also, he can use the last option to present users with the nearest printer through profile settings (this functionality, known as Proximity Printing, is explained later).

Finally, he applies the policy to a group of users (or other filtered objects).

Modifying settings of session printers

William can modify default printer settings like paper size, copy count, print quality, and orientation.

On the **Session printers settings** page, he selects the name of the printer for which he wants to modify the settings and clicks on the **Settings** button.

He checks the **Apply customized settings** checkbox and then changes the required settings.

He needs to select the **Apply customized settings at every logon** checkbox to ensure that these settings are restored in future sessions (even if users modify them):

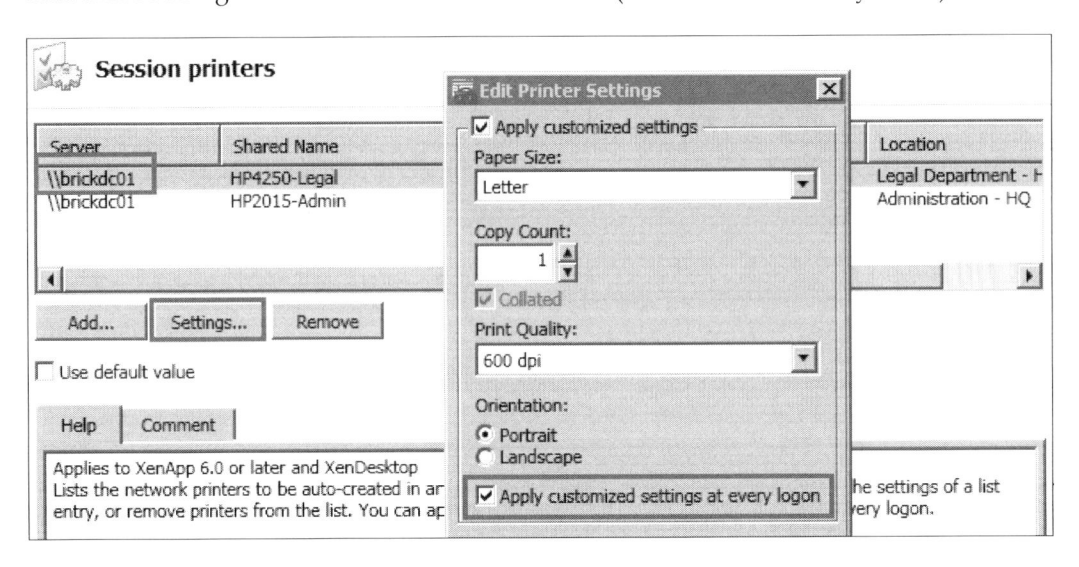

After clicking on the **OK** button, the settings value in the list of printers on the session printers page changes to **Modified**.

Server local printers

Server local printers are printers installed locally on the XenApp server. Server local printers are shared printers that are connected to a XenApp server.

This option is not popular in medium to large enterprise environments because they require managing printers and drivers on XenApp servers and printing jobs can cause an overhead on the servers, but it is a good option for small XenApp environments without print servers.

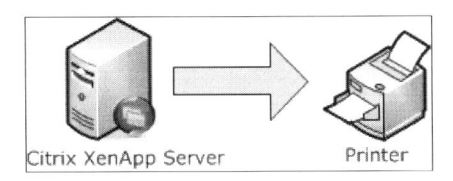

> To use a locally attached printer as a server local printer in a XenApp farm, the printer must be shared; otherwise XenApp does not recognize it.

Configuring server local printers

To let our users print from a printer installed locally on the XenApp server, William needs to share it as follows:

On the server where the printer is physically connected, in **Control Panel | Hardware | Devices and Printers**, he right-clicks on the printer he wants to share.

He chooses **Printer Properties**.

In the **Sharing** tab, he enables these two checkboxes:

- **Share this printer**
- **Render print jobs on client computers**

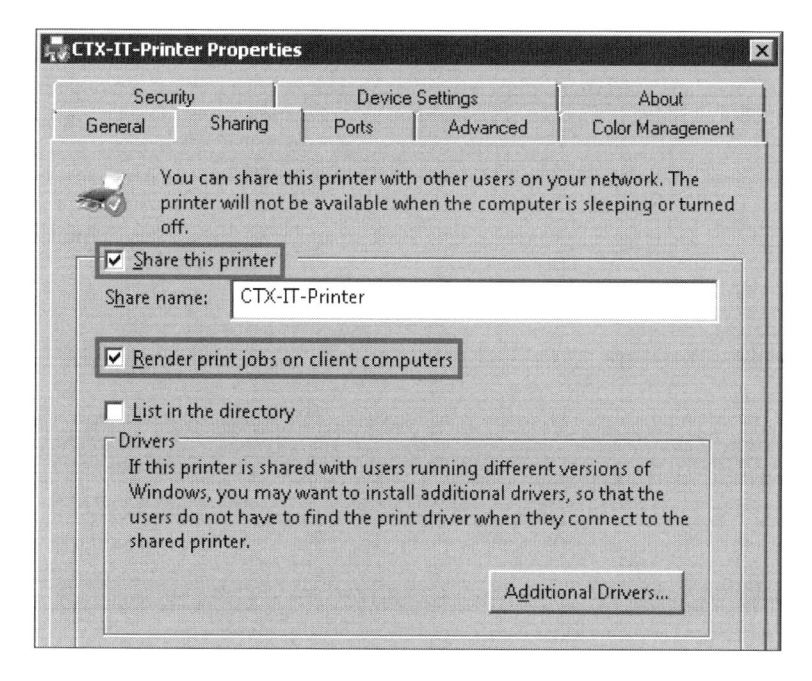

Sharing the printer allows creation of the printer when a session on that XenApp server is launched.

Managing printer drivers

As users in a XenApp environment do not have a persistent workspace, drivers cannot be stored on the client machine. To print, XenApp must find the correct driver on the client machine or the XenApp server.

The printer driver on the XenApp server and the driver used by the client machine must match exactly. If not, printing fails.

Missing drivers can prevent users from printing successfully. If a non-native or manufacturer printer driver has multiple or inconsistent names across our XenApp farm, a session might not be able to find the right driver and a user's job may fail to print.

Printing to a client printer with a defective driver can cause a fatal system error on a server. Number one cause of issues and blue screens on XenApp servers is printer drivers.

XenApp servers do not download any drivers, including printer drivers, from the print server. We need to install the correct device-specific printer driver for the XenApp server's operating system, for both version and architecture (32- or 64-bit).

Advise: Test your printer drivers and do not install any non-native or manufacturer printer driver if you don't need it. If a defective driver is replicated throughout a XenApp farm, it is a difficult and time consuming task to remove it from every XenApp server and always check the printer manufacturer's websites before any printer purchase.

> Download `CtxCertifyPrinters` from `http://ctxadmtools.musumeci.com.ar`. This FREE tool will scan your servers or Citrix Farm for non-native or manufacturer drivers and export the results to an Excel file.
>
> Also, we can use Citrix StressPrinters tool to test our printer drivers. The tool is available at `http://support.citrix.com/article/CTX109374`.

Controlling printer driver automatic installation

Managing printer drivers is critical for a successful printing experience. When XenApp autocreates printers, it determines if their corresponding drivers are missing. By default, XenApp installs any missing printer drivers from the Windows native printer driver set. If a problematic printer driver is installed automatically, it can cause issues.

We can either prevent printer drivers from being installed automatically, or, if we want to have them installed automatically, we can control what drivers are installed on XenApp servers by specifying the drivers on a compatibility list.

When users log on:

- The XenApp server checks the client machine printer driver compatibility list before it sets up the client printers
- If a printer driver is on the list of drivers that are not allowed, XenApp does not set up the printer unless the **Universal Printing** feature is enabled
- When the compatibility list prevents setup of a client printer, XenApp writes a message in the server's Event log

To prevent drivers from being installed automatically, William can configure the Citrix User policy setting **Automatic Installation of in-box printer drivers**, available at **Printing | Drivers**.

The **Enabled** option allows Windows native drivers to automatically install on the XenApp server. This is the default option. Disabling this setting prevents the automatic installation of printer drivers (recommended option):

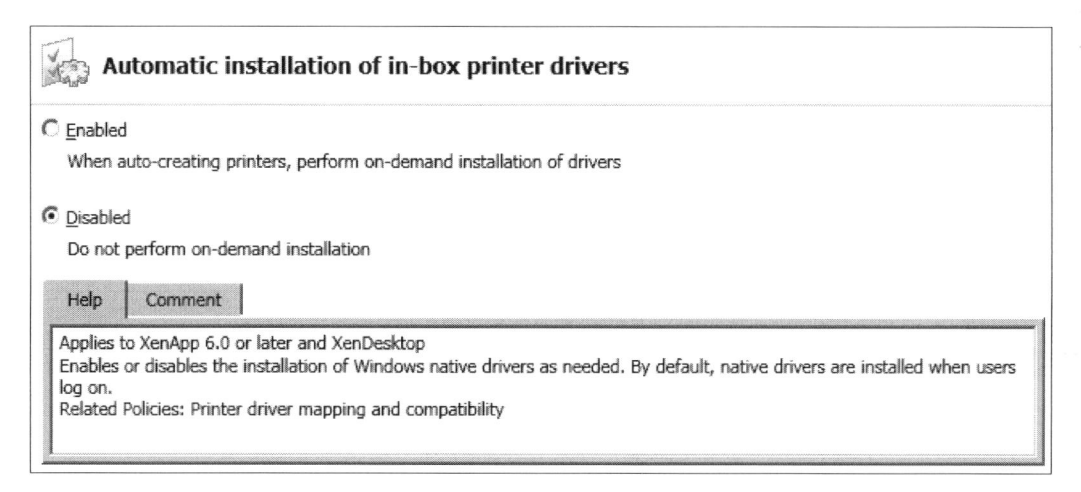

```
Automatic installation of in-box printer drivers

○ Enabled
   When auto-creating printers, perform on-demand installation of drivers

● Disabled
   Do not perform on-demand installation

Help    Comment
Applies to XenApp 6.0 or later and XenDesktop
Enables or disables the installation of Windows native drivers as needed. By default, native drivers are installed when users log on.
Related Policies: Printer driver mapping and compatibility
```

Modifying the printer driver compatibility list

William can configure the Citrix policy setting **Printing | Drivers | Printer driver mapping and compatibility** to specify whether printers can be created with specific drivers or not, or with universal printer drivers. He can use this setting to add driver mapping, edit an existing mapping, remove a mapping, or change the order of driver entries in the list.

- **Allow** option enables the use of printer driver
- **Do not create** option blocks the printer driver

- **Create with universal driver only** option forces the printer to use the universal driver
- **Replace with** option allows us to use a different print driver

Here, William will force printers using the HP LaserJet 1320 (driver famous for causing a lot of print issues on XenApp) to use the universal driver:

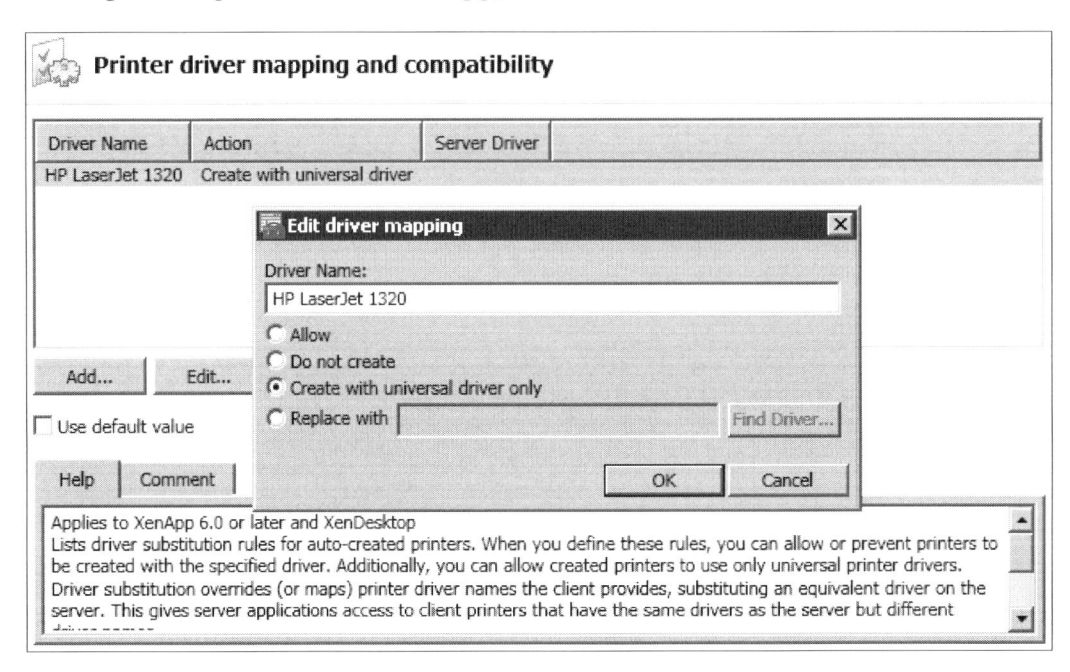

If client machines and XenApp servers use the same drivers but with a different name, for example, "HP LaserJet P2055" on client machines and "HP LaserJet P2055DN" on XenApp, XenApp may not recognize the drivers causing printer autocreation failures.

William can resolve this issue by mapping the printer driver name on the client machine to a similar driver on the XenApp server.

Here William will map the **HP LaserJet 4250 PCL5** driver on client machines to **HP LaserJet 4250 PCL6** on XenApp servers. Unlike previous versions of Windows, Microsoft provides only a certified PCL6 driver for the popular HP LaserJet 4250 printer on Windows Server 2008 R2:

Chapter 9

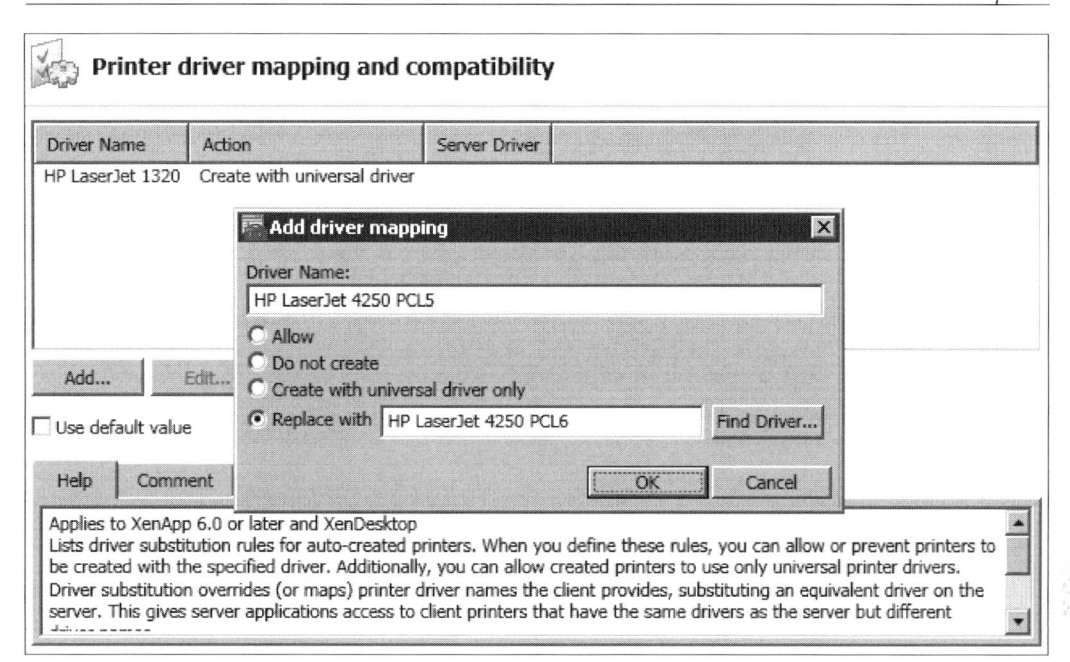

![Screenshot of Printer driver mapping and compatibility dialog with Add driver mapping subdialog showing Driver Name "HP LaserJet 4250 PCL5", options Allow, Do not create, Create with universal driver only, Replace with "HP LaserJet 4250 PCL6"]

> We can use wildcards in print driver mapping. For example, William can force all HP printers to use a specific driver by specifying HP* in the driver name.

Replicating print drivers in XenApp

XenApp 5 and previous versions allow print driver replication in the Citrix Management Console. However, in XenApp 6.5 (and 6.0), this feature has been replaced by PowerShell commands and other methods in the Windows operating system.

In XenApp, we replicate print drivers with the following PowerShell commands:

- `Get-XAPrinterDriver`: Retrieves farm printer drivers
- `Start-XAPrinterDriverReplication`: Replicates printer drivers
- `Update-XAPrinterDriver`: Updates printer driver information

> More information about using PowerShell commands to replicate printer drivers is available at CTX126125 at http://support.citrix.com/article/CTX126125.

[251]

In Windows Server 2008 R2, the printer driver replication can be managed using **Print Management Administrative Tool** (`printmanagement.msc`) or `PrintBrmUI.EXE` to export and import print drivers and printing settings.

Optionally, `PrintBrm.EXE` can also be used to create scripts to export and import print drivers.

`PrintBrm.EXE` is located in the `%systemroot%\System32\Spool\Tools` folder. Installing the **Print Management Console** is required to access the console or `PrintBrm` tools. To install the feature, open **Server Manager** | **Add Features** | **Remote Server Administration Tools** | **Role Administration Tools** | **Print and Document Services Tools**.

Using the Citrix Universal Printer

The Citrix Universal Printer is a generic printer created at the beginning of sessions that can be used with almost any printer. Using a single print driver simplifies the deployment of a XenApp farm.

The Citrix Universal Printer name doesn't change when users reconnect; this is good because changing printer names can cause issues on some applications.

When the Citrix Universal Printer is enabled, an extra printer is created in each session with the name Citrix UNIVERSAL Printer in the session #number of session, where #number of session is ID of the client connected.

Using Citrix Universal printers provides two benefits:

- Reduce print management complexity
- Increase the speed of starting a session

Often, Citrix Universal printing can't work in our environment, for example:

- A few printer models can't work properly as they are incompatible with the Citrix Universal driver
- Some users require access to advanced printer options which are not available; for example, duplexing
- The Citrix Universal Printer and printer driver solution require the Citrix Receiver (formerly known as Citrix Online Plug-in) or the Citrix Offline Plug-in
- If the users are using the Citrix Offline Plug-in and streaming applications to the client machine, or not connecting through the ICA channel, the Citrix Universal Printer doesn't work in this scenario

When we talk about the Citrix Universal Printer, we find that XenApp provides:

- **Citrix Universal Printer**: This is the generic printer object that replaces the printers during users' sessions. This printer can be used with almost any printer model.
- **Citrix Universal Printer Drivers**: These Windows-native Printer drivers are generic drivers that work with almost any printer and even with non-Windows clients. Citrix-created Universal printer drivers consist of the Citrix XPS Universal Printer driver and the EMF-based Citrix Universal Printer Driver. We will talk about this later.

We can use the Citrix Universal Printer Driver in the following ways:

- Auto-Created Citrix Universal Printer with a Citrix Universal Printer Driver: When the session starts, just one Citrix Universal Printer is auto-created. The session uses the Citrix Universal Printer Driver to communicate with the driver on the client machine and the print job is processed locally.
- Auto-Created Device Printers, Auto-Created Citrix Universal Printer with a Citrix Universal Printer Driver: When the session starts, both the Citrix Universal Printer and local printers are auto-created using the Citrix Universal Printer Driver.
- Auto-Created Device Printer with Citrix Universal Printer Driver: Local printers are auto-created using the Citrix Universal printer driver and the print job is processed locally.

The Citrix Universal Printer Driver provides a lot of benefits, but we need to *test* it with each printer in our environment. Sometimes it might be better to use a device-specific driver or another Universal Printer solution like HP Universal Printer Driver, because the driver might be able to optimize print jobs for the printer or create smaller print jobs.

> Citrix Universal Printer is available in the Presentation Server 4.0 to XenApp 6.5 Supported clients including: Citrix Presentation Server Client, Version 9.x or 10.x, Citrix XenApp Plug-in 11.x or later, Citrix Online Plug-in 12.x or later, Citrix XenApp Plug-in for Streamed Apps, Citrix Offline Plug-in and Citrix Receiver.

Now we will walk William through all settings used to configure the Universal Printing using the **Printing | Universal Printing** and **Printing | Drivers** policy settings.

XenApp 6.0 RTM (Release To Manufacturer, the original version of XenApp 6.0), included four Universal Printing policies.

By the end of October 2010, Citrix released the XenApp Printing Optimization Pack for XenApp 6.0, designed to improve printing speed, reduce printing bandwidth, and more. This pack is included by default on XenApp 6.5 and includes four more Universal Printing policies.

> If we are using XenApp 6.0 servers and we need to install XenApp Printing Optimization Pack for XenApp 6.0, we need to download the package from the Citrix Web site.
>
> After we download and decompress the file `XA6PrintPack.zip`, we will find three files inside it:
>
> `XA600W2K8R2X64010.msp`: This file installs the XenApp Printing Optimization Pack on the XenApp server
>
> `XenAppGPMX64.msi` and `XenAppGPMX86.msi`: This is an updated version of the Citrix XenApp Group Policy Management Experience for each platform (64-bit and 32-bit)

Universal Printing includes multiple rules:

- **Auto-create generic universal printer**: This rule enables or disables the auto-creation of the Citrix Universal Printer. By default, generic universal printers are not auto-created. This policy is located at **Printing | Client Printers** in XenApp 6.5 and under **Printing | Universal Printing** in XenApp 6.0.

- **Universal driver preference** (called **Universal driver priority** in XenApp 6.0): This rule specifies the order in which XenApp tries to use universal printer drivers, starting with the first entry in the list. He can add, edit, or remove drivers and change the order of the drivers in the list. This policy is located at **Printing | Drivers** in XenApp 6.5 and under **Printing | Universal Printing** in XenApp 6.0.

- **Universal print driver usage** (called **Universal printing** in XenApp 6.0): This rule specifies when to use universal printing. This policy is located at **Printing | Drivers** in XenApp 6.5 and under **Printing | Universal Printing** in XenApp 6.0.

- **Universal printing preview preference**: This rule specifies whether to use the print preview function for auto-created or generic universal printers. This policy is located under **Printing | Universal Printing** in both XenApp 6.5 and XenApp 6.0.

- **Universal printing EMF processing mode**: This policy allows us to send the EMF spool file directly into the spooler on the client machine or reprocess the EMF records on the client machine. This policy is located under **Printing | Universal Printing** in both XenApp 6.5 and XenApp 6.0.

- **Universal printing image compression limit**: This policy is located under **Printing | Universal Printing** in both XenApp 6.5 and XenApp 6.0.
- **Universal printing optimization defaults**: This policy is located under **Printing | Universal Printing** in both XenApp 6.5 and XenApp 6.0.
- **Universal printing print quality limit**: This policy is located under **Printing | Universal Printing** in both XenApp 6.5 and XenApp 6.0.

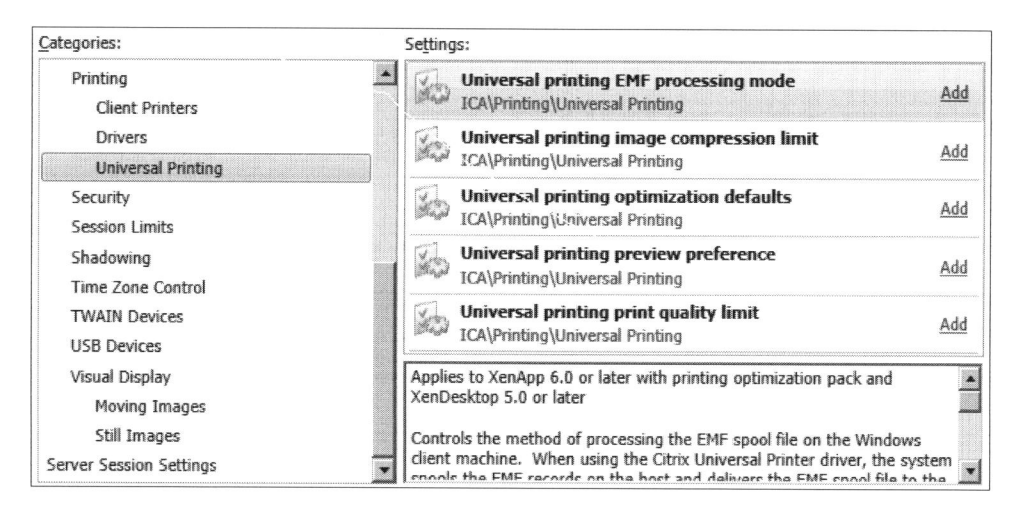

Setting up an auto-create generic universal printer

By default, Universal Printers are not auto-created. William can use this setting to enable or disable auto-creation of the Citrix Universal Printer.

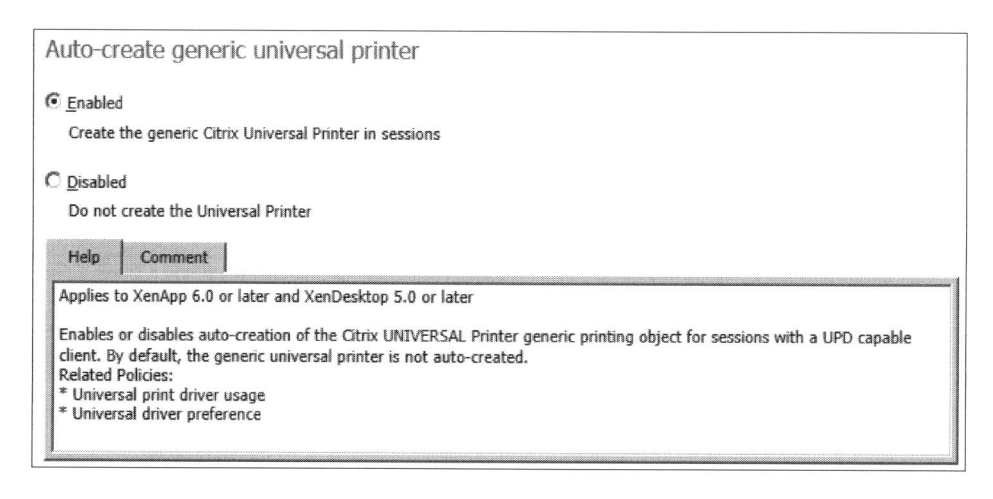

Setting up universal driver preference

This policy is called universal driver priority in XenApp 6.0. There are several different Universal Print Drivers, but the two more popular versions are:

- Citrix Universal Printer driver (EMF-based)
- Citrix XPS (XML Paper Specification) Universal Printer Driver

Now William will change the order in which UPD drivers are used, assigning XPS as a preferred option. He needs to modify the Citrix policy setting by going to **Printing | Drivers | Universal driver preference** (**Printing | Universal Printer | Universal driver priority** on XenApp 6.0) and move XPS to the top of the list.

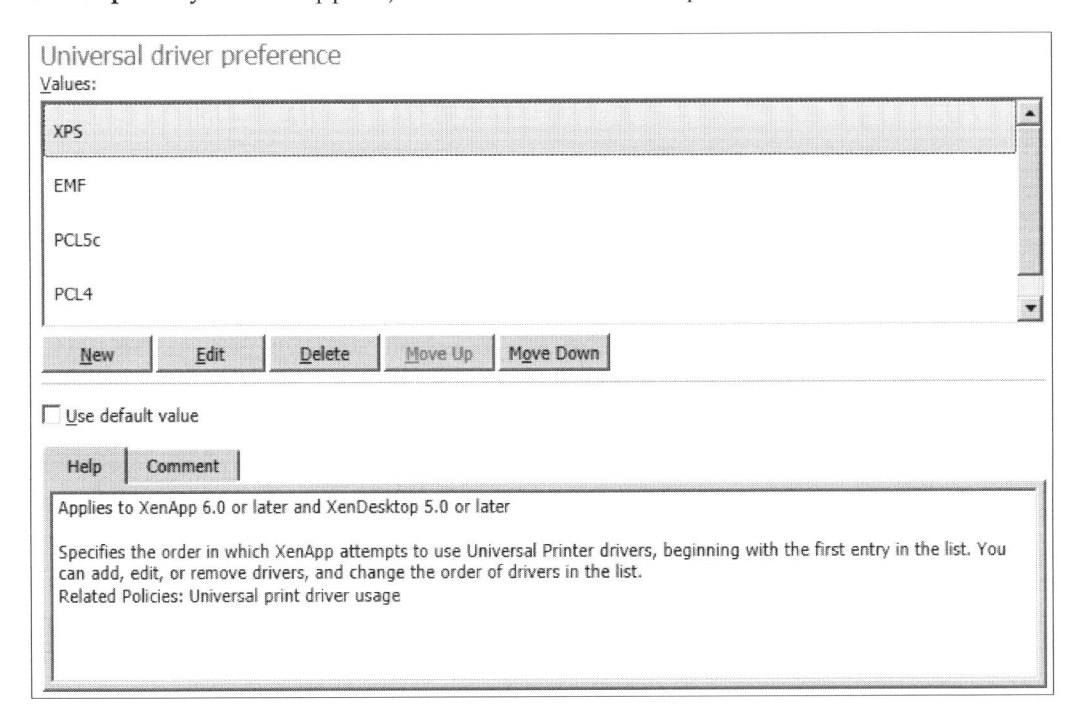

There are several versions of the Citrix Universal Print Driver:

- EMF (Enhanced Metafile Format): EMF is the default and preferred option, because it provides several benefits including the reduction of the size of some print jobs, faster printing, reduction of load on the server, and printing delays on high latency connections
- XML Paper Specification: XML Paper Specification (XPS) is a platform-independent printing language and is a new feature in Windows server 2008

- **PCL5c**: This printer command language is based on the HP Color LaserJet 4500 PCL 5 driver
- **PCL4**: This printer command language is based on the HP LaserJet Series II driver
- **PS (PostScript)**: PS is based on the HP Color LaserJet 4500 PS driver

Here we can see the Citrix Universal Printer Drivers listed in the Print Management MMC snap-in:

- **Citrix Universal Printer**, which is the EMF driver
- **Citrix XPS Universal Printer**
- **HP Color LaserJet 2800 PS** (Citrix PS Universal Printer Driver)

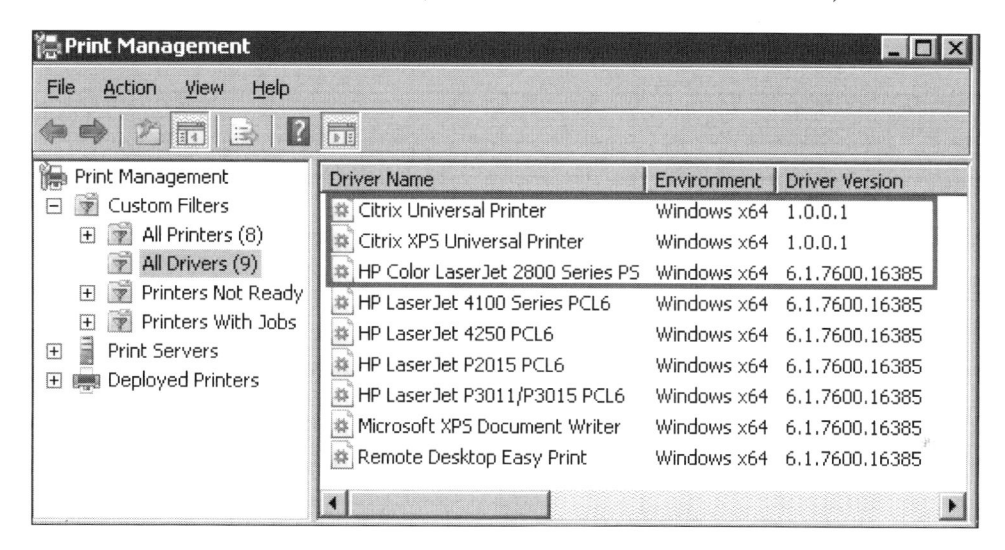

Configuring the Universal printer driver usage on sessions

The **Universal printer driver usage** (called **Universal Printing** in XenApp 6.0) is located at **Printing | Drivers** in XenApp 6.5 and under **Printing | Universal Printing** in XenApp 6.0. We can configure the Universal printing Citrix policy setting by choosing one of the following:

- **Use only printer model specific drivers**: Client printer uses only the native drivers that are auto-created at logon. The client printer cannot be auto-created, if the native driver of the printer is unavailable on the XenApp server.

- **Use universal printing only**: Client printer uses the Universal Printer Driver only.
- **Use universal printing only if requested driver is unavailable**: The client printer uses native drivers if they are available. If they are not available in the XenApp server, the client printer uses the universal driver, based on Universal driver priority policy setting.
- **Use printer model specific drivers only if universal printing is unavailable**: The client printer uses the Universal Printer Driver. If the driver is not available in the XenApp server, the client printer is created with the native printer driver.

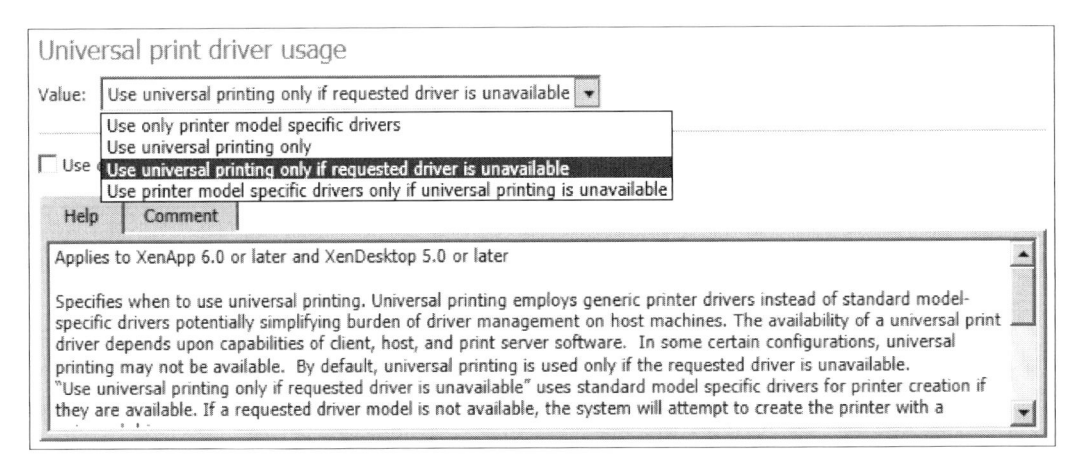

> Configuring only a universal printer driver will not improve session start time (printers on the client device are still enumerated and auto-created at the beginning of sessions), but configuring a universal printer driver does improve printer driver performance.

Setting up universal printing preview preference

This setting allows William to enable or disable the print preview function for the auto created and/or generic universal printers. This option is disabled by default.

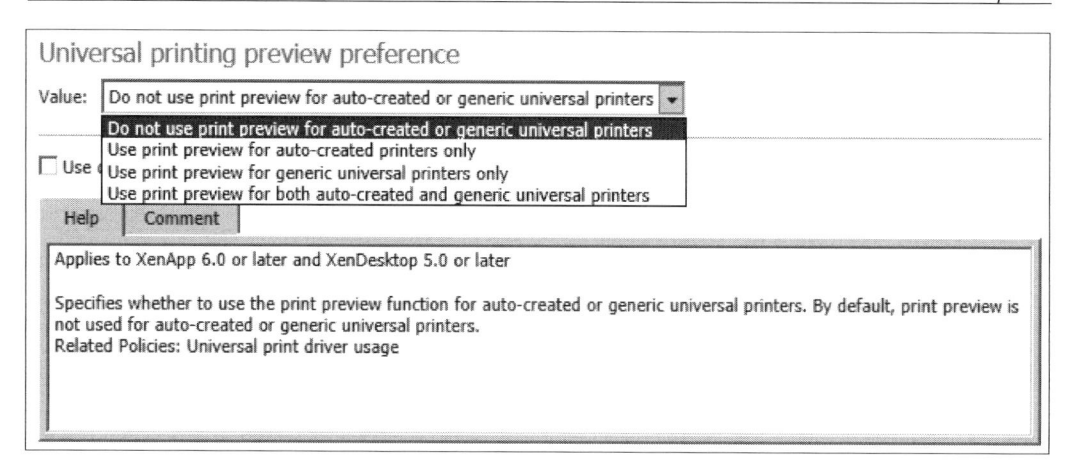

Universal printing EMF processing mode

This policy allows us to send the EMF spool file directly into the spooler on the client machine (default option) or reprocess the EMF records on the client machine. By default, EMF records are spooled directly to the printer.

Reprocessing EMF records on the client machine allows some printer drivers to prompt users for additional information when generating printed output.

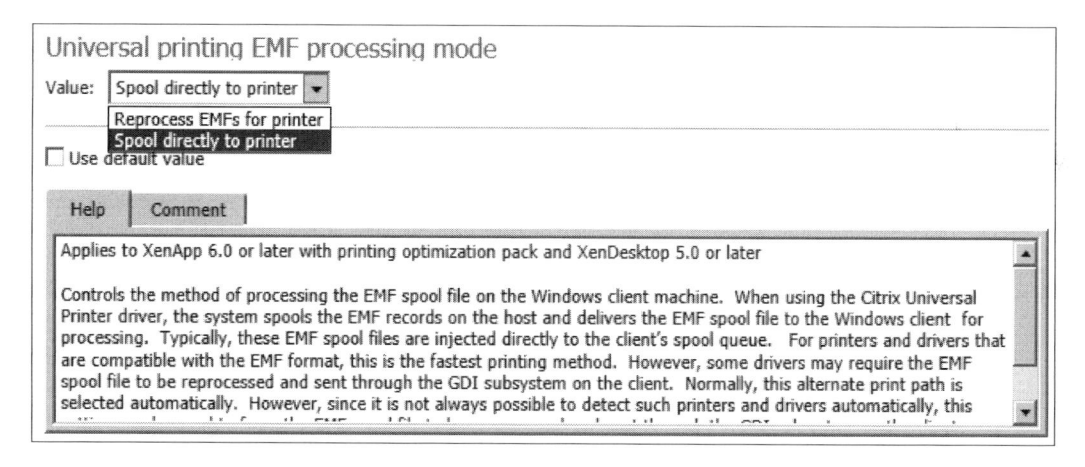

Universal printing image compression limit

This policy allows us to set the maximum quality and the minimum compression level available for images printed with the Universal Printer Driver. By default, the image compression limit is set to **Best quality (lossless compression)**.

If we select the **No compression** option, compression is disabled for EMF printing only; this option doesn't apply for XPS printing.

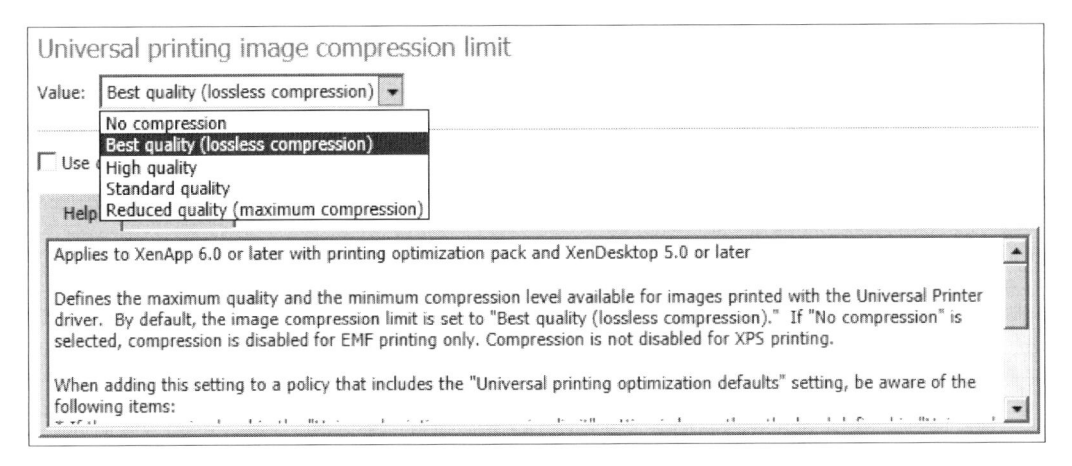

Universal printing optimization defaults

This rule specifies the default settings for the Universal Printer when it is created for a session, including the following options:

- **Desired image quality**: Sets the level of image compression. By default, the **Standard quality** option is selected.
- **Enable heavyweight compression**: This option enables or disables (default option) reducing bandwidth beyond the **Desired image quality** compression level without losing image quality.
- **Allow caching of embedded images**: This option allows (default option) or prevents embedded images to be cached.
- **Allow caching of embedded fonts**: This option allows (default option) or prevents embedded fonts to be cached.
- **Allow non-administrators to modify these settings**: This option allows or prevents (default option) standard users from modifying any of these options through the printer driver's advanced print settings.

Please note that all these options are supported for EMF printing; only the **Desired image quality** option is supported for XPS printing.

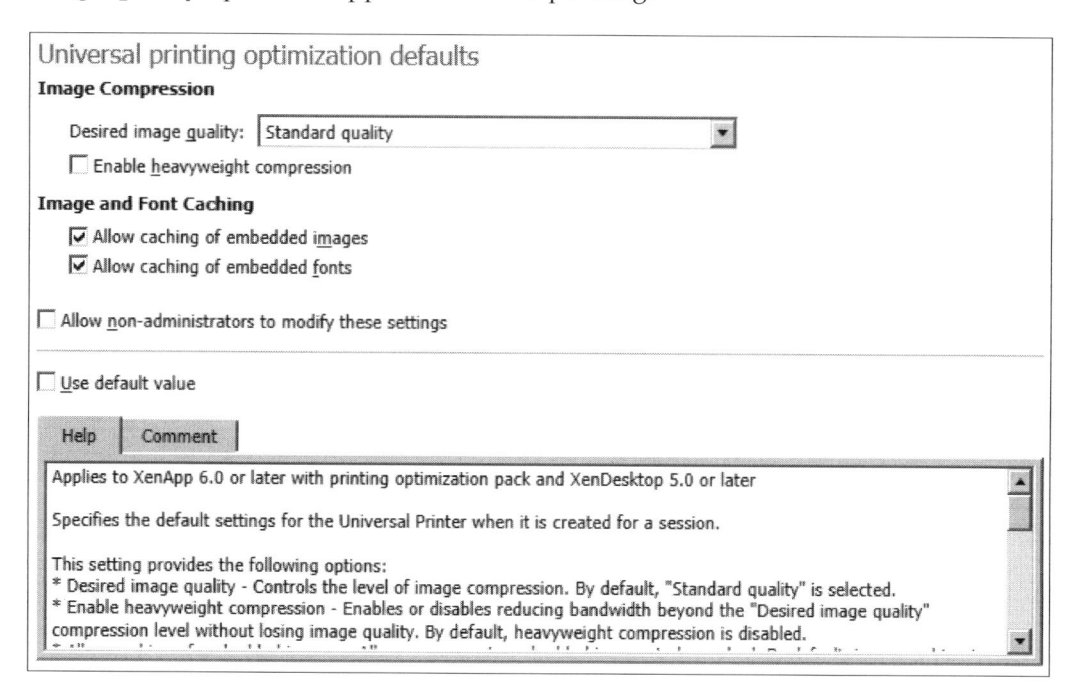

```
Universal printing optimization defaults
Image Compression
    Desired image quality:  [Standard quality         ▼]
        ☐ Enable heavyweight compression
Image and Font Caching
    ☑ Allow caching of embedded images
    ☑ Allow caching of embedded fonts

☐ Allow non-administrators to modify these settings

☐ Use default value

[ Help ][ Comment ]
Applies to XenApp 6.0 or later with printing optimization pack and XenDesktop 5.0 or later

Specifies the default settings for the Universal Printer when it is created for a session.

This setting provides the following options:
* Desired image quality - Controls the level of image compression. By default, "Standard quality" is selected.
* Enable heavyweight compression - Enables or disables reducing bandwidth beyond the "Desired image quality" compression level without losing image quality. By default, heavyweight compression is disabled.
```

Universal printing print quality limit

This setting sets the maximum DPI (dots per inch) available for generating printed output in the session. By default, no limit is specified.

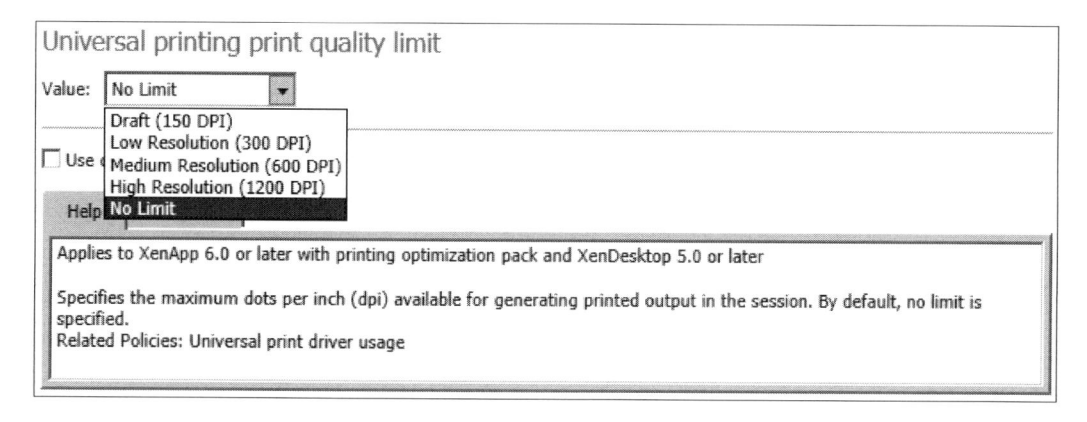

```
Universal printing print quality limit
Value:  [No Limit                ▼]
         Draft (150 DPI)
         Low Resolution (300 DPI)
☐ Use   Medium Resolution (600 DPI)
         High Resolution (1200 DPI)
 Help   No Limit
Applies to XenApp 6.0 or later with printing optimization pack and XenDesktop 5.0 or later

Specifies the maximum dots per inch (dpi) available for generating printed output in the session. By default, no limit is specified.
Related Policies: Universal print driver usage
```

Changing the default settings on the Universal Printer

We can change the default settings for the Citrix Universal Printer, including settings for paper size, paper width, print quality, color, duplex, and the number of copies. We can override the default settings of the Citrix Universal Printer and modify these settings manually using the following registry key:

HKEY_LOCAL_MACHINE\SOFTWARE\Citrix\Print\UPDDevmode

More information on the default settings is available at http://support.citrix.com/article/CTX113148.

Implementing Printers

Another important concept on XenApp printer deployment is Printer Provisioning. This is the process by which XenApp makes printers available in a session. We can find two types of printer provisioning:

- **Static**: When we connect to a server's local printer in a session, printers are provisioned once and always created in the sessions with the same properties.
- **Dynamic**: When our users start a session, printers are created dynamically. Two of the most common methods of dynamic printer provisioning are Auto-creation, where printers are created automatically based on Citrix policies and User Provisioning, where users self-provision their printers.

As static printer provisioning is pretty easy to understand, we are going to talk about dynamic provisioning.

Auto-creation

The auto-creation of printer policy allows us to configure whether printers are automatically created within a user session or not, and allows us to configure which types of printers are automatically created.

By default, XenApp makes printers available in sessions by creating all printers configured on the client machine automatically, including locally attached and network printers. When the user closes the session, all printers for that session are deleted.

When the user logs in, the auto-creation feature creates a list of printers, their print drivers will be installed, and all printers in this list will be available.

XenApp can auto-create redirects to client printers in two ways:

- By creating a one-to-one match with printers on the client machine
- By creating one Citrix Universal Printer which represents all printers on the client machine

In several environments, especially medium and large ones, it is a common (and good) practice to auto-create only the default printer. Auto-creating a smaller number of printers creates less overhead on the XenApp server and reduces CPU utilization.

However, in small environments or locations where users need to print to several local printers, we may want to leave the default auto-creation setting so that all printers are created on logon.

Auto-creating client machine printers

At the start of a session, XenApp auto-creates all printers on the client machine by default. We can manage what types of printers are provisioned to users or prevent auto-creation entirely using the Auto-create client printers policy (explained in the following section).

When configuring policies for printer auto-creation, we need to check if:

- User accounts are not shared
- Users are not members of local power user or administrators group on the client machine
- Microsoft native or fully tested drivers only are used
- Users have write access on the XenApp server to the folder `%systemroot%\system32\spool`

Auto-creating network printers

By default, any network printer on the client machine is created automatically at the beginning of a session.

The preferred method to create network printers is using the session printers on Citrix policies, rather than auto-create all the network printers available in the client machine.

Session printers are easy to manage and apply to several users using Citrix policies. For example, they are very useful if we want to assign printers to users located on the same floor of one building or in a branch office using the IP address of client machines.

Configuring printer auto-creation settings

Now William will use the **Auto-create client printers** policy to configure the way printers are created automatically at the beginning of sessions. By default, XenApp creates all printers on the client machine.

To change the printer auto-creation policy, William needs to configure the **Printing | Client Printers | Auto-Create Client Printers** policy, using one of the following settings:

- **Do not auto-create client printers**: Printers in the client machine are not mapped
- **Auto-create the client's default printer only**: Only the client machine's default printer is auto-created in the session
- **Auto-create local (non-network) client printers only**: Only locally attached (non-network) printers are auto-created in the session
- **Auto-create all client printers**: Both local and network printers connected to the client machine are auto-created in the session

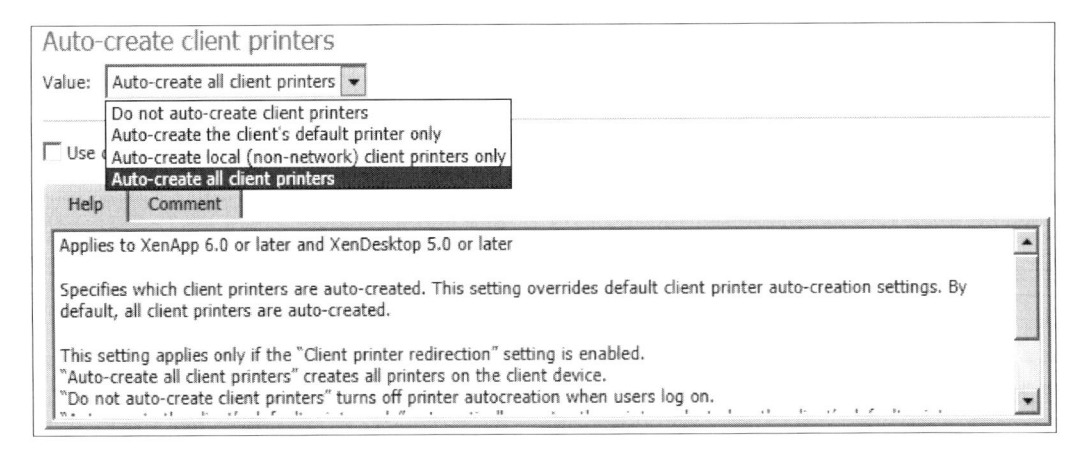

Configuring legacy client printer support

The **Client printer names** policy enables the use of legacy client printer names. This setting allows us to preserve backward compatibility for users or groups using Citrix MetaFrame 3.0 or earlier.

We need to use the setting **Legacy printer names** option from the **Printing | Client Printers | Client Printer Names** policy to auto-create client printers with legacy printer names and Standard printer names to use the default name based on Terminal Server.

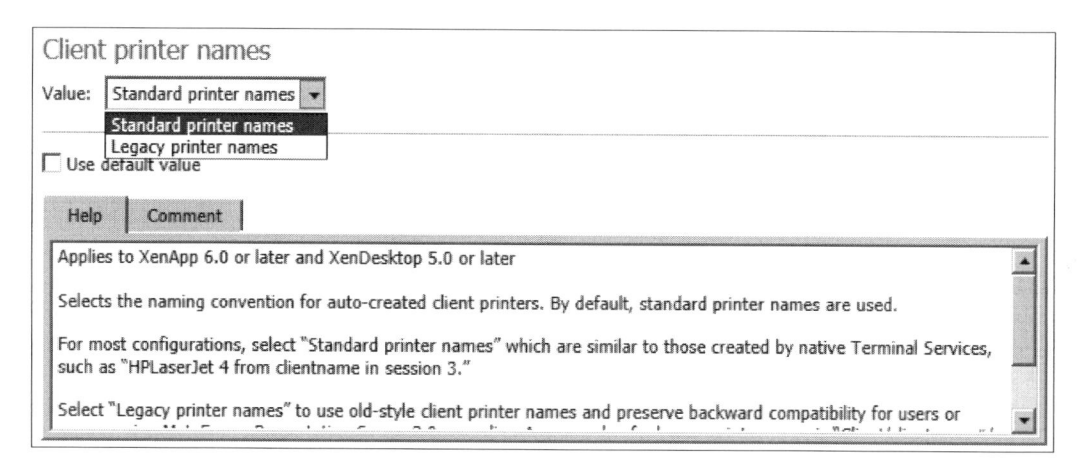

```
Client printer names
Value:  Standard printer names ▼
        Standard printer names
        Legacy printer names
☐ Use default value

  Help    Comment
Applies to XenApp 6.0 or later and XenDesktop 5.0 or later

Selects the naming convention for auto-created client printers. By default, standard printer names are used.

For most configurations, select "Standard printer names" which are similar to those created by native Terminal Services, such as "HPLaserJet 4 from clientname in session 3."

Select "Legacy printer names" to use old-style client printer names and preserve backward compatibility for users or
```

User provisioning

We can also allow users to add printers to their sessions on their own. Users can map client printers that are not auto-created by a policy manually in a user session through the **Windows Add Printer** wizard on the server (in their sessions). If users have thin clients or they don't have permissions in their client devices machines, they can self-provision printers by running the ICA Client Printer Configuration tool (PrintCfg.exe).

We need to publish PrintCfg.exe or the Add Printer wizard on our farm to allow users to self-provision their own printers or after a user adds a printer using either of these methods, XenApp retains the printer information for future sessions from that client machine. Client printers created using this process are called retained printers.

Printing in XenApp Environments

Publishing the Windows Add Printer wizard

Now, we help William to publish the **Add Printer** wizard.

He creates the following folder at the root level of one of the XenApp server's drives, `C:\Printers.{2227A280-3AEA-1069-A2DE-08002B30309D}`, where C represents a drive on the XenApp server; then when he presses *Enter*, the folder icon changes to a printer icon.

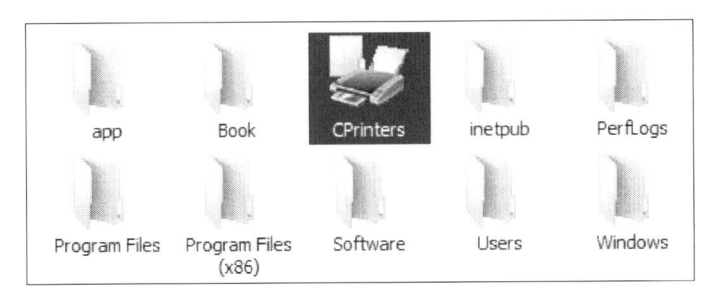

Then he needs to create a published application with the following properties in the command line and the path where `explorer.exe` is located as a working directory:

`C:\windows\explorer.exe C:\Printers.{2227A280-3AEA-1069-A2DE-08002B30309D}`

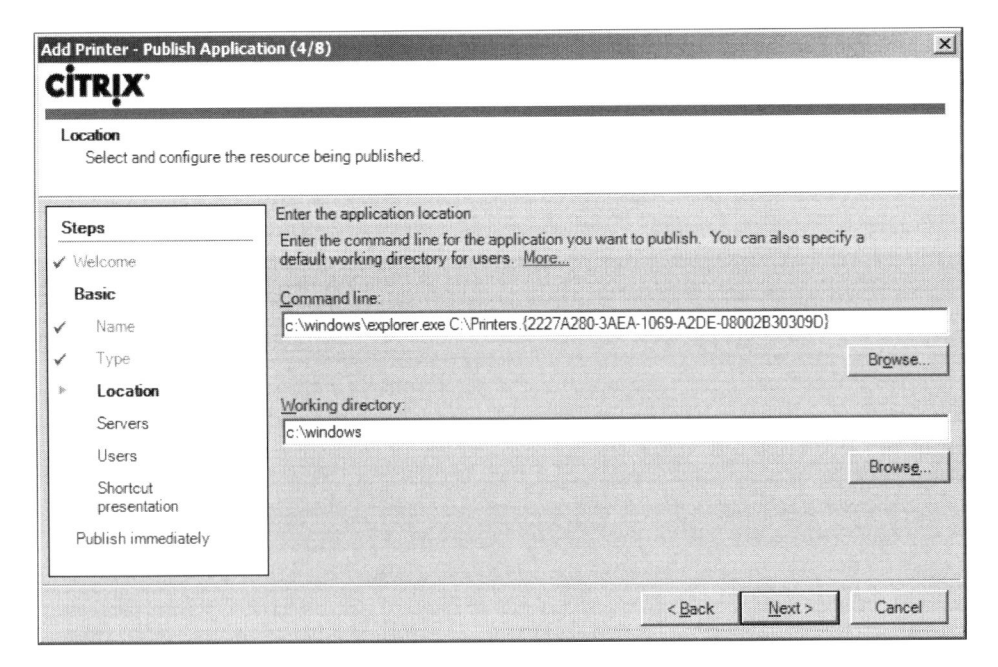

Publishing the ICA Client Printer Configuration tool

To publish the ICA Client Printer Configuration tool, William needs to follow the instructions for publishing an application using the **Publish Application** wizard (explained in *Chapter 6, Application Publishing*).

On the **Location** page, he needs to enter the path for the **ICA Client Printer Configuration tool** (printcfg.exe) on the XenApp server.

By default, the tool is located in C:\Program Files (x86)\Citrix\system32\printcfg.exe.

Storing users' printer properties

After publishing any of the tools, William wants to keep the user printer's settings. To retain the user printer properties, he needs to configure the **Printing | Client Printers | Printer Properties Retention** policy by choosing from the following settings:

- **Retained in user profile only**: This option reduces logon time and network traffic, but only works if a Remote Desktop Services roaming profile is used. Recommended if the users use legacy Citrix Plug-ins like MetaFrame Presentation Server Client 8.x, or earlier.
- **Saved on the client device only**: This option stores printer properties only on the client machine. This is the preferred option if the users use Remote Desktop Services mandatory profile or roaming profile.
- **Held in profile only if not saved on client**: This is the default option and allows XenApp to determine the method. It tries to store printer properties on the client machine if available, or if not, in the user profile. This option increases logon time and uses extra bandwidth to check. Usually, this version is used for backward compatibility with prior versions of XenApp.

- **Do not retain printer properties**: Does not retain printer properties.

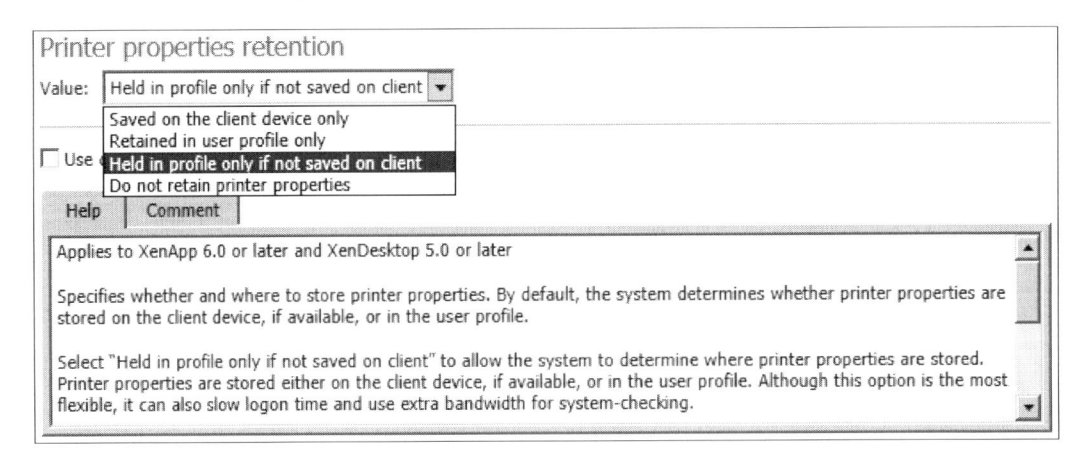

```
Printer properties retention
Value:  Held in profile only if not saved on client ▼
        Saved on the client device only
        Retained in user profile only
  Use   Held in profile only if not saved on client
        Do not retain printer properties
   Help    Comment

Applies to XenApp 6.0 or later and XenDesktop 5.0 or later

Specifies whether and where to store printer properties. By default, the system determines whether printer properties are
stored on the client device, if available, or in the user profile.

Select "Held in profile only if not saved on client" to allow the system to determine where printer properties are stored.
Printer properties are stored either on the client device, if available, or in the user profile. Although this option is the most
flexible, it can also slow logon time and use extra bandwidth for system-checking.
```

As we mentioned earlier, XenApp attempts to store printing settings on the client machine. If the client does not support this operation, XenApp stores printing properties in the user profile for that specific user.

Sessions from non-Windows XenApp Plug-ins or even older Windows XenApp Plug-ins use the user profiles on the server for properties retention.

We can use the **Printer Properties Retention** policy rule to force properties to be saved on either the client machine or on the XenApp server.

If the users have trouble saving printer information, we need to check items in the following list and sometimes reconfigure how XenApp stores user printing preferences:

- **Client version**: Users must be running Citrix Presentation Server Client 9.x and higher to store user-modified printer properties on the client machine. Not all XenApp Plug-ins allow users to store printer properties on a client machine.
- **Type of Windows user profile**: If we are using a mandatory profile and we want to retain the user's printer properties, we must store the properties on the client machine.
- **Type of users**: If we have remote or mobile users using roaming profiles, we need to save the printer properties to the user's profile and not the client machine.

> A mandatory user profile is a special type of preconfigured roaming user profile that we can use to specify settings for users. With mandatory user profiles, a user can modify his or her desktop, but the changes are not saved when the user logs off. The next time the user logs on, the mandatory user profile created by us is downloaded.

If none of these factors apply to us or we don't have any issues, Citrix recommends no change where the printer properties are stored and keeps the default setting, which saves the printer properties on the client machine and is the easiest way to guarantee consistent printing properties.

If we want to keep changes to the printer settings the users make locally outside of a session or offline with locally attached printers, we need to modify the registry key in the client and create and set the `Win32FavorRetainedPrinterSettings` registry key to False. This registry key is located at:

- `HKEY_LOCAL_MACHINE\SOFTWARE\Citrix\ICA Client\Engine\Lockdown Profiles\All Regions\Lockdown\Virtual Channels\Printing`
- `HKEY_CURRENT_USER\Software\Citrix\ICA Client\Engine\Lockdown Profiles\All Regions\Lockdown\Virtual Channels\Printing`

When we create this registry key, the Plug-in gives priority to settings from the printer, rather than retained settings

The client must have the same print driver installed on the client machine and server. If we don't have it, only the same settings are exchanged between the real printer and the virtual printer in the session.

Settings in the session stay synchronized with settings on the printing device. If the user makes a change in the printer inside the session, the Plug-in attempts to write the change back to the printer on the client machine when logging off. If a user makes a change outside a session, the Plug-in will update the printer configuration inside the session.

General locations of printing preferences

When we work in Windows, changes made to printing preferences can be stored on the client machine or in a document. However, in a XenApp environment, settings can be stored in three locations:

- **On the client machine**: Settings are stored on the client machine. Depending on the version of the operating systems, these settings are available in **Control Panel | Device and Printers | Printing Preferences**.

- **Inside a document**: Mostly applications store settings are inside documents and these settings are known as Document Settings. One example is Microsoft Office applications that typically store the printing preferences inside the document. These settings appear by default the next time we print that document.
- **On the XenApp server**: Some settings associated with a specific printer driver are stored on the XenApp server.

As printing preferences can be stored in multiple places, XenApp processes them according to a specific priority.

XenApp searches for settings in this order:

- XenApp checks for retained printer settings. If XenApp detects retained settings, it applies these settings when the user prints.
- If there are no retained printer settings, XenApp searches for any changes to the printer settings for the default printer for the client machine. If XenApp detects any changes to printer settings on the client machine, it applies these settings when the user prints.
- If there are no retained or client printer settings, XenApp applies the default printer settings stored on the XenApp server when the user prints.

Generally, XenApp merges any retained settings and the settings inherited from the client machine with the settings for the default printer driver on the server.

By default, XenApp always applies any printer settings modified by the user during a session, that is, the retained settings, before considering any other settings.

Printing for mobile users

Sometimes we have users moving between different workstations, floors in the building, or even branch offices, and we need to present them to the closest printers.

XenApp provides two features designed for mobile users:

- Smooth Roaming
- Proximity Printing

Smooth Roaming

This feature, also known as Workspace control, lets a user disconnect from one session, move to a different client machine, and reconnect to continue that same session. The printers assigned on the first client machine are replaced on the reconnection with printers appropriate for the second client machine.

Proximity printing

The proximity printing feature is based on the use of two Citrix policies: Session printer and Default printer. We can use the location of the client machine to assign the closer network printer.

Proximity printing requires that we filter the policy using a location setting like:

- Network's IP addresses, if they are related to user locations
- The name of the client machine, if the name relates to the location.

Configuring printers for mobile users

We need to configure the proximity printing solution, if we want to make sure that our users always have access to the closest printer to their client machine. Proximity printing allows users within a specified IP address segment to automatically access network printers within that same IP address segment.

The HQ (headquarters) of Brick Unit Construction is a large building with ten floors. Each floor holds multiple departments. Several users move between offices to have meetings or work on the same projects, so they need access to a closer printer.

William deployed two network printers on each floor, one at each side of the floor.

To configure proximity printing in the Brick Unit building, William needs to:

- Set up the DHCP server to assign IP addresses to each floor of the building.
- He needs to assign a unique designated IP address segment to each floor within the company. For example, he will assign segment 172.16.31.xxx to the first floor, 172.16.32.xxx to the second floor, and so on.
- He needs to provide IP addresses to each network printer within the range of IP addresses for the floor in which they are located. He will reserve the first ten IP addresses for network printers. So, for example, he will assign IP addresses 172.16.31.2 and 172.16.31.3 to network printers on the first floor.

- Then he needs to create a separate Citrix policy for each floor and add the printers in that to the session printers setting.
- Set the default printer setting to **Do not adjust the user's default printer**.
- Filter the policies by Client IP address.

Improving printing performance

By default, XenApp routes jobs to network printers from the XenApp server directly to the print server using the network printing pathway.

Print jobs sent over the network printing pathway are not compressed. When routing printing jobs across a network with limited bandwidth, we can disable the **Direct connection to print servers** policy, so we route jobs through the client machine, and the ICA protocol compresses the jobs.

Also, we can limit the bandwidth used by the client printing to avoid performance issues caused by using multiple virtual channels at the same time (like printing and multimedia applications).

When we limit the data transmission rate for printing, we can make more bandwidth available for video, keystrokes, and mouse data. More available bandwidth can help prevent degradation of the user experience during printing.

> The printer bandwidth limit is always enforced, even when no other channels are in use.

There are two ways we can limit printing bandwidth in client sessions using printer settings in the **Bandwidth** category:

- We can use the Citrix policy bandwidth printer settings in the **Citrix AppCenter Console** to enable and disable the printing bandwidth session limit for the XenApp farm.
- Use individual server settings to limit printing bandwidth in the farm. We can perform this task using `gpedit.msc` locally on each server to configure the Citrix policy Bandwidth printer settings.

Limit printing bandwidth

William can configure one of the following options in the Citrix User policy **ICA | Bandwidth** setting. If he enters values for both settings, the most restrictive setting (with the lower value) is applied.

- **Printer redirection bandwidth limit**: Specifies the bandwidth available for printing in kbps
- **Printer redirection bandwidth limit percent**: Sets the percentage of the overall bandwidth available for printing

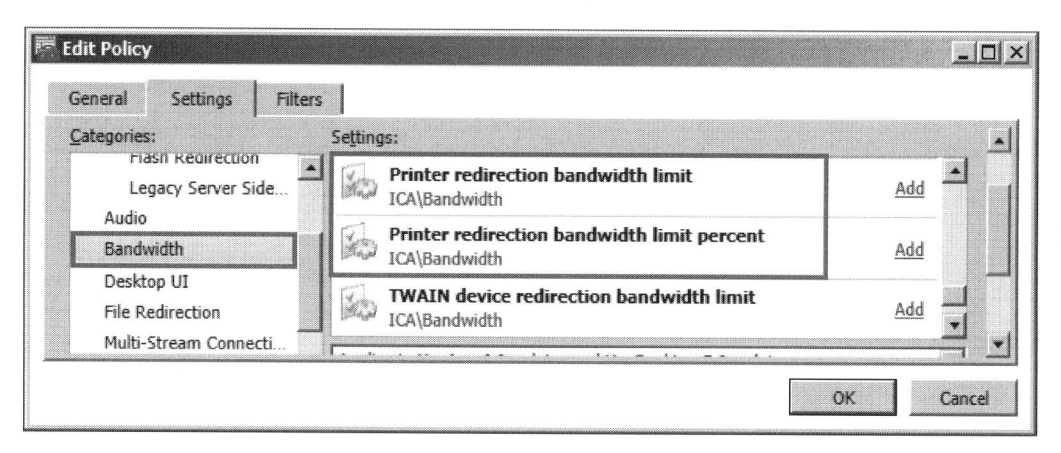

Third-party printing solutions

There are two Citrix partners that provide third-party solutions for printing. They provide a simple printer driver, great performance, fast printing, and more. We can find more info at:

- ThinPrint: www.thinprint.com
- UniPrint: www.uniprint.com

Summary

In this chapter, we learned about printing in XenApp environments, in particular:

- Windows and Citrix XenApp printing concepts
- Assigning network printers to users using Citrix policies
- Managing printer drivers
- Using the Citrix universal printer
- Implementing printers
- Printing for mobile users

In the next chapter, we are going to talk about Multimedia Content on XenApp.

10
Multimedia Content in XenApp

In the last chapter, we learned about printing in XenApp environments, starting with Windows, XenApp printing concepts, and how to use Citrix policies to manage printing. In this chapter, we will discuss how to improve the multimedia experience of users using Citrix HDX technologies. HDX stands for **High Definition eXperience**.

Citrix HDX is a big set of technology that enables better multimedia and peripheral support, and provides improvements in audio quality, enabling us to deliver multimedia and conference applications on XenApp 6.5 and 6.0 farms.

In this chapter we will talk about:

- Description of HDX technologies
- Using HDX 3D technologies to improve image display
- Reduce CPU use by moving processing to GPU
- Using HDX Broadcast Display settings
- Using HDX MediaStream Multimedia Acceleration
- Using Citrix policies to configure multimedia settings (HDX MediaStream)
- Configuring echo cancellation
- Using HDX MediaStream for Flash to optimize Flash content
- Installing HDX Monitor

Description of Citrix HDX technologies

XenApp includes various HDX technologies that allows us to improve user experience and session responsiveness. In this chapter, we are going to help William Empire from Brick Unit Construction to install and configure Citrix HDX technologies on his XenApp farm.

We have two major issues affecting the performance of playback Multimedia applications or content. These two issues are network latency and bandwidth availability.

Using Citrix HDX technologies will help us to deal with these two issues.

Using HDX 3D technologies to improve image display

Citrix provides HDX 3D technologies to improve image display and reduce the CPU load of graphics-intensive applications.

In environments with intensive use of graphics applications, such as image editing or manipulation applications, large images are transferred between XenApp servers and client machines.

This is a common issue at Brick Unit Construction, where large images of building plans or presentations with a lot of graphics are used every day. William wants to enable HDX 3D technologies to reduce bandwidth and improve image display.

XenApp includes Citrix **User** policies to manage image compression and improve image display:

- **Lossy compression**, located under **ICA** | **Visual Display** | **Still Images**
- **Progressive compression**, located under **ICA** | **Visual Display** | **Moving Images**

Both policies are located under **ICA** | **Graphics** | **Image Compression** policy settings in XenApp 6.0.

Using HDX 3D Image Acceleration to reduce bandwidth

The first HDX 3D technology William wants to implement is SpeedScreen Image Acceleration. This technology uses compression to reduce the size of image files that the XenApp server sends to the client machine.

This feature, enabled by default, uses compression to remove redundant data from the files before the transfer to a client machine.

He can configure the **Lossy Compression** policy located under **User | ICA | Visual Display | Still Images**, with one of the following options:

- **High**: Provides low image quality
- **Medium (default option)**: Provides good image quality
- **Low**: Provides high image quality
- **None**: No compression is applied and quality is almost the same as the original file

William can set up multiple policies depending on user membership or application and assign different levels of compression. He needs to choose **None** or **Low** compression for users who need to view images at the original or near the original quality levels.

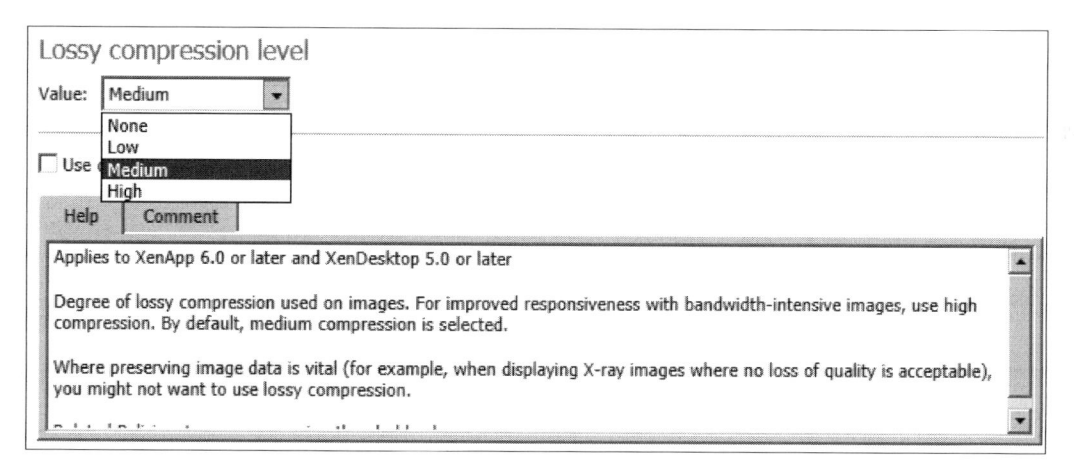

Multimedia Content in XenApp

Another important setting in this policy is the **Lossy Compression Threshold Value**. This setting represents the maximum bandwidth in kilobits per second for a connection to which lossy compression is applied. By default, the threshold value is 2,000 kilobits per second.

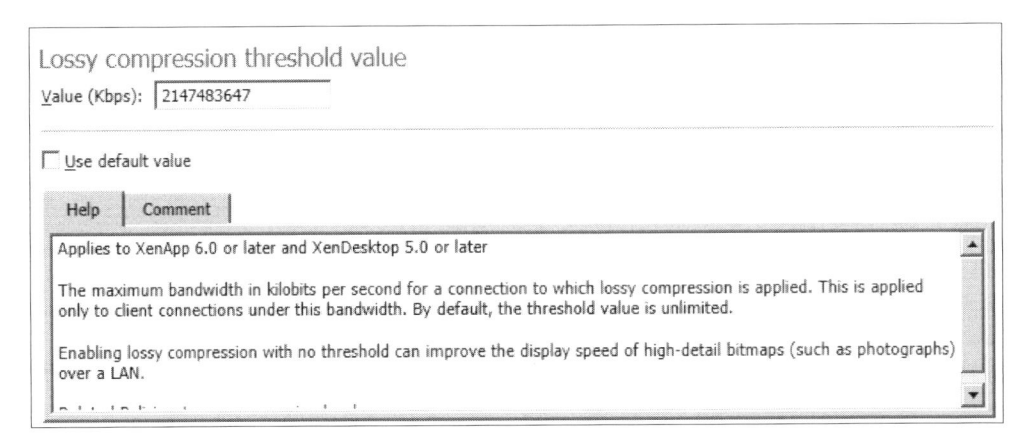

```
Lossy compression threshold value
Value (Kbps): 2147483647

☐ Use default value

[ Help ] [ Comment ]
Applies to XenApp 6.0 or later and XenDesktop 5.0 or later

The maximum bandwidth in kilobits per second for a connection to which lossy compression is applied. This is applied
only to client connections under this bandwidth. By default, the threshold value is unlimited.

Enabling lossy compression with no threshold can improve the display speed of high-detail bitmaps (such as photographs)
over a LAN.
```

The **Heavyweight compression** (called **Progressive heavyweight compression** in XenApp 6.0) uses an advanced (and CPU-intensive) graphical algorithm to reduce bandwidth without losing image quality. By default, this setting is **Disabled**. Please note that this setting is supported on the Citrix Receiver (formerly known as Citrix Online Plug-in), but has no effect on other plug-ins.

```
Heavyweight compression
○ Enabled
    Reduce bandwidth beyond normal progressive compression, without losing image quality, by using a CPU-intensive algorithm

● Disabled
    Do not perform heavy compression

[ Help ] [ Comment ]
Applies to XenApp 6.0 or later and XenDesktop 5.0 or later

Reduces bandwidth further without losing image quality by using a more advanced, but more CPU-intensive graphic
algorithm. If enabled, it applies to all lossy compression settings. By default, heavyweight compression is not used. This
setting is supported on Citrix Receiver but has no effect on other plug-ins.

Related Policies:
* Progressive compression level
```

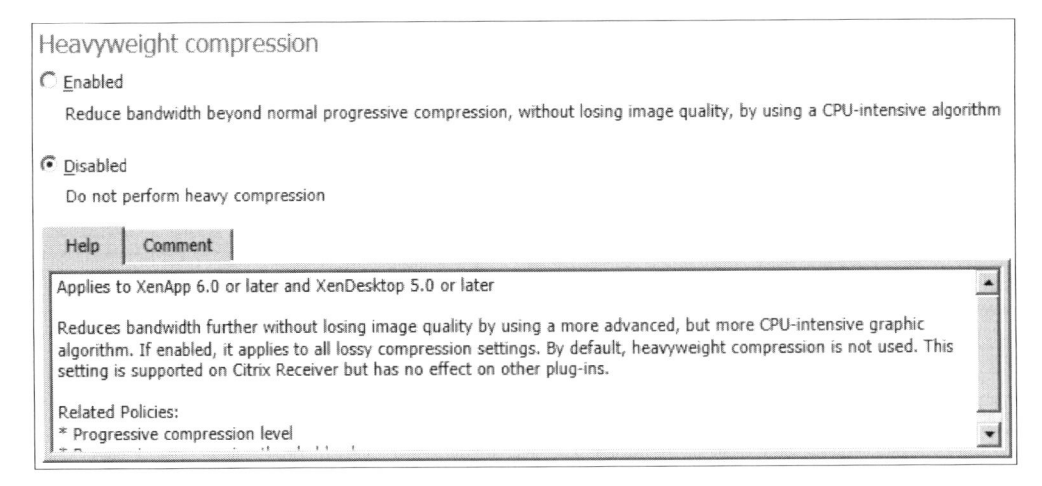

Using HDX 3D Progressive Display to improve the display of images

Citrix HDX 3D Progressive Display helps us to improve the performance of an application, showing an initial compressed version of an image file, and if the image doesn't change, the image is processed in the background and replaced by a high quality image.

If **Lossy compression** is enabled, the progressive compression must be higher than the **Lossy compression level** setting.

William can set the level at **User | ICA | Visual Display | Progressive Compression Level** to provide a less detailed, but faster, display of images. By default, progressive compression is not applied.

He needs to use the **Very High** or **Ultra-High** option to enable viewing of bandwidth-intensive graphics such as building pictures or detailed building plans.

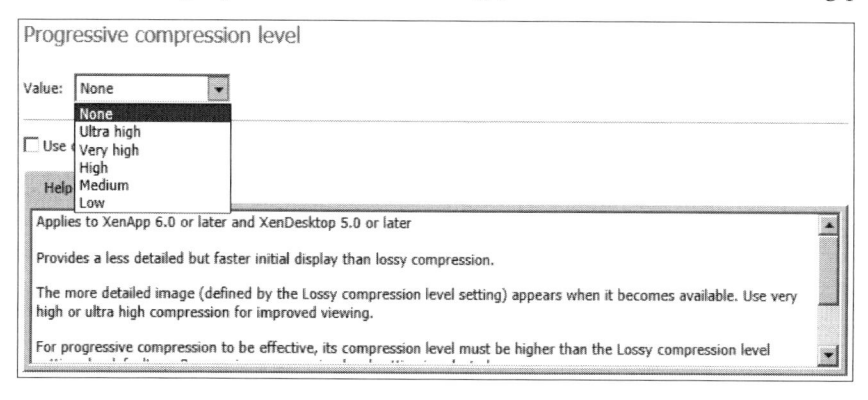

Another related setting is the **Progressive compression threshold** found at **User | ICA | Visual Display | Progressive compression threshold**. This setting sets the maximum bandwidth in Kbps for client machine connections. This setting is applied to connections below this bandwidth. By default, the threshold value is **1440 Kbps**.

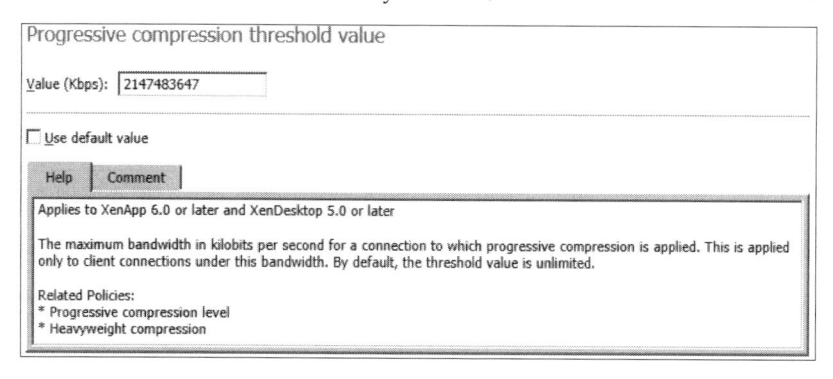

Multimedia Content in XenApp

On November 2011, Citrix introduced a new feature called **Adaptive Display** in XenApp 6.5 (available on XenDesktop before) through Hotfix XA650W2K8R2X64002. This Hotfix was replaced later by the Hotfix XA650W2K8R2X64025 (available at `http://support.citrix.com/article/CTX132912`).

Adaptive Display automatically adjusts the image quality of videos and transitional slides in slide shows based on available bandwidth. This feature allows users to watch videos in high quality and see smooth-running presentations with no reduction in quality.

Adaptive Display eliminates the need for **Progressive Display complex configurations** and provides a fantastic out-of-the-box experience for XenApp 6.5 farms. XenApp 6.0 farms must use **Progressive Display**.

This new feature is enabled by default, after William installs the Hotfix, and reboots the XenApp server. He can verify if **Adaptive Display** was enabled properly by running HDX Experience Monitor v2.0 inside an ICA session. More details about HDX Experience Monitor are available at the end of this chapter. If **Adaptive Display** is not showing as enabled, he needs to remove any **Progressive Display** settings from policies or GPOs.

If William wants to disable or re-enable **Adaptive Display**, he can use the **User | ICA | Visual Display | Moving Images | Moving Image Compression** policy.

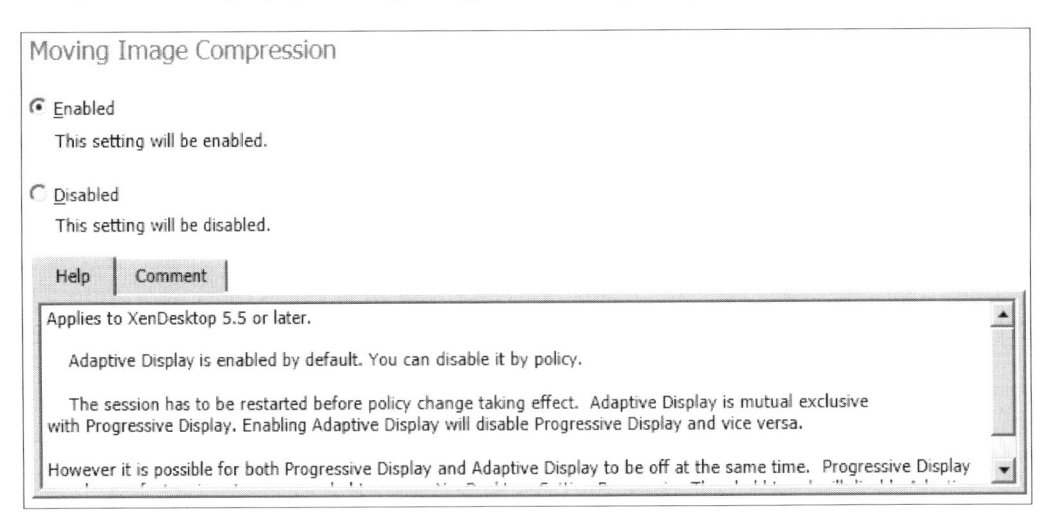

[280]

Reducing CPU usage by moving processing to GPU

Using HDX 3D, we can move graphics-intensive processing from CPU to GPU (Graphics Processing Unit). Moving processing to the GPU will upload compressing and rendering operations from CPU, reducing the CPU's use. This feature is only available on physical servers with a GPU (HDX 3D can't run on Virtual Machines) that support DDI (Display Driver Interface) Versions 9 or later.

William can enable published applications to render using the physical server's GPU, adding the `EnableWPFHook` key (type `REG_DWORD`) and set its value to `1` in the following registry key on our XenApp server:

`HKLM\SOFTWARE\Wow6432Node\Citrix\CtxHook\AppInit_Dlls\Multiple Monitor Hook`

Using HDX Broadcast Display settings

HDX Broadcast Display settings are used to improve the response when graphics are sent to the client machine. William can configure HDX Broadcast Display settings using the Citrix **Computer** | **ICA** | **Graphics** policy. This policy manages how images are handled in user sessions.

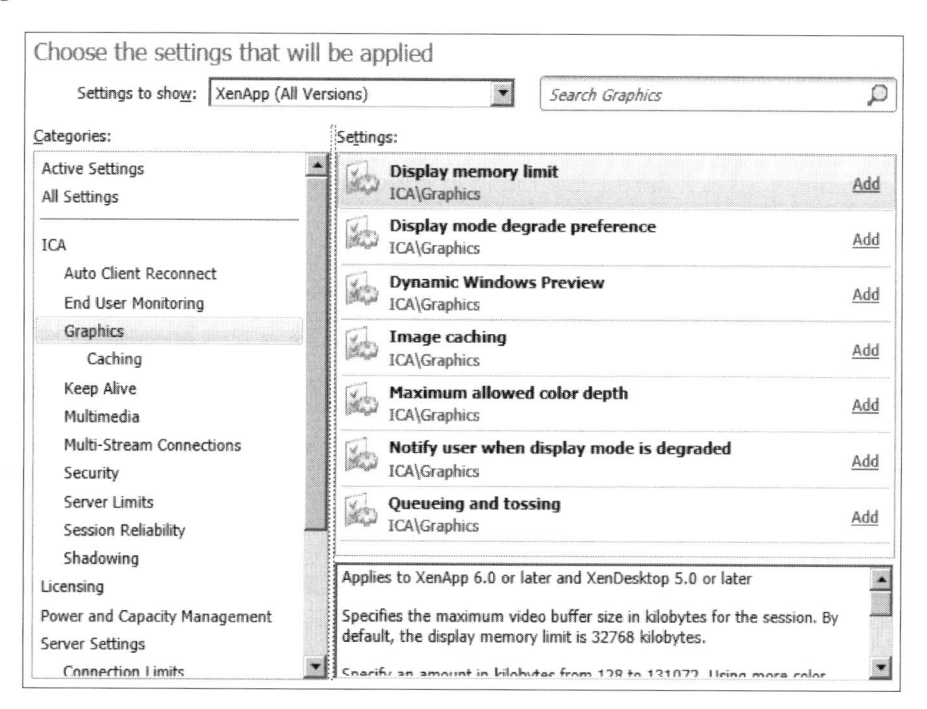

[281]

Multimedia Content in XenApp

William can use the **Display Memory Limit** setting to change the maximum video buffer size for the session. By default, the display memory limit is **32768 KB**. He can specify an amount between 128 and 65536 KB. If the memory limit is reached, the display degrades according to the **Display Mode Degrade Preference** setting, described here. If Brick Unit has several users using large resolutions or dual monitor on the client, William needs to create a policy with an increase value and assign it to these users.

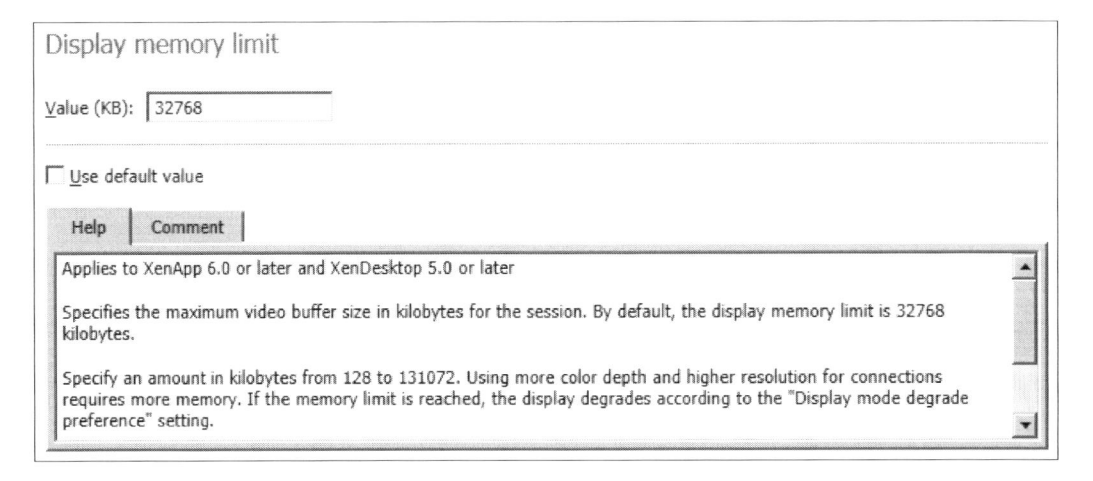

```
Display memory limit

Value (KB):  32768

☐ Use default value

  Help  | Comment

Applies to XenApp 6.0 or later and XenDesktop 5.0 or later

Specifies the maximum video buffer size in kilobytes for the session. By default, the display memory limit is 32768
kilobytes.

Specify an amount in kilobytes from 128 to 131072. Using more color depth and higher resolution for connections
requires more memory. If the memory limit is reached, the display degrades according to the "Display mode degrade
preference" setting.
```

The **Display Mode Degrade Preference** setting specifies color depth or resolution degrades first when the session display memory limits are reached. By default, color depth is degraded first. William also can notify users when either color depth or resolution is degraded, using the **Notify user when display mode is degraded** setting, described here.

```
Display mode degrade preference

Value:  Degrade color depth first ▼
        Degrade color depth first
        Degrade resolution first
☐ Use default value

  Help  | Comment

Applies to XenApp 6.0 or later and XenDesktop 5.0 or later

Degrades either color depth or resolution first when the session display memory limit is reached.

When the session memory limit is reached, you can reduce the quality of displayed images by choosing whether color
depth or resolution is degraded first. When you allow color depth to be degraded first, displayed images use fewer colors.
When you allow resolution to be degraded first, the size (in pixels) of your session is reduced. By default, color depth is
degraded first.
```

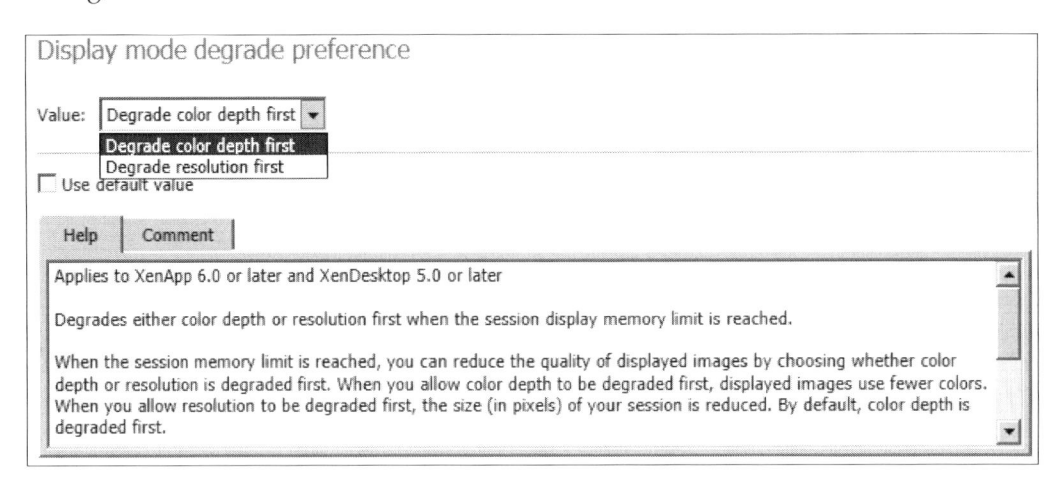

Chapter 10

William can use the **Image caching** setting to enable (default option) or disable caching of images in sessions. This setting, when enabled, makes scrolling smoother.

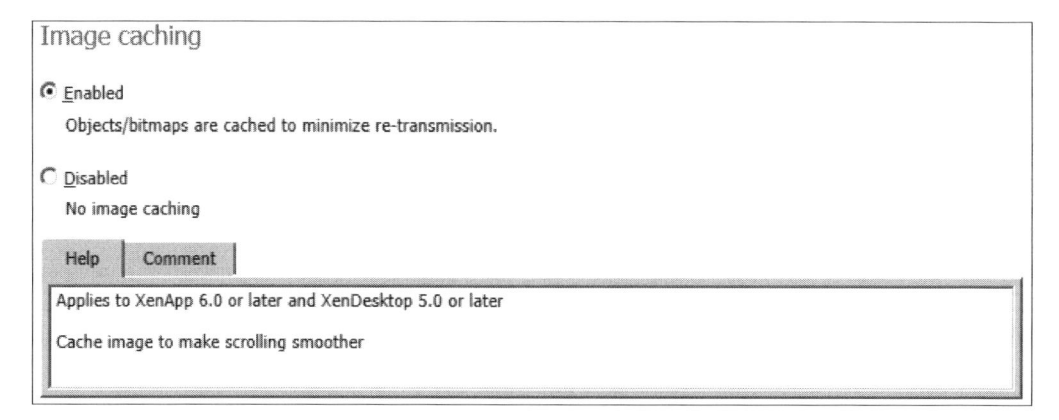

```
Image caching

(•) Enabled
    Objects/bitmaps are cached to minimize re-transmission.

( ) Disabled
    No image caching

  Help    Comment
  Applies to XenApp 6.0 or later and XenDesktop 5.0 or later
  Cache image to make scrolling smoother
```

The **Maximum allowed color depth** setting specifies the maximum color depth allowed for a session. By default, the maximum allowed color depth is 32 Bits per Pixel. William can reduce high color depth to save memory.

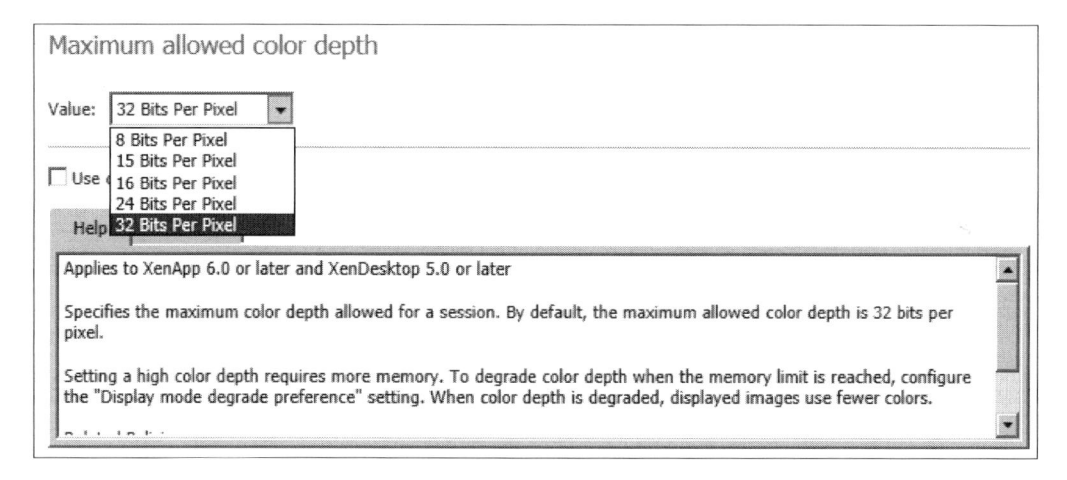

```
Maximum allowed color depth

Value:  [ 32 Bits Per Pixel  ▼ ]
         8 Bits Per Pixel
         15 Bits Per Pixel
  Use    16 Bits Per Pixel
         24 Bits Per Pixel
  Help   32 Bits Per Pixel

Applies to XenApp 6.0 or later and XenDesktop 5.0 or later

Specifies the maximum color depth allowed for a session. By default, the maximum allowed color depth is 32 bits per pixel.

Setting a high color depth requires more memory. To degrade color depth when the memory limit is reached, configure the "Display mode degrade preference" setting. When color depth is degraded, displayed images use fewer colors.
```

The **Notify user when display mode is degraded** setting shows a message to the user when the color depth or resolution is degraded. By default, this option is **Disabled**.

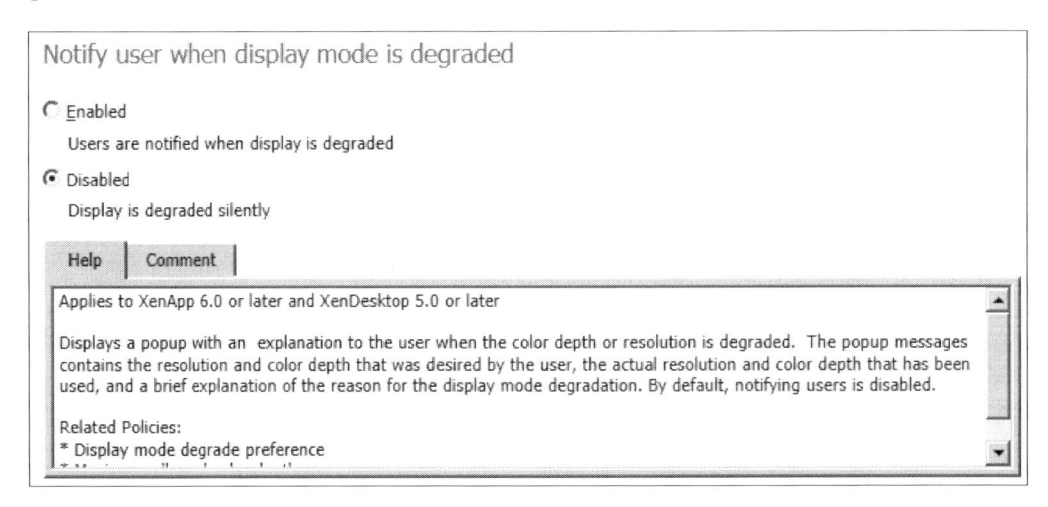

The **Queueing and tossing** setting is enabled by default. This setting discards queued images that are replaced by another image. This improves the response when graphics are sent to the client machine.

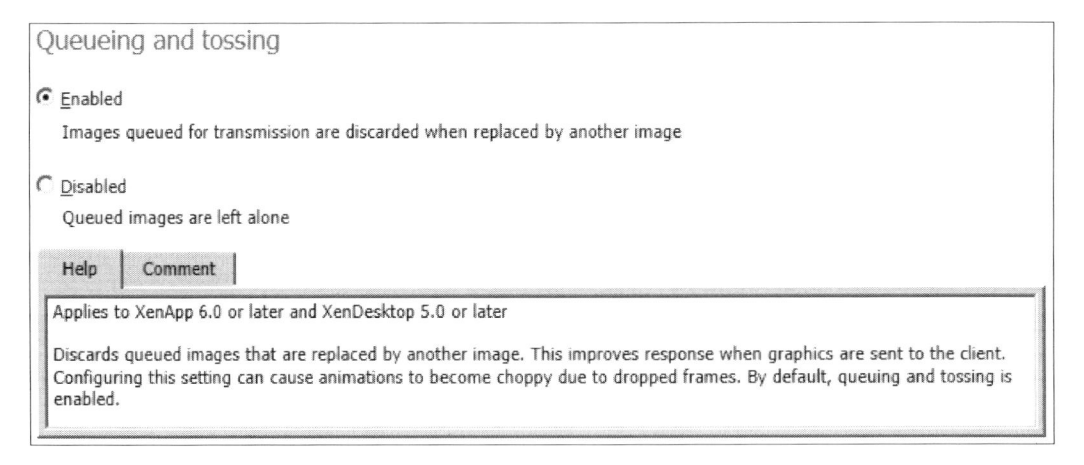

Using HDX MediaStream Multimedia Acceleration

William can improve the multimedia experience of the users by enabling the HDX MediaStream Multimedia Acceleration feature. This feature optimizes multimedia playback running in Internet Explorer, Windows Media Player, and RealOne Player, and offers significant performance improvements in these areas:

- **CPU use**: William can reduce the CPU use of XenApp servers by moving the multimedia content process to the client machine. Without HDX, when users play multimedia content in a session, XenApp decompresses and renders the multimedia file, increasing the server's CPU use.

- **Network bandwidth**: The multimedia content is compressed and delivered to client machines, reducing bandwidth consumption. Without HDX MediaStream Multimedia Acceleration, XenApp delivers the file uncompressed over the network, using more bandwidth.

HDX MediaStream Multimedia Acceleration optimizes playback of multimedia files that are encoded with codecs (programs used to encode or compress files) compatible with Microsoft's DirectShow and DirectX. A codec, compatible with the encoding format of the multimedia file, must be present on the client machine.

The following are the client machine's requirements to use HDX MediaStream Multimedia Acceleration:

- The codec required to decompress and play the multimedia file must be installed on the client machine. Audio and video are not synchronized, or only video or audio played are signs of most missing or wrong codec.

- Citrix Receiver or Online Plug-in must be installed on the client machine.

- The client must have enough memory and CPU available to process multimedia playback. A desktop computer is recommended because almost thin clients can't support multimedia playback.

> Playback of multimedia files protected with Digital **Rights Management (DRM)** is not supported by HDX MediaStream Multimedia Acceleration.

Multimedia Content in XenApp

By default, Windows Server 2008 R2 doesn't install Windows Media Player. If William wants to play multimedia content on the XenApp farm, he needs to install the feature **Desktop Experience**. This feature is installed by XenApp 6.5, when we install the XenApp server role. If we are deploying XenApp 6.0, we need to install this feature.

To install **Desktop Experience**, William needs to open **Server Manager** (located in **Administrative Tools**), select **Features**, and choose **Desktop Experience**.

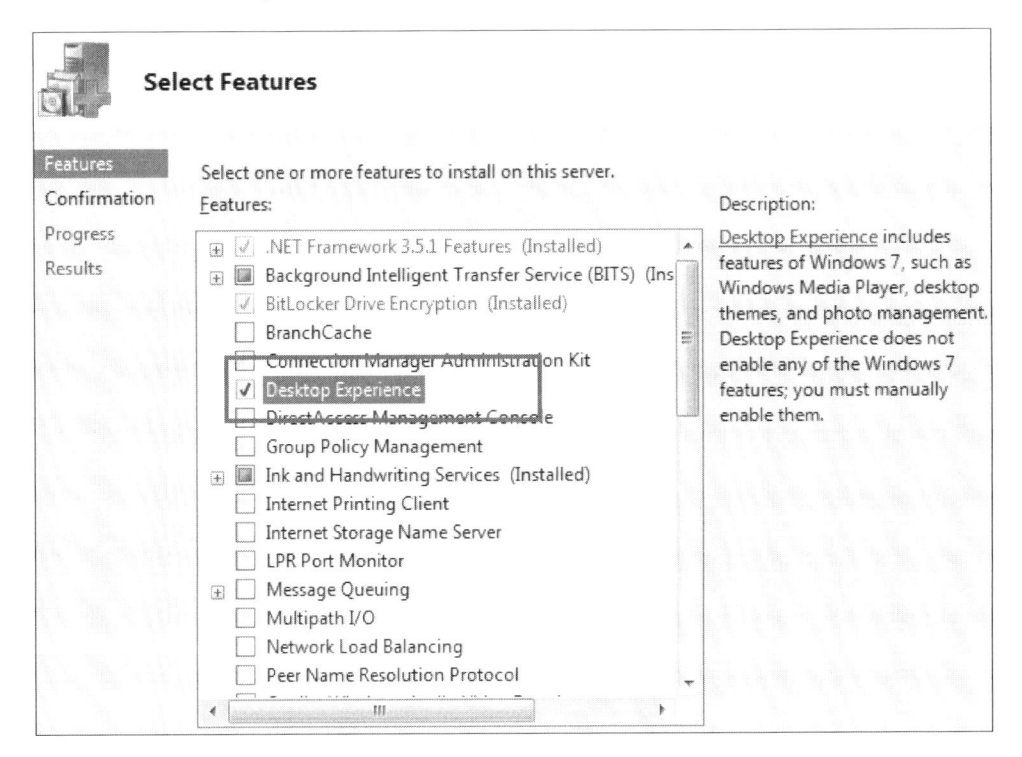

Using Citrix policies to configure multimedia settings (HDX MediaStream)

William can manage **Multimedia** settings (called **HDX MediaStream** settings in XenApp 6.0) using the **Computer | ICA | Multimedia** policy. This section contains policy settings for managing streaming audio and video in user sessions.

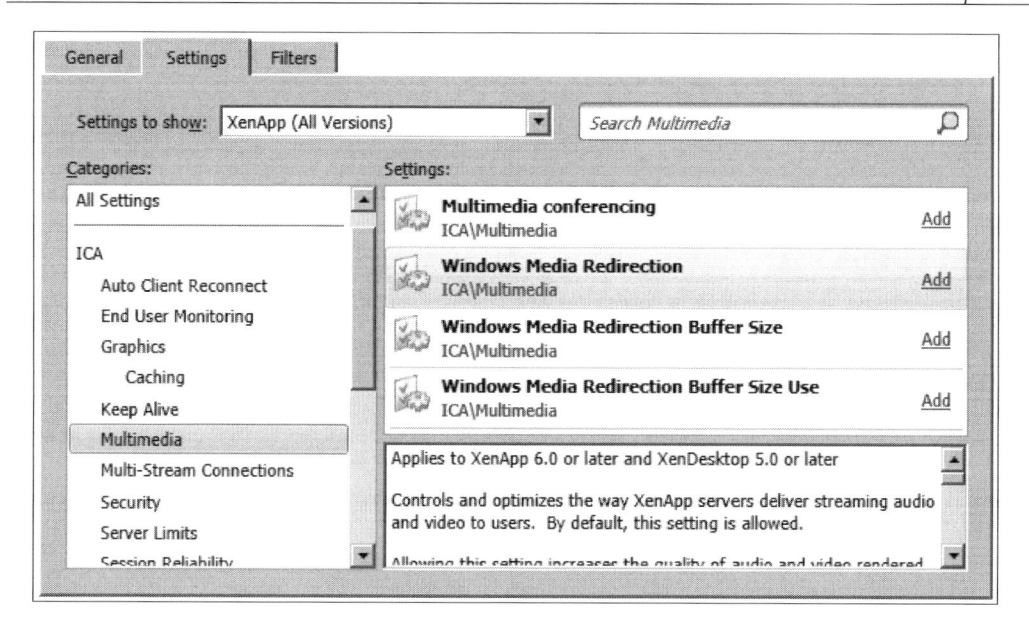

William can use the **Windows Media Redirection** setting (called **HDX MediaStream Multimedia Acceleration** setting in XenApp 6.0) to enable (default option) or disable **Windows Media Redirection**. This setting controls and optimizes the way XenApp servers deliver streaming audio and video to clients.

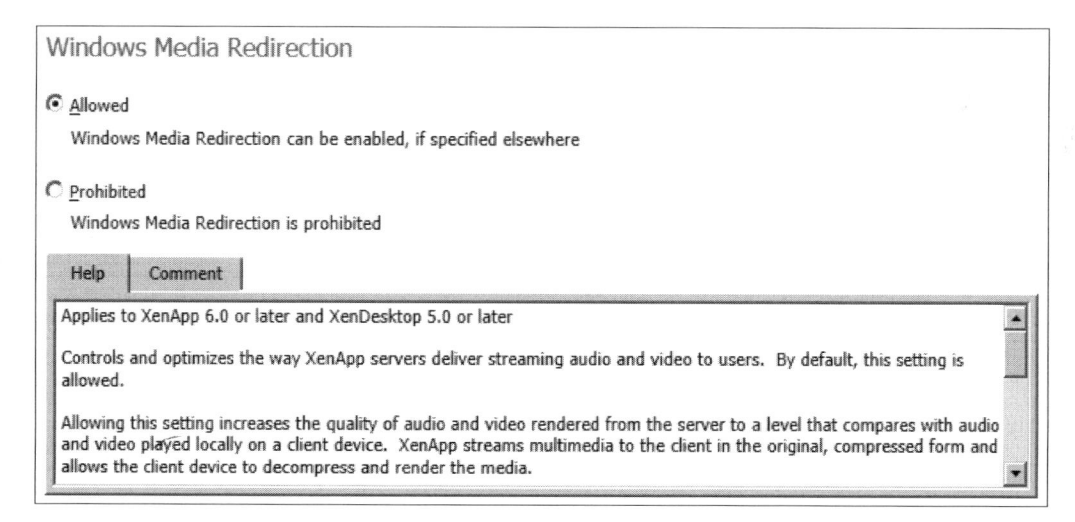

The **Windows Media Redirection Buffer Size** setting (called **HDX MediaStream Multimedia Acceleration default buffer size** setting in XenApp 6.0) specifies a buffer size (from 1 to 10 seconds) used for multimedia acceleration. By default, the buffer size is **5** seconds. William can increase this setting in high latency networks.

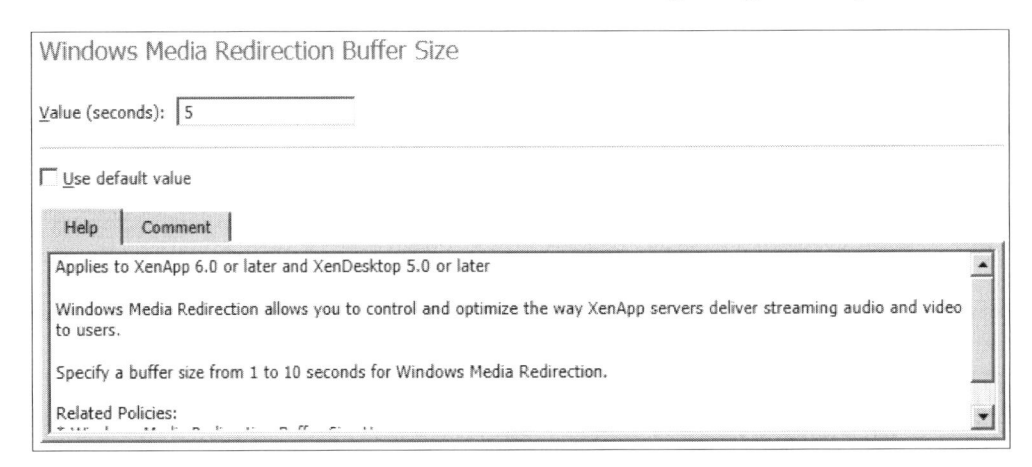

The **Windows Media Redirection Buffer Size Use** setting (called **HDX MediaStream Multimedia Acceleration default buffer size use** setting in XenApp 6.0) enables (default option in XenApp 6.0) or disables (default option in XenApp 6.5) using the buffer size specified in the **Windows Media Redirection Buffer Size (HDX MediaStream Multimedia Acceleration default buffer size)** setting.

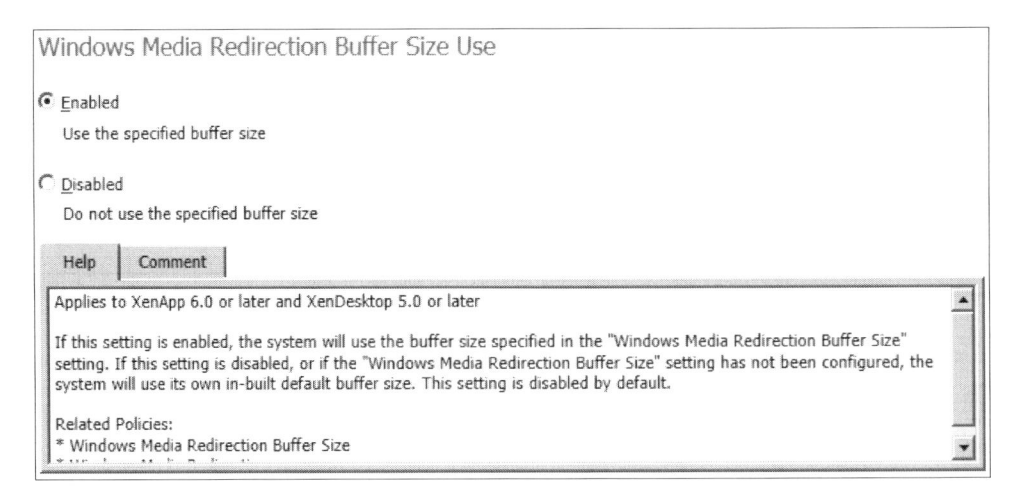

The **Multimedia conferencing** setting allows or prevents support for video conferencing applications. By default, video conferencing support is **Enabled**. William needs to set the **Windows Media Redirection** setting (**HDX MediaStream Multimedia Acceleration** setting in XenApp 6.0) to **Allowed** to enable multimedia conferencing.

Before using multimedia conferencing, also calling HDX RealTime, William needs to check the following conditions:

- Drivers for the webcam used for multimedia conferencing are installed on the client machines. Drivers are not required on XenApp.
- The webcam is connected to the client machine before starting a video conferencing session.
- Microsoft Office Communicator 2007 client software must be published on the XenApp server.
- The Office Communicator server must be present in the XenApp farm environment (but not installed on any XenApp server).
- Enable the following policies settings:
    - **User | ICA | Audio | Client audio redirection**
    - **User | ICA | Audio | Client microphone redirection**
    - **Computer | ICA | Multimedia | Windows Media Redirection**
- Citrix recommends assigning one CPU (virtual or physical) per user.

The Hotfix XA650W2K8R2X64002, replaced by Hotfix XA650W2K8R2X64025 (available at http://support.citrix.com/article/CTX132912), mentioned before on the **Progressive Display** section, also added support for the following communication software:

- Microsoft Lync
- Citrix GoToMeeting with HD Faces
- Skype
- Adobe Connect

Multimedia Content in XenApp

Citrix added great enhancements on the audio virtual channels to help reduce latency, improving performance of communications applications.

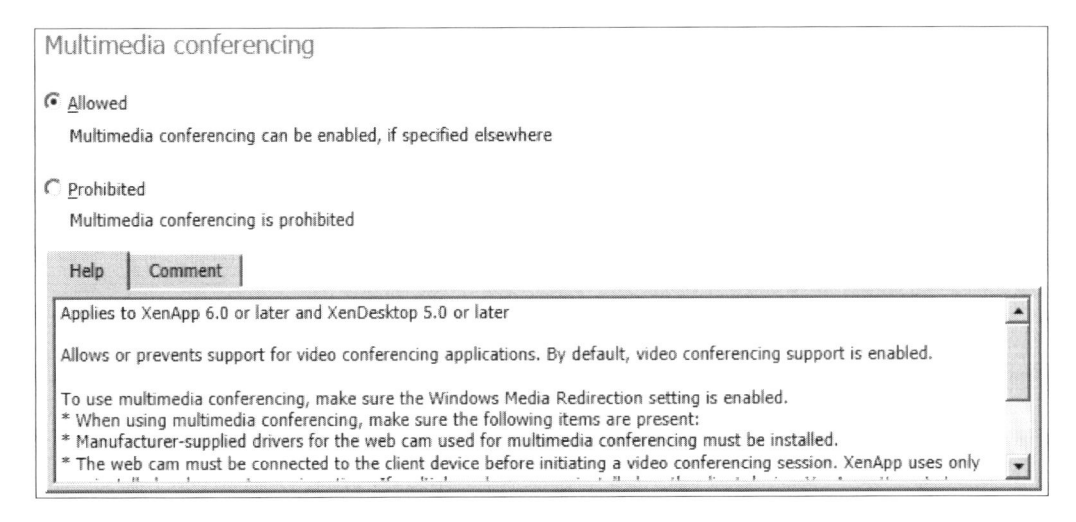

When users take part in audio or video conferences, they may hear an echo in their audio. Echoes usually occur when speakers and microphones are too close to each other. For that reason, Citrix recommends the use of headsets for audio and video conferences.

The success of echo cancellation is related to the distance between the microphone and the speakers. These devices must not be too close to each other or too far from each other.

Echo cancellation is available with only Citrix Receiver 3.0 or later, Citrix Online Plug-in 12.0 for Windows or later, and Web Interface 5.3 or later.

Configuring echo cancellation

When William enables HDX RealTime, echo cancellation is enabled by default, which minimizes echo during a conference. He needs to set audio quality to **Medium - optimized for speech** or **Low - for low-speed connections**. The **High - high definition audio** setting is NOT recommended because it is planned for music playback.

William needs to open the registry editor on the client machine and navigate to the following key:

- 32-bit machines: `HKEY_LOCAL_MACHINE\SOFTWARE\Citrix\ICA Client\Engine\Configuration\Advanced\Modules\ClientAudio\EchoCancellation`
- 64-bit machines: `HKEY_LOCAL_MACHINE\SOFTWARE\Wow6432Node\Citrix\ICA Client\Engine\Configuration\Advanced\Modules\ClientAudio\EchoCancellation`

William needs to set the **Value** data field to **TRUE** to enable or **FALSE** to disable echo cancellation.

Using HDX MediaStream for Flash to optimize Flash content

William can enable HDX MediaStream for Flash to move or redirect the processing of Adobe Flash content to the client machine rather than using network resources, reducing the XenApp server and network load, and improving the amount of sessions per server. HDX produces a high-definition experience when users are using Microsoft Internet Explorer to access Flash content, including animations, videos, and applications.

Playing Flash content on a XenApp server usually is slow because the Adobe Flash Player renders the content on the server, by default, in high-quality mode. This causes high bandwidth use.

On XenApp 6.5, Citrix included the second generation of HDX MediaStream for Flash, which includes new features, including:

- Support for users using WAN connections.
- The new second generation of Flash and legacy versions of Flash Redirection will run in separate virtual channels.
- **Intelligent Fallback** decides if a more efficient Flash content is rendered on the client or the XenApp server.
- The **Flash URL Blacklist** setting included in XenApp 6.0 is now replaced on XenApp 6.5 by the **Flash URL Compatibility List** setting. This allows us to block URLs or decide to render on the client machine or XenApp server.

System requirements for HDX MediaStream for Flash

The following is a list of the requirements:

- Windows-based client machine with Citrix Receiver 3.0 (formerly known as Citrix Online Plug-in) or later installed.
- Adobe Flash Player 10.1 for Windows or above installed on the XenApp servers. If an earlier version of the Flash Player is installed, or the Flash Player is not installed on the client machine, the Flash content is rendered on the XenApp server.
- Microsoft Internet Explorer 7.0, 8.0, or 9.0.

Internet Explorer 9.0 is not supported by default and William needs to add the following registry key on the XenApp server to enable the support.

```
HKEY_LOCAL_MACHINE\SOFTWARE\Wow6432Node\Citrix\HdxMediaStreamForFlash\Server\PseudoServer
```

He needs to add a new **DWORD** value called **IEBrowserMaximumMajorVersion** and set value to **00000009**.

Enabling HDX MediaStream at server side

William can configure HDX MediaStream server-side Flash functionality using Citrix policies. He needs to open the **User | ICA | Adobe Flash Delivery | Flash Redirection** policy in XenApp 6.5.

HDX MediaStream for Flash requires installation on the XenApp 6.0 server (explained in the following section).

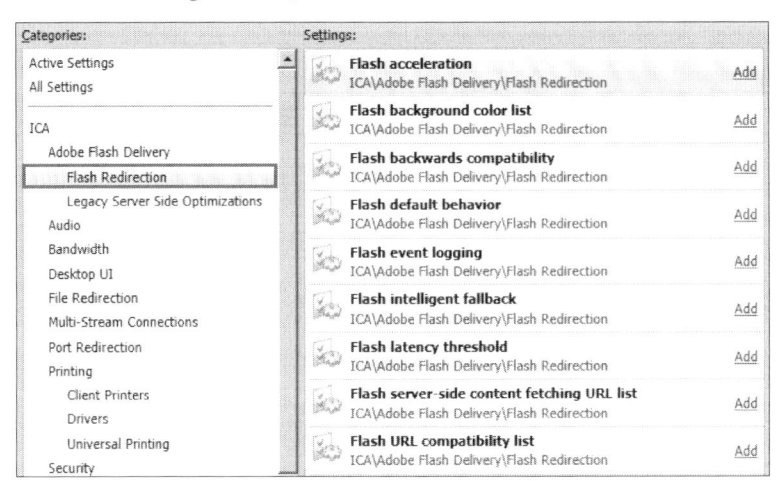

William can configure Flash redirection using one of these **Flash default behavior** settings:

- **Block Flash player**: This option doesn't allow the user to reproduce any Flash content. Second generation, Legacy mode Flash Redirection, and server-side rendering are not used.
- **Disable Flash acceleration**: This option allows reproducing Flash content on the XenApp server. Second generation and Legacy mode Flash Redirection is not used and the Flash Player for Windows Internet Explorer is required on the XenApp server.
- **Enable Flash acceleration**: The **default** option enables the Flash Redirection. If requirements are met the second generation is used. Also, William can use Legacy mode when backwards compatibility is enabled.

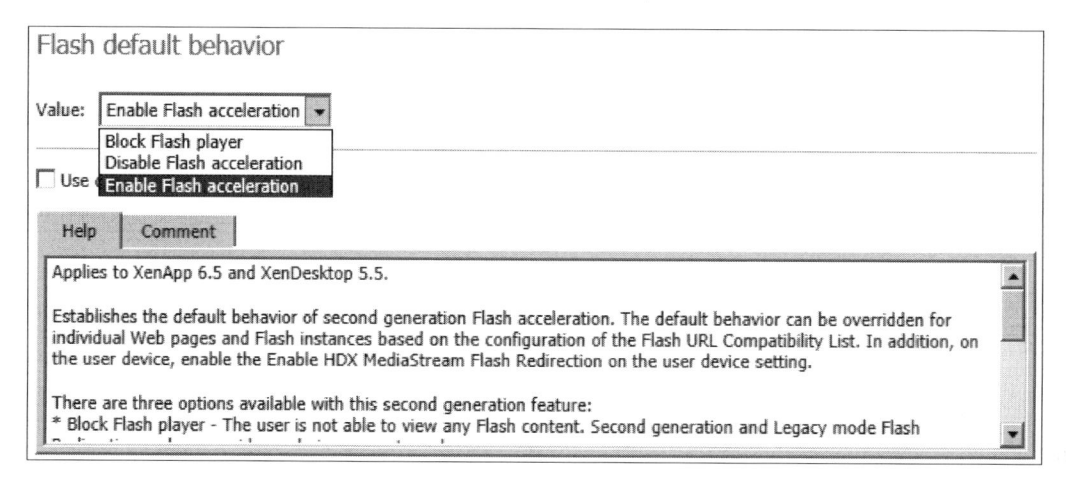

William can configure the **Flash quality adjustment** setting to adjust the quality of Flash content rendered on session hosts to improve performance.

Multimedia Content in XenApp

This setting is located under the **User | ICA | Adobe Flash Delivery | Legacy Server Side Optimizations** in XenApp 6.5 and in the **User | ICA | Multimedia | HDX Multimedia For Flash (server side)** setting on XenApp 6.0.

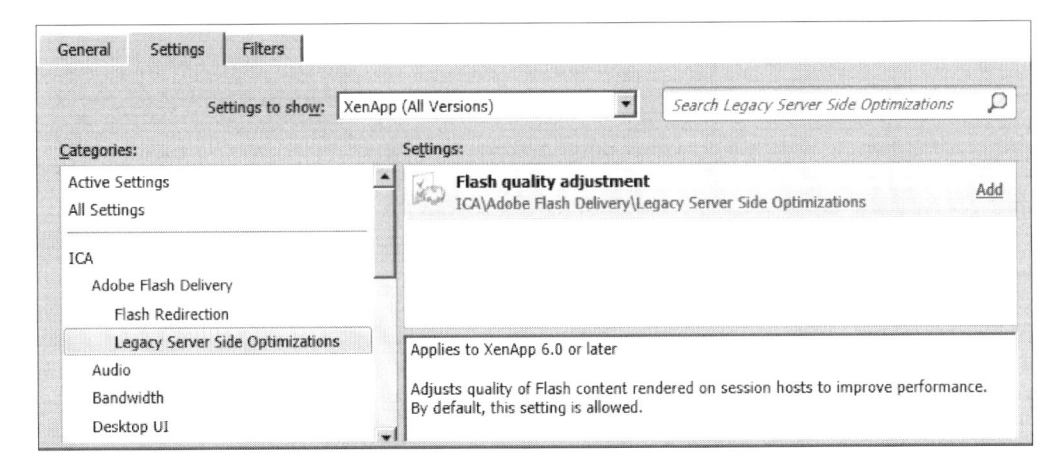

He can configure the Flash quality adjustment setting, located at **User | ICA | HDX MediaStream for Flash (server side)** policy with one of the following options:

- **Do not optimize Adobe Flash animation options**: This option plays all Flash content in high-quality mode.

- **Optimize Adobe Flash animation options for all connections**: This option reduces the CPU use and the amount of Flash data sent to users.

- **Optimize Adobe Flash animation options for low bandwidth connections only**: This option improves client responsiveness when Flash content is sent to users on connections with low bandwidth (below 150Kbps). When our users are located on a LAN where bandwidth is not limited, Flash content is played in high-quality mode.

By default, Flash content is optimized for low bandwidth connections only.

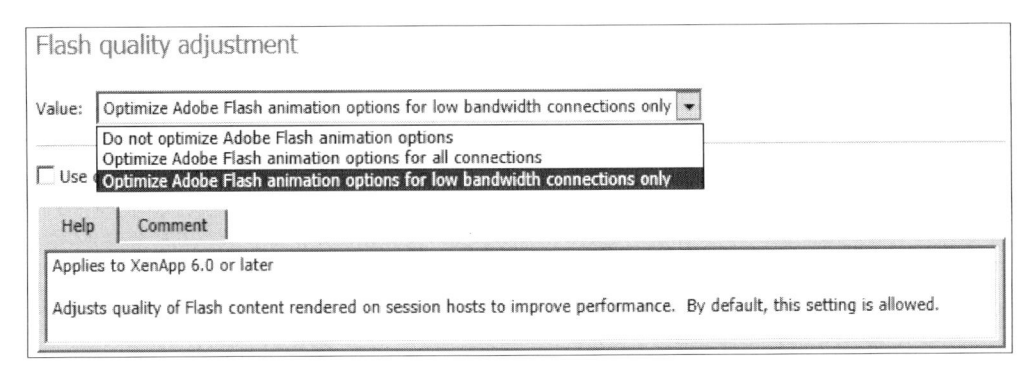

[294]

Configuring HDX MediaStream for Flash settings

William can configure HDX MediaStream for Flash settings for handling Flash content in user sessions on the XenApp server using the Policies node of the Citrix AppCenter (or Citrix Delivery Services Console in XenApp 6.0). He can control the settings for the HDX MediaStream for Flash features through the following Citrix policy settings, under **User | ICA | Adobe Flash Delivery | Flash Redirection** policy in XenApp 6.5 and **User | ICA | HDX MediaStream for Flash (client side)** policy in XenApp 6.0:

- Flash acceleration (available on both XenApp 6.5 and XenApp 6.0)
- Flash background color list (new in XenApp 6.5)
- Flash backwards compatibility (new in XenApp 6.5)
- Flash event logging (available on both XenApp 6.5 and XenApp 6.0)
- Flash intelligent fallback (new in XenApp 6.5)
- Flash latency threshold (available on both XenApp 6.5 and XenApp 6.0)
- Flash server-side content fetching URL list (new in XenApp 6.5)
- Flash server-side content fetching whitelist (XenApp 6.0)
- Flash URL blacklist (XenApp 6.0)
- Flash URL compatibility list (new in XenApp 6.5)

Setting up Flash Acceleration

William can use the Flash acceleration setting, available on both XenApp 6.5 and XenApp 6.0, to enable (default option) or disable Flash content rendering on client machines instead of the XenApp server.

The policy is located under **User | ICA | Adobe Flash Delivery | Flash Redirection | Flash acceleration** policy in XenApp 6.5 and **User | ICA | HDX MediaStream for Flash (client side) | Flash acceleration** policy in XenApp 6.0.

- When this setting is **Enabled**, it reduces network and server load by rendering Flash content on the client machine. Also, William can use Flash URL blacklist setting (described in the following section) or the Flash URL compatibility list (new in XenApp 6.5) to force Flash content from specific websites to be rendered on the XenApp server.

- When this setting is **Disabled**, Flash content from all websites, regardless of the URL, is rendered on the XenApp server. William can configure the Flash server-side content fetching whitelist setting to allow only certain websites to render Flash content on the client machine.

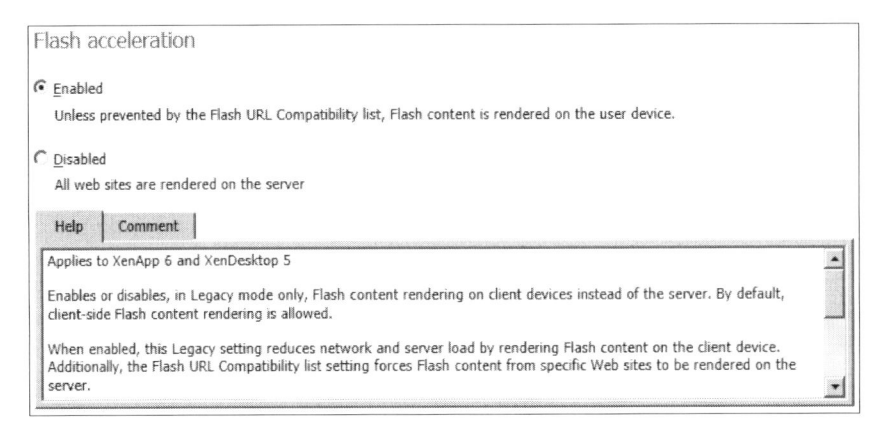

Setting up Flash background color list

William can use this new XenApp 6.5 policy to assign colors to specific URLs. These colors appear behind client-rendered Flash and help provide visible region detection.

This policy is located under **User | ICA | Adobe Flash Delivery | Flash Redirection | Flash background color list**.

He can add a new entry using the **New** button and adding the URL followed by a 24-bit RGB color hex code. The URLs can include optional wildcards at the beginning and end.

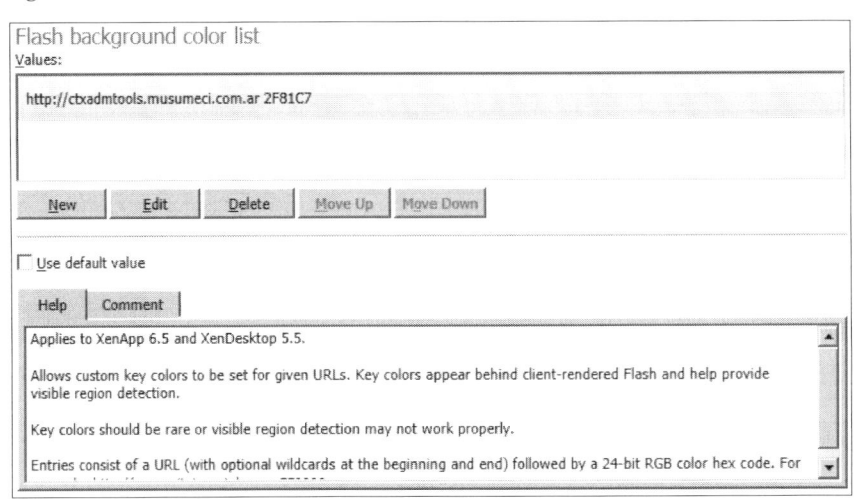

Setting up Flash backwards compatibility

The second generation Flash Redirection included in XenApp 6.5 works with Citrix Receiver 3.0 or later. If William is still using earlier versions of Citrix Receiver, he needs to enable Flash backwards compatibility to work with the legacy Flash Redirection.

The **Enable HDX MediaStream Flash Redirection** option on the user device setting must also be enabled.

This is a new XenApp 6.5 policy and is located under **User | ICA | Adobe Flash Delivery | Flash Redirection | Flash backwards compatibility**.

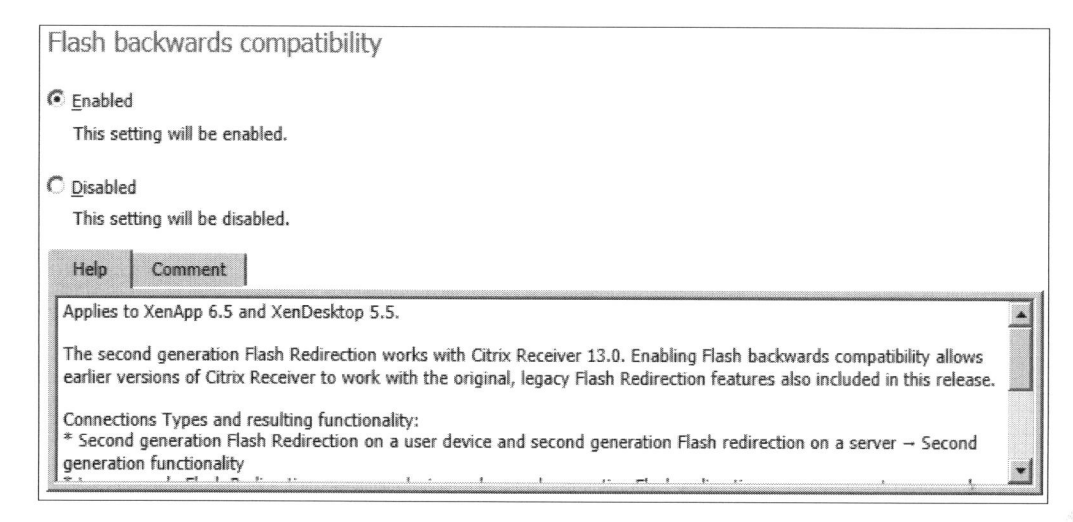

Enable Flash event logging

HDX MediaStream for Flash uses Windows event logging on the XenApp server to log events. William can review the **Windows Event Log** to check the usage or troubleshoot issues with HDX MediaStream for Flash.

The following are common to all events logged by HDX MediaStream for Flash:

- HDX MediaStream for Flash reports events to the Application log
- The **Source** value is **Flash**
- The **Category** value is **None**

Multimedia Content in XenApp

An HDX MediaStream for a Flash-specific log appears in the Applications and Services Logs node on the servers running Windows Server 2008 R2.

The **Flash event logging** setting, located under the **User | ICA | Adobe Flash Delivery | Flash Redirection | Flash event logging** policy in XenApp 6.5 and **User | ICA | HDX MediaStream for Flash (client side) | Flash event logging** policy in XenApp 6.0, allows (default setting), or prevents, Flash events to be recorded in the Windows application event log.

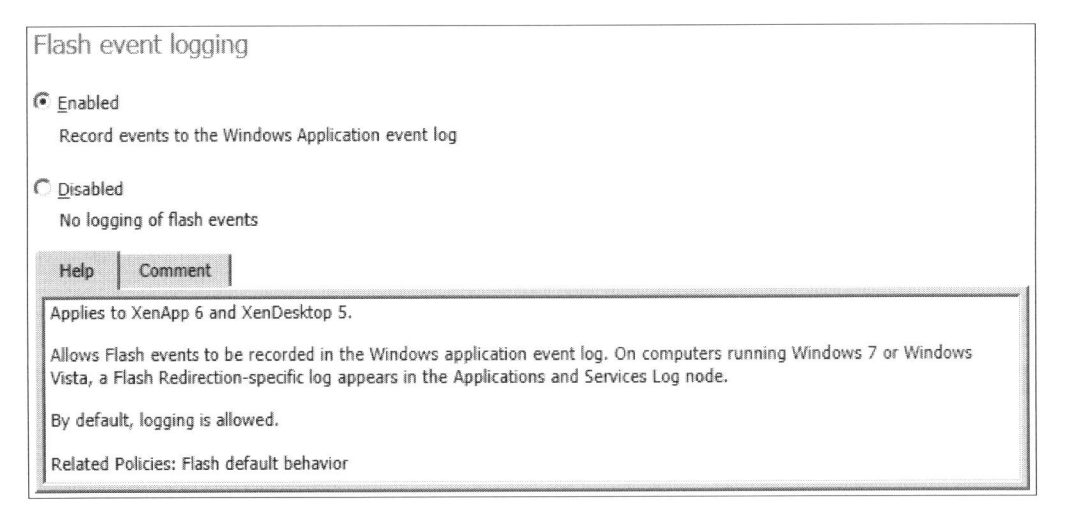

Setting up Flash intelligent fallback

This new XenApp 6.5 policy, located under **User | ICA | Adobe Flash Delivery | Flash Redirection | Flash intelligent fallback** tries to automatically revert client-side rendering to server-side rendering for Flash Player instances when it is redundant or provides a poor experience, when the policy is enabled.

> **Flash intelligent fallback**
>
> ⦿ Enabled
>   This setting will be enabled.
>
> ○ Disabled
>   This setting will be disabled.
>
> | Help | Comment |
>
> Applies to XenApp 6.5 and XenDesktop 5.5.
>
> If enabled, the system attempts to automatically revert to server-side rendering for Flash Player instances for which client-side rendering is unnecessary or would provide a poor experience

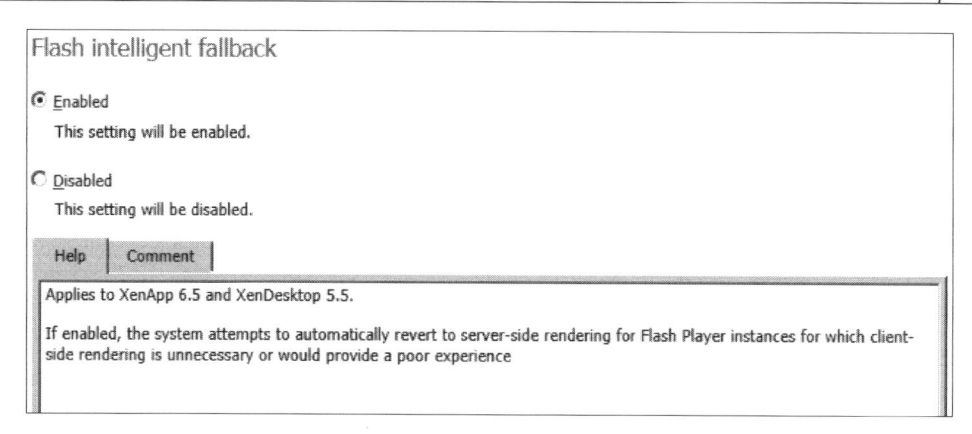

Setting up Flash latency threshold

The **Flash latency threshold** setting, located under the **User | ICA | Adobe Flash Delivery | Flash Redirection | Flash latency threshold** policy in XenApp 6.5 and **User | ICA | HDX MediaStream for Flash (client side) | Flash latency threshold** policy in XenApp 6.0, specifies a threshold between 0 and 5,000 milliseconds to determine where Adobe Flash content is rendered. By default, the threshold is 30 milliseconds.

On XenApp 6.5 this policy only applies to **Legacy mode features** and **Flash backwards compatibility** must be enabled.

During start up, HDX MediaStream for Flash analyses the current latency between the server and client machine, and if the latency is below the **Flash latency threshold** value, HDX MediaStream for Flash is used to render Flash content on the client machine.

A latency maximum threshold to determine when Adobe Flash content is rendered is specified. By default, the threshold is 30 milliseconds.

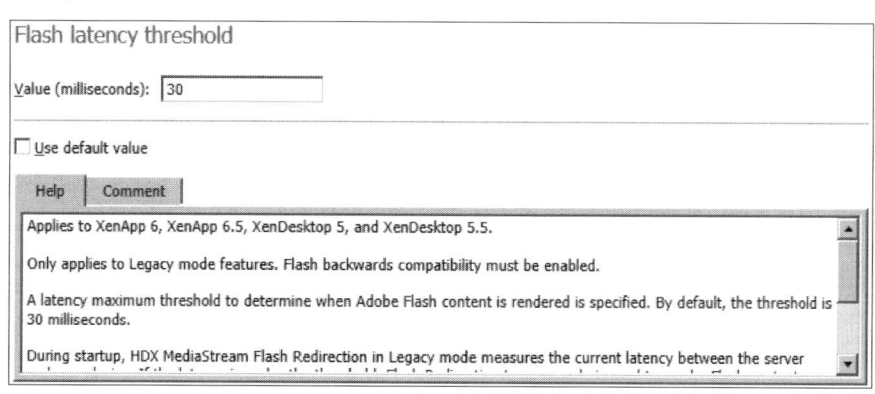

> **Flash latency threshold**
>
> Value (milliseconds): 30
>
> ☐ Use default value
>
> | Help | Comment |
>
> Applies to XenApp 6, XenApp 6.5, XenDesktop 5, and XenDesktop 5.5.
>
> Only applies to Legacy mode features. Flash backwards compatibility must be enabled.
>
> A latency maximum threshold to determine when Adobe Flash content is rendered is specified. By default, the threshold is 30 milliseconds.
>
> During startup, HDX MediaStream Flash Redirection in Legacy mode measures the current latency between the server

Setting up Flash server-side content fetching URL list

The Flash server-side content fetching URL list policy (called Flash server-side content fetching whitelist in XenApp 6.0) specifies websites whose Flash content is allowed to be rendered on the client machine and unlisted websites are rendered on the XenApp server.

William needs to set the **Flash acceleration** setting to **Enabled**, otherwise websites listed on the whitelist are ignored.

Note that listed URL strings do not need the `https://` prefix. These prefixes are used, if found, but not required. Wildcards (*) are valid at the beginning and end of a URL.

The second generation of Flash redirection introduces a server-side content fetching fallback for Flash's `.swf` files. When client machine is not capable to play the Flash content from a site and the Flash server-side content fetching URL list is configured and enabled, server-side content fetching seamlessly takes over.

This policy setting is located under the **User | ICA | Adobe Flash Delivery | Flash Redirection | Flash server-side content fetching URL list** policy in XenApp 6.5 and **User | ICA | HDX MediaStream for Flash (client side) | Flash server-side content fetching whitelist** policy in XenApp 6.0.

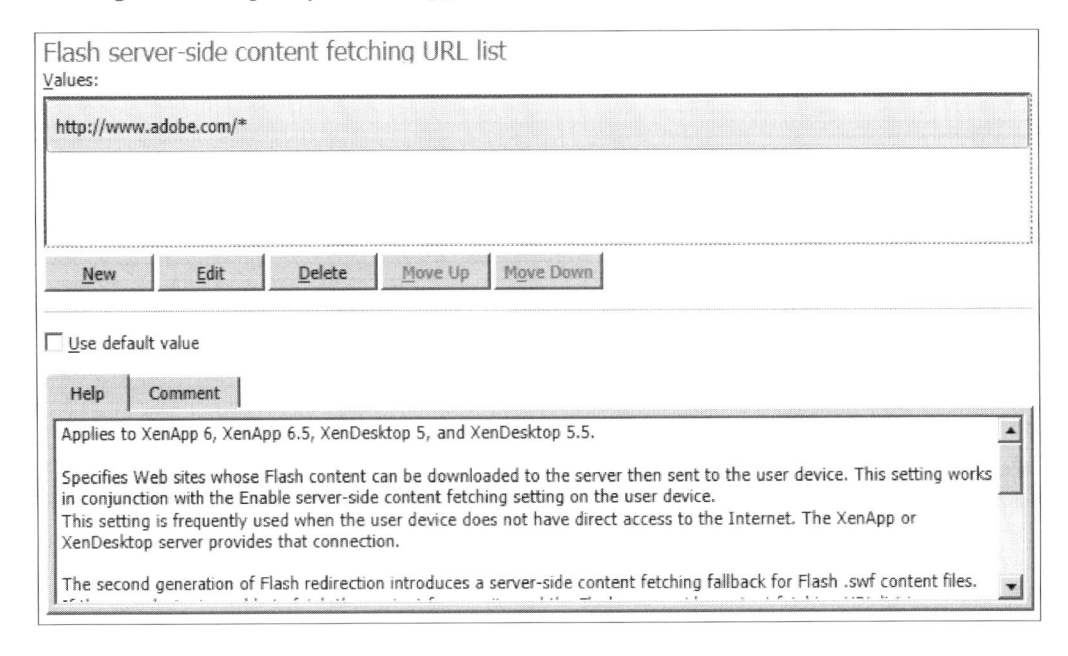

Setting up Flash URL Blacklist

The Flash URL Blacklist setting, only available in XenApp 6.0, is used by websites whose Flash content is rendered on the XenApp server. Flash content on unlisted websites is rendered on the client machine.

William needs to set the **Flash acceleration** setting to **Enabled**, otherwise websites listed in the URL blacklist are ignored.

Listed URL strings do not need the `https://` prefix. These prefixes are ignored, if found. Wildcards (*) are valid at the beginning and end of a URL.

This policy setting is located under **User | ICA | HDX MediaStream for Flash (client side) | Flash URL Blacklist**.

Setting up Flash URL compatibility list

This new policy available on XenApp 6.5 is pretty similar to the **Flash URL Blacklist** policy available on XenApp 6.0, but easy to use and provides more features.

To use it, William needs to type the URL of website and choose the action:

- **Render on Client**: Flash content is rendered on the client machine
- **Render on Server**: Flash content is rendered on server (this is the only option available in Legacy mode)

- **Blocked**: Flash content is blocked from rendering

> Arrange the URL list with the most used or important URLs at the top.

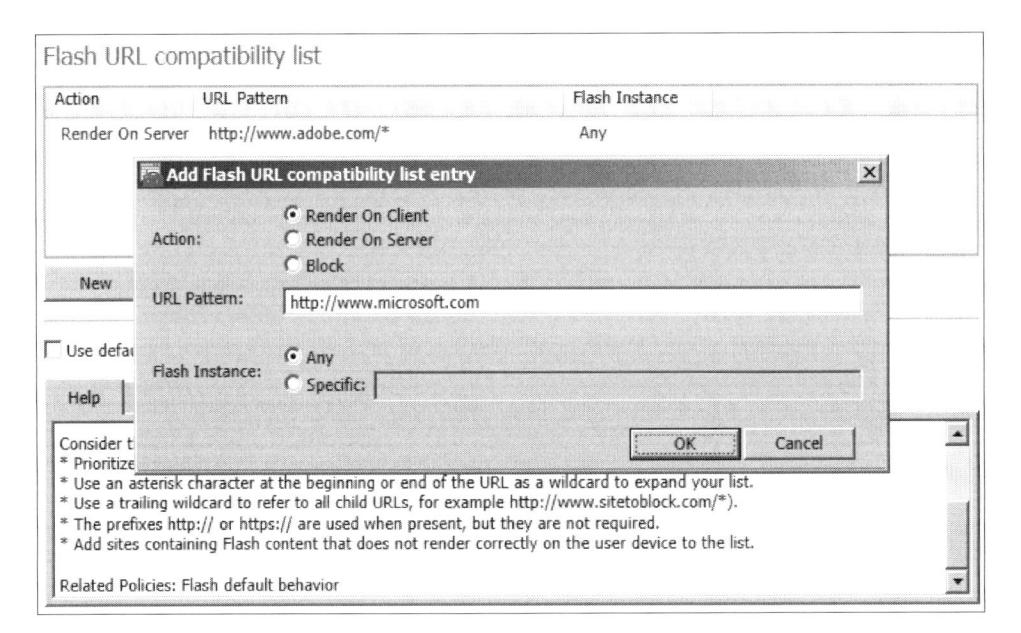

Configuring HDX MediaStream for Flash on the client machine

William can configure HDX MediaStream for Flash on client machines locally using **Group Policy Management Editor** and apply it to a group of machines using the following procedure:

1. Open **Group Policy Object Editor**.
2. Open **Computer Configuration | Policies | Administrative Templates**.
3. Right-click on **Administrative Templates** and select **Add/Remove Templates**.
4. Import and add the HDX MediaStream for Flash - Client administrative template (`HdxFlash-Client.adm`) available, depending on CPU platform:
    - 32-bit: `%ProgramFiles%\Citrix\ICA Client\Configuration\language`
    - 64-bit: `%ProgramFiles(x86)%\Citrix\ICA Client\Configuration\language`

Language represents the two letter folder, for example: EN for English template, ES for Spanish template, and so on.

After installation of HDX MediaStream for Flash, William can see following policies:

- Enable HDX MediaStream for Flash on the user device
- Enable synchronization of the client-side HTTP cookies with the server side
- Enable server-side content fetching
- URL rewriting rules for client-side content fetching

> Only first three options are available on XenApp 6.0.

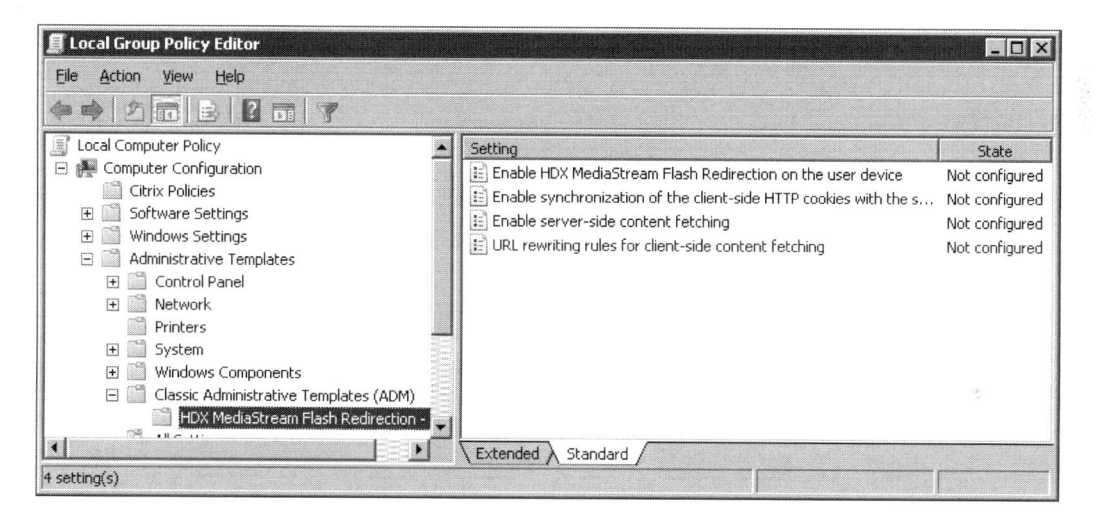

William can configure the HDX MediaStream for Flash on the client machine, by editing the **Enable HDX MediaStream for Flash** on the user device policy and selecting **Not Configured**, **Enabled**, or **Disabled**.

If he selected **Enabled**, from the **Use HDX MediaStream for Flash** list, he can select **Always**, **Ask**, **Never**, or **Only with Second Generation** options.

- **Always**: This option uses HDX MediaStream for Flash to play Flash content on the client machine
- **Ask**: Users will receive a dialog box the first time they access Flash content in each XenApp session

Multimedia Content in XenApp

- **Never**: Uses HDX MediaStream for Flash and has Flash content play on the XenApp server
- **Only with Second Generation**: Allow client-side rendering using Flash Redirection Second Generation only.

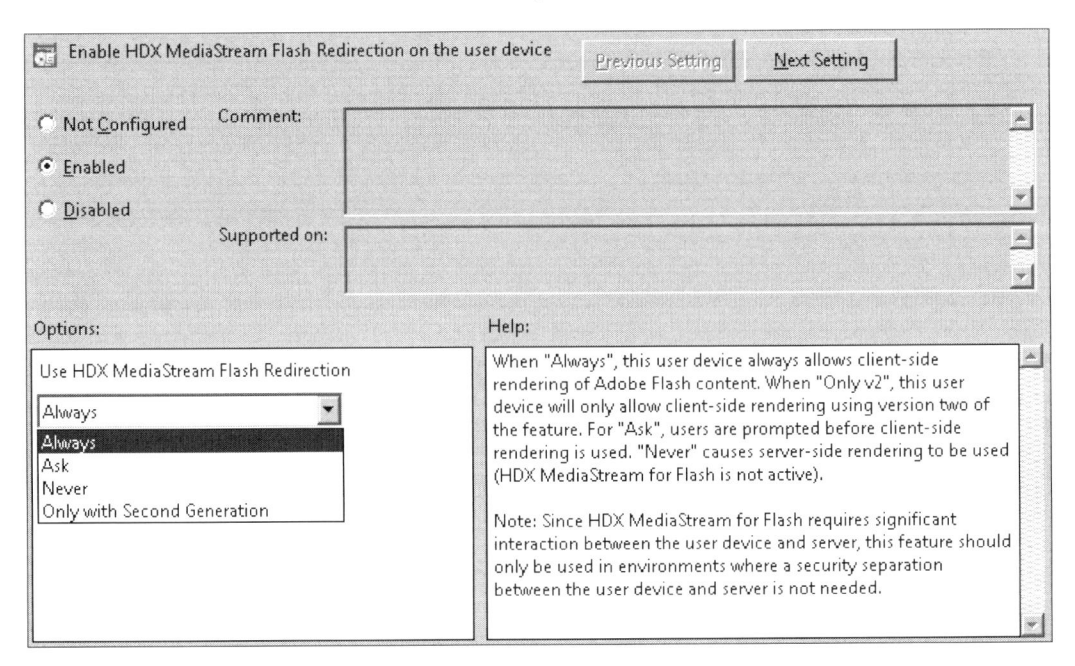

By default, HDX MediaStream for Flash downloads Adobe Flash content and plays the content on the client machine. Enabling server-side content fetching causes it to download the Flash content to the XenApp server and then sends it to the client machine. William can configure this setting using the **Enable server-side content fetching** policy.

> The Flash server-side content fetching whitelist setting on the XenApp server must be enabled and be populated with target URLs for server-side content fetching to work.

Install/uninstall HDX MediaStream for Flash

Installing Citrix HDX MediaStream for Flash is a very straightforward process. We just need to run the file `CitrixHDXMediaStreamForFlash-ServerInstall-x64.msi`, located in the folder `HDX MediaStream for Flash\X64` on the root of the DVD.

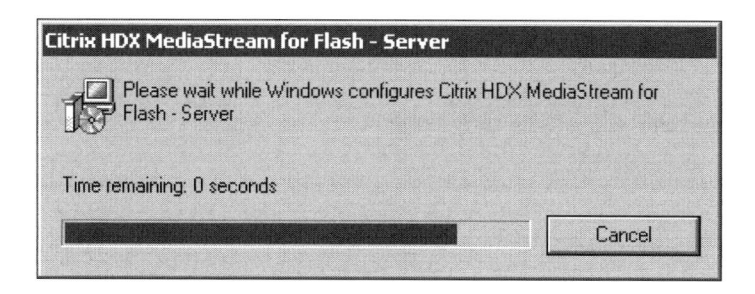

To remove HDX MediaStream for Flash from the XenApp server, we need to use the **Uninstall a program** option accessed in the **Control Panel**, under **Programs** and then select **Citrix HDX MediaStream for Flash - Server**.

Configuring audio using policies

William can configure audio through the **Policies** node of the **Citrix AppCenter Console** on XenApp 6.5 or **Citrix Delivery Services Console** on XenApp 6.0. He can control the audio settings using two policies located under the **ICA** policy: **Audio** and **Bandwidth**.

William can use the **Audio** policy to enable client machines to send and receive audio in sessions.

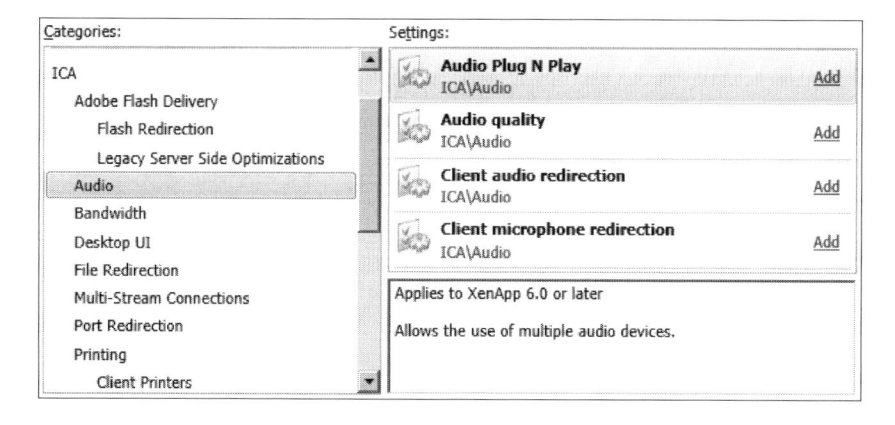

Enabling Audio Plug N Play

The **Audio Plug N Play** setting is a new policy available in XenApp 6.5 and allows the use of multiple audio devices, when it is **Enabled**.

Setting up audio quality

The **Audio quality** setting controls sound quality; available options are **Low**, **Medium**, and **High** (default option).

- **Low (low speed connections for low-bandwidth connections)**: Sounds delivered to the client machine are compressed up to 16 Kbps, causing a significant decrease in the quality of the sound, but providing a good performance for a low-bandwidth connection. With both audio playback and recording, the total bandwidth consumption is 22 Kbps at maximum.

- **Medium (optimized for speech for most LAN-based connections)**: Sounds delivered to the client machine are compressed up to 64 Kbps. With both audio playback and recording, the total bandwidth consumption is 33.6 Kbps at maximum.

- **High (high definition audio for LAN connections where sound quality is important)**: This setting can cause high CPU and bandwidth utilization because client machines play sound at its native rate. Sounds can use up to 1.3 MBps of bandwidth.

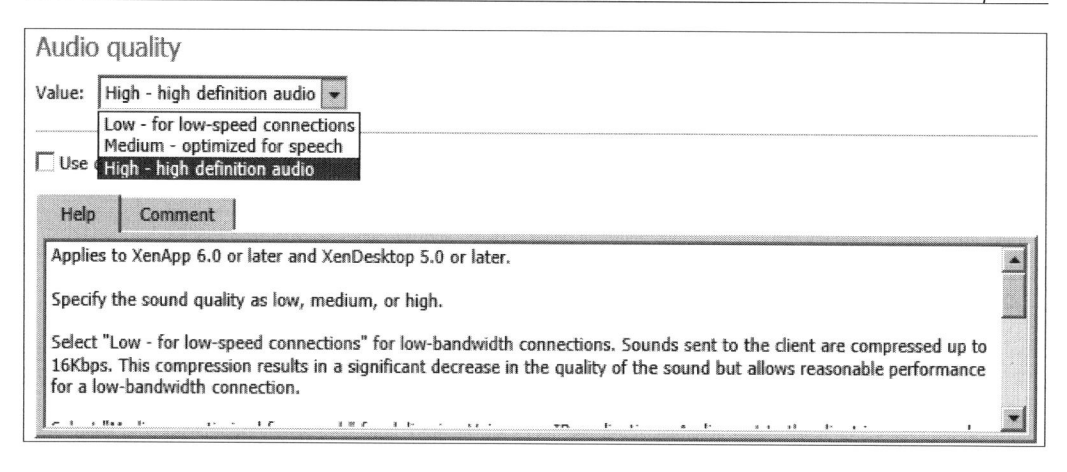

Chapter 10

[Screenshot: Audio quality setting with dropdown showing "Low - for low-speed connections", "Medium - optimized for speech", "High - high definition audio"]

Setting up Client audio redirection

The **Client audio redirection** setting allows (default option) or prevents applications hosted on the XenApp server to play sounds through a sound device installed on the client machine. It also allows or prevents users from recording audio input. After enabling this setting, we can limit the bandwidth consumed by playing or recording audio, using the **Audio redirection bandwidth limit** or the **Audio redirection bandwidth limit percent** settings (explained later, under *Bandwidth policy settings*). When William limits the amount of bandwidth consumed by audio, using previously-mentioned policies, audio quality decreases, but application performance increases.

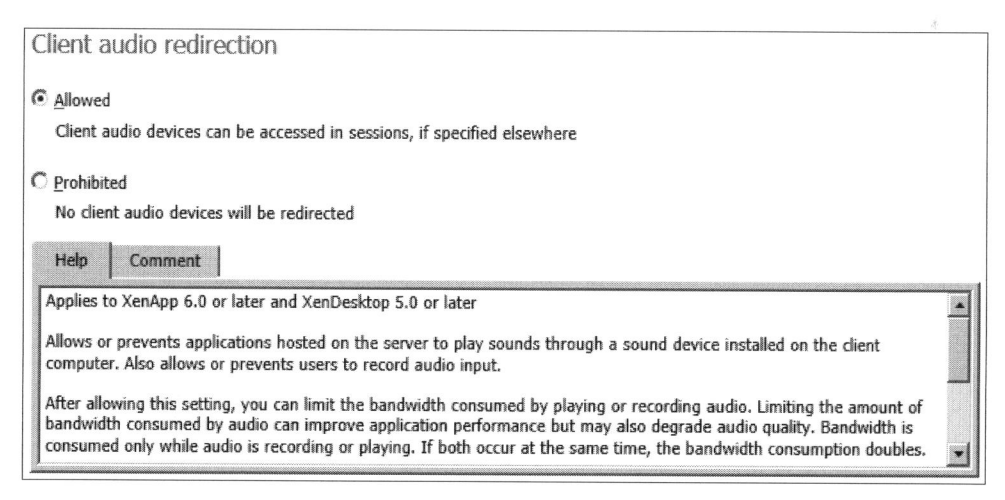

[Screenshot: Client audio redirection settings with "Allowed" selected and "Prohibited" option]

[307]

Setting up Client microphone redirection

The **Client microphone redirection** policy allows (default option) or prohibits users from recording audio using input devices such as a microphone on the client machine. The client machine needs either a built-in microphone or a device that can be plugged into the microphone jack.

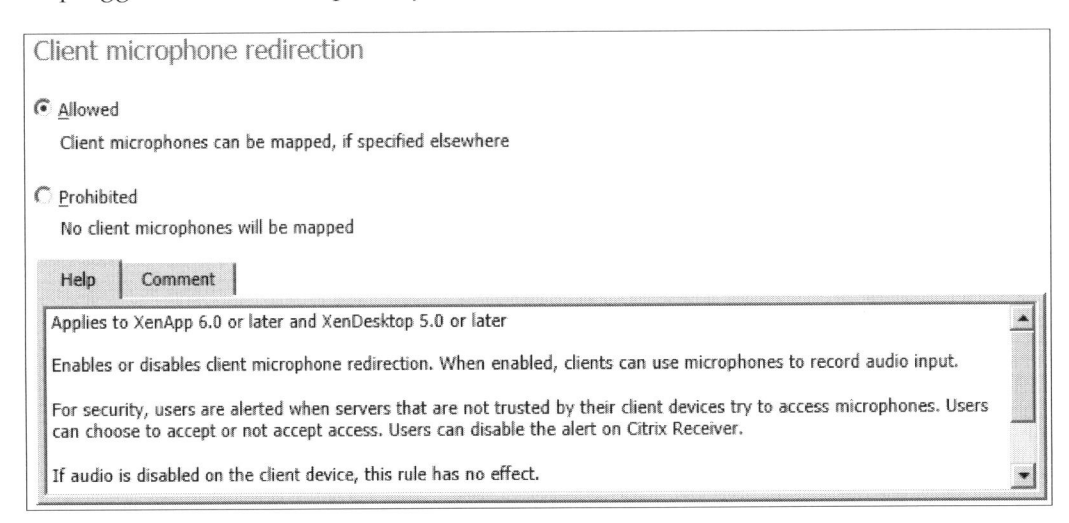

Bandwidth policy settings

The **Bandwidth** section contains policy settings that William can configure to reduce performance problems related to client session bandwidth use. There are several policies, but William will configure four bandwidth policies related to multimedia:

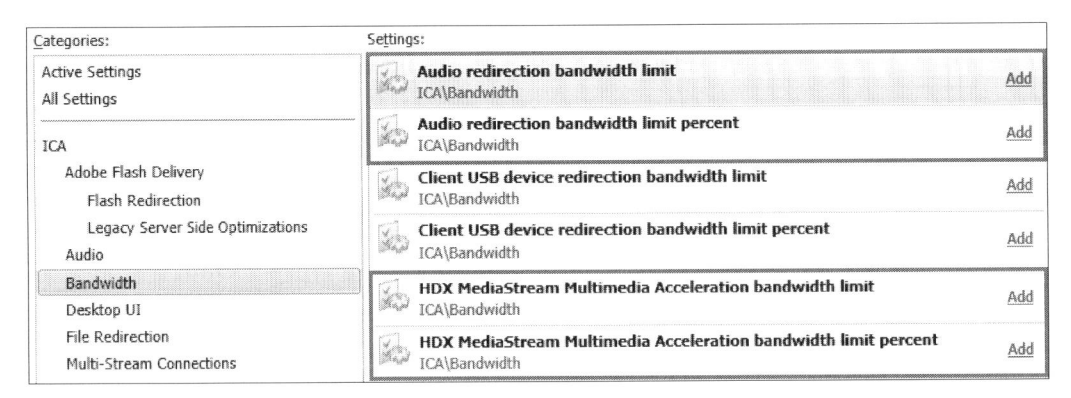

Setting up Audio redirection bandwidth limit

William can configure the **Audio redirection bandwidth limit** setting (available in both XenApp 6.5 and XenApp 6.0) to set the maximum allowed bandwidth in Kbps for playing or recording audio in a user session. If William enters a value for both these settings and the **Audio redirection bandwidth limit percent** setting, the most restrictive setting (with the lower value) is applied.

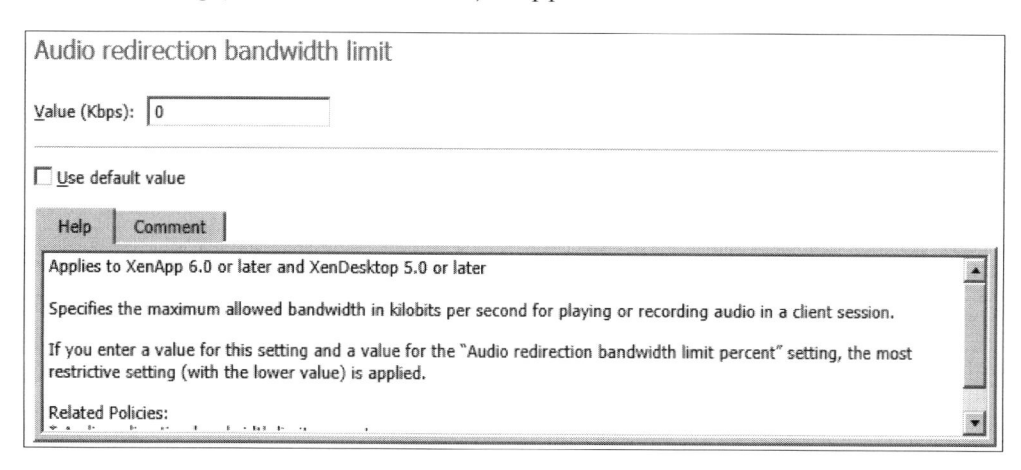

Setting up Audio redirection bandwidth limit percent

This **Audio redirection bandwidth limit percent** setting helps William to set the maximum allowed bandwidth limit for playing or recording audio as a percent of the total session bandwidth. This policy is available in both XenApp 6.5 and XenApp 6.0.

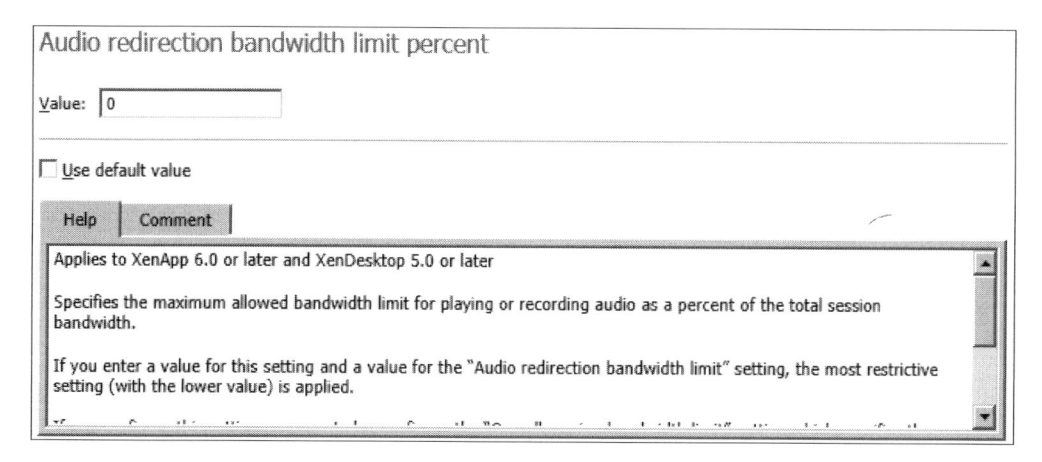

Setting up HDX MediaStream Multimedia Acceleration bandwidth limit

William can use this new policy introduced in XenApp 6.5 to set the maximum allowed bandwidth in Kbps to deliver streaming audio and video to users using HDX MediaStream Multimedia Acceleration. If William enters a value for **HDX MediaStream Multimedia Acceleration bandwidth limit percent** setting, the most restrictive setting (with the lower value) is applied.

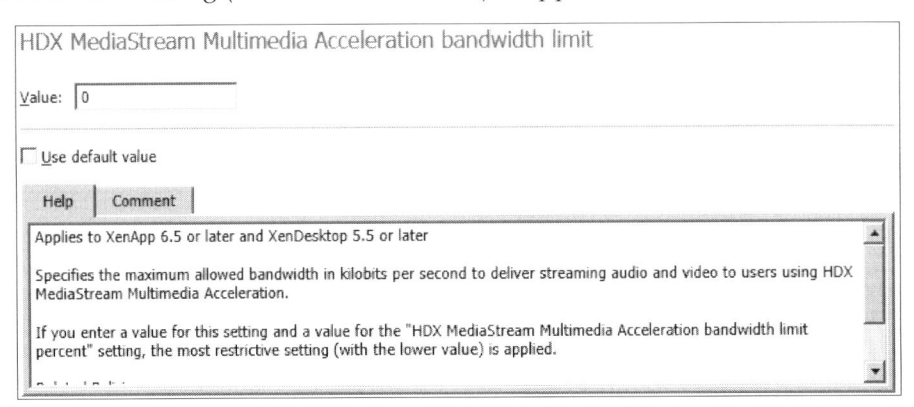

Setting up HDX MediaStream Multimedia Acceleration bandwidth limit percent

This new XenApp 6.5 policy can be used by William to set the maximum allowed bandwidth, as a percent of the total session bandwidth, to deliver streaming audio and video to users using HDX MediaStream Multimedia Acceleration.

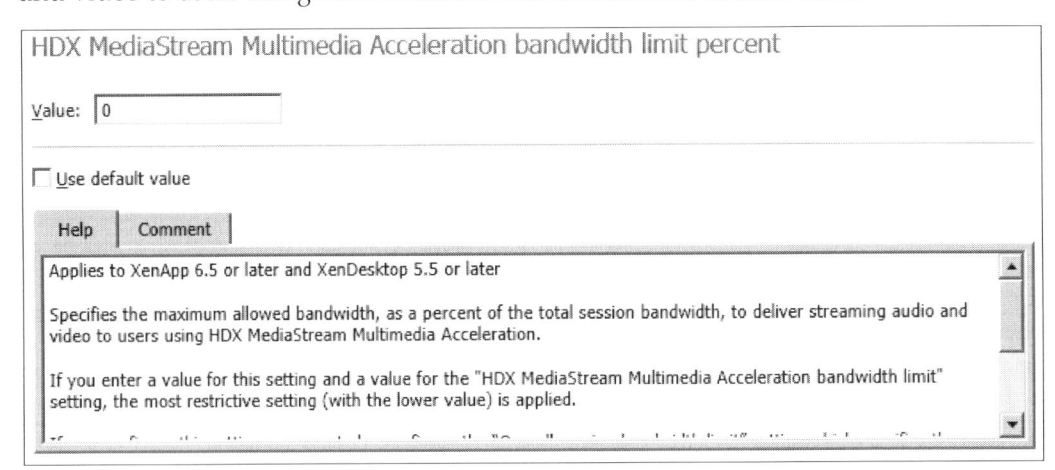

Configuring audio for user sessions

If William disables audio for a published application, then audio will not be available within the application under any condition. If he enables audio for an application, then he can use policy settings to set the conditions where audio is available within the application.

In the **Citrix AppCenter Console** (or **Citrix Delivery Services Console** in XenApp 6.0), William needs to select the published application for which he wants to enable or disable audio and select it from **Action | Application Properties**.

In the **Application Properties** dialog box, he clicks on **Advanced | Client options**.

Then he checks or clears the **Enable legacy audio** checkbox.

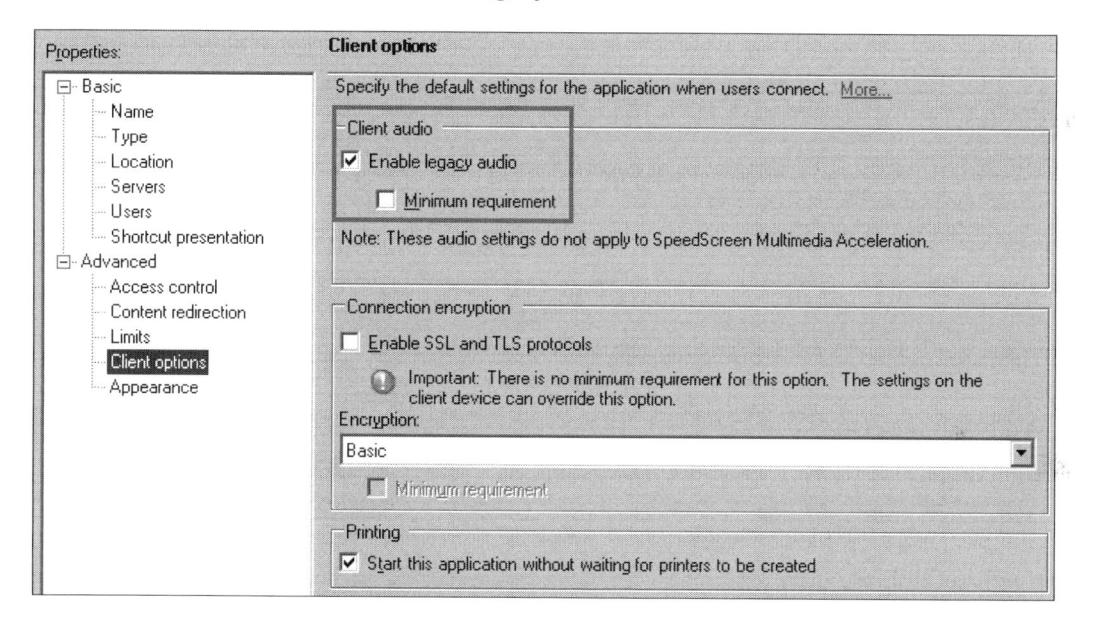

HDX Experience Monitor for XenApp

Citrix released in August 2010 Citrix released the first version (1.0) of HDX Experience Monitor for XenApp 6.0. After the release of XenApp 6.5, Citrix released version 2.0. This tool provides detailed information about the various HDX technologies, including performance and diagnostics information, for the following items:

- Graphics (Version 1.0 and 2.0)
- Network (New in version 2.0)
- Audio (New in version 2.0)

Multimedia Content in XenApp

- Windows Media (New in version 2.0)
- Adobe Flash (Version 1.0 and 2.0)
- Mapped Client Drives (New in version 2.0)
- Scanner (New in version 2.0)
- Smart cards (Version 1.0 and 2.0)
- Printing (Version 1.0 and 2.0)
- System Information (New in version 2.0)
- USB Devices (Version 1.0 only)
- Branch Repeater (Version 1.0 only)
- Session Reliability (Version 1.0 only)

The HDX Monitor is available at `http://hdx.citrix.com/hdx-monitor/downloads`.

After William completes the simple setup, he can run HDX Monitor. This tool must run inside an ICA session. If he tries to run in the XenApp server console or in an RDP session, the version 1.0 will exit after showing a warning message.

The home page of HDX Monitor v2.0 shows a summary of technologies installed and their statuses.

Here is the home page of HDX Monitor v1.0 for XenApp 6.0. This version is recommended only if you are running a XenApp 6.0 farm and is not recommended on XenApp 6.5.

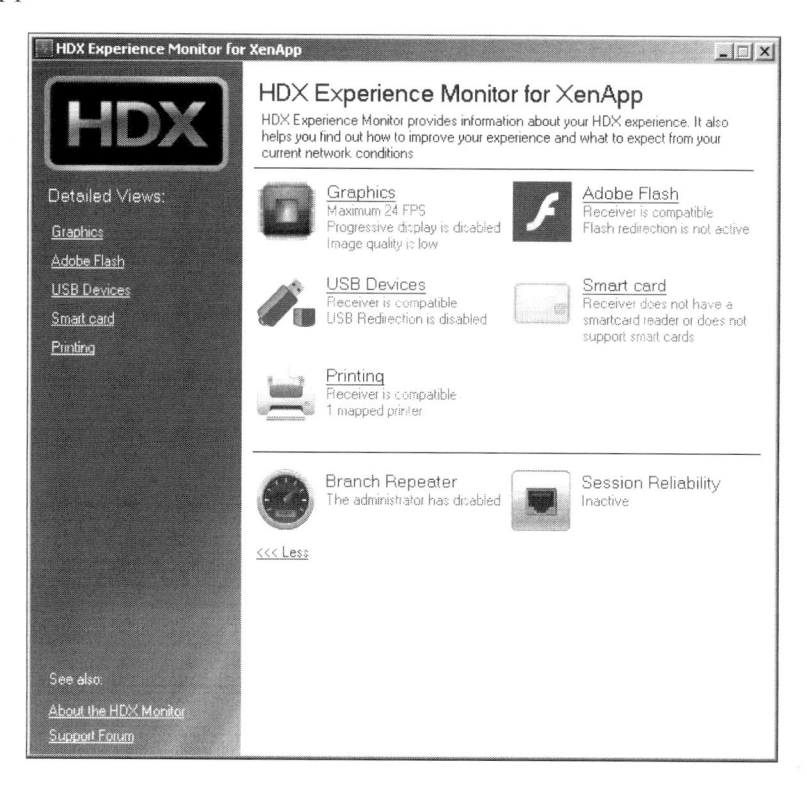

Summary

In this chapter, we learned about multimedia on XenApp farms. In particular, we talked about optimizing user sessions for XenApp using different Citrix HDX features such as:

- HDX MediaStream Multimedia Acceleration
- HDX 3D Image Acceleration
- HDX 3D Progressive Display
- HDX MediaStream for Flash, and more.

We learned in detail how to set up HDX MediaStream for Flash on the Server and configure different multimedia, audio, and video settings using Citrix policies.

In the next chapter, we will learn how to manage sessions.

11
Managing Sessions

In the last chapter, we learned how to improve the multimedia experience of users using Citrix HDX technologies. Citrix HDX enables better multimedia and peripheral support, provides improvements in audio quality, and enables us to deliver multimedia and conference applications on XenApp farms. In this chapter, we will discuss Citrix sessions and how to manage session environments, and in particular, we will talk about:

- Understanding sessions
- Managing and monitoring sessions using Citrix AppCenter console
- Viewing and shadowing sessions
- Maintaining session activity using Session Reliability, Auto Client Reconnect, and ICA Keep-Alive
- Customizing user environments in XenApp
- Limiting concurrent connections
- Optimizing user sessions for XenApp
- Redirection of local special folders in sessions

Understanding sessions

Each time we establish a session with a XenApp server, we use a protocol called **Citrix ICA (Independent Computing Architecture)**, created by Citrix. ICA uses virtual channels to transmit keyboard strokes and mouse movements, printing, video and audio traffic, and more from the client machine to the XenApp server and the response back from the XenApp server to the client machine.

ICA uses port 1494 by default, but when we enable the **XenApp Session Reliability** feature in our XenApp farm, port 2598 is used instead of port 1494.

Managing Sessions

When a client machine initiates communication to the XenApp server with an ICA client and the user is successfully authenticated against the XenApp farm, a session is created on the server. The session is the core of the XenApp experience.

We can find a session in three main states: active, idle, and disconnected.

Let's use an example to understand these states. Our friend William Empire at Brick Unit Construction starts a session in XenApp. He opens Microsoft Word and starts working on a letter, now the session is considered to be in an active state.

The active state is maintained as long as there is a communication between the client machine and the XenApp server. If William left his machine for a few minutes to get a coffee, the session state changes to idle.

While a session is in an idle state, communication channels are kept open, but the communication between the client machine and the XenApp server is stopped.

When William returns and continues using the Word document, the session moves back to the active state.

When a session is open and idle on the server, the applications (and the environment) still use resources (and a license!) on the XenApp servers. To avoid wastage of the server's resources, it is best practice to establish an idle timeout value. If a session has remained idle longer than the allowed threshold, the session will change states.

Here, we can decide to change idle sessions to a disconnected or terminated state. When the XenApp server retains an open session but the user is no longer actively connected this is a disconnected session. Also, disconnected sessions can happen for other reasons such as network issues or loss of network connectivity.

Some applications that rely on virtual channels, such as media players, may act differently. For example, if we disconnect a user from a session running multimedia applications while playing audio, the audio stops playing because the audio virtual channel is no longer available. If the user then connects to the same XenApp server running the disconnected session, the disconnected session is reconnected.

Similar to an idle session, a disconnected session remains running on the XenApp server consuming resources, until the disconnected session is terminated, using the disconnected timeout value.

We can customize users' environments, including whether or not users can access mapped drives, printers available, bandwidth used for audio and redirect, or limited access to special folders. We can use policies or script to detect the location of users and apply different settings on the session.

> If we keep multiple versions of Citrix XenApp farm running, we need to avoid our users logging in to different versions at the same time. This can cause a lot of unexpected results. Also, if we are using roaming profiles, we need to keep multiple versions of profiles and policies for Windows 2003 and Windows 2008. Profiles are different and can cause profile corruption (an administrator's number one nightmare!).

Citrix provides the ability of monitoring or troubleshooting users' sessions, using shadowing and keeping sessions running on high latency network connections.

Keeping the Citrix Receiver or Citrix Plug-In (formerly known as Citrix Client) updated is very important. This ensures our users are able to use the latest features in their sessions and makes session troubleshooting a lot easier (one of the first questions from Citrix Technical Support is which version of Citrix Receiver or Citrix Plug-In our users are running). The next chapter provides a lot of information about the Citrix Receiver or Citrix Plug-In.

Monitoring XenApp sessions

In this chapter, we are going to help William Empire and his team to manage sessions on the Brick Unit Construction farm, using the **Citrix AppCenter** Console (formerly known as **Citrix Delivery Services** Console in XenApp 6.0) and the following procedure:

He opens the console, and selects the XenApp server on which he wants to monitor sessions.

In the **Results** pane, he clicks on the **Sessions** tab. This tab shows sessions running on the XenApp server:

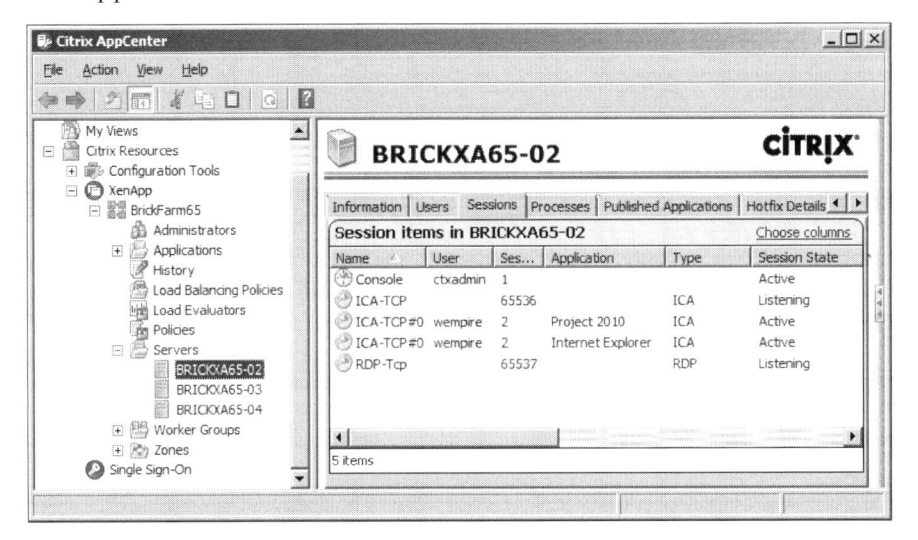

> The **Citrix AppCenter** Console included in XenApp 6.5 is extremely similar to **Citrix Delivery Services** Console in XenApp 6.0, so most of the procedures included in this chapter can be reproduced on both Citrix XenApp 6.5 and XenApp 6.0.

By default, the **Results** pane shows the following information for all sessions (William can click on the **Choose columns** link to specify which columns to display and the display order):

- **User**: Username that initiated the session. The username of anonymous connections begins with "Anon" followed by a session number.
- **Session ID**: This is a unique number that begins with 0 for the first connection to the console. Listener sessions are numbered from 65,537 and numbered backward sequentially.
- **Application Name**: Name of the published application running in the session.
- **Type**: Session type, ICA, or RDP.
- **State**: Active, listen, idle, disconnected, or down.
- **Client Name**: Name of the client machine running the session.
- **Logon Time**: When the user started the session.
- **Idle Time**: Shows how long the session has been idle.
- **Server**: XenApp server on which the application is running.

William can select a session and depending on the session, some tasks become available in the **Actions** pane; these can include **Reset**, **Log off**, **Disconnect**, and **Send Message**.

The lower portion of the results pane displays tabs containing additional information such as **Information**, **Client Cache**, **Session Information**, **Client Modules**, and **Processes** tabs.

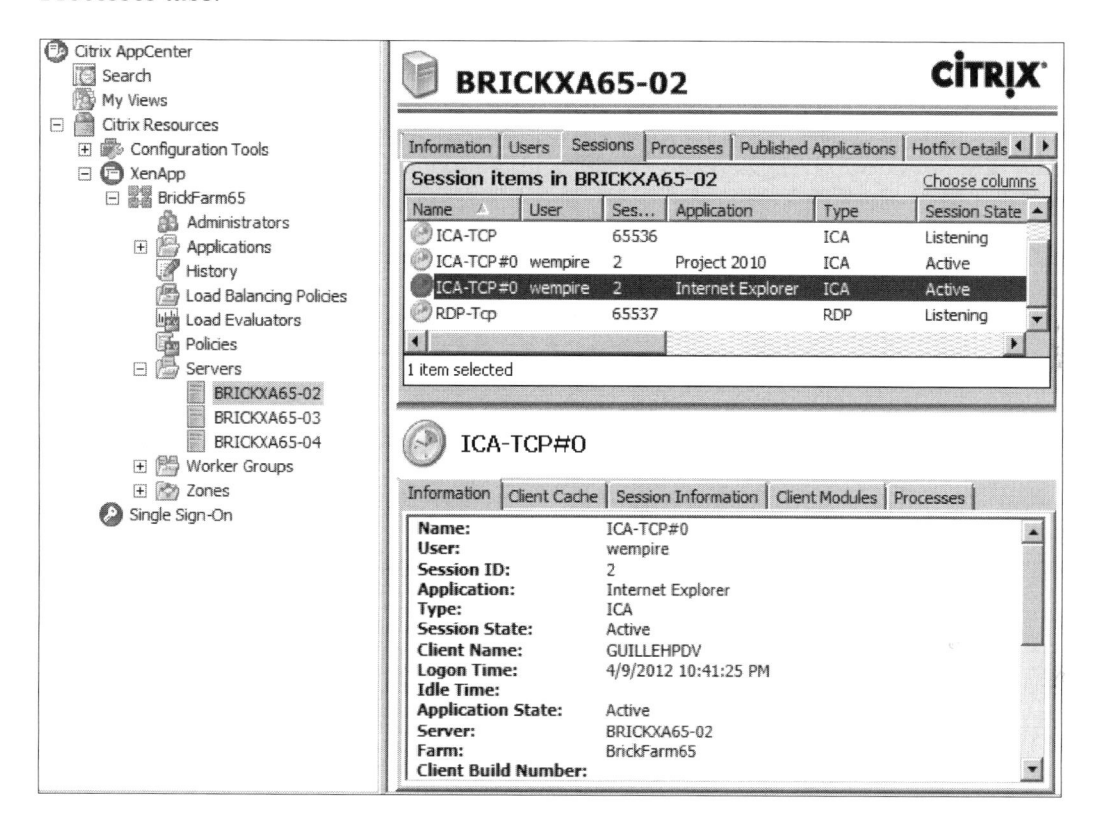

Managing XenApp sessions

Administrators and help desk specialists interact with sessions by resetting, disconnecting, logging off sessions, shadowing, or sending messages to users.

Detailed information to provide permissions to manage sessions on **Citrix AppCenter** Console (or **Citrix Delivery Services** Console in XenApp 6.0) is provided in the section *Managing Citrix Administrators* in Chapter 5, *Using Management Tools*.

Managing Sessions

Disconnecting, resetting, and logging off sessions

William can log off users or reset a user's active or disconnected session.

Resetting a session terminates all processes that are running in that session. He can reset a session to remove the remaining processes in the case of a session error or sometimes because users left the sessions open. However, resetting a session can cause applications to close without saving data.

When he resets a disconnected session, the **Session State** shows **Down**. When he refreshes the console or when the next automatic refresh occurs, the session no longer appears in the list of sessions.

He can select one or multiple sessions, right-click over it (or them), and select one of the options, **Reset**, **Log off**, or **Disconnect** from the drop-down menu. He can also use the same menu to send messages or shadow a user's sessions. Another option is using the **Action** panel, located at the right-hand side of the screen.

Note that we cannot send messages to disconnected sessions, so if there are such sessions selected, the option is not available.

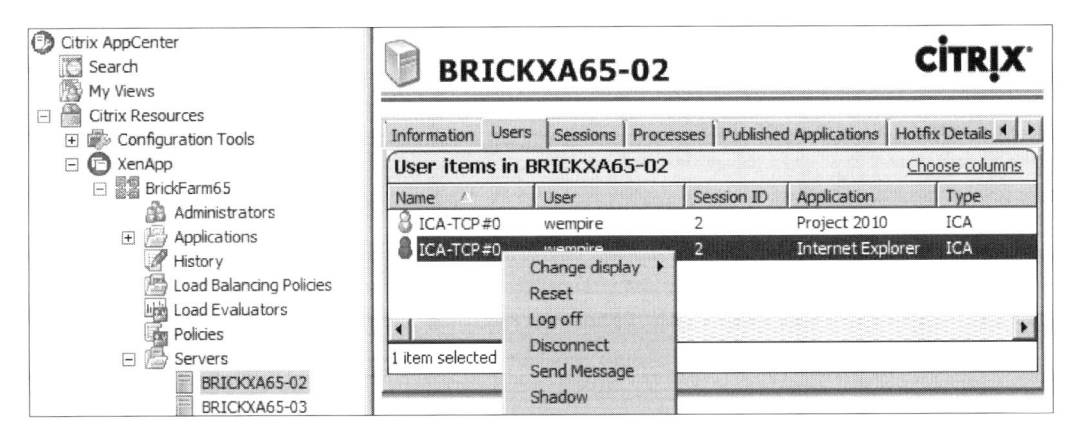

The process to reset, disconnect, or log off a session is pretty similar.

1. William selects the XenApp server to which the user is connected and in the **Results** pane, he then clicks on the **Sessions** tab.

2. Then he selects the session he wants to reset/disconnect/log off (he can select one or more sessions).

3. In the **Actions** pane, he selects **Reset**, **Disconnect**, or **Log off**.

Chapter 11

> Resetting or ending user sessions using **Log off** can result in a loss of data, if users do not close their applications first.

When William clicks on the **Sessions** tab, he will find two special sessions (**ICA-TCP** and **RDP-TCP**) displaying **Listening** in the **Session State**. If he resets a listener session, the server resets all sessions that use the protocol associated with the listener.

For example, if he resets the ICA listener session (**ICA-TCP**), he resets the ICA sessions of all users connected to the XenApp server.

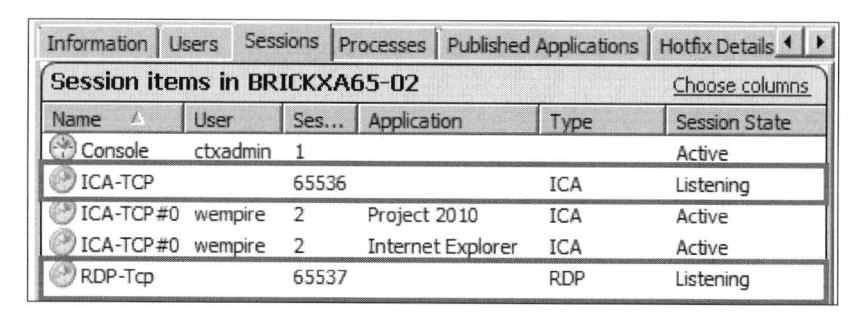

Name	User	Ses...	Application	Type	Session State
Console	ctxadmin	1			Active
ICA-TCP		65536		ICA	Listening
ICA-TCP#0	wempire	2	Project 2010	ICA	Active
ICA-TCP#0	wempire	2	Internet Explorer	ICA	Active
RDP-Tcp		65537		RDP	Listening

Session items in BRICKXA65-02

Terminating processes in a user session

Sometimes, a process inside a session is hung. This happens when the application calls another application, and the second one is not responding. William can kill the process for the second application without affecting the first one or resetting the session, using the following process:

1. William selects the XenApp server to which the user is connected and in the **Results** pane, he selects the session from the **Users** tab.
2. In the lower portion of the **Results** pane, he clicks on the **Processes** tab and selects the process he wants to terminate.

Managing Sessions

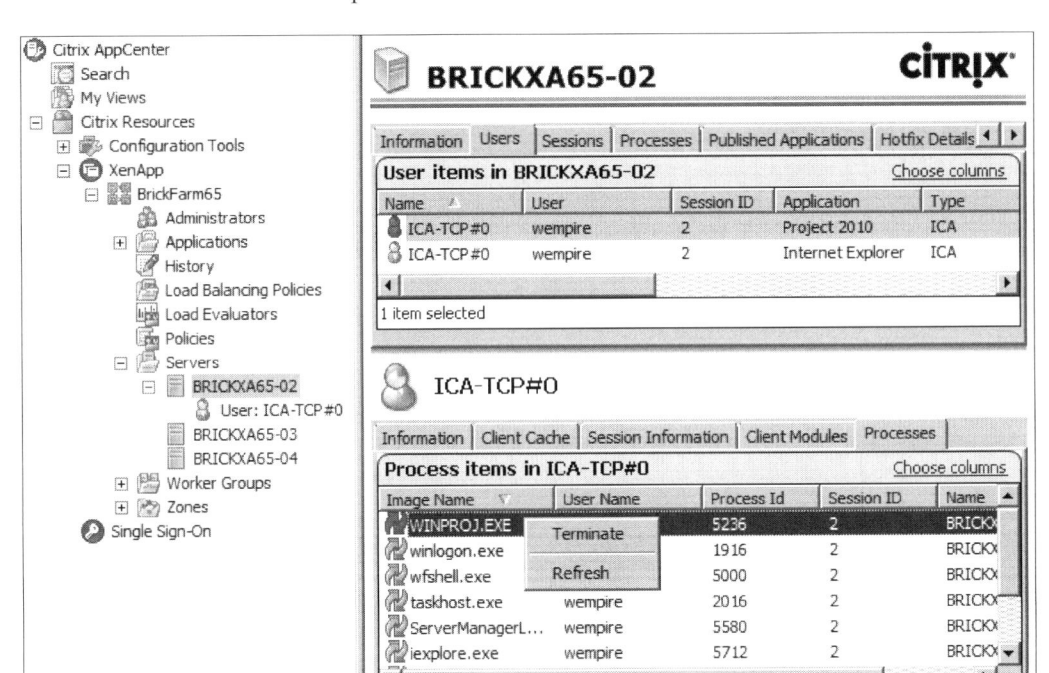

3. Then in the **Actions** pane, he selects **Terminate**:

> Terminating a process may abruptly end a critical process and leave the XenApp server in an unusable state.

Sending messages to users

Sending a message to user sessions is a common practice to notify users of the XenApp server reboots, to alert users about issues with published applications, or requesting a shadowing session to a user. The following is the procedure used by William:

1. From the **Citrix AppCenter** Console (or **Citrix Delivery Services** Console in XenApp 6.0), he selects the XenApp server to which the users are connected. Also, he can send a message to all user sessions in the XenApp farm, selecting a farm node instead of a XenApp server.

2. In the **Results** pane, he clicks on the **Users** tab and then he selects one or more sessions.

3. In the **Actions** pane, he chooses **Send Message**. The **Send Message** dialog box appears.
4. He can edit the title of the message, if required, and enter the message text:

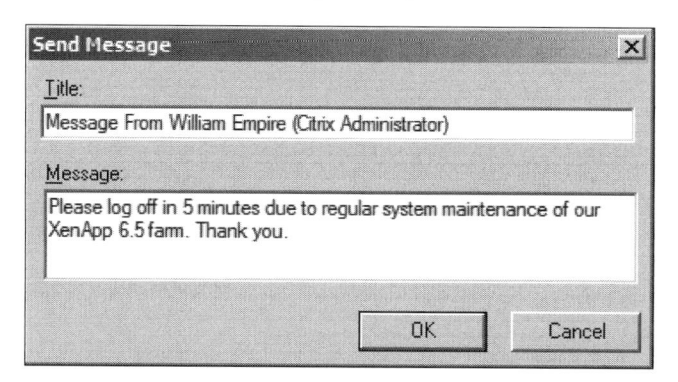

Viewing XenApp sessions

William can view another user's session running on a remote machine by using shadowing. When shadowing is enabled, he can monitor the session activity, and if configured, he can also use our keyboard and mouse to control the user's keyboard and mouse remotely in the shadowed session. Shadowing a session provides a powerful tool to assist and monitor users.

Shadowing is a very useful option for the Brick Unit Construction help desk staff who can use it to help users. They can view a user's screen or actions to troubleshoot problems and can demonstrate correct procedures. Also, it is possible to use shadowing for remote diagnosis and as a training tool.

They can shadow using both the **Citrix AppCenter Console** and the **Shadow Taskbar**.

> Shadow is not going to work if the user has enabled Dual Monitor or Aero (Desktop Experience) on the XenApp server. Refer to the article http://support.citrix.com/article/CTX125693 for more information.

We enable shadowing on a XenApp server when we configure XenApp and select the default option, which allows shadowing on all connections on the server. If we do not leave the shadowing option enabled during configuration, we need to reinstall XenApp to get the shadowing functionality.

Managing Sessions

The following screenshot explains the installation and configuration process (more details about the setup process are available in *Chapter 3, Installing XenApp 6.5*).

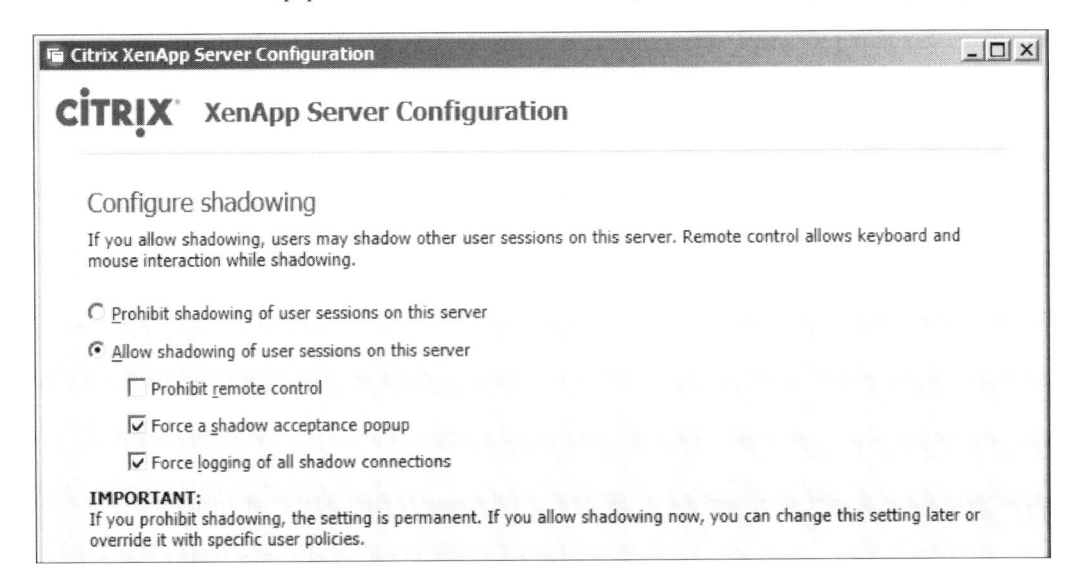

Citrix XenApp Server Configuration

Configure shadowing

If you allow shadowing, users may shadow other user sessions on this server. Remote control allows keyboard and mouse interaction while shadowing.

○ Prohibit shadowing of user sessions on this server

● Allow shadowing of user sessions on this server

☐ Prohibit remote control
☑ Force a shadow acceptance popup
☑ Force logging of all shadow connections

IMPORTANT:
If you prohibit shadowing, the setting is permanent. If you allow shadowing now, you can change this setting later or override it with specific user policies.

By default, the user is notified of the pending shadowing and asked to allow or deny shadowing.

> Our client device machine and shadowing ICA session must support the video resolution of the user's ICA session (the shadowed session), if not, the operation fails. Also, we cannot shadow a system console from another session.

Viewing sessions using the Shadow Taskbar

William and his team can use the **Shadow Taskbar** to shadow multiple ICA sessions from a single location, including the XenApp server console.

He can use the **Shadow** button to start shadowing one or more users. The **Shadow Taskbar** uses the client to launch an ICA session to monitor a user. A separate ICA session is started for each shadowed user.

William needs to enter his username and password to start an ICA session on the XenApp server running the **Shadow Taskbar**.

Please note:

- The administrator or help desk engineer uses a license to log on to the XenApp server and start shadowing a user.
- The **Shadow Taskbar** shows sessions on the server or domain we are logged in to. If we are using multiple domains, we need to log on with an account of the same domain users are connected to.
- Each shadow session consumes memory on the XenApp server, so we need to avoid wastage of resources on XenApp servers and limit the number of simultaneous shadow sessions.
- Each shadowed session is represented by a task button on the **Shadow Taskbar**. We can use this button to switch quickly between the shadowing sessions we have opened.

Starting the Shadow Taskbar

From the **Start** menu, William needs to choose **All Programs | Citrix | Administration Tools | Shadow Taskbar**.

To configure shadowing options, he needs to right-click on an empty area of the **Shadow Taskbar** or press *Shift + F10*. He can switch between shadow sessions, using buttons in the **Shadow Taskbar**.

To close the **Shadow Taskbar**, he needs to right-click on an empty area of the **Shadow Taskbar** and select **Exit**.

Initiating shadowing

On the **Shadow Taskbar**, William clicks on the **Shadow** button. The **Shadow Session** dialog box appears.

The **Available users** list shows user sessions that can be selected for shadowing in the current domain. User sessions are organized by XenApp servers, published applications, and users.

The **Shadowed users** list shows user sessions selected for shadowing and existing shadow sessions; it also displays the username of currently shadowed users next to the shadow icon.

Managing Sessions

In the **Available users** list, he needs to select one or more users to shadow and then click on the **Add** button. At that moment, the selected users move to the **Shadowed users** list. Clicking on the **OK** button will cause shadowing initiated for all users in the **Shadowed users** list.

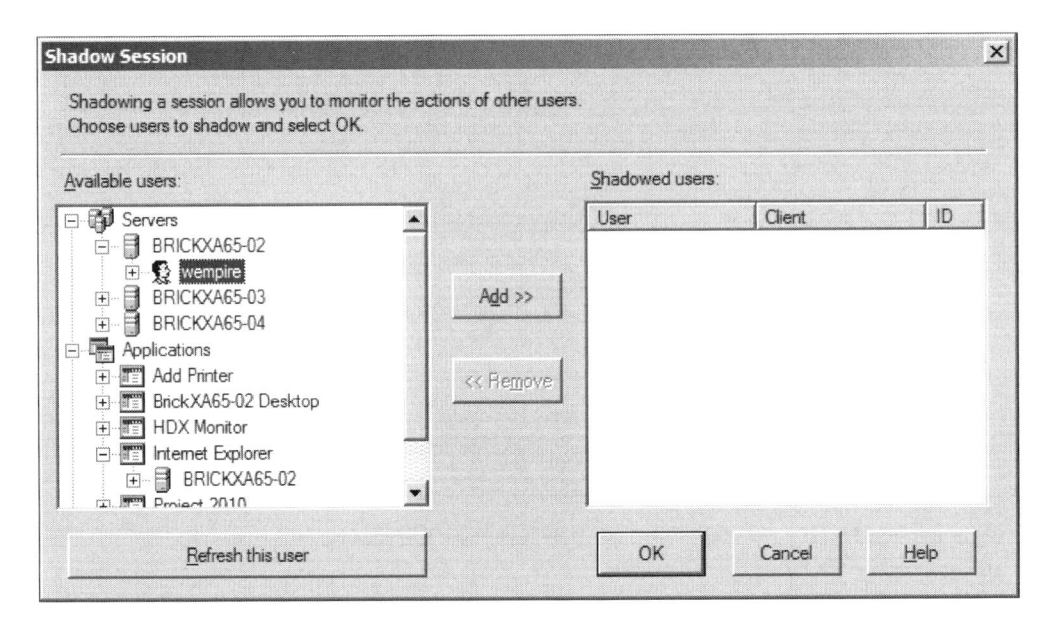

Ending a shadowing session

On the **Shadow Taskbar**, William needs to click on the **Shadow** button. The **Shadow Session** dialog box appears.

In the **Shadowed users** list he needs to select the users to stop shadowing and click on **Remove**.

> We can end a shadow session by right-clicking on the session's task button on the **Shadow Taskbar** and clicking **Stop Shadow**. We can end all shadow sessions by right-clicking the **Shadow Taskbar** and clicking on **Stop All Shadowed Sessions**.

Enabling logging for shadowing

After configuring XenApp, William can enable shadow logging and configure shadow logging output to one of two locations on the XenApp server:

- **In a Central File**: This option records a limited number of logging events, such as date and user being shadowed. When he configures shadow logging through the **Shadow Taskbar**, logged events are not recorded in the **Windows Event Log** and they go to the file specified.
- **Windows Event Log**: This option logs events in the **Application log** of the **Windows Event Log**. These include user shadowing requests, such as when users stop shadowing, failure to launch shadowing, and access to shadowing denied.

Logging events **In a Central File** makes the management of a log easy. Because just shadowing events go in to this file, they are easy to review.

William can use the following process to configure shadow logging **In a Central File**:

1. He clicks on an empty area of the **Shadow Taskbar** and presses *Shift + F10*.
2. Then he clicks on **Logging Options**.
3. He enables the **Enable Logging** checkbox and specifies a log file path.
4. Finally, he clicks on the **Clear Log** button to empty the current log file.

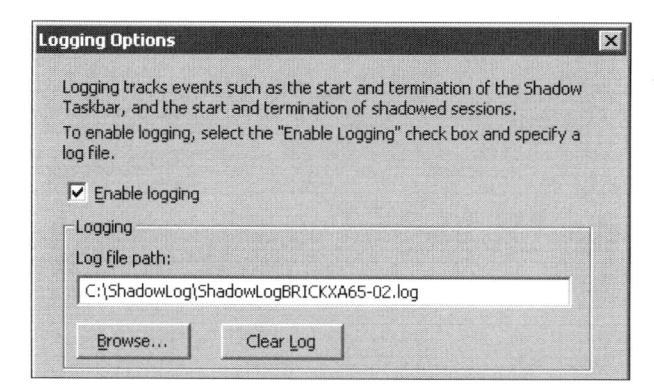

Managing Sessions

Also, William can enable shadow logging in the **Windows Event Log** by configuring the **Citrix User policy**: **Log shadow attempts** set to **Enabled**:

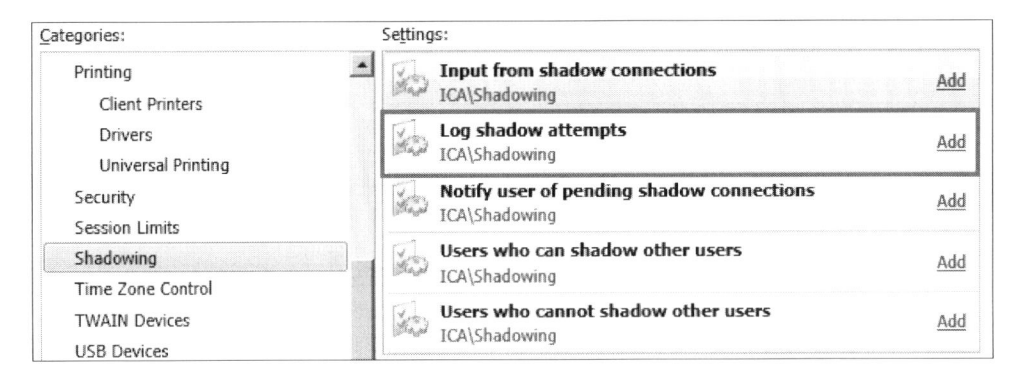

Enabling user-to-user shadowing

William can create a user policy to enable user-to-user shadowing, which allows users to shadow other users without requiring them to be members of the Citrix administrator group. With user-to-user shadowing, multiple users from different locations can view present and training sessions, allowing one-to-many, many-to-one, and many-to-many online collaborations.

Also, William can enable Help Desk personnel to shadow users' sessions or allow Brick Unit Project Managers and Architects to hold online meetings to review the current project status.

William enables user-to-user shadowing by creating policies that define users who can and cannot shadow, then he assigns these policies to the users to be shadowed.

Creating a shadowing policy

Creating a policy requires us to go through the following steps:

1. Create a user policy that lists the users who can shadow other users' sessions.
2. Assign the policy to the users to be shadowed.
3. Publish the Citrix **Shadow Taskbar** and assign it to the users who will shadow.

> The **Shadow Taskbar** cannot function in seamless mode.

Now we are going to help William to enable Brick Unit Help Desk staff shadow the Project Manager group, using the following procedure:

1. William creates a new **User policy** named **Project Manager Shadowing**:

New Policy

Enter basic policy information

Name: Project Manager Shadowing

Description: This is a USER policy to manage Project Manager Shadowing

Remaining Steps

- Settings - what will be applied by this policy
- Filters - when to apply this policy
- Enable - whether to immediately enable this policy

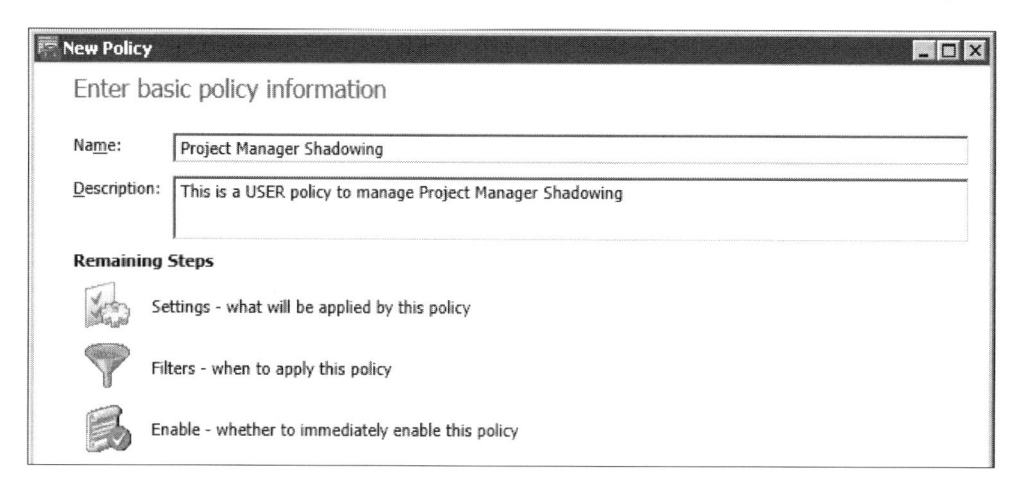

2. As the Project Managers may work with sensitive data, William wants to add the **Notify user of pending shadow connections Citrix User policy** setting and set it to **Enabled**. Also, because the Project Managers group does not want other users to take control of their mouse and keyboard, he adds the **Input from shadow connections Citrix User policy** setting and sets it to **Prohibited**.

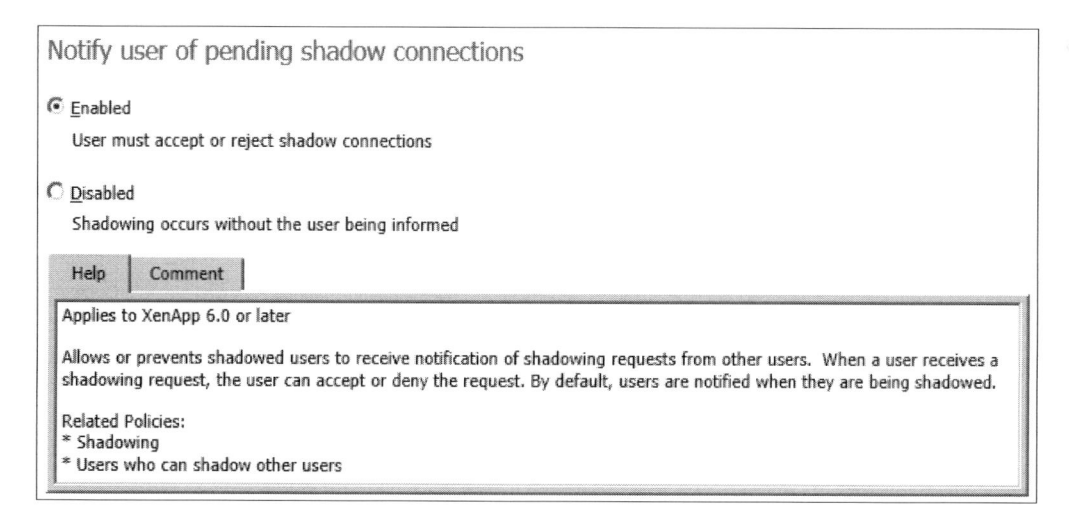

Notify user of pending shadow connections

⦿ Enabled
User must accept or reject shadow connections

○ Disabled
Shadowing occurs without the user being informed

| Help | Comment |

Applies to XenApp 6.0 or later

Allows or prevents shadowed users to receive notification of shadowing requests from other users. When a user receives a shadowing request, the user can accept or deny the request. By default, users are notified when they are being shadowed.

Related Policies:
* Shadowing
* Users who can shadow other users

Managing Sessions

3. Now he needs to add users to the **Users who can shadow other users** setting and select the users who can shadow the **Project Managers group**: Help Desk staff and Domain Admins in Brick Unit.

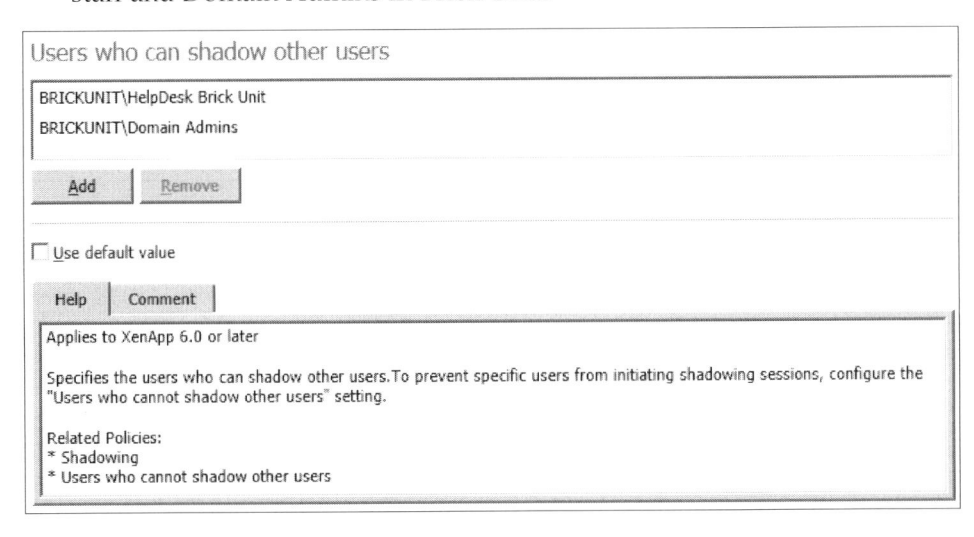

```
Users who can shadow other users

BRICKUNIT\HelpDesk Brick Unit
BRICKUNIT\Domain Admins

   Add      Remove

☐ Use default value

  Help  |  Comment
Applies to XenApp 6.0 or later

Specifies the users who can shadow other users. To prevent specific users from initiating shadowing sessions, configure the
"Users who cannot shadow other users" setting.

Related Policies:
* Shadowing
* Users who cannot shadow other users
```

4. He adds the user filter and selects the users who can receive shadowing requests. Here William adds the **Project Managers group**.

```
Choose when to apply the settings using filters

Filters to show: XenApp (All Versions)    ▼    Search All Filters    🔍

Categories:              Filters:
Active Filters           ▽  Access Control                              Add
All Filters
                         ▽  Branch Repeater                             Add

                         ▽  Client IP Address                           Add

                         ▽  Client Name                                 Add

                         ▽  Organizational Unit                         Add

                         ▽  User or Group                          Edit Remove
                            Allow - BRICKUNIT\BU Project Managers

                         ▽  Worker Group                                Add

Applies to XenApp 6.0 or later and XenDesktop 5.0 or later

The User filter allows you to apply policies based on the user or group membership
of the user connecting to the session.

If no filters are configured for an enabled policy then all of the configured settings
```

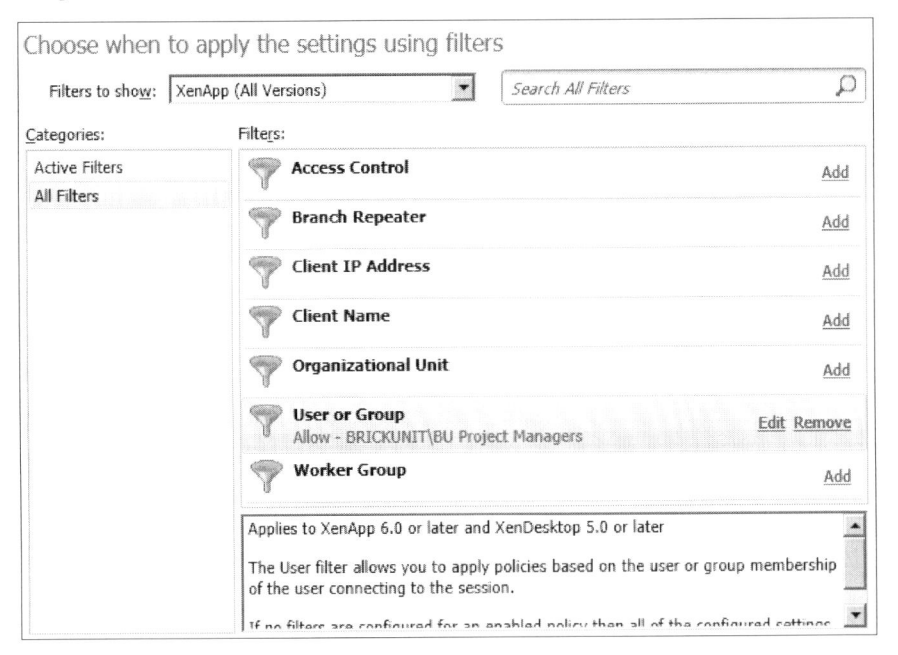

5. Finally, he finishes the wizard, enabling and saving the policy.

Maintaining session activity

Users can lose network connectivity for various reasons, including unreliable networks, and change of wireless network for mobile users. We can increase the reliability of sessions and reduce the amount of inconvenience, downtime, and loss of productivity using the following features:

- **Session Reliability**
- **Auto Client Reconnect**
- **ICA Keep-Alive**

Configuring Session Reliability

When we enable Session Reliability, any temporary disconnection from the network keeps the session active, allowing users to remain connected but with the screen frozen and the cursor changed to the hourglass; it will continue to queue keyboard input until network connectivity resumes or the timeout is reached.

This feature was originally designed to help users connected to their application sessions on low bandwidth conditions, such as remote locations, but now this feature is especially useful for mobile users with wireless connections.

For example, one Brick Unit project manager with a wireless connection is taking notes in a construction site and momentarily loses connectivity. Usually, the session is disconnected and disappears from the user's screen, and the user has to reconnect to the disconnected session.

Session Reliability reconnects users without re-authentication prompts.

> We can use Session Reliability with Secure Sockets Layer (SSL).

By default, Session Reliability is enabled through policy settings. William can set the port on which XenApp listens for session reliability traffic and the amount of time Session Reliability keeps an interrupted session connected using Citrix policies.

The Citrix **Computer** policy **Session reliability connections** setting allows or prevents session reliability.

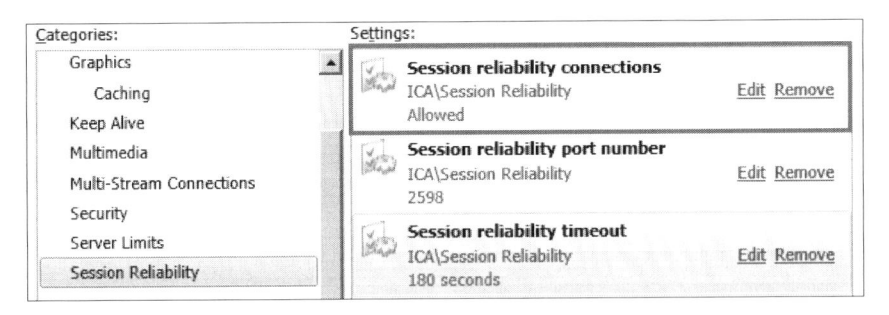

Categories:	Settings:	
Graphics	**Session reliability connections** ICA\Session Reliability Allowed	Edit Remove
Caching		
Keep Alive		
Multimedia	**Session reliability port number** ICA\Session Reliability 2598	Edit Remove
Multi-Stream Connections		
Security		
Server Limits	**Session reliability timeout** ICA\Session Reliability 180 seconds	Edit Remove
Session Reliability		

The **Session reliability connections** policy setting lets us allow or prohibit the Session Reliability feature.

Incoming session reliability connections use the default port 2598, unless we change the port number using the **Session reliability port number** policy setting.

The **Session reliability timeout** setting has a default of 180 seconds, or three minutes.

This is the time allowed before the session is disconnected. If we do not want users to be able to reconnect to the interrupted sessions without having to re-authenticate, we can use the **Auto client reconnect** feature.

If we use both Session Reliability and Auto Client Reconnect, the two features work in sequence.

Session Reliability closes, or disconnects, the user session after the amount of time we specify in the Citrix **Computer** policy **Session reliability timeout** setting. After that, the **Auto client reconnect** policy setting takes effect, attempting to reconnect the user to the disconnected session.

Configuring automatic client reconnection

The Auto Client Reconnect feature allows Citrix Receiver or Citrix Plug-In for Windows and Java to detect broken connections and automatically reconnect users to disconnected sessions. When the Citrix Receiver or Plug-In running on client machine detects an unintentional disconnection of a session, it tries to reconnect the user to the session until a successful reconnection, or the user cancels the reconnection attempts.

William can configure **Auto Client Reconnect** with the following Citrix **Computer** policy settings:

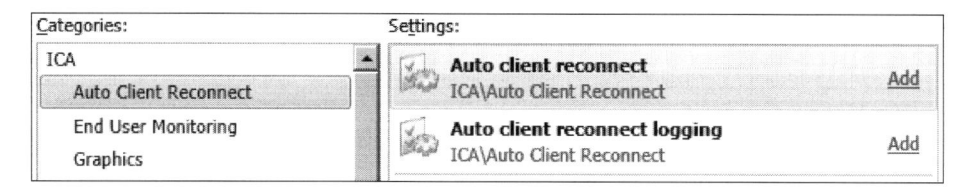

Categories:	Settings:	
ICA	Auto client reconnect	Add
Auto Client Reconnect	ICA\Auto Client Reconnect	
End User Monitoring	Auto client reconnect logging	Add
Graphics	ICA\Auto Client Reconnect	

- **Auto client reconnect**: Enables or disables automatic reconnection by the same client after a connection has been interrupted.
- **Auto client reconnect logging**: Enables or disables (default setting) logging of reconnection events in the Windows event log.
- **Auto client reconnect authentication** (only available in XenApp 6.0): Enables or disables the requirement for user authentication upon automatic reconnection.

The **Auto Client Reconnect** incorporates an authentication mechanism based on encrypted user credentials. When a user initially logs on to a server farm, XenApp encrypts and stores the user credentials in memory, and creates and sends a cookie containing the encryption key to the Citrix Receiver or Plug-In. The Receiver or Plug-In submits the key to the XenApp server for reconnection. The server decrypts the credentials and submits them to Windows log in for authentication. When cookies expire, users must reauthenticate to reconnect to sessions.

Cookies are not used if we enable the **Auto client reconnection authentication** setting. Instead, XenApp displays a dialog box to the users requesting credentials when the Citrix Receiver or Plug-In attempts to reconnect automatically.

We can disable **Auto Client Reconnect** on the Citrix Receiver or Plug-In for Windows by using the `icaclient.adm` file. Detailed instructions to import the `icaclient.adm` file are available at `http://xenapp6.musumeci.com.ar`.

Managing Sessions

After we import the `icaclient.adm` file, we can modify the **Session Reliability** and **Automatic Reconnection** setting, located under **User Configuration | Policies | Administrative Templates: Policy definitions (ADMX) | Classic Administrative Templates (ADM) | Citrix Components | Citrix Receiver | Networking routing**.

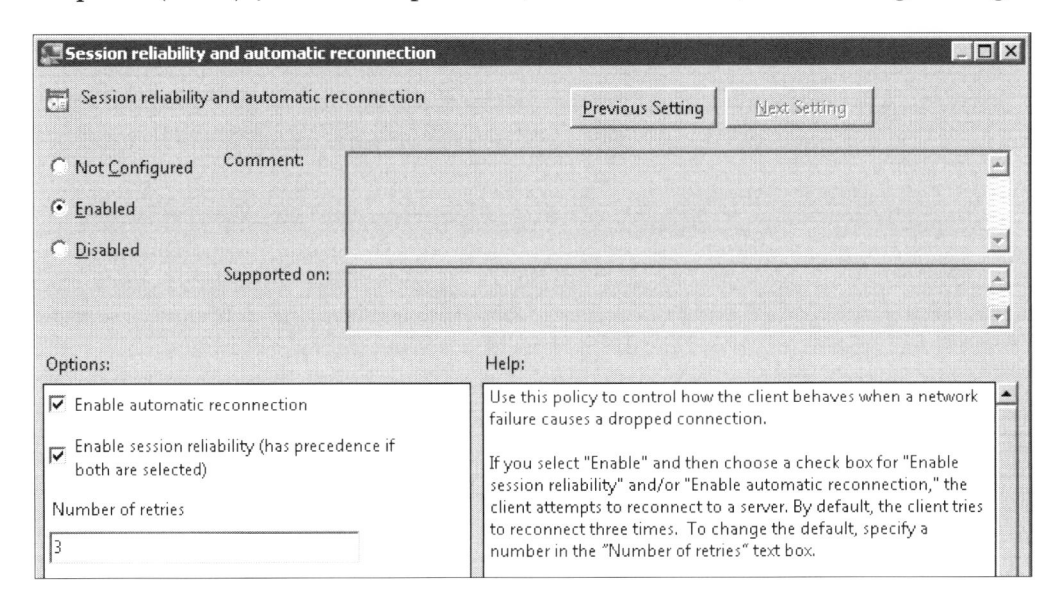

By default, **Auto Client Reconnect** is enabled through policy settings on the farm level.

By default, the ICA TCP connection on a XenApp server is set to disconnect sessions with broken or timed out connections. Disconnected sessions remain intact in system memory and are available for reconnection by the Citrix Receiver or Plug-In. We need to keep in mind all disconnected sessions still running and use resources.

However, if a XenApp server's ICA TCP connection is configured to reset sessions with a broken communication link, automatic reconnection does not occur. Auto **Client Reconnect** works only if the XenApp server disconnects sessions when there is a broken or timed out connection.

The connection can be configured to reset, or log off, sessions with broken, or timed out connections. When a session is reset, attempting to reconnect initiates a new session; thus, rather than restoring a user to the same place in the application in use, the application is restarted.

If XenApp server is configured to reset sessions, **Auto Client Reconnect** creates a new session.

[334]

Configuring ICA Keep-Alive

Enabling the **ICA Keep-Alive** feature prevents broken connections from being disconnected. When we enable it, if XenApp notices no activity (for example, no clock change, no mouse movement, no screen updates), this feature prevents **Remote Desktop Services** from disconnecting that session. XenApp sends keep-alive packets every few seconds to detect if the session is active. If the session is no longer active, XenApp marks the session as disconnected.

The **ICA Keep-Alive** feature does not work if you are using **Session Reliability**. **Session Reliability** has its own mechanisms to handle this issue. We need to configure only **ICA Keep-Alive** for connections that do not use **Session Reliability**.

ICA Keep-Alive settings override keep-alive settings that are configured in Microsoft Windows Group Policy.

Configure the following Citrix **Computer** policy settings:

- **ICA keep alive timeout**: Specifies the interval (1 to 3,600 seconds) used to send ICA Keep-Alive messages. In environments where broken connections are infrequent, enabling keep-alive is not required. The 60-second default interval causes ICA Keep-Alive packets to be sent to client devices' machines every 60 seconds. If a client device does not respond in 60 seconds, the status of the ICA sessions changes to disconnected.

- **ICA keep alives**: Enables or disables sending ICA Keep-Alive messages periodically.

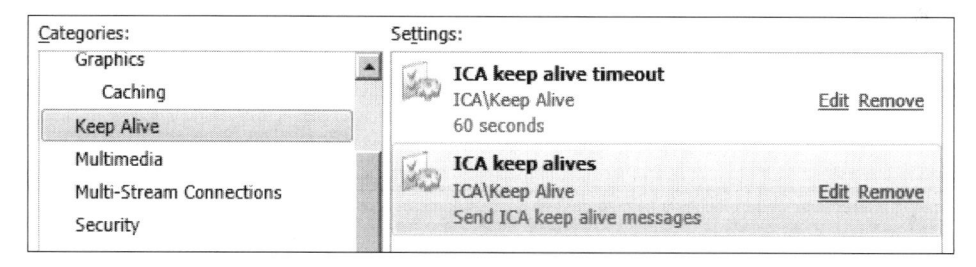

> Servers running the **Citrix Access Gateway** intercept packets being sent from XenApp servers to client machines. We need to set keep-alive values on the **Access Gateway** servers to match **ICA Keep-Alive** values on XenApp servers. This allows ICA sessions to be changed from active to disconnected.

[335]

Customizing user environments in XenApp

XenApp provides different ways to control what users experience in their session environments. We can customize user environments including suppressing or hiding login progress bars, allowing or restricting users from accessing their local devices, port, multimedia content (audio, video), or applications, and more.

We can also customize the user's experience by choosing whether we want published applications and desktops to appear in a window within a **Remote Desktop** window or "seamlessly". In seamless window mode, published applications and desktops appear in separate resizable windows, which make the application seem to be installed locally.

Controlling the appearance of user logons

When users connect to a XenApp server, they can see all connection and login status information in a sequence of screens, from the time they double-click a published application icon on the client machine, through the authentication process, to the moment the published application launches in the session.

XenApp achieves this logon look-and-feel by suppressing the status screens generated by a server's Windows operating system when a user connects. To do this, XenApp setup enables the following Windows local group policies on the XenApp server on which we install the product:

- **Administrative Templates** | **System** | **Remove Boot** | **Shutdown** | **Logon** | **Logoff status messages**
- **Administrative Templates** | **System** | **Verbose versus normal status messages**

Active Directory group policies take precedence over equivalent local group policies on servers. So, if we enable these specific policies in our domain, this will override the Citrix local policies. We can disable these local GPOs for troubleshooting but it is recommended to keep them enabled on production environments.

Controlling access to devices and ports

The Citrix Receiver or Citrix Plug-In provides mapping disks or devices on the client machine so users can access their own devices within sessions. Client device mapping provides:

- Access to local drives and ports
- Cut-and-paste data between the client machine and the session
- Multimedia playback inside the session

During logon, the Citrix Receiver or Plug-In lists the available client drives and COM ports and sends the list to the XenApp server. By default, client drives appear as network resources, so the drives appear to be directly connected to the server. The client's drives are displayed with descriptive names so they are easy to locate among other network resources.

In general, XenApp displays client drive letters as they appear on the client machine; for example, the user device's hard disk drive appears as `C:` on `ClientName`, where `ClientName` is the name of the client machine. This allows the user to access client drive letters in the same way locally and within sessions.

These drives are used by Windows Explorer and other published applications like a network drive.

The following example shows the administrator using Windows Explorer running on a XenApp session. The hard drive `C:` is the drive in the XenApp server and CD/DVD and other disks are local disks on the client machine (note the label Local Disk).

We can use GPO to hide the server's hard drive from users and avoid confusion.

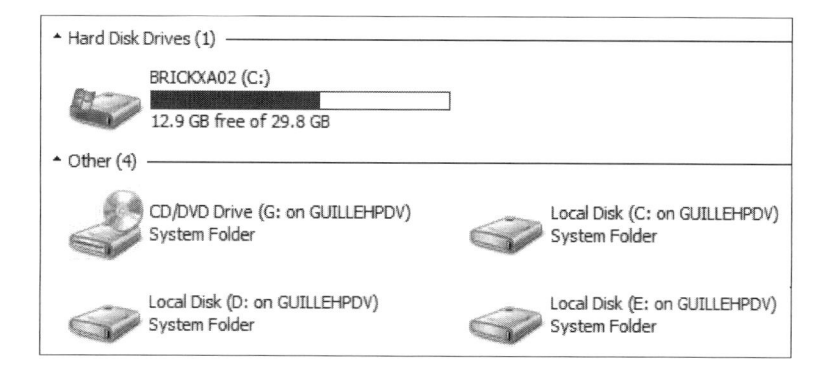

Managing Sessions

Mapping drives

We can use Citrix policies to allow or prevent device mapping. We can use the **File Redirection (User)** policy to enable or disable mapping to client floppy disk drives, hard drives, CD/DVD drives, or remote drives.

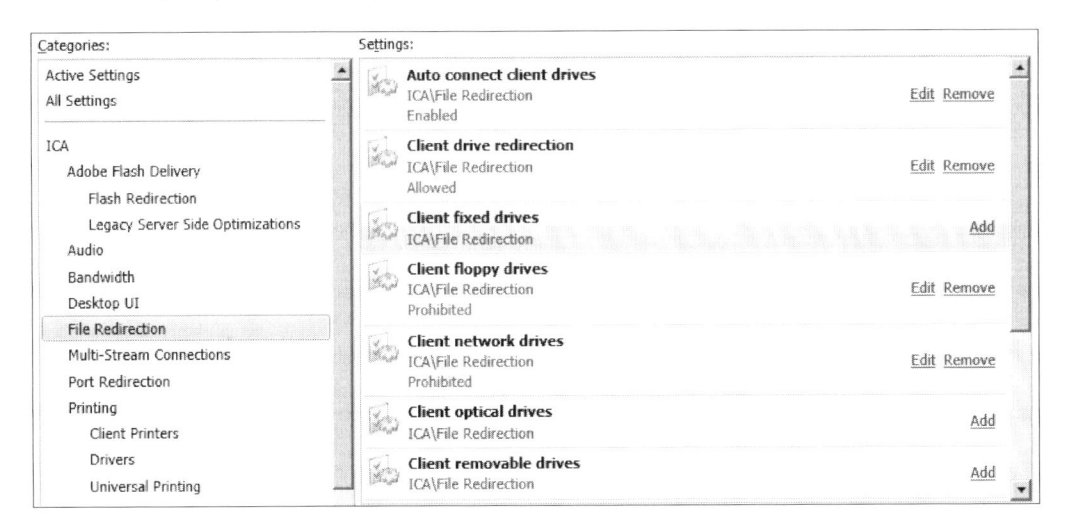

Redirecting COM ports and audio

Client COM port redirection allows a remote application running on the XenApp server to access devices attached to COM ports on the client machine. Both COM port and audio redirection are configured with the **Port Redirection (User)** policy or **Ports (User)** policy on XenApp 6.0.

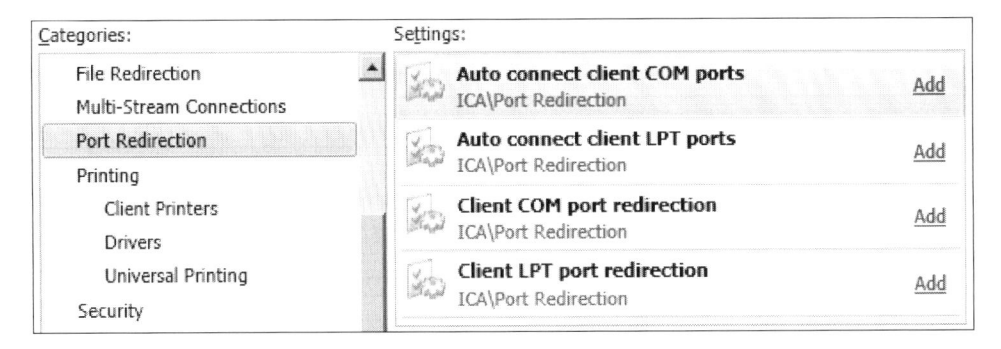

Limiting concurrent connections

William Empire can limit the number of connections to reduce the use of XenApp server resources, like CPU and memory, and increase the amount of concurrent users per server.

William can set a limit of two concurrent connections for users. If a user tries to establish more than two connections, a message tells the user that a new connection is not allowed. This is a common practice to reduce resource and license use.

We can also enable session sharing to limit the number of connections on a XenApp farm. Session sharing is a mode in which more than one published application runs on a single connection.

Session sharing occurs when a user has an open session and launches another application that is published on the same XenApp server; the result is that the two applications run in the same session. For session sharing to occur, both applications must be hosted on the same XenApp server. Session sharing is configured by default when we specify that applications appear in seamless window mode. If a user runs multiple applications with session sharing, the session counts as one connection.

Limiting the number of sessions per server

When this setting is used, users can start sessions until the limit has been reached.

William can configure the **Server Settings | Connection Limits (Computer)** policy using the following settings:

- **Limit user sessions**: Sets the maximum number of concurrent connections, in the range 0 to 8192 per user. A value of 0 indicates no connections allowed.
- **Limits on administrator sessions**: Enables or disables connection limit enforcement for Citrix administrators. This setting affects their ability to shadow other users. Local administrators are exempted from the limit so they can establish as many connections as necessary.

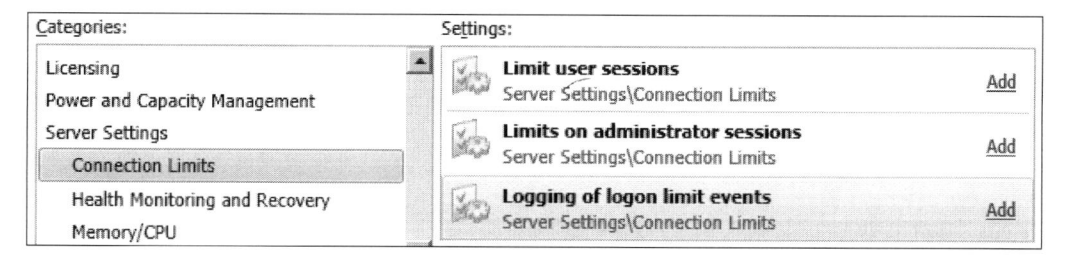

Limiting application instances

By default, XenApp does not limit the number of instances of a published application that can run at one time in a farm. By default, a user can launch more than one instance of a published application at the same time.

William can specify the maximum number of instances that a published application can run at one time or concurrently in the XenApp farm.

Brick Unit Construction bought 25 licenses of Adobe Acrobat Professional; they can publish the Acrobat application and set a limit of 25 concurrent instances in the farm. Once 25 concurrent users are running the application, no more users can launch it.

Another connection control option lets us prevent any user from running multiple instances of a particular published application. With some applications, running more than one instance in a single user context can cause errors.

Brick Unit Construction notices some issues with Outlook. Some are related to Outlook profiles being corrupted. They don't want to rebuild profiles every time users open Outlook to improve login times. Sometimes, users use a .PST file to receive error messages. Help Desk staff found that the same issues occur when users run multiple copies of Outlook in different sessions and XenApp servers. Brick Unit Construction decided to limit users to run only one session of Outlook at the same time. This setting will reduce Help Desk calls (and wastage of resources in the XenApp farm).

> Connection control options apply only to published applications and published desktops and do not affect published content, such as documents and media Files that execute on the client device machine.

To set a limit for a published application or desktop, William needs to use the following procedure:

1. William needs to open the **Citrix AppCenter Console** in XenApp 6.5 or **Citrix Delivery Services Console** in XenApp 6.0, select the farm, and then select **Applications**.
2. He needs to select the application or desktop he wants to modify. In the **Action** menu, he chooses **Application properties**.

3. In the **Properties** tree, he selects **Limits**, then he chooses one or both of the following options:
    - **Limit instances allowed to run in server farm**: He needs to enter the maximum number of instances that can run at one time in the XenApp farm
    - **Allow only one instance of application for each user**: Prevents any user from running more than one instance of this application at the same time

Here, William limits concurrent sessions of Microsoft Project 2010 to 35 users. When a user tries to launch the application when 35 instances are running, XenApp denies the connection request and records the time and the name of the published application in the System log (if logging is enabled). See the following section to enable logging.

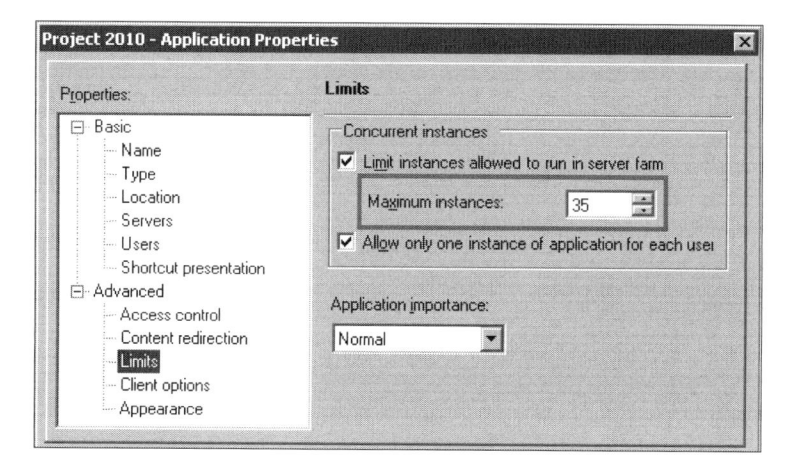

Logging connection denial events

William can enable event logging in the **Windows Event Viewer System log** each time a XenApp server denies a user connection because of a connection control limit. Each XenApp server records the data in its own System log. By default, this type of event logging is disabled.

William can configure XenApp to log when limits are reached (and connections are denied) for the following:

- Maximum connections per user
- Application instance limits
- Application instances per user

Managing Sessions

He needs to configure the **Logging of logon limit events** under the **Server Settings | Connection Limits (Computer)** policy setting to enable or disable logging of connection denial events.

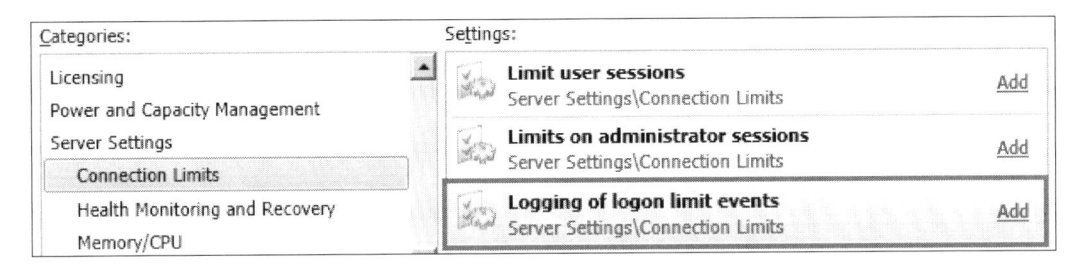

Categories:	Settings:	
Licensing	Limit user sessions Server Settings\Connection Limits	Add
Power and Capacity Management		
Server Settings	Limits on administrator sessions Server Settings\Connection Limits	Add
Connection Limits		
Health Monitoring and Recovery	**Logging of logon limit events** Server Settings\Connection Limits	Add
Memory/CPU		

Sharing sessions and connections

Depending on the Citrix Receiver or Plug-In version, when a user opens an application, it can either appear in a seamless or non-seamless window. These window modes are available for most Receivers or Plug-Ins, including the Web Interface and Citrix Receiver or Citrix Online Plug-In.

- **Non-seamless window Mode**: Published applications and desktops are contained within an ICA session window. Desktops are typically published in non-seamless window mode. Publishing Desktop is the preferred option for thin clients or kiosks.

- **Seamless window Mode**: Published applications and desktops are not contained within an ICA session window. Each published application and desktop appears in its own resizable window, and looks like the application is installed on the client machine. Users can switch between published applications and the local desktop. This is the preferred mode to publish individual applications. Publishing individual applications is a preferred option for desktop computers or laptops.

When a user launches a published application, the Citrix Receiver or Citrix Plug-In establishes a connection to a XenApp server and initiates a session. If session sharing is not configured, a new session is opened on the XenApp server each time a user opens an application.

If we want to share sessions, we need to ensure all applications are published with the same configuration, like encryption; unexpected results may occur when applications are configured for different requirements.

Session sharing always takes precedence over load balancing. Enabling session sharing can cause overload of XenApp servers, if our users have one application running on a server, and they launch a second application that is published on the same XenApp server and the server is at capacity, XenApp still opens the second application on that server.

William needs to use a policy to configure the client handling of remote applications. When this policy is enabled, it uses the list in the Application box to determine which published applications can be directly launched by the client.

This setting is not available by default. William needs to import the `icaclient.adm` and then access the policy located on **Citrix Components | Citrix Receiver | User experience | Remote applications**.

The session sharing feature can be enabled or disabled using the **Session sharing** checkbox.

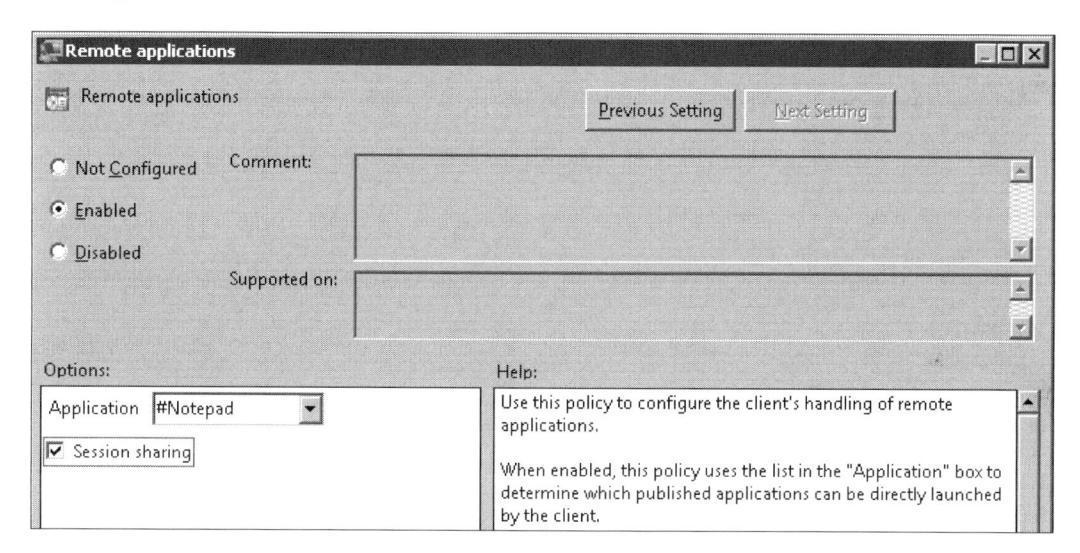

> If we import the `icaclient.adm` from **Citrix Online Plug-In**, the policy is located under **Citrix Components | Citrix Online Plugin | User experience | Remote applications**.

Preventing user connections during farm maintenance

William wants to prevent logons to a XenApp server when he performs maintenance or configuration tasks or installing applications.

By default, logons are enabled when we install XenApp and users can launch an unlimited number of sessions and instances of published applications. He can prevent users from connecting to a server in the farm by disabling logons, using the following procedure:

1. He opens the **Citrix AppCenter Console** (or **Citrix Delivery Services Console** in XenApp 6.0) and selects the **XenApp server**.
2. In the **Actions** pane, he selects **Other Tasks | Disable logon**.
3. To re-enable disabled logons, he selects **Other Tasks | Enable logon**.

Optimizing user sessions for XenApp

XenApp includes various features to improve user experience by improving keyboard and mouse responsiveness.

SpeedScreen Latency Reduction is a collective term used to describe features such as **Local text echo** and **Mouse click feedback** that help enhance user experience on a slow network.

Mouse click feedback

On high latency connections, users often click the mouse multiple times because there is no visual feedback showing that a mouse click resulted in an action. Mouse click feedback, which is enabled by default, changes the appearance of the pointer from idle to busy after the user clicks a link, indicating that the system is processing the user's request.

William can enable and disable mouse click feedback at the server level.

He needs to use SpeedScreen Latency Reduction Manager, located at **Start | All Programs | Citrix | Administration Tools**.

Then from the **Application** menu, he selects **Server Properties** to enable or disable mouse click feedback.

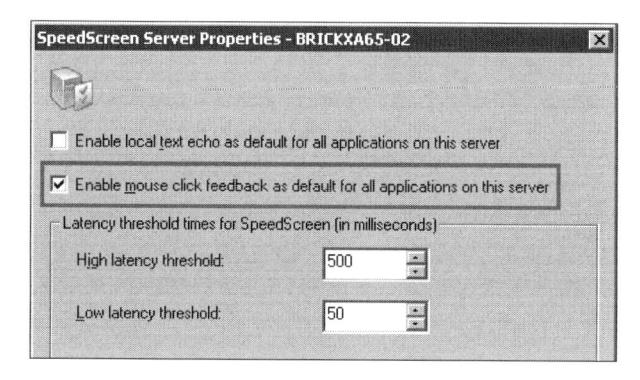

Local text echo

On high latency connections, our users frequently experience significant delays between typing text and when it is displayed (echoed) on the screen. When a user types text, the keystrokes are sent to the XenApp server, which renders the fonts and returns the updated screen to the client machine.

By default, local text echo is disabled. William can enable and disable this feature both at the XenApp server and application level. Also, he can configure local text echo settings for individual input fields within an application.

He needs to open **SpeedScreen Latency Reduction Manager**, located at **Start | All Programs | Citrix | Administration Tools**.

Then from the **Application** menu, select **Server Properties** to enable or disable local text echo.

Only Windows applications that use the standard Windows APIs for displaying text support local text echo.

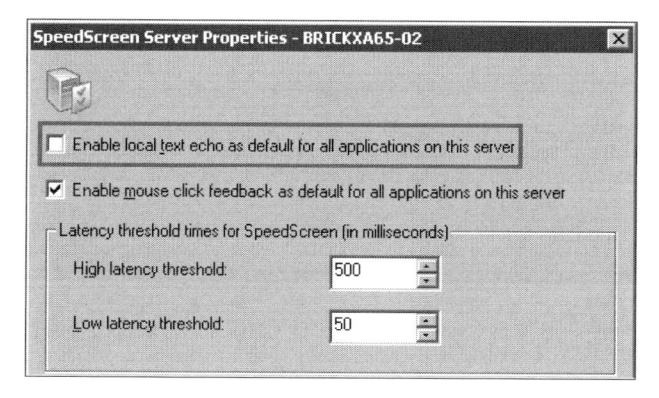

Configuring SpeedScreen Latency Reduction

William can use the **SpeedScreen Latency Reduction Manager** to configure **SpeedScreen Latency Reduction** settings for a XenApp server, for single or multiple instances of an application, as well as for individual input fields within an application. He can also use it as a troubleshooting tool to improve SpeedScreen Latency Reduction behavior for applications.

To launch the tool, William needs to select **SpeedScreen Latency Reduction Manager**, located at **Start | All Programs | Citrix | Administration Tools**.

William can configure common **SpeedScreen Latency Reduction** settings for all applications on a XenApp server or select custom settings for individual applications.

He can use the **Add New Application** wizard, included with the **SpeedScreen Latency Reduction Manager**, to adjust latency reduction functionality for a published application showing abnormal behavior after it is configured to use **SpeedScreen Latency Reduction**.

To optimize usability of the application, he needs to use the following procedure to adjust, turn on, or turn off **SpeedScreen Latency Reduction** for the application:

1. William needs to open the application. The application must be running before he can use this wizard to modify existing settings.
2. He launches **SpeedScreen Latency Reduction Manager** from **Start | All Programs | Citrix | Administration Tools**.
3. From the **Applications** menu, he selects **New** to start the wizard.
4. He uses the **Define the Application** screen to select an application instance on the XenApp server. To specify the application, he clicks the icon at the bottom of the page and drags the pointer onto the window of an application or uses the **Browse** button and navigates to the application.
5. He can disable local text echo by selecting or clearing the **Enable local text echo for this application** checkbox.

6. Finally, he chooses to apply settings to all instances of the application on the XenApp server or just the instance selected.

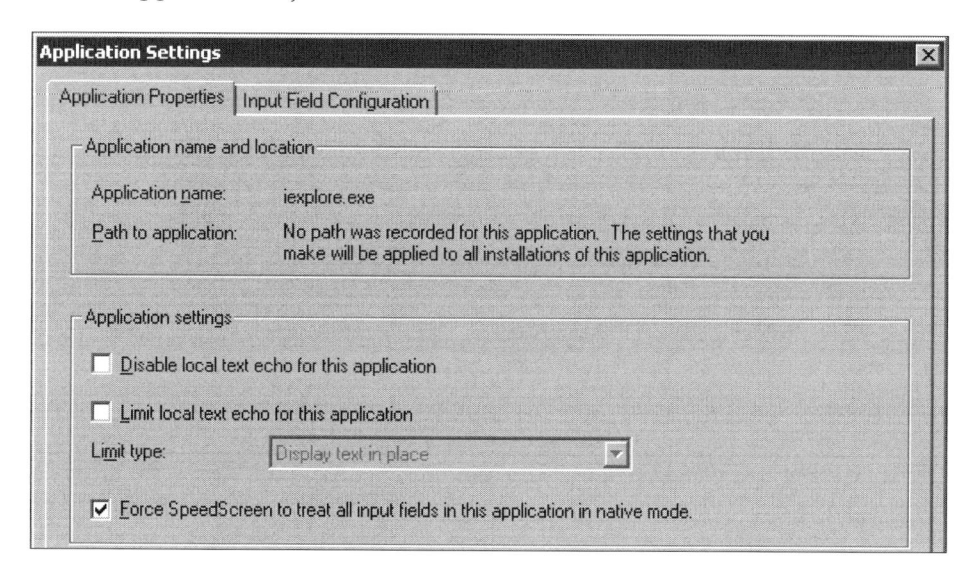

> When we configure the **SpeedScreen Latency Reduction Manager** on a particular XenApp server, settings are saved in the `ss3config` folder in the Citrix installation directory of that server. We can replicate settings to other servers by copying this folder and its contents to the same location on the other servers.

Redirection of Local Special Folders in sessions

William can enable **Special Folder Redirection** to simplify the way Brick Unit's users save Files to their special folders locally. Special folders are Windows folders such as Documents, Computer, and the Desktop.

When **Special Folder Redirection** is disabled, the Documents and Desktop icons that appear in a session point to the user's Documents and Desktop folders on the XenApp server.

Managing Sessions

When **Special Folder Redirection** redirects is enabled, and users open or save a File from special folders, they are accessing the special folder on a File server (the preferred option) instead of their local computers.

There are two scenarios where enabling **Special Folders Redirection** to client machine is not recommended: when users connect to the same session from multiple client machines simultaneously or when remote users are accessing through Access Gateway or VPN.

For **Special Folder Redirection** to work, the user must log off from the session on the first client machine and start a new session on the second client machine, or we need to use roaming profiles or set a home folder for that user in the **User Properties** in the **Active Directory**. These are the preferred options for most Citrix deployments.

Currently, for seamless and published desktops, **Special Folder** Redirection to the client machine works only for the Documents folder.

For seamless applications, **Special Folder Redirection** only works for the Desktop and Documents folders. Citrix does not recommend using **Special Folder Redirection** with published Windows Explorer.

If we need to provide **Special Folder Redirection** for all folders such as Favorites or Music; for example, we need to use roaming profiles and network File share.

Using roaming profiles is a best practice because it allows users to have a consistent experience, they can see and save files and settings all the time, but also reduce the storage wastage on local XenApp hard drives.

Special Folder Redirection support is enabled by default, but we must configure this feature for users through the Citrix Receiver or the Citrix Online Plug-In and Citrix Web Interface. We can either enable **Special Folder Redirection** for all users or configure that users must enable the feature themselves in their client settings.

Also, we can allow or prevent specific users from having redirected special folders with the **Special folders Redirection** user policy setting located at **ICA | File Redirection**.

We can create a policy to use the **Special Folder Redirection** policy setting. Then we can apply Filters to provide or disable access to the users accessing local special folders.

Enabling Special Folder Redirection in the Web Interface

The following is the procedure used by William to enable **Special Folder Redirection**. This requires a XenApp website. Detailed instructions to create and configure a XenApp website are available in *Chapter 3, Installing XenApp 6.5*.

1. He opens the **Citrix Web interface Management** on the server hosting the Web Interface and selects the XenApp website name.
2. From the **Action** menu, he chooses **Session Settings**.
3. In the **Managing Session Preferences** page, he selects **Remote Connection | Local Resources**.

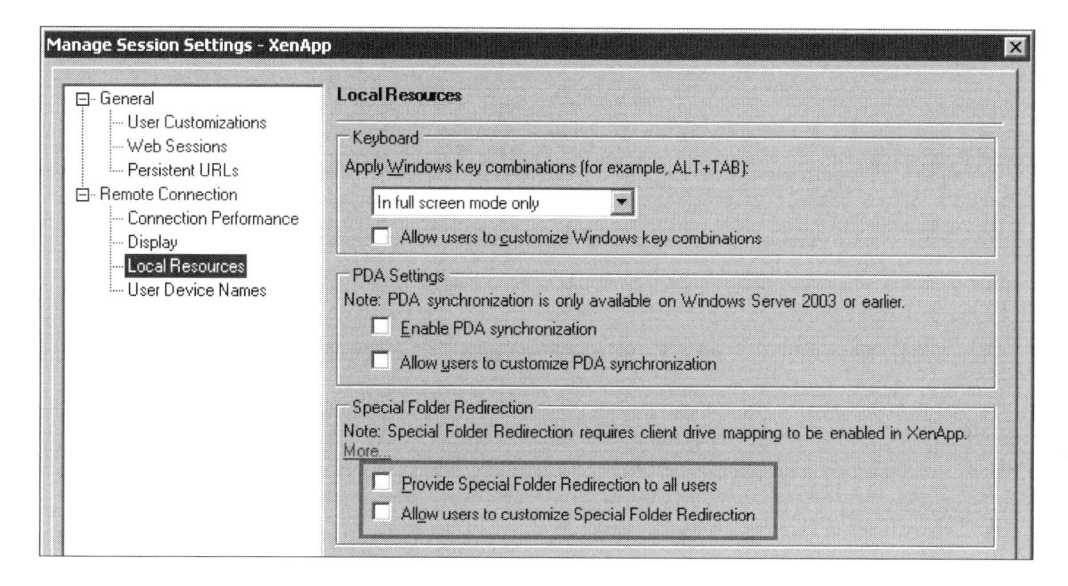

Now he can choose:

- **Provide Special Folder Redirection to all users**: Enables **Special Folder Redirection** to all users
- **Allow users to customize Special Folder Redirection**: Disables **Special Folder Redirection**, by default, but lets users turn it on in their session options

Enabling Special Folder Redirection for the Citrix Receiver or Citrix Online Plug-In

The following procedure is used by William to enable **Special Folder Redirection** for the Citrix Receiver or the Citrix Online Plug-In. This procedure requires a XenApp Services site. Detailed instructions to create and configure a XenApp website are available in *Chapter 3, Installing XenApp 6.5*.

1. He opens the **Citrix Web interface Management** on the server hosting the Web Interface and selects the XenApp services site name.
2. From the **Action** menu, he chooses **Session Options**.
3. In the **Change Session Options** page, he selects **Remote Connection | Local Resources**.

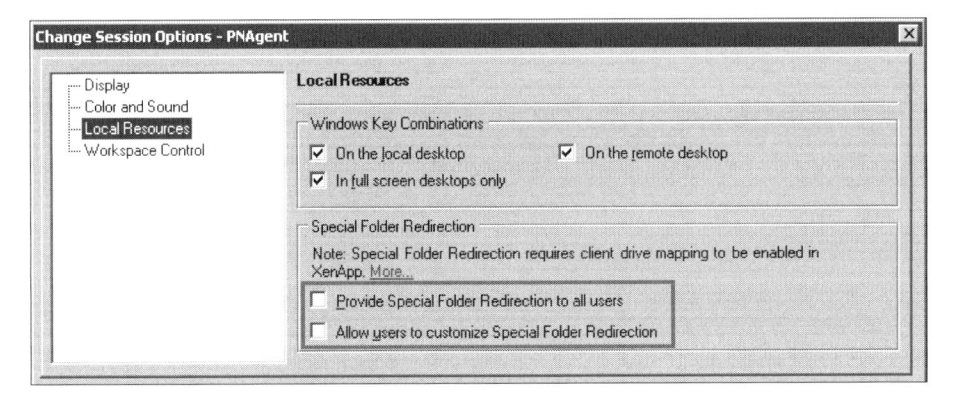

Now he can choose:

- **Provide Special Folder Redirection to all users**: Enables **Special Folder Redirection** by default
- **Allow users to customize Special Folder Redirection**: Disables **Special Folder Redirection**, by default, but lets users turn it on in their session options

Using Group Policy to redirect Special Folders

We can use GPO (Group Policies) and Windows Roaming Profiles to redirect Citrix or Terminal Server profiles to a network file server. This is a common scenario in almost all Citrix implementations. There are plenty of options to redirect profiles, including several profile tools, scripts, or GPOs.

> If we have a XenApp Enterprise or Platinum editions licens, we can deploy Citrix Profile Management. This tool is extremely powerful to manage and optimize loading profiles. Learn more about Citrix Profile Management at www.citrix.com/ppm. Also, there are great (and more expensive) third-party user profile solutions like AppSense Environment Manager.

Now let's take a look at how Brick Unit Construction will use GPO to redirect profiles.

William Empire decided to use **Special Folder redirection** to a **File Server**. Implementing file redirection will provide a lot of benefits to the company, including centralization of all documents in one place, simplification of backup of data, and so on.

1. The First step is creating a GPO in the OU where the Citrix servers are located, using the **Group Policy Management Console**.
2. He opens the console and then he expands **User Configuration | Policies | Windows Settings | Folder Redirection**.

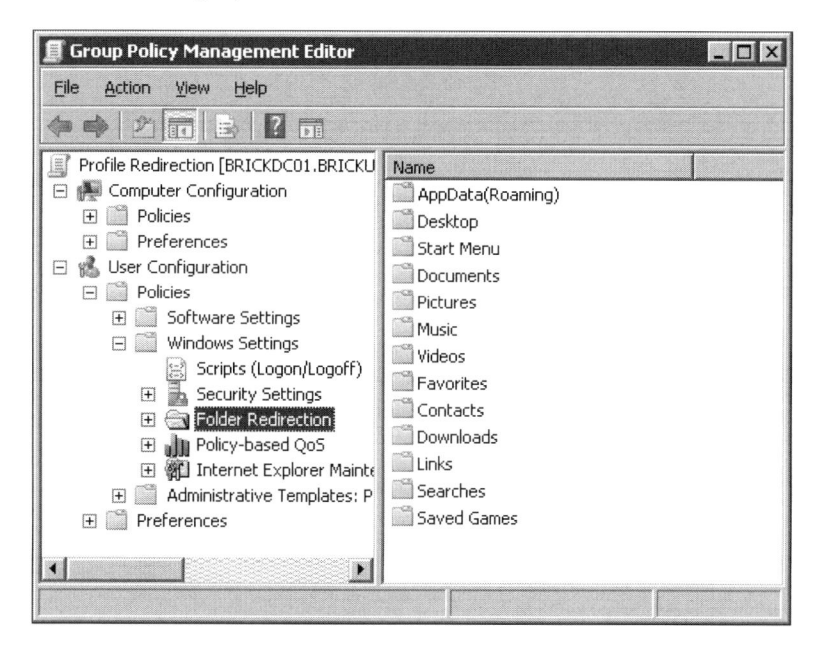

Managing Sessions

3. He right-clicks the special folder that he wants to redirect (for example, My Documents or Desktop) and then clicks on **Properties**.

4. He clicks the **Target** tab, and then in the **Settings** box, selects **Basic - Redirect everyone's folder to the same location**.

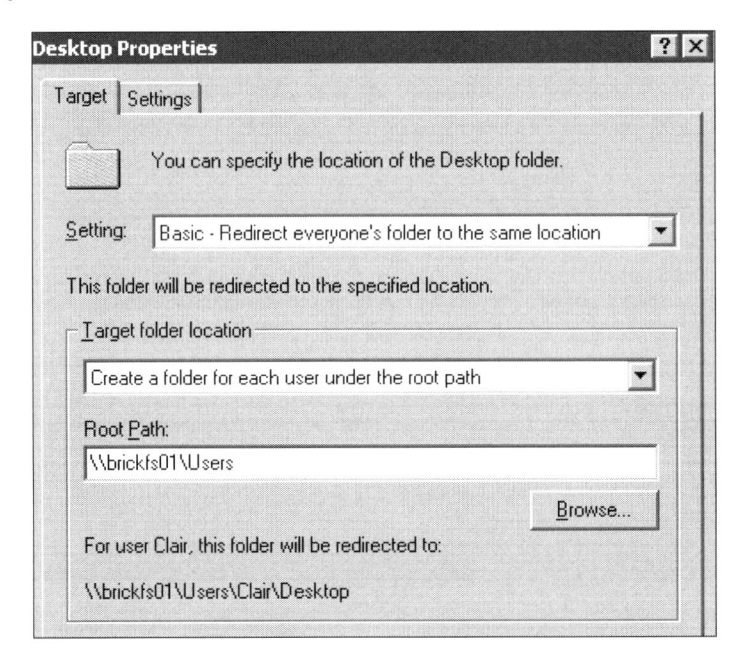

![Desktop Properties dialog box showing Target tab with Setting set to "Basic - Redirect everyone's folder to the same location", Target folder location set to "Create a folder for each user under the root path", Root Path: \\brickfs01\Users, and the redirection path \\brickfs01\Users\Clair\Desktop for user Clair.]

5. Under **Target folder location**, he selects **Create a folder for each user under the root path**.

6. In the **Root Path** box, he enters the UNC (Universal Naming Convention) path of the File Server, here it is `\\brickfs01\Users`, and then he clicks on **OK**.

7. In the **Properties** dialog box for the special folder, he clicks on **OK** to finish the process.

Summary

In this chapter, we learned about Managing Sessions on XenApp farms. In particular, we talked about:

- Understanding XenApp sessions
- Managing and monitoring sessions using Citrix Delivery Services Console, including disconnecting, resetting, and logoff sessions, and sending messages to users
- Viewing and shadowing sessions, using Shadow Taskbar
- Maintaining session activity using Session Reliability, Auto client reconnect, and ICA keep-alive features
- Customizing user environments in XenApp, including controlling the appearance of user logons and access to devices and ports, mapping drives, and redirecting COM Ports and Audio
- Limiting concurrent connections per server and limiting application instances and sharing sessions and connections
- Optimizing user sessions for XenApp, using local text echo, and mouse click feedback
- Redirection of Local Special Folders in Sessions, including setup of Special Folders
- Folder Redirection on web interface and using GPO

In the next chapter, we will learn about Citrix Receiver and Plug-In Management, including installing Citrix Receiver for Windows and Macintosh and deploying and configuring Citrix Merchandising Server on VMware and XenServer Virtual Machines.

12
Scripting Programming

In the last chapter, we discussed Managing Sessions on XenApp farms. In this chapter, we will learn how to automate common tasks using PowerShell scripts. This powerful scripting language combined with the Citrix XenApp Commands package will help us to create scripts to manage our XenApp farm. We can automate common and simple tasks, such as publishing or enabling/disabling applications, assign/remove users or disable logon on servers; however, we can use PowerShell for more complex tasks such as generating CPU usage reports, creating backup of policies, or migrating applications between XenApp farms.

In this chapter we will cover:

- Installing and configuring PowerShell to manage XenApp farms
- Use of cmdlets to manage XenApp servers
- Using PowerShell commands from inside .NET code
- Converting our MFCOM scripts to PowerShell to manage XenApp 6.5
- Accessing MFCOM objects and managing previous versions of XenApp from PowerShell

MFCOM and PowerShell

Before XenApp 6.0 was released, MFCOM was used by developers and administrators to create utilities and scripts to automate administration tasks on Citrix XenApp farms.

MFCOM is very powerful and can be used from inside .VBS files (Visual Basic scripts), .WSH files (Windows Scripting Host), Visual Studio, Visual Studio.NET, and more.

Starting from XenApp 6.0, Citrix dropped support for MFCOM and moved scripting capabilities to Microsoft PowerShell. MFCOM-based scripts need to be completely re-written using XenApp cmdlets. A cmdlet is a command that is used in the Windows PowerShell.

On previous versions of XenApp, we can use multiple scripting or development languages to manage XenApp, but now on version 6.5 (and version 6.0), we have only one option: PowerShell; later we can learn how to run PowerShell commands from inside .NET code.

Microsoft is using PowerShell for management of different infrastructure products (Windows Server, Exchange Server, SQL Server, and so on), so the transition to PowerShell provides standardization across different Windows-based products.

William can use PowerShell with Citrix XenApp Commands to configure and administer XenApp servers and farms. For example, he can use PowerShell to publish an application or add users to published applications, like the console.

Installing XenApp Commands on XenApp Servers

Windows Server 2008 R2 includes Microsoft PowerShell 2.0 preinstalled, so we just need to install XenApp Command to start using it. If we are using a previous version of Windows, we need to download (for free) and install Microsoft PowerShell 2.0 from the Microsoft website.

We have two options to install XenApp Commands:

- Download the **Citrix XenApp 6.5 PowerShell SDK** (which includes the XenApp Command cmdlets), the SDK helps us to manage XenApp 6.5 farms using PowerShell, and also provides PowerShell cmdlets to manage common Citrix components and group policies. This is the recommended option. If we have a XenApp 6.0 farm, we need to download the **Citrix XenApp 6.0 PowerShell SDK**.
- Download **Citrix XenApp Commands**. This pack allows PowerShell to manage XenApp 4.5, 5.0, and 6.0 farms.

All these tools are available for download at `http://community.citrix.com/display/xa/Download+SDKS`.

Installing Citrix XenApp 6.5 PowerShell SDK

William needs to decompress the downloaded `.zip` file using WinZip, WinRAR, or a similar utility, and then run the `.exe` file.

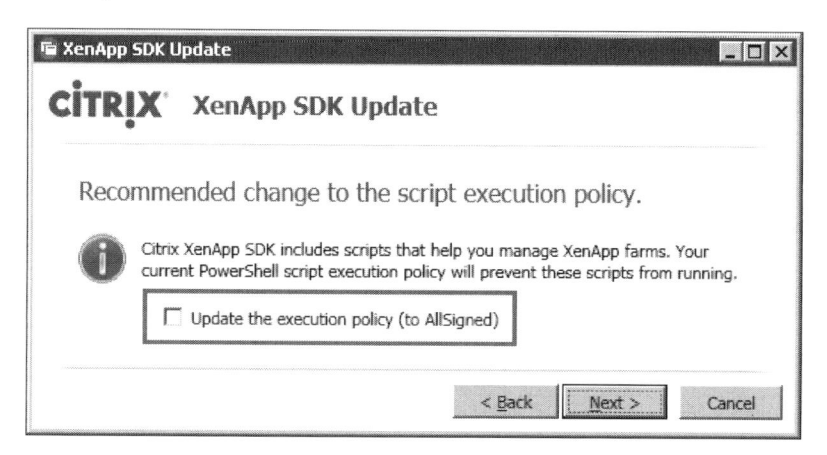

He needs to enable the option **Update the execution policy (to AllSigned)**. This is required so all scripts and configuration files are signed by a trusted publisher, including scripts that we write on the local computer.

The XenApp 6.5 PowerShell SDK includes multiple components: Citrix Common Commands, Citrix XenApp Commands, Citrix XenApp Server SDK, and Citrix Group Policy Management.

Installing PowerShell XenApp Commands

William needs to decompress the downloaded `.zip` file using WinZip, WinRAR, or similar utility, and then run the appropriate `.msi` file:

- `Citrix.XenApp.Commands.Install_x64.msi` for 64-bit systems
- `Citrix.XenApp.Commands.Install_x86.msi` for 32-bit systems

He can only install the XenApp Commands on systems with XenApp 4.5 or later installed.

> The PowerShell sample code in this chapter is based on Citrix XenApp Command CTP3, this version of Citrix XenApp Command is not the final release, so some code or commands may change when the final version is released.

Using PowerShell for basic administrative tasks

This chapter requires that we are familiar with Microsoft PowerShell. If you are not familiar with it, I recommend downloading **Windows PowerShell Graphical Help File** and **Windows PowerShell Quick Reference**. Both the files are located in the **Download** section of this page at http://technet.microsoft.com/en-us/scriptcenter.

Also, you can review the Citrix XenApp 6.5 Server SDK Help, available in **Start** | **All Programs** | **Citrix** | **XenApp 6.5 Server SDK**:

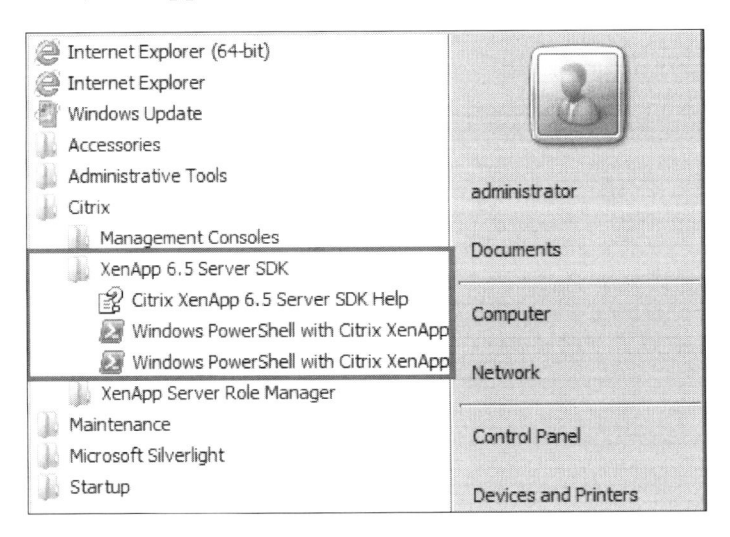

Installing Citrix XenApp Commands snap-in

The Citrix XenApp Command snap-in is an add-on developed by Citrix to manage XenApp from PowerShell.

To open the PowerShell Citrix Commands console, William needs to use the Windows PowerShell with Citrix XenApp 6.5 Server SDK shortcut available at **Start | All Programs | Citrix | XenApp Commands**.

Another option is to open the PowerShell shortcut and load the Citrix XenApp snap-in. This option is required when William wants to use a PowerShell to manage multiple products or he is using the PowerShell console version 1.0.

```
Add-PSSnapin Citrix.XenApp.Commands
```

To verify that the XenApp Commands are working properly, he needs to type:

```
Get-command -psSnapin Citrix.XenApp.Commands
```

This command will generate the following output:

```
PS C:\Users\administrator.BRICKUNIT> Get-command -psSnapin Citrix.XenApp.Commands

CommandType     Name                                    Definition
-----------     ----                                    ----------
Cmdlet          Add-XAAdministratorPrivilege            Add-XAAdministratorPrivilege [-Admin
Cmdlet          Add-XAApplicationAccount                Add-XAApplicationAccount [-BrowserNa
Cmdlet          Add-XAApplicationFileType               Add-XAApplicationFileType [-BrowserN
Cmdlet          Add-XAApplicationServer                 Add-XAApplicationServer [-BrowserNam
Cmdlet          Add-XAApplicationWorkerGroup            Add-XAApplicationWorkerGroup [-Brows
Cmdlet          Add-XAAutoReplicatedPrinterDriver       Add-XAAutoReplicatedPrinterDriver [-
Cmdlet          Add-XAWorkerGroupServer                 Add-XAWorkerGroupServer [-WorkerGrou
Cmdlet          Clear-XAApplicationLoadEvaluator        Clear-XAApplicationLoadEvaluator [-B
Cmdlet          Clear-XAConfigurationLog                Clear-XAConfigurationLog [-Credentia
Cmdlet          Clear-XADefaultComputerName             Clear-XADefaultComputerName [-Scope]
Cmdlet          Connect-XASession                       Connect-XASession [[-ServerName] <St
Cmdlet          Copy-XAApplication                      Copy-XAApplication [-BrowserName] <S
Cmdlet          Copy-XAFolder                           Copy-XAFolder [-FolderPath] <String[
Cmdlet          Copy-XALoadBalancingPolicy              Copy-XALoadBalancingPolicy [-PolicyN
Cmdlet          Copy-XALoadEvaluator                    Copy-XALoadEvaluator [-LoadEvaluatorN
Cmdlet          Copy-XAWorkerGroup                      Copy-XAWorkerGroup [-WorkerGroupName
Cmdlet          Disable-XAAdministrator                 Disable-XAAdministrator [-Administra
Cmdlet          Disable-XAApplication                   Disable-XAApplication [-BrowserName]
Cmdlet          Disable-XALoadBalancingPolicy           Disable-XALoadBalancingPolicy [-Poli
Cmdlet          Disable-XAServerLogOn                   Disable-XAServerLogOn [-ServerName]
Cmdlet          Disconnect-XASession                    Disconnect-XASession [-SessionId] <I
```

The `Get-Command` cmdlet gets commands in the session, such as aliases, functions, filters, scripts, and applications.

Also, William can use the following command to check if the snap-in is installed:

```
Get-command -psSnapin Citrix*
```

Scripting Programming

He can use the `Get-Help` command to show information about a command.

This command will generate the following output:

```
PS C:\Users\administrator.BRICKUNIT> Get-help Get-XAServer
NAME
    Get-XAServer
SYNOPSIS
    Retrieves Citrix servers.

SYNTAX
    Get-XAServer [[-ServerName] <String[]>] [-Full] [-ComputerName <String>] [<CommonParameters>]
    Get-XAServer -BrowserName <String[]> [-Full] [-ComputerName <String>] [<CommonParameters>]
    Get-XAServer -FolderPath <String[]> [-Full] [-ComputerName <String>] [<CommonParameters>]
    Get-XAServer -ZoneName <String[]> [-OnlineOnly] [-Full] [-ComputerName <String>] [<CommonParam
    Get-XAServer -AccountAuthorityName <String[]> [-Full] [-ComputerName <String>] [<CommonParamet
    Get-XAServer -LoadEvaluatorName <String[]> [-Full] [-ComputerName <String>] [<CommonParameters
    Get-XAServer -DriverName <String[]> [-Full] [-ComputerName <String>] [<CommonParameters>]
    Get-XAServer -WorkerGroupName <String[]> [-ExplicitOnly] [-Full] [-ComputerName <String>] [<Co
    Get-XAServer -LocalhostOnly [-Full] [-ComputerName <String>] [<CommonParameters>]
    Get-XAServer -InputObject <XAServer[]> [-Full] [-ComputerName <String>] [<CommonParameters>]
```

Note the new `-ComputerName` parameter included on XenApp 6.5. All the PowerShell commands on XenApp 6.5 now support the `-ComputerName` parameter that makes the cmdlet execute remotely on the machine specified.

Using PowerShell for farm management

William can use the following command to show farm information:

`Get-XAFarm`

In the following example, he will run the command from a remote server using the `-ComputerName` parameter.

```
PS C:\> Get-XAFarm -ComputerName BRICKXA65-02

FarmName          : BrickFarm65
ServerVersion     : 6.5.0
AdministratorType : Full
SessionCount      : 0
MachineName       : BRICKXA65-02
```

He can also use the `Get-XAFarmConfiguration` cmdlet for more detailed information about the farm.

Chapter 12

To show the list of XenApp servers in his XenApp farm, he can use the following cmdlet:

`Get-XAServer`

This command will generate this output.

```
PS C:\> Get-XAServer

ServerName                  : BRICKXA65-02
ServerFqdn                  :
ServerId                    : 247E-000C-0000011E
FolderPath                  : Servers
ZoneName                    : Frederick
ElectionPreference          : MostPreferred
IPAddresses                 : {192.168.2.222}
OSVersion                   : 6.1.7601
OSServicePack               : Service Pack 1
Is64Bit                     : True
CitrixProductName           : Citrix Presentation Server
CitrixVersion               : 6.5.6682
CitrixEdition               : Platinum
CitrixEditionString         : PLT
CitrixServicePack           : 0
CitrixInstallDate           : 12/8/2011 4:50:36 AM
CitrixInstallPath           : C:\Program Files (x86)\Citrix\
LicenseServerName           : brickxa65-01
LicenseServerPortNumber     : 27000
LogOnsEnabled               : True
IsSpoolerHealthy            :
LogOnMode                   : AllowLogOns
PcmMode                     : Normal
IcaPortNumber               : 1494
RdpPortNumber               :
SessionCount                :
MachineName                 : BRICKXA65-02
```

Now he can use a pipeline character (|) to pass the output generated by one command to another command. He can filter specific information about his XenApp servers, for example, if he wants to see a list with the server name and the logon enabled, he can use `Select` to filter commands.

`Get-XAServer | select ServerName, LogOnsEnabled`

Also, William can order the results using `Sort` and extra pipe. The following example orders the results based on the `LogOnsEnabled`:

`Get-XAServer | select ServerName, LogOnsEnabled | Sort LogOnsEnabled`

```
PS C:\> Get-XAServer | select ServerName, LogOnsEnabled | Sort LogOnsEnabled

ServerName                                                    LogOnsEnabled
----------                                                    -------------
BRICKXA65-04                                                          False
BRICKXA65-02                                                           True
BRICKXA65-03                                                           True
```

Scripting Programming

William can disable logons on a specific XenApp server using the following command:

```
Disable-XAServerLogOn -ServerName "BRICKXA65-02"
```

If he needs to enable logons on a specific XenApp server, he can use the following command:

```
Enable-XAServerLogOn -ServerName "BRICKXA65-02"
```

To show application information, he can use:

```
Get-XAApplication
```

```
PS C:\> Get-XAApplication

ApplicationType                   : ServerInstalled
PreLaunch                         : False
DisplayName                       : Project 2010
ApplicationId                     : 247e-0006-00000251
Description                       : Project 2010
FolderPath                        : Applications
BrowserName                       : Project 2010
Enabled                           : True
HideWhenDisabled                  : False
SequenceNumber                    : 1327403758
LoadBalancingApplicationCheckEnabled : True
ContentAddress                    :
CommandLineExecutable             : "C:\Program Files\Microsoft Office\Office14\WINPROJ.EXE" "%*"
WorkingDirectory                  : C:\Program Files\Microsoft Office\Office14
ProfileLocation                   :
ProfileProgramName                :
ProfileProgramArguments           :
AnonymousConnectionsAllowed       : False
ClientFolder                      :
AddToClientStartMenu              : False
StartMenuFolder                   :
AddToClientDesktop                : False
ConnectionsThroughAccessGatewayAllowed : True
OtherConnectionsAllowed           : True
AccessSessionConditionsEnabled    : False
AccessSessionConditions           : {}
InstanceLimit                     : 35
MultipleInstancesPerUserAllowed   : False
CpuPriorityLevel                  : Normal
AudioType                         : None
AudioRequired                     : False
SslConnectionEnabled              : False
EncryptionLevel                   : Basic
EncryptionRequired                : False
WaitOnPrinterCreation             : False
WindowType                        : 1024x768
ColorDepth                        : Colors32Bit
TitleBarHidden                    : False
MaximizedOnStartup                : False
OfflineAccessAllowed              :
CachingOption                     :
AlternateProfiles                 :
RunAsLeastPrivilegedUser          :
MachineName                       : BRICKXA65-02
```

Now William can use pipes, `Select`, and `Sort` to filter some commands:

```
Get-XAApplication | Select DisplayName, ApplicationType, Enabled | Sort DisplayName
```

```
PS C:\> Get-XAApplication | Select DisplayName, ApplicationType, Enabled | Sort DisplayName

DisplayName              ApplicationType         Enabled
-----------              ---------------         -------
Add Printer              ServerInstalled         True
BrickXA65-02 Desktop     ServerDesktop           True
CtxAdmTools Web Site     Content                 True
HDX Monitor              ServerInstalled         True
Internet Explorer        ServerInstalled         True
Project 2010             ServerInstalled         True
Visio 2010               StreamedToClient        True
```

He can use the `Export-CSV` command to save the result to a CSV file (comma separated values text file). He can open the CSV file using Excel:

```
Get-XAApplication | Select DisplayName, ApplicationType, Enabled | Sort DisplayName | Export-CSV C:\farm-apps.csv
```

	A	B	C
1	DisplayName	ApplicationType	Enabled
2	Add Printer	ServerInstalled	TRUE
3	BrickXA65-02 Desktop	ServerDesktop	TRUE
4	CtxAdmTools Web Site	Content	TRUE
5	HDX Monitor	ServerInstalled	TRUE
6	Internet Explorer	ServerInstalled	TRUE
7	Project 2010	ServerInstalled	TRUE
8	Visio 2010	StreamedToClient	TRUE

Also, he can use the `ConvertTo-HTML` command to generate an HTML file, then he needs to redirect the output using the `Out-File` command. He can open the HTML file using Internet Explorer, Firefox, or any other Internet browser:

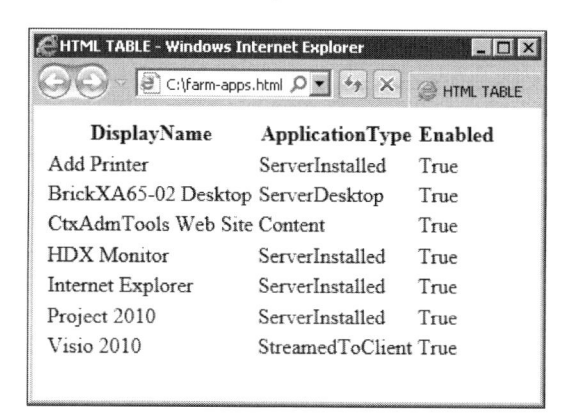

DisplayName	ApplicationType	Enabled
Add Printer	ServerInstalled	True
BrickXA65-02 Desktop	ServerDesktop	True
CtxAdmTools Web Site	Content	True
HDX Monitor	ServerInstalled	True
Internet Explorer	ServerInstalled	True
Project 2010	ServerInstalled	True
Visio 2010	StreamedToClient	True

To list sessions on his XenApp farm, he can use:

```
Get-XASession
```

Scripting Programming

The following command will generate a lot of information in the XenApp farm. William is going to use pipeline to limit the information shown. In the following example, he is going to use the `Select` command to show the XenApp server (ServerName), username (AccountName), application (BrowserName), and session state.

```
Get-XASession | Select ServerName, AccountName, BrowserName, State
```

```
PS W:\> Get-XASession | select ServerName, AccountName, BrowserName, State

ServerName          AccountName           BrowserName      State
----------          -----------           -----------      -----
BRICKXA65-01        BRICKUNIT\ecadoret    XEN Desktop      Active
BRICKXA65-02        BRICKUNIT\djones      XEN Desktop      Active
BRICKXA65-02        BRICKUNIT\cjenkins    XEN Desktop      Active
BRICKXA65-01        BRICKUNIT\emendenh    XEN Desktop      Active
BRICKXA65-01        BRICKUNIT\agill       XEN Desktop      Active
BRICKXA65-02        BRICKUNIT\ddike       XEN Desktop      Disconnected
BRICKXA65-03        BRICKUNIT\jstone      XEN Desktop      Disconnected
BRICKXA65-02        BRICKUNIT\jserfass    XEN Desktop      Disconnected
```

Now he can add an extra pipeline to filter the `Disconnected` sessions.

```
Get-XASession | Select ServerName, AccountName, BrowseName, State |
Where-Object {$_.State -eq "Disconnected"}
```

```
PS W:\> Get-XASession | select ServerName, AccountName, BrowserName,
State | Where-Object { $_.State -eq "Disconnected" }

ServerName          AccountName           BrowserName      State
----------          -----------           -----------      -----
BRICKXA65-02        BRICKUNIT\ddike       XEN Desktop      Disconnected
BRICKXA65-03        BRICKUNIT\jstone      XEN Desktop      Disconnected
BRICKXA65-02        BRICKUNIT\jserfass    XEN Desktop      Disconnected
```

To close all disconnected sessions, he adds an extra pipeline and the `Stop-XASession` command:

```
Get-XASession | Select ServerName, AccountName, BrowseName, State |
Where-Object {$_.State -eq "Disconnected"} | Stop-XASession
```

Now William is going to learn how to publish an application using cmdlets. The following example will publish WordPad on servers BRICKXA65-02 and BRICKXA65-03:

```
New-XAApplication -BrowserName "WordPad" -ApplicationType
"ServerInstalled" -DisplayName "WordPad" -FolderPath "Applications"
-Enabled $true -CommandLineExecutable "C:\Program Files\Windows NT\
Accessories\wordpad.exe" -WorkingDirectory "C:\Program Files\Windows
NT\Accessories" -AnonymousConnectionsAllowed $false -ServerNames
BRICKXA65-02, BRICKXA65-03 -Accounts "BRICKUNIT\Domain Admins"
```

Let's review this command in detail:

- `BrowserName`: Specifies the browser name of the published application. The browser name must be unique among all published applications.
- `ApplicationType`: Specifies the application type. Options are `ServerInstalled`, `ServerDesktop`, `Content`, `StreamedToServer`, `StreamedToClient`, `StreamedToClientOrInstalled`, and `StreamedToClientOrStreamedToServer`.
- `DisplayName`: Specifies the display name of the published application. The display name needs to be unique.
- `FolderPath`: Specifies the parent folder name of the published application.
- `Enabled`: Specifies whether to enable or disable the published application. Valid parameters are `$true` and `$false`.
- `CommandLineExecutable`: Specifies the application full path.
- `WorkingDirectory`: Specifies the default working directory for the application.
- `ServerNames`: Specifies a list of servers where the published application is installed.
- `Accounts`: Specifies the user accounts that can access the published application.

William can add extra users to an existing published application using the following command line:

```
Add-XAApplicationAccount -BrowserName "WordPad" -Accounts "BRICKUNIT\wempire"
```

He can add extra XenApp servers to an existing published application using the following command line:

```
Add-XAApplicationServer -BrowserName "WordPad" -ServerNames "BRICKXA65-04"
```

The following command will remove specific XenApp servers from the WordPad application:

```
Remove-XAApplicationServer –BrowserName "WordPad" -ServerNames "BRICKXA65-03"
```

He can disable the application WordPad using the following command:

```
Set-XAApplication -BrowserName"WordPad" -Enabled $false –HideWhenDisabled $true
```

The `HideWhenDisabled` parameter can hide or show the application.

Using PowerShell Commands from .NET applications

Now we are going to learn how to develop simple .NET applications to call Citrix PowerShell cmdlets on both Visual Basic.NET (VB.NET) and C#.NET.

Requirement to develop applications:

- Citrix XenApp 6.5 PowerShell SDK or Citrix XenApp Commands
- Microsoft Visual C#.NET and/or Visual Basic.NET. Microsoft provides the Express Edition of Visual Studio.NET, Visual C#.NET, and Visual Basic.NET for free at www.microsoft.com/visualstudio

Creating a sample VB.NET application

Now we are going to create a sample application to list all XenApp servers in our XenApp farm using Citrix XenApp Commands with managed code.

The first step is to start VB.NET. Samples contained in this book are developed in **Microsoft Visual Basic 2010 Express Edition**.

Chapter 12

Go to **File** | **New Project** | **Windows Forms Application**.

Enter the desired name for our project and click on the **OK** button.

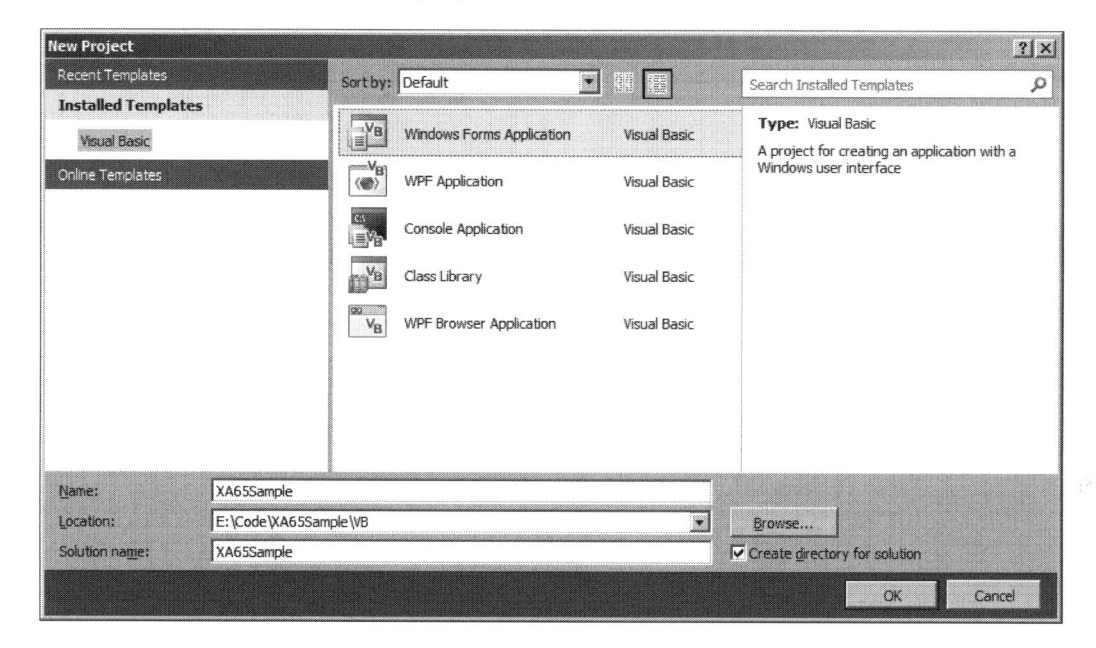

Adding references

The next step is to add a reference to the `System.Management.Automation.dll` assembly. Adding this assembly is tricky; first, we need to copy the assembly file to our application folder using the following command:

`Copy %windir%\assembly\GAC_MSIL\System.Management.Automation\1.0.0.0__31b f3856ad364e35\System.Management.Automation.dll C:\Code\XA65Sample`

where `C:\Code\XA65Sample` is the folder of our application.

Then we need to add the reference to the assembly.

In the **Project** menu, select **Add Reference**, click on the **Browse** tab, search and select the file `System.Management.Automation.dll`.

After referencing the assembly, we need to add the following directive statements to our code:

```
Imports System.Management.Automation
Imports System.Management.Automation.Host
Imports System.Management.Automation.Runspaces
```

Scripting Programming

> **Downloading the example code**
>
> You can download the example code files for all Packt books you have purchased from your account at http://www.PacktPub.com. If you purchased this book elsewhere, you can visit http://www.PacktPub.com/support and register to have the files e-mailed directly to you.

Also, adding the following directive statements will make it easier to work with the collections returned from the commands:

```
Imports System.Collections.Generic
Imports System.Collections.ObjectModel
```

Creating and opening a runspace

To use the Microsoft Windows PowerShell and Citrix XenApp Commands from managed code, we must first create and open a runspace. A runspace provides a way for the application to execute pipelines programmatically. Runspaces construct a logical model of execution using pipelines that contain cmdlets, native commands, and language elements.

So let's go and create a new sub called ShowXAServers for the new runspace:

```
Private Sub ShowXAServers()
```

Then the following code creates a new instance of a runspace and opens it:

```
Dim myRunspace As Runspace
myRunspace = RunspaceFactory.CreateRunspace()
myRunspace.Open()
```

The preceding piece of code only provides access to the cmdlets that come with the default Windows PowerShell installation. To use the cmdlets included with XenApp Commands, we must call it using an instance of the RunspaceConfiguration class. The following code creates a runspace that has access to the XenApp Commands:

```
Dim rsConfig As RunspaceConfiguration
rsConfig = RunspaceConfiguration.Create()
Dim info As PSSnapInInfo
Dim snapInException As New PSSnapInException
info = rsConfig.AddPSSnapIn("Citrix.XenApp.Commands", snapInException)
Dim myRunSpace As Runspace
myRunSpace = RunspaceFactory.CreateRunspace(rsConfig)
myRunSpace.Open()
```

This code specifies that we want to use Windows PowerShell in the XenApp Command context. This step gives us access to Windows PowerShell cmdlets and Citrix-specific cmdlets.

Running a cmdlet

Next, we need to create an instance of the Command class by using the name of the cmdlet that we want to run. The following code creates an instance of the Command class that will run the Get-XAServer cmdlet, add the command to the Commands collection of the pipeline, and finally run the command calling the Pipeline.Invoke method:

```
Dim pipeLine As Pipeline
pipeLine = myRunSpace.CreatePipeline()
Dim myCommand As New Command("Get-XAServer")
pipeLine.Commands.Add(myCommand)
Dim commandResults As Collection(Of PSObject)
commandResults = pipeLine.Invoke()
```

Displaying results

Now we run the command Get-XAServer on the shell to get this output:

```
PS C:\Users\ctxadmin> get-xaserver

ServerName              : BRICKXA65-02
ServerFqdn              :
ServerId                : 247E-000C-0000011E
FolderPath              : Servers
ZoneName                : Frederick
ElectionPreference      : MostPreferred
IPAddresses             : {192.168.2.222}
OSVersion               : 6.1.7601
OSServicePack           : Service Pack 1
Is64Bit                 : True
CitrixProductName       : Citrix Presentation Server
CitrixVersion           : 6.5.6682
CitrixEdition           : Platinum
```

The left column displays the properties of the cmdlet, and in this case, we are looking for the first one, the ServerName, so we are going to redirect the output of the ServerName property to a listbox.

Scripting Programming

So the next step will be to add a `ListBox` and `Button` controls. The `ListBox` will show the list of XenApp servers when we click the button.

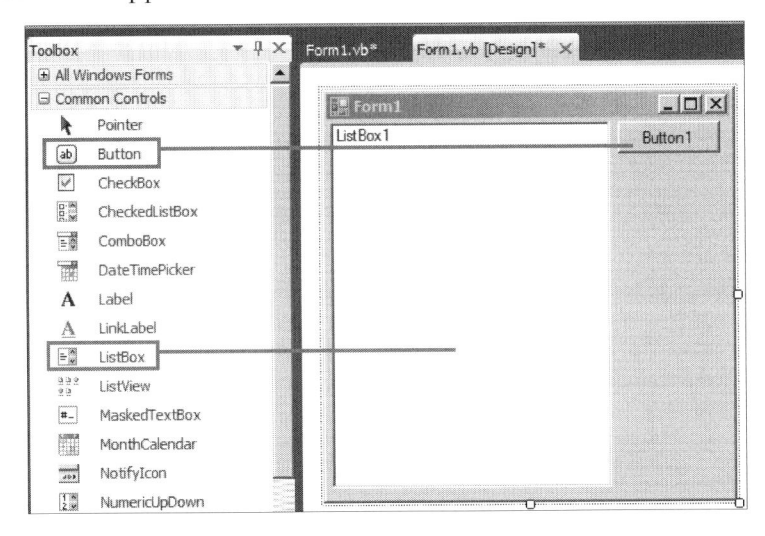

Then we need to add the following code at the end of Sub `ShowXAServers`:

```
For Each cmdlet As PSObject In commandResults
   ListBox1.Items.Add(cmdlet.Properties("Servername").Value.ToString())
Next
```

The full code of the sample will look like this:

```vb
Imports System.Management.Automation
Imports System.Management.Automation.Host
Imports System.Management.Automation.Runspaces
Imports System.Collections.Generic
Imports System.Collections.ObjectModel

Public Class Form1
    Private Sub ShowXAServers()
        Dim rsConfig As RunspaceConfiguration
        rsConfig = RunspaceConfiguration.Create()
        Dim info As PSSnapInInfo
        Dim snapInException As New PSSnapInException
        info = rsConfig.AddPSSnapIn("Citrix.XenApp.Commands", snapInException)
        Dim myRunSpace As Runspace
        myRunSpace = RunspaceFactory.CreateRunspace(rsConfig)
        myRunSpace.Open()
        Dim pipeLine As Pipeline
        pipeLine = myRunSpace.CreatePipeline()
        Dim myCommand As New Command("Get-XAServer")
        pipeLine.Commands.Add(myCommand)
        Dim commandResults As Collection(Of PSObject)
        commandResults = pipeLine.Invoke()
        For Each cmdlet As PSObject In commandResults
            ListBox1.Items.Add(cmdlet.Properties("Servername").Value.ToString())
        Next
    End Sub

    Private Sub Button1_Click(sender As System.Object, e As System.EventArgs) Handles Button1.Click
        ShowXAServers()
    End Sub
End Class
```

And this is the final output of the application when we run it:

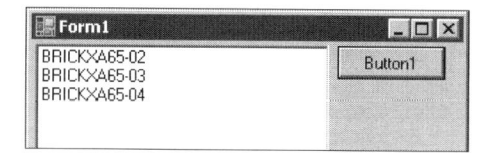

Passing parameters to cmdlets

We can pass parameters to cmdlets using the `Parameters.Add` option. We can add multiple parameters. Each parameter will require a line. For example, we can add the `ZoneName` parameter to filter server members of the US-Zone zone:

```
Dim myCommand As New Command("Get-XAServer")
myCommand.Parameters.Add("ZoneName", "US-ZONE")
pipeLine.Commands.Add(myCommand)
```

Creating a sample C#.NET application

Now we will create a sample application to list all XenApp servers in our farm using Citrix XenApp Commands with managed code. This sample is exactly the same as the VB.NET application. Open C#.NET. Samples contained in this book are developed in Microsoft C# 2010 Express Edition.

Then we need to go to **File** | **New Project** | **Windows Form Applications**. Type the desired name for our project and click on the **OK** button.

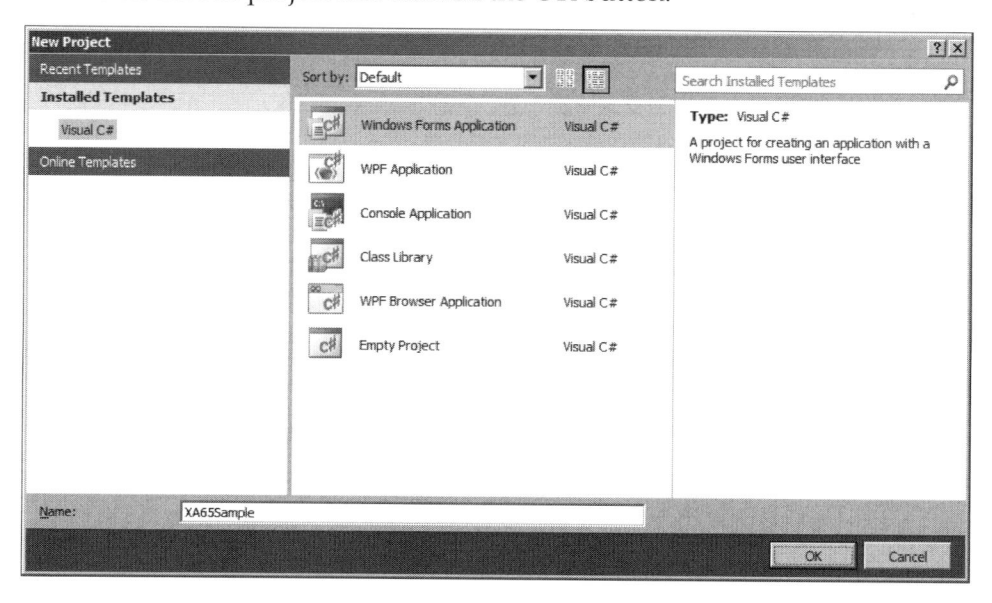

Adding references

We need to add a reference to the `System.Management.Automation.dll` assembly. Adding this assembly is tricky; first, we need to copy the assembly file to our application folder using the following command:

```
Copy %windir%\assembly\GAC_MSIL\System.Management.Automation\1.0.0.0__31b
f3856ad364e35\System.Management.Automation.dll C:\Code\XA65Sample
```

where `C:\Code\XA65Sample` is the folder of our application.

Then we need to add the reference to the assembly. In the **Project** menu, we need to select **Add Reference**, click on the **Browse** tab, search and select the file `System.Management.Automation.dll`.

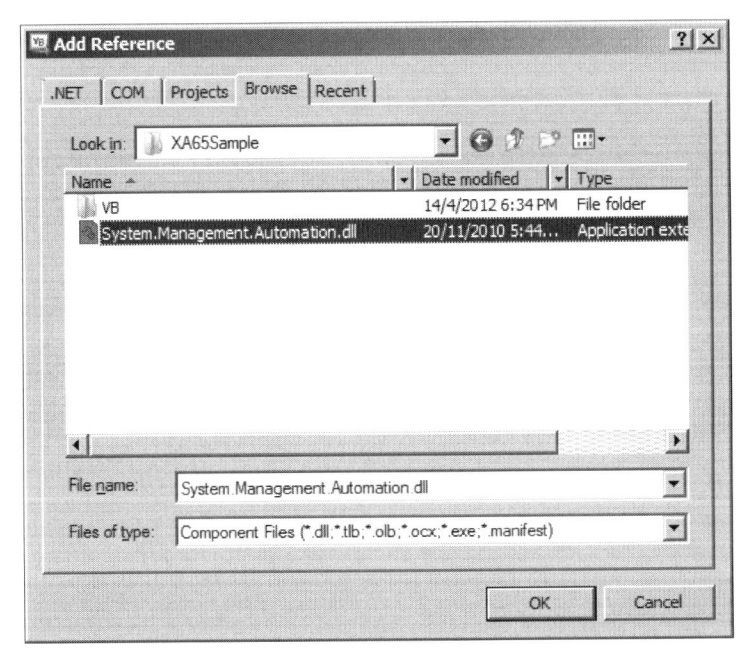

After referencing the assembly, we need to add the following directive statements to our code:

```
using System.Management.Automation;
using System.Management.Automation.Host;
using System.Management.Automation.Runspaces;
```

Also, adding the following directive statements will make it easier to work with the collections returned from the commands:

```
using System.Collections.Generic;
using System.Collections.ObjectModel;
```

Creating and opening a runspace

To use the Microsoft Windows PowerShell and Citrix XenApp Commands from managed code, we must first create and open a runspace. A runspace provides a way for the application to execute pipelines programmatically. Runspaces construct a logical model of execution using pipelines that contains cmdlets, native commands, and language elements.

So let's go and create a new function called `ShowXAServers` for the new runspace:

```
void ShowXAServers()
```

Then the following code creates a new instance of a runspace and opens it:

```
Runspace myRunspace = RunspaceFactory.CreateRunspace();
myRunspace.Open();
```

The preceding piece of code provides access only to the cmdlets that come with the default Windows PowerShell installation. To use the cmdlets included with XenApp Commands, we must call it using an instance of the `RunspaceConfiguration` class. The following code creates a runspace that has access to the XenApp Commands:

```
RunspaceConfiguration rsConfig = RunspaceConfiguration.Create();
PSSnapInException snapInException=null;
PSSnapInInfo info = rsConfig.AddPSSnapIn ("Citrix.XenApp.Commands", out snapInException);
Runspace myRunSpace = RunspaceFactory.CreateRunspace(rsConfig);
myRunSpace.Open();
```

This code specifies that we want to use Windows PowerShell in the XenApp Command context. This step gives us access to Windows PowerShell cmdlets and Citrix-specific cmdlets.

Running a cmdlet

Next, we need to create an instance of the `Command` class by using the name of the cmdlet that we want to run. The following code creates an instance of the `Command` class that will run the `Get-XAServer` cmdlet, add the command to the Commands collection of the pipeline, and finally run the command calling the `Pipeline.Invoke` method:

```
Pipeline pipeLine = myRunSpace.CreatePipeline();
Command myCommand = newCommand("Get-XAServer");
pipeLine.Commands.Add(myCommand);
Collection<PSObject> commandResults = pipeLine.Invoke();
```

Scripting Programming

Displaying results

Now we run the command `Get-XAServer` on the shell and get this output:

```
PS C:\Users\ctxadmin> get-xaserver

ServerName              : BRICKXA65-02
ServerFqdn              :
ServerId                : 247E-000C-0000011E
FolderPath              : Servers
ZoneName                : Frederick
ElectionPreference      : MostPreferred
IPAddresses             : {192.168.2.222}
OSVersion               : 6.1.7601
OSServicePack           : Service Pack 1
Is64Bit                 : True
CitrixProductName       : Citrix Presentation Server
CitrixVersion           : 6.5.6682
CitrixEdition           : Platinum
```

In the left-hand side column, the properties of the cmdlet are located, and in this case, we are looking for the first one, the ServerName, so we are going to redirect the output of the ServerName property to a ListBox.

So the next step will be to add a ListBox and Button controls. The ListBox will show the list of XenApp servers when we click the button.

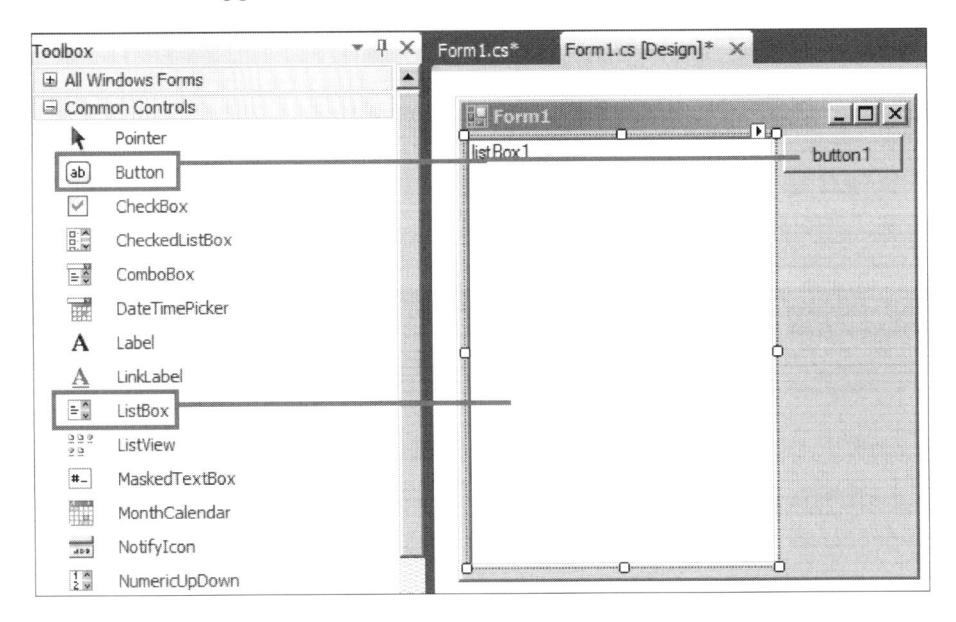

Then we need to add the following code at the end of Function `ShowXAServers`:

```
foreach (PSObject cmdlet in commandResults)
{
  string cmdletName = cmdlet.Properties["ServerName"].Value.
  ToString();
  listBox1.Items.Add (cmdletName);
}
```

The full code of the sample will look like this:

```csharp
using System;
using System.Collections.Generic;
using System.ComponentModel;
using System.Data;
using System.Drawing;
using System.Linq;
using System.Text;
using System.Windows.Forms;
using System.Management.Automation;
using System.Management.Automation.Host;
using System.Management.Automation.Runspaces;
using System.Collections.ObjectModel;
namespace XA65Sample
{
    public partial class Form1 : Form
    {
        public Form1()
        {
            InitializeComponent();
        }

        void ShowXAServers()
        {
            RunspaceConfiguration rsConfig = RunspaceConfiguration.Create();
            PSSnapInException snapInException = null;
            PSSnapInInfo info = rsConfig.AddPSSnapIn("Citrix.XenApp.Commands", out snapInException);
            Runspace myRunSpace = RunspaceFactory.CreateRunspace(rsConfig);
            myRunSpace.Open();
            Pipeline pipeLine = myRunSpace.CreatePipeline();
            Command myCommand = new Command("Get-XAServer");
            pipeLine.Commands.Add(myCommand);
            Collection<PSObject> commandResults = pipeLine.Invoke();
            foreach (PSObject cmdlet in commandResults)
            {
                string cmdletName = cmdlet.Properties["ServerName"].
                Value.ToString();
                listBox1.Items.Add(cmdletName);
            }
        }

        private void button1_Click(object sender, EventArgs e)
        {
            ShowXAServers();
        }
    }
}
```

And this is the final output of the application when we run it:

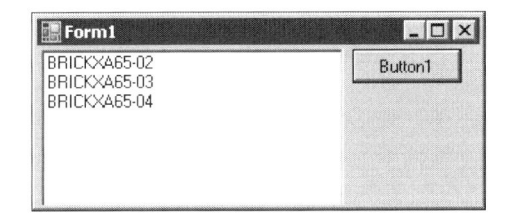

Passing parameters to cmdlets

We can pass parameters to cmdlets, using the `Parameters.Add` option. We can add multiple parameters. Each parameter will require a line. For example, we can add the `ZoneName` parameter to filter server members of the US-Zone zone:

```
Command myCommand = newCommand("Get-XAServer");
myCommand.Parameters.Add("ZoneName", "US-ZONE")
pipeLine.Commands.Add(myCommand);
```

Using MFCOM on XenApp

We can use PowerShell to call MFCOM objects on XenApp 5.0 farms or older versions. This is useful when we want to use PowerShell to manage multiple versions of XenApp farms or migrate data from previous versions of XenApp.

The following is a simple example of how to call an MFCOM object, inside a PowerShell script. The script shows the XenApp farm name on a XenApp 5.0 or earlier version. This example will fail in XenApp 6.5 (and XenApp 6.0):

```
$CtxXA = New-Object -ComObject "MetaFrameCOM.MetaFrameFarm"
$CtxXA.Initialize(1)
$CtxXA.FarmName
```

Convert MFCOM scripts to PowerShell

We can convert our MFCOM Scripts to PowerShell using the MFCOM Script Searcher tool, available for download at http://support.citrix.com/article/CTX125089.

Chapter 12

This tool will help us to search existing MFCOM scripts and provide us with an alternative PowerShell cmdlet to perform a similar function. Also, the tool will show the syntax of the PowerShell and some examples.

To use the tool, download the file, decompress the `.zip` file, and run the `.exe` file.

We need to set the location to search for the script file. Select the type of scripts we would like to search. Click on the **Search Files** button. The application inspects the files located in the folder (and subfolders, if we enable the **Search Subfolders** checkbox) and returns PowerShell commands and examples.

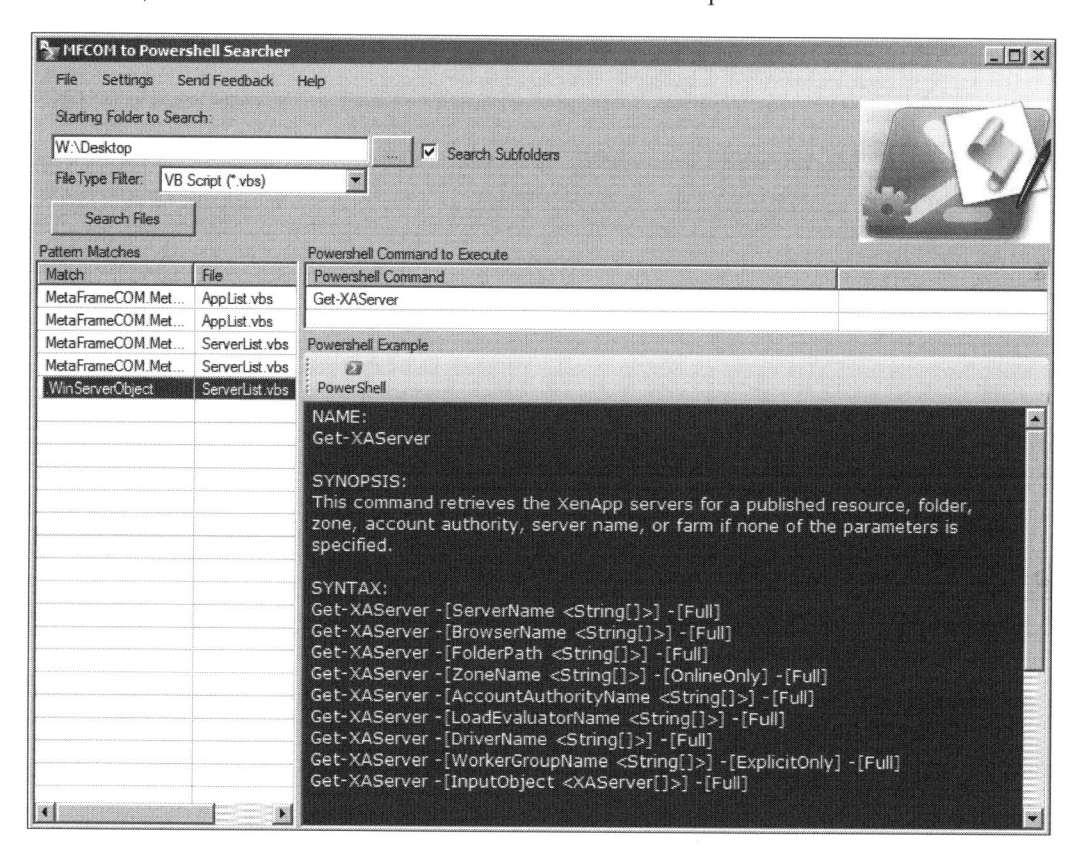

[377]

Summary

In this chapter, we have learned about managing XenApp with Windows PowerShell and developed sample .NET applications to call Citrix PowerShell cmdlets, on both Visual Basic.NET (VB.NET) and C#.NET. Specially:

- Difference between MFCOM and PowerShell scripts
- Installing XenApp Commands on XenApp servers
- Using PowerShell for basic administrative tasks
- Using PowerShell commands from .NET applications (VB.NET and C#.NET)
- Converting MFCOM scripts to PowerShell

In the next chapter, we will learn about Receiver and Plug-in Management, including installing Citrix Receiver for Windows and Macintosh, and deploying and configuring Citrix Merchandising Server on VMware and XenServer Virtual Machines.

13
Receiver and Plug-Ins Management

In the previous chapter, we learned about scripting programming, which included the installation of XenApp Commands on XenApp servers and the use of PowerShell for basic administrative tasks. We also learned how to use PowerShell commands from inside .NET applications (VB.NET and C#.NET). In this chapter, we will talk about Citrix Receiver and Plug-Ins Management.

Citrix Receiver turns any device, from a PC running Windows or Linux, Macintosh, thin client, tablet like iPad or Android devices, or Smartphone, (like Android, Blackberry), and iPhones into a powerful business tool, providing the ability to work from anywhere, any time. In this chapter, we will talk about Citrix Receiver and Plug-Ins management, including:

- Introduction to Citrix Receiver, including features and compatibility
- Installing Citrix Receiver for Windows and Macintosh
- Deploying Citrix Merchandising Server on VMware and XenServer Virtual Machines
- Setting up Merchandising Server and Receiver Plug-Ins

Introduction to Citrix Receiver

Citrix Receiver is a light software client that makes accessing virtual applications and desktops possible on almost any client machine, including Windows and Macintosh computers and mobile devices such as Android, Blackberry, Apple iPhones, and iPad devices.

Citrix describes the Citrix Receiver as similar to a satellite or cable TV receiver in a broadcast media service. Citrix Receiver allows IT organizations to deliver desktops and applications as an on-demand service to any device in any location with a rich "high-definition" experience.

The information in this chapter is based on Citrix Receiver 3.2 and Merchandising Server 2.2.

Citrix Receiver features

The following are Citrix Receiver's features:

- Secure access to any Windows or web application or virtual desktop on any network or device
- Universal browser support
- Centralized administrative control of virtual and physical desktops; applications and IT services distribute automatic updates to users based on preferences and credentials
- A complete SDK that offers a simple, extensible, architectural framework; allows third-party software and technology vendors to integrate new customized services

Citrix Receiver Plug-In compatibility

The following table lists the Plug-Ins compatible with the Merchandising Server and required operating systems:

Plug-Ins name	Compatible operating systems
Acceleration Plug-In 5.5.2 or later	Microsoft Windows XP (32-bit), Windows Vista (32- and 64-bit)
Acceleration Plug-In 5.5.4 or later	Microsoft Windows XP (32-bit), Windows Vista (32- and 64-bit), Windows 7 (32- and 64-bit)
Citrix Receiver for Mac 2.x or later	Apple Mac OSX 10.5 Leopard and 10.6 Snow Leopard (32- and 64-bit)
Citrix Receiver for Mac 11.x or later	Apple Mac OSX 10.6 Snow Leopard and 10.7 Lion (32- and 64-bit)
Citrix Receiver for Windows 2.x or later	Microsoft Windows XP, Windows Vista, Windows 7, Windows Server 2003 and 2008 (32- and 64-bit)

Plug-Ins name	Compatible operating systems
Citrix Receiver for Windows 3.x or later	Microsoft Windows XP, Windows Vista, Windows 7, Windows Server 2003 and 2008 (32 and 64-bit)
Communication Plug-In for Mac 3.0 or later	Apple Mac OSX 10.5 Leopard, 10.6 Snow Leopard and 10.7 Lion (32 and 64-bit)
Dazzle Plug-In 1.1.2 or later	Microsoft Windows XP, Windows Vista, and Windows 7 (32 and 64-bit)
EasyCall 3.x or later	Microsoft Windows XP, Windows Vista, Windows 7, Windows Server 2003 and 2008 (32 and 64-bit)
MS Application Virtualization Desktop Client 4.5 or later	Microsoft Windows XP (32-bit), Windows Vista (32 and 64-bit), Windows 7 (32 and 64-bit)
Offline Plug-In 5.x	Microsoft Windows XP, Windows Vista, Windows 7, Windows Server 2003 and 2008 (32 and 64-bit)
Online Plug-In for Mac 11.x or later	Apple Mac OSX 10.5 Leopard and 10.6 Snow Leopard (32 and 64-bit)
Online Plug-In for Windows 11.x, 12.x and Citrix Receiver 13.x	Microsoft Windows XP, Windows Vista, Windows 7, Windows Server 2003 and 2008 (32 and 64-bit)
Profile Management Plug-In 2.0 or later	Microsoft Windows XP, Windows Vista, Windows Server 2003 and 2008 (32 and 64-bit)
Secure Access for Mac Plug-In 1.2 or later	Apple Mac OSX 10.5 Leopard and 10.6 Snow Leopard (32 and 64-bit)
Secure Access for Windows Plug-In 4.6.2 or later	Microsoft Windows XP, Windows Vista, and Windows 7 (32 and 64-bit)
Secure Access Plug-In 9.1	Microsoft Windows XP, Windows Vista, and Windows 7 (32 and 64-bit)
Single Sign-On Plug-In 5.0	Microsoft Windows XP, Windows Vista, Windows 7, Windows 2003 and 2008 (32 and 64-bit)
Service Monitoring Plug-In 5.3 or later	Microsoft Windows XP, Windows Vista, Windows 7(32 and 64-bit)

Citrix Receiver system requirements and compatibility

The following are the system requirements for Windows and Macintosh users:

Citrix Receiver for Windows

To install Citrix Receiver on a Windows machine, we need:

- .NET Framework version 2.0 or later.
- Administrator privileges on the user's computer. Users must have administrator privileges on their client machines to install Receiver for Windows manually. The recommended option is deploying Citrix Receiver for Windows using Active directory GPOs, SCCM (Microsoft System Center Configuration Manager), or similar tools to users' client machines.

The following browser versions are required to download Receiver for Windows:

- Microsoft Internet Explorer v6.x or later
- Mozilla Firefox v1.x or later
- Google Chrome v 10.0 and later
- Apple Safari (this browser is not supported by Citrix Merchandising Server Administrator Console)

The following operating systems are supported by Citrix Receiver for Windows:

- Microsoft Windows XP Professional SP3 (32 and 64-bit)
- Microsoft Windows Vista SP2 (32 and 64-bit)
- Microsoft Windows 7 (32 and 64-bit)
- Microsoft Windows Server 2003 SP2 (32 and 64-bit)
- Microsoft Windows Server 2008 SP2 (32 and 64-bit)
- Microsoft Windows Server 2008 R2 (64-bit)

Citrix Receiver for Macintosh

Our users must run the following operating systems and versions to install Citrix Receiver for Mac:

- Apple Mac OSX 10.5 Leopard for Intel CPUs (32 and 64-bit)
- Apple Mac OSX 10.6 Snow Leopard (32 and 64-bit)
- Apple Mac OSX 10.7 Lion (32 and 64-bit)

Setting up Citrix Merchandising Server 2.2

Citrix Receiver for Windows, Receiver for Macintosh, and Merchandising Server are components of the Citrix Delivery Center solution. Citrix Merchandising Server and Citrix Receiver work together to update the installation and management of application delivery to the user desktops.

Merchandising Server is an administrative tool for configuring, delivering, and upgrading Plug-Ins for our users' devices and provides a great end-user experience on laptops and desktops.

Merchandising Server currently is supported on Citrix XenServer and VMware Servers.

Installing Merchandising Server software

The Merchandising Server software is delivered as a virtual appliance image that contains all of the software necessary for running the Merchandising Server.

William can download the virtual appliance image from `www.citrix.com` and then import the virtual machine into Citrix XenServer or VMware servers.

Two images are available under Receiver options:

- **XenServer**: The image name is similar to `citrix-merchandising-server-[releaseNumber].bz2`
- **VMware**: The image name is similar to `citrix-merchandising-server-VMware[releaseNumber].ova`

Merchandising Server System requirements

The following are the requirements to install and use the Merchandising Server:

Hypervisors (virtualization software) supported:

- Citrix XenServer 5.x or later. XenServer is available for free at `www.citrix.com`
- VMware ESX 3.5, VMware vSphere 4.x or later, and VMware Server 2.x. We can download VMware ESXi or VMware Server 2.x for free at `www.vmware.com`

Browsers required for the Citrix Merchandising Server Administrator Console:

- Microsoft Internet Explorer 7.x or later
- Mozilla Firefox version 3.x or later

Browsers supported for Citrix Receiver download pages:

- Microsoft Internet Explorer 7.x or later
- Mozilla Firefox version 4.x or later
- Apple Safari
- Google Chrome

Other requirements:

- Active Directory based on Windows 2003 or later is required

Based on the amount of users, the Merchandising Server virtual appliance will require more Memory or vCPU (virtual CPUs). Citrix recommends setting up at least 4 GB of RAM and 2 vCPUs to the virtual appliance, except in small deployments or testing environments.

Importing the virtual appliance into VMware vSphere

To deploy Merchandising Server on VMware, William must:

1. Start VMware vSphere Client and enter the IP address or host name of the VMware host or VMware vCenter server and then enter the username, password, and click on **Login**.

2. He chooses the **File and Deploy OVF Template** option. The **Deploy OVF Template** window appears and he needs to click on the **Browse** button, then selects the .ova file, and clicks on the **Next** button:

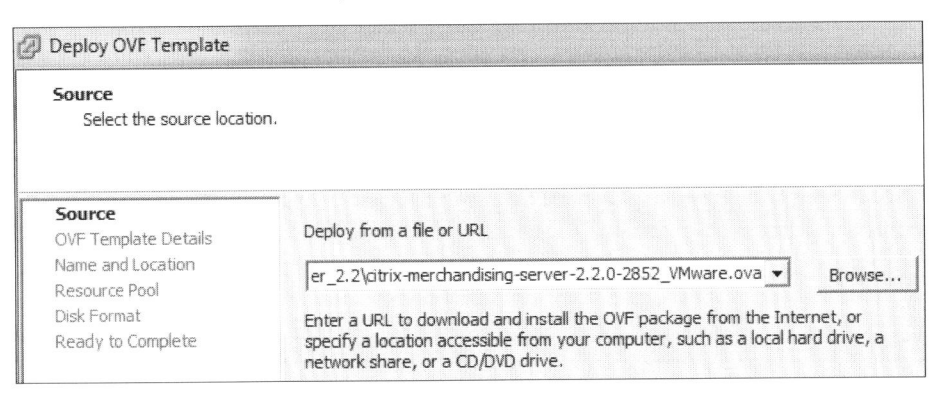

Chapter 13

3. He verifies the OVF template details and then he clicks on the Next button.
4. He clicks on the **Accept** button to accept the EULA agreement and clicks on the **Next** button.
5. He needs to enter the name of the Merchandising Server virtual machine and clicks on the **Next** button:

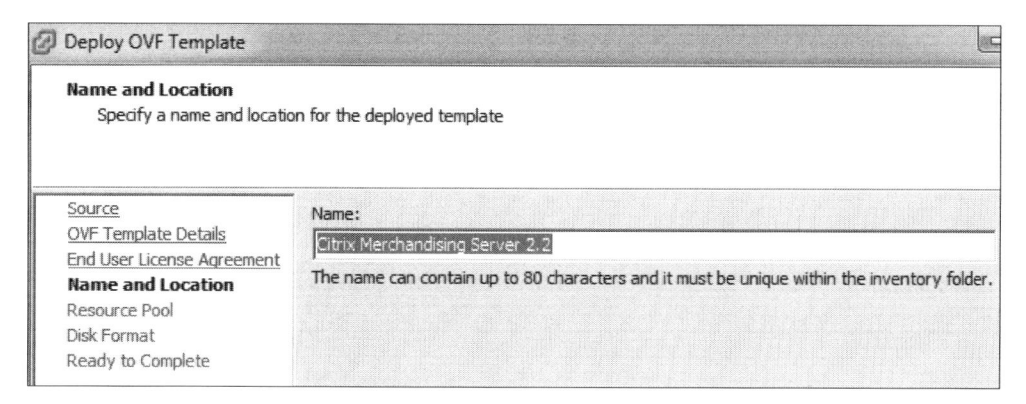

6. William chooses a datastore and then he clicks on the **Next** button.
7. He reviews the deployment settings and then he clicks on the **Finish** button.
8. After the Virtual Machine build is complete, he chooses the Merchandising Server virtual machine name in the inventory and then in the **Getting Started** tab, he clicks on **Edit virtual machine** settings. A properties pop-up window appears.
9. In the **Hardware** tab, William needs to select **Memory** and change the memory Size to 4 GB. Then he chooses **CPUs** and changes the **Number of virtual processors** to **2**. Citrix recommends allocating at least 4 GB of memory and configuring 2 vCPUs:

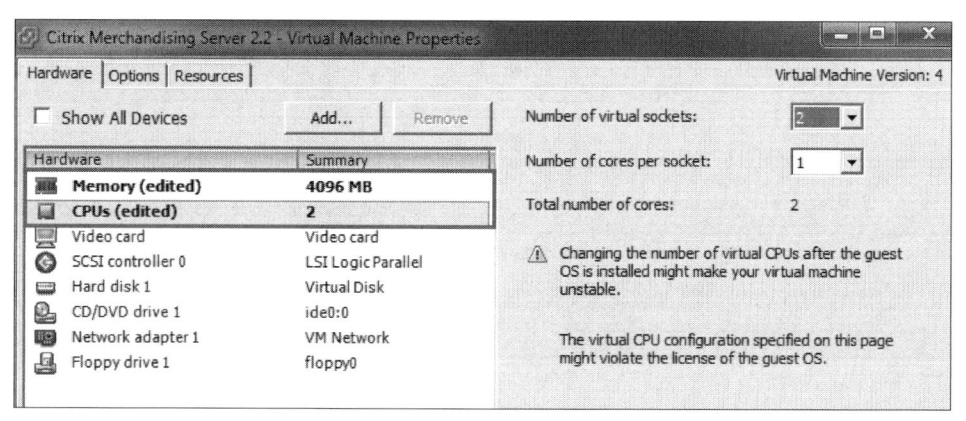

Importing the virtual appliance into Citrix XenServer

The following is the procedure to install the virtual appliance in Citrix XenServer, followed by William:

1. William uses WinRAR or a similar tool to decompress the .bz2 file.
2. He starts the **Citrix XenCenter**, selects **File** and then the **Import VM** option. The **Import VM** pop-up window displays, he clicks on the **Browse** button, navigates to the **.xva** file, and clicks on **Open**:

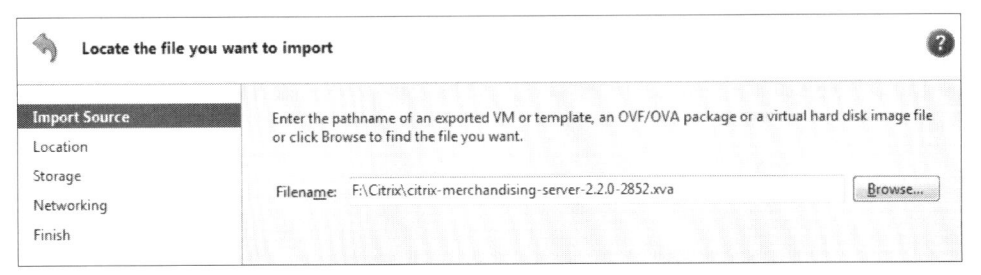

3. He selects **Exported VM** as the **Import Type** and then he clicks on the **Next** button.
4. In the **Home Server** screen of the wizard, William selects the XenServer instance where this VM should be imported and then he clicks on the **Next** button:

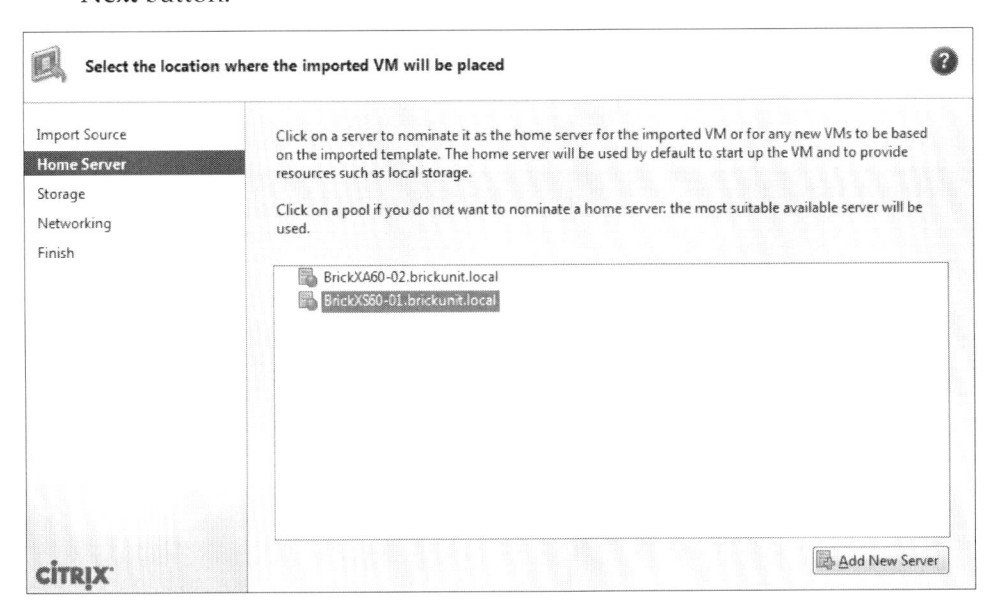

Chapter 13

5. In the **Storage** screen, William selects the storage repository to store the Virtual Machine and then he clicks on the **Import** button.

6. The import begins and the **Networking** screen opens. In the **Networking** screen, William needs to select the appropriate network and then he clicks on the **Next** button:

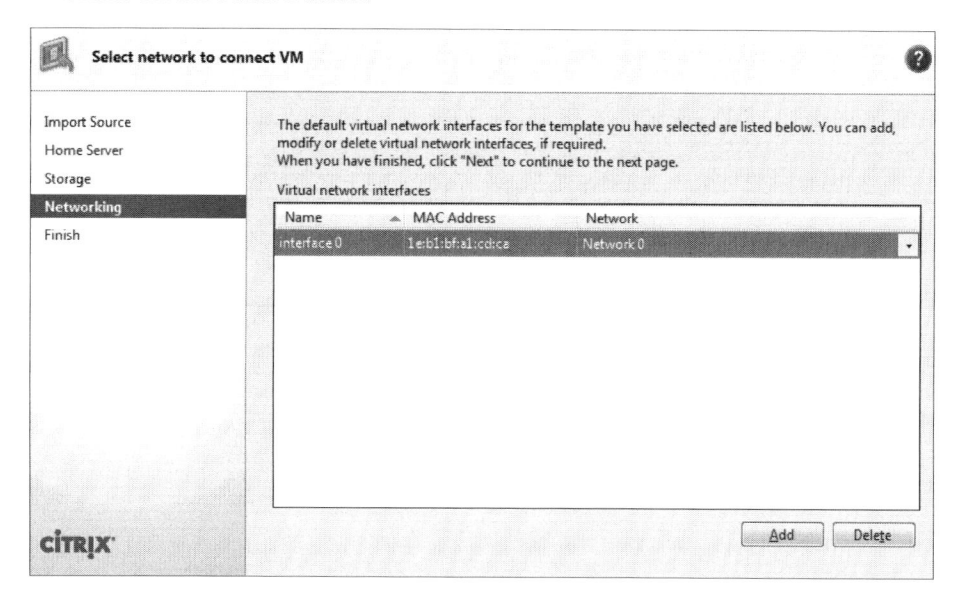

7. In the **Finish** screen, William clears the checkbox for **Start VM(s) after import** and he clicks on the **Finish** button:

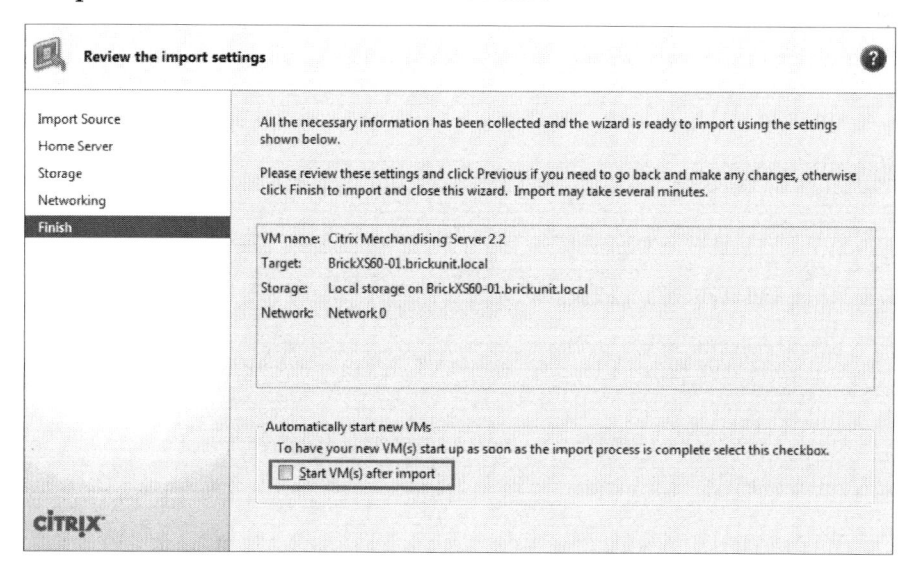

[387]

Receiver and Plug-Ins Management

8. After the import process completes, William needs to right-click the **Virtual Machine** and choose **Properties**.

9. He needs to click on the **CPU and Memory** tab and adjust the amount of memory and the number of vCPUs. Citrix recommends allocating at least 4 GB of memory and 2 vCPUs:

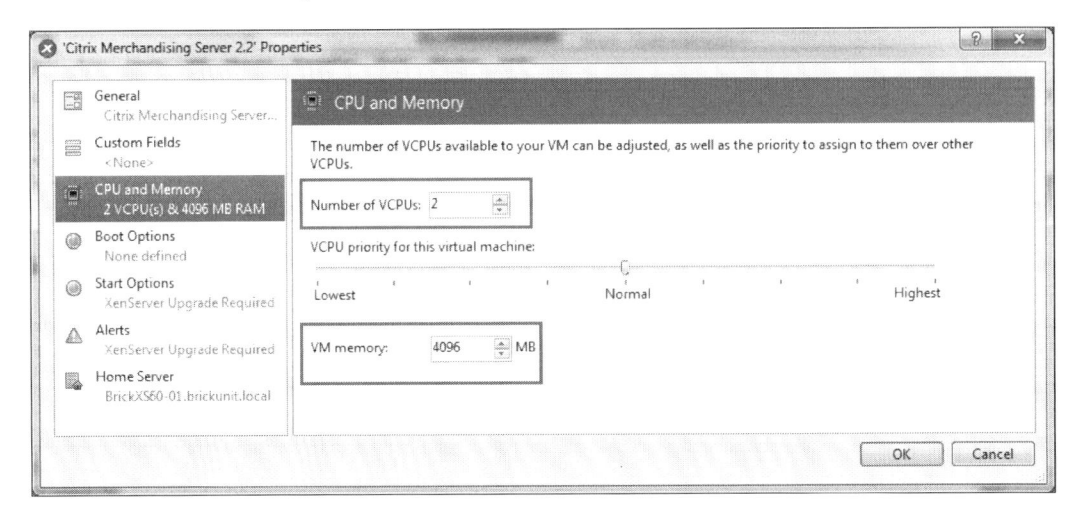

10. He clicks on the **OK** button. He then selects the VM and clicks on the **Network** tab.

11. Finally, he clicks on the **Properties** button, selects **Auto-generate**, and clicks on **OK**.

Setting up Merchandising Server

As soon as William finishes adjusting memory and CPU settings, he is ready to start the virtual machine.

- In VMware, using the **Getting Started** tab, he clicks on **Power on the virtual machine**. Then he needs to open the console by clicking on the **Console** tab or opening an independent console.

- In XenServer he needs to right-click the VM and choose **Start**, then he needs to select the **Console** tab.

[388]

Now he will configure network settings and enters **9** to save the configuration:

```
###############################################
#                                             #
#        Citrix Merchandising Server          #
#                                             #
#           Network Configuration             #
#                                             #
###############################################

   [1]* Hostname (receiver.brickunit.local)
   [2]* IP (192.168.1.37)
   [3]  Netmask (255.255.255.0)
   [4]* Gateway (192.168.1.1)
   [5]* Domain Name System
         nameserver 192.168.1.30
         nameserver 192.168.1.1
         search brickunit.local

   [8]  Diagnostics
   [9]  Save Changes
   [0]  Discard Changes

   * Changes that need to be saved.
```

When prompted, he needs to enter a new password for the virtual appliance:

```
###############################################
#                                             #
#         New password for root user.         #
#                                             #
###############################################
New UNIX password: _
```

When this process is completed, he needs to reboot the virtual appliance to apply settings.

Receiver and Plug-Ins Management

Configuring administrator users

The next step for William is configuring the virtual appliance to connect to Active Directory and provide access to his account and other administrators to the Administrator Console, using the following procedure:

1. He needs to open a browser window and enter the Administrator Console URL. The URL is similar to `https://[server_address]/appliance`, where `server_address` is the Merchandising Server host name or IP address. For example, he needs to enter `https://receiver.brickunit.local/appliance` and the login window will appear:

2. Now he needs to enter the default administrator console account, the default username is root, and the default password is `C1trix321`. Clicking on **Log on** will give him access to the console:

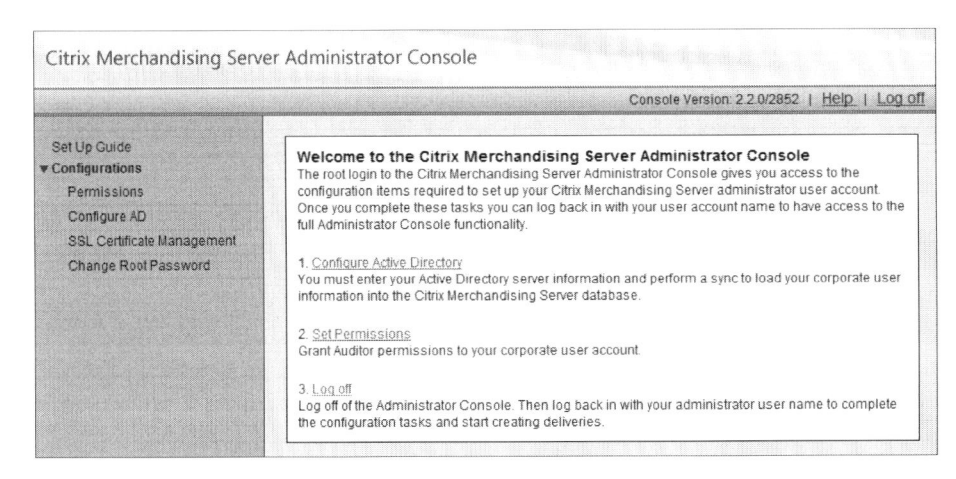

[390]

3. He needs to select the **Configurations** option, then the **Configure Active Directory** option, and provide the Active Directory server information:

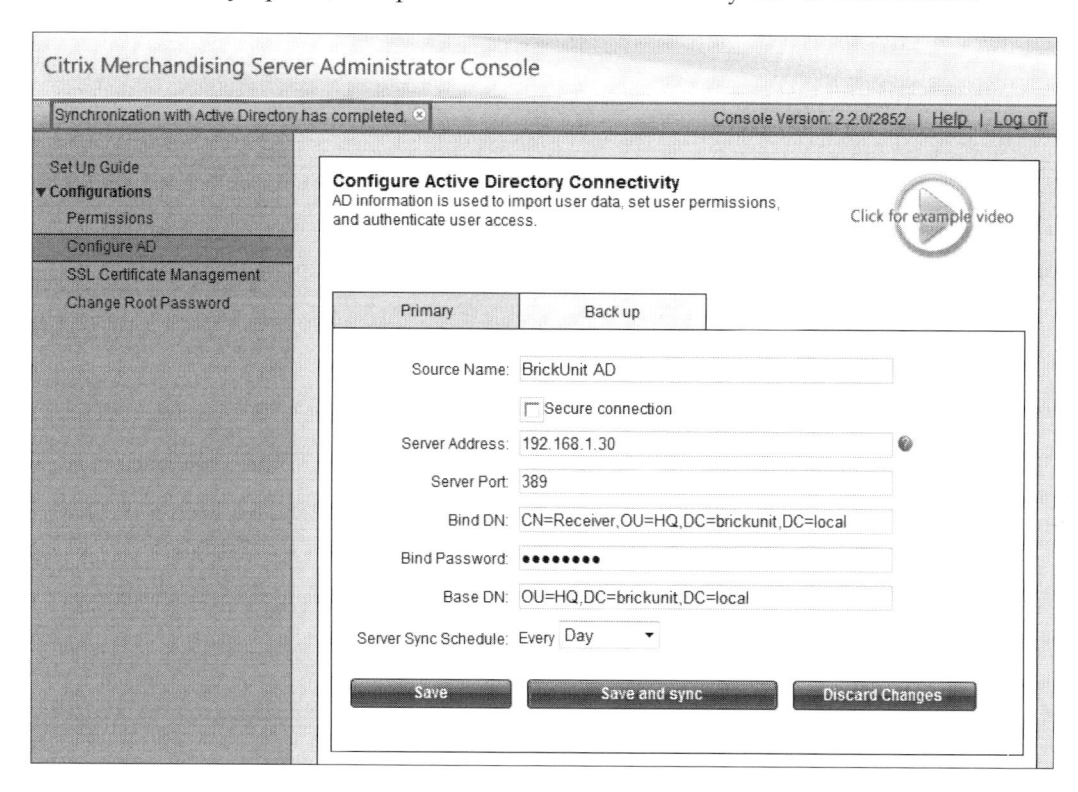

![Citrix Merchandising Server Administrator Console showing Configure Active Directory Connectivity screen with fields for Source Name: BrickUnit AD, Server Address: 192.168.1.30, Server Port: 389, Bind DN: CN=Receiver,OU=HQ,DC=brickunit,DC=local, Bind Password, Base DN: OU=HQ,DC=brickunit,DC=local, Server Sync Schedule: Every Day]

4. He clicks on the **Save and sync** button to load users into the Merchandising Server database.

5. The next step is choosing administrators; he needs to select the **Configurations** option and then the **Permissions** option.

6. He needs to enter the username, first or last name in the **Search Users** text box, and click on **Search**. He chooses the name in the search results list and clicks the **Edit** button. He selects the **Administrator** role and clicks on the **Save** button:

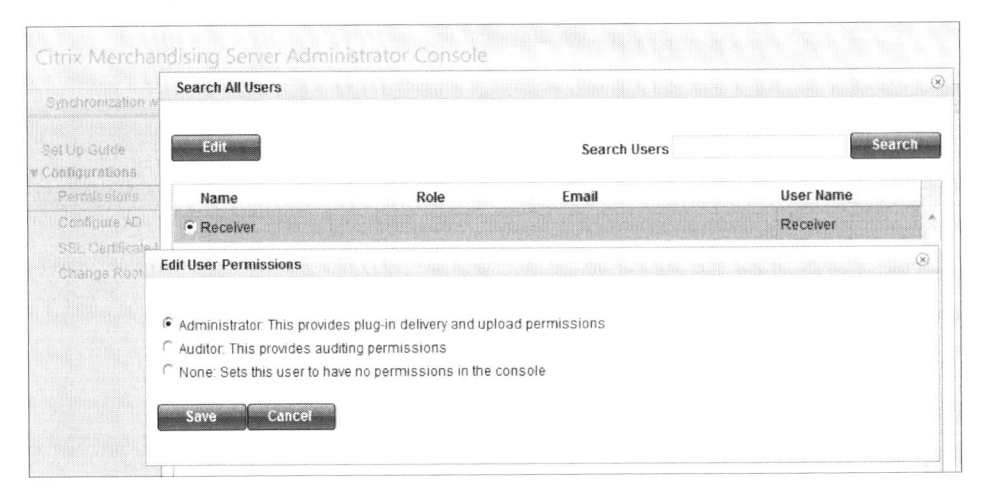

7. He needs to repeat the process for each of the users who will need **Administrator** or **Auditor** permissions.
8. Finally, he needs to log out of the **Administrator Console**.

Installing Plug-Ins

Now, William is ready to download Plug-Ins and create delivery rules.

The first step is to log in to the Merchandising Console using his Active Directory username and password, and then he has two different options to access Plug-Ins.

As this is the first time William has accessed the console, the home page will show the total number of new Plug-Ins available to download:

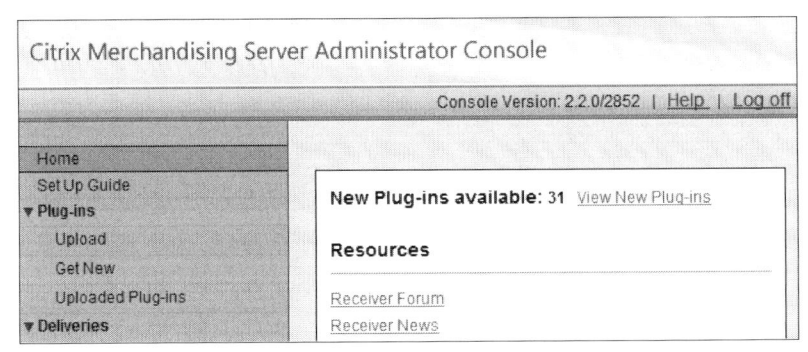

William can click on the **View New Plug-ins** link to access the list of Plug-Ins available to install. Also, he can click on the **Plug-ins | Get New** menu.

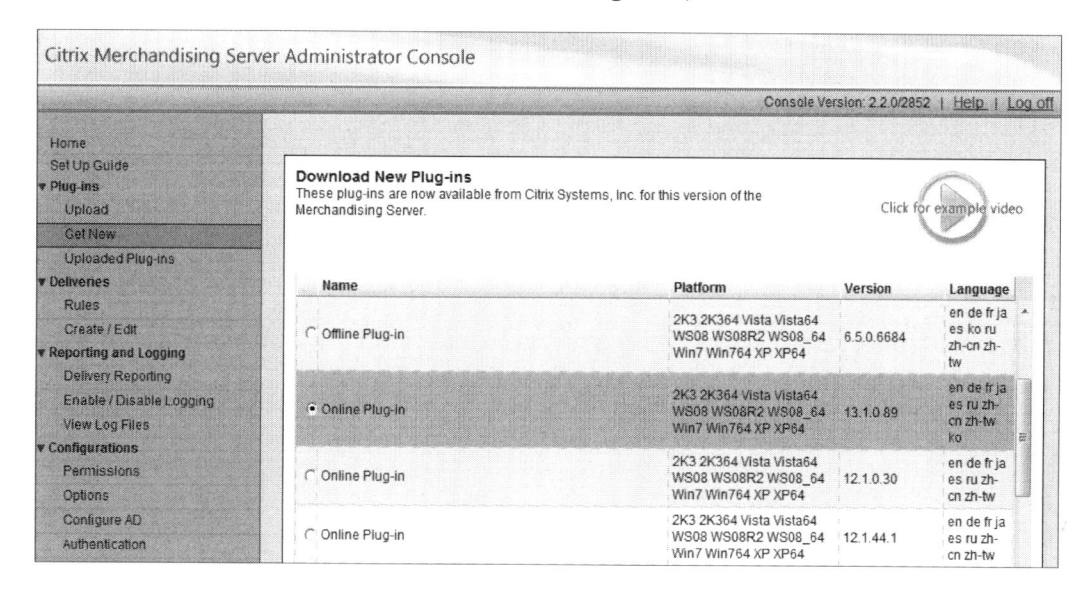

Now he can select the Plug-In from the list and click on the **Download to Server** or the **Download All button** to download all available Plug-Ins. When the **Success** dialog box appears, he clicks on the **Close** button.

He can repeat the process until he downloads all the Plug-Ins he wants to distribute to Brick Unit's users.

Creating recipient rules

Delivery recipients are created based on the rules William will create. Rules can be based by User Name, User Group, User Domain, Machine Name, IP Address, or Operating System. William can create as many rules as he needs and use them individually or in combination to define a set of delivery recipients, but only one delivery can be defined as the default delivery. The default delivery cannot contain rules.

Receiver and Plug-Ins Management

This is the procedure used by William to create rules:

1. In the **Administrator Console**, William chooses the **Deliveries | Rules** option.
2. He clicks on the **Create** button (located at the bottom of the page). Also, he can use the **Edit** button to edit any existing rule.

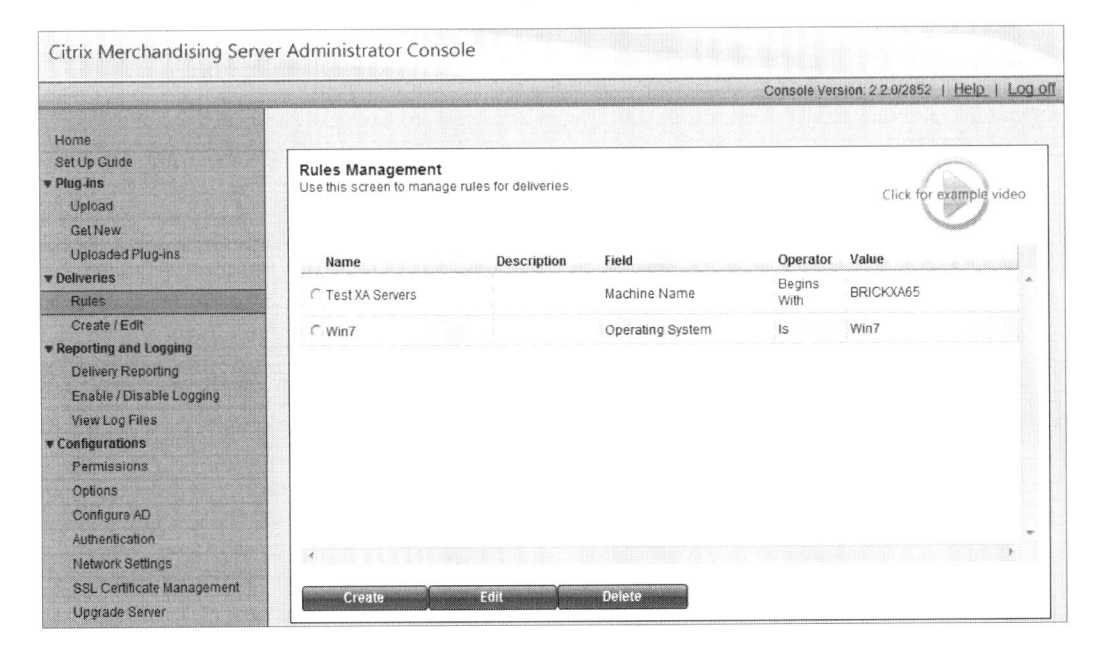

3. He types the rule **Name** and optionally the **Description**.
4. Then he chooses the rule type from the **Field** menu, from the list of available values: Machine Name, User Domain Membership, Computer Domain Membership, Operating System, LDAP User, and LDAP Group, Machine Name, and IP Address Range. Based on the **Field** he selects, different options are available:

    ○ The Search functionality is available when he selects LDAP User or LDAP Groups

    ○ If he chooses User Domain Membership, Machine Domain Membership, Operating System, or IP Address Range, he needs to select **Is** or **Is Not** for the **Operator** field and type the appropriate **Value** entry

    ○ If he selects Machine Name, he can choose **Begins With**, **Contains**, or **Is Exactly**, and type the appropriate **Value** entry

Chapter 13

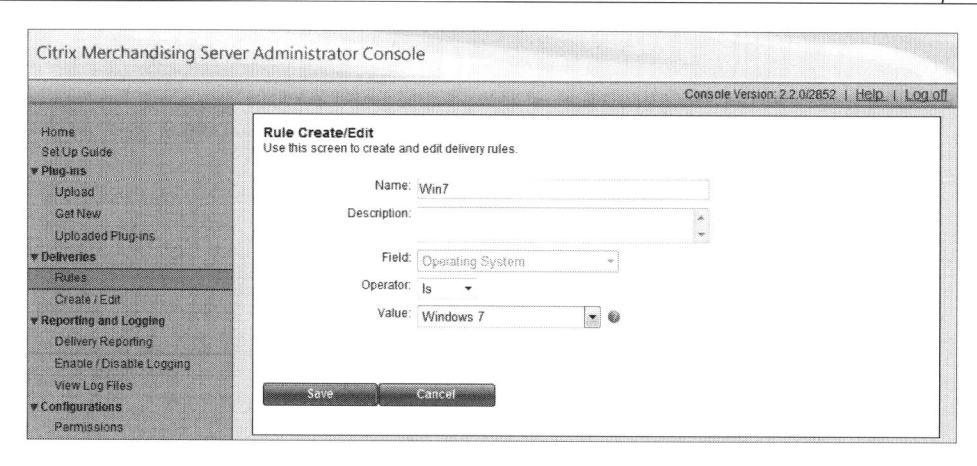

5. Finally, when the rule is ready, he needs to click on the **Save** button to save the rule.

Creating deliveries

Deliveries are used to deploy and update the Plug-In to a client machine or device. To create deliveries, William has to:

1. Open the **Administrator Console**, and choose **Deliveries | Create / Edit**.
2. Click on the **Create** button, located at the bottom of the page.
3. In the **General** tab, he enters the general information for the delivery:

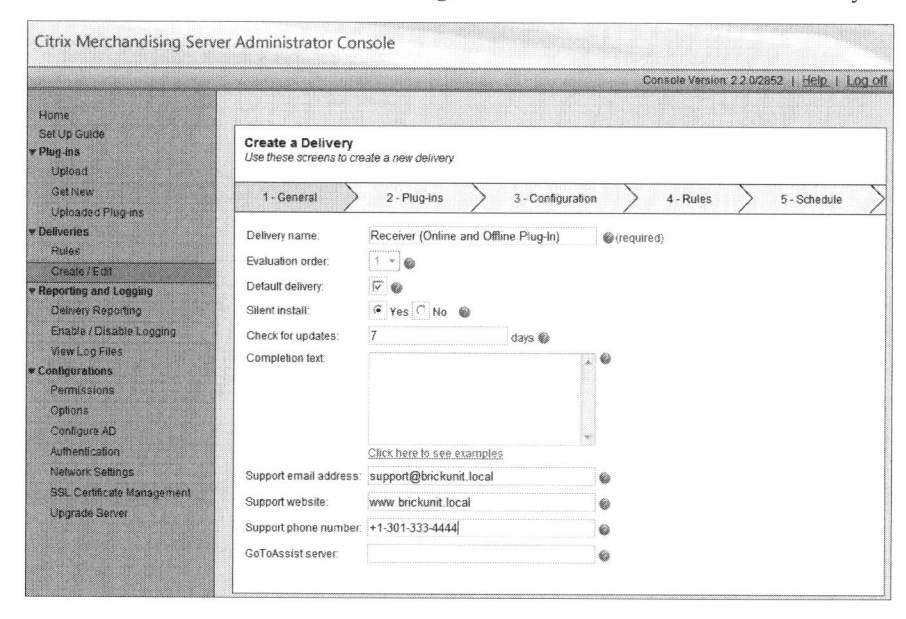

[395]

Receiver and Plug-Ins Management

4. In the **Plug-Ins** tab, he chooses Plug-Ins to deliver, using the **Add** and **Remove** buttons:

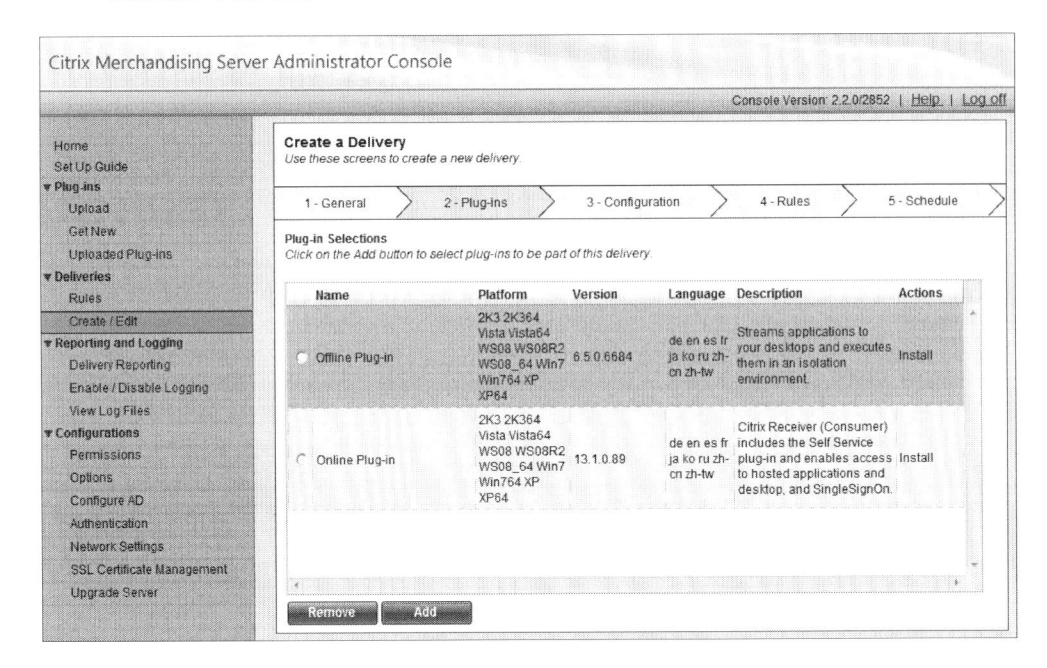

5. In the **Configuration** tab, he can modify Plug-In settings:

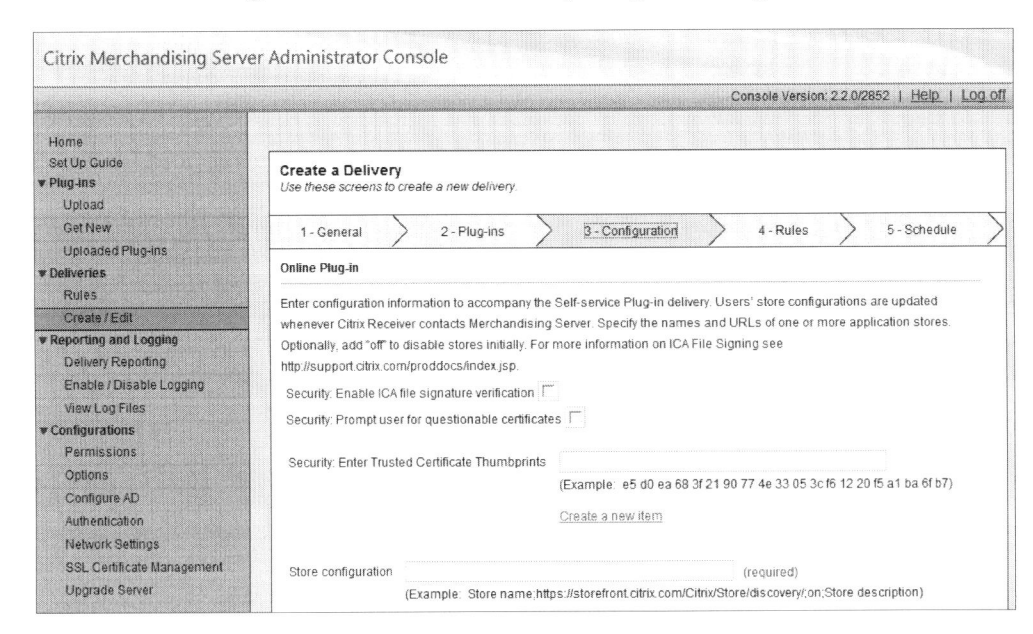

6. In the **Rules** tab, he can set up rules to apply in the delivery (note: in the default delivery, the option is not available).

7. In the **Schedule** tab, William can set the delivery schedule time and date or choose the **Deliver Now** option. Then he clicks on the **Schedule** button to complete the process:

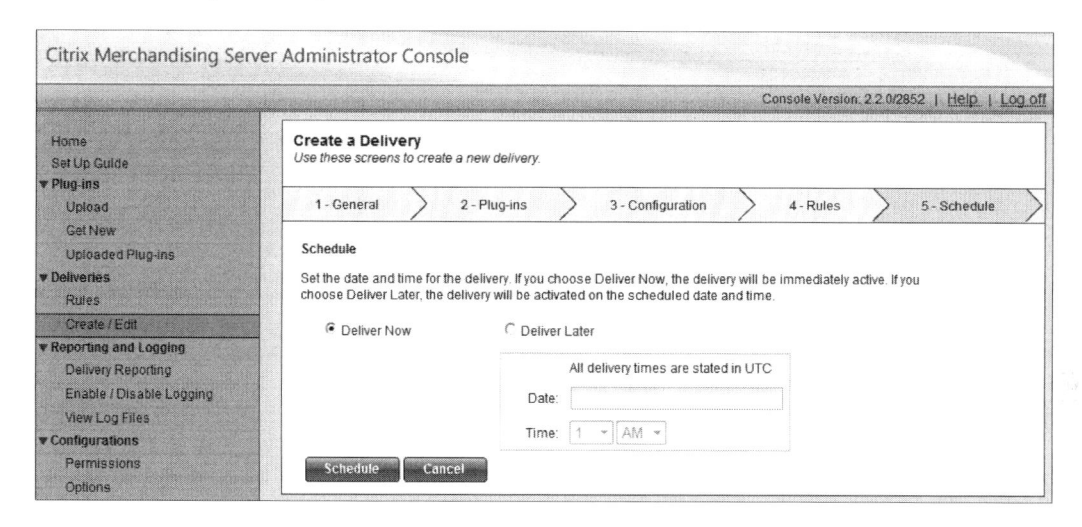

8. After the delivery is completed, he can review deliveries and modify, suspend, or resume any of them:

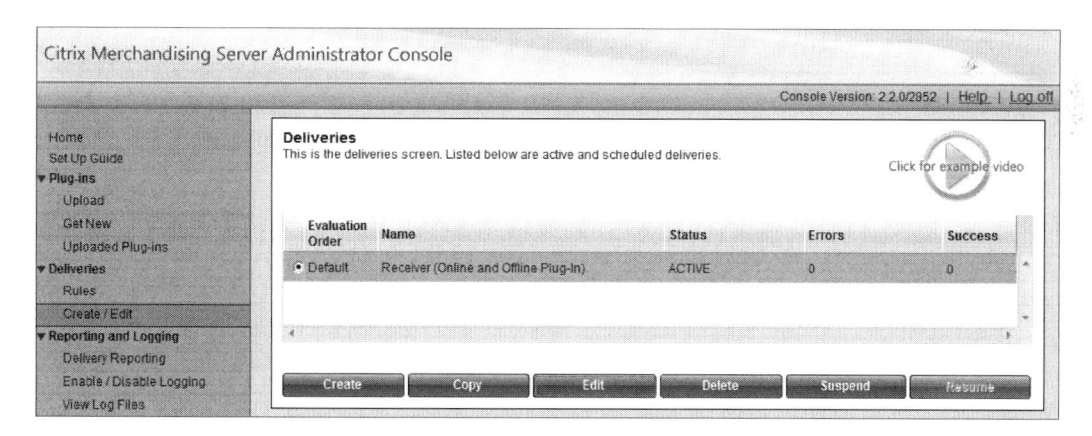

9. Merchandising Server setup now is complete. Brick Unit Construction users are ready to download and install Citrix Receiver. Once they have downloaded Receiver, Merchandising Server will install Plug-Ins based on the schedule created before.

Configuring SSL certificates

By default, Merchandising Server uses SSL to encrypt communication with Receiver clients. This requires installing and configuring an SSL certificate for the Merchandising server.

The Merchandising Server includes a temporary 30-day certificate. William needs to replace or renew this certificate within 30 days to ensure continuous communication between the server and client machines.

> Merchandising Server 2.2 supports 2048-bit or greater SSL certificates, when previous versions support only 1024-bit SSL certificates. This can be a great reason to update your Merchandising Server to version 2.2

William can use the following options to create the SSL certificate:

- Creating a Self-Signed SSL Certificate: Every 30 days he can renew installed certificate. This is the less preferred option.
- Use an Existing SSL Certificate: William can import an existing certificate, like a wildcard certificate generated in another server, using a private key file.
- SSL Certificate using a Certificate Signing Request from the Merchandising Server: William needs to send the certificate signing request to public certificate authority or use an internal one.
- Internal certificates: Generated using Microsoft Certificate Services.

Also, William can enable or disable the SSL communication with the HTTPS redirection option. By default, any attempt to access the Merchandising Server through HTTP protocol is automatically redirected to HTTPS.

William can change this setting using the **HTTPS Redirection** option, available at **Administrator Console**, under **Configurations | Options**.

Disabling SSL can be useful in some scenarios like multiple Merchandising Servers in different geographical areas or when the Merchandising Server is deployed behind NetScaler. William can use NetScaler in "Transparent SSL" or "SSL Offload" mode.

Receiver for Windows communicates with NetScaler using SSL and the NetScaler sends commands using HTTP protocol to the Merchandising Server.

Creating a self-signed SSL certificate

A self-signed certificate valid for 30 days is already installed on the Merchandising Server. If William chooses this option, he must renew it every 30 days by generating it again. The following is the procedure to generate the certificate:

1. He logs on to the **Administrator Console** and selects **Configurations | SSL Certificate Management**.
2. He chooses **Generate self-signed certificate** from the **Select an action** drop-down box.
3. In the **Common Name** field, William needs to enter the host name or IP address of the Merchandising Server and then he needs to complete the rest of the fields.
4. He clicks on the **Submit** button to generate a self-signed certificate for the Merchandising Server. After that, the server will reboot.

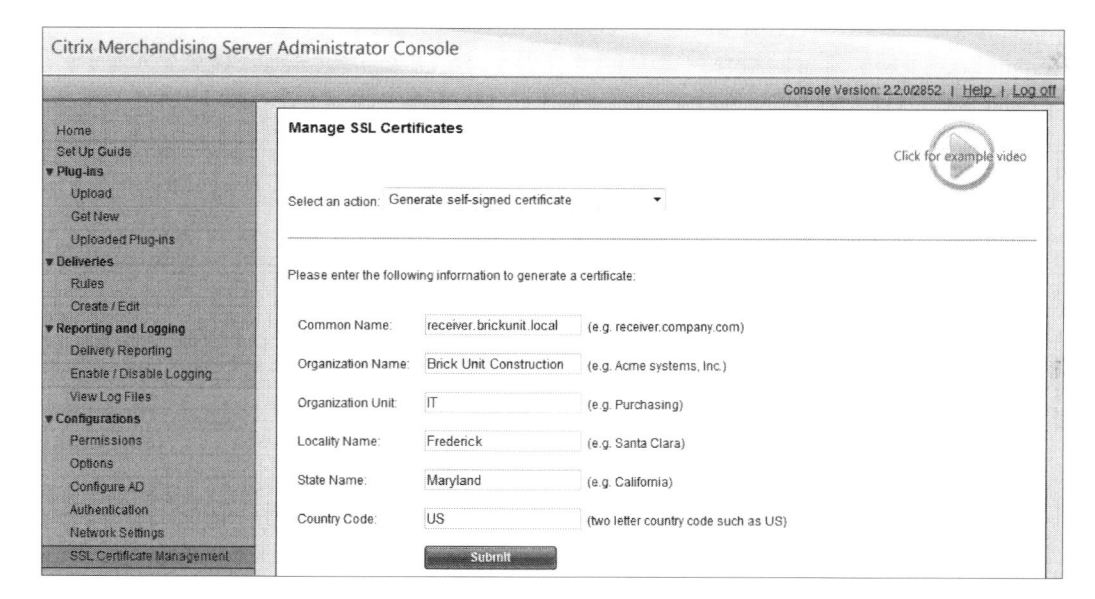

> This certificate requires that users accept a security exception for a certificate that was not issued by a trusted certificate authority.

Creating a Certificate Signing Request

William needs a CSR (Certificate Signing Request) to obtain an SSL certificate from a certificate authority. He can use the Administrator Console to generate the CSR required by the CA (Certificate Authority).

Then he can obtain a certificate from the CA by providing the completed CSR. Also, the Merchandising Server supports certificates whose CSR was generated by other servers.

1. He logs on to the **Administrator Console** and chooses **Configurations | SSL Certificate Management**.
2. He chooses **Export certificate signing request** from the **Select an action** drop-down box to create the CSR.
3. In the **Common Name** field, William needs to enter the host name or IP address for the Merchandising Server and then he needs to complete the rest of the fields.
4. He clicks on the **Export** button to generate and download the `server.csr` file that he needs to provide to the CA to obtain a certificate.
5. He contacts the CA and follows the required procedure to acquire a certificate. He needs to provide the `.csr` file generated in the previous step to the CA and sometimes the platform information (Note: The server platform is Apache and the certificate usage is WebServer).
6. Finally, the CA sends an SSL server certificate and the root certificate.

Importing SSL certificates

The following procedure is used by William to import certificates and private key files:

1. He logs on to the **Administrator Console** and chooses **Configurations | SSL Certificate Management**.

Chapter 13

2. He chooses **Import certificate from a certificate authority** from the **Select an action** drop-down box:

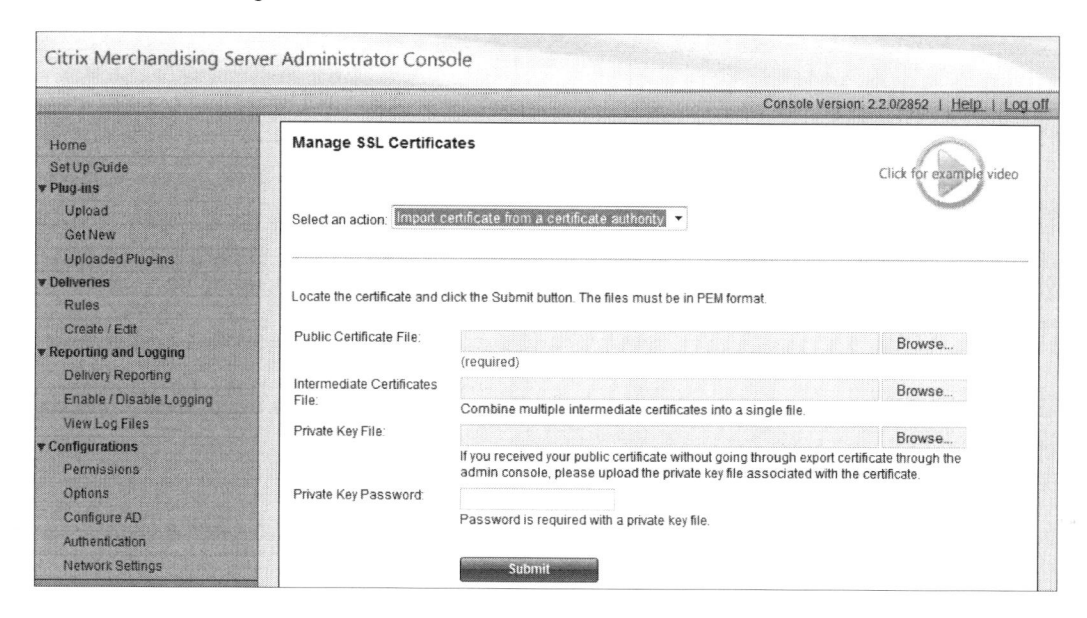

3. Now he needs to specify the files to be imported, based on the type of certificates he is using:
   - **Certificates Generated from the Merchandising Server**: He needs to use the **Browse...** button next to the **Public Certificate File** field. The Merchandising Server already has the private key file needed for the certificate requests, so he does not need to upload a private key file.
   - **Intermediate Certificates File**: He needs to use the **Browse...** button next to the **Intermediate Certificates File** field.
   - **Certificates Generated from the Merchandising Server or Certificates Generated from Other Servers**: William uses the **Browse...** button next to the **Public Certificate File** field. Then he uses the **Browse...** button next to the **Private Key File** field to locate the private key file for the certificate. After that, he types the Private Key password (also known as the pass phrase) for the private key file.
4. He clicks on the **Submit** button to finish the procedure.

The **Certificate Status** textbox displays information about the certificate after the successful completion of this process and Merchandising Server restarts.

Creating a signing request for Microsoft certificate services

The following is the procedure for requesting and downloading a signed certificate from an internal signing authority:

1. William opens the Internet browser and enters the company's certificate services URL.
2. He chooses the link to request a certificate.
3. He chooses the link to submit a request using a **Base 64 encoded CMC** or **PKS #10** file or a renewal request by using a **Base-64 encoded PKSCS #7** file.
4. He pastes the contents of the signed certificate request into the **Saved Request** field.
5. He selects the web server in the certificate template field.
6. He clicks on the **Submit** button to finish the procedure.

When the certificate is issued, he selects the **Base 64 encoding** method and downloads the signed certificate.

Installing SSL certificates on client machines

Merchandising Server uses SSL to encrypt communications with Receiver. William needs a root certificate on the client machine that can verify the signature of the Certificate Authority on the Merchandising Server certificate.

Using an external Certificate Authority, like VeriSign or similar, will automatically be trusted by most client machines.

If William chooses to use SSL certificates from an internal Certificate Authority, he needs to distribute root certificates so that they are available for all users in the centralized local computer certificate store. If the root certificates are not available in the centralized local computer certificate store, Receiver for Windows cannot receive updates from the Merchandising Server.

William can use Active Directory Group Policies to distribute Certificates to client machines. The document that provides detailed instructions to install certificates using GPOs can be found at `http://technet.microsoft.com/en-us/library/cc731253(WS.10).aspx`.

Installing Citrix Receiver

Depending on our environment, we can use different methods for installing Citrix Receiver:

- **Internal Users with Administrative Rights**: Installs Receiver for Windows or Receiver for Macintosh through the **Download** page at the Merchandising Server.
- **Internal Windows users without Administrative Rights**: Needs to push the Receiver for Windows installation to client machines.
- **Remote Users**: Needs to publish the **Download** page of the Merchandising Server to an external site and users need to connect to this site to download and install the Receiver for Windows or Receiver for Macintosh.

Now it's time to help William Empire, from Brick Unit Constructions, install Citrix Receiver and implement Citrix Merchandising Server on his network.

Deploying Citrix Receiver for internal users with administrative rights

A majority of internal users at Brick Unit Constructions are local administrators of their client machines as they generally need to connect devices like cameras or install applications that require administrative rights.

William will notify a few test users, with an e-mail, with the URL of the Merchandising server. The URL is similar to `https://[serverAddress]/appliance/download`, where `[serverAddress]` is the Merchandising server address or host name, for example, the URL at Brick Unit is `https://receiver.brickunit.local/appliance/download`.

Installing Citrix Receiver for Windows

Brick Unit's users must connect to the Merchandising Server URL, agree to the terms of use, and then click on the **Download** button to start the download:

Then Receiver for Windows prompts to log on, and users must enter their Active Directory credentials and click on the **Log On** button.

The Receiver for Windows starts the initial delivery from the Merchandising Server and installs Plug-Ins. The user may be asked to reboot their client machine, depending on the Plug-Ins installed.

When the process is complete, the Receiver icon is present in the notification area.

> If we install Citrix Receiver for Windows in a Windows server with Remote Desktop Services (formerly known as Terminal Services), users will notice that the status of the service under **Preferences | About** is shown in red. Plug-In updates are disabled: This is caused because when the Receiver client detects Remote Desktop Services, it automatically disables the Plug-In to avoid disrupting the sessions of active users. We can re-enable updates when we want to update the server by adding the `allowadminTSupdates` switch to the Receiver command line.

Installing Citrix Receiver on XenApp servers

Sometimes, to publish XenApp desktops, we need to install Citrix Receiver and Plug-Ins to simplify management and keep all servers at the same version level. Citrix Receiver will disable automatic installation of Plug-Ins, so we need to manually trigger updates.

To install Citrix Receiver on a XenApp server William must:

1. Log on to the XenApp server as administrator.
2. Download and install Citrix Receiver for Windows from the Merchandising Server. Receiver is installed on the server.
3. Close the Receiver, right-click the Citrix Receiver icon in the notification area and select Exit.
4. Open a command prompt window and run Citrix Receiver in the updating mode using the following command:

   `C:\Program Files\Citrix\Receiver\Receiver.exe  -autoupdate -allowadminTSupdates`

Once the updates have been installed, a reboot may be required.

Installing Citrix Receiver for Macintosh

Similar to the installation on a Windows system, Mac users must connect to the Merchandising Server URL, agree to the terms of use, and then click the **Download** button to start the download.

1. Once the installation succeeds, the Receiver will start the connection with the Merchandising Server to install Plug-Ins and requires the user to enter the Active Directory user authentication credentials.

2. After the user enters credentials, he needs to select **Standard** and click on the **Continue** button.
3. The Receiver for Windows starts the initial delivery from the Merchandising Server and installs Plug-Ins.
4. The user may be asked the password, depending on the Plug-Ins installed.

When the process is complete, the Receiver icon is shown in the menu bar as shown in the following screenshot:

Deploying Citrix Receiver for internal Windows users without administrative rights

The next step that William Empire will take is to push the Citrix Receiver client to some users' workstations without administrative rights, like training machines and a few information kiosks.

Options include deploying the .MSI file using Active Directory or Microsoft SCCM (System Center Configuration Manager, formerly known as SMS) or similar tools.

William needs to use the following installation options, if he wants to push the Receiver installation to his users:

- SERVER_LOCATION: This is the server address (with or without the HTTP prefix).
- AUTOUPDATE: Controls whether the Receiver checks the Merchandising Server for updates automatically or not. Options are True or False.
- VERBOSE: Controls the level of debug information produced by Citrix Receiver. Options are True or False.

- TOKEN: The value from the **Token Value** field in the Merchandising Server Administrator Console (Configurations, Authentication). This value is generated when we click on the **Generate Token** button:

Based on the following information, William creates a script to install Receiver, Plug-Ins, and asks a user to reboot the machine (if required). As we mentioned before, this script can be used in unattended deployment:

```
msiexec /i "Receiver.msi" /qn ALLUSERS=1 REBOOT="ReallySuppress"
SERVER_LOCATION=https://receiver.brickunit.local/appliance/services/
applianceService VERBOSE=true AUTOUPDATE=true TOKEN=S7uoeHOc7bvAY74izODqU
g0T+JSkB61HMQYCmbTIovCWwOoIGCIx94xNoiFO/W40
```

Summary

In this chapter, we learned about Citrix Receiver for Windows and Macintosh, and how to install and use Merchandising Server to configure, deliver, and upgrade Plug-Ins for our users' devices.

In the next (and last) chapter, we will talk about deploying XenApp 6.5 in a virtualized environment (VMware vSphere, Citrix XenServer, and Microsoft Hyper-V).

14
Virtualizing XenApp Farms

In the previous chapter, we learned about Citrix Receiver for Windows and Macintosh and how to use Citrix Merchandising Server for plug-ins management. In this chapter, we will cover the basics of virtualization of Citrix XenApp farms. We have been hearing a lot about virtualization over the last few years and implementing XenApp in a virtualized environment is a very popular option today.

Running XenApp on virtual machines helps reduce datacenter size and costs, cuts down on server deployment time, and saves (a lot of) money. In this chapter, we will learn more about implementing XenApp on virtual machines including:

- Deploying XenApp 6.5 in a virtualized environment
- Advantages and disadvantages of virtualization, virtual machine performance and host scalability, and more
- Deploying XenApp 6.5 on Citrix XenServer, Microsoft Hyper-V, and VMware vSphere virtual machines
- Cloning XenApp 6.5 virtual machines

Deploying XenApp 6.5 in a virtualized environment

Deploying virtualized XenApp farms today is a common scenario for any Citrix environment. In this chapter, we will help William Empire from Brick Unit Construction to evaluate XenApp 6.5 on leading bare metal hypervisors in the market: Citrix XenServer, VMware ESX vSphere, and Microsoft Hyper-V.

Hypervisors allow multiple operating systems, called guests, to run concurrently on a host computer, a feature called hardware virtualization. The hypervisor presents to the guest operating systems a virtual operating platform and monitors the execution of the guest operating systems. Multiple instances of a variety of operating systems may share the virtualized hardware resources. Bare metal hypervisors run directly on the host's hardware to control the hardware and to monitor guest operating systems.

There are many good reasons to virtualize XenApp 6.5 farms, including:

- **Faster server and application provisioning**: In a (standard) non-virtualized environment, deploying new servers and increasing farm capability can take days. In a virtualized environment, we can create templates and scripts to deploy VMs (virtual machines) in a few minutes.
- **Server consolidation**: Virtualization improves server utilization. The average server utilization in the datacenter is usually between 5 to 25 percent. The application silos utilization ratio is lower and can be around 5 percent to 10 percent. Consolidating multiple servers and application silos allows us to maximize the utilization of our hardware resources and reduce datacenter expenses such as energy and rack space. Also, we can consolidate multiple operating systems into the same host.
- **Improved disaster recovery**: By using snapshots, we can replicate production VMs to disaster recovery datacenters in a few minutes and keep our environment updated.
- **Zero-downtime for hardware maintenance**: In a virtualized environment, we can move VMs between hosts without service interruption, to update the hardware of our hosts' servers.
- **Dynamic workload management**: We can use VMs to support dynamic workload management, moving VMs to accommodate spikes in demand.
- **Improved solution for test environment**: We can build multiple copies of similar environments, and test new applications and hotfixes before we apply changes on production. Also, virtualized environments are great for training and development environments.

A few disadvantages of implementing virtualization:

- **Server consolidation**: Consolidation of servers and storage virtualization may create a larger, single point of failure, tuning storage (SAN, NAS, and so on), and networking (switches, for example) in critical elements in our datacenter. A switch failure can affect our storage and may cause a virtual machine Datastore failure. This issue can cause the downtime of virtual machines located in this Datastore.

- **Performance**: Some applications can run slow on virtual machines. The performance of the applications sometimes is related to hardware used to host our virtual machines. For example, using the SAS (Serial Attached SCSI) disk can provide better performance for critical applications than SATA (Serial ATA) disks.
- **Licensing**: We can definitely save (a lot of) money on licenses, but virtualization licensing is complex. We need to analyze the cost of hypervisor, hypervisor management tools, operating systems, and applications.

Virtual machine performance and host scalability

When we start a VM deployment, there are multiple questions that should be addressed to pin down the most appropriate host configuration:

- How many VMs should be deployed on a single host?
- Which CPU must be chosen and how many CPU cores must be used for the host?
- How much memory and NIC ports should be installed on the host?
- How many virtual CPUs and how much memory should be allocated to each VM?
- Do we have to use internal storage or shared storage to store the VM disks?

The key for a successful deployment is always testing. Our applications and users will determine the appropriate VM configuration. When we test applications on XenApp VMs, we can find VMs that require a lot of memory and just a single vCPU. Others VMs require a normal amount of memory (4 GB of RAM for 32-bit and 8 GB of RAM for 64-bit VMs), but many vCPUs (usually two or more vCPUs).

Usually, XenApp servers use more memory than CPU but again each environment is different.

Too many vCPUs can affect the performance of VM because they create an overhead on the virtualization host. We need to avoid assigning more than 2 vCPUs to VMs except when we have a reason. It is always recommended to scale out (add more VMs) than scale up (create large VMs).

One of the keys to improved performance is to avoid oversubscribed vCPUs, which means allocate more vCPUs than the number of cores. For example, if we have a server with two CPUs and each of them have six cores, we have 12 cores. On Intel CPUs with Hyper-Threading (HT) technology, each physical core behaves like two logical processors, so if we have 12 cores and we use Intel HT CPUs, we have 24 threads or logical processors, so in this example, it is recommended to avoid using more than 24 vCPUs. This will cause VMs to share CPUs, which will eventually lead to performance degradation.

Again, each environment is unique and this is a best practice, particularly for enterprise or mission critical environments, so we need to test and test until we find the right amount of vCPU to be allocated per virtualization host.

Another key is to avoid oversubscribed memory, which in some hypervisors is not allowed. That means, William must assign less memory to VMs than existing physical memory and allocate enough memory on the host to run all VMs, plus 1 GB for the host and extra memory for the memory overhead caused for 64-bit.

Storage is one of most critical components on a VM deployment. In medium to large production environments, it is always advisable to use shared storage such as SAN (Storage Area Network) or NAS (Network Attached Storage). Using local storage is a cheaper solution and a valid option for PoC (Proof of Concepts), pilots, or small environments, but medium to large environments must use storage technologies such as SAN (iSCSI or FC) or NAS (NFS).

Also, storage is crucial for the performance of VMs. As I mentioned before, using a SAS (Serial Attached SCSI) disk can provide better performance for critical applications than SATA (Serial ATA) disks. These technologies provide the ability to move VMs between hosts without any downtime (live migration), high availability, and better performance than local disks. Some storage systems also provide extra functionality, like snapshots, deduplication, thin provisioning, and more.

The major consideration in any shared storage system is cost. FC (Fibre Channel) SAN are the preferred option for large or enterprise environments, but the cost of HBA cards and FC switches will increase the final cost of the deployment.

The cost of iSCSI SAN is lower because it uses standard NIC cards and switches instead of HBA cards and FC switches, which provides a similar performance, but on the other hand causes higher CPU utilization on the virtualization host and dedicated network switches are recommend for better performance and to avoid traffic interference with LAN traffic.

Another option is to use NFS NAS, which uses standard Ethernet network to transport file-level traffic (read/write) from storage device to our virtualization hosts. NFS causes high CPU utilization of the virtualization host (but less than iSCSI). Also, dedicated network switches are recommended for better performance and to avoid traffic interference with LAN traffic.

Networking is important for the success and performance of our virtualization deployment, so we need to have enough network ports to avoid performance issues. Usually, XenApp requires a solid network infrastructure. Most of the environments store Windows roaming profiles on file servers, and every time a user logs into the XenApp farm, the profile is copied from the network to the XenApp server.

Also, depending on our applications and type of storage, we will need less or more network ports. For example, if we are using iSCSI, we need at least one dedicated network port (two for redundancy) to connect with the storage. Also, it is very important to choose a server to have enough expansion slots, just in case we need to add more network ports.

Choosing the right CPU is also very important. AMD Opteron and Intel Xeon processors provide on-chip instructions to handle direct hardware calls from the hypervisor, minimizing the associated overhead. We need to choose a CPU that supports virtualization technologies like AMD-V or Intel-VT.

As we mention before, Intel Hyper-Threading (HT) provides great benefit to virtualization; Hyper-Threading allows a single physical processor core to appear to behave like two logical processors. So for example, if we choose an Intel Xeon CPU with four cores and enabled Hyper-Threading, the operating system or hypervisor will see eight cores. Enabling Hyper-Threading allows us to use eight vCPUs per physical CPU. The performance is not the same as having a CPU with eight "real cores", but is pretty good.

Choosing the right virtualization platform

Which is the best platform to deploy XenApp on virtual machines: Citrix, Microsoft, or VMware? The response: it depends. If we have the time and resources, building a test lab is a good option. Also, we can find some reviews on the Internet from independent professionals (for example, Virtual reality Check Project www.virtualrealitycheck.net) and some from hypervisor companies and hardware vendors. These tests show results based on simulated tests. A real environment can show the same or opposite results.

Every implementation is unique, and server loads are different, based on users and applications. My recommendation is to build a small PoC or Pilot with these three platforms and evaluate the best option for our needs, except in the case our company chose a virtualization platform before.

> A good practice recommended by Citrix is do not P2V (convert a physical server into a virtual machine) Citrix production servers into VMs. Build VMs from scratch, except when you don't have any options. The P2V process does not remove drivers and applications from hardware vendors. If you don't have any choice, remove all hardware tools such as HP Proliant Support Pack or Dell OpenManage after the P2V process. If you are using HP Proliant servers, you can use the HP Proliant Support Pack Cleaner tool (available for free at http://ctxadmtools.musumeci.com.ar) to remove all HP Proliant Support Pack tools.

Deploying XenApp 6.5 on Citrix XenServer

XenServer is an open and powerful server virtualization solution that cuts datacenter costs by transforming static and complex datacenter environments into more dynamic, easy-to-manage delivery centers.

XenServer, the Citrix server virtualization solution, is based on Xen, an open-source virtualization project that supports both Intel Virtualization Technology (INTEL VT) and AMD Virtualization (AMD-V) capabilities. Xen allows a single machine to host multiple isolated environments, each running on a different operating system.

In 2004, the Xen project released the first version of its hypervisor and in 2007 Citrix purchased XenSource, renaming Xen products as XenServer Standard Edition and XenServer Enterprise Edition.

Citrix XenServer free edition is available for free at www.citrix.com/xenserver.

Also, we can buy the Advanced, Enterprise, or Platinum Editions. These versions provide different features such as high availability, workload balancing, storage links, provisioning services, lab and stage management, and site recovery.

The installation of XenServer 6.0 is relatively simple. Refer to the following XenServer documentation for details:

- XenServer 6.0 Installation Guide (http://support.citrix.com/article/CTX130421)
- XenServer 6.0 Administrator's Guide (http://support.citrix.com/article/CTX130420)
- XenServer 6.0 Virtual Machine Installation Guide (http://support.citrix.com/article/CTX130422)

> The information in this chapter is based on Citrix XenServer 6.0.2.

Creating a new XenApp 6.5 VM in XenServer

The process to create a new VM for XenApp 6.5 is very straightforward. The following is the process used by William to install a XenApp 6.5 VM in XenServer:

1. In the **XenCenter** console, William clicks on the **VM** menu and selects **New VM**. Also, he can right-click on the XenServer host and click on the **New VM** option.

2. The creation of VM wizard starts. On the **Template** page, he needs to choose the **Citrix XenApp on Windows Server 2008 R2 (64-bit)** option. This will set up the VM with optimal settings for XenApp.

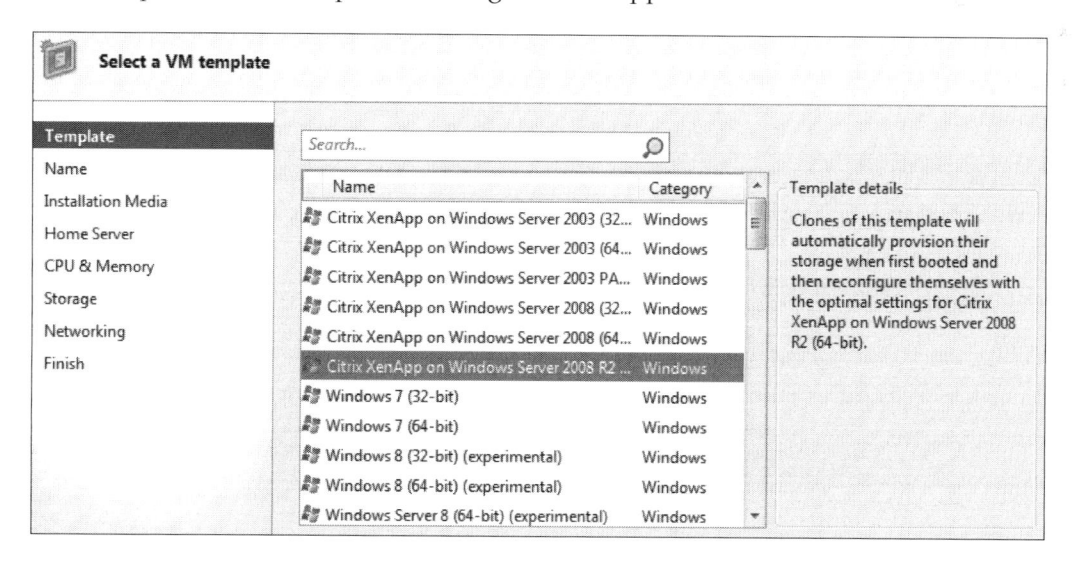

[415]

Virtualizing XenApp Farms

3. On the **Name** page, he needs to enter a VM name. He can change this name later, if he needs to. Also, he can enter a description for the VM.

4. On the **Installation Media** page, he can choose the location of operating system files. By default, he can boot from the host DVD or from the network. He can click on the **New ISO library** link to create an ISO Library to store operating systems disks in ISO format. In the following screenshot, he selects a Windows Server 2008 R2 ISO image from their ISO library:

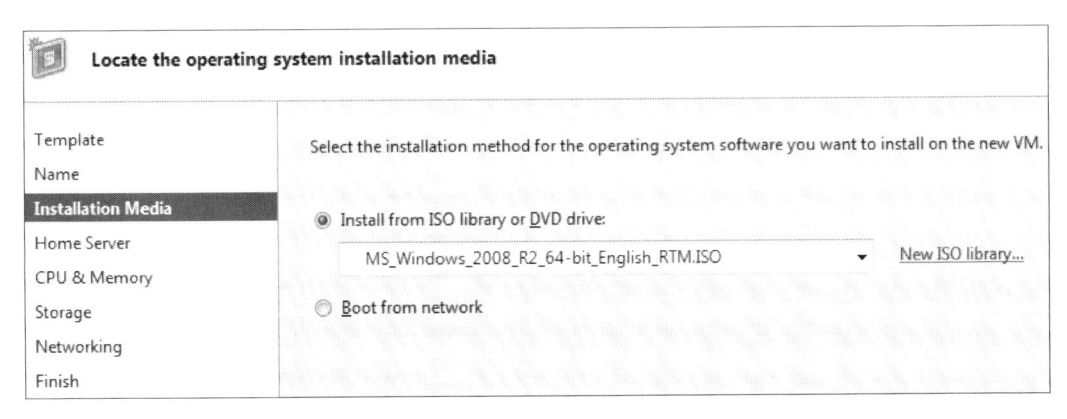

Locate the operating system installation media

| Template |
| Name |
| **Installation Media** |
| Home Server |
| CPU & Memory |
| Storage |
| Networking |
| Finish |

Select the installation method for the operating system software you want to install on the new VM.

◉ Install from ISO library or DVD drive:
MS_Windows_2008_R2_64-bit_English_RTM.ISO   New ISO library...

○ Boot from network

5. On the **Home Server** page, he needs to select the XenServer where he is going to place the VM.

6. On the **CPU & Memory** page, he will set the number of vCPUs and the amount of memory for the VM. Also, he can adjust both values later.

7. On the **Storage** page, he can select the size and location of the VM's disk or disks. Also, he selects to create a diskless VM that can be booted from the network.

8. On the **Networking** page, William can set up the network card of the VM. He can add or remove network cards and choose the appropriate network host:

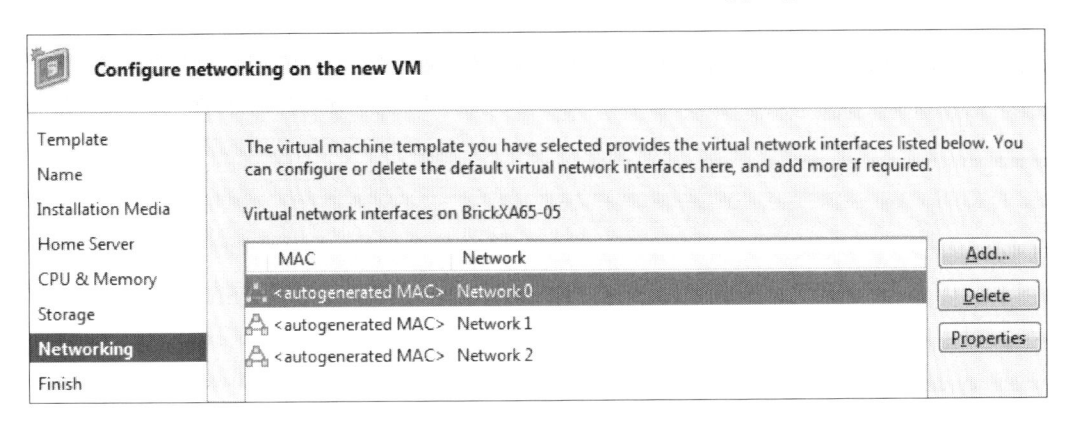

Configure networking on the new VM

| Template |
| Name |
| Installation Media |
| Home Server |
| CPU & Memory |
| Storage |
| **Networking** |
| Finish |

The virtual machine template you have selected provides the virtual network interfaces listed below. You can configure or delete the default virtual network interfaces here, and add more if required.

Virtual network interfaces on BrickXA65-05

MAC	Network
<autogenerated MAC>	Network 0
<autogenerated MAC>	Network 1
<autogenerated MAC>	Network 2

[Add...] [Delete] [Properties]

9. On the **Finish** page, he reviews all settings of the VM machine and he clicks the **Finish** button to start the VM build process.

10. Once the build process is complete and the virtual machine is started, the installation of Windows Server 2008 R2 starts.

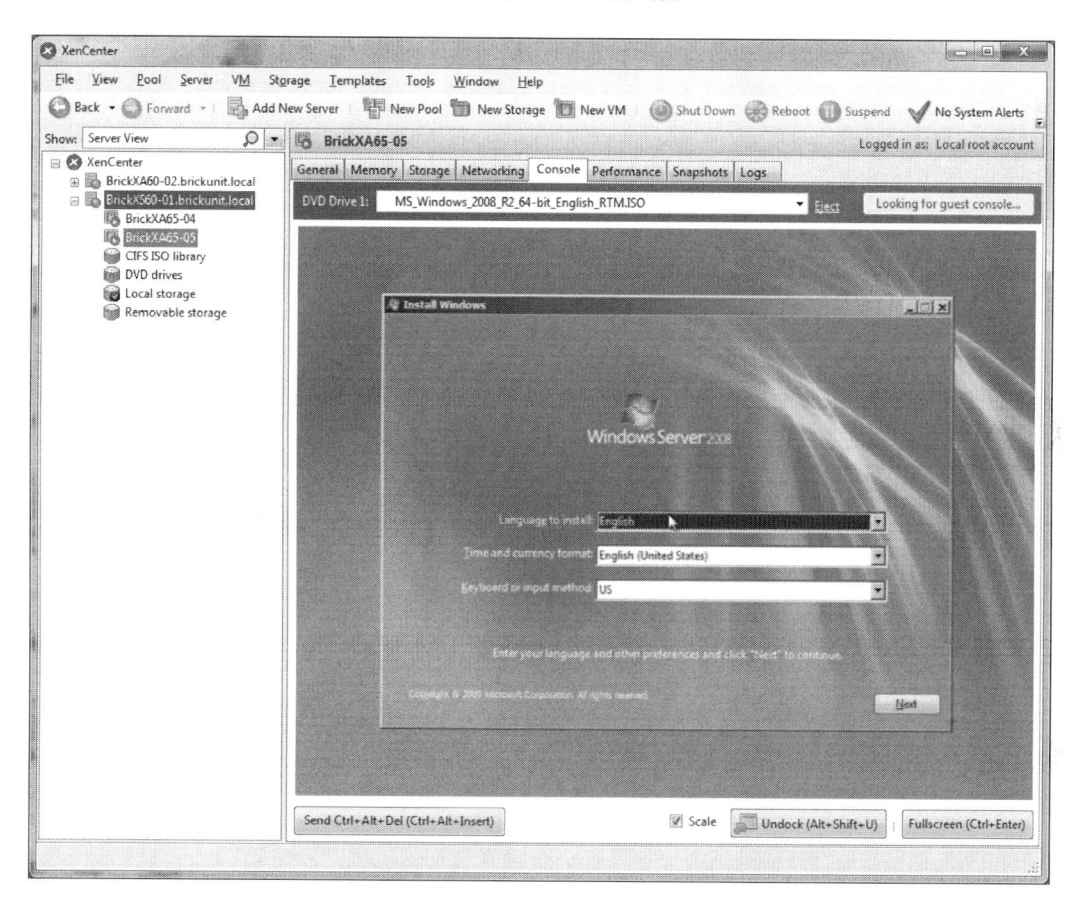

Virtualizing XenApp Farms

11. William also can change the **Advanced Options** (available on the **VM** menu, **Properties**) to set the **Optimize for Citrix XenApp** setting. Citrix recommends to select this option on servers using pre-Nehalem processors because this setting provides increased scalability. After the release of the Nehalem processors, this functionality is provided at the hardware layer (Intel EPT / AMD RVI), so this option should not be enabled.

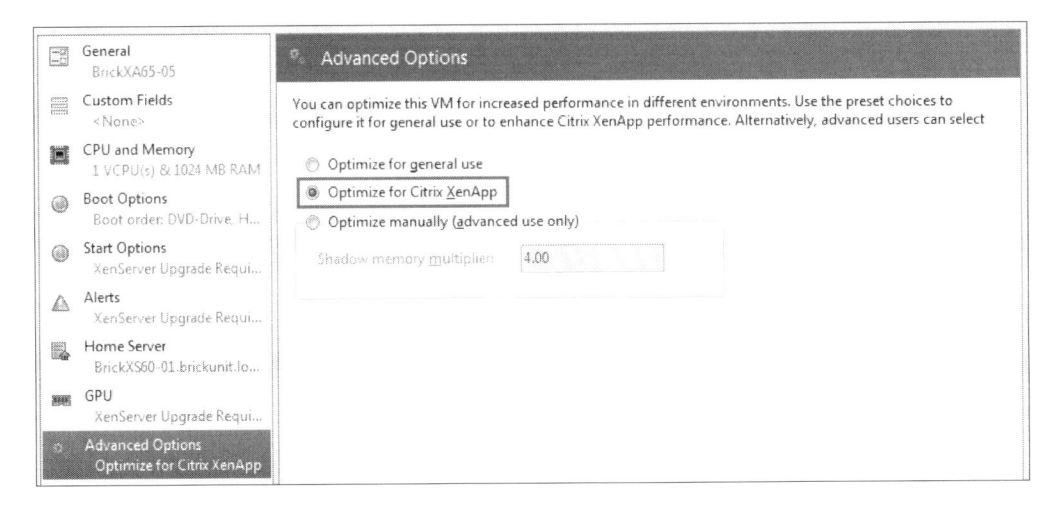

12. Once the setup of the operating system is complete, William can install XenServer tools in the VM, using the **VM** menu, **Install XenServer Tools...** option. XenServer tools provide high performance Windows drivers and a management agent (this is a recommended step).

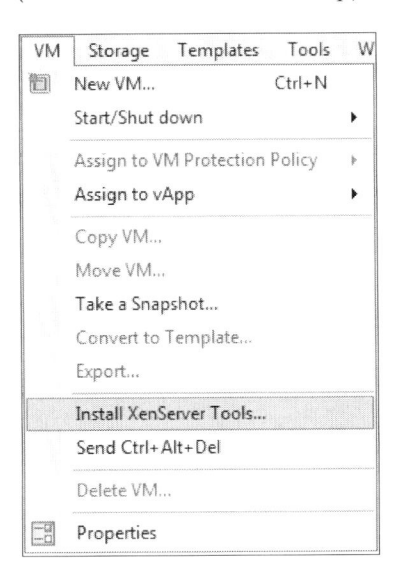

After XenServer tools are installed and the server is rebooted, William is ready to configure the VM.

He needs to configure the IP Address, install Remote Desktop Services (optional step), and reboot the server.

> Take a VM snapshot before any step of the install and setup process, until you are familiar with the procedure, just in case. You can always roll back changes.

Now, William is ready to set up XenApp on the VM! He needs to follow the instructions discussed in *Chapter 3, Installing XenApp 6.5* to set up the first server XenApp 6.5 on the farm. Also, you can read the section *Cloning XenApp 6.5 virtual machines* later in this chapter, to know how to prepare our VM for cloning.

Deploying XenApp 6.5 on Microsoft Hyper-V

Microsoft Windows Server 2008 Hyper-V R2 (Hyper-V), the next-generation hypervisor-based server virtualization technology, is available as an integral feature of Windows Server 2008 R2 and enables you to implement server virtualization with ease.

Hyper-V allows us to make the best use of the server hardware investments by consolidating multiple server roles as separate virtual machines (VMs) running on a single physical machine.

Hyper-V requires 64-bit machines with AMD-V or Intel VT-enabled processors

Hyper-V is not available for the Itanium edition or Windows Server 2008 R1 32-bit editions.

Hyper-V is available as two different versions:

- A standalone product called Microsoft Hyper-V Server 2008 R2: This version is free and available for download at `www.microsoft.com`. This version is a limited version of Windows Server 2008 R2 Core with the Hyper-V role enabled and other roles disabled. This version can be managed using command line, PowerShell, or using the managing console from a Windows Server 2008, Windows 7, or Windows Vista machine.
- As part of Microsoft Windows Server 2008 R2. We need to have a license of Windows Server 2008 Standard, Enterprise, or Datacenter editions (Windows Server 2008 Web Edition is not supported) and install the Hyper-V role.

Virtualizing XenApp Farms

For more information about Microsoft Server 2008 Hyper-V R2, check this link: `www.microsoft.com/hyper-v-server/en/us/default.aspx`.

> The information in this chapter is based on Microsoft Windows Server 2008 R2 with the Hyper-V R2 role installed.

A management tool is required to manage the (free) standalone edition of Hyper-V or for specific features like Live Migration or cloning on the Windows Server 2008 edition.

Microsoft offers System Center Virtual Machine Manager 2008 R2, available for evaluation at `www.microsoft.com/systemcenter/en/us/virtualmachine-manager.aspx`.

Creating a new XenApp 6.5 VM in Hyper-V

The process to create a new VM for XenApp 6 is pretty simple. The following is the process used by William to install a XenApp 6 VM in Hyper-V:

1. He opens **Hyper-V Manager**, clicks on the **Actions** menu, and chooses **New** and then **Virtual Machine**. Also, he can right-click on the hostname, select **New**, and then **Virtual Machine**.

2. On the **Specify Name and Location** page, William types the VM name, chooses the location to store the VM, and clicks on the **Next** button:

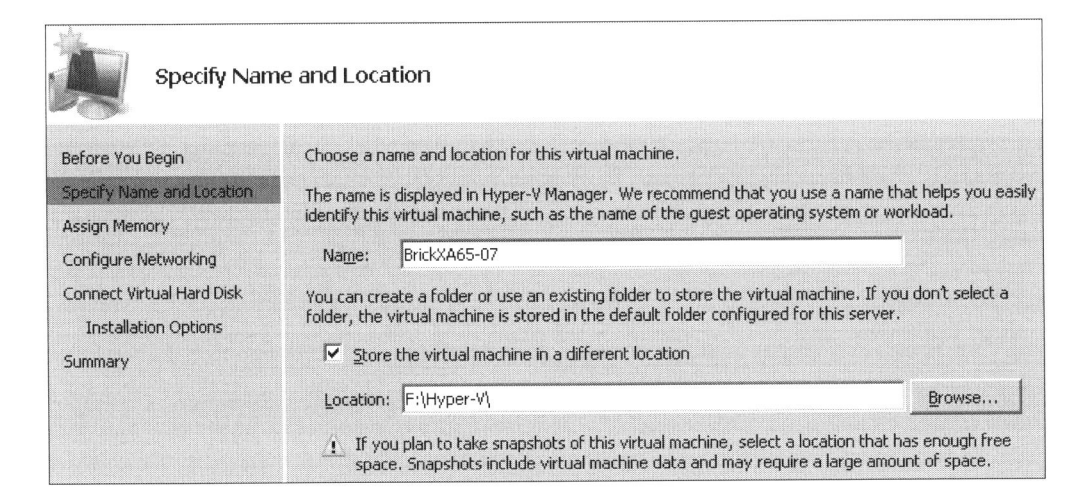

Chapter 14

3. On the **Assign Memory** page, he enters the amount of memory for the VM and clicks on the **Next** button.

4. On the **Configure Networking** page, he selects the appropriate network connection and clicks on the **Next** button. The default network adapter called synthetic network adapter (called **Network Adapter** on the Hyper-V Manager) is loaded by the **Host Integration Services** after the operating system loads inside the virtual machine. This network adapter is preferred because it provides better performance, but it is only available when the OS is loaded, so if we are planning to use Citrix Provisioning Server with PXE, it is not going to work. For PXE boot, the preferred option is use the **Legacy Network Adapter**.

5. On the **Connect Virtual Hard Disk** page, he selects the **Create a virtual hard disk** option, uses the **Browse** button to select the folder to store the .VXD file, sets the **Size** of the disk, and then clicks on the **Next** button.

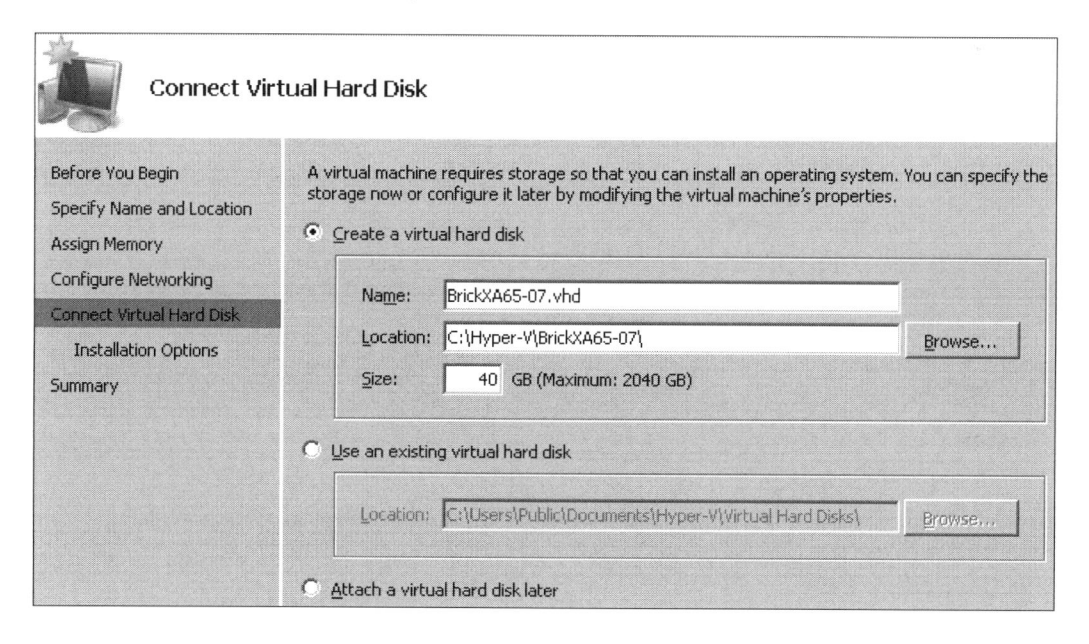

6. On the **Installation Options** page, William can select the **Install an operating system from a boot CD/DVD-ROM** option to boot from CD/DVD in the host or using an .ISO image. This is the most common scenario. Also, he can select the **Install an operating system from a boot floppy disk option** or the **Install an operating system from a network-based installation server** option.

7. On the **Summary** page, he clicks on the **Finish** button to complete the process and creates the VM.

Virtualizing XenApp Farms

8. After the build process is complete and the virtual machine is ready, he right-clicks over the VM name and selects the **Properties** to edit the settings of the VM. He can modify the amount of vCPUs (this is an optional step—he can keep the default 1 vCPU option).

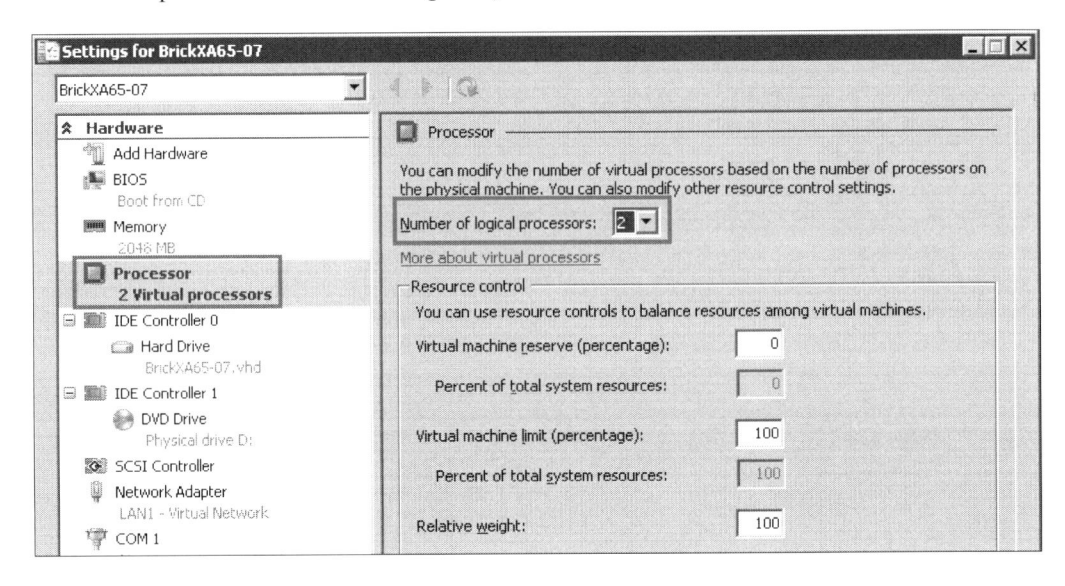

9. The next (and optional) step is converting the default dynamic disk format to fixed format. The Dynamic VHDs can be useful for test environments because they allow us to save lot of space, but they are *not* recommend for production environments. When dynamic VHDs expand, they generate lot of overhead on disk systems because they use an expansion algorithm (in 2 MB blocks). When dynamic drive expands, the allocation table is updated and the drive's header and footer sections are rewritten for each of the file extension operations. Also, dynamic VHDs include a single byte at the end of the file that causes the file to be out of alignment with the disk subsystem. When a file is out of alignment, it causes the disk subsystem to perform extra I/O operations for each file change and degrades performance considerably. Using a fixed disk VHD will not include the extra byte at the end of the file.

> For more information about VHDs, please refer to the Microsoft Whitepaper Virtual Hard Disk Performance, located at `http://download.microsoft.com/download/0/7/7/0778C0BB-5281-4390-92CD-EC138A18F2F9/WS08_R2_VHD_Performance_WhitePaper.docx`.

Chapter 14

To convert dynamic disks to fixed, on the **VM settings** page, William clicks on the **IDE Controller | Hard Drive** and clicks on the **Edit** button.

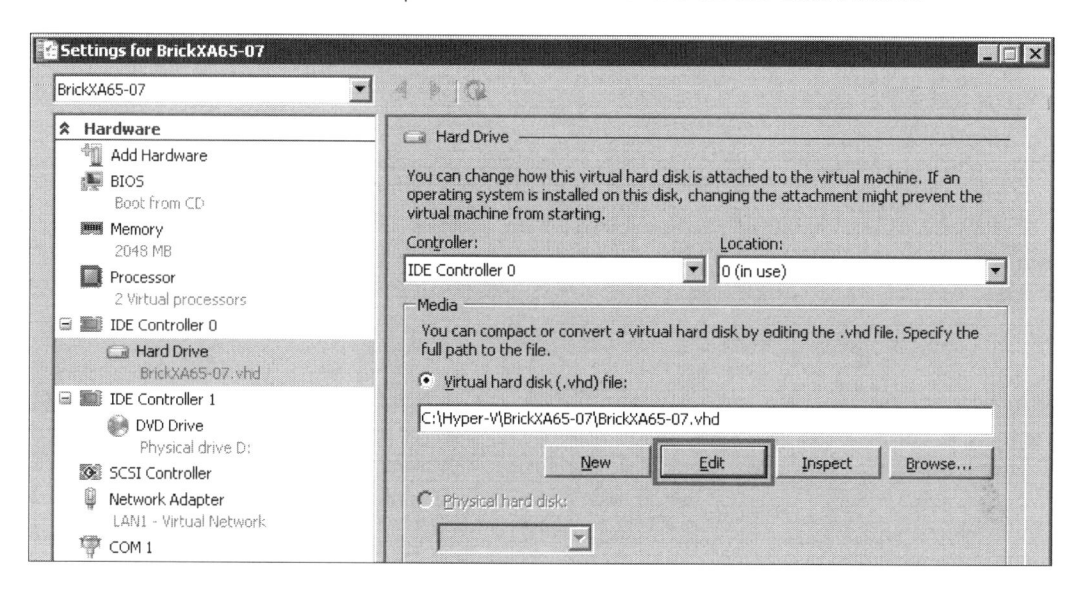

Then on the **Choose Action** page, he selects the **Convert** option and then on the **Finish** button.

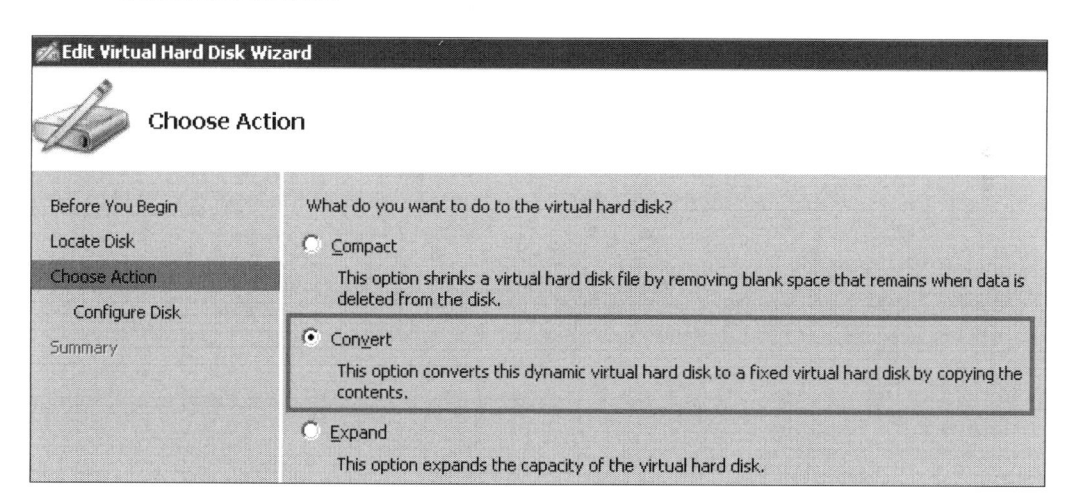

[423]

10. After that, William is ready to install Windows Server 2008 R2 operating system. When the setup of the operating system is complete, he is ready to configure the VM. He needs to configure the IP Address, install Remote Desktop Services (optional step), and reboot the server.

> Take a VM snapshot before any step of the install and setup process, until you are familiar with the procedure, just in case. You can roll over any change.

Now William is ready to set up XenApp on the VM! He needs to follow the instructions discussed in *Chapter 3*, *Installing XenApp 6.5* to set up the first server XenApp 6.5 on the farm. Also, you can read the section *Cloning XenApp 6.5 virtual machines* later in this chapter, to know how to prepare our VM for cloning.

Deploying XenApp 6.5 on VMware vSphere

VMware vSphere leverages the power of virtualization to transform datacenters into dramatically simplified cloud computing infrastructures, and enables IT organizations to deliver the next generation of flexible and reliable IT services, using internal and external resources, securely and with low risk.

VMware vSphere (formerly known as VMware ESX Server) is available in these versions:

- **VMware vSphere Hypervisor (ESXi)**: This is the free version of vSphere. Perfect for testing, evaluating the platform, remote offices, and small environments.
- **VMware vSphere for Enterprise**: This is the full version of the hypervisor. Available in multiple versions, it provides different features, depending on the cost of every product.

Some limitations of ESXi:

- **Limited management capabilities**: We need to buy a VMware vCenter Server license if we want to create templates or copy VMs from a GUI.
- **Limited scripting capabilities**: We can't create scripts for unattended installations. Also, VMware locks access to several APIs, so we can't manage all types of functionality using scripts.
- **Host Active Directory Integration**: ESXi doesn't support AD integration.

Choosing the right VMware vSphere product will depend on our environment, but I will give some advice based on my experience of implementing XenApp on VMware.

First of all, if there are no budget constraints build a dedicated cluster just for XenApp application servers' VMs. We can use a different cluster for infrastructure servers, like Edgesight, Web interface servers, and so on.

The best version for most of the XenApp environments is vSphere Standard edition; this decision will depend on the hardware with which we choose to build our vSphere servers.

Standard edition provides the ability to build clusters with high availability, vMotion, thin provisioning, and more.

One of the features not supported by Standard Edition is VMware DRS (only available at Enterprise and Enterprise Plus). VMware DRS dynamically balances computing capacity across multiple VMware hosts. VMware DRS is a great feature when we have multiple VMs with different resource requirements, but because XenApp VMs are highly resource-intensive, there is no need for VMware DRS.

Also, I do not recommend using vMotion to move XenApp production VMs, except for a host emergency or maintenance tasks. Usually, XenApp server load is similar between VMs and host, therefore there is no reason to move VMs between hosts. Moving VMs causes an overhead on the VM.

The new licensing of vSphere 5 turns the product into the most expensive hypervisor in the market, sometimes the same environment can cost three times as much as vSphere 4.x, so take your time to choose the right license for your implementation.

[The information in this chapter is based on VMware vSphere v5.0]

Virtualizing XenApp Farms

Creating a new XenApp 6.5 VM in VMware vSphere

The process to create a new VM for XenApp 6.5 in vSphere is a little bit more complicated than in Citrix XenServer and Microsoft Hyper-V because vSphere provides more options. Now we are going to help William to configure a VM to run XenApp:

1. On the **Configuration** page, he chooses **Custom** and clicks on the **Next** button:

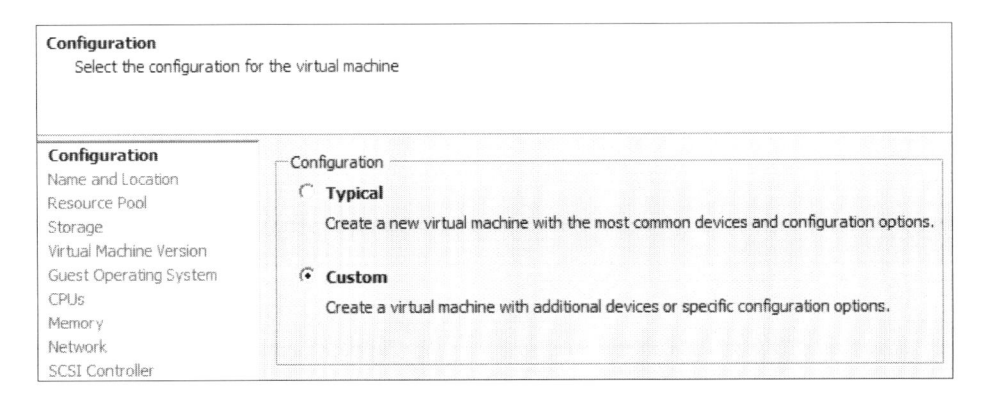

2. On the **Name and Location** page, he needs to type the name and the location of the VM and then click on the **Next** button.

3. On the **Resource Pool** page, William selects the VMware resource pool to host the VM.

4. On the **Storage** page, he needs to choose the datastore in which to store the VM and then click on the **Next** button:

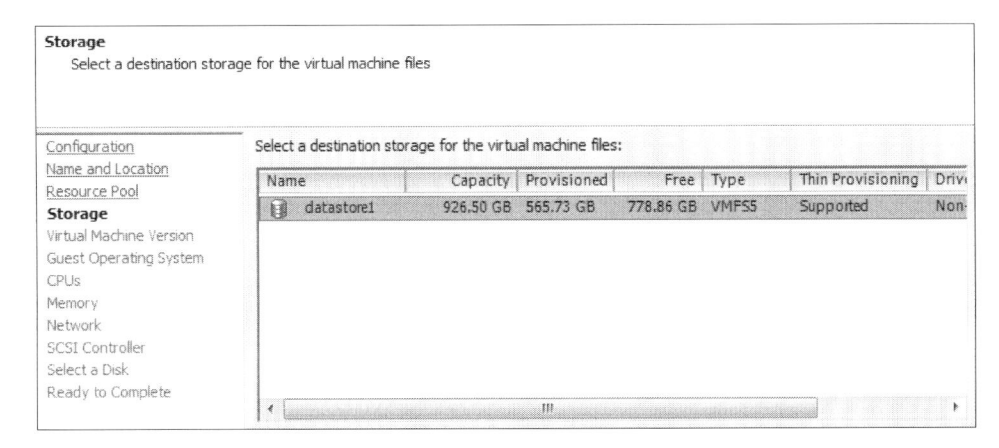

Chapter 14

5. On the **Virtual Machine Version** page, he selects the **Virtual Machine Version 8** and clicks on the **Next** button.

6. In the **Guest Operating System** page, William needs to choose **Microsoft Windows Server 2008 R2 (64-bit)** and click on the **Next** button:

```
Guest Operating System                              Virtual Machine Version: 8
    Specify the guest operating system to use with this virtual machine

Configuration
Name and Location       Guest Operating System:
Resource Pool
Storage                     (•) Windows
Virtual Machine Version     ( ) Linux
Guest Operating System      ( ) Other
CPUs
Memory                  Version:
Network                 [Microsoft Windows Server 2008 R2 (64-bit)         ▼]
SCSI Controller
```

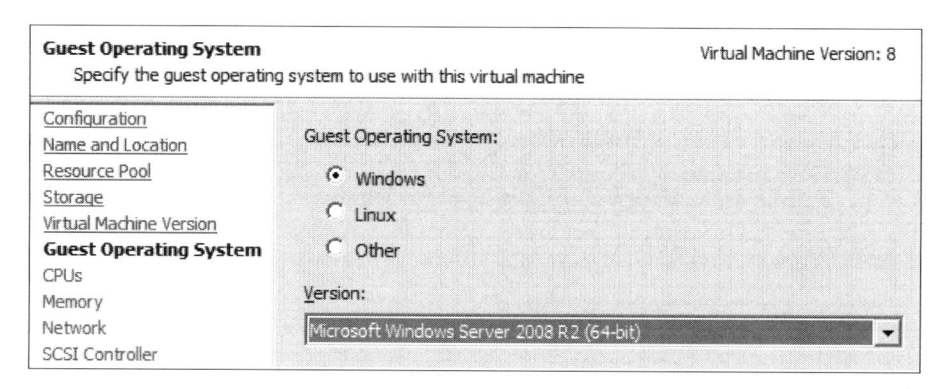

7. On the **CPUs** page, he needs to assign the number of vCPUs he wants and then click on the **Next** button.

8. On the **Memory** page, he needs to assign the amount of memory he wants and then click on the **Next** button:

```
Memory                                              Virtual Machine Version: 8
    Configure the virtual machine's memory size.

Configuration           ┌─Memory Configuration─────────────────────────────
Name and Location       │ 1011 GB ◄
Resource Pool           │              Memory Size:     [  4 ▲▼] [GB ▼]
Storage                 │  512 GB
Virtual Machine Version │              Maximum recommended for this
                        │  256 GB  ◄   guest OS: 1011 GB.
Guest Operating System  │  128 GB  ◄   Maximum recommended for best performance: 16300 MB.
CPUs
Memory                  │   64 GB      Default recommended for this
Network                 │   32 GB  ◄   guest OS: 4 GB.
SCSI Controller         │              Minimum recommended for this
Select a Disk           │   16 GB  ◄   guest OS: 512 MB.
Ready to Complete       │    8 GB
                        │    4 GB  ◄
                        │    2 GB
                        │    1 GB
                        │  512 MB  ◄
                        │  256 MB
                        │  128 MB
                        │   64 MB
                        │   32 MB
                        │   16 MB
                        │    8 MB
                        │    4 MB
```

[427]

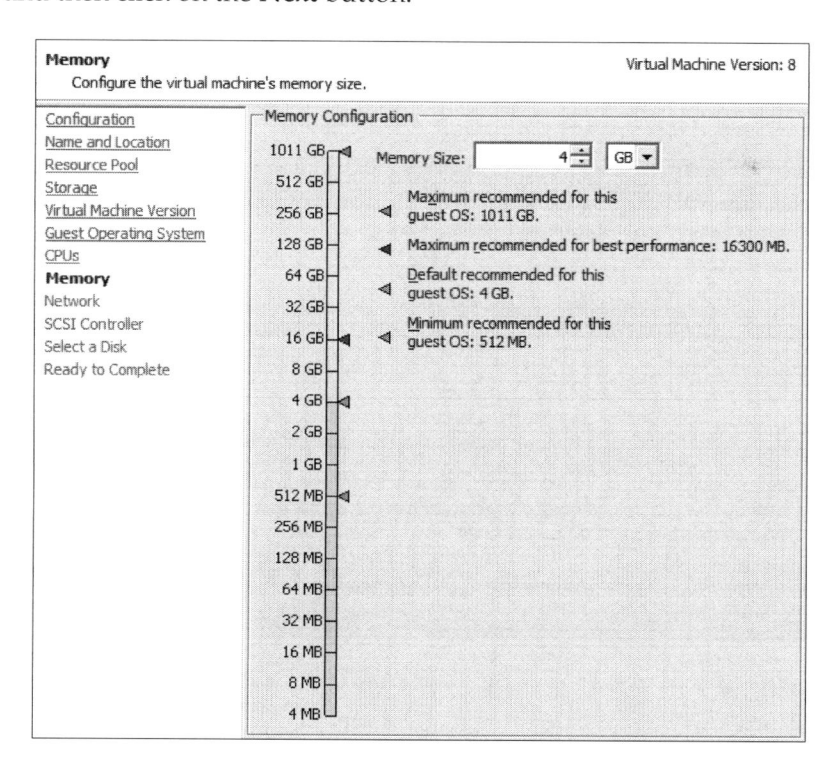

9. In the **Network** page, William can add one or more network cards, choose the right network, and click on the **Next** button. The **VMXNet3 NIC** is recommended option because it reduces CPU utilization and improves network throughput.

> The **VMXNet3 NIC** can cause Blue Screen when we use it with Citrix Provisioning. We need to choose a different NIC or check CTX125361 – Target Device Fails to Start with VMXNet3 Drivers.

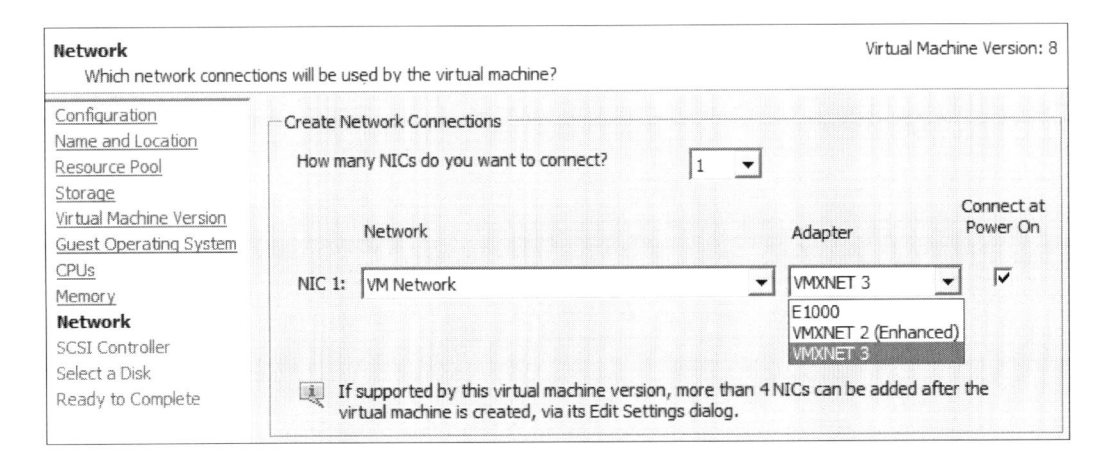

10. On the **SCSI Controller** page, William needs to select the **SCSI Controller**, and depending on the VM configuration, he has multiple options. If he has a single disk for both operating systems and application, **LSI Logic SAS** is the recommended option. If he has two or multiple disks, it is recommended to set the first disk (where the operating system resides) to the **LSI Logic SAS** controller and the **VMware Paravirtual controller** for all remaining data disks.

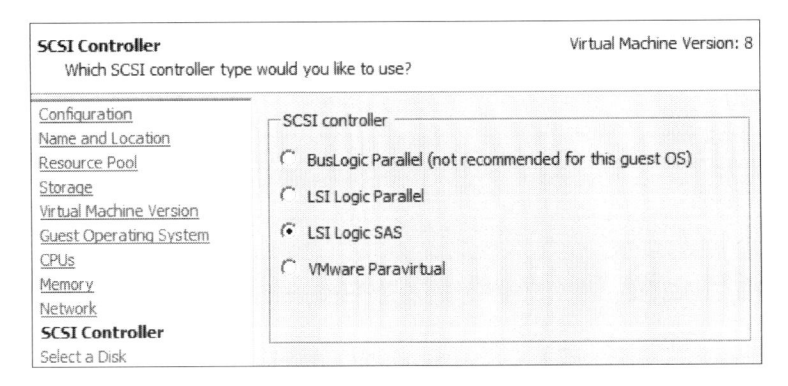

Chapter 14

11. On the **Select a Disk** page, he chooses the **Create a new virtual disk option** and then clicks on the **Next** button.

12. On the **Create a Disk** page, he sets the **Disk Size**, selects the **Disk Provisioning** format and then clicks on the **Next** button.

    Disk provisioning mode can affect the performance of the VM, so William needs to choose the right option:

    - **Thick Provision Lazy Zeroed**: Create a virtual disk in the default thick format. The space required for the virtual disk is allocated during creation. This is the faster method to create a VM. This is the default option.
    - **Thick Provision Eager Zeroed**: Create a thick disk that supports clustering features such as Fault Tolerance. Space required for the virtual disk is allocated at creation time. This format takes much longer to create than other types of disks.
    - **Thin Provision**: The thin provisioned disk uses only as much datastore space as the disk originally needs. When the thin disk needs more space later, it can grow to the maximum capacity allocated to it. This is not recommended for production environments because it causes a lot of overhead on the storage system.

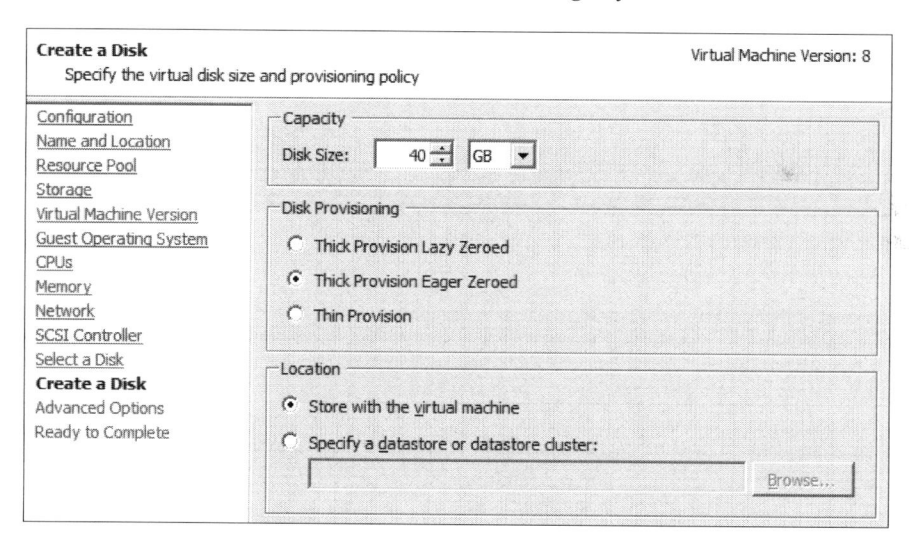

13. On the **Advanced Options** page, he keeps the default settings, and clicks on the **Next** button.

Virtualizing XenApp Farms

14. On the **Ready to Complete** page, William enables the **Edit the virtual machine settings before completion** checkbox and clicks on the **Continue** button:

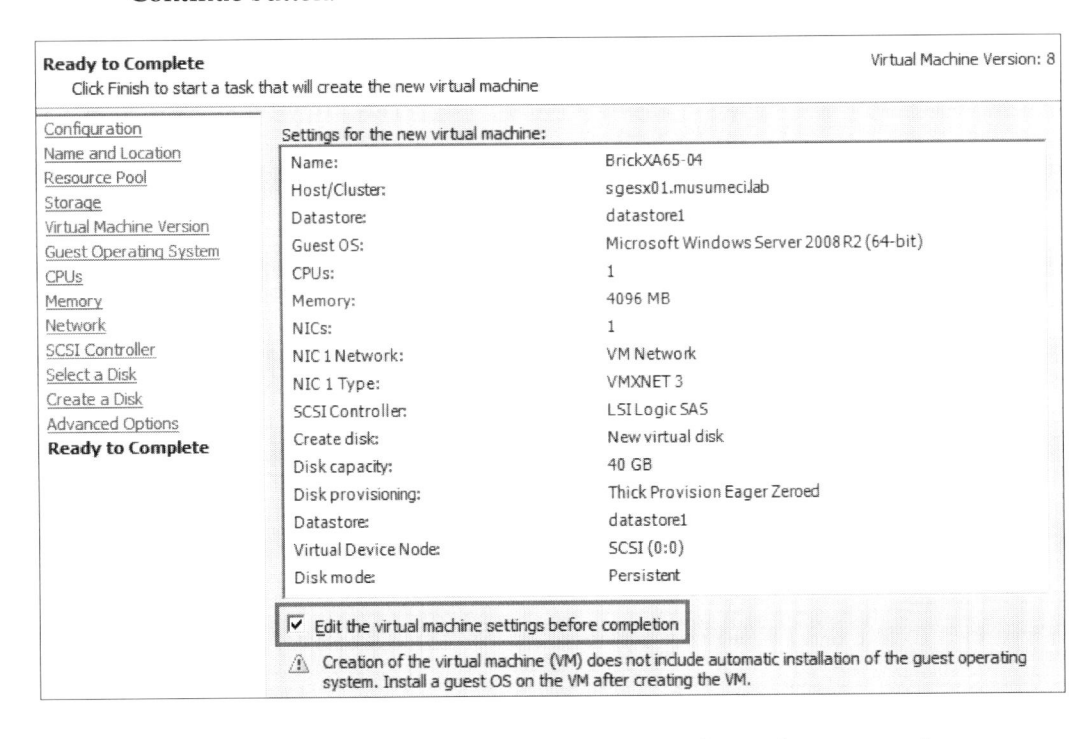

15. To remove the floppy disk, he selects it and clicks on the **Remove** button:

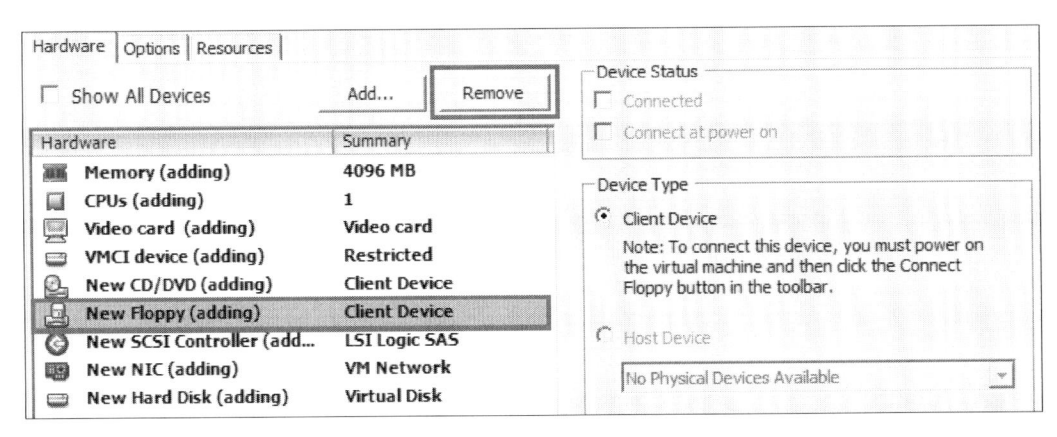

16. **Optional**: To add an extra disk, William needs to click on the **Add** button and choose **Hard Disk**. He chooses **SCSI (1:0)** in the **Virtual Device Node**. This step will add a New SCSI Controller too. Change the New SCSI controller to **Paravirtual**:

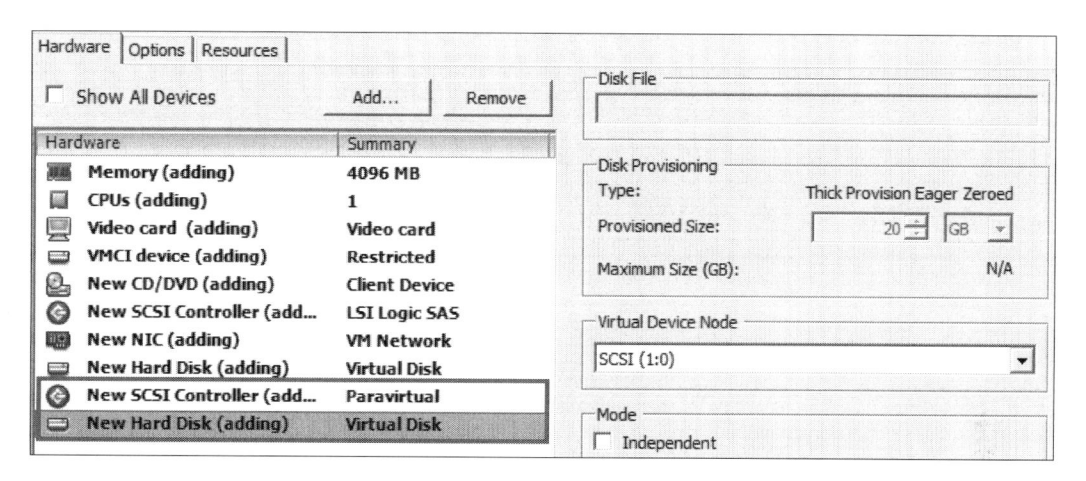

17. **Optional**: In the **Options** tab, he selects **Memory/CPU Hotplug**. This option allows him to increase the amount of memory and CPU without powering off the VM. This option only works on Windows Server 2008 Enterprise and Datacenter editions.

> This option can be useful on some specific scenarios, but it is not recommended to enable it if we don't have a real need because it causes an overhead on the host server

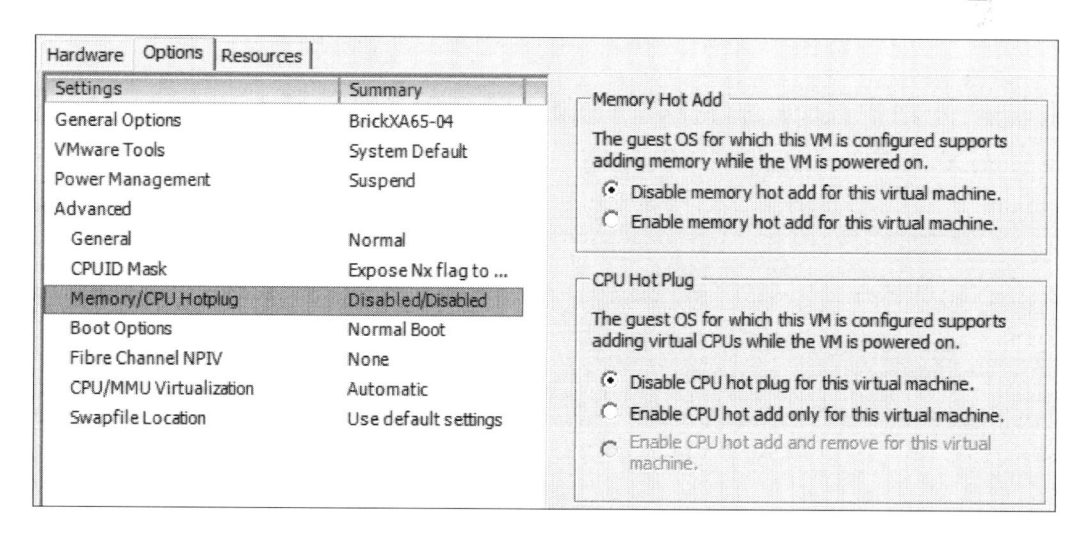

18. In the **Options** tab, he selects **CPU/MMU Virtualization**. Enabling this option will provide a significant increase in the performance of VM. Hardware-assisted MMU (Memory Management Unit) virtualization requires specific CPUs models like Intel Xeon 5500 Series or later, or AMD Opteron 4000 or 6000 Series or subsequent processors.

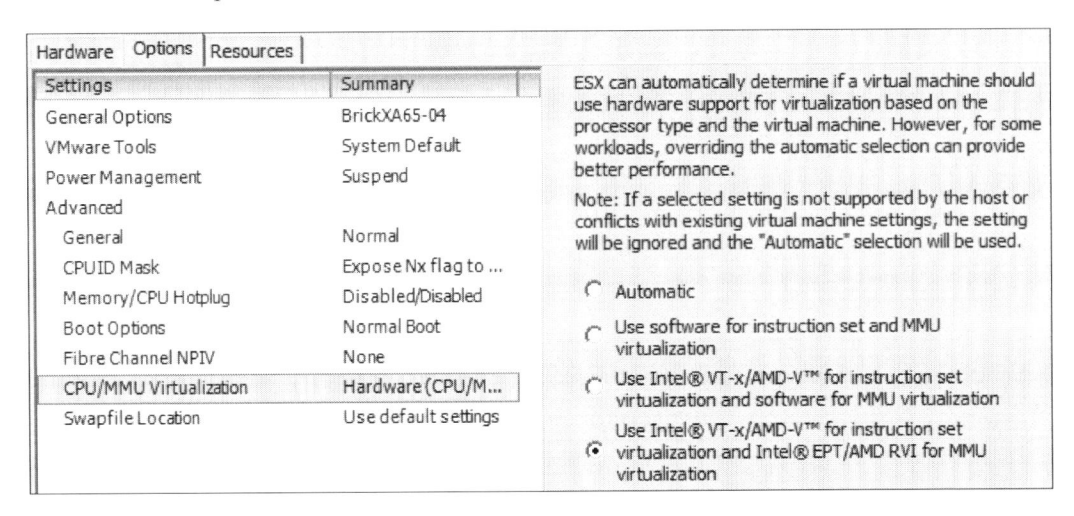

19. Now, he is ready to install the Windows Server 2008 R2 operating system.

20. Once the setup of the operating system is complete, William needs to install VMware Tools. To install VMware Tools, in the **VM console**, he clicks on the **VM** menu, selects **Guest** and then **Install/Upgrade VMware Tools**, follows the instructions, and restarts the server:

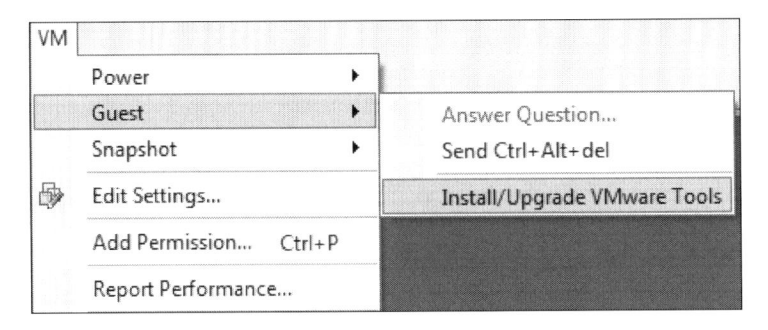

21. After VMware Tools is installed, he needs to configure the IP Address, install Remote Desktop Services (optional step), and reboot the server.

> Take a VM snapshot before any step of the install and setup process, until you are familiar with the procedure, just in case. You can always roll back any change.

Now William is ready to set up XenApp on the VM! He needs to follow the instructions discussed in *Chapter 3, Installing XenApp 6.5*, to set up the first server XenApp 6.5 on the farm. Also, you can read the next section, *Cloning XenApp 6.5 virtual machines*, to know how to prepare our VM for cloning.

Virtual machines optimizations

There are lot of optimizations to apply to virtual machines. We provide some basic optimizations for hypervisors. For more virtual machines optimizations please take a look to following documents:

- Citrix XenApp on VMware Best Practices Guide, at `http://www.vmware.com/files/pdf/solutions/vmware-citrix-xenapp-best-practices-EN.pdf`
- Performance Tuning Guidelines for Windows Server 2008, at `http://go.microsoft.com/fwlink/?LinkID=135682`
- XenApp 6.x (Windows 2008 R2) — Optimization Guide, at `http://support.citrix.com/article/CTX131577`

Cloning XenApp 6.5 virtual machines

After William creates the first XenApp 6.5 virtual machine and creates a XenApp farm (or joins an existing XenApp 6.5 farm), he is ready to start the cloning process.

Cloning is not supported for the first server in the farm (the server where we created the XenApp farm).

Virtualizing XenApp Farms

> The procedure to clone XenApp 6.0 VM is similar to XenApp 6.5, but requires you to download (and install) the updated XenApp Server Configuration Tool for Citrix XenApp 6 for Microsoft Windows Server 2008 R2 from http://support.citrix.com/article/CTX124981.

1. William needs to open **XenApp Server Role Manager** (**Start | All Programs | Citrix | XenApp Server Role Manager**).
2. The wizard starts and he needs to click on the **Edit Configuration** link:

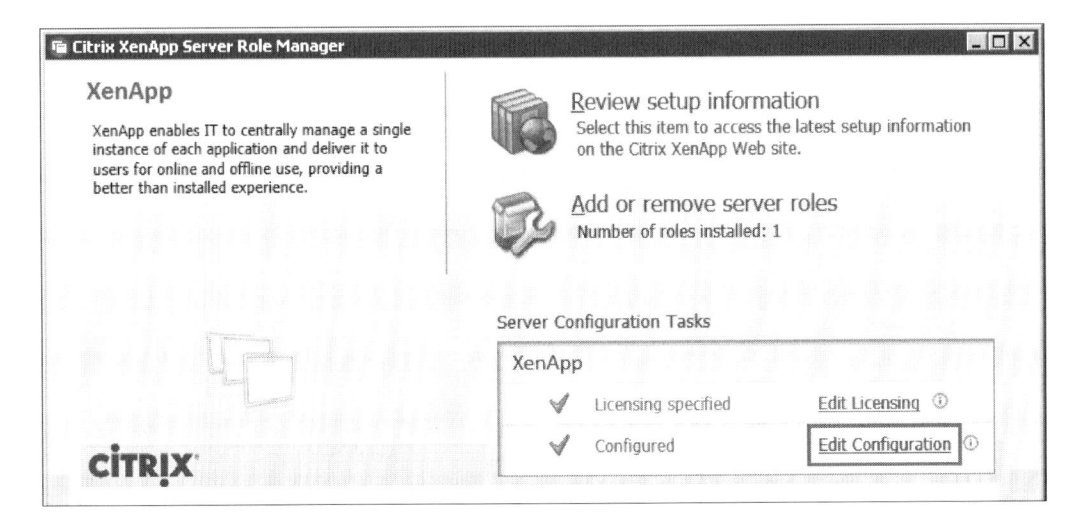

3. Then he needs to select the **Prepare this server for imaging and provisioning** option:

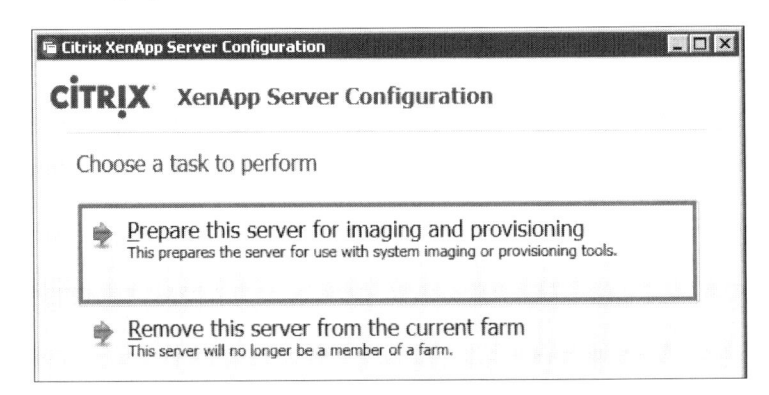

Chapter 14

4. He selects the **Remove this current server instance from the farm** checkbox and clicks on the **Next** button:

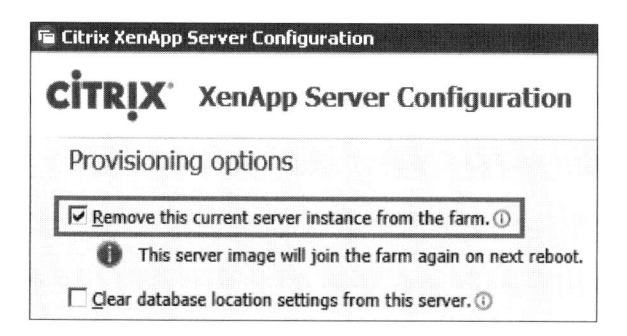

5. William clicks on the **Apply** button to start the process.
6. This page shows the result of the process. William clicks on the **Finish** button to close the wizard.

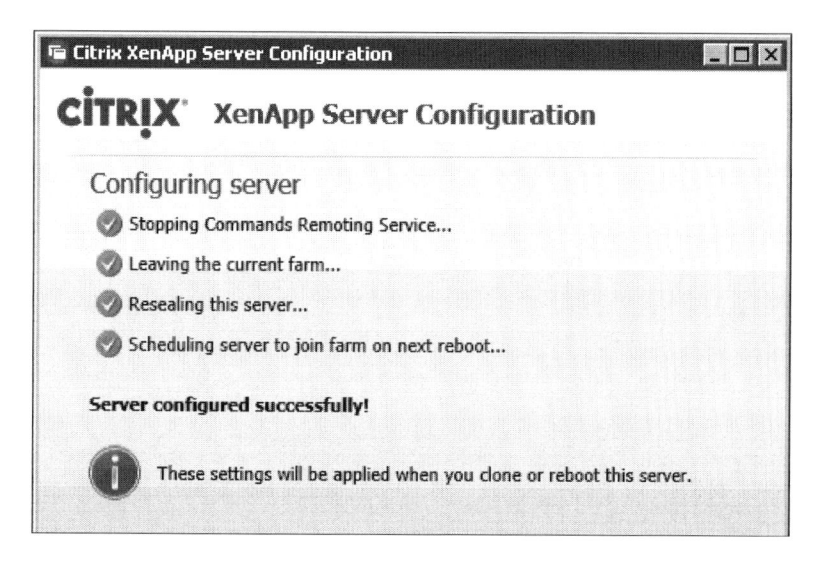

7. When the wizard is closed, he returns to the **XenApp Server Role Manager**, where he can choose to close the window or reboot the virtual machine. He needs to close the window, so he can run SYSPREP before cloning the virtual machine.

[435]

> The **System Preparation Tool (SYSPREP)** is a tool used to remove system-specific data from Windows, such as the Computer SID. Also, SYSPREP resets other machine-specific information that, if duplicated, can cause problems for certain applications like Windows Server Update Services (WSUS).
>
> Microsoft recommends to SYSPREP the image before cloning, but we can skip this step and replace a process like reset WSUS settings by scripts, if we want.
>
> To understand the SYSPREP tool, I recommend reading Mark Russinovich's article The Machine SID Duplication Myth at `http://blogs.technet.com/b/markrussinovich/archive/2009/11/03/3291024.aspx`

8. William is going to run SYSPREP before the cloning process. He needs to choose the **Enter System Out-of-Box Experience (OOBE)** option, enable the **Generalize** checkbox, select **Shutdown** in the **Shutdown Options**, and click on the **OK** button:

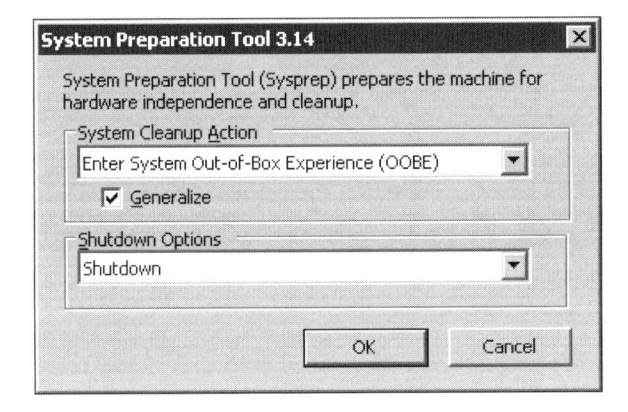

9. When the **SYSPREP** process is complete, the virtual machine is turned off. Now William is ready to copy the virtual machine.

10. When he turns on the VM, the setup process starts and after he chooses the language and keyboard, he is ready to configure the VM. He needs to rename the server, assign an IP address (optional), and join it to the domain. Once the setup is complete, the new VM is joined to the XenApp farm and the server is ready.

11. Remaining steps for unattended setup of XenApp are available in *Chapter 4, Advanced XenApp Deployment*.

Summary

In this chapter, we learned about Virtualization of XenApp farms. In particular, we talked about:

- Deploying XenApp 6.5 in a virtualized environment, including advantages and disadvantages, Virtual machine performance and host scalability and more
- Deploying XenApp 6.5 on Citrix XenServer, Microsoft Hyper-V, and VMware vSphere virtual machines
- Cloning XenApp 6.5 virtual machines

This is the last piece of advice. Virtualization will provide a lot of benefits and savings. However, one of my preferred reasons to implement VM over physical servers is not related to performance or management, it is related with reliability. Let's use an example to clarify the idea:

We have two identical servers. One is the physical server running XenApp. This server can support 120-140 users. Now we have the second server, running a hypervisor with four virtual machines. Each virtual machine can support 25 to 35 users, depending on the load. So the hypervisor can support around 100-140 users.

If the physical server hangs or crashes, all users are affected. However, if only one virtual machine crashes or hangs, only one-fourth of the users are affected.

Remember to scale out instead of scaling up. Add more machines instead of adding more users per server.

Another benefit of scale out is maintenance. Let's go back to previous example. We can disable logon on two VMs, and when no users are on these servers, we can update, and re-enable logon. After that, we can disable the logon of two remaining VMs. Updating a single server with 100+ users is more complicated.

Index

Symbols

.NET applications, PowerShell Commands
  sample C#.NET application, creating 371
  sample VB.NET application, creating 366
.WSH files (Windows Scripting Host) 355

A

access gateway (optional) 25
access infrastructure
  about 23
  access gateway (optional) 25
  secure gateway (optional) 26
  web interface 25
Active Directory Federation Services
    Support. *See* ADFS
Active Directory Group Policies (GPO)
  used, for configuring Windows Firewall 41
Active Directory integration
  designing 30
Adaptive Display 280
Add shortcut to the client's desktop option
    140
ADFS 12
administration (server farm) component,
    application streaming 175
administrator users, Citrix Merchandising
    Server 2.2
  configuring 390-392
Aero (Desktop Experience) 323
Alert Configuration tab 102
Allow caching of embedded fonts option
    260
Allow caching of embedded images option
    260

Allow non-administrators to modify these
    settings option 260
alternate, access method 107
Always option 303
AMD Virtualization (AMD-V) 414
AppCenter Console 209, 210
application gateway 12
Application Properties dialog box 311
applications 20
applications, publishing
  application compatibility 124
  client machine type 123
  multiple versions 124
  network connectivity 123
  patching and upgrading 123
application streaming
  about 171
  benefits 172
  system requisites 173, 174
application streaming, components
  administration (server farm) component
      175
  citrix plug-ins component 176
  citrix streaming profiler component 175
  licensing component 175
application streaming, plug-ins
  about 176
  server, accessed from 177
  streamed to client desktops 176
Apply customized settings checkbox 245
Ask option 303
audio
  client audio redirection, setting up 307
  client microphone redirection, setting up
      308

configuring, for user sessions 311
configuring, policies used 305
quality, setting up 306
Audio Plug N Play
enabling 306
Audio quality setting
high 306
low 306
medium 306
Audio redirection bandwidth limit
setting up 309
Audio redirection bandwidth limit percent
setting up 309
Authentication Methods option 107
Auto client reconnect authentication feature 333
Auto client reconnect feature 332, 333
Auto client reconnect logging feature 333
Auto-create all client printers 264
auto-create generic universal printer
about 254
setting up 255
Auto-create local (non-network) client printers only 264
Auto-create the client's default printer only 264
auto-creation, printer policy 262
automatic client reconnection, session activity
configuring 332, 334
automatic installation, printer drivers
controlling 248
AUTOUPDATE 406
Available users list 325, 326

B

bandwidth
reducing, HDX 3D Image Acceleration used 277, 278
Bandwidth policy settings
about 308
Audio redirection bandwidth limit percent, setting up 309
Audio redirection bandwidth limit, setting up 309
HDX MediaStream Multimedia Acceleration bandwidth limit percent, setting up 310
HDX MediaStream Multimedia Acceleration bandwidth limit, setting up 310
BrickDocProject 34, 38
BrickExpenses 34
BrickFin 37
BrickTime 34
Brick Unit Constructions, case study 19
BRICKXA65-01 server
license server, installing 47
web interface roles, installing 47
BRICKXA65-02
XenApp 6.5 configuring, Wizard-Based Server Role Manager used 53-55
XenApp 6.5 installing, Wizard-Based Server Role Manager used 53-55
BRICKXA65-03
XenApp 6.5, configuring 65-67
XenApp 6.5, installing 65-67

C

cache application at launch time 139
Certificate Signing Request, Citrix Merchandising Server 2.2
creating 400
Citrix Access Management Console 95
Citrix Administrators
adding 114-117
disabling 118
managing 114
properties, modifying 119
Citrix AppCenter Console
about 16, 95-97, 122, 317, 318
Disable Authenticode signature checking option 96
Citrix Client. *See* **Citrix Receiver**
Citrix Client. *See* **Citrix Plug-In**
Citrix Dazzle
about 12
and the Self-service storefront 23
Citrix Delivery Services Console. *See* **Citrix AppCenter Console** 16
Citrix Edgesight 25

Citrix HDX technologies
  about 10
  description 276
Citrix High Definition User Experience templates 221
Citrix High Server Scalability templates 221
Citrix ICA (Independent Computing Architecture) 315
Citrix Licenses
  installing 50-52
  managing, License Administration Console used 98-103
Citrix License Server
  about 17
  configuring 48-52
Citrix Licensing 24
Citrix Merchandising Server 2.2
  administrator users, configuring 390-392
  Certificate Signing Request (CSR), creating 400
  deliveries, creating 395-397
  plug-ins, installing 392, 393
  recipient rules, creating 393, 394
  self-signed SSL certificate, creating 399
  setting up 383-389
  signing request, creating for Microsoft certificate services 402
  software, installing 383
  SSL certificates, configuring 398
  SSL certificates, importing 400, 401
  SSL certificates, installing on client machines 402
  system requisites 383
  virtual appliance, importing into Citrix XenServer 386, 387, 388
  virtual appliance, importing into VMware vSphere 384, 385
Citrix Online Plug-in. *See also* Citrix Receiver
Citrix Online Plug-In
  Special Folder Redirection, enabling 350
Citrix Optimized Bandwidth for WAN templates 221
Citrix Plug-In. *See also* Citrix XenApp Receiver
Citrix Plug-In 317

citrix plug-ins component, application streaming 176
Citrix policies
  session printers settings, adding 244
  using, to configure multimedia settings (HDX MediaStream) 286-290
Citrix Policies Templates
  exporting 222, 223
  importing 222, 223
  new Citrix Policies Templates, creating 221, 222
  using 220, 221
Citrix Receiver
  about 11, 22, 104, 317, 379, 380
  features 380
  installing, for Macintosh 382, 405
  installing, on Windows 382
  installing, on XenApp servers 405
  plug-In compatibility 380
  Special Folder Redirection, enabling 350
  system requisites 382
Citrix Receiver installation
  about 403
  Citrix Receiver deploying for internal users, with administrative rights 403
  Citrix Receiver deploying for internal Windows users, without administrative rights 406, 407
  for Macintosh 405
  for Windows 404
  on XenApp servers 405
Citrix Receiver, system requisites
  about 382
  Citrix Receiver, installing on Windows 382
  installing, for Macintosh 382
Citrix Security and Control templates 221
Citrix SSL Relay Configuration Tool 112
Citrix Streaming Profiler
  installing 179
citrix streaming profiler component, application streaming 175
Citrix Universal Printer
  about 252, 253
  auto-create generic universal printer, creating 255
  benefits 252-254

[441]

default settings, changing 262
drawbacks 252
rules 254, 255
universal driver preference, setting up 256
universal printer driver usage on sessions, configuring 257, 258
universal printing EMF processing mode 259
universal printing image compression limit 259
universal printing optimization defaults 260, 261
universal printing preview preference, setting up 258
universal printing print quality limit 261
using, ways 253
Citrix User policy, categories
Bandwidth 240
Printing | Client Printers 240
Printing | Drivers 240
Printing | Universal Printing 240
Citrix Web Interface Management Console 104-111
Citrix Web Interface server
configuring 67
Citrix Web Interface server configuration
XenApp Services site, creating 73, 74
XenApp Services Sites 67
XenApp website, creating 68
XenApp Web Sites 67
Citrix Web Interface Server, customizing
about 86, 87
devices image, changing 90
footer Citrix logo, changing 92
footer section, changing 93, 94
HDX logo, changing 93
header Citrix logo, changing 88
header section color, changing 88
horizontal page lower section color, changing 91
horizontal page upper section color, changing 89
product name image, changing 89, 90
tagline text, changing 91, 92
Citrix XenApp
about 7
printing on 239, 240

Citrix XenApp 6.5 PowerShell SDK
installing 357
Citrix XenApp 6 Migration Tool
URL 236
Citrix XenApp Commands snap-in
installing 359, 360
Citrix XenApp Migration Center 235
Citrix XenApp on VMware Best Practices Guide
URL 433
Citrix XenApp, printing on
printing pathway 240, 241
Citrix XenApp Receiver 17, 18
Citrix XenServer
virtual appliance, importing 386-388
XenApp 6.5, deploying 414
Citrix XenServer free edition
URL 414
Citrix XML Broker 24
Citrix XML Service 24
client audio redirection
setting up 307
Client COM port redirection 338
client local printing
about 241, 242
print job, spooling 241, 242
client machine
HDX MediaStream for Flash, configuring 302-304
client machine printers
auto-creating 263
client machine type 123
client microphone redirection
setting up 308
client network printing
about 242
print job, spooling 242
client printing pathway 241
cloning
XenApp 6.5 virtual machines 433-436
computer policy settings, XenApp policies 206
concurrent connections
application instances, limiting 340
connection denial events, logging 341
limiting 339

number of sessions per server, limiting 339
sessions and connections, sharing 342, 343
user connections, preventing during farm
    maintenance 344
configuring
  Citrix Licenses 50-52
  Citrix License Server 48, 49
  Citrix Web Interface server 67
  IE ESC 43
  Remote Desktop licensing 74-76
  Windows components 40
  XenApp 6.5 39, 40
  XenApp 6.5, on BRICKXA65-03 65-67
Connection Limits (Computer) policy 339
consoles
  used, for creating XenApp policies 213-217
content
  about 122
  publishing, publish application wizard
      used 147-152
content redirection
  configuring 162
  configuring, from server to client 163
  disabling 168, 175
  enabling 167, 168
  enabling, from server to client 162
Controller. *See* **Session-Host and Controller**
CPU usage, reducing
  by moving processing to GPU, HDX 3D
      used 281
CPU Utilization Management 12
CTX114501
  URL 58
CTX126125
  URL 251
CtxAdmTools 147

D

data collector 22
data store database 15, 24
data stores, installing
  Microsoft SQL Server 2008 database server
      60, 61
  Microsoft SQL Server 2008 Express database server 59, 60

options 58
Oracle database server 62, 63, 64
default printer
  setting, for session 244, 245
deliveries, Citrix Merchandising Server 2.2
  creating 395, 396
design validation farm 21
Desired image quality option 260
Desktop Experience 286
devices and ports
  access, controlling 337
devices image, Citrix Web Interface Server
  changing 90
Diagnostic Logging task 112
direct, access method 107
Disable Authenticode signature checking
    option 96
Display Mode Degrade Preference setting
    282
Do not adjust the user's d efault printer 245
Do not auto-create client printers 264
Do not retain printer properties option 268
drives
  mapping 338
Dual Monitor 323
dynamic printer provisioning 262
Dynamic VHDs 422

E

echo cancellation
  configuring 290, 291
EdgeSightServer option 82
Edit Settings pane 107
EMF (Enhanced Metafile Format) 256
Enable heavyweight compression option
    260
Enhanced Security Configuration. *See* **IE**
    ESC
ESXi
  about 424
  limitations 425
Existing Oracle database option 59

F

farm
  Office 2010, publishing 197-201
farm, architecture
  about 21
  data collector 22
  server roles 22
  worker group 22
  zones 21
farm management
  PowerShell, using 360
farm, XenApp 6.5
  about 20
  applications, selecting 33
  multi-user environment 20
  remote desktop services 20
  test farm, building 30, 31
  XenApp application servers 20
  XenApp infrastructure servers 20
  XenApp server 20
FC (Fibre Channel) 412
file type associations
  updating 165, 167
file types
  published application, associating with 163-165
Flash Acceleration
  setting up 295, 296
Flash acceleration setting 301
Flash background color list
  setting up 296
Flash backwards compatibility
  setting up 297
Flash content
  optimizing, HDX MediaStream for Flash used 291
Flash default behavior setting
  Block Flash player 293
  Disable Flash acceleration 293
  Enable Flash acceleration 293
Flash event logging
  enabling 297, 298
Flash event logging setting 298
Flash intelligent fallback
  setting up 298

Flash latency threshold
  setting up 299
Flash quality adjustment setting 293
Flash server-side content fetching URL list
  setting up 300
Flash URL Blacklist
  setting up 301
Flash URL Blacklist setting 291
Flash URL compatibility list
  setting up 301
footer Citrix logo, Citrix Web Interface Server
  changing 92
footer section, Citrix Web Interface Server
  changing 93

G

gateway, access method 107
gateway alternate, access method 107
gateway translated, access method 108
Get-XAPrinterDriver command 251
GPMC 77
Group Policy (GPO)
  used, for configuring Remote Desktop licensing mode 76, 77
  used, for Special Folder Redirection 350, 352
Group Policy Management Console. *See* GPMC 209
Guest Operating System page 427

H

HDX 3D
  used to reduce CPU usage, by moving processing to GPU 281
HDX 3D Image Acceleration
  using, to reduce bandwidth 277, 278
HDX 3D Progressive Display
  using, to improve image display 279, 280
HDX 3D technologies
  using, to improve image display 276
HDX Broadcast Display settings
  using 281-284
HDX Experience Monitor
  for XenApp 311

HDX logo, Citrix Web Interface Server
  changing 93
HDX MediaStream for Flash
  enabling, at server side 292-294
  Flash Acceleration, setting up 295, 296
  Flash background color list, setting up 296
  Flash backwards compatibility, setting up 297
  Flash event logging, enabling 297, 298
  Flash intelligent fallback, setting up 298
  Flash latency threshold, setting up 299
  Flash server-side content fetching URL list, setting up 300
  Flash URL Blacklist, setting up 301
  Flash URL compatibility list, setting up 301
  installing 304
  on client machine, configuring 302-304
  settings, configuring 295
  system requisites 292
  uninstalling 305
  using, to optimize Flash content 291
HDX MediaStream Multimedia Acceleration
  configuring, Citrix policies used 286-290
  using 285
HDX MediaStream Multimedia Acceleration bandwidth limit
  setting up 310
HDX MediaStream Multimedia Acceleration bandwidth limit percent
  setting up 310
HDX MediaStream Multimedia Acceleration default buffer size setting 288
HDX MediaStream Multimedia Acceleration default buffer size use setting 288
HDX MediaStream Multimedia Acceleration setting 287
HDX Monitor
  URL 312
header Citrix logo, Citrix Web Interface Server
  changing 88
header section color, Citrix Web Interface Server
  changing 88

heavyweight compression. *See* Progressive heavyweight compression
Held in profile only if not saved on client option 267
horizontal page lower section color, Citrix Web Interface Server
  changing 91
horizontal page upper section color, Citrix Web Interface Server
  changing 89
hosted application
  publishing, publish application wizard used 124-136
hosted applications 121
Hotfix 280
Hotfix XA650W2K8R2X64002 280
Hotfix XA650W2K8R2X64025 280
HQ (headquarters) 271
HTTP (Hypertext Transfer Protocol) 162
HTTPS (Secure Hypertext Transfer Protocol) 162
Hydra 7
Hyper-Threading (HT) technology 412
Hyper-V
  Microsoft Hyper-V Server 2008 R2 419
  Microsoft Windows Server 2008 R2 419
  versions 419
  VM for XenApp 6, creating 420-424
Hypervisors 410

I

ICA Client. *See* Citrix XenApp Receiver
ICA Client Printer Configuration tool
  publishing 267
ICA Keep-Alive, session activity
  configuring 335
ICA keep alive timeout 335
IE ESC
  configuring 43
  disabling 43
IMA 122
Image caching setting 283
image display
  improving, HDX 3D Progressive Display used 279, 280
  improving, HDX 3D technologies used 276

Independent Management Architecture. *See* IMA
infrastructure server
  about 23
  access infrastructure 25, 26
  virtualization infrastructure 24, 25
Installation Manager 12
installing
  license server, in BRICKXA65-01 server 47
  web interface roles, in BRICKXA65-01 server 47
  XenApp 6.5 39, 40
  XenApp 6.5, on BRICKXA65-03 65-67
  XenApp, Wizard-based Server Role Manager used 44, 45
Instant App Access 9
Intelligent Fallback 291
Intel Virtualization Technology (INTEL VT) 414

J

Java 37

K

Key Management Service (KMS) 177

L

legacy client printer support
  configuring 265
Legacy printer names option 265
License Administration Console
  controlling, Citrix licenses used 98-103
license server
  installing, in BRICKXA65-01 server 47
License-server-IP-Address 98
License-server-name 98
licensing component, application streaming 175
Licensing option 82
Local Group Policy Editor 77, 211, 212
local text echo 114, 345
locations, printing references 269
logging
  enabling, for shadowing 327, 328
Log On button 404

Lossy compression 279

M

Macintosh
  Citrix Receiver for 382
  Citrix Receiver, installing for 382, 405
Manage IIS Hosting task 111, 112
management consoles
  about 208
  AppCenter Console 209, 210
  Group Policy Management Console 209
  Local Group Policy Editor 211-213
Maximum allowed color depth setting 283
merchandising server 23
MerchandisingServer option 82
MFCOM
  and PowerShell 355, 356
  using, on XenApp 376
MFCOM scripts
  converting, to PowerShell 376
Microsoft App-V integration 11
Microsoft certificate services, Citrix Merchandising Server 2.2
  signing request, creating 402
Microsoft Hyper-V. *See also* Hyper-V
Microsoft Hyper-V
  XenApp 6.5, deploying 419
Microsoft Hyper-V Server 2008 R2 419
Microsoft Management Console (MMC) 95
Microsoft Office 2010
  profiling 177, 187-196
  issues 37
Microsoft Office applications 36, 37
Microsoft Office suite 37
Microsoft Server 2008 Hyper-V R2
  URL 420
Microsoft SQL Server 2008 database server 60, 61
Microsoft SQL Server 2008 Express database server 59, 60
Microsoft System Center Configuration Manager (SCCM) 123
Microsoft Systems Management Server (SMS). *See* Microsoft System Center Configuration Manager (SCCM)
MMS (Microsoft Media Format) 162

mobile users printing
  printers, configuring 271
  printing bandwidth, limiting 273
  printing performance, improving 272
  proximity printing, feature 271
  smooth roaming, feature 271
mouse click feedback 344
Mouse Click Feedback technology 114
MUI 11
Multi-lingual User Interface. *See* MUI
Multimedia conferencing setting 289
multimedia settings (HDX MediaStream) settings
  configuring, Citrix policies used 286-290
Multiple Activation Key (MAK) 177
multiple policies 219
Multi-stream ICA 11

N

Name and Location page 426
NAS (Network Attached Storage) 26, 412
NAS (NFS) 412
NDS Support 12
network connectivity 123
Network Management Console Integration 12
network printers
  about 238
  assigning, to users 243
  auto-creating 263
  default printer, setting for session 244, 245
  session printers settings, adding to Citrix policy 244
  session printers settings, modifying 245, 246
network printing pathway 241
Never option 304
nodes 205
non-seamless window mode 342
Notify user when display mode is degraded setting 284
Novell eDirectory 12

O

Office 2010
  publishing, on farm 197-201

Office 2010 installation
  customizing 179-186
One printer created by a session printer rule 244
Only with Second Generation option 304
Optimize for XenApp setting 418
Oracle database server 62, 63, 64

P

password manager. *See* Single Sign-On
PCL4 257
PCL5c 257
PCMAdmin option 82
Performance Tuning Guidelines for Windows Server 2008
  URL 433
pilot farm 21
  deploying 40
pilot plan
  about 28, 29
  Active Directory integration, designing 30
  application list, creating 33, 34
  application list, testing 34, 35
  Java 37, 38
  Microsoft Office applications 36, 37
  small test farm, building 30-32
plug-In compatibility, Citrix Receiver
  Acceleration Plug-In 5.5.2 or later 380
  Acceleration Plug-In 5.5.4 or later 380
  Citrix Receiver for Mac 2.x or later 380
  Citrix Receiver for Mac 11.x or later 380
  Citrix Receiver for Windows 2.x or later 380
  Citrix Receiver for Windows 3.x or later 381
  Communication Plug-In for Mac 3.0 or later 381
  Dazzle Plug-In 1.1.2 or later 381
  EasyCall 3.x or later 381
  MS Application Virtualization Desktop Client 4.5 or later 381
  Offline Plug-In 5.x 381
  Online Plug-In for Mac 11.x or later 381
  Online Plug-In for Windows 11.x, 12.x and Citrix Receiver 13.x 381
  Profile Management Plug-In 2.0 or later 381

Secure Access for Mac Plug-In 1.2 or later 381
Secure Access for Windows Plug-In 4.6.2 or later 381
Secure Access Plug-In 9.1 381
Service Monitoring Plug-In 5.3 or later 381
Single Sign-On Plug-In 5.0 381
PNM (Legacy Real Player) 162
port 98
Power and Capacity Management feature 13
Power and Capacity Management (optional) 25
PowerShell
  and MFCOM 355, 356
  MFCOM scripts, converting 376, 377
  using, for basic administrative tasks 358
  using, for farm management 360
PowerShell Commands
  using, from .NET applications 366
PowerShell Support 9
PowerShell XenApp Commands
  installing 357
pre-cache application at login 139
printer auto-creation settings
  configuring 264
printer driver compatibility list
  modifying 249, 250
printer drivers
  about 238
  automatic installation, controlling 248
  compatibility list, modifying 249-251
  managing 247, 248
  replicating, in XenApp 251, 252
printer policy
  auto-creating 262
printers
  about 237
  auto-creation policy 262
  client machine printers. auto-creating 263
  configuring, for mobile users 271
  ICA Client Printer Configuration tool, publishing 267
  implementing 262
  legacy client printer support, configuring 265
  network printers. auto-creating 263, 264
  printer auto-creation settings, configuring 264
  printing preferences, locations 269, 270
  provisioning, types 262
  user printer properties, storing 267-269
  user provisioning 265
  Windows Add Printer wizard, publishing 266
printers provisioning, types
  dynamic 262
  static 262
printing
  bandwidth, limiting 273
  on Citrix XenApp 239, 240
  performance, improving 272
  references, general locations 269
printing, concepts
  about 237
  network printer 238
  printer driver 238
  printers 237
  printing device 237
  print job 238
  print queue 238
  print server 238
  print spooler 238
printing device 237
Printing Optimization Pack 10
printing pathway 240
print job
  about 238
  spooling 238, 239
  spooling, printing process 239
print queue 238
print servers 238
print spooler 238
production farm 21
product name image, Citrix Web Interface Server
  changing 89, 90
profiler workstation
  installing 178
Progressive Display 280
Progressive heavyweight compression 278
provisioning option 83
Provisioning Services (optional) 25
proximity roaming 271

[448]

PS (PostScript) 257
publish application wizard
  used, for publishing content 147-152
  used, for publishing hosted application 124-136
  used, for publishing server desktop 152-161
  used, for publishing streaming application 136-146
Publish Application wizard 126
published applications
  associating, with file types 163-165
Publish immediately page 130, 157

Q

Queueing and tossing setting 284

R

Receiver options, images
  VMware 383
  XenServer 383
recipient rules, Citrix Merchandising Server 2.2
  creating 393, 394
Remote Desktop licensing configuration
  about 74-76
  Group Policy used 76, 77
Remote Desktop Services 20, 121, 405
Repair Site task 111
Resource Pool page 426
Resource Types option 108
Retained in user profile only option 267
Role-based Setup Wizard 8
RTSP (Real Player and QuickTime) 162
RTSPU (Real Player and QuickTime) 162

S

sample C#.NET application
  cmdlet, running 373
  creating 371
  parameters, passing to cmdlets 376
  references, adding 372
  results, displaying 374-376
  runspace, creating 373
  runspace, opening 373

sample VB.NET application
  cmdlet, running 369
  creating 366
  parameters, passing to cmdlets 371
  references, adding 367, 368
  results, displaying 369, 370
  runspace, creating 368
  runspace, opening 368
SAN (iSCSI or FC) 412
SAN (Storage Area Network) 412
SAS (Serial Attached SCSI) 412
SATA (Serial ATA) disk 412
Saved on the client device only option 267
Script Searcher tool, MFCOM
  URL 376
seamless window mode 342
Search Files button 377
Secure Access option 107
SecureGateway option 83
secure gateway (optional) 26
Select Install Option page 189
self-signed SSL certificate, Citrix Merchandising Server 2.2
  creating 399
Server Configuration tab 102
server consolidation 410
server desktop
  about 122
  publishing, publish application wizard used 152-161
server local printers
  about 246
  configuring, steps for 247
SERVER_LOCATION 406
server network printing
  about 243
  print job, spooling 243
server roles 22
server-side application virtualization 21
server to client
  content redirection, configuring from 163
  content redirection, enabling from 162
Service Monitoring (optional) 25
session activity
  automatic client reconnection, configuring 332, 334

ICA Keep-Alive, configuring 335
maintaining 331
session reliability, configuring 331, 332
Session-Host and Controller 97, 106
Session Pre-Launch feature 9, 28
session printers
 default printer, setting for 244, 245
 settings, adding to Citrix policy 244
 settings, modifying 245
Session printers settings page 245
Session reliability connections setting 332
session reliability, session activity
 configuring 331, 332
Session reliability timeout setting 332
sessions. *See also* **XenApp sessions**
sessions
 Special Folder Redirection 347
 XenApp policies, applying 217, 218
Set default printer to the client's main printer 245
Shadow button 324
Shadowed users list 325
shadowing
 initiating 325, 326
 logging, enabling 327, 328
 policy, creating 328-330
 session, ending 326
 user-to-user shadowing, enabling 328
shadow taskbar
 about 113
 shadowing, initiating 325, 326
 starting 325
 used, for viewing sessions 324, 325
Shortcut presentation page 156
silent installation. *See* **unattended installation**
Single Sign-On 13
Single Sign-on (optional) 24
SmartAuditor 13
SmartAuditor (optional) 25
SmartAuditorServer option 83
smooth roaming 271
Special Folder Redirection
 disabled 347
 enabled 348
 enabling, in Citrix Online Plug-In 350
 enabling, in Citrix Receiver 350

enabling, in web interface 349
for seamless applications 348
Group Policy (GPO) used 350, 352
in sessions 347
policy setting 348
working 348
SpeedScreen Latency Reduction Manager
 about 114
 configuring 346, 347
 Local Text Echo technology 114
 Mouse Click Feedback technology 114
spooling
 print job 238, 239
SSL certificates, Citrix Merchandising Server 2.2
 configuring 398
 importing 400, 401
 installing, on client machines 402
SsonService option 83
Start-XAPrinterDriverReplication command 251
static printer provisioning 262
streamed applications 122
streamed profiles
 trusted servers, specifying 202, 203
streamed services
 trusted servers, specifying 202, 203
streaming application
 publishing, publish application wizard used 136-146
Sysinternals tools
 URL 36
SYSPREP Tool 436
System Center Virtual Machine Manager 2008 R2
 URL 420
System Preparation Tool. *See* **SYSPREP Tool**

T

tagline text, Citrix Web Interface Server
 changing 91, 92
Terminal Server. *See* **Remote Desktop Services**
terminal services. *See* **Remote Desktop Services**

Thick Provision Eager Zeroed 429
Thick Provision Lazy Zeroed 429
ThinPrint
  URL 273
Thin Provision 429
third-party printing solutions 273
TOKEN 407
translated, access method 107
troubleshooting policies
  Citrix Policy Modeling Wizard, using 228
  Citrix settings, precedence over Windows settings 233
  connection scenarios 228-231
  existing policies, importing 235, 236
  existing policies, migrating 235, 236
  policies, searching 233, 234
  settings, searching 233, 234
trusted servers
  specifying, for streamed profiles 202, 203
  specifying, for streamed services 202, 203

U

Ultra-High option 279
unattended installation
  of XenApp 6.5 79
  of XenApp components 80-86
unfiltered policies 218, 219
Uninstall Site task 111
UniPrint
  URL 273
universal driver preference. *See* universal driver priority
  setting up 256
universal driver priority 254
universal print driver usage. *See* universal printing
universal printer
  default settings, changing 262
universal printer driver
  usage on sessions, configuring 257, 258
universal printing 254
universal printing EMF processing mode 254, 259
universal printing image compression limit 255

universal printing image compression limit 259
universal printing optimization defaults 255, 260, 261
universal printing preview preference
  about 254
  setting up 258
universal printing print quality limit 255, 261
Update-XAPrinterDriver command 251
use only printer model specific drivers 257
Use printer model specific drivers only if universal printing is unavailable 258
User Configuration tab 100
user environments
  audio, redirecting 338
  COM ports, redirecting 338
  customizing 336
  device access, controlling 337
  drives, mapping 338
  ports access, controlling 337
  user logons appearance, controlling 336
user logons
  appearance, controlling 336
user policy settings, XenApp policies 206
user provisioning 265
users
  network printers, assigning 243
  printer properties, storing 267-269
user sessions
  audio, configuring for 311
user sessions optimization
  about 344
  local text echo 345
  mouse click feedback 344
  SpeedScreen Latency Reduction, configuring 346, 347
user-to-user shadowing, enabling 328
use universal printing only 258
use universal printing only if requested driver is unavailable 258

V

VBS files (Visual Basic scripts) 355
vCPUs 412
Vendor Daemon Configuration tab 103

VERBOSE 406
Very High option 279
virtual appliance
  importing, into Citrix XenServer 386-388
  importing, into VMware vSphere 384, 385
Virtual Hard Disk (VHD) page 194
virtualization
  disadvantages 410, 411
  host scalability 411-413
  platform, selecting 413, 414
  virtual machine performance 411-413
  XenApp 6.5 farms, need for 410
virtualization infrastructure
  about 23
  Citrix Licensing 24
  Citrix XML Broker 24
  Citrix XML Service 24
  Data Store database 24
  Power and Capacity Management (optional) 25
  Provisioning Services (optional) 25
  Service Monitoring (optional) 25
  Single Sign-on (optional) 24
  SmartAuditor (optional) 25
virtualized environment
  disadvantages 410, 411
  host scalability 411-413
  platform, selecting 413, 414
  virtual machine performance 411-413
  XenApp 6.5, deploying 409, 410
virtual machine, optimizations
  Citrix XenApp on VMware Best Practices Guide, URL 433
  Performance Tuning Guidelines for Windows Server 2008, URL 433
  XenApp 6.x (Windows 2008 R2), URL 433
Virtual reality Check Project
  URL 413
Visual Basic for Applications (VBA) 37
VM hosted application virtualization 21
VMware 383
VMware ESX Server. See VMware vSphere
VMware vSphere
  virtual appliance, importing 384, 385
  VM for XenApp 6.5, creating 426-433
  XenApp 6.5, deploying 424, 425
VMware vSphere for Enterprise 424

VMware vSphere Hypervisor. See ESXi
VM, XenApp 6
  creating, in Hyper-V 420-424
VM, XenApp 6.5
  creating, in VMware vSphere 426-433
  creating, in XenServer 415-419
VMXNet3 NIC 428
Volume Activation (VA) 177

W

web applications 38
web interface 25
  Special Folder Redirection, enabling 349
WebInterface option 13, 83
web interface roles
  installing, in BRICKXA65-01 server 47
Windows
  Citrix Receiver for 382
  Citrix Receiver, installing for 404
  Citrix Receiver, installing on 382
Windows 32-bit on Windows 64-bit. See WOW64
Windows Add Printer wizard
  publishing 266
Windows components
  configuring 40
Windows components configuration
  IE ESC 43
  Windows Firewall, configuring 41, 42
Windows Desktop Experience Integration 9
Windows Event Log 327
Windows Firewall
  configuring 41, 42
  configuring, Active Directory Group Policies (GPO) used 41
  configuring, for XenApp 42
  disabling 41, 42
Windows Media Redirection Buffer Size setting. See HDX MediaStream Multimedia Acceleration
Windows Media Redirection Buffer Size Use. See HDX MediaStream Multimedia Acceleration default buffer size use setting

Windows Media Redirection setting. *See*
   HDX MediaStream Multimedia
   Acceleration setting
WinFrame 7
WinView 7
Wizard-based Server configuration tool
  used, for configuring XenApp 56, 57
Wizard-Based Server Role Manager
  used for configuring XenApp 6.5, on
     BRICKXA65-02 53-55
  used, for installing XenApp 44, 45
  used for installing XenApp 6.5, on
     BRICKXA65-02 53-55
worker group 22
Worker Groups
  creating 224-227
  using, to assign policies 223, 224
WOW64 34

X

XA600W2K8R2X64010.msp file 254
XA_Console 83
XA_IISIntegration 83
XenApp
  architecture 26-28
  client-side application virtualization 21
  configuring, Wizard-based Server
     configuration tool used 56, 57
  features 12
  for HDX Experience Monitor 311
  installing, Wizard-Based Server Role
     Manager used 44, 45
  MFCOM, using 376
  mobile users, printing for 270
  server-side application virtualization 21
  VM hosted application virtualization 21
XenApp 6.5
  about 8
  Active Directory group policy integration
     11
  Citrix Dazzle 12
  Citrix HDX Technologies 10
  Citrix Receiver 3.0 11
  configuring 39, 40
  configuring on BRICKXA65-02, Wizard-
     Based Server Role Manager used 53-55

  configuring, on BRICKXA65-03 65-67
  deploying, in virtualized environment 409,
     410
  deploying, on Citrix XenServer 414
  deploying, on Microsoft Hyper-V 419
  deploying, on VMware vSphere 424, 425
  highlights 8
  installing 39, 40
  installing on BRICKXA65-02, Wizard-Based
     Server Role Manager used 53-55
  installing, on BRICKXA65-03 65-67
  Instant App Access 9
  Microsoft App-V integration 11
  Multi-lingual User Interface (MUI) 11
  Multi-stream ICA 11
  New Management Console 10
  pilot farm, deploying 40
  PowerShell Support 9
  printing pathway 240
  Printing Performance 10
  Role-based Setup Wizard 8
  system requisites 13, 14
  unattended installation 79, 80
  Windows Desktop Experience Integration 9
  Windows Portable USB Devices, support
     for 11
  Windows Service Isolation, for streamed
     applications 11
XenApp 6.5 farms
  virtualizing, need for 410
XenApp 6.5, system requsites
  about 13, 14
  Citrix AppCenter console 16
  data store database 15
  license server 17
  XenApp Server Role Manager 14
XenApp 6.5 virtual machines
  cloning 433-436
XenApp 6.x (Windows 2008 R2)
  URL 433
XenApp application server 20
XenApp, architecture 26-28
XenApp Commands
  installing, on XenApp Servers 356
  installing, options 356

[453]

XenApp Commands, installing on XenApp
        Servers
    Citrix XenApp 6.5 PowerShell SDK,
        installing 357
    PowerShell XenApp Commands, installing
        357, 358
XenApp components
    unattended installation 80-86
XenAppConfigConsole.exe 80
XenApp configuration, Wizard-based Server
        Configuration tool used
    about 56, 57
    data stores, installing 58
    first XenApp server, configuring 57, 58
XenApp design validation farm 28
XenAppEnhancedDesktopExperience 83
XenApp farms
    managing 77, 78
XenApp, features 12, 13
XenAppGPMX64.msi file 254
XenAppGPMX86.msi file 254
XenApp infrastructure servers 20
XenApp policies
    about 205, 206
    applying, to sessions 217, 218
    assigning, worker groups used 223
    computer policy settings 206
    creating 213
    creating, best practices for 207, 208
    creating, consoles used 213-217
    guidelines 208
    importing 235, 236
    migrating 235, 236
    multiple policies, ussing 219, 220
    unfiltered policies 218, 219
    user policy settings 206
    working with 206, 207
XenApp server farm
    about 21
    design validation farm 21
    pilot farm 21
    production farm 21

XenApp servers
    about 20
    Citrix Receiver, installing 405
XenApp Services Site
    about 67
    creating 73
XenApp Session Reliability 315
XenApp sessions
    disconnecting 320, 321
    logging off 320, 321
    managing 319
    messages, sending to users 322, 323
    monitoring 317-319
    processes in user session, terminating 321,
        322
    resetting 320, 321
    shadowing, initiating 325, 326
    shadowing, logging enabling for 327
    shadowing policy, creating 328-330
    shadowing session, ending 326
    Shadow Taskbar, starting 325
    user-to-user shadowing, enabling 328
    viewing 323, 324
    viewing, Shadow Taskbar used 324, 325
XenAppSetupConsole.exe 80
XenApp Web Site
    about 67
    creating 68-72
XenServer
    about 383
    new XenApp 6.5 VM, creating 416-419
    XenApp 6.5 VM, creating 415
XenServer 6.0 Administrator's Guide
    URL 415
XenServer 6.0 Installation Guide
    URL 415
XenServer 6.0 Virtual Machine Installation
        Guide
    URL 415
XML Paper Specification 256

Z

zones 21

[PACKT] PUBLISHING enterprise
professional expertise distilled

Thank you for buying
Getting Started with Citrix XenApp 6.5

About Packt Publishing

Packt, pronounced 'packed', published its first book "Mastering phpMyAdmin for Effective MySQL Management" in April 2004 and subsequently continued to specialize in publishing highly focused books on specific technologies and solutions.

Our books and publications share the experiences of your fellow IT professionals in adapting and customizing today's systems, applications, and frameworks. Our solution based books give you the knowledge and power to customize the software and technologies you're using to get the job done. Packt books are more specific and less general than the IT books you have seen in the past. Our unique business model allows us to bring you more focused information, giving you more of what you need to know, and less of what you don't.

Packt is a modern, yet unique publishing company, which focuses on producing quality, cutting-edge books for communities of developers, administrators, and newbies alike. For more information, please visit our website: www.packtpub.com.

About Packt Enterprise

In 2010, Packt launched two new brands, Packt Enterprise and Packt Open Source, in order to continue its focus on specialization. This book is part of the Packt Enterprise brand, home to books published on enterprise software – software created by major vendors, including (but not limited to) IBM, Microsoft and Oracle, often for use in other corporations. Its titles will offer information relevant to a range of users of this software, including administrators, developers, architects, and end users.

Writing for Packt

We welcome all inquiries from people who are interested in authoring. Book proposals should be sent to author@packtpub.com. If your book idea is still at an early stage and you would like to discuss it first before writing a formal book proposal, contact us; one of our commissioning editors will get in touch with you.

We're not just looking for published authors; if you have strong technical skills but no writing experience, our experienced editors can help you develop a writing career, or simply get some additional reward for your expertise.

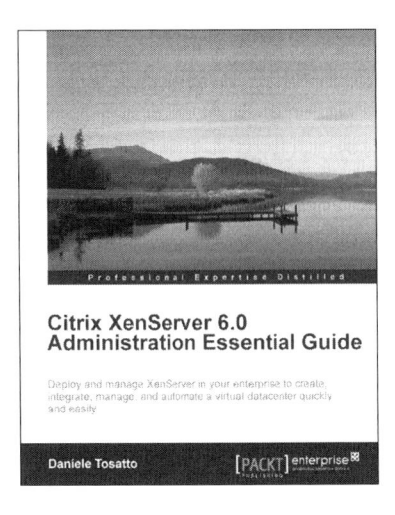

Citrix XenServer 6.0 Administration Essential Guide

ISBN: 978-1-84968-616-7 Paperback: 364 pages

Deploy and manage XenServer in your enterprise to create, integrate, manage, and automate a virtual datacenter quickly and easily

1. This book and eBook will take you through deploying XenServer in your enterprise, and teach you how to create and maintain your datacenter

2. Manage XenServer and virtual machines using Citrix management tools and the command line

3. Organize secure access to your infrastructure using role-based access control

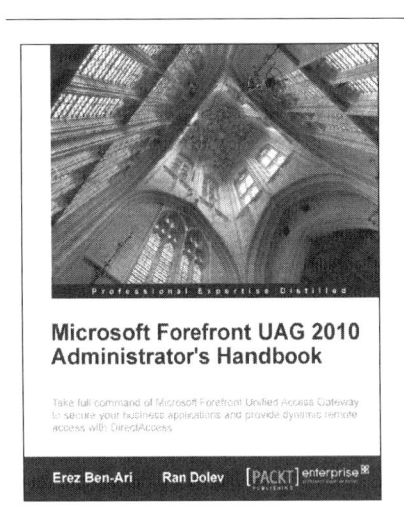

Microsoft Forefront UAG 2010 Administrator's Handbook

ISBN: 978-1-84968-162-9 Paperback: 484 pages

Take full command of Microsoft Forefront Unified Access Gateway to secure your business applications and provide dynamic remote access with DirectAccess

1. Maximize your business results by fully understanding how to plan your UAG integration

2. Consistently be ahead of the game by taking control of your server with backup and advanced monitoring

3. An essential tutorial for new users and a great resource for veterans

Please check **www.PacktPub.com** for information on our titles

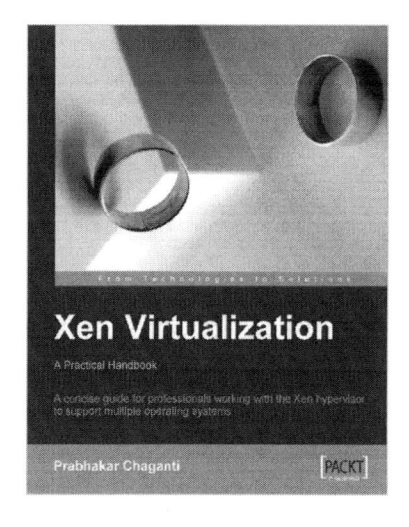

Xen Virtualization

ISBN: 978-1-84719-248-6   Paperback: 148 pages

A concise guide for professionals working with the Xen hypervisor to support multiple operating systems

1. Installing and configuring Xen
2. Managing and administering Xen servers and virtual machines
3. Setting up networking, storage, and encryption
4. Backup and migration

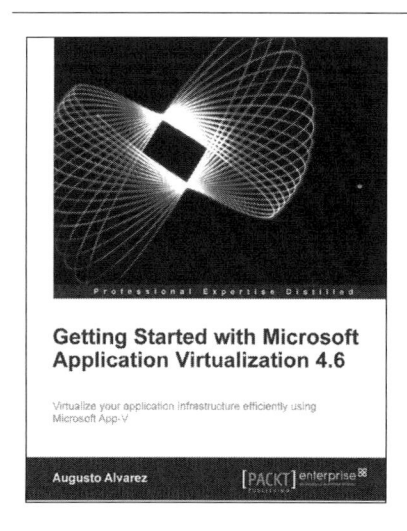

Getting Started with Microsoft Application Virtualization 4.6

ISBN: 978-1-84968-126-1   Paperback: 308 pages

Virtualize your application infrastructure efficiently using Microsoft App-V

1. Publish, deploy, and manage your virtual applications with App-V
2. Understand how Microsoft App-V can fit into your company
3. Guidelines for planning and designing an App-V environment
4. Step-by-step explanations to plan and implement the virtualization of your application infrastructure

Please check **www.PacktPub.com** for information on our titles

Made in the USA
San Bernardino, CA
27 November 2013